Dweller in Shadows:
A Life of Ivor Gurney

2

and who loves joy as he ... that dwells in shadows

Do not for --- get me quite ---

a Se --- vern mea --- dows

Only the wanderer
   Knows England's graces
Or can anew see clear
   Familiar faces.

And who loves joy as he
   That dwells in shadows?
Do not forget me quite,
   O Severn meadows.

—Ivor Gurney

Forget not thyself and the world will not forget thee—forget thyself and the world will willingly forget thee till thou art nothing but a living-dead man dwelling among shadows and falsehood.

from 'Self-identity' (1841) by John Clare: poet, asylum patient

Dweller in Shadows:
A Life of Ivor Gurney

WAR POET, COMPOSER, ASYLUM PATIENT

Kate Kennedy

PRINCETON UNIVERSITY PRESS

Princeton and Oxford

Published by Princeton University Press
41 William Street, Princeton, New Jersey 08540
6 Oxford Street, Woodstock, Oxfordshire OX20 1TR

press.princeton.edu

Library of Congress Cataloging-in-Publication Data
Names: Kennedy, Kate, 1977- author.
Title: Dweller in shadows : a life of Ivor Gurney : war poet, composer, asylum patient /
Kate Kennedy.
Description: [Princeton] : [Princeton University Press], [2021] |
Includes bibliographical references and index.
Identifiers: LCCN 2020034534 (print) | LCCN 2020034535 (ebook) |
ISBN 9780691212784 (hardback) | ISBN 9780691218540 (ebook)
Subjects: LCSH: Gurney, Ivor, 1890-1937. | Poets, English—20th century—Biography. |
Composers—England—20th century—Biography.
Classification: LCC PR6013.U693 Z78 2021 (print) | LCC PR6013.U693 (ebook) |
DDC 821/.912 [B]—dc23
LC record available at https://lccn.loc.gov/2020034534
LC ebook record available at https://lccn.loc.gov/2020034535

British Library Cataloging-in-Publication Data is available

Editorial: Ben Tate and Josh Drake
Production Editorial: Ellen Foos
Text Design: Carmina Alvarez
Jacket Design: Pamela Schnitter
Production: Danielle Amatucci
Publicity: Jodi Price and Amy Stewart

Jacket art: (1) Piano in the main hall, City of London Mental Hospital, Dartford.
It was taken in 2010, after the hospital had been closed. Photo by Martin Frankcom.
(2) Portrait © The Ivor Gurney Trust, 2020

This book has been composed in Arno Pro with Joanna MT

Printed on acid-free paper. ∞

Printed in the United States of America

1 3 5 7 9 10 8 6 4 2

This book is dedicated with much love to Simon Over,

and to the memory of James Allum.

Contents

PART III: CIVILIAN

PART IV: ASYLUM

Illustrations

Maps

Pictures

Gurney's People: A Checklist

Family

Florence and David Gurney—parents
Ronald, Dorothy and Winifred Gurney—siblings
Ethel Gurney—Ronald's wife, Ivor's sister-in-law
Marie Gurney—Ivor's aunt (with whom he lived at her house in Longford,
 Gloucester)

Gloucestershire Friends

Herbert Howells (composer, and companion from Gloucester Cathedral days to
 the Royal College of Music)
Frederick William Harvey (Gurney's greatest friend; poet and soldier in the
 1/5th Gloucesters)
Matilda Harvey (Will Harvey's mother, with whom Gurney stayed at The Redlands, in Minsterworth)
Eric Harvey (Will Harvey's younger brother, who was a chorister with Gurney, and
 was killed in France)
J. W. (Jack) Haines (solicitor and poet, friend of Edward Thomas, Gurney's
 walking companion)
W. P. (William Pat) Kerr (tax inspector, critic and poet who obtained a brief post
 for Gurney in the tax office)
Margaret and Emily Hunt (sisters who played the violin and piano and were
 supportive friends)
Canon Alfred Cheesman (Gurney's godfather, who introduced him to literature)
James Harris (a lockkeeper, with whom Gurney convalesced by the river at
 Framilode)

London Friends

Marion Scott (Gurney's literary and musical executor, and lifelong friend)
Ethel Voynich (novelist and a friend of Scott's with whom Gurney holidayed in
 1918)
Sydney Shimmin (organist, contemporary of Gurney at the Royal College of Music)

Arthur Benjamin (pianist and composer, contemporary of Gurney)

Arthur Bliss (composer, wounded on the Somme, also studied at the RCM with Gurney)

Francis Purcell Warren (RCM student, violinist, violist and composer, killed in France)

Eugene Goossens (contemporary composition student at the RCM)

High Wycombe Friends

The Chapman family: Matilda and Edward—parents; Kitty (Catherine), Winnie (Winifred), Arthur and Micky (Marjorie)—siblings (Gurney proposed marriage to Kitty)

Literary Friends

Harold Monro (poet and owner of the famous Poetry Bookshop in Charing Cross)

W. W. Gibson

Lascelles Abercrombie and his wife Catherine

John Masefield

Walter de la Mare

Helen Thomas (writer, and wife of poet Edward Thomas, who was killed in France)

Hilaire Belloc

J. C. Squire (poet and editor of the *London Mercury*)

C. K. Scott Moncrieff (friend of Wilfred Owen, critic, and secretary to Lord Northcliffe at *The Times*)

Edward (Eddie) Marsh (private secretary to Winston Churchill, editor of the hugely successful *Georgian Poetry* series)

Teachers

Sir Herbert Brewer (Director of Music and Master of the Choristers at Gloucester Cathedral)

Sir Hubert Parry (Founder-President of the Royal College of Music)

Sir Charles Villiers Stanford (Cofounder of RCM and Gurney's prewar teacher)

Ralph Vaughan Williams (Gurney's teacher on his postwar return to the RCM and supporter thereafter)

Medical Staff

VAD nurse Annie Nelson Drummond (to whom Gurney was briefly and unofficially engaged)

Dr Terry (Gurney's GP in Gloucester, who certified him)

Dr Soutar (the second GP who certified him, and treated him in Barnwood House asylum)

Dr Townsend (Superintendent of Barnwood House asylum, Gloucester)

Dr Steen (Superintendent of Stone House Hospital, Dartford)

Dr W. L. Templeton (responsible for Gurney's experimental malaria treatments at Dartford)

Dr E. W. Anderson (Junior Medical Assistant at Dartford, later an eminent psychiatrist)

Dr Randolph Davis (Junior Medical Assistant at Dartford)

Dr Robinson (Superintendent of Stone House Hospital after Dr Steen's retirement)

Prologue

The Farringdon Metropolitan Archive contains many thousands of documents recording the details of the noble, sordid or mundane lives of London's past residents. Among them is a rather unprepossessing brown register, listing the names of patients in the City of London Mental Hospital. Whenever a patient received a visit, the event was marked by a red cross. Many of the patients' names are followed by years of blank boxes. The register's yellowing graph paper offers us a glimpse into the forgotten lives of these asylum patients, but it withholds so much more than it reveals. Against one name there is a smattering of crosses: not many, and sometimes with months in between the visits. The register does not tell us the identity of the visitors, nor how long their visits lasted, but we know that the patient who received them was named Ivor Gurney.

It is often the silence and space between the facts that is the most resonant for the biographer, and Gurney's journey as a poet and composer from the trenches to the asylum is full of such lacunae. For instance, Gurney's story raises questions that probe the uncertain relationship between madness and creativity. He was equally gifted as a poet and a composer, a dual career so unusual that the only other models are Renaissance figures such as John Dowland and Thomas Campion. Gurney was seen by the writers and musicians who knew his work as one of the greatest of his generation; but beyond the intellectual circles of London, his name was hardly known, and few of the visitors to the asylum in which he was held would have known his work. His studies at the Royal College of Music had been interrupted by the outbreak of the First World War, and only four years after his return from the trenches, he had been certified insane and removed from the public gaze for the rest of his life.

Gurney's achievements were read through the narrow lens of war damage: he was seen, by those who remembered him at all, as a tragic victim of shell shock, whose voice from within an asylum became increasingly deranged and nonsensical. This book attempts to establish a new relationship to Ivor Gurney. It reclaims him as an important cultural figure, whose work helps us understand something about the intersections between mental illness, human relationships, landscape and the traumatic experience of war. Above all, to use a much-favoured phrase of Gurney's, it aims to 'pay homage' to him and his work.

I have tried to pull Gurney back from the uneasy territory of a diagnosed madness. Such a diagnosis leaves the subject unfairly flattened by a medical language still grappling to make sense of the complex relationship between a gifted sensibility and mental illness. Perhaps the crucial question to any biographer, trying to rethink Gurney's life, is this: how 'mad' would Gurney's later work have seemed to us if it had not been written inside an asylum? Boxes of his asylum manuscripts were destroyed on the grounds that they were 'incoherent'. However, the manuscripts that do survive from this period are complex, poignant testimonies that speak of a man who was distressed, certainly, but mostly lucid. As the decades pass, our thinking changes as to whether Gurney was eccentric to the point of insanity, or rather, a man passionately engaged with creative innovation. His poetic and harmonic experimentation sometimes sits uneasily with his fundamental conservatism. Is it possible, or even helpful, to try to delineate between forms of intense creativity and madness with any certainty?

Gurney was a man to whom conventional rules seemed not to apply. Before his incarceration he would work and walk at night, at times sleeping in barns, or by the sides of rivers. When police tried to move a hunched figure from his improvised bed on the Thames Embankment, they found they had apprehended not a tramp but a scholarship student of the Royal College of Music. Gurney could be described as an egotist, writing his first collection of poetry, unashamedly, about 'Myself'. But when he believed that he would never return from the trenches, his plea was not for immortal fame, but only that the Severn meadows might not quite forget him. Gurney lavished on the Gloucestershire landscape a passion that is usually reserved for the most intense human relationships, and relationships for Gurney were almost always ambiguous. Many of his friends, including Herbert Howells, were convinced that he was heterosexual. Others hinted heavily at his homosexuality, a 'secret confusion' at the heart of Gurney's personality, which only psychoanalysis could manage. Gurney was briefly engaged to be married, but most of his attachments to women were to those old enough to be his mother.

The person dearest to him was the Gloucestershire poet F. W. (Will) Harvey. It is, of course, a coincidence that the name given to the dedicatee of Shakespeare's sonnets when they were first printed was William Harvey.[1] Gurney (who at times believed he *was* Shakespeare) and Harvey were joined by their poetry, and Harvey runs like a ghostly theme through Gurney's life: a reference point and a signifier of dedication, influencing both his work and his relationships. However, we have no evidence that Harvey visited Gurney more than a handful of times in fifteen years when he was confined to the asylum. He found the experience simply too painful and could not meet his friend's needs. Whatever Gurney's sexual predilection, the defining feature of his relationships was his continual search for connection. His friends and loves move through his story in a constant stream, many real, some imaginary. His networks of affection range from his comrades in the trenches to the landscape of home, from devoted friends such as the music critic Marion Scott to fantastical encounters with the spirit of Beethoven.

As both a poet and composer, Gurney defies categorisation. Was one discipline stronger than the other in his imagination, and how do they compare in the work he produces? The answers are complex and vary during the course of his career. Gurney's musical idiom is essentially traditional, in that he yoked harmonies together that our ears would recognise as logical, if sometimes surprising. On the page, his chord progressions often look unfathomable, and it can be a leap of faith to play them. He moves deftly between the simplest chord patterns and a post-Wagnerian harmonic world, creating work that can be jarring and wrong-footing. But however far he pushed harmony (and why not? He was, after all, writing at the same time as Stravinsky and Schoenberg), there is always a sense of internal logic.

As a writer, he identified strongly with the Georgian poets. At the same time, the poetry he was writing from the early 1920s onwards had more in common with the modernist experiments of Joyce, Eliot and Pound, combined with elements of Edward Thomas and Walt Whitman. His writing could be profoundly experimental, but always with the air of organic spontaneity, and a lack of self-consciousness. In later years, his creativity frequently took unrecognised and 'unacceptable' forms: letters that were poems, poems that were letters, a transmission between forms that reflects Gurney's poetic method. His work across letters, essays and poetry meticulously documents locations and experiences. This might be as a result of his perpetual yearning for rootedness, in terms of finding both people and places that accepted and understood him.

I have taken his attention to the documentation of detail as the cue for my own methodology in writing this biography. By charting the places and events of Gurney's life, and by attempting to be as attentive as possible to the porous details of his story, I have tried both to reflect and to honour Gurney's work, and to situate it in a context that will enhance our understanding of it. Gurney's progress through life was halting and difficult, and the war years (in particular) read as a series of often anguished and disrupted fits and starts in locations and between groups of people. He struggled to attach himself to the fleeting wartime communities that might offer him affection and inclusion, among comrades as well as networks of lovers, admirers and friends. His letters and poems document this rich mix of emotional life-forms that often seem to threaten to spin out of control.

> I am gone
> Out of myself into pain, into delirium alone.
> And my mind is tortured and my tale changed,
> Truth itself turned against truth and ranged

Against itself, everything worthy gone
To a past that's pain, and now all's clear alone.[2]

From his incarceration in 1922, Gurney began a committed campaign to revise his own role and identity, returning often to the imperative to tell the 'truth'. Gurney believed his calling was to continue to document the circumstances of his suffering both in the present and the remembered suffering of the war years. His writing is characterised by his tendency to think and feel communally—shifting through time from the present back through past wars, to Ancient Rome and Greece.

His imagination became boundless. Refusing to be limited by the confines not only of his time period but of his own identity, he preferred, instead, to imagine himself as Shakespeare, Brahms or Schubert. Such role-plays smack of hubris, and a certain lack of reality (the two are surely related), but they also remind us that Gurney's work poses direct challenges as to how we might evaluate and process states of creativity. His life and work ask us to reconsider the many creative relationships he makes between music and literature. Should we, for example, read a single poem as an individual entity? So many of Gurney's poems shuffle kaleidoscopically through the same themes, words and ideas, to make new but related patterns.

During his years in the asylum, his very identity was under threat from an institution that defined him only as patient number 6420, noting with suspicion that 'The patient is said to be musical'. Definitions and boundaries were things Gurney strongly resisted, and in his fight against anonymity, and in defiance of the institution, he insisted on defining himself by his own set of designated titles: 'First War Poet' and 'A Soldier and a Maker' among them.

Gurney recognised that it was his very instability that allowed him to see more clearly. When, in 1918, he believed he had communed with the spirit of Beethoven, he was fully aware of how this transcendental experience would be read by 'professionals': 'What would the doctors say to that? A Ticket, certainly, for insanity. No, it is the beginning of a new life, a new vision.'[3] Gurney's life was a painful negotiation between inspiration and mental anguish, but it was a struggle he knew, on some level, to be unavoidable, and even essential, to an artist intent on forging new forms.

Kate Kennedy
Oxford Centre for Life-Writing at Wolfson College, 2020

Acknowledgements

During the course of the research for this book I have received help and encouragement from many sources, for which I am most grateful. In particular I would like to thank the staff at the Soldiers of Gloucestershire Museum, the Gloucester Public Records Office, Royal College of Music, Gloucester Cathedral, Imperial War Museum, Metropolitan Records Office, Kew Records Office, British Library, Bodleian Library and Cambridge University Library. Also Piet Chielens, Director of the In Flanders Museum in Ypres; Nicholas Anderson, whose psychiatrist father treated Gurney; Francine Payne, a nurse at Dartford Asylum; and Professors Kate Saunders of Oxford University and Edgar Jones of Kings College, London and the Maudsley Hospital for their professional opinions on Gurney's illness.

I'm grateful for the support and advice of biographers Hermione Lee and Max Saunders; historians and literary critics Santanu Das, Johnathan Clinch, Mark Lee and Trudi Tate; composers Tim Watts and John Hopkins; poet John Fuller; Gurney scholars Eleanor Rawlings, Pamela Blevins and Anthony Boden; Noel Hayward (a relative of Gurney's); editors Ben Tate, Kim Hastings, Josh Drake, Ellen Foos and Philippa Brewster; my agent Georgina Capel; and composer Ian Venables for his personal support as well as his expert direction of the Gurney Trust. I am especially grateful to Philip Lancaster for colluding on exact dates of many manuscripts, discussing the transcription of Gurney's challenging handwriting, and compiling the appendices to this book. Musicians Iain Burnside, Sarah Connolly and Julius Drake have collaborated on performances involving Gurney's music and performed dramatised versions of this book.

I have been generously supported by the Mistress and Fellowship of Girton College, Cambridge during my Fellowship there, and by Wolfson College, Oxford, in particular the Oxford Centre for Life-Writing and its inspiring and intellectually stimulating community of biographers. Above all, a heartfelt thanks to critic Alison Hennegan and Gurney scholar and editor R.K.R. Thornton; I am indebted to them both for their friendship, critical reading and wisdom.

PART I

Youth

Great Malvern ●

MALVERN
HILLS

● Ledbury

R.Leadon

Forthhampton ● ● Tewkesbury

R.Avon

BREDON
HILL

Foscombe Hill ● ● Cleeve Hill
Hartpury ● ● Ashleworth

R.Chelt

Maisemore ● Cheltenham ● ● Cirencester
● Longford

Highnam ● ● Chosen Hill
Minsterworth ● Dryhill ●
R.Twyver ● Crickley Hill
Gloucester Coopers Hill ● Cold Slad
Newnham ● Cranham
upon
Severn ● Longney COTSWOLDS

Framilode ● Painswick
Frampton
upon Severn
R.Frome ● Stroud

R.Severn

Dursley ●

0 _____ 5 mi
0 _____ 5 km

● Edinburgh
● Bangour War Hospital

● Seaton Delaval
● Newcastle upon Tyne
Brancepeth ●

● Warrington

GREAT BRITAIN

Gloucester ● St. Albans
High ●
Wycombe ● **London** ● Dartford

● Gurnard's Head

CHAPTER ONE

'The Young Genius'

In Room 53 of the Royal College of Music, with oil paintings of composers lining its walls and a view of the Royal Albert Hall through its large windows, sits the great Sir Charles Villiers Stanford, frowning through his pince nez as he marks a composition with 'his gold propelling pencil'. He shakes his head, shakes it again, hums a little, then, with a flourish, holds up the altered song. 'There, m'boy', he exclaims to one of the two students eagerly watching him. 'That'll be half a crown'. An unkempt, dark-haired student in a rather shapeless blue coat takes one look at the corrections and leaps to his feet. 'But Sir—you've jiggered the whole thing!'

Stanford looks at him in silence, slowly rises from his seat, takes his student firmly by the ear, and expels him from the room. The other observer, the young composer Herbert Howells, looks on aghast. With his back to the door, Stanford smiles. 'I love Gurney more and more. He's the greatest among you all, but the least teachable.'[1] He returns to look at some of Howells's immaculately presented musical offerings as the sound of footsteps stamping on the stone stairs rings down the corridor.

By the time the twenty-year-old 'young genius', as Gurney referred to himself (with only partial irony), reached the imposing marble entrance hall of the Royal College of Music on 8 May 1911, he was hardly a child prodigy. His compositions showed promise and flair, but they were a long way from remarkable. Gurney knew he had hardly begun to investigate the depth of his gift, and he had a deep conviction that he possessed the capability to write something extraordinary, if only he could discipline and train himself. These were early days, and his education was just beginning. For now, with the real possibility of future greatness, and a capital city full of world-class music-making to explore, optimism outweighed anxiety.

One year before, Gurney had been sitting in the draughty pews of Gloucester Cathedral. He had watched the many colours the stained glass cast across the great

FIG. 1.1: Ivor Gurney at the Royal College of Music, from Herbert Howells's personal collection. © Gurney Trust.

building as the sun set, as he listened with rapt attention to a piece that was unlike anything he had ever heard. Both he and Howells were organ scholars, and Gurney had practically grown up in the cathedral, having been a chorister there from the age of ten. Howells sat by Gurney's side, the two overawed by the importance of what they were hearing. Dr Herbert Brewer, the cathedral's music director, had announced to the choir that there would be a premiere of a 'queer mad work' by an 'odd fellow from Chelsea'.[2] His curmudgeonly description had hardly prepared them for the sheer magnitude of what they were now experiencing, with string writing that sounded simultaneously new and ancient, the sound appearing to rise from the very building as if it had been hewn from its stone. This was the premiere of Ralph Vaughan Williams's *Fantasia on a Theme by Thomas Tallis*.

After the final applause had ended, and a starstruck seventeen-year-old Howells had obtained Vaughan Williams's autograph, the two young organists walked out of the cathedral, unable to speak. The cathedral was only a stone's throw from Gurney's home on Barton Street, above the family's tailoring business. From his glass-fronted shop, with counters piled high with rolls of plaid and corduroy, Gurney's father David served customers, cut cloth and took measurements for the gentlemen of Gloucester who required suits; he was assisted by his rather truculent wife, Florence. Their son Ivor jostled for space in the handful of gloomy rooms upstairs,

FIG. 1.2: Gurney's father's tailor shop in Barton Street, Gloucester. © Gurney Trust.

alongside his sister Winifred, who was his senior by three years; Ronald, who was four years younger than Ivor; and Dorothy, the baby of the family, who was born when Ivor was ten.[3]

That night Ivor Gurney did not go straight home. Instead he and Howells walked, for hour after hour. They strode through the cobbled streets around the cathedral cloister where during the day Gurney often perused the secondhand books that were piled high on wooden barrows. They passed the crossroads where the straight Roman roads of Westgate and Eastgate meet at the city's centre, past the darkened windows of the tailor's shop at 19 Barton Street, past the ancient sign of the grocers—a great brass grasshopper which stretched the length of the shop front—and the battered façade of a disused eighteenth-century theatre that had once hosted the royalty of the acting profession. A few hours earlier the streets had been bustling with horses and drays, ambling farmers in leggings with corduroy coats and bowler hats, clergymen on bicycles and red-faced women in from the countryside with gossiping voices and bulging shopping baskets. Now the only sound was the boys' footfall as they walked on. Little Howells, immaculately dressed, was obliged almost to run to keep up with the typically furious pace set by his friend. After a while the initial shock of the *Tallis Fantasia* wore off, and as they walked, they talked animatedly about what they had just heard. They knew that these new sounds meant something momentous for British music, and they were equally determined to have a role in shaping its future.

For the past decade, Vaughan Williams had been trying to establish a new English music through folk song and the amalgamation of ancient church music and modern harmonies.[4] Both Gurney and Howells felt the calling to be part of this 'New English Musical Renaissance', as it was to become known, and knew that the Royal College of Music in London was certainly the best place to begin preparing for the challenge. The College, far more than the Royal Academy, flourished as a centre of composition in the years before the war. A look through the generally adventurous Queen's Hall Promenade Concert programmes in the autumn of 1913 shows the Royal College to be impressively overrepresented: in one season audiences could hear works by Stanford, Walford Davies, Vaughan Williams, Landon Ronald, Thomas Dunhill, Frank Bridge, Harry Keyser, Eugene Goossens and Coleridge Taylor—all either teachers or alumni.

Three years after hearing Vaughan Williams's music ringing round the pillars of Gloucester Cathedral, both Gurney and Howells were enrolled at the College. The teachers there quickly found that Gurney was no ordinary student. He was enchanting and frustrating in equal measure.[5] Exceptionally talented, his ambitiousness could occasionally slip over into a naïve arrogance, which, coupled with his stubbornness, led to frequent clashes with his teachers. The compositions Gurney had brought with him from Gloucester showed great potential, but were really only charming, well-crafted Edwardian parlour pieces. How would an inexperienced, provincial boy with a general disregard for convention progress in the professional musical world?

He had written his juvenile piano and violin works for sisters Margaret and Emily Hunt, music teachers who lived close to the family's shop. They had practically adopted the lonely teenager, who was keen to escape from the frequent arguments at home, in search of music and inspiration. In turn, Gurney adored them. Imagining himself perhaps as a Brahms secretly serenading his Clara Schumann, he had written a piano waltz for Emily's birthday in 1918, with her initials as a musical monogram. There is no doubt that Emily meant a great deal to him, but it was always Margaret who inspired his most passionate devotion. The diminutive, dark-haired 'Madge' was his earliest muse, despite the sixteen years between their ages.[6] This was not a romantic relationship in the conventional sense. When Gurney visited Margaret during what was to be her final illness, he described her as a 'brave little woman', a phrase redolent of respect and deep affection, but not of a love affair. During the years in which he might have been considered to be in love with her, he did not feel it inappropriate to propose to two other girls and continue an almost daily correspondence with another older woman. If Margaret was indeed his 'love', then he loved her for providing him with an audience and beneficiary to whom he could direct his work, when his own family had neither time nor inclination to listen.

FIG. 1.3: Gurney at the piano, September 1905. © Gurney Trust.

The Gurney family home was not entirely devoid of music, however. There was a piano on which Gurney learnt, and both his father David and mother Florence sang in local choirs. Florence, always keen for social advancement, had insisted that all the Gurney children learn an instrument, but practising was a challenge; there was little opportunity for quiet in the parlour, and no music to study. The Hunt sisters provided both, and Gurney learnt a great deal from leafing through books of Schubert's Lieder at their Bechstein. Gurney soon aspired first to copy, then to rival Schubert.

On arrival in South Kensington, Gurney found the Royal College to be an elegant red brick affair, with a glass and iron portico and distinguished-looking miniature towers—a monument to proud Victorian prosperity. It nestles between Imperial College and the Royal School of Mines. Overlooking the Royal Albert Hall, it is surrounded everywhere by testaments to the Victorian penchant for the lavish and impressive. Behind the Albert Hall is Regent's Park, with the outrageously golden Prince Albert memorial. This was an area of London in which the very pavements leaked confidence, and every new museum and academic establishment (largely funded by the triumph of the Great Exhibition) boasted artistic and intellectual achievement. It was, in short, the perfect destination for a young man with a clear sense of his own self-importance.

The College itself, whilst impressive, was then crammed into a site of only an acre. The limitations of the site necessitated building upwards, but there were no lifts. To get from lunch back to the organ room, Gurney had a climb of 186 steps. When he took up his scholarship, the College was still comparatively new, and proud of its illustrious beginnings (it had opened, in a flapping extravaganza of bunting, in 1894). In 1911 it was an exciting place to be. Moreover, it was dominated by two of the most influential men in musical Britain.

Sir Hubert Parry had long been established as the College principal, and was unanimously respected, and his colleague Sir Charles Villiers Stanford was the most eminent composition teacher in the institution. They were both to play a large part in Gurney's student life, and to take an interest in him far beyond that of an average undergraduate. Parry gave four lectures a term on music history, as an attempt to broaden the horizons of performers, who were often focused on their instrumental skills to the exclusion of all else. He was a farsighted and inspiring man, in favour of students 'talking wild', by which he meant the exuberant bandying about of big ideas, and thinking widely and ambitiously.[7] Gurney, who had wild talking down to a fine art, held an instant attraction for him, and the feeling was mutual. 'Sir Hubert is a great man.[...] He speaks with authority, not as one of the scribes', Gurney wrote.[8] The friendship was not simply deferential, but warmly affectionate: 'Sir Hubert, of course, was a darling.'[9] It was a popularly held view; Howells also revered him, and with good reason: Parry was to be generous enough to pay all Howells's substantial medical bills when he became dangerously ill with Graves' disease in 1916.

Two years younger than Gurney, Howells had also begun his life above a shop, although not in the cramped city centre. The Howells family lived in the Gloucestershire village of Lydney, surrounded by the Forest of Dean. Their home was larger than Gurney's, but Howells was obliged to share it with seven older siblings. His father's painting and decorating business had gone bankrupt, and like Gurney, Howells grew up impecunious. Howells's father played the organ in Lydney church at the weekends, and although he was not particularly proficient a musician, his enthusiasm led him to make regular musical expeditions with his son to churches and to Gloucester Cathedral. They would have seen Gurney, one of ten choristers, in his red cassock in evensong, or running at the flocks of overfed pigeons in the cathedral close, in Eton suit and mortarboard, black gown flapping behind him.

In 1909, at sixteen, Howells was to take his place as one of three teenage boys in the cathedral organ loft, where his friendship with Gurney began. With spectacular incongruity, the third of their party was the young Ivor Novello. From their vantage point, Herbert and the two Ivors looked down on the choir and on Dr Brewer, a rather humourless man with a forbidding moustache, round spectacles and neatly swept back hair. As articled pupils and later assistants, the three boys accompanied services and studied theory and harmony, and Howells quickly warmed to the gregarious, spontaneous Gurney. Whereas Ivor Novello (or David Ivor Davies as he was known then) was charming but prodigiously lazy, Gurney was positively bursting with ambition. He was also somewhat guileless, and his drive to better himself could sometimes brim over into boastful arrogance; a trait his friends forgave but which was guaranteed to challenge even the most amiable teacher. Brewer was not known for his amiability, and he did nothing to help Gurney with the next steps in his fledgling career. When Gurney decided against an organ scholarship to Durham University and announced instead that he wanted to try for the composition scholarship to the Royal College, Brewer chose not to use his personal friendship with Hubert Parry on his pupil's behalf, remarking grudgingly (and inaccurately), 'why does he bother? He can get all he wants here.'[10]

Gurney was never going to be cut out for life in a provincial cathedral organ loft, and despite his outward appearance of a lack of faith in Gurney, Brewer knew that he was no ordinary pupil. He later admitted to Gurney's father that he would have been 'proud if the music that Ivor had written was his.'[11] This was a generous admission, but Gurney's family was far from able to offer the financial and emotional support their son needed in order to nurture such a talent. Had he decided to help, Brewer could have been an influential and powerful supporter of his young student. It took Gurney's godfather, Alfred Cheesman, to step in with financial assistance to make it possible for Gurney to study in London. Canon Cheesman had become Gurney's godfather by default when David and Florence had brought baby Ivor to their local church to be baptised by him but had omitted to bring a sponsor. In lieu of any other options, Cheesman volunteered himself. It was a stroke of great serendipity for Gurney. Cheesman was a sensitive, educated man who lived alone among his poetry and botany books. He had travelled Europe and had the great distinction of an acquaintance with Rudyard Kipling. If Gurney's parents had tried, they could not have chosen a more suitable godfather than this genteel Victorian intellectual. As Gurney matured, he spent more and more time with Cheesman, listening in delight as he read to him from the great poets, and walking the country lanes together, pointing out the different species of flowers and birds. Gurney dearly loved his own quietly spoken father, with whom he shared his passion for the countryside, but through Cheesman he caught a tantalising glimpse of a world of education and culture that was alien to his own family.

As the teenage Gurney matured, so his relationship with Cheesman intensified. Despite the deep complexities and contradictions riven through his personality,

FIG. 1.4: Gurney's godfather, Canon Cheesman. © Gurney Trust.

Gurney had a great talent for friendship, and could be a hilarious and stimulating companion. He was eager to absorb what he could from those who would give him their time and wisdom, and was always sensible of the emotional and financial debts he was incurring. Cheesman procured the seventeen-year-old Gurney his very first paid job: as organist at nearby Whitminster church. Gurney was generous to a fault, when his limited means allowed, and in gratitude, he spent much of his first earnings on a book to give to his godfather: a copy of Ernest Rhys's *Fairy Gold: A Book of Old English Fairy Tales*. He inscribed it:

> That he who loved Hans Andersen
> His trees and flowers, his sun and rain
> May remember tales from his childhood known
> And read with his childhood's heart again.
> Easter 1907.

A rather touching little rhyme, this is the first surviving evidence of Gurney's own inclination towards verse. It was an inscription aptly tailored for its recipient. Cheesman, like his young protégé, did indeed love trees and flowers, sun and rain;

and his reading reflected it. Cheesman's library constituted Gurney's first exposure to literature, and books on nature and botany far outweighed any other category. Gurney browsed titles such as *The Plant-Lore and Garden-Craft of Shakespeare, Our Woodlands, Heaths, and Hedges* and *The Rivers and Streams of England*. In his own copy of Helen Milman's *In the Garden of Peace*, Cheesman had written:

> How much more lovely & worthy of love flowers are than human beings . . . If I had been the Creator, I think I would have given the flowers immortal souls, rather than to men.[12]

Under Cheesman's influence, Gurney was brought up on a diet of literary flowers.

Gurney shared his love 'of natural things and simplicity' with Cheesman, and when he had taken leave of him to move to London, it became a close bond between Gurney and Howells, two Gloucestershire scholarship boys a long way from the countryside of home.[13] Gurney and Howells also shared a fierce sense of ambition. They were both blessed with ability in abundance, but only Howells had a clear sense of how to make use of his gift. As soon as he reached South Kensington, he began to establish himself as a model student, building a reputation that would secure his place firmly within the establishment. In Howells, Gurney found both a lifelong rival and someone for whom he had sincere and deep affection. The origins of their relationship were bound up in his memory with the magisterial Gloucester Cathedral. The little dominion of the organ loft had been the setting for their burgeoning friendship; and the fabric of the cathedral, with its constantly changing light and shadows, formed the backdrop to their early years together.

Howells recalled an incident in which Gurney had been so inspired by the light filling up the east window of the cathedral that he had sprung down from the organ loft, exclaiming, 'God, I must go to Framilode!' (a picturesque little village on a bend of the River Severn), and subsequently vanished for three days. This was not even particularly remarkable. He would frequently disappear from home with no explanation, which, understandably, his family found somewhat disturbing. His sister Winifred recognised that

> The truth was, he did not seem to belong to us and he had so many intellectual friends who recognised his gifts and who encouraged him in every way, that we really did not attain his standards or understand his genius. It was only when I learned from outsiders of the high opinion people had of him, did I realise that he was outstanding—and that was how we, as a family had to regard him. He had so many homes to spend his time with friends, that he simply called upon us briefly and left again without a word.[14]

Rather than being inspired by Howells's example, the teenage Gurney in fact led the way in their fledgling compositional careers. He was the first of the two friends

FIG. 1.5: Gurney and Howells together. © Gurney Trust.

to begin to write, with two songs written in 1904 when he was fourteen, along with seven piano pieces, organ works and settings of Rudyard Kipling's poems 'Who Hath Desired the Sea' and 'Mandalay' already to his name.[15] In total, he had been writing for four years by the time Howells began to compose, and his example may well have helped to nudge Howells into attempting more than the odd hymn descant or psalm chant. Whilst Howells experimented with 'Four Romantic Piano Pieces' and a 'Marching Song', Gurney was writing violin pieces for the Hunt sisters: a 'Romance' for violin in 1909, along with a 'Folk Tale' for violin and piano—an unexceptional, pleasant little piece in compound time, beginning 'plaintively and simply', with a whispered, lilting quaver pattern in the violin, and a lightly textured piano accompaniment.

Howells made a tentative foray into song composition with a setting of Robert Louis Stevenson, but Gurney was already ahead of him, and developing a particular affinity with song. He found inspiration in the Elizabethan poet Robert Herrick's 'Passing By', and A. E. Housman's 'On Your Midnight Pallet Lying' in 1907. He also set five poems by the recently deceased W. E. Henley (another Gloucester poet) in the spring of 1908, and Elizabeth Barrett Browning's 'The Crown' in May 1909. These songs are charming, textbook creations, relying on circles of fifths, and with little or no hint of the harmonic adventurousness of his later work. Chromaticism, when it is present, as in Henley's 'Gulls in an Aëry Morrice', is decorative, rather than destabilising, although this is one of the first works in which he establishes what would become a penchant for juxtaposing remotely related keys. There are even hints of the stylistic world of Ivor Novello in the Henley setting 'Dear Hands, So Many Times', and it is fun (if rather fanciful) to imagine the two Ivors vamping away, swapping musical ideas in the organ loft or at the piano in the choir room.

From his earliest attempts at composition, Gurney knew he did not want to limit himself solely to songwriting. Between 1910 and 1911 he wrote what was probably his first orchestral piece: Coronation March in B flat. It was a competent, conservative work, owing a debt to Elgar's *Pomp and Circumstance* marches. Despite the work being intended as a triumphant coronation piece, Gurney gave it a rather inappropriately subdued quotation from *The Merchant of Venice*: 'Then, if he lose, he makes a swan-like end, Fading in music.'

King Edward VII had died on 6 May 1910, and the coronation of George V had taken place on 22 June 1911. The music for the coronation service in Westminster Abbey was chosen by the Abbey's organist, Frederick Bridge. The service was a feast of English composers, from Orlando Gibbons and Thomas Tallis to Charles Stanford, Edward Elgar and Hubert Parry's anthem *I Was Glad*, which he had written for Edward VII. The Worshipful Company of Musicians ran a competition for composers to write a march for inclusion in the celebrations. Despite some two hundred entries, they decided not to award a prize, much to Gurney's disappointment. But the competition had given him the incentive to experiment with orchestral writing, and the opportunity, in fantasy at least, to picture his music being heard alongside the great names of English music. Beginning his studies at the Royal College in daily contact with the great Dr Parry meant that he was one significant step closer to realising his dream.

On the whole, Gurney was on better terms with his teachers at the Royal College than he had been with Dr Brewer at the cathedral. Sidney Waddington taught him harmony and counterpoint, and Walter Alcock oversaw his organ studies. Howells considered Alcock one of the greatest organists in the country, and as assistant organist at Westminster Abbey he was to have the unique privilege of playing for three coronations.[16] He was an endearing figure; when he left the College for the organ loft of Salisbury Cathedral in 1916, he built a model railway in his garden and let the choristers ride on it. Gurney also had lessons with the gentle and undemanding

Charles Wood, and the composer Sir Henry Walford Davies, who was at the height of his prolific career and held the post of director of music at the Temple Church on The Strand.[17] Gurney was scathing about Walford Davies's work, with a superiority that was the least likeable side of his character:

> Could you possibly let me have a look at Walford Davies' Violin Sonatas next term, and early? I have fell designs on a V.S. and the pleasant consciousness of superiority which those Sonatas would probably give me, might be in the highest degree valuable.[18]

Gurney took classes in German as a second study alongside piano and organ, an obvious choice at that point as the College was steeped in the influence of Brahms and Beethoven, but not such a popular option by 1914. The formidable Stanford, Gurney's principal composition teacher, was to be his most formative influence. With his walrus moustache, Stanford was an eminent Victorian in a proud Victorian institution. He had a sense of inheritance and entitlement—he had been the organ scholar at Trinity College, Cambridge, and had come from a well-off Irish family. He gave the impression, with some justification, of owning the College, as at the age of twenty-nine he had helped to found the institution with Parry. He was sure of himself and not particularly inclined to be flexible, which made for some challenging encounters with his equally stubborn and opinionated pupil. He and Gurney fought from the start.

Stanford's pupils were divided about the benefits of his teaching; Sir Arthur Bliss later recalled Stanford having a 'devitalising effect' on him.[19] But there is no doubt that Stanford was a major figure in English music, and a great teacher, for those who re-sponded to his methods. He insisted on 'sound craftsmanship, economy and clarity of thought and self-criticism'.[20] His rule was authoritarian, but he did allow pupils to write whatever they wanted, once they had cut their teeth on a year of Palestrinian counter-point and modes.[21] Howells got on with him famously, which was perhaps rather pre-dictable, whereas the more problematic Frank Bridge, who had studied with Stanford and now taught at the College himself, unflatteringly described his 'years in the nursery' with Stanford as like 'imbibing water through a straw instead of Glaxo and Bovril'.[22] Even the humble and amenable Vaughan Williams found that Stanford made him feel that he was 'unteachable'.[23] Both Bridge and Vaughan Williams were great technicians, and, like Gurney, recognised the importance of a sound musical grounding. It would be easy to assume from Gurney's battles with his teacher that he was ill disciplined or too truculent to be educated. This would not be entirely fair. It is more likely that Stanford had a somewhat 'devitalising effect' on many of the young composers who came under his tutelage in the last decades of his teaching career, particularly if they felt they wanted to establish a new musical voice that did not fit with his famously narrow views of what was musically acceptable, and what was beyond the harmonic pale.

Gurney respected him, despite their troubled relationship. He knew him to be a great man, and later wrote that Stanford was a 'born poet'.[24] Both Stanford and Parry revered the great German Romantics, and all composition students were obliged to study Beethoven and Brahms. Gurney was perfectly capable of rejecting Stanford's very considerable musical prejudices, but his own musical tastes were to remain largely within the idiom of his teacher's, and he was to turn to Beethoven repeatedly in later years. However, Gurney's music would later explore a chromaticism to which a horrified Stanford would have liberally applied his infamous red pencil. Benjamin recalled Stanford's harmonic 'bigotry', as he termed it:

> Those of us who, having indulged in a 'spice' of modern harmony, were not angrily ejected from his room, were considered by our fellows, after all, mere fogeys. Displeased, Stanford would foam with rage, stab viciously with his pencil at an offending chord, point to the door with a long arm and utter the command: 'Leave the room, me bhoy, and don't come back till ye can write something beautiful!'[25]

Despite Stanford's best efforts, his young pupils' harmonic explorations continued regardless, and Gurney, Bliss, Howells and Benjamin all explored new musical territory. As Gurney's confidence grew, his work began to embrace both beauty and eccentricity in equal measure, and he built on the forms and textures he had learnt from Schubert, Brahms and Beethoven's songs and chamber music, rather than considering his conservative training a hindrance.

Gurney began his studies with Stanford in May 1912. With the £40 scholarship that he had been awarded, and a further £40 from Cheesman, he was able to pay the rent on a modest flat in Fulham and have a very little to spare. The paint was peeling from the walls, and the light shades were dingy and torn, but Gurney, in true student style, pinned up pictures from magazines to brighten the rooms, and filled what little space he had with piles of books. London might have seemed a vast and potentially overwhelming place for a country boy who was more at home in the daffodil meadows and hills of Gloucestershire than suburban London. But he had Howells to remind him of his roots, and he spent much of his time in the company of his greatest friend, the Gloucestershire poet Will Harvey, with whom he could talk about the landscape he loved, in its absence.

Their friendship began in 1908, when, sitting on a tram in Gloucester one day, Gurney had recognised the stocky, thick-set young man in spectacles opposite him. It was Frederick William Harvey, who had overlapped with him at the Cathedral School for two years. Theirs was to become the closest and most intense friendship Gurney would ever experience. Although they had barely been acquainted at school, Gurney already knew Harvey's younger brother Eric well, as they had been choristers together. It was enough common ground for him to strike up a conversation

FIG. 1.6: F. W. (Will) Harvey. Reproduced with kind permission of the
Anthony Boden Private Collection, published in *F. W. Harvey: Soldier, Poet*
(Phillimore & Co., 2016).

with Will. It did not take them long to find they shared a passion for music and literature, and so, quite by chance, each discovered a kindred spirit. At the time of the
meeting, Gurney was serving out his rather torturous apprenticeship with Brewer in
the organ loft, and Harvey was reluctantly studying to be a lawyer in an office overlooking the cathedral, so it was easy for them to fall into each other's company, and
offer some mutual comfort. Harvey was more than happy to escape from his office
into the countryside, and Gurney was delighted to have a walking companion, especially one who wrote poetry about the landscape he loved.

Will Harvey was full of charisma and charm: an eloquent and witty conversational-
ist, and a natural performer. But each saw in the other something darker that they tacitly
understood. Harvey had a self-destructive streak, a carelessness regarding his own
safety and well-being, and Gurney recognised like for like.[26] He was later to describe it
as Harvey's only flaw, calling it introspection, or self-absorption; a curse he himself understood well, along with the misery it could cause. Both boys would grow into adult-
hood seeking the serenity and peace that continually eluded them. It was to be the bond
that would elevate their friendship to something more than companions with shared
interests. Both possessed a sensitive, artistic nature, but it was through their various
struggles to write, or to stave off depression, that each truly understood the other.

Harvey lived in a Georgian farmhouse called The Redlands, in the village of Minsterworth. He came from a family of farmers and grew up surrounded by pigs, cattle and poultry. The Redlands was a beautiful spot, with large gardens and an orchard in which Gurney helped to pick apples. Will Harvey's childhood was nothing short of idyllic, and friendship with Harvey offered the perfect rural home life that Gurney craved. Harvey was Gurney's first real contact with a living poet, albeit a young, burgeoning one, and it was as a writer that he made the greatest impression on the adolescent Gurney. Gurney read Harvey's work, discussed his poems with him, and began to gain confidence from the fact that even a humble boy from Gloucester might aspire to see his verse in print. If Harvey could do it, then so could he; and as his affection for Harvey grew, so he felt the first stirrings of a fruitfully competitive relationship with his new friend. Harvey's poem 'Ducks' is one of his finest and frequently included in poetry anthologies. It begins:

From troubles of the world I turn to ducks,
Beautiful comical things
Sleeping or curled
Their heads beneath white wings
By water cool,
Or finding curious things
To eat in various mucks
Beneath the pool,[27]

'Ducks' exemplifies Harvey's whimsical light touch at its best. Much of the rest of his work was written for popular appeal. His verse is humorous, often touching, as might be expected from the pen of a sensitive, perceptive man. Over the course of the following years, Gurney realised that Harvey's work, even in maturity, was limited. At the same time, he respected Harvey's talent and maintained that at his best, his work could rival the best of his generation.[28] This pleasant, accessible poetry would exert a huge influence over Gurney at the start of his journey as a poet, before he had discovered the far greater possibilities that the work of Walt Whitman, Edward Thomas and Gerard Manley Hopkins offered him, and was able to take his own poetry into territory that left his friend far behind.

Many of the interests and poetic ideas that were to become trademarks of Gurney's verse were encouraged and moulded by Harvey's example. He passed on to Gurney his interest in all things Roman; a passion easy for Gurney to cultivate in the historic Gloucestershire landscape, peppered with Roman settlements. Harvey was a stickler for personal discipline, and Gurney also grew to find that order and routine were essential to his health and creativity, although he could rarely achieve the levels he required to function. In short, Harvey and Gurney were temperamentally a perfect match. Both felt themselves observers, watching from the shadows and turning what they saw into music and verse. Harvey later described himself as

A thick-set dark haired dreamy little man
Uncouth to see
Revolving ever this preposterous plan—
Within a web of words spread cunningly
To tangle life—no less.
(Could he expect success?)

Of life he craves not much, except to watch.

Being forced to act,
He walks behind himself, as if to catch
The motive:—An accessory to the fact
Faintly amused, it seems,
Behind his dreams.[29]

When Harvey failed his law exams, which came as a surprise to no one, he moved to London to start a six-month crammer course at Lincoln's Inn Fields. For a brief while, Gurney was actually ahead of his sophisticated friend, and in the unusual position of being able to offer *him* support. Harvey was utterly despondent. Publisher after publisher had rejected his poetry. He hated studying law, and his exam results did nothing to encourage him, but so far his literary ambitions had come to nothing, and he was left with no alternative. Gurney, however, was finding himself surrounded by young, vivacious and prodigiously talented musicians, amongst whom it was difficult not to feel inspired.

The camp and cheeky 'Benjee', otherwise known as Arthur Benjamin, a brilliant young pianist and composer from Brisbane, Australia, had started at the College three months before Gurney (in February 1911), and quickly became a close companion. Three years Gurney's junior, he was a bright, attractive boy, with dark hair swept to one side and a wide smile. His warm and generous personality was coupled with the supreme confidence of the child prodigy (he had given his first recital at the age of six). The result of such a spectacular childhood was an easy air of sophistication at which Gurney, whom Benjee found endearingly gauche, marvelled. He also had the luxury of a generous private income. Benjamin's comfortable digs in upmarket Bayswater were a far cry from Gurney's shabby lodgings.

When Howells came to join the group a year later, Benjamin was smitten. Howells looked like a little boy, terribly young and slightly built, with, as Benjamin observed, a 'beautiful head'.[30] He immediately asked Howells out to lunch; and so a friendship began, which for Benjamin at least, was far more than platonic. Benjamin and Howells, the one flamboyant and charismatic, the other serious and conscientious, in their different ways fitted perfectly into undergraduate life at the College. Gurney, just as musically gifted, combined his talent with a nature that pulled always towards the chaotic; in his dress, his behaviour and his music. His was a personality that was uncontained and lacked both the capacity and inclination to conform.

In November 1913 the group of friends was joined by Arthur Bliss. Gurney's year was a bumper crop of interesting composers, with ambitions to match his own. Howells wrote a five-movement orchestral suite which he called *The B's* as a celebration of their friendship. It was a deftly orchestrated, ambitious answer to Elgar's *Enigma Variations*; a tribute to an extraordinarily talented group of young men, rendered all the more poignant by the fact that only months later they would be separated by war. Howells gave the overture of *The B's* his own nickname: Bublum. Gurney's movement, a lament (in itself an interesting choice), was dubbed 'Bartholomew' as Gurney's middle name was Bertie. Arthur 'Blissy' had a brief scherzo; there was a mazurka alias minuet for 'Bunny'; and the final movement, an exuberant march, was 'Benjee', dedicated to the flamboyant Benjamin.

The dedicatee of the penultimate movement was a friend to whom Howells was particularly devoted. Francis Purcell Warren (affectionately known as 'Bunny') was a quiet boy, whose understated charm and modesty made him a great favourite. He was an exceptional violinist and violist and had just begun to compose. He had only a handful of songs to his name: a beautiful little suite of miniatures for cello, a piano caprice, the adagio of a cello sonata and a string quartet. When Bunny was killed on the Somme in 1916, Howells poured his grief into an elegy in his memory.[31] In the years preceding the war, however, there was little more to worry about than whether Stanford would approve of their latest compositional offerings. The friends shared their work and their leisure time, experiencing as much of London life as they could afford, visiting bookshops (a particular passion of Gurney's), accompanying each other to concerts, and vociferously sharing their opinions of the new works they were discovering.

Gurney's contemporaries found his combination of unpredictability, naivety and enthusiasm compelling, and many of the friendships he made at the College were to be lifelong. But the institution itself had not been designed to foster sociability. There were no communal spaces and no sports clubs. In 1905 the RCM Union had been founded as a central focus for students' social lives, and the *RCM Magazine* first appeared in the Christmas term of 1904, aimed at instilling a sense of identity and unity amongst the students. It would later be one of the first publications to print Gurney's poetry. Alongside negotiating lesson timetables and finding their way around the maze of stairs and corridors, signing up for the Union was one of the jobs for first years in Freshers' Week. Gurney duly did so, and was interviewed by a quietly spoken, genteel violinist in her thirties. Her name was Marion Scott.

Scott had first seen Gurney walking in the corridors, and, if not love, it was certainly fascination at first sight. He was a striking figure and instantly intrigued her.

FIG. 1.7: Marion Scott. © Gurney Trust.

The romantic terms in which she would later cast her first impressions of him are as revealing as the details she recalls:

> The boy was wearing a thick, dark blue Severn pilot's coat, more suggestive of an out-door life than the composition lesson with Sir Charles Stanford for which (by the manuscript tucked under his arm) he was clearly bound. But what struck me more was the look of latent force in him, the fine head with its profusion of light brown hair (not too well brushed!) and the eyes, behind their spectacles, were of the mixed colouring—in Gurney's case hazel, grey, green and agate—which Erasmus once said was regarded by the English as denoting genius.[32]

Scott lived a quiet, single life with her parents in their respectable Kensington home. This unpredictable and exciting young composer was to become the centre of her world. Her devotion to him was unswerving, and her practicality and generosity were to prove invaluable to him in the coming years.

Straitlaced, and with her parents' zealous passion for causes (the family were advocates for abstention), Scott took life rather seriously. With intelligent dark eyes and long hair wound in a bun, her appearance had something of a pre-Raphaelite quality. She was petite, dark and attractive, in many respects rather like the music teacher Margaret Hunt whom Gurney had left behind in Gloucester. Scott was intellectual and, like many academic women of her generation, had to create her own opportunities. She knew how to make things happen, how to work publicity for her own ends, and was driven by a strong sense of ambition and determination. She had studied composition alongside the violin at the College, and had been one of Stanford's first female pupils at a time when the College was so new it still smelt of fresh paint. She failed to make much impression as a professional violinist but became known as an editor and musicologist as well as an advocate for struggling female musicians. At the point at which she first met Gurney, Scott was becoming a well-known figure in the London musical world, and her musical journalism later became widely respected. Her true legacy, however, would lie in the work she did on behalf of Gurney as the curator and preserver of his manuscripts, and as his supporter and friend.

Her personal life was marked by disappointment. She devoted herself to the men she cared for, whether or not the relationship was physical, and found it hard to recover from her disappointment if they did not return her affections. Gurney was not the first scholarship composition student to whom she had become passionately attached. The composer Ernest Farrar, a reserved, gently spoken Yorkshireman, had until recently been her recital partner. It was a relationship based on practical music-making, but for her, it was a passion that went far beyond the love of music. When, in January 1911, Farrar told Scott the news of his engagement to another woman, he was bemused to find that she was mortified, and had resolved never to speak to him again. She succeeded, as after seven years of estrangement from Scott, he was killed almost as soon as he entered the trenches in 1918. It was in the spring of 1911, only a few months after Farrar's announcement of his engagement, that the lonely and embittered Scott encountered the new scholarship boy in the corridors of the College.

There were thirteen years between Gurney and Scott, but Gurney had already established his penchant for seeking out the friendship of older women with his devotion to the Hunt sisters, and Scott was an obvious successor to Margaret and Emily.[33] From his teenage years onwards Gurney was to crave sympathetic maternal figures, compensating perhaps for the inadequacies of his actual mother. The earliest surviving photographs of Gurney's mother Florence capture a young woman with an expression that suggests a sense of vision and optimism, despite the restrictions of artificial posed photographic portraiture. The mother Ivor knew bore little resemblance to these early images. As the years passed, Florence had grown into a severe and disillusioned woman, whose thin face was uncompromisingly unsmiling. Her husband David was far gentler in appearance, a genial Victorian

FIG. 1.8: Gurney's mother, Florence, c. 1915. Courtesy of Noel Hayward, from the photograph album belonging to Dorothy Gurney.

gentleman, 'properly' placed in the period's own social hierarchies, and with a slight resemblance to Edward Elgar. But Florence was not a woman who embraced life and all its challenges, and the larger her family grew, the more the demands overwhelmed her.

Florence thought of herself as superior to the Gurneys' working-class relatives, but the family had little money to show for it, and finances were a constant worry. The family was very isolated, but needlessly so. With a father who was one of seven, they were surrounded by local cousins, but Florence forbade Ivor and his siblings from fraternising with most of their relatives. Her intense sense of pride and snobbery made it unthinkable for her to associate with builders, who were further down the social ladder than tailors, and so the Gurney children were obliged to maintain a haughty distance. David was too dreamy and casual to be left in charge of money, so it was Florence who ran the business accounts. She managed to keep the family out of debt, but there was very little to spare. One Christmas, when finances were particularly critical, David tried to maintain some semblance of jollity by playing Father

Christmas and filling the children's stockings with a penny, an orange, a Brussels sprout, and a potato—the full extent of their presents that year—only to be attacked by his wife for his extravagance.[34]

As a child, Gurney was already aware of his mother's limitations, and her humourlessness and histrionics meant that she was a prime candidate for affectionate teasing. When at mealtimes he was about to be admonished for refusing to eat his food, he would anticipate her catchphrase in an exaggerated parody: 'Ah! There are *lots* of little boys in London who would only be too *glad* to eat it!' Winifred remembered that their mother would smile at this, in spite of herself. On other occasions, when Florence was too furious with the children to catch her breath to threaten and scold them, Gurney would pipe up on her behalf, slowly and deliberately and with the *h*'s well aspirated: 'I shall *hit* you on the *head* with a *hammer*', reducing his brothers and sisters to fits of laughter, and outraging his mother yet further.[35]

Gurney was a quick-witted, humorous and ebullient child, and he soon became conscious that he was a misfit in his emotionally restricted family. He loathed conflict and antagonism, and as he grew older he chose to absent himself at every opportunity rather than stay for an argument. He could not bear the tense atmosphere of repressed grievances that dominated the household. Whenever his father tried to intervene between Florence and her children, he exacerbated the situation, and Gurney realised that the only way for him to find any peace was to avoid the family as much as possible. When cornered, he would take up an armful of books and disappear, either into the hills or to the comforts of his godfather's library and the Hunt sisters' music room.[36]

His adult friends had been his refuge and support through his teenage years, and it was natural that when in London he would seek an equivalent to the Hunt sisters. He needed someone to lavish attention and adoration on him, and Scott was prepared to provide both in abundance. She made herself invaluable to Gurney, moulding her life around his. She became involved in his circle of friends at the College, and later befriended the Hunt sisters back in Gloucester. Her relationship with Howells was particularly intense, to the point of infatuation. She wrote to him pleading repeatedly for him to visit her, but her keenness was not reciprocated. However much she might have invested in her relationships with Howells and 'Benjee', it was Gurney who really needed her and to whom she would remain truly devoted.

She was less than impressed with the Fulham 'slums' where Gurney dwelt among the great unwashed.[37] But Gurney had grown up in dark, cramped rooms, and unlike Marion, he was no snob. He was able to find enough beauty in Fulham, taking evening walks around the neighbourhood when he needed a break from work. His flat was on a pleasant enough street; part of a row of Victorian terraced houses set in a tree-lined avenue. He was near the railway, but on the other side of the track were large fields, so even in the metropolis he had some sense of space. It reminded him of home; and in some respects was much like the townhouse he had left back in Gloucester, which overlooked a busy street, but with fields only a short cycle ride beyond, visible on the horizon. He would sit at his London desk, looking out at the shadowy shapes of the plane trees outside his window, and work late into the night at harmony and counterpoint exercises. There were moments when both he and Howells missed Gloucester with an intensity that was almost physical pain. When things got really bleak, Howells would go to Paddington station, not to travel, but only to watch the trains departing for the southwest, imagining them passing through the landscape he loved. He did not have enough money for a ticket.

This was a brave new world for the two provincial scholarship boys, and they were certainly not pining all the time. The London cityscape inspired Gurney in new ways. Initially he found that the stalls on the North End Road were a good term-time substitute for the bustle of Gloucester's market, 'Flaring with many a coloured stall / Of apples and oranges decked-out.'[38] But as the weeks in London passed, he became increasingly jaded. Then he would long for the serenity of the Gloucestershire countryside and imagine himself tramping the hard winter roads in deep morning frost, or sailing his little boat down the River Severn as the waves lapped at the rushes on the banks. Once home, he used his walks to develop the musical ideas he had had in London, planning big projects for the next term, and discussing them in animated conversation with Cheesman and the Hunts. He still relied on them for their friendship, but as the terms progressed, the distance between their amateur music-making and the standards to which he was now accustomed became more apparent. He was conscious he had begun to outgrow them, and by the end of the holidays he was restless to return to the College again.

Gurney was full of excitement at the musical possibilities London had to offer, and secure in the sympathetic and stimulating friendships he had made in his first few terms as a student. He had soon written a handful of songs. One of his very first offerings for Stanford was a setting of a text by Ethna Carbery called 'Song of Ciabhan', written in June 1911. Perhaps he thought he might appeal to Stanford's fiercely patriotic feelings for Ireland. There is no record of Stanford's reaction to any specific piece by Gurney, but he would have been churlish not to be impressed—the song was good enough for publication by Oxford University Press (although Gurney did not see it in print in his lifetime).[39] For his next ventures Gurney turned to the poet Robert Bridges, whom he had already begun to set to music in 1908. Now he composed 'I Praise the Tender Flower' and 'I Love All Beauteous Things' in June, alongside 'Fate' by Francis Brett Harte (written in the summer term of 1911 and revised in 1912).

He also continued to develop his instrumental writing. Taking Brahms's sonatas as his model (he joked that Brahms was the one person he would want to take as his date to a dinner party), he tentatively had high hopes for his own violin sonata in G.

'On second thoughts, perhaps my V.S. *won't* be better than the Brahms. But who knows what the third thoughts may be?'[40]

By any standards, Gurney had made a promising start. He had even begun work on a string quartet (in A minor) in January, and managed to complete it in June, but by the summer of 1912 he had to admit that some kind of illness was starting to affect his work and make 'all things gray'.[41] 'The Young Genius does not feel very well and His brain won't move as He wishes it to,' he wrote to Scott.[42] It was to be the first manifestation of a lifelong pattern of moods that swung between crippling depression to periods of manic energy. Gurney assumed that his symptoms were due to a digestive problem or overwork. If he did suspect something more sinister, he did not voice his concerns in any correspondence, but these were in fact the first signs of a condition that would eventually claim his sanity entirely. For now, he knew only that something was very wrong, and he could do no more than follow his doctor's orders and embark on a regime of exercise and recuperation. He affected a tongue-in-cheek, lighthearted tone when discussing his affliction. Although he must have been alarmed at his sudden incapacitation, a small part of him could also enjoy playing the role of the suffering genius and aligning himself with the tortured Romantic poets.

Gurney struggled on despite this first real taste of illness, and managed to finish his string quartet over the spring and summer terms of 1912.[43] Scott was keen to perform it with her all-female quartet that summer, but the premiere was not to happen until the winter of 1913, when it was played at a meeting of the Society of Women Musicians, as Scott was their chairwoman. Gurney's depression tainted everything, even his feelings about the piece, which had initially been a source of great pride. 'But oh, so sick of everything, and by no means looking forward to work. I will allow anyone to say anything against my Scherzo, my slow Movement even, which shows to what depths I have descended.'[44]

He might have been sick of work, but he was still as fiercely ambitious as ever. He had not yet written any vocal work larger than a song, but in 1912 he began to plan a cycle of operas, to be based on the short plays of W. B. Yeats. He was also entertaining the idea of a 'Riders to the Sea' opera based on J. M. Synge's play. Ralph Vaughan Williams was to work on his own operatic version of the same text in 1925 (it may be that it was Gurney who had suggested the subject matter to him). Gurney never wrote his projected operas; he soon realised, as Stanford would doubtless have pointed out to him, that multiple operas were rather too ambitious an undertaking for an undergraduate still learning his craft, and he sensibly turned his attention to more realistic projects.

Gurney had already established his natural inclination towards poetry as a source of musical inspiration, but now, for the first time, he began to write his own poetry as well as music. It is not possible to know exactly when Gurney moved from reading poetry to trying it himself, but in May 1912 he felt confident enough to send a poem, 'The Irish Sea', to the popular political weekly the *Eye Witness*, in the hope of seeing his name in print. He also posted a copy of the poem to Harvey for approval. It was a daring first attempt; the *Eye Witness* sold over 100,000 copies a week. It was its editor, the 'Georgian' poet Hilaire Belloc, who had attracted Gurney. Both Gurney and Harvey were great admirers of Belloc's verse, and his 1902 memoir *The Path to Rome* was one of Gurney's favourite books.

Gurney longed to write the 'oldest kind of song' (as Belloc put it) about the River Severn and his native Gloucestershire. His abilities as a composer were developing fast, but he had by no means found the technique to achieve it in poetry, if 'The Irish Sea' was anything to go by.

> The afterglow slid out of Heaven,
> Heavily arched the vault above,
> Then round my bows, and in my gleaming
> Wake, dim presences 'gan to move.
>
> My boat sailed softly all the night,
> Through wraiths and shapes of mystery,
> But dawn brought once again to sight
> The friendly and familiar sea.[45]

It is an attractive, musical little poem, but there is little hint of the idiosyncratic, deeply personal tone that would resonate through his later work. The examples of Harvey and Belloc imprint themselves on this rather conventional verse, with a simple rhyme scheme that offers only a little hint of the experimental, Hopkins-influenced half-rhymes he would later use (here Gurney rhymes 'Heaven' and 'gleaming'). 'Squareness' and order were hallmarks of the Georgian poets, whose first, hugely successful collective anthology *Georgian Poetry* had been published in 1912, just as Gurney was beginning to think about writing his own verse. He devoured their work, and with the added influence of Thomas Hardy's short, orderly stanzas, it was inevitable that his early poems would be structured in a similar manner to his role models. As Gurney began to formulate his views on art, he drew repeatedly on the image of the four-square to describe symmetry and beauty in music, poetry and architecture (the square tower of Gloucester's St Peter's Cathedral, under whose shadow he grew up, was to be a recurring image). Gurney considered squareness as a metaphor for good structure and balance rather than a limitation, but he had yet to develop the skill to find a freedom and originality of tone within the restrictions of form.

The manuscript version of 'The Irish Sea' bears a hopeful if sycophantic annotation: 'Hommage à Belloc' (Belloc was born in France). He paid a musical homage in the form of an unpublished song setting of Belloc's curious, swaggering poem 'Heretics All', written the same year (1912). It would have been a long shot for an unknown student poet to find immediate publication, and predictably perhaps, Belloc refused 'The Irish Sea' outright. It must have been expected, but still it was Gurney's first, tentative attempt at making an impression on the poetry world, and he had failed. His fragile mental health was in no state to cope with a rejection from his hero, and the episode resulted in a 'terrific attack of the blues.'[46] It was a major setback in Gurney's efforts to include himself among contemporary poets. The first of a series of rejections which were to feed into a lowered sense of 'faith' in himself, it marked the beginning of a slow road of attrition of self-confidence and belief.

Gurney began to write and compose at a time in which British poetry and music were unequally matched. The 'land without music', which had only begun to rectify its reputation at the turn of the century, was beginning to find its musical identity with the help of only a handful of leading lights—Vaughan Williams, Parry, Stanford, Elgar and Holst. Whilst they forged ahead, building on scant foundations and fighting to emerge from the shadow cast by the musical achievements on the continent, British poetry had been enjoying a golden age. Robert Browning, Matthew Arnold and Tennyson had died just before Gurney was born, marking the end of the old school of Victorian poets. The new generation were free to reject or take what they chose from their work. Hardy and Yeats still reigned supreme, and the Edwardians Henry Newbolt and Alfred Austin provided a short-lived interlude in which Empire and poetry met and mingled with memorable but sometimes rather unsavoury results. Of the younger generation of poets, Rupert Brooke was just beginning to establish his reputation, Edward Thomas was still writing journalism rather than poetry by 1912, and Robert Frost was still waiting impatiently for recognition. It was an exciting time to be a poet. Gurney had already established that his creative impulse was the celebration and creation of beauty, with the contours of the hills of Gloucestershire etched into his soul. Now, in London, he had begun to cast around for models for his own embryonic poetry and found that the refreshingly simple imagery and direct syntax of the new Georgian poets offered a near-perfect match for the voice he wanted to develop.

There would be five volumes of *Georgian Poetry* anthologies published between 1912 and 1922, showcasing the work of Rupert Brooke, W. H. Davies, John Drinkwater, W. W. Gibson and John Masefield, among others. Gurney's discovery of the Georgians was a moment of epiphany, his literary equivalent to hearing Vaughan Williams's *Fantasia on a Theme by Thomas Tallis* back in 1910. Over the coming years, Gurney was to enjoy friendships with the poets themselves, and expand upon their work in his own poetry, sharing their interest in reflecting the pastoral and the urban in simple language and resonant, vivid verse. As a composer, Gurney could relate to language in a manner that was inaccessible to other poets. He found the lyricism of the Georgians lent itself to song setting, and turned many of Gibson's, Masefield's and Brooke's poems into songs. This intense, creative engagement with others' work, interpreting it and inhabiting it from within, was perhaps the most fruitful way for Gurney to develop as a poet in his own right. He learnt to understand the rhythms of others' lines from within, developing and colouring them with musical nuance; augmenting and framing poems he admired by transmuting them into song.

To some writers and critics at the time, the Georgians were an anachronism, their style obsolete even as they wrote. But to Gurney they were gods. He had found his poetic soulmates, but by the winter of 1912, Gurney was still a long way from joining their ranks. His depression had entirely incapacitated him, and he was unable to write either poetry or music. Not even Scott's premiere of his quartet could revive him. There was one bright point in the wintry gloom, however; in February 1913 Vaughan Williams's *A Sea Symphony* received its first London performance, and Gurney, Benjamin, Scott and Howells all had tickets.

> I crawled out of bed to hear it, and afterwards went back for three days more— but it was worth it. A Third is Nonsense, but the other two thirds simply great.[47]

Three days at a time spent in bed was not sustainable during term time, and Gurney knew it could not continue. He managed to get himself out to Threadneedle Street in Piccadilly, to consult a Dr Harper. This was to be the first of a great many medical opinions on his condition, and it made a deep impression on him, largely because Dr Harper offered the advice he wanted to hear; he was to return to Gloucester to convalesce.

Recuperation above the shop with his impatient brother and neurotic mother was out of the question, so he arranged to stay as a self-catering guest in a cottage called The Lock House, by the junction of the Severn and the Stroudwater canal, at Framilode. It was owned by the lockkeeper, a marvellous old character called James Harris, whom Gurney adored.

> That dark face lit with bright bird-eyes, his stride
> Manner most friendly courteous, stubborn pride,
> I shall not forget, not yet his patience
> With me, unapt, though many a far league hence
> I'll travel for many a year, [. . .][48]

Gurney and Harvey had previously bought a leaky little boat from Harris for the princely sum of £5, and named it *The Dorothy*, after Gurney's sister.

> this most treacherous and fine sailing
> Vessel of mine, so leaky—but never failing . . . [49]

FIG. 1.9: Gurney's sisters: Dorothy, the dedicatee of the boat, and Winifred
(the older of the two). Courtesy of Noel Hayward, from the photograph album
belonging to Dorothy Gurney.

The vigour of sailing, coupled with the serenity and simplicity of life with the lock-keeper, was the perfect restorative combination. Gurney's days were spent looking out at the constantly changing water, watching the wildlife and the passing boats during the day, and sailing when his health allowed it. In the evenings, he accompanied Harris to the pub and listened to the conversation that was so far removed from the world of books and music he had temporarily left behind. Life there could hardly have been more different from the daily grind of London studies.

Almost as soon as he had arrived, his mood had brightened. Writing from his bed, he was soon exhorting Scott to come sailing with him. Scott was herself frequently ill, and Gurney was evangelical on the delights of simple country life as a cure for almost any ailment: 'I have been here a week. And oh! What a difference. And oh! Framilode on good behaviour! What you want is sailing, I am sure. And if you came here I would give it you.'[50] Scott did not take him up on the offer, but he did manage to persuade Margaret and Emily Hunt to go out on a daring expedition with him. He took them from Framilode to Bollo Pool and back, and was delighted to see that, whatever secret anxieties they harboured about putting their lives in the hands of someone who prided himself on his dangerous sailing, they showed no outward signs of fear.

In the years to come, Gurney would often use poetry as a medium to reflect in meticulous detail on key events that had taken place years before, writing verse as a form of journaling. His time on the riverside was to be the inspiration for two poems, both entitled 'The Lock Keeper', written between 1918 and 1922.[51] Either would have been a highly respectable addition to any *Georgian Poetry* anthology. The 1922 version is a long, uneven ramble of a poem (only Gurney can get away with using the word 'tentaculous' twice), but its peculiar quality lies in its power of evocation, its honesty and earnestness. The poem cannot be rushed; it captures in its lengthy unfolding the slow progress of the convalescent student, as he relearns the unhurried pace of rural living. The natural rhythm of life by the river is built into the ebb and flow of the verse:

> The lowering of the waters, the quick inflow,
> The trouble and the turmoil; characteristic row
> Of exits and of river entrances;

Finding beauty in the commonplace was a part of Gurney's nature. By 1918, when this poem was published, he had learnt to translate his instincts into verse.

Gurney had left London with ambivalent emotions, however relieved he was to be escaping. He longed for the peace of the Gloucestershire countryside, but he felt his retreat to be a sign of weakness and berated himself for his inability to cope with cosmopolitan life. 'Gloucester received me full of shame', he later remembered. He was looking to regain not only his health but his self-confidence:

> Boat sailing did save me I rushed life till self respect came, and the sweet
> air and blowing March tempest of Gloucester County
> gave me again first health;[52]

He resented the illness that had precipitated his stay, but quickly realised that the move to Gloucestershire was his salvation. He had pined for *The Dorothy*, and the exhilaration and freedom he felt when sailing her. He longed for 'such joy as to see sails quiver', 'seeing the cleaving water before prow scatter, and the moving surface so wonderful like bright floors.'[53] This was a freedom forbidden to him when in London. He had even gone to the docks at Rotherhithe to try to replicate his Severn sailing, and petitioned a boat owner to sell him a craft, but without the £20 required to buy the cheapest one, a *Dorothy* equivalent for the Thames was out of the question.

It was not just the river that was significant in Gurney's recovery. In his friendship with the lockkeeper James Harris, Gurney found an antidote to the rather negative influence of Stanford, the most dominant older man in his life at the time. Now Gurney could study the glorious secrets of ferret-keeping and the rhythms of the Severn instead of the rules of harmony and counterpoint. Both lockkeeper and composition teacher were experts in their respective fields, and Gurney admired their compendious knowledge, but the two pedagogues represented a fundamental strug-gle between the opposite poles that tormented him. He had somehow to reconcile his craving for a simple, outdoors life with the torturous 'book-poring' of the intel-lectual. He was stuck in a double bind. His artistry stemmed from a desire to express his love of nature, but in order to be able to write well of rivers and hillsides in music and verse, he was obliged to spend years studying his craft. This sojourn by the river was quite literally a breath of fresh air, but it could not last. Gurney longed for the lockkeeper's serenity and lifestyle, but he was always the observer, not the partici-pant. For now at least, his place was back in London, under Stanford's stern and un-forgiving gaze.

His student years ought to have been the starting point from which the rest of his career would be launched. For the generation who were able-bodied students in 1914, a straightforward career was to be out of the question. But Gurney's challenges were both personal and political. As he struggled to make relationships between two forms, and between his two identities as Gloucestershire lad and metropolitan intellectual, the war loomed as one of the most punishing obstacles ahead.

CHAPTER TWO

'A Waste of Spirit in an Expense of Shame'

It really does not do for one who so much desires freedom as
myself to think of the general conditions of the last few months [in training].
A waste of spirit in an expense of shame.[1]

Life as a music student is an isolated, unstructured affair, and composition is probably the loneliest way to make music. By the summer term of 1913 Gurney was once
more reluctantly back in his dark, shabby flat in Fulham, surrounded by piles of
manuscript paper, and with little to take his mind off his worryingly unstable behaviour. He knew he was different from his friends. He felt trapped within his own skin,
longing for their physical and mental freedom. For 'six weeks of almost complete
solitary confinement' he battled on, returning again to the words of Hilaire Belloc
with a setting of 'West Sussex Drinking Song', despite his knockback from the poet.[2]
He set one of Harvey's poems the day after receiving it: 'the result is excellent for its
purpose I think.'[3] Nevertheless, he knew he was still struggling, and was far from
working to capacity. He exhorted Marion Scott not to 'expect any immortal imaginings from me yet. I am a pricked bladder still. So that Strauss may lie quiet for a
while.'[4] By the summer holidays he was again in desperate need of a break and
planned 'two months of abstention from music' with another large dose of therapeutic boat sailing with Harvey, who was temporarily freed from law studies. He
wrote an enigmatic, pathetic little statement to Scott:

I'm glad
I've got to hate it.
Music, that is.[5]

Whilst Gurney was struggling to write at all, Howells was fast establishing himself as a prominent member of the College. Howells was to win no fewer than eight prizes in two years, including the Tagore Gold Medal, one of the College's most prestigious recognitions of excellence. Apparently, there was nothing at which he could not excel. The Director's History Prize went to Mr Herbert Howells with embarrassing regularity. He even seemed to be more readily associated with poetry than Gurney at this point, being asked to review a collection of the poems of Fritz Hart for the *RCM Magazine*. Howells was firmly set on his destined course for success and fame, whilst Gurney was already torn between his ambition and the illness that was seriously beginning to impede him. He felt he was a genuine talent awaiting recognition, with the capacity to write the masterpiece for which he would be remembered. But in order to write he had to fight the bouts of debilitating illness that he hardly yet understood. He sat staring at a blank page until he was sick at heart, his brain slow, his head heavy.[6] Having Howells as a constant yardstick against whom he could never quite measure up only made matters worse.

By the summer of 1913 writing music was proving too difficult and painful, and Gurney found solace in literature. Back in Gloucester, he wrote poetry, sending a piece of blank verse to Harvey for his thoughts ('You don't know what Portway was today—you don't know! I could only sing for joy, and cry in my heart with pure happiness.').[7] He immersed himself in the novels of Thomas Hardy. He had been unimpressed with *Jude the Obscure* and *Tess* ('Alec is not credible, neither is Clare; coincidence is wrested rather; it is in fact a flagrant piece of special pleading. But oh, Tess herself!').[8] But *The Dynasts* was in a different league—'colossally good!'[9] Something about the poetic drama spoke directly to him, and his enthusiasm for literature fed quickly into musical inspiration. Although he had nominally 'renounced' music, the two genres were already so interlinked that if one inspired him to creativity, the other often followed. He was particularly taken with a song from *The Dynasts*, 'The Night of Trafalgar', which he set to music in his head. By the end of September he had written it down, anxious to show it to Marion Scott. He could not abstain from composition for long. When literature did not spark ideas for songs, then the landscape would wring melodies from him, as he tramped through fields, or watched the green rushes of the Severn's banks slip past his boat. Before long he had ideas for a violin sonata in his head.[10]

That September it was Gloucester's turn to host the Three Choirs Festival.[11] Gurney's teachers past and present were all represented. The choir performed a rewritten and expanded version of Parry's *Te Deum*, Stanford's motet *Ye Holy Angels Bright*, and two new pieces by Brewer. But whilst Gurney was back in the familiar settings of the cathedral to listen to the rehearsals, his two closest college friends had 'eloped' in secret. Arthur Benjamin had whisked Howells off to ramble through the mountains in Switzerland. Not only was Gurney not invited, but he had not even been told about the trip. Benjamin's initial attraction to Howells had by now developed into something of an infatuation. The heterosexual Howells did not reciprocate with anything other than friendship, but he was fond of Benjee, and happy enough to accompany him abroad (Benjee was, of course, paying for the trip). Benjamin was practically hugging himself with glee as he wrote to Howells:

> But old chap, fancy going to Switzerland! Bloody nice! [. . .] Don't let Gurney know that I'm taking you abroad, because I don't want it to get round college that I took you. Do try and keep it quiet and tell your people not to say anything.[12]

He even went so far as to add a postscript that Howells should arrange to stay in London on their return, rather than go back to Gloucester (and by implication, to Gurney) before term started in late September. Gurney must have found out about the trip soon after, as Howells broke the silence by winning yet another prize, this time for his holiday essay, which coyly mentioned being accompanied by 'a friend'.

Gurney had never been abroad. He had undertaken a rather more modest holiday: ten days in Southwold with another Royal College colleague, the amiable and unassuming young organist Sydney Shimmin. He had come to visit Gurney and Howells in Gloucester, and to see the places Gurney had described to him with his trademark enthusiasm bordering on obsession—the villages of Crickley, Maisemore, Birdlip and Minsterworth. Gurney and Shimmin had then travelled to the Suffolk coast, where they stayed with two sisters, Jill and Daisy Levetus, who were friends of Marion Scott. The fashionable seaside resort had beautiful walks along the coast to the little rowing boat that ferried walkers to the flint-pebbled village of Walberswick, and the crumbling town of Dunwich was nearby, with the remains of its abbey clinging spectacularly to the top of the eroding cliffs. It wasn't exactly the Matterhorn, but it was at least a change of scene before term began.

A summer thinking about Hardy's Dynasts rekindled Gurney's own dreams of writing a large-scale poetic drama. He began to devise a Mussorgsky-like music-drama, taking Simon de Montfort, the controversial thirteenth-century Earl of Leicester, as his subject.[13] The project did not get very far, but the fact that he was beginning to think in large-scale dramatic terms is in itself revealing.

Gurney was introduced to opera for the first time at the College. In November 1913 the students staged Verdi's Falstaff at His Majesty's Theatre, as it was one of Stanford's favourite works.[14] Howells observed that Gurney's declamatory, dramatic ballad 'Edward, Edward' owed a debt to these early flirtations with opera, although

Gurney never actually turned any of his vastly ambitious plans for music-dramas into reality. But like Schubert, his idol, he came to understand that a miniature form could encompass high drama and emotion on an ambitious scale.

In fact, his keenness to identify himself with Schubert took a rather quirky turn whilst Gurney was at the College. Finding himself thrown from provincial obscurity into the company of the capital's musical elite, he was naturally drawn to question his own identity, and his place in this new world. This developed into a driving need to find out about his ancestry. Could he *really* only be the product of an undistinguished family of tailors and builders? The romantic allure of having been raised by the wrong parents or having a noble lineage somewhere in the background was tantalising for him.

When Gurney had presented himself for his interview at the College, the panel members were struck by his similarity to Schubert. They had perused his songs in advance and had already remarked on the Schubertian influence in his music. Even his handwriting bore an uncanny resemblance to the great man. When Gurney himself appeared in front of them, Parry took one look at his tousled hair and round spectacles and exclaimed, 'By God! it *is* Schubert!'[15] Now, determined to prove a link between himself and the greatest composer of song, Gurney took time off from the College to search in the public archives in Somerset House on The Strand in the hopes of tracing his ancestry.

His immediate family was undistinguished; his father David had been born in Maisemore, a quiet village close to Gloucester. Five of David's brothers went into the building trade and 'Gurney Bros' had become a well-known firm of builders in the area. His sixth brother was a waiter, and their mother had wanted David to have a different profession, so he trained as a tailor. It was through his work that David met his future wife and Gurney's mother, the seamstress Florence Lugg, who lived in the village of Bisley near Stroud and originated from a long line of Huguenot weavers.

It was Gurney's grandfather, however, who was something of a mystery. It was believed he had been the illegitimate child of Priscilla Gurney, the daughter of the wealthy and devoutely Quaker banking family who lived in Earlham Hall, a grand stately home near Norwich. Priscilla died within a year of his birth, but her baby son was taken by his aunt, the great prison reformer Elizabeth Fry (née Gurney), to Maisemore to be brought up by relatives. It is hard to corroborate. The identity of Gurney's great-grandfather was never discovered, but Gurney believed that Schubert had visited Earlham Hall on a trip to England, and Priscilla had subsequently visited him in Austria. Priscilla was born in 1785, undertook a lengthy trip to Nice, and then spent some months in Ireland; her tribulations and suffering there are frequently but enigmatically referred to. There is no evidence that she encountered Schubert, but she did die at the child-bearing age of thirty-six. In the 1850s a heavily edited version of her memoirs was published; it is almost defensive in its tone, proving re-petitively to the reader that her moral character was beyond reproach. If we are to take the work at its word, it appears she spent most of the time on her foreign trips handing out Bibles and preaching. If there was an illegitimate baby, the scandal was well concealed by the family. It is highly unlikely that there was any truth to the ru-mour, but the idea of being related to one of his heroes, particularly to the master of Lieder, was irresistible.

Gurney's debt to Schubert was certainly a musical one, even if the bloodline was perhaps a rather fanciful notion. In 1937, Howells wrote what has become the defin-ing commentary on Gurney's early music. He described:

> piano preludes thick with untamed chords; violin sonatas strewn with ecstatic crises . . . an essay for orchestra that strained a chaotic technique to breaking point.[16]

A critical reading of the early manuscripts of Gurney's songs shows no sign of the ecstatic crises or the untamed chords Howells thought he remembered. A setting of Robert Louis Stevenson's 'Song and Singer' would have been one of the bundle of manuscripts tucked under his arm as Gurney bounded up the stone stairs to his first lesson with Stanford. It was a setting he had made that January, only four months before he matriculated, and is entirely typical of his early songs. It bears no relation to the impression Howells gives of his work at this time. In fact, this is Gurney on his best behaviour with little hint of the quirky modulations or modal harmonies that were later to become his trademarks.

Gurney's early songs were well structured, conservative Edwardian drawing room pieces, which would not have caused his teacher so much as to raise an eye-brow. Neither does Howells's description apply to the songs Gurney was to publish from 1914 onwards. But this unchallenged critique is one of the bases for the as-sumption that there was something inherent about both Gurney's writing and per-sonality that would let him down. Howells had (perhaps inadvertently) established the narrative that Gurney was destroyed from the inside, and that a fatal flaw, a mole of nature, not only was already eating away at his mental stability but was present in his music from the very beginning. It is a compelling myth—the tragedy of a man whose mind and body rebel against his talent, and somehow take revenge on his art. It is dramatic—but it is not true.

As so little of Gurney's music is published to date, and none of the early manu-scripts, there is no reason this myth should have been questioned. Howells was there; surely he ought to know his friend's work. But there is no evidence in his music at the time to substantiate this limiting view of Gurney's trajectory. Howells made the comment in the year of Gurney's death, looking back in the knowledge of the mental disintegration of his final years. In the light of his friend's by then uncontained personality, Howells erroneously projected the traits of instability in his music back onto his earliest works, thereby condemning him to the category of 'flawed genius' from the start. In reality, these early songs are well crafted, eminently sane, and organised, and bear comparison with the very best of Howells's own work at the time.

By the spring term of 1914, the pattern of Gurney's moods had already become well established. He would begin a new term with enthusiasm, but quickly flounder, becoming overwhelmed by crippling depression. Within weeks he would be longing to escape from London. He knew he needed a way of stabilising himself, and of breaking the destructive cycle. Casting around for some form of framework with which he could structure his day and hold himself together, he hit on a book called *My System,* by the cult Danish exercise mogul J. P. Muller. Now forgotten, it was a popular book of physical 'jerks', advocating a regime to cleanse the body and hopefully, as a consequence, the mind.

My System was the Pilates of its time and became the equivalent of a self-help manual for Gurney. It built up core muscles in a series of exercises that were something between yoga and aerobics, but also concerned itself with the general well-being of the body. Muller recommended sleep, diet and fresh air; a rigid routine was essential. He had served with the Royal Engineers as a lieutenant (a title the civilian Gurney struggled to spell but was clearly impressed by), and his exercises were effectively a military training by book. Muller and his family stare out of photographs in the opening pages, ruddy with Danish wholesomeness and glowing health, and the first brisk chapters take no prisoners: 'Why be weakly?' the first demands. 'Illness is generally one's own fault', the second unsympathetically claims. By adhering to these exercises with such zeal, Gurney was already making steps towards a quasi-militarisation of his lifestyle, months before political events were to catch up with him.

The book offered more than an exercise regime. It appealed to Gurney's love of the Classical world by drawing on the Greeks as an ideal of physical and mental health, and featured a section addressing 'Literary and Scientific men and artists'. It was as if Muller were talking directly to Gurney:

> If the body is not looked after it will eventually rebel against the mind and prevent it from attaining its high goal. Many of the great composers and many poets died in their thirties. How many treasures of sound and how many valuable literary productions the world has lost simply because they took no thought for the health of their bodies![17]

Gurney was twenty-four; it was a sobering caution. With the help of Muller, he could cure himself for the good of music and literature.

The regime dominated the early months of 1914, and the optimism and purpose it gave him seemed to have a beneficial effect on his health. He was evangelical on the subject, recommending it to his Gloucestershire friend the solicitor and poet Jack Haines as being 'excellent all ways'.[18] He wrote to Harvey that 'the bloody indigestion is slowly quitting! 3 hours writing today!! Dawn of hope!!! May be well by Midsummer!!!! Do Mullers Exercises. Please do.'[19] Trapped in his office, Harvey might well have benefitted from the routine, but by August he would be in full-time training with the 1/5th Gloucestershire Regiment, and fifteen minutes of stretches would be replaced by twenty-mile route marches with a heavy pack to carry.

By early 1914, Gurney's mood had swung from miserable lethargy to an equally extreme state of exaltation; a sign of an inherent instability, perhaps, but it was a euphoria that was eminently justifiable. He had taken his Associateship Diploma of the Royal College of Organists in late January, and came second place out of the 184 students who entered. Only twenty passed at all. The exams were designed to show that the candidate had achieved a professional level of competency, assessing keyboard skills, general musicianship and composition. The exams were dominated by the presence of Bach, which was certainly no hardship as far as Gurney was concerned. Candidates had to complete Bach chorales, play some Bach, annotate a fugue, and even compose two pieces themselves, one of which should take a chorale prelude as a starting point. It is likely that Gurney's chorale prelude on the theme 'St Mary', written the previous October, had been composed in preparation. Gurney came to develop a lifelong appreciation of Bach as a craftsman, and his veneration influenced both his own music and his poetry. Only a student who has had to learn to write fugues and weave their own contrapuntal lines in the style of the master could go on to write 'Bach—Under Torment' in the early 1920s: a poem likening Bach to a hedge-layer, a craft involving intricate interweaving branches. To Gurney, Bach's works were living, breathing entities capable of emotion:[20]

> Lovely, brave, affectionate things they were,
> Strong handled and sure touched to their strong end,
> Protestant devoutness loved out all fear,
> Youthful remembrance to a grown man still friend.
> Artist of four strands, eight, with a hedger's deft
> Sure-moving purpose [...][21]

The principle of taming the natural and beautiful, of weaving together separate lines with skill to create structure and pattern was to become a central tenet of Gurney's music and poetry. He may have given Stanford the impression that he was ungovernable, but he had no intention of his work lacking craftsmanship or discipline.

Passing his ARCO had helped to boost his mood, and as his depression and indigestion had temporarily ceased to torment him, he could compose once more. The result was a set of songs that was of such quality that it alone would have been enough to make his name. Almost despite himself, Gurney seemed drawn to small-scale compositions. Howells was to go on to glory with his high-profile premieres of long works, but the degree of freshness and originality that Gurney could achieve in his miniatures was just as impressive, if less obviously glamorous. In 1914 the combination of his inspiring friends, the new music on offer in London, and his own technical development conspired to set all the pieces in place for what would be perhaps his greatest legacy. The 'Elizas' (as they were affectionately referred to by their composer) were a set of Elizabethan songs that would surpass all previous examples of English song and set the standard for the genre. They were an immense achievement for an undergraduate, chaotic or otherwise.

Over the Christmas holidays of 1913–14 Gurney had sketched out five songs with Elizabethan texts, probably worked out in the peaceful atmosphere of the Hunt sisters' music room, as he had dedicated them to Emmy Hunt. As soon as he returned to London, he wrote them up. *Five Elizabethan Songs*: a set for mezzo, two flutes, two clarinets, harp and two bassoons: 'Orpheus', 'Tears', 'Under the Greenwood Tree', 'Sleep' and 'Spring'.[22] The Elizas were a triumph, and he knew it. The accompanist Frederick Kiddle would later say of 'Sleep' that it could have been written 'by Brahms himself!'[23] But the triumph of Gurney's creation was equalled by the relief that he appeared finally to be winning the fight against his depression. His first instinct was to write to Harvey, who he knew would appreciate the magnitude of his achievement:

> It's going, Willy. It's going. Gradually the cloud passes, and Beauty is a present thing, not merely an abstraction poets feign to honour. Willy, Willy. I have done 5 of the most delightful and beautiful songs you ever cast your beaming eyes upon. They are all Elizabethan—the words—and blister my kidneys, bisurate my magnesia if the music is not as English, as joyful, as tender as any lyric of all that noble host. Technique all right, and as to word setting— models. [. . .] How did such an undigested clod as I make them?[24]

Every sentence of Gurney's letter speaks of his justifiable pride. Finally, against the odds, he had written something of which Stanford would have to take note; something to rival (perhaps even to beat?) Howells's many successes. Harvey did not wait until he was home to reply but tore a strip off some of the work on his desk at the solicitor's office to scribble congratulations to his friend.

The Elizas show how Gurney had learnt to set a poem in such a way that the text could breathe. The first song, 'Orpheus', has space built into the music, contrasting a bubbling configuration of semiquavers (suggesting the strings of a lute) with moments of stasis. This ability to create a breathing pattern for the song itself was something he would exploit further in 'By a Bierside' and 'Severn Meadows' two years later. Few songs achieve an inner pulse that is drawn from the exigencies of the text without the music itself becoming a second-class citizen; Howells's delicate 'King David' (1919) is an exception perhaps. The accompaniment Gurney creates for

'Orpheus' is muscular when required, but its primary purpose is to paint a picture deftly around the text. It demonstrates what was to be one of Gurney's defining musical characteristics: a preference for first inversion chords that, rarely lingering on the tonic, create a sense of airy rootlessness (singularly appropriate from a composer who was so often 'rootless', and continually sought the security of locating himself in time and place).

The second song of the set, 'Tears', has the same space around the text and sensitivity of accompaniment as 'Orpheus', but it has an Elgarian sweep to it. The bass is firmly present for the first five bars as a pedal note, suggesting something of the depth and mournfulness of a tolling bell. In the repeated pattern of Brahmsian parallel sixths that descend, weeping, in the right hand of the piano, Gurney has achieved absolute unity of intention and utterance, a quality that was to become another of his chief strengths.

The gravity of 'Tears' is swept away by the cheeky syncopations of 'Under the Greenwood Tree', with its faux-Tudor dance elements. But it is 'Sleep', Gurney's most enduringly famous song, that holds the listener spellbound. It is a cri de coeur, a profound expression of longing, written with the weight of the knowledge of what it meant to yearn for an escape from suffering. The set ends with a burst of sunshine, to alleviate the profundity of the gloom of 'Sleep'. Gurney had experienced despair, but he was also equally familiar with the joys of 'Spring'—both season and song. His setting of the poem is prefaced by these quotes:

> 'Cuckoo, he cries, and fills my soul
> With all that's rich and beautiful'
> (W. H. Davies)

> 'In Spring the cuckoo shall
> Alter his interval'
> (Mrs. Meynell).[25]

In playful and boisterous mood he wrote a spoof review from the 'Daily Tootler' on the manuscript of the full score of 'Spring':

> Beethoven was the first to tune his drums to an octave. Gurney was the first to alter the cuckoo's interval to such an extent. It is probable that no cuckoo could perform this feat without internal rupture.

Nineteen fourteen was to be Gurney's year. It was also the year in which his generation would be disrupted, and in great measure destroyed. By the time Gavrilo Princip fired two fatal shots in Sarajevo that June, Gurney had written a number of the songs for which he would be remembered. He felt that he was closer than he had ever yet been to establishing a permanent place in the history of English music, despite his recent battles with his health.

Alongside his composition, he was consciously training up his body and mind. He was studying contemporary poetry, and even advising Harvey on what to read: 'Remember—Daily Telegraph on Wed and Fri, and Academy every week, and Bookman every month.'[26] His poetic career had not yet begun in earnest, but he was preparing his mind for his next step towards his development as a poet, just as he was beginning to realise he had attained a degree of mastery over notes.

Free from the College for the summer holidays, he and Harvey wandered through the fields of Gloucestershire, seemingly oblivious to the heightening political tension in Europe. It was a golden time, and one to which he would return in many of his letters throughout the war.

> My thoughts of England are first and foremost of the line of Cotswold ending with Bredon Hill, near Tewkesbury, and seen with him. Or the blue Malverns seen at a queer angle, from the hayfield, talking when War seemed imminent, and the whole air seemed charged with fateful beauty.[27]

The first few days of the war were memorable for Gurney, but not for their political significance. On the second day there was a particularly beautiful sunset:

> one most magical afterglow at Framilode when I was alone; and the evening before I rode in late to find England had declared war. Great billowy clouds hung over distant Malvern, and the poplars, black against the glowing West, sang music unto me, which someday I may fit myself to sing to others.[28]

It was a prophetic image. Just as the clouds seemed to be lifting for Gurney, storm clouds had burst over Europe.

This 'charged' and 'fateful' beauty found its way into his music. At some point in 1914 he wrote a turbulent setting of W. H. Davies's 'Dreams of the Sea', which combined the compelling beauty of nature with the darkness of the times. He created a piano part that rolled like breakers, and a ghastly middle section in which the singer contemplates the body of a drowned boy, but still cannot relinquish his obsession with the sea, despite its barbarity.[29] The inexorable pull of Gurney's deadly sea resembles Arthur Bliss's experience of the outbreak of the war: 'The crash of a European war on our very beaches sucked me into its undertow without my ever probing the consequences.'[30]

From that summer onwards, men of Gurney's age were bombarded with propaganda to encourage them to sign up for the armed services. It was an institution for which Gurney had no real passion. Eight years later, he remembered the moment he decided to enlist:

> Though some reluctant were to the first going—
> and to answer the all imperative

Call of honour, being bound as few were to a service
Asking devotion, dawn to dawn, love and pain's sacrifice—
The young makers went, and I myself—shamed on
        such terms to remain safe or alive.[31]

Gurney was not belligerent by nature; neither did he 'respond to the call' out of patriotic fervour. He *was* patriotic, but his relationship to his country was not reducible to the slogans of recruitment campaigns; it was a complex, deeply personal relationship, and the inspiration for many of his most sophisticated poems.[32] As he was to write after months in the trenches,

If it were not for England, who would bear
This heavy servitude one moment more?[33]

As his sister Winifred rather wryly observed, 'IG would have been alright in the army, it would have been good for him, had he not had to go to war.'[34] He knew this to be true. The structure of life in the army offered something to which Gurney instinctively responded. Some of the burden of autonomy that he found so crushing as a student was alleviated by a system in which thinking for oneself was actively discouraged. It was not a difficult decision. He had gone to the local recruiting station to enlist as soon as war was declared, knowing that by joining the army in Gloucester and not in London, he would be put with a Gloucestershire regiment. He hoped to be given a place in the 1/5th Gloucesters along with Harvey, who was already in training at Chelmsford, but it was not to be. The medical officer rejected him because of his poor eyesight. This was a stage of the war when the army could still afford to be particular about its recruits. By 1915, they would not be so picky, and Gurney would pass muster, glasses and all. For now, he had to return rather ignominiously to the College, whilst Harvey prepared for war.

Of the students who had left for the summer holidays in July, those who did return found London life changed almost beyond recognition. Of Gurney's friends and fellow students, 'Bunny' Warren, Arthur Bliss and Arthur Benjamin had all enlisted. Sydney Shimmin joined the Royal Army Medical Corps in 1915. Howells was saved, rather ironically, by serious ill health. The College's student population was dramatically reduced, and Parry faced the painful task of addressing a depleted, female-dominated student body at the start of the autumn term.

One thing which concerns us deeply is that quite a lot of our happy family party have been honourably inspired to go and chance the risks of a military life; and among them are some very distinguished musicians.

We feel a thrill of regard for them. . . . But then we must also face the facts with open minds. The College in relation to war is in a different position from other educational institutions. Our pupils are made of different stuff from the pupils of ordinary schools. They are gifted in a rare and special way. Some of them are so gifted that their loss could hardly be made good.[35]

This deeply felt, fatherly speech had its grounds in a very real fear, soon to be realised, that some of the best musicians would be killed. However, the assumption that students could be divided up between dispensable and indispensable is difficult to stomach. Was Gurney's departure a loss that 'could hardly be made good'? Apart from the Elizas, he could count his musical successes on the fingers of one hand.[36]

One benefit Gurney had missed out on by being rejected for military service was a regular salary. He had not written enough songs to make any money from his composition, and his allowance was meagre, to say the least. He managed to obtain a post as an organist at Christ Church, a rather undistinguished red brick church in High Wycombe, a short train journey from London. Gurney spent his weekends there, and whilst the money for playing for services was useful, it was the friendship of the church warden Edward Chapman and his beneficent wife Matilda (to be renamed 'La Comtesse' by Gurney) that was to prove of far more enduring value. He lunched with them regularly after the service, and had soon established a routine of ping-pong, cricket and general romping and gallivanting with their children: Kitty (Catherine), Winnie (Winifred), Arthur and Micky (Marjorie). In fact, Gurney found their company so congenial that he impetuously proposed marriage to Kitty, who was only seventeen. The matter went no further and was handled graciously enough that he could continue his friendship with the family. No doubt there was a genuine attraction, but it was the action of an unsettled and impulsive man, seeking a stability that eluded him.

Gurney reluctantly stuck it out for the autumn term at the College, but he still believed that the army was the only real course of action for him. Remaining a student when he was able-bodied and by nature an outdoors, adventurous type seemed impossible, and his thoughts turned enviously to Harvey in training. When he returned home for Christmas, he tried his luck at the recruiting office again. By 9 February 2015 he could proudly report that his new identity was Private no. 3895, of the 2/5ths: the 2nd Reserve Regiment of the 5th Battalion of Gloucesters.

He would not be with Harvey, who was in the 1/5th Gloucesters. The 1/5ths were a fighting division and only needed one thousand men. Many of these had already been Regular Army members when the war broke out.[37] Almost as soon as recruitment began, the battalion was complete, and as the hundreds of surplus new volunteers needed to be placed somewhere, the 2/5th was hastily created to absorb them. Its purpose would be to 'fill up gaps, and generally stop up holes' in the 1/5th.[38] Thus Gurney was assigned to an untried and untested reserve battalion that was made up of spare parts. The 2/5ths absorbed anyone wounded in training, and any new recruits not physically fit enough to be considered for the 1/5th, which,

FIG. 2.1: Gurney in uniform, 1915. © Gurney Trust.

FIG. 2.2: Gurney with the 2/5ths in an official photograph. © Gurney Trust.

boasting half the Gloucester rugby team and the UK captain of rugby, had had the pick of the crop.

> About one-third were mere lads, 17 years of age, and what grit they had—they wore ammunition, boots, belt and bayonet, pouches across the chest, great-coat rolled high up on the shoulders, and carried a rifle, which when the bayonet was fixed was as tall as themselves. From Marlow to Chelmsford not one of them fell out—they used to say that if they did 'they won't take us with them when they go'.[39]

Gurney's education qualified him for officer status, but he felt more at ease with privates than with the officer class and had no desire for promotion. He found himself surrounded by a wonderfully eclectic range of characters: bakers, drapers, conjurers, butchers, sugar magnates, farm labourers and artisans of every sort. It was an impressively diverse mix, both musically as well as socially:

> The less that is said of our musical taste the better; but in full chestedness and knowledge of ragtime etc we excel. [. . .] And our talk is rough, a dialect telling of days in the open air and no books.[40]

At the other end of the social scale was the commanding officer, Lieutenant-Colonel The Honourable A. B. Bathurst (affectionately known as 'Benny'), who in peacetime was an MP in the good old tradition of local squires, and who had formerly commanded the 5th Battalion. The Bathursts were well beyond Gurney's social milieu, but he did have an indirect connection to them through Howells, as the family had funded his studies with Brewer at the cathedral. Gurney seemed impressed enough with the senior ranks, particularly as they could boast some sporting prowess: 'Our Captain is Sewell of some note as a cricketer; S. African and Gloucestershire.'[41]

As soon as he was in uniform and waiting to start his training, Gurney began casting around for literary role models; writers whose voice he could adopt, or whose work he might build on to express his emotions. He turned once more to his copy of *Georgian Poetry*, hit upon John Masefield as a model, and wrote to Harvey:

> Tonight I have been reading the *Georgian Poetry Book*, and it is this that has made me write to you. Our young poets think very much as we, or rather as we shall when body and mind are tranquil. Masefield's feeling of beauty and its meaning strike chords very responsive in ourselves. I found myself remembering old things, old times together as I read 'Biography', and it brought you very near.[42]

Masefield, twelve years Gurney's senior, had much in common with Gurney. He too had suffered a largely unhappy childhood and had had a chequered start to his career. Both were also avid readers. Rather to Gurney's envy, Masefield had gone to sea, in part to cure himself of his voracious reading. The only poem of his that featured in the first *Georgian Poetry* anthology is the lengthy 'Biography', a musing on the poet's own life. It is similar in structure, length and tone to the many autobiographical poems and letters Gurney would later write himself.

> I have known golden instants and bright days;
> The day on which, beneath an arching sail,
> I saw the Cordilleras and gave hail;
> The summer day on which in heart's delight
> I saw the Swansea Mumbles bursting white,
> The glittering day when all the waves wore flags
> And the ship Wanderer came with sails in rags; [. . .][43]

Gurney had come to this poem at a seminal moment, on the brink both of war and of discovering his own poetic identity. Masefield learnt much of his craft as poet whilst at sea. Gurney, learning to become a poet whilst soldiering, would have related to this unconventional training. Masefield described making sense of one's life through the act of writing. 'Biography' described wandering through London, learning from nature and through suffering, and coming to understand a sense of history through landscape. Masefield asked the questions that were uppermost in Gurney's thoughts, poised between the world of the civilian and the soldier; aware of his own mortality, and of the legacy he was leaving.

Even as he was beginning his career in the infantry, Gurney was yearning for the sea. There seems to have been a brief moment in February 1915 when enlisting in the navy was a possibility, although there is no record of why he did not ultimately make this choice:

> The Sea, the Sea will be my home for a while, and the hard friendly life of that wrestle with that most untameable, unknowable element of God.[44]

He had loved his brief time as organist at the tiny Mariners' Chapel on the docks in Gloucester, where the organ sounds mingled with the cries of seagulls outside and the rhythmic slapping of rigging against wood. It was a miniature haven of peace amidst the bustle, surrounded by the masts of the tall ships, and with its own unique and ever-changing multinational congregation; a heady mix for a young and romantically inclined musician.

Gurney's military service was part of his Masefield-inspired master plan. Rather than struggle on at the College, he would learn from practical experience, tire out his body, and be a wanderer and adventurer. The result would be both great art and eventual recognition.

Harvey and the 1/5ths had only just vacated the training camp at Danbury near Chelmsford when the 2/5ths arrived in April 1915. The camp consisted of a number

FIG. 2.3: Some of the 2/5ths outside the bell tents (Gurney is standing second from the right).

of large white bell tents, with around fourteen men in each tent, which was more than they could comfortably hold.[45] The tents were poor-quality affairs and freely let in the elements. Larger rectangular marquees housed the messes, but they were far too cramped, and dinner was often eaten squatting in the field.[46] Those who were lucky were billeted in the village hall, or in one of the nearby farms or houses. Gurney had often chosen to sleep rough when on long nocturnal rambles, but for the more conventional among the recruits, conditions must have come as a shock. There was more opportunity for comfortable living than there would be in France, however. For those who could afford it, local restaurants could provide an alternative to the mess.[47] There was also a much beloved and frequented pub, and a library, which Gurney eagerly singled out. At one point he found himself billeted in a bric-a-brac shop, along with a member of the 1/5ths who was still on leave in the area. Gurney was eager to glean any news of Harvey and found that the soldier did indeed know him. He reported that Harvey was a most personable character, but that he had a disconcerting habit of using long words that 'flummoxed' him. Gurney reported the comment to Harvey with some mirth.

Gurney's days were filled with outpost training, route marches, sham fighting, lectures and rifle drill.[48] One of the first basic skills a formation of recruits could learn was how to achieve neat left and right turns. Then they could progress to foot and rifle drill; it was tedious enough for the newcomers, but doubly so for those who had transferred from the 1/5ths and were going over old ground. Soon the new

FIG. 2.4: Gurney (see arrow) in a somewhat staged bayonet practise.
© Soldiers of Gloucestershire Museum.

recruits were ready to begin bayonet practise, which Gurney quickly found to be both stultifying and exhausting. Attempting to muster some semblance of hatred for a sack, he was repeatedly required to 'dash up and jab a bag of straw'.[49]

Uniform was issued, usually after training had begun, and the first parade in full kit bore greater resemblance to a scarecrow parade or fancy-dress ball than an impressive fighting unit. After their first motley appearance, the men then swapped clothing between them until they had something approximating the correct sizes in caps, boots and tunics.[50] They were also issued with their khaki webbing, designed to hold up to fifty or sixty rounds of ammunition, which was a considerable weight. As soon as kit had been issued, the endless rounds of inspections began, and Gurney quickly realised that brass button polishing was never going to be his strong point.

Locals did their best for the new soldiers. There was an improvised 'Soldier's Hall' where volunteers served coffee and buns at an affordable price and put on almost nightly concerts for the men. Whatever the standard of the performers, their shows were a welcome break in the routine.

Training was tough, but Gurney had not been at it long enough to be worn down by the monotony of the life. He was disgusted by the 'grey neurasthenic' weather, and cursed Essex and its miserable, colourless skies. He even wrote a little doggerel verse berating the place for the amusement of Harvey, in which he suggested Essex ought to be sent West to learn how to be a 'proper' county. Fundamentally he was in stoic mood, ready to embrace his new life, and make the best of it:

I am well; in the sense that I am able to hang on in everything they have done as yet, but in the sense of feeling well there is improvement but nothing else. But fatigue from the body brings rest to the soul—not so mental fatigue.

Gurney was heartily proud of his battalion, and even tried out some soldierly fighting talk:

Do you know that the Glosters have the second best roll of battle honours in the British Army? So it is. And though we are a rough lot in some ways, (and the Bosches will discover some of them,) we have no end of a good domestic reputation, so to speak.[51]

Brief interludes in the routine included a week or so on anti-aircraft picket, camping out in Galley Wood, a mile from the official camp. Their instructions were to watch for zeppelins from dusk to early morning, with only an hour guard duty each, so there was plenty of time to relax in the surrounding woodland and enjoy the spring sunshine. The job was entirely futile, but Gurney could lie in the opening to his tent and admire the sunsets and sunrises as he stared into the sky through binoculars.[52]

In early May Gurney was made a signaller. It was a controversial move; signallers were often referred to as the 'suicide club' by those who had seen them in action in France. Harvey had tried to warn him that it was a particularly dangerous specialism, but either Gurney had not listened or it may not have been his decision. Training for signallers was at least marginally more interesting than the standard training. Gurney began with flags, learning through repetitious drills how to signal the alphabet. This surprisingly tiring exercise resulted in a great deal of arm ache. Morse code was next and involved less physical exertion. After three weeks the fledgling signallers were given a buzzer test, being expected to be able to read at a speed of thirty letters or six words per minute. Then there was a telephony course, which lasted around a fortnight, and Gurney was sent on route marches to learn how to lay cables, hanging them from trees, and suspending them from poles when roads needed to be crossed. It gave him little sense of the difficulties signallers actually faced in maintaining these primitive communications at the front. Shells easily cut through a wire, and signallers were obliged to expose themselves above the parapet to make the repairs.

In June, just as Gurney was beginning to become heartily sick of the training camp, the 2/5ths were sent to Epping Forest for two months. It was fortuitous timing—he had been due to be confined to barracks for having a dirty rifle on parade, and the punishment was forgotten in the move. The 2/5ths were to help in the creation of a huge trench system circling the periphery of London. This was being dug by soldiers who happened to be training in the area, as a defence against German invasion. It was hardly any more exciting than Chelmsford, but at the very least it was something new. Digging, combined with drills, marches and mock attacks, was extremely arduous, and Gurney developed lumbago.

Stanford wrote Gurney a letter in June, which was much appreciated, despite handwriting that bore more resemblance to hieroglyphs than letters. Beneath the gruff exterior Stanford was a kindly man, and he was concerned about his pupil. So was Parry. 'The thought of so many very gifted boys being in danger, such as Gurney and Fox and Benjamin and even Vaughan Williams, is always present with me [. . .] Gurney's case I feel to be quite a special martyrdom. His mind is so full of thoughts and feeling far removed from crude barbarities that it seems almost monstrous.'[53]

Gurney had eschewed all music-writing for the time being, but he still kept close links to the Royal College of Music. Scott acted as a regular source of College news and made sure that Gurney was not forgotten by the College during his absence. Howells did his bit, and performed Gurney's songs there on at least two occasions.[54] The first, in early April 1915, caused Gurney to write to his friend in consternation: 'Well, if you and Miss Higgs could make out "I Praise the Tender Flower" to CHH P[arry]'s satisfaction, you are very deserving of praise—I did not mean that to be sung; there were corners to be rounded off, too. But still, if "Edward" went well, I am content.'[55] The song was finished in 1911, but he had intended to revise it before it was performed. No one had consulted him. A year later, he was equally frustrated by the circumstances in which 'The Twa Corbies' was heard at the College. It was clearly a song intended for a male voice, but, again, Gurney wasn't consulted, and as men were scarce, it was performed by a woman.[56] This time Gurney was incandescent with rage. 'But of course, "The Twa Corbies" is a man's song, if there were any left to sing it, and that's all the comment Sir CHHP will get when I write.'[57]

Gurney hoped that it would not be long before he was fit enough in body and mind to begin composing again, with a view to returning to the College a more mature and stable student after the war. By the middle of June 1915 he optimistically observed that his military 'cure' seemed to be working:

> health is still slowly improving; and as my mind clears, and as the need for self-expression grows less weak; the thought of leaving all I have to say unsaid, makes me cold.[58]

Gurney's phraseology is revealing: he articulates his 'need for self-expression' as if it were his pulse. The more robust his health, the greater the drive to create. Writing and good mental and physical health are synonymous.

The Epping camp began to pack up at the start of August, and the men of the 2/5ths started to feel that their involvement in the war might finally be getting closer. Gurney had been inoculated against typhoid in June whilst still at Chelmsford, an indication that they were shortly to be off for the 'real thing'. There were other soldiers in Epping working on parts of the trench, many of whom had been to the front already and were retraining prior to being sent back. Gurney became used to hearing them talking about 'real' trench experience. As the 2/5ths watched other regiments move off to overseas action, they waited expectantly to be told it was their turn. They had cheered off one hundred reinforcements on 28 June, shortly followed by another departing wave. 'And so the Brigade gradually dribbles out to the Front.'[59]

Gurney had found the send-off overwhelming, and turned to music to find the analogy with which to do justice to the experience:

> The cheering was immense, overwhelming, cataractic [*sic*]. The only things that can give you an idea of that sound are either elemental sounds like the war of winds and waves or the greatest moment in music—the end of the development in the 1st movement of the Choral Symphony. Like the creative word of God.[60]

It was to be the first of many moments of high emotion during his war service: of terror, misery, desperation and elation, and already he was finding himself drawn naturally towards a combination of music, natural imagery and poetic language to express himself. It would be a short step indeed to work such a memory into a poem, or song.

As the camp was being disassembled around him, Gurney found himself with time and inspiration enough to begin to write his first 'war' poems. On 3 August he sent Scott his sonnet 'To the Poet before Battle'.

> Now, Youth, the hour of thy dread passion comes;
> Thy lovely things must all be laid away,
> And thou, as others, must face the riven day
> Unstirred by the tattle and rattle of rolling drums
> Or bugle's strident cry. When mere noise numbs
> The sense of being, the fearsick soul doth sway,
> Remember thy great craft's honour, that they may say
> Nothing in shame of Poets. Then the crumbs
> Of praise the little versemen joyed to take
> Shall be forgotten; then they must know we are,
> For all our skill in words, equal in might
> And strong in mettle, as those we honoured. Make
> The name of Poet terrible in just War;
> And like a crown of honour upon the fight.

At the start of his time in Epping, Gurney had been impressed by Rupert Brooke's sonnet 'Peace'. It begins, 'Now, God be thanked that has matched us with this hour', and Gurney's first attempt at a sonnet clearly owes a debt to Brooke's example. Brooke had died only two months before, on 23 April 1915, aboard a troop ship on his way to the Dardanelles. Gurney believed that he too was most likely to be destined for the Aegean, following the tracks of the poet whom he believed had written the only enduring work to come out of the war so far. Brooke had been mythologised as a poet-hero, positioned in a tradition stretching back to Homer of lyrical warriors whose names were 'terrible' in war. How tempting it would be for Gurney, brought up on the classics as a schoolboy, to attempt to join their ranks, in verse at least, imagining himself as part of a superrace, 'equal in might / And strong in mettle, as those we honoured.'

> It is curious how little great youthful-seeming poetry has been written; and sonnets seem especially fated to be the work of 'solemn whiskered men, pillars of the state'.[61]

Brooke's friend the poet Harold Monro believed that 'A long war would reduce most writers to a condition of elementary candour; there would be so much to express that the tricks and affectations of the past few years would seem as useless as tattered clothes.'[62] Gurney was already heartily sick of the mindless and exhausting routine, the terrible food, and the weather. Had he written about what he knew, his first sonnet might have made more of an impression. As it was, this early attempt has a ring of youthful authenticity about it, but none of the clarity and searing honesty that would become his hallmark. The war poetry Gurney was emulating was, at this early stage of the conflict, still largely self-conscious. It was too much steeped in the 'tricks and affectations' that Monro notes. As a result, Gurney turned to an archaic, overblown language more redolent of Shakespeare's Agincourt than of a twentieth-century soldier about to enter the trenches.

Gurney was aware of the sonnets with which his work might invite comparison: 'Wordsworth is too much of the master to read and allow confidence overmuch in oneself.' On the one hand he was coy about his achievement—'oh bashfulness and blushes!'—but on the other, would think nothing of putting himself up for comparison with the great masters.[63] Gurney's split self-regard was to remain complex, and hard to pin down. He often vacillated between blushing and bragging, using his correspondence to strike different poses, playing disingenuously at confidence (but with a degree of genuine and justifiable self-belief underlying it), or giving an exaggerated, pantomime performance of modesty, with a very real sense of self-doubt at its core.

His principal means of absorbing contemporary writing was the newspapers. Scott forwarded him the *Times Literary Supplement* (published separately from 1915 as a periodical in its own right, and diligently supplied by Scott throughout the war). The *Daily Chronicle*, for which Edward Thomas was writing, was another excellent source of snippets of contemporary poetry, and served to cement his lifelong veneration of Thomas's work.

In the same letter in which Gurney sent Scott 'To the Poet before Battle', he also praised Harvey's new poem, the mischievous 'Ballade of Beelzebub'. It seems that, in part at least, the spur to begin to write was an unstated competitive subtext; if Harvey could rattle off verse with such apparent ease, then could not Gurney also write? Harvey's 'Ballade' had been published in the Gloucesters' trench paper, the *Fifth Gloster Gazette*: 'Have I not right to be proud of him? Is it not gorgeously *meaty*?' Gurney gloated.[64] The poem was a rather neat little tongue-in-cheek piece of humorous verse cursing the devil as the 'God of Flies', which were his personal bête noire of trench life.[65]

The whisperings of Gurney's own move to the trenches turned out, for the time being, to be a false alarm. The 2/5ths were in fact heading back to the old Chelmsford camp for yet more months of 'stunting around', as Gurney put it with a note of disgust. But even as they returned to their depressingly familiar haunts, there was still a sense that this was only a preliminary stay before France.

> Well, we have practically finished our Training; have been inspected and are to hold ourselves ready to move. There have been rumours of India, but the wording of the announcement makes that very unlikely, though sweet to my mind. If I am to leave earth shortly, a trip to India would make no bad preliminary.[66]

It was frustrating to return to camp, but it did guarantee time to write in safety. 'To the Poet before Battle' had given him enough of a sense of achievement to want to carry on, and throughout September Scott received a steady trickle of poems from him. Gurney had often found that he could write songs quickly, and that they cost him comparatively little effort, whereas longer works were far more of a grind. Now, as he embraced his new identity as poet, he found to his delight that he had hit upon a yet more fluid and fluent outlet for his creativity. The poetry flowed '(as R.L.S. [Robert Louis Stevenson] said) like buttermilk from a jug.'[67]

Soon the poetic buttermilk was flowing in earnest, with 'Satan above the Battle', 'Afterwards' and 'A Ballad of the Cotswolds'. 'Satan above the Battle' sets out a view of war that depicts a titanic struggle, observed from a height. Gurney presents war as a battle between Satan and God, the rather distancing archaic language made more immediate by the righteous anger that fuels it. There are overtones of Thomas Hardy here (we might think of the darkly whimsical 'Channel Firing', for instance, in which the dead are mistakenly awoken for judgement day by the gunfire over the channel). But Hardy has mastered the touch of humanity, humour and intimacy that makes his poem so darkly ironical. Gurney was at the early stages of experimentation, trying too earnestly to emulate his poetic heroes, and failing to find himself in the process.

Satan above the Battle

Think you that he who made the skies was ever
Able before to make a scene accurst
As this one? Nay; now God hath done his worst,
His keenest spite hath poured on Man's endeavour
To live and dream—like Him! Nor would he sever
His countenancing help from Man, nor burst
That bubble of Love, till those, his creatures, had first
Near equalled Him in might. O clever! Clever!
But, Son of God, and Man, what think you of this?
What is your Passion worth? Three days in Hell
Under protection. Poverty. Judas' kiss?
(O Sentiment!) Or can it be you came
Too soon? These taunting triumphs of Science . . . ! Well,
That's all; but were I you I'd burn with shame.[68]

He had been trying to memorise the beginning of Milton's *Paradise Lost* in August, so the theme was fresh in his mind. Projecting a source of trauma onto a large-scale scene was a trope to which Gurney was to return in the 1920s, when his writing would depict his own suffering through a hyperbolic stage set of God and man. He would evoke vague images of black tides of evil and unspecified torture, drawing on Old Testament Hebrew, 'belial', to describe his tormentors as wicked and worthless. But this was still to come. Here, Gurney portrays something like this titanic struggle for the first time, as evil in the abstract grapples with good and honour. With the exception of 'Satan above the Battle', his writing during the war years would tend to steer away from grand dramatisations of conflict, focusing instead on the soldiers themselves, and the minutiae of their lives.

Alongside these September 1915 poems, Gurney also sent Scott a song she had not previously seen. He does not mention its title, but it may well have been a first draft of his setting of Harvey's poem 'In Flanders'. He was clearly pleased with it, instructing Scott to show it to Parry.[69] Harvey had just won the DCM (Distinguished Conduct Medal), and Gurney admired his poetic and military achievements in equal measure.

It must, with some justification, have seemed to Gurney that Harvey and Howells were always one step ahead. Harvey was proving his worth on the Somme with the 1/5ths, whilst Gurney was wasting time in England. In Chelmsford the biggest danger Gurney faced was a minor zeppelin raid, with two bombs dropped near his camp.

The damage was about £5 worth. It cured an old lady of muscular rheumatism, indeed it made an athlete, a sprinter of her—she went down the street in her nightgown like a comet or some gravity-defying ghost. One of the bombs was terrifying and must severely have shocked the elm tree which it mostly affected.[70]

Harvey's DCM had been awarded for a skirmish a little more impressive than Gurney's comic farce. The official citation reads:

> For conspicuous gallantry on the night of Aug. 3–4, 1915, near Hébuterne, when, with a patrol, he and another non-commissioned officer went out to reconnoitre in the direction of a suspected listening-post. In advancing they encountered the hostile post, evidently covering a working party in the rear. Corporal Knight at once shot one of the enemy, and, with Lance-Corporal Harvey, rushed the post, shooting two others, and, assistance arriving, the enemy fled. Lance-Corporal Harvey pursued, felling one of the retreating Germans with a bludgeon. He seized him, but, finding his revolver empty and the enemy having opened fire, he was called back by Corporal Knight, and the prisoner escaped.[71]

If Gurney's setting of 'In Flanders' was indeed written that summer, it might be read as a poignant tribute to his dearest friend. Gurney deeply admired Harvey's bravery, but he was concerned for him; his reckless actions had cost him dearly. Harvey, like Gurney, was a highly strung, sensitive character, and his nerves were affected by this first experience of point-blank killing.[72]

The rest of the year crawled slowly on. Gurney was bored and frustrated, but not in danger, and the brief rest periods could be put to good use. In August, he amused himself by stopping up a gap in the regiment's marching band. He taught himself the baryton (a three-valved brass instrument, similar to a bass cornet) at great speed, and became rather taken with it: 'It is a fine instrument, and three days practise— even to me—are inadequate to do it justice.' It was a diversion at least, and although he was rather impressed with the instrument (he had a keen sense of the absurd), it did not take him long to tire of band practise, which was beginning to 'bore me like Billyoh.' By November he was already dreaming ruefully of Mozart, and of music-making at the College. He was also struggling with the early morning parades, reporting to Sydney Shimmin that 'I believe my mind and body improve little by little constantly; but would to God that power would be given me from on high to wake up earlier. 'Tis truly distressing to miss 5 parades in one week, chiefly through that reason. I deserved the V.C. but, Lord knows how, they either did not miss me or someone answered my name, for the slimy dungeon has not yet received me.'[73]

The 2/5ths languished for month after month in Chelmsford, as they waited for their youngest members to become old enough for overseas duty. Gurney had time to read and rediscovered the poetry of Walt Whitman. He found it utterly

Fig. 2.5: The 2/5ths band, including Gurney with his baryton
(back row, fourth from right). © Gurney Trust.

compelling in its self-belief, exuberance and gusto. Whitman refused to be bound
by traditional forms, and Gurney found in him a model for composition by the flow
of the phrase rather than by form. He realised the immensity of what he was reading,
but he was not yet confident enough to incorporate such freedom and certainty of
tone into his own work. He returned repeatedly to Whitman over the next few
months, until by the summer he was ready to assimilate some of his influence.

Finally, orders came for a move. But it was still not France. Instead, they were
being transferred to the vast training camp on Salisbury Plain. On 19 February 1916
the battalion moved to the station at Tidworth village, fifteen miles northeast of
Salisbury. Salisbury Plain had been used to train the regular army since 1897 and is
still in use today. By the time Gurney was sent there, it was well established as a
major training centre, with the army having taken over forty-three thousand acres of
the Plain. Trenches were dug across swathes of ground which, in only a pale imitation of what was to come, quickly filled up with water. They were shallower than the
real thing, as it was impossible to dig deeply enough into the white chalky soil, but
they allowed for both live firing and the firing of blanks, and a little taste of the practise of undermining trenches.

From Tidworth station Gurney marched to Perham Down on the Plain, where
the battalion was housed in row upon row of the prefabricated huts that constituted
Park House 'A' Camp. The huts, each of which accommodated around thirty men,
were 'seventh heaven' compared with the tents they'd left behind.[74] It was a lucky
stroke of timing, as snow lay on the ground in drifts of up to eight inches. Park House

Camp was strongly rooted in the army's history; the barracks were all distinguished by campaigns in Afghanistan and India. Names such as Aliwal, Assaye and Lucknow contrived to make the new civilian recruit feel either part of a greater whole with a prestigious military history or, in Gurney's case, utterly out of his depth in an environment that was foreign to him both metaphorically and in reality.

Gurney slept on bare boards, conditions which represented an upgrade from the palliasses on the ground, back in Chelmsford. The blankets were damp, and frostbite was averted by keeping a fire lit in the stove in each hut. Despite the cold, Gurney was relatively upbeat. He was enjoying the scenery, and found his location in the middle of the Downs to be a 'charming spot'.[75] The daytime activities were just as monotonous and exhausting as ever, but he was composing, and engrossed in reading Shakespeare, whenever he could sufficiently block out the noise in the overcrowded, smoky hut to concentrate. 'I am sure either to be killed or cured by this, hein?'[76] The camps on Salisbury Plain were known for sending wave after wave of newly trained recruits directly out to the battlefields. The 2/5ths had been in training for over a year, and the 1/5ths, now seasoned fighters, had had a year of casualties who needed to be replaced. Surely Gurney's channel crossing was imminent. His letters to Howells were full of swagger and bravado, but in the quiet moments when he had time to reflect, he had to admit to himself that he was terrified. He found some solace in the final volume of Tolstoy's *War and Peace*, which had the desired effect of calming him, and stemming the rising panic when thoughts of a German bayonet ending his fledgling career became too unbearable.[77]

He tried to amuse himself by playing chess to keep his brain active. His mind turned from Shakespeare to Beethoven and back again; the slow movement of the C major Razumovsky Quartet (or Rasoumoffsky Quartett, to use Gurney's spelling) was very much in his thoughts, as one of the 'loveliest things in music'.[78] Whenever he could, he played Beethoven and Bach on the two decayed camp pianos, but most of his time for these first few weeks on the Plain was occupied in firing and marking. Bayonet fighting, squad drill and fatigues were dull and seemingly 'eternal'. 'It would tax Shakespeare's mind to conceive the monotony'.[79] It was in this state of mind that he received a well meant but unfortunate letter from the Royal College:

> It has been brought to the notice of the RCM Union General Committee that some of the Members who are on Active Service may have experienced difficulties in arranging for the maintenance of their professional musical interest during their enforced absence, and may be glad to know where to apply in the event of their wanting a temporary teacher for their pupils, a reliable deputy to take over their position, or a responsible representative to gather any royalties from publishers that may accrue.

He scribbled a reply on the back, for want of paper:

> *I have experienced no great difficulty in arranging for the maintenance of my professional interests, for at best they were only slightly more than nil. As for requiring a temporary teacher, you could serve me little in this; but for any temporary pupils—a half a guinea a lesson of 20 minutes—I should feel most grateful. Your remark about collecting royalties happens merely to be ironic, and does not give me anything like the pleasure the other offer does—that offer to provide a responsible deputy for my position. My position is at present that of a private in the 2nd/5th Battalion of the Glosters, who are about to move into huts on Salisbury Plain. Any deputy, trustworthy or otherwise, would be most gratefully welcomed and fulsomely flattered, receive all my military decorations and valuable insight into the best method of mud cleaning with vocal accompaniment.*
>
> *Yours truly,*
>
> *Ivor Gurney.*[80]

On 22 February, only three days after Gurney had arrived at the training camp, Sir John French (then the commander in chief of the British Expeditionary Force) inspected the 2/5th, along with the 7th and 9th Gloucesters, who were training alongside them. Gurney was always rather impressed by dignitaries, and found French to be a 'short, kind faced gentleman'. However, it was the sight of so many of Gloucestershire's boys, lined up to parade on the Plain with an unknown future ahead, that left a lasting impression on him.[81]

Spring blossomed around the camp, as in April 1916 Gurney was given his final leave—five blissful days of cycling and walking the Gloucestershire lanes, trying to forget the now imminent prospect of France. Returning to one's family for what might well be the last time was an emotionally charged experience for any soldier. For Gurney, it was fraught with particular complexity.

It is perhaps a little too tempting to point to Gurney's mother Florence as the source of many of Gurney's later difficulties. The pseudo-Freudian biographical trend is to look to the mother as the explanation for a subject's eccentricities, and to point the oversimplified finger of blame at poor parenting, or a dysfunctional early childhood. The reality is rarely as simple as that. However, Gurney's patterns of behaviour and his adult relationships all indicate this early, most important relationship to be somewhere near the heart of his later disturbance.

It is difficult to gain any sense of his mother from Gurney himself, who hardly mentions her in his adult writing. Perhaps this in itself is significant. His sister Winifred is far more vocal on the subject. The years of bitter wrangling and familial injustices had left their mark, and her memories of her childhood are dominated by the vitriol with which she pours out her grievances against Florence. At best, we can

safely say that Florence Gurney was a woman unlikely to produce stable and functional offspring. She has been described as being on the schizoid spectrum, and the
few existing examples of her writing have been treated as a case study in themselves—
streams of consciousness, flitting from subject to subject, delightful but rambling.

> Now to tell you some of his little sayings he was learning his Collect for Sun-
> day School he was conning it over about twice he always knew a thing directly
> and I thought how reverent he sounded and thought I believe Ivor is going to
> be a good boy and he clapped the book together and said all men no women
> good gracious what a come down and there was a scrubbing brush with made
> in England on it and he wrote what a wonder till it was worn out the others
> were curly Ronald was Bubbles but Ivor's was straight and silver theirs was
> gold and he used to look up at people so affectionate but they wouldn't take
> any notice of him and he was a lovely boy and the others people offered so
> much money for them he cut every tooth with Bronchitis and his teeth grew
> projecting out and that was very painful pulling them in besides the teeth cant
> bite as well because they are not opposite and then they took out his teeth to
> try to make him better and made it worse.[82]

Her writing is are certainly hard to follow, and appear uncontained and devoid of
structure. But if we assume that Florence, a seamstress, had had only a basic education, and little opportunity or necessity to write well, we might be more circumspect
about judging her state of mind from written evidence alone. If we add the punctuation that she would naturally have implied when speaking, this monologue not only
becomes reasonable but also reveals moments of beauty. She was clearly a woman
with a strongly instinctive aesthetic sense, and whilst her children remembered her
as cold and unloving, it was not for want of emotion. However tortured Gurney's
relationship with his mother might have been, it is to her credit that she remembered him as having been 'a lovely boy'.

The best of her represented an appreciation of nature, and an innate musicality.
She would often sing to the children when they were very young, and Gurney's enduring love of folk song may well have stemmed from these few positive memories
of her. She may have given the gifts of music and an aesthetic sensibility to her
children, but it was what she *withheld* from them that had such a detrimental effect
on their development. According to Winifred, Florence was incapable of love—a
heavy accusation, and one that, if true, would have had a devastating impact on a
child's emotional development.

On the second day of his leave, Gurney cycled down 'the noblest road I know—
the Gloucester-Malvern Road' towards the village of Redmarley. There, daffodils
and cowslips grew abundantly in the orchards and fields. Even in this rural idyll, he
could see the damage war was inflicting on the landscape, as wood was being claimed

for the war effort. Telegraph poles had been removed to be taken to the front, or re-cycled, and he was horrified to see 'great trees lying stricken and low forever'. He cycled on towards the Malverns, stopping only for a 'foaming beaker of gingerbeer', when suddenly he hit upon the idea of visiting the Georgian poets Lascelles Aber-crombie and Wilfrid Gibson, who lived in the nearby village of Ryton. He had never met either, but he knew he may well never set foot in England again, and necessity made him bold. He asked directions to Abercrombie's house:

> A double cottage with a sort of courtyard. I stood hesitating for long with my eyes fixed on its white front; made up my mind, went up and knocked. Let it suffice to say that I spent 6 very full hours of joy with Mrs Abercrombie, her husband is munition-making in Liverpool, and acquired a rich memory. I wheeled the pram, I did feats of daring to amuse the three children, and talked books and music with Mrs Abercrombie, the genius of the place; all set in blue of the sky, green of the fields and leaves, and that red, that red of the soil.[83]

Catherine Abercrombie wrote to him as soon as he got to France, sending him a copy of Lascelles's play *Deborah*. It is a dark, claustrophobic work, in which the curse of one boy being saved from cholera at the expense of others in his plagued village serves to ruin his life. The darkness of the narrative, and the precariousness of life in the diseased fenland village, must have made for topical if not cheery reading in the trenches.

Before the camp packed up and all were given the final orders to 'fall in', Gurney returned to the Harveys' home in the Gloucestershire village of Minsterworth, The Redlands, for one last evening. It was a house in which he had spent many happy childhood days, and he was saddened, if not surprised, to find the atmosphere bleak and sombre. Harvey's father had died, and instead of his jovial welcome, Matilda received Gurney alone. She was a shadow of the genial, motherly figure he remem-bered from his teenage visits.

With all three sons away fighting, Matilda was in a state of perpetual anxiety. Gurney played her some Bach, as much for old time's sake as for her entertainment. It was a particularly resonant choice, invoking the prewar evenings when Will had thrown himself down on the sofa, cigarette in one hand, book in the other, to listen to Gurney's renditions of preludes and fugues at the keyboard. Whenever he thought of Harvey, it was Bach that Gurney imagined playing to him. He bid Matilda farewell, and as he cycled back home through the dark country lanes, he looked up to admire the stars—'Venus high in the air and black vault studded with stars not so fair as she but dear to me; most dear.'[84] Perhaps he wondered whether, from be-tween the parapets of their trenches, the Harvey brothers were also looking up at the night sky.

PART II

War

CHAPTER THREE

'First Time In'

At the end of May 1916, a whole fifteen months after Gurney had enlisted, he and the 2/5ths were finally off to 'somewhere in France'. They did not know their destination, but they were in fact bound for Flanders, the area bordering France and Belgium. It had been continually fought over since the beginning of the war, as the Allies tried to defend what was left of the once beautiful medieval town of Ypres. The strategically important Channel seaports west of the town would, if captured, have provided the Germans with easy access to Britain. Since the early months of the war, when 58,000 British had been killed in the First Battle of Ypres, it had become a place synonymous with heavy casualties for little gain.[1] Its association with poison gas made it even less enticing. All in all, Ypres was no soft option, and every infantryman knew it.

Gurney wrote a rather poignant postcard to 'little Howler', as he fondly referred to Howells. It has the air of a final benediction, despite the optimistic *au revoir* with which he signed off.[2] Secretly, he had a fatalistic conviction that this was in fact a final farewell. He believed he would never fulfil the part he could have played in the story of British music; Howells must speak for them both, with his blessing.

Dear Howler,

Finis est, or rather, Inceptus est (?). We go tomorrow. Little Howler, continue in thy path of life, blessing others and being blest, creating music and joy, never ceasing from the attempt to make English music what it should be, and calmly scornful-heedless of the critics. Go on and prosper, and Au revoir.

I.B.G.

However excited Gurney may have been about going abroad, and his general appearance of high spirits implied that he was bored enough to embrace any change, all the men who waited in the camp that final evening would have been aware of how slim their chances were of returning to Britain again. When the bugle sounded the final 'fall in', the routine remark 'All present and correct, Sir' was heard for the last time on English soil. 'Many a time before the same words had been uttered, but now they seemed to bear a new significance. Who, it was wondered, would be present when the roll was called on some not far distant date?'[3] On the brilliant spring morning of 24 May, the day before compulsory conscription came into force in Britain, the company made the hot and dusty three-mile march to Tidworth station. Laden down with their equipment, they looked like a load of 'well stocked Christmas trees', as one soldier rather whimsically observed.[4] They crammed themselves into wooden-seated carriages, to the wistful accompaniment of a band playing 'Auld Lang Syne'. The mood was subdued, with little talking or attempt at banter. No flag-waving children or flower-strewing girls were there to see them off—only a handful of moist-eyed relatives waved from the platform.

The regiment arrived at Southampton at dusk, to be greeted with a view of their ship, the unromantically named HMT 861, looming beyond the gloomy platform. The Gloucesters were left to their own devices to wander around the port for a few hours before boarding their boat in the dark. Throughout May Gurney had been reading W. H. Davies, another poet who, like Masefield, had a complicated love affair with the sea.[5] The industrial port, crammed with cold, silent soldiers, certainly did not have the romance of Davies's sea adventures, nor indeed of Gurney's own sailing of the beloved but leaky *Dorothy* back in Gloucestershire. Here, danger presented itself more in the form of submarines than old fashioned shipwrecks, thoroughly unnerving for the men who had never been to war before, and probably, like Gurney, had never made a channel crossing.

Gurney waited with nearly eight hundred officers and men for several hours at the docks—enough time to pick up more information than they would have liked about torpedoed ships, and attacks on the East Coast. One newsboy was rather enterprising: 'Three German Submarines gone down', he cried, and as he pocketed two pence from an unsuspecting patron, he added with a wink, 'and they all came up again.'[6] They were issued with their life belts, the siren sounded for departure, and in the growing dark, the ship set off. Men huddled together on deck, perhaps as much for comfort as for warmth, but the crossing proved uneventful, and the boat docked at Le Havre in the early morning of 25 May.

Gurney was delighted with his first experience of a foreign country, despite the inauspicious circumstances for his adventure. He declared Le Havre to be 'the most noble town he'd ever seen' (and this despite his slavish devotion to Gloucester!).[7] Architecture alone could not entirely make up for physical discomfort, however. The battalion was cold, and ready for a rest. They marched, confusingly, on the right-hand side of the road, up to a temporary camp on the hillside nearby. The local French civilians paid them little or no attention. A year ago, the same journey would have seen the troops besieged by well-wishers and curious children, but by spring 1916 the inhabitants of Le Havre had seen too many troop ships disembarking to be impressed by yet another.

After two days the battalion moved on, again by train, but this time their final destination was the front line. They were met by a trainload of old hands going on leave. "'Are we down-hearted?" they called. "No," came the chorus from the 2/5th led by the Padre. A laconic voice rejoined, "Then you ****** soon will be."[8] It did not take long for the prophesy to come true. For twenty-four hours their train crawled at a torturously slow pace up the line through northern France to the Belgian border. The language used when reaching a stop, only to find there was still a seven-mile march to their destination, was unprintable. They eventually reached the little village of Le Sart, where they spent the night. They were near enough the front line to be able to see the eerily beautiful flares known as Very lights in the distance, and to hear their first distinct gunfire, although Gurney does not record the impression these first sounds of war made on his highly sensitive musician's ear.[9] The next day, 29 May, the order came to move up into the trenches. The battalion was to receive instruction from the London Welsh, who were occupying the trenches in front of Riez Bailleul.

Riez Bailleul is not on any modern map; it was a tiny hamlet, now without a name, near the small town of Bailleul and the village of La Gorgue. Its name is resonant with meaning today only because Gurney's repeated mentions of it in poems have immortalised a place that would otherwise have been entirely forgotten. It was roughly nine miles behind the British front line, below the town of Ypres, and level with Ploegsteert Wood.[10] The regimental history recalls this sector of the line:

> The curious names of the lanes, Eton Road, Cheltenham Road, Rugby Road—then the main road running from Estaires to La Bassee—then Rouge Croix with its red Crucifix (still standing to this day) and the sentry standing at the cross roads, then, after a long wait the splitting up into small parties and proceeding at intervals along a duckboarded trench—the Very lights in the near distance, the tat-tat of machine-guns and the occasional whistle of a stray bullet and the instinct to duck.[11]

Six years later Gurney looked back on his time there, and recalled the domestic details of life lived in the fields immediately behind the trenches:

> Behind the line there mending reserve posts, looking
>   On the cabbage fields with other men carefully tending cooking;
> Hearing the boiling;[12]

He was full of energy at the change of environment and the anticipation of what was to come. He found constant reminders of Gloucestershire in the French landscape, hardly surprising as he had little experience of travelling, and Gloucester was his touchstone of excellence. It was to be the first of many poetic convergences of the two worlds.

> Some of the country we passed through was very beautiful—rather like the
> Stroud valley only far longer, and there was later a river, most serenely set in
> trees, long lines of trees.[13]

In his letters he observes the 'natives' closely, finding the French children a 'joy to
watch for their grace and independence', and the French women's faces very different, 'full of character!'[14]

The sector of trench they were to occupy (known as the Fauquissart Sector—the
Gloucesters were to be in the right subsection) had been heavily shelled on 30 May.
Happily they missed the drama, but arriving the day after the bombardment they found
that the atmosphere amongst the men occupying the trenches was still very tense.

> Snipers were continually firing, and rockets—fairy lights they call them; fired
> from a pistol—lit up the night outside. Every now and again a distant rumble
> of guns reminded us of the reason we were foregathered. They spoke of their
> friends dead or maimed in the bombardment, a bad one, of the night before.[15]

The 13th London Welsh Regiment, who were holding the sector, were given the
job of instructing the anxious newcomers. Gurney's 'first night in' was to become
one of the most iconic moments of his life; he seemed to be self-consciously aware
of its importance even as he was experiencing it. He turned it into literature almost
immediately, writing descriptions of it to at least three of his friends:

> We went up through the interminable communication trenches, watching the
> West when we halted, our minds filled with thoughts that are naturally the
> raw soldier's [. . .] I crawled into a candle lit dugout, and so met four of the
> nicest young men you could meet, possibly.[16]

Something about this night, his very first experience of trench life, held him especially in thrall. His narrations of his encounter with the Welsh regiment exude a
childlike delight:

> But O what luck! Here am I in a signal dugout with some of the nicest, and
> most handsome young men I ever met. And would you believe it? my luck I
> mean; they talk their native language and sing their own folksongs with sweet
> natural voices. I did not sleep at all for the first day in the dugout—there was
> too much to be said, asked, and experienced; and pleasure in watching their
> quick expressions for oblivion. It was one of the notable evenings of my life.[17]

As the experience worked its way into poetry, Gurney evoked, with the lightest
of touches, the strange beauty he found in this most unlikely of settings—the flickering candlelight, glimpsed through slits in oil sheets; the soft whispering of the
boys, whose strange but familiar melodiousness replaced the harsher possibilities of
trench life that had until that moment filled his mind.

First Time In

After the dread tales and red yarns of the Line
Anything might have come to us; but the divine
Afterglow brought us up to a Welsh colony
Hiding in sandbag ditches, whispering consolatory
Soft foreign things. Then we were taken in
To low huts candle-lit shaded close by slitten
Oilsheets, and there but boys gave us kind welcome;
So that we looked out as from the edge of home.
Sang us Welsh things, and changed all former notions
To human hopeful things. And the next day's guns
Nor any Line-pangs ever quite could blot out
That strangely beautiful entry to War's rout,
Candles they gave us precious and share over-rations—
Ulysses found little more in his wanderings without doubt.
'David of the White Rock', the 'Slumber Song' so soft, and that
Beautiful tune to which roguish words by Welsh pit boys
Are sung—but never more beautiful than here under the guns' noise.[18]

Gurney's poetic accounts of his first night in the trenches became a tender and intimate celebration of communality, music and artistic expression in the face of misery. He would not be drawn on the 'thoughts that are naturally the raw soldier's', but substituted these thoughts for his joy in the strange beauty of the occasion, just as he drew the focus away from the sounds of the guns to the singing. This unlikely juxtaposition of sound was the beginning of many letters, songs and poems that sought to understand the war through placing such different soundscapes side by side both to escape, but also to embed himself in the experience of war.

By writing down the sounds of the trenches, and layering them into his descriptions of his life in France, he arranged the soundscape around him into potential material for poetry and music. The birdsong, the exact differences in sound of particular guns, the patterns of machine gun fire, the singing of the men and the accents of their speech, all become potential music in Gurney's hands. Left uncomposed, the noise of war could become unbearable, and threaten to overwhelm him. Wrestling all the sounds he heard into his own shapes, he could maintain some control over both the beautiful and the obscene, and by doing so manufacture a degree of mastery over an environment that might expose him to anything from the song of a lark to the screams of dying men at any moment.

For many, the first few days in trenches often felt like the longest; the numbness and resignation of the seasoned trench soldier had not yet been cultivated. The trenches had improved significantly since the first year of the war. Drainage, a huge problem in the clay soil around Ypres, had been developed; duckboards and sandbags had become more available than they were in the early months, and soldiers had learnt on the job how to improve and fortify trenches. Nonetheless, conditions were still appalling. The water table had been destroyed by the incessant shelling and posed a perennial problem for those fighting in the waterlogged and mud-soaked trenches.

Two men from the 2/5ths were killed during this first week, and a handful wounded, the kind of casualty numbers that spoke of a 'very quiet time'. However, on 6 June Gurney was to experience his first 'strafe' (or bombardment), reporting that

> As I was in a signallers' dugout, a bombardment means little else but noise and apprehension—as yet. But a whizz-bang missed me and a tin of Maconachie (my dinner) by ten yards; a shower of dirt no more.[19]

He did not go into how he responded to this 'noise and apprehension', and did not attempt to describe it, a telling omission for a man whose world was so often interpreted through sound. Other writers did try to describe the sound of a bombardment through language, even if it was only to exclude the reader from the possibility of imagining it. For Robert Graves, the noise was incommunicable. It 'never stopped for one moment—ever.'[20] Ford Madox Ford tried to explain the sound in visual terms: 'There was so much noise it seemed to grow dark. It was a mental darkness. You could not think. A Dark Age!'[21]

Four days later Gurney was obliged to leave his beloved Welshmen, and moved forward to Laventie, a little town near the Belgian border. Marching continually within the reach of the guns, he marvelled at the continuity of rural life under such extraordinary conditions:

> It is surprising to see everything as usual very well within reach of the guns. They used to shell the villages but do not seem to now. There is quite a fine church a few yards from me shattered but still noble, and under the shadow of it the estaminets are doing good trade—maybe with windows shattered, the children play; and the country a mile or so behind the firing line is green and peaceful as our Dear England's.[22]

Such juxtapositions were to become one of Gurney's hallmarks. His most powerful work, in both music and poetry, would arise from the blurring and jarring of these experiential boundaries, these located and abstract states of being—Severn and Somme, peace and war, beauty and abjection. Already, only days after reaching the front, he had begun to think in the patterns that would be played out in his work for years to come.

Laventie itself, with its quaint cobbled streets, was 'a place of happy memories to many' for the regiment, and this was certainly true for Gurney.[23] He returned to it repeatedly in his later poems, with some fondness. It was an unusual little town, built in the form of a cross, with its red brick church in the centre. Though it was only a mile or so from the front line of the Fauquissart Sector, civilians continued to live there and farmed a certain amount of the land around. The town had suffered considerably in 1915, when it was partially destroyed during house-to-house fighting, but the billets were fairly habitable, and the plane trees still stood in the streets—a reminder perhaps of the view he had left behind from the window of his Fulham flat. There were even beautiful lawns and gardens behind some of the big houses. But it was not quite the sleepy rural retreat it once was. The nights at Laventie were distinctly noisy, since the village was surrounded with eighteen-pounder batteries and a fifteen-inch railway gun.[24] It was to be bombarded only a few weeks after Gurney arrived, on 28 June, and by spring 1917 it had been heavily battered.

The Gloucesters were on their way to relieve the 2/1st Bucks in trenches nearby. Getting a regiment of men and their equipment into the trenches around Laventie was a challenge. The land was so distinctly flat that 'it was easy to spot any movement, which, as the German trenches were unusually close to the British line, inevitably meant being bombarded by field guns' although they were 'quiet' once the battalion was in.[25]

The 2/1st Bucks would continue to exchange duties with the Gloucesters in the months to come, alternating stints in the front line. This was the start of what felt like an interminable pattern of moving in a cycle between front line, reserve trenches and rest billets. Whilst the period of rest was always gratefully welcomed, the rest billets could be between one and three miles behind the front line, over terrain that was virtually impassable if it had rained. Once the men were there, they were often still in range of the guns.

The battalion had to send all its equipment and supplies back behind the lines and wait for the relieving battalion to be fully installed before the men themselves could leave. The equipment included such cumbersome objects as machine guns and trench mortars, and was heavy and awkward to transport. Gurney spent hours stumbling, shuffling and cursing in the dark as he helped to drag the guns back out of the line onto limbers brought up from three or four miles away. The twists and turns of an unfamiliar trench were a major challenge, and the shell hole–pitted track back to the reserve billets could be potentially lethal when negotiated in total darkness.

Once at 'rest' Gurney found the term to be used rather loosely. Rest could often entail parade after parade, drills, exercises, fatigues and route marches, although he did find the longer periods of unoccupied time in which he was free to wander more conducive to writing than his stints at the front. Most of his poetry and songs written during the next fifteen months would stem from these rest periods.

Gurney explored the countryside around Ypres and found it was characterised by small, red-roofed hamlets and farms, windmills, estaminets, and endlessly flat fields, some given over to hop production, others to cabbages. Villages behind the front line were mostly requisitioned by the army for rest billets. Often farmers were tenaciously holding on to their livelihoods, and in many cases, charging as much as possible for any food or service they could persuade their British houseguests to buy. Gurney returned to these memories in later years:

> Water and wine and beer and citron—
> Drinks grateful all to the frame well used;
> Taken as precious, or quickly gone—
> Such goodness as never right mind refused.
>
> By farms and homesteads of coloured frames there,
> And fields of coloured squares many a sort,
> A march took past, and the foreign names there
> Took well the mind, and at fancy caught.[26]

Looking back from the vantage point of 1923, Gurney plays here with the idea of framing; the human frame becoming linked to the artistic rendering of this memory as a highly coloured painting of squares. The 'frames' of humans are set alongside the timber frames of buildings and the typically French square fields, all presented within the 'picture' of the poem. Gurney succinctly captures a sense of fleeting impressions in a few impressionistic brushstrokes. As the soldiers pass, so in his recollections he marches his reader past his list of drinks, of foreign names, and of the patchwork of fields, in panoramic glimpses of the Ypres landscape and its inhabitants. This is memory, ordered within lists and squares, transferred and transported as a form of verbal and visual patterning. By ordering his memories into different coloured frames, Gurney diverts himself away from horror towards the imaginative shapes of storytelling, enacting in the very form of the poem the moment of imaginative connection, when 'fancy caught'.

The town of Ypres itself was almost entirely destroyed; legend has it that a man sitting on a horse could see across the city by the end of the war, with not a building left standing. It never saw street fighting, as the Allied front line remained outside its outer walls, but the town was so heavily and frequently shelled that it could hardly provide a restful break for a wandering soldier.

The skyline of Ypres was dominated by the ruins of its Cloth Hall, a monument of medieval craftsmanship. Its destruction had been entirely gratuitous. Ypres itself was not a strategic city. Had the Germans managed to push through the defences that held it, they would have had no problem sweeping through the little market town to the far more important port of Calais 'as easily as a hyena through a rice-crop', as Arnold Bennett vividly put it.[27] The city's desecration served no other purpose, according to Bennett, than to offer psychological relief for the frustration of the Germans whose advance had foundered near its walls. By April 1915, it was already being described as a dead city, and when Gurney first saw it, it had suffered a further year of bombardment. It was the subject of paintings, poems and stories, and the pathetic ruins of the town

FIG. 3.1: The medieval Cloth Hall in Ypres. © Soldiers of Gloucestershire Museum.

became an iconic image of the ruin of Belgium. Gurney, along with many others, was captivated by the place. He fully understood the human cost of such shelling, and the futility of it, but he could also impose upon the city a tragic romance, animating the rubble with imaginings of regal glamour and drama. He imagined 'proud Ypres' at dawn, with

> [. . .] pale besmeared face
> A little colour took from pride
> In her past beauty, and her race
> Of heroes that like princes died.[28]

Ypres was of more use to Gurney as a symbol of noble suffering than a place of recreation. Armentières and Bailleul were nearby, and these became his regular haunts when on rest, with the estaminets still doing a thriving trade in exhausted soldiers, eager to spend their money.[29] Estaminets were havens of normality, despite being often only a few miles behind the lines. Gurney spent some of his happiest hours in their crowded rooms 'loud with song and story' and 'blue with tales and smoke', playing cards, and drinking wine and café au lait.[30] They were also Gurney's only contact with women while out in France, and although many men did return to England with venereal disease, there is no clue as to whether Gurney ever engaged in any pleasures less innocent than cigarettes and coffee.[31] Of course, if he did, Marion Scott would have been the last person to whom he would confide and his letters to her are the main source of information about his actions in France. There was one 'delightful' girl in Laventie, who particularly caught Gurney's attention. She ran a café with her mother, within range of the guns—'evidently born to be the mother of dauntless men'.[32] She made enough of an impression on him to inspire a paean of praise. However, in a poem whose final stanza owes a debt to the hypnotically compelling rhyme scheme Alfred Noyes had used in 'The Highwayman', it is his love of his British comrades, not the local girls, that Gurney evocatively recalls:

> O I may get to Blighty,
>   Or hell, without a sign
> Of all the love that filled me,
>   Leave dumb the love that filled me,
> The flood of love that filled me
>   For these dear comrades of mine.[33]

Rest billets usually had the advantage of better and more varied food, especially when soldiers were billeted to local homes. As in any institution where life was unvaried, food played an overly dominant part in a soldier's day, and Gurney was as excited by changes to his diet as any other bored soldier. Food in the front line was monotonous, to say the least. Plum and apple jam was apparently considered the only possible variety of preserve suitable for the army, and Gurney spread it onto dry, hard biscuits, which were only marginally improved by being dipped in tea. There was an unending supply of unpalatable Maconochie stew, and bully (corned) beef. This repetitive diet could on occasion be brightened by a fry-up of bacon on a Tommy cooker in a trench, if conditions and supplies allowed.[34]

Dismal though the food was, for Gurney it was a temporary relief from a troubled relationship with eating, which was always a feature of his periods of depression. As a teenager, Gurney would eat only sweets or butter, starve himself, then buy as many cakes as he could afford, and devour them all. Rejecting food and regular meals had begun as a way of rebelling against his mother's authoritarian control. Later on, eating would become part of his illness, and what began as a teenage eating disorder became 'a terrible and contemptuous torture of eating', as he described it.[35] For now at least, when food in France was scarce and rationed, and he was perpetually hungry from honest physical exertion, he found fate had relieved him of the burden of disordered eating. He could enjoy the smell of bacon frying without any sense of guilt, and celebrate it in his poetry.

Bread was a constant source of consternation, and Gurney's letters to Scott return obsessively to the subject:

> The food in trenches is curiously arranged, apparently. I don't know whether the A S C [Army Service Corps] steal it, but nobody gets more than a third of a loaf ever, and as a rule only a quarter. This is serious to a battalion that has innocently trusted to the army and spent all its money, before knowing how fickle and uncertain is the day of pay.[36]

The postal service offered sustenance for both mind and stomach. Gurney eagerly anticipated food parcels, both as a link to normality and home, and as a practical supplement to his very limited diet. Cakes, sweets and cigarettes were usually shared with egalitarian fairness around dugouts and friends, and many of B Company benefitted from Scott's generosity. Gurney ensured he made the most of her benevolence, giving her shopping lists of purchases she might make for him, often written whilst still consuming the contents of the most recent parcel. His humour and charm made his demands hard to resist, and Scott was by now well established as his supporter in all things practical and emotional.

> But look here about that parcel, and my pencil moves decidedly quicker at
>   the thought of it.
> Here's how. (And I've lost my well prepared curiously conned syllabus.)
> Fowl. (since you insist on such a lofty height.)
> Cafe au lait. (Tin, you know?)
> Cake. Stodgy and Sustaining.
> Tommy's cooker and tin of refills (can't get this here somehow.)
> Lemonade crystals or powder or such like.
> Chocolate. (*Plain*)
> Biscuits. *Oatmeal.*
> Tin of Butter.
> *One book.*
> *cheap.*
> Any old *interesting* papers.
> A candle or two (somebody's always short.)
> Acid Drops. Peppermint Bulleyes Toffee or such.
> [. . .]

I should have remembered about the matches. A piano would also be acceptable, but is not insisted on. One must not push about trifles. We could get some of this on reserve but not here so well. Part of the cake is lying on the first part of this letter so excuse grease marks.[37]

By 15 June 1916 Gurney was back in the frontline trenches near Laventie, and on the third night he endured the worst bombardment he had yet experienced. Seventy-five minutes of shattering explosions rocked the dugout where he cowered, huddled together with a veteran of trench warfare who claimed the strafe was 'worse than Loos'.[38] It was Gurney's first real 'test', and he was unsure how he would react to the strain. Would he be able to prove himself? Back in the summer of 1915, he had anxiously imagined such a moment in 'To the Poet before Battle':

> . . . When mere noise numbs
> The sense of being, the fear-sick soul doth sway,
> Remember thy great craft's honour, that they may say
> Nothing in shame of poets.[39]

There was more at stake for him than for the average new recruit. He recognised his own instability and had joined the army to cure it. His first real experiences of heavy fighting were a test of the efficacy of his self-imposed experimental treatment. If he broke down, it would mean acknowledging to himself that the problems with which he had struggled back at the Royal College were systemic, not a temporary state brought on by the exigencies of life as a solitary student.

After five days in the front line, the 2/5ths planned a raid on enemy trenches, prefaced by the usual bombardment. Unfortunately, the Germans began their own strafe twenty minutes before the British guns were due to start. They knew what was about to happen and were ready for the attackers. After thirty-five minutes of heavy bombardment from both sides, the Gloucesters' A Company sent a raiding party over the top, only to be held up by the wire which had hardly been touched by their shells. They were stranded, exposed to the Germans' machine guns, and the survivors were forced to return to their own trenches. Gurney and the other signallers tried to establish lamp signal communication between the front line and battalion headquarters. They quickly learnt the difference between a dress rehearsal on Salisbury Plain and the real thing, disorientated by the explosions and dazzled by the Very lights. Both signallers and raiding party found themselves entirely out of their depth.

So far, Gurney's nerves had seemed to withstand bombardment; now he had an active role to play.

> I was out mending wires part of the time, but they were not so bad then. 10 high explosives were sailing over the signaller dugout and the bay where I was in front of it. A foot would have made a considerable difference to us I think. They burst about 30 yards behind.[40]

That night, his attempts to keep communications intact under fire brought him the closest he would come during his war service to being recognised for bravery—in rather vague tones he reported back to Marion Scott that he was 'nearly' recommended for a DCM 'for something or other that was done chiefly by other men'. The relief that he had not 'funked it' was palpable. He reported back with his usual mix of egotism and humour that he found he had as little fear as a 'stolid cow'. Gurney's version of events, as he chose to tell it for Scott, was that

> everything went wrong, and there was a tiny panic at first—but everybody, save the officers, were doing what they ought to do, and settled down later to the proper job, but if Fritz expected us as much as we expected them, he must have been in a funk.

The raid was an unmitigated disaster, and Gurney began to question the wisdom of army authority:

When I return to England I am going to lie in wait for all men who have been officers, and very craftily question them on several subjects, and if the answers to my questions do not satisfy me, they may look out for squalls. This is deadly serious. Talk of the need of 'dithipline' won't suit me.[41]

Thus began a 'red' streak in Gurney's politics, which was to become increasingly prominent after the war. He was fighting alongside thousands of his generation who had no say in the battle plans and tactics. It was hardly unreasonable that many, including Gurney, felt that when operations were shambolic, those who had directed them should be held to account.

For now, though, he was confident that the war would not be prolonged much longer. Such experiences as the raid were traumatic, but not yet part of the agonising pattern of betrayal and mismanagement Gurney would later come to experience, both within the army and in postwar Britain. Previously, he had written of his most intense emotional experiences in musical terms, such as his first night in the trenches and the send-off of troops from Epping. Here, again, he characterised his description of the attack through song, filtering his retelling of the night through the music and sounds around and within him. It was almost as if he 'composed' these seminal moments when relaying them to Marion Scott in his letters, setting experiences to music much in the same way as he might translate a poem into song. He set his account of the attack to an eclectic variety of music.

one bay filled with signallers and stretcher bearers [from C Company] sang lustily awhile a song called 'I want to go home' [. . .]

Whilst:

The machine guns are the most terrifying of sound, like an awful pack of hell hounds at one's back.[42]

To escape the noise, he turned to Bach—forcing himself to take refuge in his memories of the sublime G minor prelude from part 2 of *The Well-Tempered Clavier*. Gurney had begun to place music 'in competition' with the noise of war, dramatising the internal conflict between Gurney the musician and Gurney the fighting man through quasi-musical settings of his experiences.[43]

Gurney's tone in his letters to Scott vacillates between his longing to escape it all, and the acknowledgement of the excitement and adrenalin: 'Floreat Gloucestriensis! It was a great time'.[44] Unlike the poet Julian Grenfell's infamous letter of October 1914, in which he stated: 'I adore war! It is like a big picnic, but without the objectlessness of a picnic',[45] Gurney does not allow himself the simplicity of naïve, gung-ho optimism, or an outright rejection of the horrors. Instead, he uncompromisingly interrogates his own response, which, typically, is far from simple. Fighting was both great and 'full of fear'. He would far rather be out of it, but to return to London and music college life would mean a potential return to depression. Even a trench mortar strafe is 'not so bad as neurasthenia.'[46]

The attack had left three officers wounded, along with thirteen other ranks. One man died of wounds at the time, and four others were reported missing.[47]

> We had a gross casualties or more—some damned good men among them. Two chaps especially, whom I hoped to meet after the war.

Two weeks after the raid, Gurney sent Scott a poem he titled 'To the Fallen'. It was dedicated first to E. S., then renamed on 16 August 'To Certain Comrades', and the dedication extended to E. S. and J. H., his two friends killed during the attack.[48]

To Certain Comrades
(E. S. and J. H.)

Living we loved you, yet withheld our praises
Before your faces;

And though we had your spirits high in honour,
After the English manner

We said no word. Yet, as such comrades would,
You understood.

Such friendship is not touched by Death's disaster,
But stands the faster;

And all the shocks and trials of time cannot
Shake it one jot.

Beside the fire at night some far December,
We shall remember

And tell men, unbegotten as yet, the story
Of your sad glory—

Of your plain strength, your truth of heart, your splendid
Coolness, all ended!

All ended, . . . yet the aching hearts of lovers
Joy overcovers,

Glad in their sorrow; hoping that if they must
Come to the dust,

An ending such as yours may be their portion,
And great good fortune—

That if we may not live to serve in peace
England, watching increase—

Then death with you, honoured, and swift, and high;
And so—not die.

Ernest Skillern and John Hall have been remembered as initials only through this poem. They were not nameless casualties to Gurney. Skillern and Hall were twenty and twenty-two when they died—Gurney, at the ripe old age of twenty-six, must have felt keenly their deaths so early in their adulthoods.

'To Certain Comrades' can technically lay claim to being Gurney's very first 'war' poem. In fact, he makes certain that readers will appreciate this, by adding 'In Trenches, July 1916' at the end of the published version. Imbued with the tone of Rupert Brooke (whom he was already quoting in May 1915) and the sentiment of Laurence Binyon, Gurney's high claims of immortality and honour were already beginning to sit uncomfortably with the rumbling uncertainties he expresses about war in his letters.[49] He set out his thoughts on himself and his relationship to the war in a letter, possibly written on the evening of the attack. His second point in this long list is particularly telling. In both his poetry and music, Gurney transposes himself from one place to another—from one culture to another, partly as escape from the present, partly to remember and redefine who he is: a creative 'maker', whose work and identity are compounded of the images and places he holds dear.

My feelings about my being connected with the whole affair are

1. It is a weird queer war—this, against unseen enemies.
2. That I have really no part in it. I wake up with a start from my dreams of books and music and home, and find I am—here, in this!
3. That I have as little fear as anyone I have seen around me. Partly because I am more or less fatalistic; partly because my training in self-control not yet finished, has been hard enough. Partly because I possess an ingrained sense of humour. (A whizz-bang missed me by inches over my head and exploded ten yards from me—and the impression it gave and gives me now is chiefly of the comic.)
4. The conviction that prayer is no use to me.
5. The fineness of the men. (The officers *may* develop.)
6. My increasing love of music.
7. An absolute belief (not so very old) that once out of the Army I can make myself fit. [. . .]
8. The conviction also, that in a hand to hand fight I shall be damned dangerous to tackle. A useful one to have; but I hope to God that He has a nice blighty ready for me and that there will be no need of such vulgar brawling—greatly against my taste as it is.[50]

Thankful but exhausted, the Gloucesters trudged out of the trenches on 21 June, and back to their billets in Laventie. They had entered the trenches as green and inexperienced recruits but left feeling like veterans. They had lost a number of their company and endured heavy fighting. However, at the beginning of summer 1916, the general atmosphere was one of optimism. There was still some hope that peace might be negotiated, and Gurney clung to it, along with positive reports from the Russian front.[51] Ninety-six kilometres south of the Gloucesters, guns were being wheeled into place for the preparatory bombardment for the battle of the Somme; the offensive that would, in theory, see the British sweeping across occupied territory within days.

By the end of June, the Gloucesters were preparing for their second attack. It took place on the night of the 29th under a huge bombardment from both sides. This time Gurney had to run at least three messages, a difficult and dangerous job. He was also ordered to act as stretcher bearer to 'one of our best men; hit in many places but none serious.'[52] As before, Gurney fell shy of describing the bombardment in any detail to Scott. Writer Charles Carrington (who fought alongside Arthur Bliss) is rather more forthcoming in his postwar memoir, remembering the high explosives used in 1916–17 near Ypres, which

> seemed to touch the pitch of the aweful, even if one watched it in safety from the next acre of ground. Looking narrowly, you could see the plunge of impact before there spouted a fountain of smoke and blackened earth, and heard the agonising split of the steel case beneath the pressure of exploding ammonal. This would fill me with terror in which my body seemed to dissolve and my spirit beat panic-stricken as a bird in the abyss of winter waves.[53]

Five Gloucesters were killed and fourteen wounded in the attack. Gurney escaped relatively unharmed, apart from injuring his back as he struggled to carry the heavy stretcher through the mud-soaked, uneven trench. He bragged to Scott with a swagger of the 'pluck' of the men, their fortitude and irreverence, in which he took enormous pride. The black humour of the trenches was one of the few mechanisms of collective self-preservation available to men in the line, and Gurney entered into it with relish. He had always possessed a rather wicked sense of humour, along with an appreciation of the absurd, and so turning his satirical eye on the more frustrating and irritating aspects of trench life came naturally to him. A strafe was trench slang for a bombardment. In his poem of the same name, he plays with sound and materiality to translate something truly terrifying into a domesticated, playful form of faux aggression.

Strafe

I strafe my shirt most regularly,
And frighten all the population.

Wonderful is my strategy!
I strafe my shirt most regularly;
(It sounds like distant musketry.)
And still I itch like red damnation!
I strafe my shirt most regularly
And—frighten all the population. . . .?[54]

Gurney had spent the last few years at the College trying to develop some kind of psychological defence against mental illness. Now he observed that these men, through their own resources, had found a way of using humour to protect themselves despite seemingly overwhelming odds, and he delighted in the security and confidence he felt, surrounded by their rebellious irreverence. 'Our men would gag before the Judgement seat and before the throne of Heaven, and not in the most refined language either, and smoking a fag the while.'[55]

There was one man in particular whom he adored: a 'gagster' whose unfailing humour, Gurney eulogised to Scott, was sure to see him through the war unscathed.

Our men are still behaving well, and are still able to 'gag' with straight faces and to some purpose. For instance last night, after the strafe had just finished, some weary eyed Signaller spoke the mind of the dugout. 'I wish this were all over.' The man on duty, a nervy-to-a-degree but plucky gagster, laughed at and loved, and one of my beloved few who have kicked and still do kick whenever possible against the Army pricks 'So do I. I've been sitting here 3 hours and my behind is sore.' An immortal joke, I think. But that's them. Jokes in unexpected places.[56]

Gurney interrupted his letter-writing to sleep and returned to it to write an additional paragraph the next day. But by the time it was light enough to continue writing, he learnt that his seemingly indestructible gagster had had a nervous breakdown during the night and been sent away.

Gurney had to acknowledge to himself that humour and camaraderie alone could not guard against madness. Sharing jokes and gags with his comrades was a form of creativity, as well as the means by which he bound himself to the men around him and created a sense of security. In losing his confidence in the power of humour to safeguard him, he needed to rely on other forms of creative expression to take its place. His reaction, so typical of what was to become a recurring pattern when in distress, was to draw music and literature to himself, along with the visual elements of the landscape, in a kaleidoscope of sound and colour.

'I need music, which means Bach, very badly, and won't be happy till I get it', he wrote, and a few sentences later:

[Elgar's *Dream of*] *Gerontius* has run very strong in my mind of late—the solemn and noble priests music especially [he writes out the passage in musical notation, which begins 'in the name of Christ who died' and ends 'that shall be poured on thee'] very beautiful that part. There is a bunch of glorious poppies perched as if they meant to astonish and delight one, on a little green knoll just back of the firing line. Blue through the rift, or one of Walt Whitman's letters from God.[57]

It was this moment, so understated in his letters home, but so very painful, that elicited a sonnet entitled 'To England—A Note', which ends the letter, with no explanatory comment.[58]

A pattern had started to emerge—the deaths of Skillern and Hall were worked out through poetry, exploring and developing what the letters skate over in one or two understated sentences. Gurney clung to music and poetry as creative substitutes, but as the former was inaccessible, he increasingly began by necessity to put his faith into poetry. He knew he needed to use his creativity in some form to guard against his own breakdown, and in the final couplet of 'To England', it is the triumph of music, not humour, on which he stakes his trust.

In one of his stronger early poems, a sonnet with a good clear turn, he explores the banality of commonplace duty and routine as the very substance of poetry. All the lads he describes are putative poets, and their work is itself a form of resistance to war. There are echoes of Gerard Manley Hopkins ('Tom's Garland', perhaps, or 'Felix Randal the Farmer') in Gurney's glorifying of the working man, whether he be labouring in the fields, or in a trench.

Are these the heroes—these? have kept from you
The power of primal savagery so long?
Shall break the devil's legions? These they are
Who do in silence what they might boast to do;
In the height of battle tell the world in song
How they do hate and fear the face of War.[59]

It marked the beginning of Gurney's attempts to establish his relationship to his comrades through his verse, positioning himself as first among his equals. By writing of the men around him, Gurney found a way to link himself to them, strengthening bonds in fantasy that might not have been so certain in reality, and turning the silent work of the Gloucesters into verse or song. His poetry built a new form of embodied experience, transferring his need for physical closeness and connection onto the page, capturing the physicality of the men around him, and by doing so, forging an indelible link with them through his writing.

By 30 June 1916 a big advance had begun 'and all things are now ready for the great Bust'.[60] Gurney was now constantly under fire but sustained by the general sense of expectation. Things were bad, but they were at least moving, and movement in a war this static was something exciting. He did not know that in the south the great offensive on the Somme was about to begin. Arthur Bliss and his younger brother Kennard would be caught up in this historic battle, which would cost Kennard his life and leave Arthur wounded, traumatised and bereaved. Gurney had his own problems further north, with a German raid on Colvin Craters (part of the line near Laventie held by 2/5th Gloucesters) which took place that night. Eighty yards of their front line were blown to pieces. A small raiding party of Germans got into the shell craters that made up the line, were there for some time, and withdrew unmolested. The signallers' wires were cut by the shelling, so messages had to be sent from each company to battalion headquarters by runners. No one was quite certain whether the Germans were actually still in the Gloucesters' line or not, so no one attacked them. Even if there had been orders to do so, all the nearby Gloucesters who had been trained as bombers had been killed. There was no one left who knew how to use bombs.

The official report into the event rather sanctimoniously set out the lessons to be learnt, and reflected on the general chaos and lack of communication:

Five signallers were found in a dug-out by the German party and killed. If it is a man's duty to be in a dugout during a bombardment, all should understand it is the most unsafe place to be in the moment the bombardment ceases. Did they have their rifles with them? Specialists often seem to have an idea that it is not their business to man the parapet, or to fight.

The confusion led to unnecessary deaths, and to a sense of general despair on the part of those in charge of the men. They were having

a devil of a time [. . .] We were made a cock-shy of for the artillery, and so have really been a part of the advance. One strafe lasted 2 ½ hours, and gave me a permanent distaste for such. We were under fire every day, and nowhere was safe. In the post where I was for half my time, there were twelve dugouts. Four have been smashed, the cookhouse a mere melancholy ruin of its former greatness, and the bomb store not what it was.[61]

Men of all description, from cooks to machine gunners, were wandering around vaguely with no instruction. Only a handful took the initiative to put themselves under the command of the nearest officer and help hold the line. Despite this temporary mayhem, Gurney felt that the offensive was going well and morale was still high, with 'surely great hopes now of an early advance.'[62]

Around this time (30 June and 1 July), Higher Command ran a series of bizarre 'stunts' to upset German morale, more redolent of a scene from the television series *Blackadder* than of serious strategy. The Gloucesters were instructed to hurl smoke bombs out into No Man's Land, then animate full-sized cardboard figures, connected by wires to the frontline trenches, drawing them up into a standing position to give the appearance of an attack. It was effectively a puppet show. At another time sandbags filled with grass were thrown over the top of the breastworks with the same purpose in view.[63] However comical and absurd these actions, the consequences were neither; the Gloucesters were heavily shelled, sustained a great many unnecessary casualties, and they cursed the generals for their antics.

By 3 July the 2/7th Worcesters arrived to relieve them, and Gurney marched back out of his worst stint in the front line so far. He was directed to billets in La Gorgue, a village roughly five kilometres to the west of Laventie. There he luxuriated in a large vat, enjoying his first hot bath in France, whilst his clothes were disinfected in a largely ineffective attempt to kill the trench lice that lived in every seam.[64]

There was a makeshift theatre at La Gorgue, and a performance on the evening of the 4 July was attended by many freshly scrubbed 2/5ths.[65] Although there was not much to see in nearby Estaires, it did have the attraction of a large, very dilapidated hotel, which still served a sad approximation of its peacetime dinners. There was even a shop opposite, run by two genteel ladies, who were rather incongruously selling scent and handkerchiefs.[66] Estaires provided Gurney with a few days' respite, and allowed him time to write, and to send his poems back to Marion Scott for safekeeping. This was to be the start of a repeating pattern. Whenever he returned to billets, with time to reflect on his recent experiences in the front line, he would either write poems or copy out any he had written in the previous days in the trenches. When he was in the front line, he was obliged to abandon his larger pack, along with notebooks and paper, as he could only take a small haversack of his belongings with him.

As the war ground on, the gulf between Gurney in France and Howells back in England became wider by the day. Gurney's first chance in months to think about writing music involved 'writ[ing] out on some dirty scraps of manuscript I always carry with me, my setting of Davis's "The Sea."'[67] His access to performance had amounted to an aborted attempt to play hymn accompaniments for 'our Wesleyan brethren', which had been frustrated by an earlier than expected transfer to the trenches at Richebourg–St Vaast. It was a long way from the vision he and Howells had shared as ambitious young organ scholars walking the streets of Gloucester only five years before.

Gurney and Howells were both experiencing critical moments in their careers, but in very different ways. The summer of 1916 represented Gurney's first real introduction to trench warfare, and his own nervous exploration of how much he could endure without breaking down. Howells, in his world of civilian safety, was also fighting for his life. At only twenty-three, he had developed a condition called Graves' disease, which affected his heart and eyes, and left him exhausted, struggling to see, and out of breath, with a dangerously high pulse. The unlikely fact of his survival was due to a highly experimental two-year course of radium treatment, which was given on the basis that he did not have long to live anyway, and any risk was worth taking. The treatment was far too expensive for the impecunious Howells family, so Hubert

Parry gallantly stepped in. His generosity quite literally saved his student's life. Despite travelling constantly between Gloucestershire and St Thomas's Hospital in London for his therapy, Howells still managed to finish a string quartet at the village of Churchdown that June. Churchdown's Chosen Hill was one of Gurney's most cherished Gloucestershire haunts, and the quartet was dedicated to Gurney. It was a poignant gesture. Both men knew that Gurney might not ever hear the piece or revisit the place of its inspiration. It was Howells's first 'mature' work, exploring beyond the Germanic influences of the Royal College, and inviting comparison with Ravel's Piano Trio. It was to become one of the most significant pieces written in England during the war. Rather wistfully admiring Howells's triumph from afar, Gurney was not to know that despite all the distractions of war, he was about to write four songs that would equal the quartet's claim to originality and significance.

By July 1916 Gurney's frustration was mounting, along with the very real anxiety that he would never have the opportunity to write any more lasting works. He had tired of his temporary 'rest' from music, boldly informing Scott that he could manage '5 or 6 hours work a day now'.[68] The irony would hardly have been wasted on him that his army 'cure' was the very thing that was now keeping him from his work.

The days wound on, as Gurney trudged from front line to reserve trench and back, the mud-clogged fields of Flanders framed by vast, depressing, grey skies. He was increasingly aware that he was trapped within the cyclic rhythm of trench life. On 6 July the 2/5ths were ordered back into the front line near Richebourg–St Vaast, this time relieving men from the famous Scottish regiment the Black Watch.[69] Richebourg, a previously prosperous and attractive village, was in ruins.[70] It was a thoroughly unsavoury place, so much so that even the war-hardened Belgian civilians had entirely deserted it. The buildings had been loopholed and sandbagged, and the rows of poplars still lining the streets had judiciously placed observation ladders running up them.

The church at Richebourg had been particularly badly hit (church towers were always an obvious target, as they provided useful surveillance posts). Edmund Blunden, stationed there only two months before, in May 1916, had been fascinated by the macabre allure of the church and its dead.

It was a district of shrines and keeps. St. Vaast had resplendent examples of both; a white marble shrine, if I remember, looked eastward there, its saints gleaming like Byron's Assyrians. . . . The large church, and the almost rococo churchyard, astonished everybody: they had been bombarded into that state of demi-ruin which discovers the strongest fascination. At the foot of the monolith-like steeple stood a fine and great bell, and against that, a rusty shell of almost the same size; the body and blood of Christ, in effigy of ochred wood, remained on the wall of the church. Men went to contemplate that group, but more to stare into the very popular tombs all round, whose vaults

FIG. 3.2: The Church at Richebourg. © Imperial War Museum.

gaped unroofed, nor could protect their charges any longer from the eye of life. Greenish water stood in some of these pits; bones and skulls and decayed cerements there attracted frequent soldiers past the 'No Loitering' notice board. Why should these mortalities lure those who ought to be trying to forget mortality, ever threatening them? Nearly corpses ourselves, by the mere fact of standing near Richebourg Church, how should we find the strange and the remote in these corpses? I remember these remarks: 'How long till dinner, Alf?' 'Half an hour, chum.' 'Well, I'll go and 'ave a squint at the churchyard.'[71]

Private Horlicks, in the same trenches as Gurney, wrote in his diary:

Mud up to our knees. Rotten trenches. In places only 80 yards apart and in others less than that. This is the place the Sussex Brigade went over. [. . .] Rumour has it only 900 came back out of the Brigade. There were a lot of dead out in front. It was terrible to see them, after they had been out there for a time. It quite upset me. We also dug up 4 or 5 when filling sandbags. Was glad to get back.[72]

Gurney chose not to mention the unburied corpses that surrounded him but focused instead on the Scottish soldiers who were now keeping the line. It was only a fleeting encounter with the historic Scottish regiment, 'but I would like a turn with some Scots we just met once. They were fine indeed.' Like his first night in with the Welsh, they left a deep impression.

It was a restless summer. With limited access to newspapers, Gurney turned to Scott and civilians in London for some idea of what was happening on the Somme. He was still hoping that the war was progressing, but it was now a month into the Somme campaign, and there was little to show for it. The initial optimism in the trenches was wearing thin, and few now believed that it might signal the beginning of the end. Gurney was becoming depressed, describing a state of 'moral washed-outness', without the will or energy even to clean his face in the old biscuit tin he was using for a sink.[73] At various points during his war service he experimented, not altogether successfully, with cultivating a moustache. Now, however, he had lost all interest in his appearance, and the stubble sprouted freely. The sergeant major seemed to have given up enforcing military standards on Gurney's appearance, at least while in the trenches. Gurney took advantage of the leniency, stopped shaving altogether, and tied sandbags round his boots to keep off as much of the mud as possible. All the men's energy had been sapped by the cripplingly heavy fatigues of the last few days, as they dragged supplies up through the network of trenches ready for the advance they all knew was imminent.

By 18 July, the battalion was on fatigue preparing for an attack near Aubers Ridge, which was scheduled to take place the next day. All they knew was that Army Corps HQ had sent a message: 'We are going to attack on this front to relieve our comrades on the Somme'. No letters survive from this time, if Gurney indeed had the opportunity to write any. It was to be a huge attack on a notorious piece of high ground. Whilst the gradient was not severe, any advantage of height, however slight, put those occupying the higher trenches in a far better position than the other side. In this instance, the Germans were well dug in, and looking down, and into, the British lines. No one gazing up at the waves of German wire ahead could have felt that the outcome of the next few days was likely to be positive.

The Gloucesters were in the support trenches by 6 am on the 20th, with the battle already raging around them. They had received some unexpectedly encouraging news on the previous evening: the Australians further up the line had taken the first and second German lines. Emboldened by this progress, it fell to the Bucks and Berkshire regiments to attack, with the Gloucesters in the trenches behind them, ready to take over. The battle went on for around four days. Gurney spent the first few days waiting for orders to move off, potentially at half an hour's notice. The hours dragged by, in a strange mixture of terror and boredom. There was nothing to do but wait passively to be ordered into the midst of the fighting. But by 4:30 on the morning of the 21st a message came that the German trenches captured by the nearby Australians had now been lost, and what was left of the Australian regiments had been obliged to retire. The 2/5ths were to finish the job for them, a less than appealing prospect, and Gurney and his friends were sent off in an incongruous convoy of requisitioned London buses to Laventie, ready to be deployed to the front line.

This was the Battle of Fromelles. The attack was one of a number planned because the Somme was thought to be going well enough that a breakthrough was imminent (which, of course, it was not). There had been sixteen months of comparative quiet since fierce fighting on the same spot the previous March had made Aubers Ridge infamous. During that time, the Germans had abandoned the flooded frontline trenches they had occupied that spring and made a strategic retreat to better trenches, digging their machine guns into well-constructed, reinforced emplacements. Any progress the Australians and British could make towards them had to involve traversing the crisscross of abandoned, waterlogged trenches, whilst under heavy fire. If, by some miracle, a small breakthrough was achieved, the attack would simply have moved the troops further towards the German guns securely dug in on the ridge. From their higher vantage point, with their well-constructed concrete pillboxes and a mire of impassable mud and wire in front of them, the Germans were invincible.

Bombardment began at 11 am on 19 July, with the infantry attack timetabled for 6 pm. The Germans retaliated with a counterbombardment that killed many of those assembled before they had even left their trenches. The assault by the 61st Division was a total failure, and German machine gun fire forced them to retreat without occupying any of the German front line. The 2/5ths waited in comparative safety at Laventie for their part in the battle. Gurney and his comrades knew precisely what the chances of success were against such an impregnable location. They waited for the order to attack with much the same anticipation as if they were waiting for an order to commit suicide, but the order never came. By the time the attack was over, the 61st Division had suffered 50 percent casualties, but by a stroke of amazing good fortune, Gurney and the 2/5ths had escaped intact. They were deeply shaken, but relatively unscathed.[74]

By 23 July 1916 the battalion was back in the trenches, thankful not to be attacking the ridge itself, but still very nearby. They were now taking over the right subsection of the rather romantically entitled Moated Grange Sector, near the village of Neuve Chapelle, to relieve some men of the 11th and 14th Yorkshire regiments.

The Grange's Tennysonian name entirely belied the reality of the flooded shell holes and poisoned landscape.[75] In fact, it was near the improbably unromantic 'Dead Horse Copse'. Gurney was certainly under no illusions about the area. His experiences there were, in his own words, 'grisly'. He spent many hours on sentry duty, staring into the darkness. He lay in No Man's Land, in front of his own trenches, in a pool of stagnant water near the wire. He endured it for an hour, counting the minutes until he heard the quiet approach of another of the 2/5ths to take their turn. After an hour off, they would swap again.

It was whilst the battalion was at Moated Grange that Will Harvey's brother Eric joined them from the 3/5ths. Gurney might not have been aware of his transfer.[76] Despite, or perhaps because of the unqualified misery of Moated Grange,

17. La Grande Guerre 1914-15
Aspect de NEUVE-CHAPELLE (P.-de-C.) après le départ des barbares   A. R.

FIG. 3.3: Neuve Chapelle in ruins. © Soldiers of Gloucestershire Museum.

late July and August proved to be a period of some experimentation and creativity for Gurney. On 27 July, he sent Scott 'Strange Service', his first attempt at 'rhymeless verse'. In the same letter, he hinted at the pain all the men felt in thinking of home: 'We are all fed up. How fed up you must gather from the fact that anyone who mentions home is howled down at once.' Homesickness was too painful to be articulated, and so it had to be internalised. 'But Gloster, like Troy in Masefield's poem, has become a city in the soul.'[77] This city in the soul, with the depth of meaning and feeling the image conveys, was to be the inspiration for some of his finest poetry so far.

Strange Service

Little did I dream, England, that you bore me
Under the Cotswold hills beside the water meadows,
To do you dreadful service, here, beyond your borders
And your enfolding seas.

I was a dreamer ever, and bound to your dear service,
Meditating deep, I thought on your secret beauty,
As through a child's face one may see the clear spirit
Miraculously shining.

Your hills not only hills, but friends of mine and kindly,
Your tiny knolls and orchards hidden beside the river
Muddy and strongly-flowing, with shy and tiny streamlets
Safe in its bosom.

Now these are memories only, and your skies and rushy sky-pools
Fragile mirrors easily broken by moving airs. . . .
In my deep heart for ever goes on your daily being,
And uses consecrate.
Think on me too, O Mother, who wrest my soul to serve you
In strange and fearful ways beyond your encircling waters;
None but you can know my heart, its tears and sacrifice;
None, but you, repay.[78]

'Strange Service' is a poem full of water, an act of imaginative transference from waterlogged trenches to English seas, ponds, rivers and lakes. It is also full of the undulations of landscape. The trenches literalised Gurney's close emotional connection with the earth; they offered both precarious shelter and potential entombment, and he was beginning to use his poetry to articulate such paradoxes. The earth is a source of both restoration (in imagination) and possible death. Its power lies in its potential for both. This combination of adoration of the landscape and anxiety about its destructive power, or the possibility of rejection, results in a powerful sense of ambivalence that drives much of Gurney's landscape poetry. His anthropomorphism of the countryside extended to the topography of his writing, both in poetry and in music: the hills and valleys become the shapes of melodic and poetic lines, both art and countryside outlining a form and body. Poetry, music and landscape together become a place through which Gurney imagines forms of physical life (and perhaps also death).

He painted these alternative landscapes whenever he was in the mood for drawing on his memories to, as he rather self-consciously refers to it, 'make' poetry and music. These reimaginings of events frequently return in his poetry to a refrain of friendship and community, building relationships in words that are often beyond the obvious and familial. Here, Gurney uses the poem 'Strange Service' to probe his own ambiguity about his relationship to the state and his war service through the lens of his deep ambivalence towards his mother. For someone with such a troubled maternal relationship, the mother as a metaphor in wartime was particularly complicated, especially when that 'mother' represented the Motherland. He found it was a theme that resonated deeply, and he returned to the trope of Mother England throughout the following year, in 'The Mother' (November 1916), 'Spring. Rouen, May 1917' and 'England the Mother' (both written in May 1917).

At the heart of Gurney's relationship with his own mother lay an unresolved paradox. She was unable to love her children, or so Gurney's siblings believed, but this loss was perhaps at the very heart of his drive to create. These poems, teasing out the complexities of the mother-child relationship, can be read as an emotional response to this early deprivation. Whatever the negative impact of Gurney's estrangement from his mother, he did inherit some essential qualities from her that were fundamental to the success of his work. Both Florence and her son possessed a keen appreciation of beauty and the environment, and a naturally expressive writing style. Gurney took his mother's underdeveloped poetic and musical gifts and offered them back to her through his own work. In doing so, he created a song of innocence in the Blakean sense: 'Strange Service' is Gurney's farewell to his childhood, and to the maternal landscape that had until now protected him, as he turned to face the horrors of human brutality and stupidity.

His conception of the mother in 'Strange Service' is indeed, as his title suggests, deliberately strange. His experiences in France had heightened his appreciation of the vexed relationship between the country in need and those who fought to defend her, and he now had the technical capacity to explore such complexities by manipulating cultural clichés in his verse. As he observed other communities, and watched the men around him group together to form familial bonds, so he began to develop his own set of tenets, and a belief structure, expressed through his work. In his poetry, Gurney was developing his own national and cultural code of allegiance, based on recreating beauty, observing and elevating the quotidian details of the everyday, and shaping his identity through his work.

As a composer, Gurney could select preexisting poetry to set as part of his continual search for a personal manifesto. The text of a song might be chosen by the composer as something to enhance, attack, or perhaps both. Gurney understood how he might inhabit someone else's words and rebalance their rhythms, or shift emphases, undermine their meaning or create an atmosphere that revealed the text in a new light. The subtlety with which he could shape and reinterpret a line of text through sound was already more advanced than many composers achieve in a lifetime.[79] In 'Strange Service' Gurney is starting to apply this principle to poetry, with the trope of 'Mother England' standing in place of a preexisting poem.

This musical experimentation might have his relationship with his mother and his beloved Gloucestershire as its inspiration, but the experience of war was one of profound contradiction, and what was a characteristic of his life as a soldier became a structuring principle in his writing. Proximity to death was experienced alongside a heightened appreciation of life; a delicate poppy could be appreciated even when plucked from next to a corpse. Such contradictions were all held in tension in the daily life of the soldier, and Gurney absorbed and transmuted them into both poetry and music. The jarringly unexpected comparison, the unpredictable, wrong-footing chord progression, are held within a larger framework. Just as Gurney the soldier was obliged to encompass an extreme range of experience and emotion, so Gurney the creator widened his horizons to develop a compositional style that embraced a bewilderingly broad range of reference.

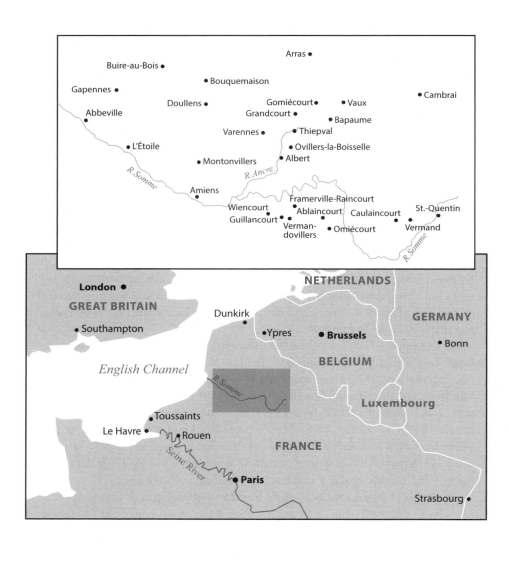

CHAPTER FOUR

'Most Grand to Die'?

One day, in the midst of the miserable summer of 1916, Gurney erected a makeshift shrine in his dugout, an altar at which to worship Gloucester. In place of an icon or crucifix he wedged a photograph taken by a friend of his in a niche in the sand-bagged wall. The sepia image represented

> a place that stands for delight with all Gloster men. It means a good tea, clean air, feminine society, a good row on a pretty stretch of river, Beauty and leisure to enjoy it; Home and all its meaning.[1]

In 'Strange Service' he had imagined consecrating the sacred memories of Glouces-tershire within his very being. Now the shrine had become literalised, and he could make his worship a communal act. But what would his congregation make of it? Would a photograph of Gloucestershire indeed 'stand for delight with all Gloster men', however homesick they might be? It seems unlikely, but he believed his little picture postcard moved others just as much as its owner.

> I lead weary men into this commodious residence, and show them this pen-nyworth of poor printing. They cannot speak, or do so in such phrases as— 'That hurts my cory.' 'My God, my God!' 'What a life!' or more explosively, 'How *Long* is this ******* War Going to *Last*?'[2]

Gurney delighted in the exquisite pain and pleasure the image aroused in his comrades. He was pining for home, but he was no longer alone in his homesickness, as he had been in London. Gurney knew that he was by nature an outsider. As a creative personality he was an observer, rather than a participator; a 'watcher in shadows', and his awareness of his different status surfaces repeatedly in his poetry. His relationship to the men around him was defined by a combination of comrade-ship and distanced observation. Few in B Company would have shared his passion for the latest poets, or could fully understand his artistic ambitions. But he had one fundamental connection to them; he adored their home county, and they were its living embodiments. Mental transference and acts of nostalgic remembrance were

Fig. 4.1: Gurney's beloved picture of Gloucester Cathedral,
'The Lighthouse of the Vale', as its photographer Sydney Pitcher entitled it.
Courtesy of the Historic England Archive.

Gurney's means of psychic survival. By showing his comrades this little picture postcard, he shared with them the very apparatus that both upheld him and inspired his work.

Gurney's happiest childhood memories were all associated with the Gloucestershire countryside. When he had been a chorister at Gloucester Cathedral, he had lived at home while many of the other boys boarded. On free Sunday afternoons, his parents would occasionally take a group of them out for a trip on the river, or, if Gurney's father was inclined to relax his observance of the Sabbath sufficiently, a game of cricket.

After the boys had returned to school, the family would embark on an eight-mile round trip to the picturesque village of Maisemore to take Gurney's paternal grandmother her weekly supplies of butter and tea. Gurney would often take a circuitous route, wandering off alone into the bluebell woods.[3] These, as Gurney's sister Winifred later remembered, were the 'pleasant days of our lives'. Gurney adored his father, and their walks together through the countryside were pure joy to him. Their mother

FIG. 4.2: Gloucester Cathedral School football team
(Gurney, seated second from right). © Gurney Trust.

went too, and nature brought out the better, more poetic side of her troubled personality. She would 'go into raptures over a beautiful sunset', whilst the more self-contained David taught his children to identify flowers and birds, teaching them to appreciate the markings on wings, or the tiny flowers half hidden at the bottom of a hedgerow.[4] The whole family was temporarily at ease in each other's company, away from the claustrophobia of home. Later, Gurney would watch with intense pity the children growing up in dark, soot-stained streets in the East End of London:

[. . .] my own young life was set in
A happier City smaller, whose four ways met in
From country; with green meadows for children's
Free pleasure, far from traffic's loud bewilderings.[5]

There are poets for whom location is not particularly important. For some, it is the act of journeying, the discovery of new landscapes, that is the source of inspiration. For Gurney, Gloucestershire's hills and meadows were the purpose of his very being. Now, in the mud fields of France, his soul ached for his home county, and his

FIG. 4.3: Gurney's grandmother, outside her house at Maisemore. Courtesy of Noel Hayward, from the photograph album belonging to Dorothy Gurney.

mind wandered the streets of the city and the country lanes, remembering the routes he knew so intimately.

By 16 August Gurney was back in the reserve trenches in the Moated Grange Sector of Fauquissart near Laventie, and delighting in the company of Will Harvey after so many months of separation. Finally, he could resume his cherished conversations about literature, if only temporarily. He was continually hungry for new books, and Harvey lent him his copy of Robert Bridges's *The Spirit of Man*, the nearest thing to a bible for Harvey and Gurney. Gurney was not without criticism of the poet laureate's selections for this new anthology, 'a good book, though very far below what it might be . . . about one third of the book is worth having, some of it foolish merely.' He missed Belloc, whom Bridges had excluded for being too conservative, and missed his favourite Yeats poems, 'Kathleen ni Houlihan' and the 'Fiddler of Dooney', again, some of the least progressive of Yeats's verse. He found the French poetry in it 'trite and dull'. 'Where is the Wordsworth, Stevenson, Whitman, Browning? And why not more Tolstoi?'[6] Gerard Manley Hopkins's verse was included, but Gurney was not yet ready, or was too weary, to understand its importance, describing him scornfully as 'Hopkins or what's his names of the crazy precious diction'. He would return to him in more auspicious surroundings, and much of his own use of language in his later poetry would be influenced by that 'crazy

FIG. 4.4: Manuscript of 'By a Bierside', complete with trench mud. © Gurney Trust.

precious diction' which was so far removed from anything he and Harvey had yet come across.

Whatever Gurney's initial reservations about the anthology, he was exhausted and starved of culture. It was balm for the soul, and an incentive to create. *The Spirit of Man* was to become a seminally important work for Gurney, both as inspiration for his own poetic development and as a source of texts to set to music. At around this time, he managed to complete one of his finest songs to date: a setting of John Masefield's poem 'By a Bierside'.[7] It was written in a disused mortar emplacement, a quiet corner of the reserve trenches which had been created for the firing of shells. He was rather proud of its genesis, a masterpiece written on a sandbag, by the light of a stump of candle.

Gurney claimed to be a composer first and foremost, but for the last few months poetry had replaced song as the more practical means of working out his impressions and thoughts in an artistic form. When access to pianos was intermittent and manuscript paper scarce, a poem scribbled in a letter or notebook was by far the more congenial way of 'composing'. Now, for the first time in his career, he was selecting poetry to set, alongside creating his own poems. In short, poetry occupied his thoughts, both as poet and composer, and the combination provides a double insight into his use of verse to articulate his experiences. 'By a Bierside' was to be the first of four songs to use others' verse to examine different approaches to death, a subject that was all too topical.

Masefield's 'By a Bierside' appears at first to be a curious choice. It insists on the grandeur of death, which, considering the conditions in the trenches at Moated Grange, was not a sentiment that might immediately spring to mind. Whilst Masefield claims it is 'most grand to die', Gurney's own verse at the time depicts the living having to 'wrest their soul' in the process of trying to stay alive.[8] Gurney was not in the habit of choosing texts lightly. He had already practically memorised the poem before going to France, and quoted it from memory in a letter to Scott in December 1915. His 'chosen identification' with the poem (as the composer Gerald Finzi would later describe the process of being drawn to a text) was not necessarily with the ideology of the text, but with a fundamental response to the emotion of it. Gurney's setting both upholds and questions the idea of grandeur in death, while exploring his own fascination with the subject.

Not only was he drawn to a poem that celebrates death (although this celebration is far from unambiguous), but he embraced the idea of the romanticised death of a hero. Even his own retelling of the inspiration for the song is surprisingly sentimental:

> In my mind I saw a picture of some poet-priest pronouncing an oration over the dead and lovely body of some young Greek hero.[9]

It is a symphony in miniature, and Gurney later offered a programmatic, symphonic explanation of it:

> The first part of the song is of course a raphsody [sic] on beauty, full of grief but not bitter, until the unreason of death closes the thought of loveliness, that Death unmakes. Then the heart grows bitter with the weight of grief and revelation of the impermanence of things—Justice and Strength turning to a

poet's theme. But, anger being futile, the mind turns to the old strangeness of the soul's wandering apart from the body, and to what tremendous mysteries! And the dimly apprehended sense of such before us all overpowers the singer, who is lost in the glory of the adventure of Death.[10]

The glory of the adventure of death finds its counterpart in the song's dramatic pauses, and richly conceived piano part. The trumpet-like fanfares repeated in the piano are grandeur at its height, but the ending, a murmured 'most grand' of both voice and piano (one of Gurney's rare and always highly significant repetitions of text), is perhaps the shadow of an alternative to this pomp and circumstance. On another occasion, Gurney claimed the song encapsulated two evenings of outstanding beauty in the summer of 1914 in Gloucestershire, just as the war was declared.[11] The country-side had 'sung' to him, and this was his interpretation of its music, in all its glory.

At the time he was drawn to Masefield's words, Gurney was at the height of an infatuation with the poetry of Walt Whitman. He equated what he found in Whitman with his own musical impulse: 'I want to write in music such stuff as "This Compost".'[12] This poem in particular seemed to exercise an especial hold over him. It reduces its hero to nothing more than dead and rotten meat, seemingly a world away from the mystical sentimentality of Masefield. 'By a Bierside' wrestles with the same contradictions—it holds the dead body and the wastefulness and disgust of death alongside ideas of nobility and grandeur, just as Gurney holds in his head Masefield's poem and Whitman's neurotic, squeamish outpouring. And at the centre of it all is the earth—both a treacherous tomb and a potentially lifesaving shelter.

On the same day that Gurney was writing musical depictions of heroism and noble death, Harvey was investigating the possibilities of both in reality. He had left Gurney in the reserve trench on the morning of 16 August, happily devouring his newly acquired Bridges anthology. Back in the front line, Harvey had decided to go out alone on patrol into No Man's Land. He was acting against advice. Finding that he had managed somehow to get as far as the German front line without meeting any resistance, he jumped down into the trench, feeling quietly triumphant. Once there, he realised it was considerably harder to get out than it had been to get in, and when he heard the sound of voices coming closer, found that he was trapped. He had no choice but to put his hands up and hope that the Germans were more interested in him as a prisoner than as a corpse. He was in luck. But whilst he was being marched back into German occupied territory to begin his long imprisonment, his company was waiting for him to return. After too many hours had passed for it to be likely that he would come back, they had to assume that he had joined the vast ranks of the 'missing presumed dead'.

It was not uncommon to get lost in No Man's Land and for a while there was some hope of his return, but by the 18th he had been recorded in the regimental war diary as officially missing. His chances of survival were lessened by the fact that there had been fighting in No Man's Land since he had disappeared. The Germans had exploded a mine that afternoon and had wired a crater during the night, along with one of the regular trench mortar strafes. The chances of anyone wounded or stranded surviving the combination of all these were very slim.

Within a few days, news of Harvey's disappearance had made its way round the company, and back to Gurney. Harvey's natural charisma and his witty poems in the battalion's unofficial newspaper, the *Gloster Gazette*, had made him a popular figure amongst the Gloucesters. But none had known him as Gurney had, or grieved his loss as deeply.

> I have had rather a blow lately, and need music to express my feelings, and let off steam. F.W.H. is almost certainly dead, and with him my deepest friendship, as far as that does pass with death; a very little with me. He went out on patrol alone, and has not returned, an unworthy ending for so fine a spirit, who should have died, if his destiny were to die in this horrible anonymous war, hot in battle, in some hopeless-brave attack.[13]

Harvey had been Gurney's dearest friend, partly perhaps because he represented the closest thing to an ideal version of himself.

After-glow
(To F. W. Harvey)

> Out of the smoke and dust of the little room
> With tea-talk loud and laughter of happy boys,
> I passed into the dusk. Suddenly the noise
> Ceased with a shock, left me alone in the gloom,
> To wonder at the miracle hanging high
> Tangled in twigs, the silver crescent clear.—
> Time passed from mind. Time died; and then we were
> Once more at home together, you and I.

> The elms with arms of love wrapped us in shade
> Who watched the ecstatic West with one desire,
> One soul uprapt; and still another fire
> Consumed us; and our joy yet greater made:
> That Bach should sing for us, mix us in one
> The joy of firelight and the sunken sun.[14]

As an adolescent, Gurney had found his own family to be hopelessly inadequate, so he'd simply adopted Harvey's. Harvey was the medal-winning, successful soldier, always surrounded by admiring men. He wasn't a shabby private like Gurney, but a respectable lieutenant, and to top it all, he was already a published poet. In short, Harvey was everything Gurney was not, even though this poetic tribute to him is arguably more assured than any poetry written by its subject. The deftness with which Gurney creates and alters atmosphere, moving from one line to another between light, smoke, dark, noise and silence, and the economy with which he conjures up a moon glimpsed through branches are already beyond the technical grasp of Harvey's polished but only intermittently profound verse.

Harvey was Gurney's first formative poetic influence, but he had been far more to him than just a poet to emulate. Now, apparently, Harvey was dead. When Gurney had received the news, he had just been reading a review of a French war poet, Paul Claudel. 'He speaks of his dead countrymen "set in the ground like corn." A most beautiful way of reference [sic] to the number of deaths and the virtue thereof.'[15] Gurney could find comfort in the image but could not bring himself to write a similarly fruitful and pacifying poem. When he later wrote of a soldier's body in one of his greatest poems, 'To His Love', it is not purposefully planted, but a bleeding corpse polluting the landscape.

By 24 August, four days before his birthday, he was relieved to be out of the trenches. He had made his way to a clearing station hospital camp 'miles away from the lines to have my spectacles and teeth mended, and to drink as much coffee as my interior may be induced to receive.'[16] Toothache had plagued Gurney since July, and now it had finally got the better of him. Despite the discomfort of having his teeth removed, Gurney found that he was in a surprisingly civilised environment in which to celebrate his twenty-sixth birthday. He had been reading Keats, and only two weeks previously had been lamenting the poet's untimely death at the age of twenty-six, before 'his pen had gleaned his teeming brain'.[17] It was unlikely that the potential parallel was lost on him, particularly as he was still deeply in mourning for Harvey. He may have been feeling morbid, but he could find a certain consolation in the luxury of personal hygiene and a proper bed to sleep in, especially as he had not had to incur a wound for the privilege. One drawback was the obligation to stay within the camp, a frustrating limitation for a man in whom the urge to roam was irrepressible. In early September he was made billet warden, a mundane post, but with the advantage of plenty of free time for reading. He was not without companions—a friend who had been in the Royal Army Medical Corps was working in the hospital. To Gurney's delight, he was impressively well connected, and could even claim to have paid a visit to Tolstoy in 'about 1902'. There was an excuse for a wheezy old harmonium in the chapel. It had 'several teeth missing, and some of the stops are mere outbursts of insensate fury'. Despite the continual dull ache of his bereavement, he was surprisingly upbeat: 'this fortnight's rest has showed me that now I am happier than ever in my life, or anyhow, for a long time.'[18]

It was not to last. By 13 September, Gurney's golden period of respite was well and truly over. The toothache was cured and he was out of hospital, and back in the line.

> Just received two delightful letters from [Sydney] Shimmin and Mr Taylor [...] Curse me, though, they both talk about Bach in a most disturbing manner, and remind me there is another world but that of war; a thing one usually realises, when the bottom of one's mind seems to fall out suddenly with the horror of it all.[19]

The last line is a particularly suggestive, dramatic image, summarising the mechanism that Gurney had developed to protect himself from breakdown. When the present became too ghastly to contemplate, and he lost his mental bearings, he could steady himself by drawing on Bach. As he was clearly well aware, the shifts in fantasy between Severn and Somme, the sights and sounds of war and the musical and natural beauty of his prewar life, were so much more than a poetic device: they were fundamental to Gurney's sanity.

The battalion had moved up to Riez Bailleul two days before, and now he rejoined them, no longer a signaller but a regular infantry soldier. His change in status meant he was likely to be given harder physical work, and he was put to work digging trenches rather than wiring.

Throughout September Gurney continued to mourn Harvey's death, whilst Harvey himself attempted to adjust to his new life in a prison camp in Germany. As the leaves on the plane trees around the camp turned to crimson and gold, the battalion started to prepare for a move from Riez Bailleul. On their penultimate day, surrounded by piles of equipment waiting to be packed onto carts, Gurney received the news for which he had hardly dared hope. His dearest friend was alive, and safe (if miserable) for the duration in a prisoner-of-war camp. It was scarcely believable.

While Harvey had been missing, his book of verse *A Gloucestershire Lad at Home and Abroad* had been passed enthusiastically around the battalion. The men were so keen to read it that Gurney could not retrieve his copy from them to send to Marion Scott, who was equally eager to have it. He was proud and perhaps a trifle envious of Harvey's success, both in the literary world and with their contemporaries in the trenches. Now, as he began once more to dare to imagine a future with Harvey as his companion, Gurney began to reassess his own verse. With a few of his own poems under his belt, perhaps he too might be ready to attempt a slim volume. He copied out a poem that Scott had not yet seen, entitled 'The Fire Kindled', speculating that he would probably need to write another fifteen or twenty to compile a small collection of verse that a publisher would consider. He even decided on the theme that these would follow, closely modelled on Harvey's example. They were to be 'chiefly of local interest', and the projected book would be called 'Songs from the Second-Fifth'.[20]

After the 2/5ths had attempted a raid, which was thwarted by two impassable machine guns, the battalion returned disconsolately to their huts at Riez Bailleul. They were short of five men, who had been wounded in the failed attack. Once again, the usual routines of smartening themselves up, marching and parading began, but this time there was a particular urgency to the buckle-polishing, as on 24 October they were inspected by Brigadier-General The Honourable R. White. By now, Gurney was feeling the strain of the army's insistence on meticulous presentation and parades. As a 'dirty civilian' he rather prided himself on his obstinate grubbiness. He kicked against a system that made a fetish of polished neatness. Being 'harried by inspections' and the 'awful crescendo of brightness in buttons and buckles' was anathema to his rebellious, anarchic nature.[21]

Inspected and approved, despite Gurney's lacklustre efforts, the battalion received its orders to march to billets at Robecq. This was to mark a new phase in Gurney's war. The Gloucesters had been on the Laventie Front from June until the end of October 1916. Now they would begin a slow move south to the Somme. Gurney keenly observed the gradual changes in the landscape as he marched, and he seemed overall to approve. 'This is a pretty place; flat, with some poplars, and always the same cultivation and red-roofs. Never a vulgar building to be seen, as usual.'[22] Robecq itself was the crowning glory. It looked exquisite in the gentle autumnal light, the 'finest of all places in Autumn'; 'the dearest place'.[23]

Having set his sights on a poetry collection of his own to rival Harvey's, Gurney soon began translating his observations into verse. 'Robecq', the first of many poems taking inspiration from specific places in France and Belgium, found its way back to Scott only a few days after he'd settled down in his new billets. It had been some time since he had been focused on an artistic task. It was his development as a poet, not as a composer, on which his efforts were concentrated, but composition was never far from his thoughts. He rather hesitantly developed something along the lines of his first manifesto as a poet-composer in a letter that October. His usual self-conscious, tongue-in-cheek pomposity was quickly set aside as he became increasingly engrossed in his topic.

Vehews on the Setting of Poems

Really, I haven't any. If I can set 'La Belle Dame sans Merci' well, the reason is; that there is something in me of Keats, able to live in the same atmosphere as that in which he wrote his poem; only—being musician, to have told my thoughts in another language. They must not be Keats' thoughts only, but mine also. It is not always necessary to read a poem through to start setting it. When one reads Elroy Flecker—

'High and solemn mountains guard Rioupéroux.'

One may start there at once. Sometimes it is necessary to be wary and fore-thoughtful, as when setting 'I praise the tender flower', but that is a difficult poem—to set it adequately is a 'stunt', I think. So is to set 'By a Bierside'. It would not do to try to set anything very big, like 'By a Bierside' at once, per-haps. But who knows? I had only the first two lines in my mind, or perhaps three, when I began to write, and did not finish till my idea was complete. I did not trouble about balance or any thing else much; it came. And after 5 years or so, I will write sonatas in the same way. The points of vital importance are

(1) A *Poem*; that is a collection of words that have inexplicable significance, and gives one visions and vistas. And
(2) You. (the right 'you'.)

Being almost devoid of patience, I am always in a hurry to get the first verse done, but that is a thing Time will correct, I hope.[24]

According to Gurney's manifesto, his first tenet of poetry is that combinations of words must allow him to shape 'visions and vistas'. This is indeed the funda-mental principle that underlines much of Gurney's work, both in music and in verse. Writing to recreate and hold close what was inaccessible to him in a trench, and later, in the asylum, his 'visions and vistas' are almost invariably those of the imagination. Poetry is, almost literally, the window through which he recalls the views (and sense of uninhibited freedom) he loves and needs. It feeds his desire for disinhibition and freedom of thought, as well as being a space in which he can imagine himself well.

As such, he is primarily the audience for whom he writes, creating the world around him that he cannot access in any other way. However, his poetry is not in-tended as a purely private exercise. He also wrote for 'the right "you"': the men around him, the approval of Scott, the countryside itself, and the recognition of those who would affirm his identity as a respected and recognised man of letters. At the same time, he acknowledges his writing is 'devoid of patience'. This hastiness is not just a fault of a slapdash approach, and certainly not the result of a lack of pas-sion for his craft. At the College, his depression had prevented him from enjoying long stretches of time in which he could guarantee he would be well enough to work methodically and consistently. In the trenches, such a luxury was a remote dream. As he reflected, he was obliged to admit, rather reluctantly, that his tendency towards mental illness was something he already acknowledged to be a fixture, and influ-enced his working method. 'The sad fact is, that I do not know what it is to feel well, and what work I do has to be done in spasms very quickly over.'[25]

Gurney had been busy during the six-day rest at Robecq, and eight poems were added to his fast-growing collection. By the time the battalion had paused at Neuvil-lette for two days, he was ready to send Scott 'Bach and the Sentry', 'Sawgint', 'Maisemore', 'The Colonel', 'Song', 'Requiem ×3', 'Acquiescence', and 'The Signaller's Vision'. His productivity was the result of free time in camp, but his burst of writing stemmed from more than opportunity. Being on the march to a new front meant movement, exhilaration and the potential for new adventure. He had trudged back and forth between the same trenches since May. Now any change was welcome, however unprepossessing the move to be 'mud hole soldiers' on the Somme might seem to be. He chanted music hall numbers with the others as they marched, passing through Toussaints where the black clothes of the peasants remembering their dead on All Souls' Day contrasted with the landscape's vivid autumnal colours. Gurney rejoiced in the unusual movement, and was to return to the memory of this moment in 1925 with sophisticated verse that enacted the moment of welcome liberation:

> (O soldiers, how your pride rots, stuck still / bearing, / waiting order!)
> We moved as soldiers of Rome moved when whim or want
> Of soldiership moved an Army across Gaul—to our / unseen, unguessed /
> Front.[26]

The soldiers whose pride rots are held within a static line that stumbles over its own consonants and halting monosyllables, only to rush in the next line across France, buoyed on a fluid tide of *m*'s and aspirated *wh*'s. They are moving not only through place but through time—synonymous with the Roman army before them in a well-used trope of telescoping the modern army into its ancient forebears (witness, although Gurney could not at this point, W. H. Auden's 'Roman Wall Blues', or the artist-poet David Jones's 'In Parenthesis'). Gurney imagines contemporary military success as a well-rehearsed historical manoeuvre, turning to ancient military orders as a way of boosting his morale.

There was a further week off at Bouquemaison, before the final three-day march south (on 16 November) to Albert, a town roughly in the centre of the Somme region. The whole place was packed with troops and transport, and the traffic along the Albert-Bapaume road was incessant. They were passed by an unending line of guns, limbers, lorries, mules and ambulances.

Gurney arrived in Albert in the pouring rain. He spent the next few days sheltering from the incessant downpour and exploring what was left of the little town. He spent many hours with his friends in the large central square of Albert, surrounded on three sides by ruined shop fronts and on the other by what remained of an incongruously large Byzantine basilica.

> Tonight we have had café au lait, our little circle; seated round a tiny hut fire; surrounded by the abomination of desolation and by day depressed by the sight of a piteously ruined church tower; once a glory. And amazed by the sight of a hanging statue.[27]

FIG. 4.5: The basilica in Albert, with its famously leaning statue.
© Imperial War Museum.

This statue was the famous Golden Virgin and Child, one of the more bizarre iconic images of the war.[28] Gurney was fascinated by the sight of the dazzling, human-size golden figure leaning over the basilica that dominated the little town. The statue had been unhinged from its base by a shell, and instead of the Virgin reaching up to heaven with her baby held up to God, she hovered horizontally, peering down over the men in the square below at an impossible ninety-degree angle over the edge of the tower. The hanging statue had already entered into the mythology of the troops on both sides. One superstition was that the war would end when the statue fell, and both German and British artillery tried at various points to knock it down. The Germans then started the myth that whoever shot it down would actually lose the war, as it was proving too hard to hit. But it was more than just a bizarre target. The attitude of the toppling statue was one of pathos, and the fact that it was even still attached seemed in itself to point to divine intervention. Some interpreted the Virgin's new attitude as a gesture of despair, throwing her child into battle, or offering him up to the fighting below as a sacrifice. Others saw a symbol of comfort as she reached out to her child. Like them, the baby was in danger, and she was protecting him. Others imagined her bowed down with grief.

The statue remained there until April 1918, after Albert had been given up to the Germans. On occupation they found that the tower, by far the tallest building left standing, was an ideal observation post from which they could see well into the British lines across the flat and unbroken landscape. Weighing up superstition against certain enemy advantage, the British had no choice but to turn their heaviest guns on it, and the statue, along with its tower, was smashed to pieces. Even in its demise, the statue proved to be a source of inspiration. The soldier and author Charles Carrington wrote an account of its fall, and Edmund Blunden wrote a poem about it as late as 1949, entitled 'When the Statue Fell', in which he imagines a veteran narrating the statue's destruction as the most miraculous sight he witnessed during the war.

Two weeks after he had first marvelled at the statue of the Virgin and child, Gurney wrote five lines of iambic pentameter, an impromptu he entitled 'The Mother'. He may have been within sight of the statue as he wrote.

We scar the earth with dreadful engin'ry;
She takes us to her bosom at the last;
Hiding our hate with love, who cannot see
Of any child the faults; and holds us fast.
We'll wait in quiet till our passion's past.[29]

Gurney's 'passion' was one of both suffering and anger (a gesture perhaps towards Milton's *Samson Agonistes*, 'calm of mind, all passion spent'). Whether or not the poem was inspired by this extraordinary symbol of hope, redemption and despair, Gurney had returned to the theme he had explored in 'Strange Service'. Mother Nature would forgive, whatever the destruction wrought upon her, just as the Virgin Mary hanging over Albert would redeem man through the sacrifice of her son.

By 2 am on 20 November, shivering and damp, the battalion were cursing the darkness as they stumbled around their new home. They were opposite Grandcourt, in trenches which were to be theirs for ten days, and it was not an appealing prospect. The conditions around Laventie had been bad, but they looked back on them with miserable nostalgia in comparison. Simply getting into the trenches themselves had been hellish. Men clung to the edges of shell holes, in mud deep enough to submerge a gun team. They were shelled continually for twelve hours as they struggled to get themselves and their equipment into position: 'dreadful Grandcourt, passing Death's Valley thigh deep, knowing no forward step—'.[30] The landscape of the Somme battlefields was almost impossible to negotiate by night. Lewis guns, needing to be carried to the front lines, were top-heavy and cumbersome. When they were transported on carts, the cart wheels would become hopelessly stuck in the

mud. The whole procedure was harrowing, laborious, and of course, highly dangerous. Troops felt that the Germans liked to 'kill two birds with one stone', and would
go out of their way to shell both incoming and outgoing battalions if they realised
that a trench was being handed over. The code phrase at the time for a successful
exchange of troops was 'another little drink won't do us any harm' (a line from an
incongruously jolly West End hit revue by the Bing Boys).[31] It would have taken
more than one drink to make life bearable under such conditions, and the incum-
bents of the trench often had only a single cup of cold tea a day. Across the fields
were strewn hundreds of unburied corpses, and when the 2/5ths finally reached the
front line, they found the trenches were merely shell holes that had been joined together.[32] Gurney was frozen, caked in mud, and hungry. 'Ration parties were held
up in the mire. . . . The shelling was so incessant that we were compelled to live more
like rats than men.'[33]

He had endured seven months in and out of trenches, with no respite, and he had
not yet broken down. Now he faced some of the worst conditions the Western Front
had to offer. The Somme region, shelled continually since the attack that began in
July, had been reduced to a state of total devastation by Christmas. It would have
pushed a soldier with nerves of steel to the limits of their endurance, and it finally
proved too much for Gurney. By 7 December he was in a state of nervous collapse,
and was sent to a rest station with what was ambiguously termed a 'cold in the stomach'. The move meant that he spent a couple of nights in a tent; hardly salubrious in
December, but a vast improvement on the trenches. He was sent back to the battalion after a few days, but it was clear to his superiors that he was not in a fit state for
frontline service. They gave him what was known as a 'soft job', manning the water
carts that supplied the regiment.[34] These could not reach the front lines as the conditions were so appalling, so their handlers had the enviable position of remaining
behind the line in reserve.

It was a particularly bleak time for Gurney. News from the wider world did nothing to raise his spirits; the entry of Austrian troops into Rumania on 6 December
dispelled any hopes for an early end to the war. His own personal unhappiness was
complicated by a combination of relief at escaping the front line and guilt at not
sharing the others' misery in full.

I am on my Soft Job [manning the water carts by the kitchens], and today my
batt: goes into the line; to stand to in frozen mud to the knees; to live 15 hours
in the dark of every 24, staring and waiting; and collecting souvenirs. To come
out so fatigued and fordone that only the knowledge that they must be left
there for hours and hours keeps them from dropping in the sludge—that and
some last grain of pluck and pride.

I spend 8 hours a day tramping about in mud and half frozen water, but
keep pretty fit notwithstanding.[35]

He did at least have the opportunity to write, and sent 'To an Unknown Lady' and 'The Strong Thing' back to Scott three days before Christmas. The first was rather a departure for him—he rarely wrote about an imagined character, but when Marion Scott enquired, perhaps with a slight hint of anxiety lest there be another woman occupying a place in his imagination, he reassured her that 'the Unknown Lady is really unknown. She's but a figment or a dream of passion.'[36]

Christmas Day came, and found Gurney back at Albert, indulging in a spot of Christmas shopping. He had become increasingly friendly with a 'little gang' of water cart drivers, from the 51st Scots Division. They had entrusted him with their combined funds, and he conscientiously scoured the ruins of Albert for food for his new friends' Christmas dinner. At the end of November the 51st Division had taken over trenches from the Canadians at Courcelette, between Albert and Bapaume. They had endured the worst conditions in their division's history, with mud waist-high during the whole period of occupation.[37] By Christmas, they were as bedraggled and jaded as the Gloucesters. Two engineers in particular became Gurney's friends: Sapper Ritchie and one other, whom he does not name.

> But I made my fastest friendship on record with two Scots Engineers lately. One of them was fine indeed. He recited To the Haggis, Tom O'Shanter, the Daisy; and sang Ae Waukin O and John Anderson, and McGregor's gathering very well.
>
> And then on Hogmanay—New Year's Eve you know, the pipers up in the village burst out in welcome for the New year with a glorious tune that set us all aching to dance.
>
> 'We've been happy a'thegither' [he quotes the tune]
>
> Over and over it went. (After the guns had finished distributing presents of iron rations) They *had* been happy a thegither, and the night resounded with it. Alas the private festivities of my pet Engineer did not altogether agree with him and the next day he was 'very poorly' as Gloster folk say. However, after the war I hope to see Sapper Ritchie again, and get folksongs off his father. O bonny Scots, après le guerre! Que le guerre soit maudit![38]

Gurney was in ecstasies about these 'best of men'. The Scots were just the therapy he needed. He had been heading rapidly towards what could have been total breakdown. Now, the guns had fallen silent for the new year celebrations, and Gurney was enjoying both the luxury of candles, and the time to write by their flickering light. He even had music of a sort, courtesy of the pipers, and an obliging clarinettist ('breath and a queer tube magicked sorrow from men').[39]

Such unexpected moments of content occasionally punctuated Gurney's general gloom, the sense of interminable monotony lifted, and he felt 'the time as tender as if green buds grew.' He turned to music with a renewed energy. In the trenches once more, near Thiepval, he picked up a song he had been working on during Christmas

Day, although he had originally begun it back in September 1915. It was a setting of Will Harvey's poem 'In Flanders', and was to be the second of Gurney's 'war' songs.[40] Harvey had written the poem while stationed in Ploegsteert Wood and had published it in the *Gloster Gazette*. Gurney had watched his comrades admire Harvey's published verses, with both a pang of pride and a little envy. Now he set it to music, adding his voice to his friend's, and signing the finished manuscript with his location 'Crucifix Corner'.

> Here it is, cast up with the flotsam and jetsam in more or less permanent form, with—'wae's me—another orchestral accompaniment, dammit.
>
> [. . .]
>
> Surely ['In Flanders'] reflects the words? But on the other hand, ought there to be a figure to bind it together? and (my usual thought) is it Oldfashioned [*sic*]? And though undoubtedly music in places, is it Immature? Or will its freshness carry it off? Is it fresh?[41]

'In Flanders' is a more intimate song than the monumental 'By a Bierside', with a spinning melodic line that appears to unfold organically. Howells later described Gurney's melodic speech as a '"kindly" human utterance—as gentle as the outline of the Malverns. But it bestows power to set the seal upon a whole song by its first phrase.'[42] Its harmonies are conservative, but when the text demanded it Gurney tentatively experimented with harmonic progressions that would not have found favour with Stanford. He hoped to get some endorsement from Howells, who was rather more open-minded: 'But what of the change from D to D minor, B flat minor, C minor in about 3 bars? Ask Herbert please.'[43]

The folk songs Gurney had shared with his Scottish companions and their talk of home had heightened his desire to create music that expressed his own nostalgia. 'In Flanders' felt to him like a breakthrough. It 'says everything for me', he wrote to Marion Scott. 'It is the perfect expression of homesickness. . . . That will be in anthologies hundreds of years hence, surely.' 'As I stand off from the song, the hills swim in sunlight like that, to the plucking of harps and a sustained sound of wood and strings.'[44]

Gurney's mood echoed the cautious optimism of the British lines during the winter of 1916. By 27 December there were even rumours of peace circulating amongst the troops. The war was expected to end at any moment, and the men were issued with instructions from officers not to run riot if peace was declared. Gurney had been behind the front line for a while, having what he described as a 'Soft Time'. He reassured Scott that 'a few days in the warm put me practically all right, and now I am expecting a call to return at any moment.' However, as sharp an eye as Scott's would have fixed instantly on the 'practically'. A few months previously Gurney had been confident that army life had cured him of his prewar neurasthenia (the term in circulation in the early twentieth century for general depression and illness of the 'nervous system'), and he was now fit for hours of hard graft at composing and poetry. The fact that he had claimed he was composing indicated that his optimism was well founded, but Scott knew that only a few weeks prior he had suffered his closest shave with mental breakdown since the Royal College. How much more could he stand? The physical labour of army life with a regimented routine might have helped him when he was back in training, but after months on the Somme, the cure was set to become the cause.

CHAPTER FIVE

'The Fool at Arms'

By the new year of 1917 the battalion had moved on to Varennes, without Gurney, who was still working on his water carts near Albert. Every day he would man the carts and look after the mules that pulled them, fill water cans to be dragged up into the lines, and make sure the huge drums of water were kept topped up from whatever local water supply could be found. By night he was sleeping in a straw-filled barn with an oil sheet to pull over himself to keep off the damp. He was bored and half-frozen, but conditions here were infinitely more conducive to writing than those in the trenches.

The congenial company of Sapper Ritchie and his pals added to the ease with which Gurney was now writing, but the little group was soon to be separated. Sir Douglas Haig was determined to keep the front active in the new year with a series of small-scale attacks, and Gurney's Scots were to be among the casualties of Haig's eagerness.[1] On 4 January they were called away, and Gurney, left alone, wrote the poem 'Scots'. It was an outcry at the war in general, but particularly at this cruel twist of fate that allowed him to find such joy in friendships only for them to be lost to him.[2]

The boys who laughed and jested with me but yesterday,
So fit for kings to speak to, so blithe and proud and gay . . .
Are now but thoughts of blind pain, and best hid away. . . .
(Over the top this morning at the dawn's first grey.)

O, if we catch the Kaiser his dirty hide to flay,
We'll hang him on a tall tree his pride to allay.
That will not bring the boys again to mountain and brae. . . .
(Over the top this morning at the dawn's first grey.)

To think—earth's best and dearest turned to red broken clay
By one devil's second! What words can we say?
Or what gift has God their mothers' anguish to repay? . . .
(Over the top this morning at the first flush of day.)[3]

His memorial to them is song-like, each verse ending with a refrain that associates his loss with the folk songs they sang him. The poem is awkward: the language is that of the folk song, absorbing the 'Scottishness' of the men it commemorates, but the length of its lines belies its suggestions of a ballad. Gurney has effectively written a folk song that cannot easily be sung but pulls the singer-reader up short with its jolting rhythmic scheme. It is strikingly uncharacteristic of him to resist his impulse towards the lyrical, and when he does so, it is always to achieve a particular effect. Here the most musical moment is the repeated refrain that condemns the men to move forwards to their deaths.

Three days after he completed 'Scots', Gurney wrote 'Purple and Black', which defensively upheld heroism as the territory of soldiers.[4] Kings may be buried with full ceremonial colour and pomp despite having lived morally dubious lives, he argued, but mothers who mourn the deaths of their truly heroic sons must do so in 'Vile black—Death's colour'. He was tacitly acknowledging his own hero worship of his Scottish friends, whilst anxiously anticipating that the 'land fit for heroes' to which they would (hopefully) return might not recognise the heroism of the sacrifices made in its name. Next came 'Communion', a particularly striking poem, and in some ways the precursor to the powerful 'To His Love', which he would write the following January (1918).[5] Both poems shock the reader by raising the dead in the final line and incongruously introducing a corpse into a peaceful landscape, but unlike the later 'To His Love', at this point Gurney seems to welcome the 'communion' with the dead.

Beauty lies so deep
On all the fields,
Nothing for the eyes
But blessing yields.

Tall elms, greedy of light,
Stand tip-toe. See
The last light linger in
Their tracery.

The guns are dumb, are still
All evil noises.
The singing heart in peace
Softly rejoices,

Only unsatisfied
With Beauty's hunger
And sacramental thirst—
Nothing of anger.

Mist wraiths haunt the path
As daylight lessens,
The stars grow clearer, and
My dead friend's presence.

There is a strong flavour of Walt Whitman here in the simplicity of the imagery. The stark, unsentimental ending chimes with Whitman's 'Reconciliation' (set by Gurney after the war), which ends with the striking image of the poet kissing the white face of his enemy's body in an open coffin. Whitman, along with Gerard Manley Hopkins, was to become one of the most formative influences on Gurney's verse, showing him ways in which he might move beyond the Georgian, four-square poetry he had surrounded himself with until now, and opening up possibilities of sprawling, expansive verse, that was as free as it was effusive.

Gurney had been absorbing Whitman that August, ever since Scott had sent him a little collection of his verse, which he was still carrying around in his pack.

> It is true that in most cases his poems are not really so much poems as raw materials for such, but dammy, it has annoyed me to find so much in so tiny a book. I will go so far as to say that no present has ever given me so much pleasure.[6]

At the time there had been no discernible alteration to his own poetry, but as the infatuation increased, and his own technique developed, Whitman's influence would gradually become more evident. He began to understand that what he had at first thought to be the 'raw materials' could in fact be legitimate poetic expressions, and that there were other possibilities beyond the more formulaic, polished verse to which he was accustomed. As he developed, Gurney took from Whitman his technique of piling up observations to make a huge picture comprising many smaller images and ideas. He shared Whitman's joyful view of life, both poets being prone to violently exuberant passions and enthusiasms. Gurney admired Whitman's shameless egocentricity, placing himself squarely at the centre of his work, the organising force that magnetically draws the material together with lines such as 'and of these one and all I weave the song of myself'.[7] That spring (1917), Gurney wrote a preface to what would become his first collection of poetry. Buoyed up by Whitman's example, he makes no apology for being the central subject of his own verse: 'Most of the book is concerned with a person named Myself'.

Gurney was becoming increasingly confident in his own poetic experimentation. Already the early rivalry with Harvey's witty, simple verse seemed an age away. Now he was assessing the wider competition, aware at a surprisingly early point in the war that a canon of poetry would emerge from the conflict, and he needed to establish his voice as one to be reckoned with alongside the burgeoning war poets. In the same letter in which he copied out 'Purple and Black', 'Song and Pain' and 'Communion', he mused: 'There are many good war poems. Harvey, [Laurence] Binyon,

Rupert Brooke, Wilfrid Gibson, and so I have been told, G K Chesterton's 'Wife of Flanders.' . . . And then there's Hardy and Captain [Julian] Grenfell.'[8]

After some rather directionless flirtations with romantic epics and Kiplingesque ballads in the form of his ambitious 'Framilode the Queen' (which Scott wisely advised him to abandon), he struck gold with a beautiful miniature he entitled 'Song' on 18 January. He was to set it to music as 'Severn Meadows' that March.

Only the wanderer
   Knows England's graces,
Or can anew see clear
   Familiar faces.

And who loves joy as he
   That dwells in shadows?
Do not forget me quite,
   O Severn meadows.[9]

Its simplicity and honesty are heart-wrenching. It came back to Scott along with 'West Country,' and the next day (19 January 1917), 'Influences' and 'Time and the Soldier' (the latter he modestly described as W. H. Davies, but better).

In the relative quiet, his thoughts turned to Binyon's 'For the Fallen', which he had been wanting to set since the previous June. He had conceived a setting of the first two verses, but not committed them to paper, as he was relying on his memory for the text. Now the ever-helpful Marion Scott had sent him a copy of the poem, but his courage began to desert him. It was too long and appeared on closer inspection to be 'altogether rather difficult to do'. He had been responding to the remembered essence of the poem, its sentiment and mood, which he found compelling. But when on the 18th he placed the poem on the music stand of a 'faint toned' piano in a nearby village (he had to pay a franc an hour for the privilege), he was stumped. However, he did have the opportunity to play 'By a Bierside' to himself for the first time, and intriguingly found the song to contain 'even more strangeness than I had thought.'

Gurney was back with the battalion by the beginning of February. He had voluntarily given up his 'soft job', in the erroneous hope that he would be entitled to some leave if he were back with the 2/5ths in the trenches. However, with one of the many ironies that characterised army life, instead of the prospect of firesides and musical chatter in London and Gloucester, he was faced with an 'orgy of cleaning', and no prospect of leave after all. It was not, retrospectively, to prove a good move: his Scottish friends were gone, and there was nothing now to detain him behind the lines. He could at least console himself with the knowledge that his absence from the 2/5ths had been well timed. Whilst he had been dispensing water to troops in comparative safety, the battalion had been almost continually under fire, and had only had respite during the last few weeks at Gapennes, where Gurney now found them.

They were supposedly enjoying a period of rest. In reality it was training and a hard grind, but Gurney was spared going straight into the front line.

It had been a particularly bitter winter. Much energy was used in trying to keep warm, with the remainder being expended on surviving the route marches and parades. Gurney quickly found that the luxury of either time or energy to write was a thing of the past. There were some small mercies—whilst cocoa might freeze in the mugs outside, there was a canteen in which one could obtain beer, eggs and chips. And there was the comfort of familiar company. Gurney turned his affections once more towards the other Gloucestershire lads with whom he shared the remains of a house. Ozzy had the 'sweetness of an angel', and Jem, an old friend from Gloucester Cathedral School days, was 'really a nut'. But it was Corporal Richard Rhodes, known as Dicky, who had the strongest hold over Gurney.[10] There was something about his eyes that captivated him, and their hypnotic power would haunt his letters and verse. Dicky had been a pit hand in civilian life, and was the only one of the group not from Gloucester. The others were an eclectic assembly, comprising an engineer, a draper's assistant, a grocer, and a tax inspector. Gurney imagined himself meeting up with the group in postwar years—a real possibility, considering they lived near each other in Gloucestershire—and talking over past miseries together. He was increasingly realising that his sense of purpose and strength came not from patriotic sentiment as he had at first assumed, but from his affection for the men around him. Watching them all by the light of the overpoweringly smoky fire they had lit in a 'contrived' chimney, Gurney found he was in love:

Firelight

Silent, bathed in firelight, in dusky light and gloom
The boys squeeze together in the smoky dirty room,
Crowded round the fireplace, a thing of bricks and tin,
They watch the shifting embers till the good dreams enter in,

That fill the low hovel with blossoms fresh with dew,
And blue sky and white clouds that sail the clear air through.
They talk of daffodillies and the bluebells' skiey bed,
Till silence thrills and murmurs at the things they have said.

And yet, they have no skill of words, whose eyes glow so deep,
They wait for night and silence and the strange power of sleep,
To lift them and drift them like sea-birds over the sea
Where some day I shall walk again, and they walk with me.[11]

Gurney was never destined to renew his friendship with little Dicky Rhodes. Soon after he had written of him with such affection, Dicky had gone on patrol in No Man's Land, lost his way, and ended up trying to enter a German trench, mistaking it for the British front line. The Germans shot him on sight. The Gloucesters did not know what had become of him until the advance later that spring. When they occupied the empty German trenches, they discovered, much to their surprise, a carefully dug grave and little wooden cross erected in honour of the 'pocket corporal', as Gurney called his diminutive friend.

I told you of the death, a little time back, of one of our most looked to corporals. Well, that was before the advance. About a fortnight after the movement started, we heard his grave had been discovered; and after tea one evening the whole company (that was fit) went down for a service there. Quite a fine little wooden cross had been erected there; the Germans had done well; it was better than we ourselves would have given him; and on the cross was
'Hier ruht ein tapferer Englander,
Richard Rhodes,' and the date.
Strange to find chivalry in the sight of the destruction we had left behind us; but so it was. They must have loved his beauty, or he must have lived a little for such a tribute. But he *was* brave, and his air always gallant and gay for all his few inches. Always I admired him and his indestructibility of energy and wonderful eyes.[12]

Dicky
(To His Memory)

They found him when the day
Was yet but gloom;
Six feet of scarréd clay
Was ample room
And wide enough domain for all desires
For him, whose glowing eyes
Made mock at lethargies,
Were not a moment still;—
Can Death, all slayer, kill
The fervent source of those exultant fires?
Nay, not so;
Somewhere that glow
And starry shine so clear astonishes yet
The wondering spirits as they come and go.
Eyes that nor they nor we shall ever forget.[13]

Both 'Firelight' and 'Dicky' are poems born of profound emotion, celebrating and preserving in memory men who are silenced either by inarticulacy or death. Their worth is communicated to Gurney in ways that will be lost unless he can preserve something of them in his verse. 'Firelight' has a truer resonance than 'Dicky', for all the sincerity of Gurney's sentiment. It is vivid and contemporary, catching something of the men through deft, subtle glimpses of flickering colour and light, with moments of sunlit countryside recalled with all the unaffected warmth of John Clare ('daffodillies' might return us to this earlier poet, to whom Gurney is in so many ways the natural successor). 'Dicky', however, has the stilted and self-conscious air of a piece written to memorialise, unable to shake itself free of a rather dusty Victorian funereal formality heard in the stiff archaisms such as 'nay' and 'scarréd'.

One of the challenges that Gurney and the other trench poets faced was to find a language that was up to the job of expressing the scale of loss and destruction without creating poetry that was too much in service to the act of mourning rather than to art. Wilfred Owen's 'Anthem for Doomed Youth' carves a space for modern commemoration that is between the reality of hasty burial in wartime and the Victorian pomp:

What passing-bells for these who die as cattle?
—Only the monstrous anger of the guns.
Only the stuttering rifles' rapid rattle
Can patter out their hasty orisons.

By juxtaposing the two extremes, Owen shapes a new way of honouring the dead. Gurney had not yet consistently reached this level of technical control in his writing, and in his eagerness to create in words the lasting memorial for Dicky Rhodes that the Germans had attempted, he ossifies him in a language that, as Owen recognises and as Gurney was slowly coming to understand, is outmoded and inadequate. Although his verse was still uneven in its originality, 'Firelight' shows him beginning to develop the ability to write about death with the devastating simplicity his poems were soon to achieve.

After only a week with the battalion, Gurney had had more than enough. He was moved onto another 'soft job' with remarkable swiftness, considering he had only just relinquished his water carts. This time he was set to work in the canteen. The few days training had 'nearly killed him', and his relief at the reprieve was immense. He knew he was not capable of heavy, frontline duty, but the fact that his failure was so obviously apparent caused him some anguish.

A colonel came to inspect the battalion on 3 February, to see the result of all the polishing and training that had been taking place. He was deeply unimpressed with Gurney. The men were all struggling against the mud, which seemed to seep into every possible corner, and cleanliness was a perpetual and largely futile battle. But Gurney stood out as being even more of a bedraggled scarecrow (as he described the men) than the rest.

But O, cleaning up! I suppose I get as much Hell as anyone in the army; and although I give the same time to rubbing and polishing as any of the others, the results—I will freely confess it—are not as they might be. Today there was an inspection by the Colonel. I waited trembling, knowing that there was six weeks of hospital and soft-job dirt and rust not yet all off; no, not by a long way. I stood there, a sheep among goats (no, vice versa) and waited the bolt and thunder. Round came He-Who-Must-Be-Obeyed. Looked at me, hesitated, looked again, hesitated, and was called off by the R.S.M. [Regimental Sergeant Major] who was afterwards heard telling the Colonel (a few paces away from me), 'A good man, sir, quite all right. Quite a good man, sir, but he's a musician, and doesn't seem able to get himself clean.' When the aforesaid RSM came round for a back view, he chuckled, and said 'Ah Gurney, I'm afraid we shall never make a soldier of you.' It is a good thing they are being converted to this way of thought at last; it has taken a long time. Anyway the R.S.M. is a brick, and deserves a Triolet.

> He backed me up once;
> I shall never forget it.
> I'm a fool and a dunce
> He backed me up once
> If there's rust I shall get it
> Your soul, you may bet it
> Yes all sorts and in tons. . . .
>   He backed me up once
> I shall never forget it.

(Triolet form quite forgotten. Please let me have it.)[14]

He may well have been thinking back to the two triolets that Harvey had published in the April and May editions of the *Fifth Gloster Gazette* in 1916, which he clearly did not have in front of him at that moment for guidance.[15] The humour and the natty little rhymes obscure the alternative picture. Gurney would have liked to present himself as a bohemian poet, for whom parade presentation was simply an amusing inconvenience. In reality, he was a man on the edge of breakdown, too depressed to keep himself clean and meet the required standard. He could not excel as a 'burnisher and brusher up', but he defensively allied himself with the great poets in his failure, and rather eccentrically imagined them in the same situation: 'Keats or Shelley could hardly make so conspicuous a failure in all that relates to kit, or equipment.'[16]

He spent his days shivering in the canteen, left alone to guard the beer, sell biscuits, and lie to hungry soldiers about the quantities of chocolate that were left so he could hold it back for his friends. In between dispensing such delicacies, he again had time and space to write. On 3 February he sent 'Hail and Farewell', an imaginary scenario in which a soldier dies as the bugle sounds the retreat. It is a little ambiguous, but it appears that the soldier he imagines is in fact himself.

> The destined bullet wounded him,
>   They brought him down to die,
> Far-off a bugle sounded him
>   "Retreat," Goodbye.
>
> Strange, that from ways so hated,
>   And tyranny so hard
> Should come this strangely fated
>   And farewell word.
>
> He thought, "Some Old Sweat might
>   Have thrilled at heart to hear,
> Gone down into the night
>   Too proud to fear!
>
> But I—the fool at arms,
>   Musician, poet to boot,
> Who hail release; what charms
>   In this salute?"
>
> He smiled—"The latest jest
>   That time on me shall play."
> And watched the dying west,
>   Went out with the day.[17]

Gurney had again been left behind by his comrades; and his preoccupation with his failure as a soldier played itself out in his verse. How inappropriate it would be for him, an unsuccessful warrior, a 'fool at arms', to have his death take place to a military soundtrack. The war's music was not *his* music. He had longed to fit in and be a comrade, to be tired 'with many men', and not suffer alone as he had in London. His failure to conform to the army and its beliefs was something he upheld with pride as a rebellious civilian, but it also troubled him deeply. He was torn between despising the army and wanting to succeed within it. Ultimately, 'Hail and Farewell' recognises that whilst he could be as superior and aloof as he liked, the army would probably have the last word over his death.

The battalion marched to L'Étoile on the day after their inspection, 'a revelation of beauty after grey desolations'. They arrived at mid-afternoon to be allocated billets in a draughty barn.[18] The place was marked with 1870 earthworks and had an odd geological feature—a huge rock that towered above the little town, slightly resembling a star, and giving the town its name. It was a beautiful spot, an oasis in the midst of unexceptional countryside and general desolation. The rock put Gurney in mind of Birdlip and Crickley, but the beauty of it did not quite compensate for the bitter temperatures.[19] The front line was unavoidable, but, for now at least, he was in his own personal 'haven of peace', with especial responsibilities for biscuit-rationing. There was also a glimmer of hope on the global stage, which had reached Gurney through his avid reading of whatever newspapers he could obtain. He anxiously questioned friends back in England: 'What difference will America's attitude make? They say today that she has declared war but the paper only speaks of broken relations. Que le guerre fait finir bientot.'[20] America had severed all links with Germany, following their return to the policy of unrestricted submarine warfare that had caused the sinking of the *Lusitania* back in 1915. America had not entered the conflict then, despite 125 Americans being drowned, but now, as Gurney hoped, President Wilson was to make a declaration of war at the beginning of April 1917. It was to be the much-needed turning point in the fortunes of the Allies.

The next few weeks shaped Gurney's 'Five Sonnets', which

> are intended to be a sort of counterblast against 'Sonnetts 1914' [by Rupert Brooke], which were written before the grind of the war and by an officer (or one who would have been an officer). They are the protest of the physical against the exalted spiritual; of the cumulative weight of small facts against the one large. Of informed opinion against uninformed (to put it coarsely and unfairly) and fill a place. Old ladies won't like them, but soldiers may.[21]

The set of five sonnets were some of the most psychologically complex work he had yet attempted and were to be placed as the final poems in his collection *Severn and Somme*. Their quality stems largely from the honesty of their position: an uneasy combination of respect for Rupert Brooke's beautifully crafted prewar work, coupled with the weariness and cynicism of an experienced soldier. Ironically, just as Gurney was beginning to stumble his way towards a rough sense of his own poetic voice, he was claiming (with a slight sense of doubt) that he would drop poetry as soon as the war was over, and he could return to his music. '[. . .] if there is a whole after-the-war for me, little enough verse will I write again—most, *most* probably, I know which is my chief game.'[22]

It appears from the body of correspondence that has survived that Marion Scott had become his main correspondent, and although her letters are lost, we can glean a sense of her anxiety for his well-being through his replies to her. Scott was Gurney's confidante, although there were some matters of the heart he chose not to share. She was also his critic, encouraging, providing alternative words or offering musical suggestions. Gurney was always conscious of his self-presentation in their correspondence. He tried not to bore her, even if the effort to remain cheerful was sometimes thinly disguised. Her replies were solicitous, her food and book parcels prompt. She gave him intellectual and practical support, and he gave her someone to adore and champion. Although they had spent a good deal of time in each other's company at various concerts in London, and at Scott's soirées in Kensington before the war, the relationship was still distant and she was always, respectfully, 'Miss Scott'. Poetry, rather than correspondence, provided the space for Gurney to explore inner conflicts that self-censorship or Scott's expectations might render unsuitable for a letter. Gurney hoped that such extremes of endurance would not have to force him to turn to poetry in peacetime. For now, in the trenches, poetry was both a record of events and emotions and an instant form of self-therapy:

> You are right about the roughness of some of my work; there is no time to revise here, and if the first impulse will not carry the thing through, then what is written gets destroyed. One virtue I know little of—that is, patience; and my mind is Hamlet's a wavering self-distrustful one, though quick and powerful at its times. Will Peace bring me peace, though?[23]

'Pain', the first of the five sonnets, was written on 7 February as an impromptu in a letter. Gurney was pleased with his rough version and copied it out neatly for Scott. He was anxious in case she should find his verse unmanly, if he spoke honestly about his despair.

Pain

Pain, pain continual; pain unending;
Hard even to the roughest, but to those
Hungry for beauty. . . . Not the wisest knows,
Nor most pitiful-hearted, what the wending
Of one hour's way meant. Grey monotony lending
Weight to the grey skies, grey mud where goes
An army of grey bedrenched scarecrows in rows
Careless at last of cruellest Fate-sending.
Seeing the pitiful eyes of men foredone,
Or horses shot, too tired merely to stir,
Dying in shell-holes, both, slain by the mud.
Men broken, shrieking even to hear a gun.—
Till pain grinds down, or lethargy numbs her,
The amazed heart cries angrily out on God.

'Pain' tells the version of the war with which we are most familiar through the writings of Owen and Sassoon. Pain is here a symbolic emotion, as well as an actual acute experience. It represents a numbness, an end of feeling, perhaps the opposite of another of Gurney's much-used shorthands for emotion: 'afterglow', the term he uses for the fading light of a sunset, and to colour his description of his 'First Time In' the trenches).[24] Afterglow as a concept often seems to stand for a freedom from the kind of pain expressed so viscerally in this sonnet, a repose after terrible physical endurance. Gurney usually balances suffering and the redemptive, the pain held alongside the beauty of an 'afterglow'. Such unmitigated suffering as the sonnet 'Pain' represents rarely found its way into either the poems or the letters Scott received. This was partly to spare her feelings, and because he was by nature (and against some odds) an optimist, and partly for more prosaic reasons. Gurney was a private, and, unlike the officer class, his correspondence was subject to censorship.

It may be that the usual tension held in play between two opposing impulses, beauty and pain, is not played out within the fabric of the text here because it is taking place in an imagined negotiation between himself and Rupert Brooke. He genuinely respected Brooke's verse, but felt that the war had made its sentiment, if not obsolete, at least representative of a different time. Gurney wanted to write the antithesis of Brooke's version of manliness and war, but worried about appearing to be too unsoldierly. He followed 'Pain' with another two sonnets, 'Beauty', and 'After-glow' (the latter dedicated to Harvey, and not ultimately included in the set of five). The final sonnet of the set, 'England the Mother', cost him more effort than any other poem. He wrote repeatedly to Scott that he was struggling with it, as there was 'too much to say'. This was a far cry from the certainty of Rupert Brooke's sonnets, in which a 'corner of a foreign field' will most certainly 'be forever England.' Here, the scarred and damaged soldier pleads with his country to recognise and heal him. It was to be one of Gurney's densest, most powerful works to date. Within the framework of the sonnet, he presents a psychologically astute examination of a dysfunctional mother-child relationship, alongside a darkening and complicating of the archetypal image of Mother England, for whom he and his comrades were expected to fight.

He had found as a child that he could rarely win his own mother's approval, so he had turned to the landscape itself to approve of his efforts as a poet and composer. It was Gloucestershire itself that he wrote to please, not his family. The two, mother and landscape, had become inextricably commingled in his early years, and the propaganda of war was to play on similar impulses. From 1914, 'Mother England' was to be fought for and defended, and in turn she would (it was assumed) honour her children's sacrifices. From the trenches in 1917 Gurney analysed his own ambivalent, intensely emotional relationship to his sacrifice on behalf of family and country. Many of the dysfunctional traits he experienced in his relationship with his mother Florence can be found here, in this destructive but adored Mother England.

England the Mother

We have done our utmost, England, terrible
And dear taskmistress, darling Mother and stern.

The unnoticed nations praise us, but we turn
Firstly, only to thee—'Have we done well?
Say, are you pleased?'—and watch your eyes that tell
To us all secrets, eyes sea-deep that burn
With love so long denied; with tears discern
The scars and haggard look of all that hell.

Thy Love, thy love shall cherish, make us whole,
Whereto the power of Death's destruction is weak.
Death impotent, by boys bemocked at, who
Will leave unblotted in the soldier-soul
Gold of the daffodil, the sunset streak,
The innocence and joy of England's blue.[25]

As a composer who could move between notes and words with ease, Gurney had a highly developed sense of metre, and of the power of juxtaposing unexpected or contradictory images. His conception of a mother was both 'terrible' and (once we have moved our eyes to the next line, thereby building in a momentary pause) 'dear'. Her eyes can burn, and again, after a pause scored in to the geography of the page, be full of love, but it is love that has been long denied. There is a clear sense that this is a relationship fraught with uncertainty, that pulls both towards and away from the mother, has a great investment in needing to believe in its security, 'Thy Love, thy love shall cherish, make us whole', and at the same time can hold in tension the possibility that this is a most unstable, troubling and compromised relationship. What as a child was a source of conflict and unhappiness, Gurney could now harness as an adult to create poetry that was capable of articulating the vulnerability, ambivalence and confusion of his childhood, alongside a tenacious belief in the redemptive powers of natural beauty. It was an intoxicating formula, but one learnt at a heavy personal cost.

Two days after he had embarked on this final set of poems there came the order to carry out a practise attack as a training exercise, usually an indication that a major attack was planned for the battalion. Sure enough, on 13 February 1917 they travelled by a torturously slow train to Wiencourt, twenty-four kilometres from Amiens.

London and the Royal College felt like another existence, but his friends had not forgotten him. Stanford sent him the odd jolly, illegible letter, full of platitudes that only 'a superannuated civilian could write—he wished he were out here.'[26] Howells had ensured that Stanford heard the two new war songs, 'In Flanders' and 'By a Bierside', and reported back that he had been enormously impressed. In one of the ironies that was to haunt Gurney's career, just as he was heading ever nearer the front and his probable death, his work was beginning to receive recognition. Not only that, but he felt his poetic voice developing in tone and confidence. His latest handful of works were his 'best yet', in his own opinion. The thought that all this would be in vain, and that it was possible that 'the Lord God should have the bad taste to delete me' just as he was coming into his prime after a lengthy and arduous apprenticeship, was almost too painful to bear.[27]

By 15 February the battalion had arrived at Framerville. Gurney had the afternoon free, and with a view to the impending battle, he finished writing the preface to the burgeoning poetry collection that would become *Severn and Somme*, but for which the working title was either 'Songs from Exile' or 'Songs from the 2/5th'. Gurney chose to dedicate his book to Margaret Hunt rather than to Marion Scott. Since he had begun his army training, Scott had written to him at least once a week, and plied him with money, food and compliments about his verse. Why dedicate the book (whose publication Scott was administering) to an old friend from Gloucester? Perhaps Margaret could not be ousted from her position as his first and therefore strongest attachment, or perhaps Scott, for all her affectionate devotion and literary discussion, was simply a friend on whom it was convenient for Gurney to depend at this point. He dedicated a number of poems to Scott and to his other friends, but whatever the explanation, the message was painfully clear—if any woman truly claimed Gurney's affections, it was Margaret, not Marion.

Gurney's preface unselfconsciously sets out the subject of the book. 'I fear that those who buy the book (or even borrow), to get information about the Gloucesters will be disappointed. Most of the book is concerned with a person named Myself'. He acknowledged the literary influences that were foremost in his mind, and whose presence can be felt behind many of the poems: 'Mr Hilaire Belloc, whose "Path to Rome" has been my trench companion, with "The Spirit of Man"; Mr Wilfrid Gibson, author of "Friends", a great little book'.[28] He even wrote to Gibson to tell him as much. His own offering was as much a homage to these poetic giants as an attempt to join their ranks.

He had enough poems now to make a slim volume, and the book was growing by the day. He wrote the 'border-ballady' 'Ballad of the Three Spectres',[29] with its strong hint of Sassoon, and bearing a striking resemblance in content, tone and form to Wilfred Owen's 'The Chances', which would be written six months later, also much under Sassoon's influence.[30] It was one of the ironies of the war that Owen, whom Gurney would later come to admire but of whom at this point he was entirely unaware, was in fact only walking distance away, undertaking a course on transport duties at Abbeville. Both Owen's and Gurney's poems play with the different fates possible for a soldier, adopting a style of colloquial soldierly wisdom, in a 'well, what's the worst that could happen?' rationalising tone. Both poems conclude that the worst would be to be left alive but insane. Both Owen and Gurney were to come close to the borderline between sanity and mental illness, but in Gurney's case, the poem was a voicing of his own worst fear. He could not bring himself to articulate the possibility of madness directly, conveying instead an indistinct horror of 'one hour of agony'.

> As I went up by Ovillers
>> In mud and water cold to the knee,
> There went three jeering, fleeing spectres,
>> That walked abreast and talked of me.
>
> The first said, "Here's a right brave soldier
>> That walks the dark unfearingly;
> Soon he'll come back on a fine stretcher,
>> And laughing for a nice Blighty."
>
> The second, "Read his face, old comrade,
>> No kind of lucky chance I see;
> One day he'll freeze in mud to the marrow,
>> Then look his last on Picardie."
>
> Though bitter the word of these first twain
>> Curses the third spat venomously;
> "He'll stay untouched till the war's last dawning
>> Then live one hour of agony."
>
> Liars the first two were. Behold me
>> At sloping arms by one—two—three;
> Waiting the time I shall discover
>> Whether the third spake verity.

The next day the gas attacks began at Framerville in earnest. At this point in the war the Germans were using chlorine and phosgene gas (mustard gas would not be developed until that summer), and British scientists, working at speed, had just had long enough to be able to develop a respirator that would offer total protection against both.[31] In the reserve trenches, only just behind the front line and within easy compass of the gas clouds rolling across, Gurney was finding life 'deucedly uncomfortable; and expecting to become still more so'; a toned-down understatement for Scott's benefit.[32] He had to endure seven days of gas, mud and thawing trenches that were becoming impassable, before being relieved by the 2/1st Bucks at dawn on 23 February. The relief attracted enemy attention, and the Bucks were welcomed to the appalling disintegrating trenches by an intense bombardment. Gurney crawled back into support trenches, no more comfortable than the positions in reserve, and hardly safer. There was no escape from the gas—the Germans were bombarding the back areas with gas shells, and by 25 February sixteen men had been evacuated.

On 27 February a further seventeen other ranks became casualties of the linger-ing gas. These were losses that the 2/5ths could not readily sustain; on average there were usually only one or two casualties per day. The men were suffering with trench foot in the mud, and the gas was straining nerves to breaking point. The next day the gassing and shelling culminated in a raid on the Oxfords nearby, with a heavy bom-bardment that lasted from 4:25 until 8:30 pm. They assumed it would become a general raid, and let off SOS rockets, but it was not the case. Gurney, along with the rest of B Company, moved into counterattack positions ready to support D Com-pany should the need arise, but it was not necessary, as the enemy retired.

By 1 March the battalion was still in support trenches near Framerville, where the conditions were nearly as bad as those in the forward zone.[33] By then, identifi-able trenches in this sector of the Somme were virtually nonexistent and movement was so difficult that the men were driven to wade across vulnerable open ground. The physical challenge of moving up a trench, particularly under bombardment, drew from Gurney some of his rare moments of despair in his letters: 'men almost weeping for exhaustion and sheer misery, stuck to the knees with some distance of torment still to traverse.'[34] He was willing himself to fall ill, for some respite in hos-pital. The line was being shelled continually, and the men were forbidden to light fires, as they would attract attention. Despite the impossible conditions, Gurney still found the opportunity to write 'Song of Pain and Beauty'. It was a desperate prayer to God.

> O may these days of pain,
>   These wasted-seeming days,
> Somewhere reflower again
>   With scent and savour of praise.
> Draw out of memory all bitterness
>   Of night with Thy sun's rays.[35]

Gurney would 'cry out angrily on God' in his poems and referred to God fre-quently (often with an air of flippancy), but it was not often that he would pray di-rectly to him. He was deeply ambivalent about Harvey's Catholic convictions, and it was beauty, not the Christian God, he most readily worshipped. Now, trapped in the nearest place on earth to hell, Gurney knew it would take a redemption beyond the powers of man to save him or make good suffering on this scale.

The battalion was back in reserve on 9 March, finding billets in amongst the ruins of Raincourt. As the Somme offensive had now died down, the Ablaincourt Sector in which the village of Raincourt fell was much quieter than it had been previously. However, there was still a good deal of shelling, and gas shells were continuing to fall. The Gloucesters speculated that the Germans were using up their artillery in preparation for the remarkably well orchestrated retreat to the Hindenburg line. By now, the war had long been at stalemate on the Western Front. News of the unprecedented movement of the Germans reached the battalion on the 17th and was cause for much excited speculation. The 2/5ths had just moved back to Guillancourt for a rest, when orders reached them to be ready to move at an hour's notice. The next day the Gloucesters were off, leaving Guillancourt just after breakfast, and marching forward to Vermandovillers by lunchtime. Their job for the next ten days was to mend roads, which had been destroyed by continuous shelling, and the systematic destruction of any billets or transport lines by the retreating Germans. The advance evinced a curious mixture of emotions. Progress was slow, and the men were constantly on the alert for traps, traversing difficult terrain that was often a wilderness. But this was still progress, and they were pathetically grateful to be out of the trenches.

The following day the battalion moved to Omiécourt (near Vermand) to begin work on the roads to enable the guns and transport to keep up the pursuit of the retreating Germans. The village of Omiécourt itself was very badly damaged, as was its once beautiful chateau. This wanton violation of the French villages heightened the protective instinct in Gurney and his comrades to defend their own rural landscapes.

On the march from Vermandovillers to Omiécourt, Gurney had written:

> This is a barren land, of flowers, that is. Once it was rich cornland, and is not much scarred by shell holes; but O my county; what tokens of your most exquisite secretest thoughts are now appearing under the hedgerows. On the march not many days ago we passed a ruined garden, and there were snowdrops, snowdrops, the first flowers my eyes had seen for long. So I plucked one each for my friends that I desire to see again, and one for Gloucestershire.[36]

Gloucestershire was a friend whose image he had used as a mental talisman on many a desperate occasion. Now his confidence in its preserving power was beginning to slip. The very structural failure of the poem 'Trees' enacts his own anxiety. Imagination was not, he now realised, enough of a defence against present horrors.

Trees

The dead land oppressed me;
    I turned my thoughts away,
And went where hill and meadow
    Are shadowless and gay.

Where Coopers stands by Cranham,
    Where the hill-gashes white
Show golden in the sunshine,
    Our sunshine—God's delight.

Beauty my feet stayed at last
    Where green was most cool,
Trees worthy of all worship
    I worshipped . . . then, O fool,

Let my thoughts slide unwitting
    To other, dreadful trees, . . .
And found me standing, staring
    Sick of heart—at these![37]

However formally controlled, the boundaries between the landscapes of home and battlefield that the poem endeavours to separate are subject to a catastrophic slippage in the spaces between words and stanzas: the silences that cannot be controlled by rhyme. The trees have become 'dreadful', not restorative, totems. There are two landscapes here, as there seem to be so often: a landscape of vitality and restoration and a landscape of moribund death.

As a composer, Gurney frequently made use of silence, in songs such as 'By a Bierside', which is characterised by its dramatic pauses, as the singer's philosophical consideration of death moves between different perspectives. Just as the silences in 'By a Bierside' are animated, moving the singer from one vision or thought to another, so in 'Trees' Gurney orchestrates the drama of the poem through dashes, ellipses and semicolons in place of musically notated pauses and rests.

As the Gloucesters marched, they found every village had been devastated, all fruit trees cut down, all crossroads mined, all wells poisoned and useless. The calculated nature and extent of the destruction left by the Germans invoked a new kind of horror in many soldiers, who had become inured to murder and desolation in the trenches themselves. There was something impersonal about shelling under orders, but what the Gloucesters now witnessed was a very personal kind of destruction. This was gratuitous vandalism, with rose bushes mutilated, and even mattresses defecated upon. Those with a deeply ingrained sense of English propriety and fair play felt particularly unnerved by the callousness of an enemy for whom they'd previously felt some sympathy, as fellow sufferers. For Gurney, who cherished his memories of the orchards of home, the sight of an ancient orchard hacked to pieces out of spite represented an unforgivable war crime.

Gurney was finding life at Omiécourt to be a 'very soft time', with

Lots of fires, enough money and a fairly satisfactory canteen; I, alas! no longer in it! sleep, a few inspections, some cleaning up; [. . .] Comradeship nourished on dangers and parcels and hardships shared, discussing Blighty, past, present and future. Copious letter writing, a little roadscraping, and mild weather to frowst in.[38]

It was a welcome contrast with the recent hard physical slog of the trenches he had just left.

> There was one night we stood to for 5 hours, and then carried rations up, in equipment, through the mud; in places, and many places, such as would stick a tank fast. It took us 8 hours there and back, and—well, I may force my neurasthenic soul to Joy one day by dwelling on contrast.[39]

He spent his days salvaging above swamps and a canal, digging in beautiful weather. At night, he returned to his billet in a partly ruined house. He was 'In Support'—a term of variable meaning. 'Here, in conquered ground it meant ration-carrying and fatigues a kilometre from the first line. Later it meant sleeping on dug-out steps, but here 9 men in a tiny dugout; But—good fires; Lots of wood—our salvation. Tea leaves were boiled 3 times, and we managed a hot drink 3 or four times every day.'[40]

At the end of March the battalion moved on to Caulaincourt. It had once been a pretty, sleepy little village, nestled on the side of a gentle, wooded hill, with a chateau on the outskirts. By the time Gurney reached it, the village was barely there. Almost all the buildings had been flattened, and the church that had stood at the centre was a ruin. Gurney had lost none of his sense of romance and drama:

> Last night's sky was gloriously tragic; I sang 'In Flanders' to myself, facing the West, alone in a lately ruined house, spoiled by that unutterable thoroughness of the German destruction; and was somewhat comforted thereby. That has all been said for me in 'In Flanders'.[41]

They arrived at Caulaincourt at nightfall, and through the gloom Gurney could make out his new billet: a dome-shaped mausoleum. It was the property of the nearby chateau, and stood alone on the brow of the hill, bizarrely intact. It had belonged to a local duke, and rumour had it that the duke had been paying the Germans to spare it. It was a 'queer' residence, as Gurney rather understatedly put it. The men were not to be deterred by their surroundings and piled into the small vaulted red brick crypt in the basement. There had been a recent issue of tin whistles and mouth organs, and the novelty had not yet worn off ('Lord, what a hell of a row in here, and what a crush!').[42] Scottish tunes, and in particular 'Annie Laurie', a favourite of Gurney's, helped to keep his spirits up. He craved good poetry. Having practically memorised the poems in Harvey's copy of *The Spirit of Man,* which he still carried with him, he asked Scott for some Browning, and a copy of the *National Song Book* (probably for more repertoire for the 'crack players' amongst the tin whistlers). For all their cheerful music-making, the whole company was feeling the strain. 'We should all relapse into neurasthenia were we not driven', Gurney wrote.[43] He took comfort in the fact that whilst his digestion was upset, and he was clearly

FIG. 5.1: Inside the mausoleum at Caulaincourt (photograph taken during its occupancy by the 21st Lancashires). © Imperial War Museum.

depressed, so was everyone else. This was neurasthenia with a sense of community. Later, in May 1917, Gurney heard a rumour that the mausoleum had been booby-trapped all the while they had slept there, and that it had blown up shortly after. 'In that mausoleum in which we slept two months ago, there was concealed—something which has sent the whole shute to glory. Good thing it had been set for a long time.'[44] It was in fact an erroneous rumour, but testament to the fragility of life and the continual series of coincidences and near misses that meant survival.

After an uncomfortable night on damp flagstones, on 31 March the battalion made the short march across the ruined fields from Caulaincourt to the little town of Vermand, which had been evacuated. They were creeping ever closer to the retreating Germans. Now they were only one and a half kilometres away, and within easy attacking range. The fighting began again the next day. A Company attacked the occupied village of Bihecourt, taking the Germans by surprise, and interrupting their shaving and breakfast preparations. It was a successful attack, with only two Gloucesters killed. They then managed to take the village and dug in at an orchard on the other side. Gurney was not involved in the attack itself but went up with B and D Companies to occupy the outpost line after dinner. This chasing and attacking the enemy across the French countryside was hard work, Gurney felt, but much better than trench life. The Gloucesters were pursuing the Hun faster than their supplies could follow them, however. Gurney was 'as weak as a rabbit' with hunger, but he could not expect much sympathy from his English correspondents. The home front was also tightening its belt. Towards the end of March, Gurney was concerned to read in the *Daily Mail* of food regulations being made more stringent.[45]

On the night of 6 April 1917, Good Friday, Gurney stood ready to go over the top. For one tense hour nothing happened, and then the Gloucesters' bombardment of the German wire began. He had heard it many times, but the 'insensate fury' of the guns was something a soldier never quite got used to. After forty minutes of deafening noise, the bombardment lifted, the whistle blew, and Gurney, along with B and D Companies, attacked. The quiet, after the guns, was eerie. Blinded by darkness, rain and mist, Gurney struggled out over a ploughed field towards the Germans' rearguard positions. The plan had been to break the wire with the bombardment, to allow the men through. It was a hard enough job just to find the wire, and when they did, a cheer went up. But their optimism was misplaced. They quickly found the German wire to still be intact and impassable, and as Gurney wryly put it, years later: 'I was not on stilts or a spectre.'[46] The senior officers did everything they could to encourage their men to continue in their suicidal mission. Lieutenant Pakeman made four efforts to get through. Although he was himself wounded, he led his men up to the wire and cut a certain amount himself. Sergeant Davis of C Company also distinguished himself cutting a gap large enough for five men to get through, but all of them were killed.

Gurney would return to this critical moment in his poetry in October 1925. In one of his most anthologised later poems, 'The Silent One', Gurney remembered the clipped, 'finicking accent', perhaps of Davis or the Cambridge graduate Pakeman, urging the men through the wire—the senior officers had their orders, even if they were, as Gurney politely pointed out, utterly unrealistic. He had no intention of joining the men who had obeyed suicidal orders. The shadow of their alternative fates, silent, hanging figures stuck on the wire, hangs over the poem as a warning to the poet.

The Silent One

Who died on the wires, and hung there, one of two—
Who for his hours of life had chattered through
Infinite lovely chatter of Bucks accent;
Yet faced unbroken wires; stepped over, and went,
A noble fool, faithful to his stripes—and ended.
But I weak, hungry, and willing only for the chance
Of line—to fight in the line, lay down under unbroken
Wires, and saw the flashes, and kept unshaken.

Till the politest voice—a finicking accent, said:
'Do you think you might crawl through, there: there's a hole?' In the afraid
Darkness, shot at; I smiled, as politely replied—
'I'm afraid not, Sir.' There was no hole no way to be seen.
Nothing but chance of death, after tearing of clothes.
Kept flat, and watched the darkness, hearing bullets whizzing—
And thought of music—and swore deep heart's deep oaths.
(Polite to God)—and retreated and came on again.
Again retreated—and a second time faced the screen.

The enduring appeal of 'The Silent One' lies in its wryly humorous recreation of a moment of intense danger through a drama of voices. In sight of the Buckinghamshire lad,[47] (we are told he is one of two) left hanging, Christ-like, in silence on the edge of our consciousness, the poem weaves together the gloriously incongruous politeness of the public school officer, Gurney's own eccentric and endearing qualification of his cursing (heartfelt, but always 'polite to God'), and the absence of speech, the silencing of the 'infinite lovely chatter' of the dead. Through its different voices, the poem dramatises the futility of maintaining codes of civility, and indeed any discourse, in the face of such pointless barbarism. The effect is a drama in miniature, encapsulating in glorious understatement the horror and futility of the last two lines—repeatedly retreating and advancing to almost certain death.

Predictably, the attack left the Gloucesters with heavy casualties. Seven officers were wounded, fifteen other ranks killed, and twenty-seven other ranks wounded. Gurney was to number amongst those twenty-seven. Shot at by the machine guns in front and in easy range of the 'friendly' fire from behind, Gurney cursed the lack of shelter. They had attempted to dig pits, but it was hard to reach any depth in the chalk soil. Gurney ran, freezing cold and wet, through the dark towards the German wire for the second time. Numbed by adrenalin and fear and hardly caring at that moment whether he would survive or not, Gurney stumbled and fell. He stretched out his arm to break his fall, and suddenly he experienced a 'bright ardour of pain'. He had been shot. 'A bullet hit me and went clean through the right arm just underneath the shoulder—the muscles opposite the biceps'.[48] For half an hour the pain was excruciating, but no artery had been hit; the bone was still intact and soon the shock blotted out the pain. Fortunately, he could think clearly enough to shelter as the attack raged around him, and even borrowed a rifle to fire a shot of indignation and revenge in the direction of the German who had jeopardised his performing career.

As a musician, his first reaction was desperation—he could not tell how serious the injury was, and whether he would ever play again. As a soldier, his relief was palpable—his only ticket out of the fighting was either death or injury, the latter being preferable. The damage to his arm was unlikely to be life-threatening, unless it became badly infected, but it could, he hoped, be serious enough to get him back to England, perhaps even out of the war altogether. He had had a premonition that this night was the end of the line: 'I do not set up to be soothsayer, but the night before my last public appearance as an active soldier, I said to a friend of mine, "I think—and do not know why—this is to finish me for a time; how or how long I do not know; but it seems to me that God had decided my limit has been pretty well reached, and I am to have a rest. I don't feel I shall see Blighty, but simply that I am to be out of it for a bit."'[49]

And I left them all, vulgar soldiers to brawl;
Passed through reserve in the sunken Road . . . Oxfords I just could
See, who asked me news 'O wires, wires, wires, sticks, wood . . .
Machine guns, machine guns, shells . . . Nothing else: goodnight'
And went off through a barrage spraying the hillside
(Machine-guns) risking so much . . . tired out and careless;
Having a Blighty; hunger; weakness; by disgust fearless;
And saw the downward slope to Blighty and new hope.[50]

CHAPTER SIX

'Even Such Is Time'

Gurney clutched his arm, a red stain spreading between his fingers as he held the ripped khaki, and stumbled cursing back through the shell holes to comparative shelter. Every soldier was issued a roll of bandages, kept tucked in a corner of their tunic. Gurney somehow managed to have his arm bandaged, enough to allow him to stagger and crawl his way back through the driving rain and darkness until he was out of the fighting. Then began a gradual process of being directed further and further away from the front line, via a string of casualty clearing stations. His ultimate destination was to be Rouen, which had been almost entirely overrun by the Allied army as a base for supplies, numerous camps, and a (relatively) safe place for hospitals to be established. No fewer than fifteen hospitals were set up there for the duration of the war, most on a racecourse on the southern outskirts of the town. There was also a cluster of hospitals to the north of the city, surrounded by beautiful countryside, and it was to these that Gurney was initially sent.[1]

There were a number of Red Cross hospitals and a convalescent depot within easy walking distance, and hospitals frequently exchanged patients as they struggled to accommodate the steady flow of casualties. Gurney spent his first days in Rouen being moved between these different hospitals. A nurse working in the nearby No. 8 General Hospital at the time of Gurney's admission described a typical scene in the surgical ward:

> If only you people would glimpse some of the suffering ones: so many of them so young too. In our ward only, there are so many with two legs clean gone with just stumps of the thigh left. Some of them in spite of it all are quite cheery. Several times a day, they have struck up singing 'just break the news to mother'.[2]

Nurse Cluett notes that the surgical cases, like Gurney, seemed able to bear their pain far more cheerily than the gas victims. The hospital had many men who had been exposed to mustard gas. Their skin had been burnt from their bodies as if they had been flayed alive, and they gasped for breath with corrupted lungs. Their suffering was almost beyond the limits of human endurance. The 'up patients', such as Gurney, were the luckier ones who were not bedbound. They were expected to help the overworked VAD nurses in their punishing rounds of bed-making and cleaning. This involved scrubbing the soot from the 'abominably' smoky stoves off the tent ceilings and endlessly sweeping and scrubbing the rough, whitewashed wooden floors, across which the rats ran freely from bed to bed once dusk had set in. Pianos were available on some of the wards. There were concerts in the nearby convalescent camp, and even an orchestra of sorts. It was to this musically promising camp (known as the No. 2 Convalescent Depot) that Gurney was eventually sent.[3] His wound was not serious enough to merit taking up a bed for any length of time in one of the hospitals.

The depot was a complex of tents and huts, each with between twenty-five and fifty-five beds. These lined the sides of the wards in long rows, each covered with a coarse brown blanket, and some with a white counterpane folded neatly over the top. On entry to the camp, Gurney was marked 'tents', as those who were housed in the draughty tented wards were generally well enough both to stand the cold and to be returned to their battalions without the luxury of a trip home.[4] It had quickly become clear that his wound was not sufficiently serious to get him back to Gloucestershire, and U-boats were seriously impeding the hospital ships, so an escape home was, for now at least, out of the question.

By the time Gurney had slept off the exhaustion and recovered from the initial shock of his injury, he was desperate for some reading material. He longed for Tolstoy. He could use his hand well enough to write, but initially there was no paper available to write on. Even if there had been, he was too depressed to be creative. With little else to distract him, he lay in his bed fretting that his inspiration was drying up: 'continual disgust has sterilised me'; language violent with horror at the possibility of losing his finer sensibilities.[5]

In an attempt to reawaken his love of beauty, he turned his thoughts to A. E. Housman's verse. Perhaps the musicality of Housman's deceptively simple lines appealed, but it was still a curious choice. Gurney was surrounded by the casualties of war, in all their pathos. There was nothing glamorous or romantic about the maimed and bandaged men around him, or about the fighting that was fresh in his mind. Gurney's response was one of blank despondency at the waste of life. Housman's enthusiasm, extolling the virtues of 'lads' who 'die in their glory and never grow old', could hardly seem less appropriate. Convoys of new recruits fresh from their channel crossing regularly marched up past the hospital to the front, sometimes with a band accompanying them. Gurney watched them from behind the barbed wire surrounding the hospital compounds. One nurse wrote, 'to watch the thousands of them sends the cold creeps all over one.'[6] The cheerful marching music struck a hollow tone. And still Gurney sought out Housman, with his winding columns of beautiful marching lads. Gurney's relationship to the war was not one that could easily be

FIG. 6.1: Gurney in convalescence at Rouen. © Gurney Trust.

defined. Romance and backbreaking misery could exist hand in hand for him. He could listen to the sounds of the groans of patients, whilst he mused on Housman's lines. It is hard to imagine that either Owen or Sassoon would have been drawn to the same poetry under the circumstances.

Once he had regained a little of his equilibrium, Gurney found moments of beauty in the spring, which until this point had been remorselessly cold and wet. The nurses made a supreme effort to fill the hospital tents with flowers. They had planted little gardens around the entrance to each tent, with flowerbeds edged with pansies, and each bedside was supplied with geraniums, asters and daisies.[7] In a later poem he gave little detail about his time in Rouen, but vividly remembered the unexpected blossoms in the nearby orchards:

> The sleet finishes, and the sun takes chance of the blue,
> And suddenly, suddenly, as if it were Gloucestershire,
> Blossoms appear on the fair orchards near.
> And a blackbird sings when the air warps warm enough—
> In an evening of rich gold like home for friendliness,[8]

By 19 April Gurney had recovered sufficiently to be moved from the camp to one of the many British army bases in the town, the 55th Infantry Base Depot, where he could make himself useful with his one good arm, while he waited to be fit enough to return to the battalion. He hoped he might be eligible for some home leave while his injury healed, but his luck was out; there were still no boats running. Men worse injured than he who had been labelled 'blighty' had waited for a fortnight for a ship, and in the meantime had recovered sufficiently enough to make them ineligible for a home convalescence. The sight of his beloved hills might have been enough to set him writing once more, but stuck in France, he could not shake off the ennui that had enveloped him. The telltale symptoms crept their way back into his letters to Scott: 'my inside has not been as placable as it might'.[9] Stomach trouble often accompanied a deterioration of Gurney's mental health. During his prewar breakdown, he had rather poetically described his digestive problems to Scott: 'the trail of the dyspeptic serpent is over me still'.[10] Now she could not fail to recognise what this fresh bout of physical illness might signify.

His mental state was hardly likely to have been helped by the knowledge that he would soon be back in the line. In the meantime he could at least amuse himself in peace and safety, whilst the Gloucesters followed their orders to move back north, and began the arduous march up to Ypres without him. Gurney was granted a week's No Duty, and he hoped he might have another three weeks' grace before he even started training again. As his arm began to heal and the physical discomfort decreased, the boredom became intense. He prowled around the camp in search of anything to alleviate it. At the depot he discovered a recreation room with a few books and magazines, and he was pleasantly surprised by the quality of the pianos, but his stiff fingers, and the lack of music, rendered it a source of pain rather than pleasure. He could hardly bear to be reminded of the music-making he was missing back in London, and of the performing career that he could already have lost:

> Yesterday someone was playing the rather good piano in the Recreation Room—toshy stuff played quite well. It was difficult to stay in the room with so many desires awakened and so poorly satisfied.[11]

Gurney needed to get out, and forget himself on long walks. Even though it was Easter it was still bitterly cold, but there was some comfort to be found in the landscape around the camp, which boasted 'some very noble pines' not far from Gurney's tent.[12]

When he finally obtained a pass to leave the depot and walk into Rouen, he found it 'a fine town, and a great rock which stands smiling and huge just out of the town and on the river is very impressive.'[13] Parts of the city were picturesque, and it was a long time since Gurney had seen a French town that was not at least partially reduced to rubble. Rouen had remained largely untouched by the war, despite being a centre of Allied activity, and life continued there roughly as normal. Shops were still open, selling souvenirs to the many soldiers on leave and nurses on their afternoons off. Cafés abounded, and enough café au lait could be obtained to satisfy Gurney's cravings for normality and comfort.

> I went into the Cathedral here two days ago, and stayed awhile in the perfect peace there. It was so still and beautiful that Bach's music mingled with the

sunlight and bathed my mind with peace, with only the joyful thought of Tea
to disturb it.[14]

It was a brief moment of serenity, but this cathedral was no real replacement for
St Peter's back in Gloucester. The 'iron spire struck me with increased horror; dreadful thing.' It could not compare with the four-square perfection of the tower he
loved. His thoughts turned to Howells, in his own quiet cathedral in Salisbury. The
gulf between their lives was ever widening; Howells's Piano Quartet in A minor,
dedicated to Gurney, with 'the hills in it and the wind blowing through', had been
selected to be published by the Carnegie Trust, an organisation set up three years
before to publish works by contemporary British composers. The trust received
many high-quality entries, and publication by it was an honour.[15] Gurney had, as
yet, achieved no such accolades. He had to make do with a performance at the Royal
College of 'By a Bierside', which was apparently murdered by a crooning 'cinema'
style baritone, who ignored all Gurney's dynamic markings ('what the foremizzen-
topmast did I write ff for?').[16] Despite the song's woeful misrepresentation, Parry
still found it to be 'the most tragic thing he knew', which went some way to relieve
Gurney's frustration at being enforcedly absent from his own premiere.[17]

Howells's congenial tranquillity in Salisbury was not actually quite as idyllic as
Gurney imagined. After only three months, his heart condition had become too severe for him to continue working, and he was obliged to resign his post as organist.[18]
Howells's luck was never far from fortune, despite the severity of his illness. His love
of the opposite sex was comparable only to his love of music, and his success and
perseverance in both were impressive. Now, in the middle of May, Gurney heard of
his engagement to the contralto Dorothy Dawe, a fellow student at the College.
Gurney was characteristically generous in congratulating the happy couple, however bitterly he felt the contrast between their situations. He sent an affectionate,
whimsical letter to Howells, but wrote two alternative biographies of his friend: a
blessing and a curse on the news of his engagement.

> So you've been and done it! Shall I congratulate you? I don't know, since
> before me there seems to lie two fat biographies, both of Herbert Howells.
> The first opens at a passage
> "At this time the composer's powers, already great, were doubled by the
> most fortunate act of his life: the engagement to and subsequent marriage to
> Miss Dorothy Dawe, a singer of miraculous endowments. From this time on-
> wards his record is one blaze of great works and huge accomplishments. The
> first 14 symphonies, the great (Sanscrit) Te Deum, for the opening of the new
> lavatory in the Dead Language Section of the British Museum; the noble set-
> ting of the genealogies in the Old Testament; of the great Bradshaw Opera,

the epic of railway life; and the whole of his masterpieces up to Op 462 which begins his Middle Period, was inspired by the remarkable lady whose exquisitely chiselled nose rendered beautiful sounds which otherwise would have been painful; for she preferred to sing through this organ only. Etc etc

And

We must here, with regret, but extenuating nothing as is our business as honest chroniclers, set down the record of the sad fact that blighted this great life; that drove a despairing man to the false comfort of spirituous liquor, and that of becoming a Plymouth Brother; bleared his eyes and upset his digestion; and in a word set his feet on the dark path that was to lead him to spiritual damnation as Harmonium Professor at the Royal College of Music. He became entangled in the fatal web of fascination spread by an unknown contralto of doubtful attainments and tone quality".[19]

Howells could not have mistaken Gurney's ambivalence. Behind the witty prose is a powerful sense of envy and bile, fuelled perhaps by Howells's neglect of his old friend. 'But why don't you write to me?' Gurney implored. It rankled that Howells apparently had time to devote to Dorothy but couldn't find a moment to send his injured friend a postcard.

Gurney had started his studies at the Royal College before Howells and had implored his friend to join him. As Howells remembered, he had known 'nothing of Stanford until Ivor Gurney fired me, in 1911, with the idea that one's only salvation lay in South Kensington'.[20] He began by following in Gurney's footsteps, but quickly overtook him. Howells was a talented, responsive and biddable pupil, and naturally became Stanford's pet.

Howells was to be associated with the College intermittently for most of his working life. He was made a fellow in 1944 and awarded an honorary doctorate by the RCM in 1982, a year before his death. The College forgot Gurney. Even during his studies there is no trace of him in College awards lists, or later in the official histories. Although their relationship was riven with rivalry and unspoken resentments, Gurney and Howells shared a deep childhood bond. In public, they were unfailingly generous about each other's work. Howells described Gurney as one of the top six songwriters in England (Gurney might have raised an eyebrow at such a long shortlist), and Gurney held Howells's work in the highest regard, pining to hear it whilst in the trenches.

Critic Stephen Banfield states the case for their antagonism: 'Who will ever know that so far from Gurney and Howells having been great friends—& any article by Marion Scott & even several loyal articles by Howells himself go to show this—that Gurney had the greatest contempt for Howells. John Haines, who knew them well in Gloucester remembered Gurney saying "Oh, Howells will just get married, & that will be the end of him, and a Dr of music which is what he is best fitted for". Both of these tragic prophecies seem to have come true.'[21]

There is no evidence other than this reminiscence that Gurney openly expressed such resentment of Howells, but alone in France, with only his polite correspondence with 'Miss Scott' to sustain him, the happiness of Howells and Dorothy could not fail to highlight his own isolation. Howells was certainly in a better position than most of Gurney's friends, despite his illness; poor Sydney Shimmin had been ill for three years and underwent a serious operation towards the end of April, followed by another a month later. Harvey languished in his prisoner-of-war camp. He was miserably depressed but had more time to write than either Gurney or Howells. He was spending the spring putting the finishing touches to his second book of poetry.

Gurney was finishing the final edits of his own first volume. He instructed Scott in the finer details of the manuscript of *Severn and Somme*, deciding on an order for the poems, and making minor changes to the poems themselves. He was becoming increasingly anxious about how it would be received. He had no full copy of the manuscript himself, and many of the poems had been written straight into letters, so he had only a tenuous grasp of them, and was in no position to make substantial or thorough revisions. He could practically hear the critics' accusations, and he began to adopt an aggressively defensive tone when talking about the book. One way to exclude those whose opinions might be negative was to aim the book at an audience he trusted to respond well: the 2/5ths themselves. With memories of the success of Harvey's book amongst his fellow soldiers, and of Harvey's reviews proudly reprinted in the *Gloster Gazette*, he suggested the title *'To Certain Comrades' and Other Poems*.

In a letter to Scott, he included a piece he intended to include at the beginning of the collection. Born of deep insecurity about the book's potential reception, it is so pugnacious it is astonishing he could have thought it would serve as an introduction and ending:

All the verses [were written overseas, except] two or three earlier pieces. This should be reason enough to excuse the roughness of the technique, and if more reason is required by the Critical Master of Words (who is rightly angry at clumsiness and botched work,) or the Arty Quibbler, (may he be poleaxed!) I would say, that it is my Royal Pleasure that it should remain rough— this book; with all its imperfections on its head. Say, O Quibbler, could You write with an empty belly and various internal disturbances? Not You; your exquisitely chiselled phrases need a velvet jacket and a crowd of imbeciles to bring them forth. Just go to Ablaincourt next November and have a look at it. (Don't forget your pack.) You people of home, and most of all, you people of Gloucester, may well be indulgent etc.

And then at the end

And if you *won't* be indulgent—why, dammy, I can do without you! I shall survive, though not as a poet perhaps.[22]

Severn and Somme, the collection Gurney's poems were to become, was indeed uneven, as Gurney feared. But it was also full of halting moments of music, where lines sing out in their originality. That May he was reading John Masefield's *Sonnets,* and his comments on them are as revealing for what they say about his own opinion of his work as for his views on Masefield: 'They are lacking in continued music and halt every now and then in a fashion strongly reminding me of my own defects.'[23]

Gurney believed there was a virtue in freshness that could be spoiled with over-revision. He was reading Yeats, and his comments are telling, finding him

Strikingly original, though the strain is occasionally apparent of the care that roots out the obvious and worn phrase, and will not be too easily pleased with first sketches.[24]

Certainly, Gurney was capable of producing miniatures that were unimprovable. 'Song', known as 'Severn Meadows' once he had set it to music, has a luminosity that overwriting would have destroyed.

He offered something of an apology for the lack of revision and care he had taken over *Severn and Somme*:

You will find that when I come to work again I also shall show much greater scrupulousness than before. It was simple lack of energy that kept me from revision, and the only method possible was to write for a minute or two at top speed, refrain from tearing it up, and return to the charge after some space of time. It won't be so, afterwards.[25]

By 30 April Gurney was passed fit for duty, although he was not yet in a presentable state; he had to spend his first church parade back at base writing letters, as his coat still had a blood-stained bullet hole in the sleeve. As he waited for orders to return to the battalion, he still had time to wander into Rouen on occasion, but the majority of his days were taken up with a return to the usual time-consuming activities of the army. He found the exercises mind-numbingly banal, but there was an element of relief; too much time gave ample opportunity for melancholy and brooding. Parades and military exercises afforded a distraction and a structure to his days.

All this week I have been down for training at the Bull-ring, as they call it— Napoleon's parade ground, a bare white sand and shingle space set among hills and surrounded by pines. It is a fine place, but a nasty job.[26]

Evenings off were spent exploring the sandy pine woods, with a pleasantly weary body and a full stomach. The supply lines to Rouen were out of reach of the Germans, so the recuperating men were well supplied with fresh, sustaining food.

No more strength had I than some decrepit rat, or seemed not to have, when we went up for the attack. But since being here, I have cherished my belly most generously, too generously some time, and hope to have a little spare energy for a month.[27]

This blessed combination of restored health, routine and leisure time all conspired to help him write freely again. The final poems of *Severn and Somme* were sent back to Scott, and Gurney had both time and equilibrium enough to compose, working on a setting of Sir Walter Raleigh's 'Even Such Is Time'. Gurney had in mind the creation of a set of war songs, to include 'By a Bierside' and 'In Flanders'. This poem, written the night before Raleigh's execution, was a pertinent text to choose as he waited to be called up for the line. The song is a brilliantly executed dramatisation of an internal monologue. From the very first words, piano and vocal line combine to evoke a tolling bell, the space between each toll inviting us to contemplate both the passing of time and imminent death. Gurney offers a counterpart to this with a spontaneous, free-flowing melodic line, a soliloquy punctuated by the bell.

Well, here is a song—the words of which you know well enough. I think it is all right now, and will go with the other two songs very well. This kind of thing is all I can do at present—things without technique and not much thought— mere wordsetting; and that is always easy to me. You may say what you like of it and not disturb me, save of the first three lines, which are as a glove to the words.[28]

After three weeks the order to return came, and with it, the end of his comparative freedom. He was freed from 'the Bull ring and marching to tyranny'. As it turned out, the return to the battalion was surprisingly jolly. Gurney left Rouen with a heavy sense of foreboding. But after a train journey to an unspecified destination, Gurney and five other Gloucesters who were also rejoining the battalion received the best possible news. They had only twenty kilometres to go, and the battalion was at rest so they were to be spared the trenches. What was more, the six men were unsupervised. They meandered along, hailed French farmers, bought newspapers and 'talked nonsense to such as would listen'. They found themselves a particularly congenial estaminet, where they consoled themselves for having missed their chances of a blighty, and revelled in the rare lack of authority. It was a glorious, unlooked-for moment of respite.[29]

When Gurney finally reached the battalion at Montonvillers, near the village of Cagny, in the Somme region on 18 May, the men were busy practising attacks. It was a preliminary to 'serious business' on the Arras front, which was only marching distance away. Whilst he had been at Rouen, Gurney had been following the offensive at Arras with great excitement, knowing that the 2/5ths had moved up there in his absence. The one-day wonder of the attack on Vimy Ridge had been enthusiastically reported in the press, and he, with many others, had begun to believe it was the beginning of the road to victory. Like so many major offensives on the Western Front, the initial breakthrough was followed by a costly stalemate, and it was hardly the sweep through the French countryside that everyone had anticipated.

The offensive had almost finished by the time Gurney arrived. The Gloucesters were employed as the 'clearing-up' troops, an activity that involved little or no chance of combat. Arras was being shelled nightly, but there were leisure and good spirits enough in daylight for entertainment. The brigade bands (presumably including Gurney, reunited with his baryton) played every day in the Grand Place, which was usually relatively safe during daylight, and makeshift entertainment troupes put on shows for the delectation of the men.

The 2/5ths suffered occasional casualties (some of their horses being victims when the transport brigade's stables took a direct hit), but the demands for medical attention were so few that the medical orderlies had time to hone their skills. Gurney played at being wounded, a welcome change from the real thing. He was bandaged up and carted around for the benefit of practise for stretcher bearers: 'Today I was twice a "casualty" . . . Is there anything in it?'[30]

After a brief and grisly stint in trenches littered with Scottish dead, Gurney and his comrades gratefully left the debris of the Arras campaign behind on 23 June. They retired to the village of Buire au Bois, chosen by Command for the Gloucester's respite camp. Gurney was in heaven. Buire au Bois was surrounded by exquisite woodland, and the farms around the village to which he and his comrades were billeted were picturesque and untouched by war. Well behind the lines, and staying with a congenial family, Gurney feasted gratefully on salad and 'deux pain-bueres'; 'perfectly wonderful to have such a dainty meal after aeons of shackles (Englished—skilly: stew)'. It was the season for strawberries, and there were gardens full of them, which appealed both to the soldiers' aesthetic sense and to their stomachs. They transported Gurney to the wild strawberries that grew 'by the million' back in Gloucestershire. 'Would I were on Coopers Hill looking over to Malvern and Wales while easing my back at times.'[31]

The homesickness was just as painful in beautiful countryside as it was in miserable trenches, but there were advantages to his current position. When he was asked to write a piece for the *Gloster Gazette*, his thoughts turned naturally to Gloucester and the beauty of summer there. Every tree at Buire au Bois reminded him of the orchards at Maisemore. The result was 'The Old City', a lengthy adoration of his native county, with a final stanza indicating that his desired poetic dialogue with Rupert Brooke still continued, as he amalgamated at least three of Brooke's *Sonnets*

FIG. 6.2: Prize-giving at the Buire au Bois camp, 1917.
© Soldiers of Gloucestershire Museum.

1914 into his own verse (there are strong echoes here of 'III The Dead', 'Safety' and 'The Soldier'):

If one must die for England, Fate has given
Generously indeed, for we have known
Before our time, the air and skies of Heaven
And Beauty more than common have been shown,
And with our last fight fought, our last strife striven
We shall enter unsurprised into our own.[32]

The army, fearful as always of the mischief that idle soldiers could dream up, kept the exhausted 2/5ths occupied with training and entertainments. It was a significant improvement on the usual dismal parades and fatigues. There was a brigade horse show, with prizes for different categories, and a flurry of polishing and brushing. Even the mules had their moment of glory with an officers' mule race, the creatures helped along by Gurney and the band who brought up the rear to encourage (or scare) any stragglers. During the course of the week, the training exercises were given a competitive edge to alleviate the boredom with bombing and shooting competitions. Years before, Gurney and Harvey had practised their marksmanship on the local rabbits in the orchards around Harvey's home. Now, Gurney's performance in the shooting earned him the status of 'crack-shot'.

In the evenings the 2/5ths were treated to performances by their own men. An enterprising lieutenant named Frank Wooster formed an entertainment troupe and named his group the 'Cheeryohs'. They were a major feature of the week and took themselves very seriously. They assembled props and costumes, wrote their own material, and even accompanied themselves on a requisitioned piano. They did not ask Gurney to be their resident 'piano puncher', as they sensitively described the role, probably because he was inappropriately highbrow, and perhaps not quite as flexible as they required. Instead, the role of accompanist was filled by a soldier named Parker, whose boast was that he could 'apparently play anything from Crown and Anchor to a classical sonata'.[33]

The makeshift stage in the orchard also hosted a performance by a visiting concert party that was touring the area, doing its bit for the morale in rest camps and Salvation Army huts. Gurney was spellbound. 'We had a concert troupe here, and its violinist played a most exquisite minuet, doubtless by Bach. It was too wonderful, and one could hear Bach in the quiet dusk and full night.'[34] It was indeed a memorable evening—Bach, performed well in an orchard at sunset on a warm summer's evening—what could be more perfect for a war-weary musician?

Sitting amongst the 2/5ths, listening to the sound of the violin resounding between the trees, Gurney could distance himself briefly from the daily routines and business of surviving and enduring, and contemplate the men around him. He was proud of their resourcefulness, and as he watched the still, 'uprapt' (to use a Gurneyism) faces of his unsophisticated companions, he was struck by the mesmeric hold the music had over them. Art music had its place, but he also had the memory of the uproarious Cheeryohs' performance fresh in his mind. He wanted these men to be moved both to laughter and to tears by the songs he could create for them, and longed to hear his melodies on their lips. The result was his own 'popular' song, a world apart from the serious, contemplative songs he had written so far. A timely request had come from Harvey to have something new and jolly to teach his comrades in captivity. Gurney still had a book of Masefield's verse in his pack and selected the poem 'Captain Stratton's Fancy', otherwise known as 'The Old Bold Mate', as its text. It is a sea shanty, taking as its subject the 'old bold mate of Henry Morgan', a celebrated sailor who ended up becoming the governor of Jamaica. Gurney set the poem as a rollicking drinking song, full of testosterone and the flushed joy of drunken camaraderie. He may well have been able to use the piano that had been acquired by the Cheeryohs for his own purposes.

A Frenchwoman told me she never heard French soldiers sing half so much as English. This pleased me, and indeed 7 Platoon has been songful of late.

'Whitewash on the Wall', 'Everybody's Happy in the Old French Trench', and Ragtimes galore ('Charlie Chaplin's Walk' being favourite), 'Rolling Home', 'Old Man Brown he had a little farm'. I hope to play 'em to you soon.[35]

It did not come naturally to him to write such popular tunes, 'the whole thing was more distasteful to me as it might have been the writing of something I loved', but he persevered, inspired by a desire to write himself into the affections of the men around him.[36] But on the day he finished it and could have begun to teach it to the Gloucesters, he received a transfer notice. He was to report to No. 1 section of the 184th Machine Gun Corps at Vaux in a week's time. They were one of the gun corps attached to the 2/5ths, but he would not be with the men whom he had come to love. He had not applied for a transfer, but as the news came only days after he had demonstrated his abilities as a marksman, it was perhaps not a coincidence that he, the 'crack-shot', was chosen. His dream of Captain Stratton being added to the Gloucesters' repertoire was not to be realised, but he sent a copy of it to Harvey in his German prison, who duly taught it to the other prisoners in Gütersloh Camp. It was an instant success. The nightly singsongs before 'lichts aus!' in the camp were a treasured part of the daily routine, and although Gurney was not there to hear it, his raucous ballad became a favourite amongst the prisoners, alongside 'Rio Grande,' 'Spanish Ladies' and 'A-Roving'. It was one of the many ironies that dogged Gurney's life that it was only Harvey, not Gurney himself, who got to witness the men's enjoyment of the ballad, and benefitted from the popularity the song brought.[37]

On 14 July 1917 Harvey's publishers Sidgwick and Jackson agreed to take Gurney's now finished first collection of poetry, *Severn and Somme*. It was one of the most significant moments in Gurney's career, and certainly the beginning of his public recognition as a poet. Gurney received the telegram with the great news on the 15th—within half an hour of receiving his notice of transfer. Naturally, he was overjoyed; finally he could hold his head up alongside the ranks of published war poets. Sidgwick and Jackson were not without their reservations about Gurney's raw and unpolished verse, however. They had had some considerable success with Harvey's first collection *A Gloucestershire Lad*, and as ever, Gurney was compared with Harvey, to his detriment. Initially, when Marion Scott had tried to interest them in Gurney's verse, they were noncommittal.

> Should we publish, I think it probable that we should like to suggest several alterations in the MS., as we did for 'A Gloucestershire Lad' . . . May I add that, speaking for myself, I agree with Mr Dunhill that Mr Gurney's work is of great interest and promise, though it lacks the easy and lyrical simplicity of Mr Harvey; and this latter characteristic has doubtless helped the popularity of 'A Gloucestershire Lad'. I do not think 'Strange Service' [the working title of

Severn and Somme, preferred by Scott] would achieve a similar success. But that is not to say that we necessarily refuse to publish it.[38]

What Sidgwick and Jackson were observing (for them an issue of sales figures, rather than literary quality) was one of the factors that elevated Gurney's verse from Harvey's more popularist writing. Too crafted and quirky to be labelled as mere doggerel, nevertheless, Harvey's poems were devoid of the singular musicality and originality of expression that already set Gurney's better works apart.

The bundle of poems that had landed on the publishers' desk, all neatly typed by Scott, was a mixed but intriguing bag. *Severn and Somme* takes its reader through the earliest stages of Gurney's development as a poet, beginning with his first derivative attempts to sound heroic ('Now, Youth, the hour of thy dread passion comes').[39] The collection charts his halting but surprisingly quick journey from a combination of pseudo-Keats and Brooke to the beginnings of a clear style and the direct, disturbingly sincere voice that rings out in poems such as 'Spring. Rouen, May 1917'. Here Gurney explores wave after wave of his most personal and precious memories in a multilayered exploration of his own homesickness and creativity. It begins with characteristic urgency and directness:

> I am dumb, I am dumb!
> And here's a Norman orchard and here's Spring
> Goading the sullen words that will not come.
> Romance, beating his distant magical drum,
> Calls to a soldier bearing alien arms,
> "Throw off your yoke and hear my darlings sing,
> Blackbirds" (by red-roofed farms)
> "More drunk than any poet with May's delight,
> Green alive to the eye, and pink and white."[40]

'Spring. Rouen, May 1917' represents a watershed moment in Gurney's poetry, resounding with the air of a speaker altogether confident within his surroundings. It is a poem awash with colour and the immediacy of place, the most dramatically present of his poems so far, and yet it is summoning the figure of Romance, who is the most elusive and fleeting (although the speaker is also romancing nature, of course). The whimsical specificity of Gurney's red-roofed farms, interrupting the imagined call of Romance with its earnest detail, is just the kind of eccentrically endearing touch that gives Gurney's mature work its vibrancy and character. Gurney is his own subject (taking his inspiration from the great egotist Walt Whitman), but he develops his range of vision to extend from his central focus on himself to take in the particular, in minute detail.

As his confidence and poetic technique develop through the volume, so he develops his own sense of what war poetry can be, and of its realism. Gurney felt, even by 1915, the year of Rupert Brooke's death, that Brooke's 'manner had become a mannerism, both in rhythm and diction.[41] Gurney's maturing vision of war poetry is not one that is particularly violent, mannered or sentimental, but raw, honest and endlessly unexpected and wrong-footing. Its virtue and strength are in fact the very qualities that cause Sidgwick's reservations—he does not court the simplicity and easy lyricism of Harvey's verse, which trips neatly off the tongue, and rarely takes the reader to unexpected places. Gurney's work, by the end of *Severn and Somme*, dwells almost perpetually in the realms of the uneasy and surprising. We might think, for example, of his masterly description of the moon in 'After-glow': '[. . .] the miracle hanging high / Tangled in twigs, the silver crescent clear.'[42] It is one of the first of the many condensed, luminous images that would come to characterise his best work.

Gurney was expansive, to the very core of his being. His urge to create and to communicate extended across words and music. His subject matter, while concerned primarily with his war experience, widens its focus quickly to dwell on beauty, in the very broadest sense. By the end of the collection it is clear that beauty is already fast becoming Gurney's watchword: beauty in landscape, in men's accents, in a quick glance or gesture, or in music. It all sprung from the same source for Gurney, and he celebrates it all in a catholic collection of observed and carefully curated moments.

The themes to which Gurney would be drawn for the rest of his poetic career can already be traced weaving their way across the forty-six poems in *Severn and Somme*, establishing the patterns that would shape his future work. His working technique would become more apparent in his later collections, but here we can see the beginnings of its development, as he takes a handful of preoccupations, and explores them across a variety of registers. Whilst there are individual gems in *Severn and Somme* ('England the Mother', and 'Trees', for instance), as would be the case in his later work, Gurney is often best understood as the sum of his parts. *Severn and Somme* is preoccupied with England, honour, beauty, war and landscape. The many different lights that he shines, and the perspectives he takes on these recurring themes, meld together collectively to create something akin to the stained glass he loved in Gloucester Cathedral—many multicoloured parts working together to reflect and refract light in a whole image.

There is a clear example of this in his three poems printed together in *Severn and Somme* all titled 'Requiem', only a quatrain each. Each represents a musing on the dead and how they should be commemorated, and on the just nature of the war in which they had fallen. The first and third 'Requiem', written with the clear influence of Whitman in the background, are riffing on the same idea. Rather than appearing as two different drafts, this series or sequence of poems manifests itself as simultaneous and varying refractions of the same idea.

Requiem

Pour out your light, O stars, and do not hold
    Your loveliest shining from earth's outworn shell—
Pure and cold your radiance, pure and cold
    My dead friend's face as well.

Requiem

Pour out your bounty, moon of radiant shining
    On all this shattered flesh, these quiet forms;
For these were slain, so strangely still reclining,
    In the noblest cause was ever waged with arms.[43]

One appeals to the stars, and one to the moon. One reflects the broken forms of the dead, the other the coldness of the dead face, and the outworn, corpse-like shell of the earth. Together they create a complementary, interlinked impression of dark, cold, broken shapes partially lit by the dim light of the night sky.

As one might expect in a collection that documents his earliest poetic attempts, *Severn and Somme* traces Gurney experimenting, more or less successfully, with different forms and styles. 'Carol', a festive work with a tight rhyme scheme and refrain for the final line of each stanza—'For Christë's joy that's born to-night'—is incongruously placed next to the deeply serious poem 'Afterwards', with its looser rhymes and lines of eleven to thirteen syllables, spilling fluidly into each other in a form of uncontained iambic pentameter. It begins

Those dreadful evidences of Man's ill-doing
The kindly Mother of all shall soon hide deep,
Covering with tender fingers her children asleep,[44]

'Carol' bears no relation to this freer verse, being a gesture back into the beautiful medieval carols of Gurney's cathedral training, complete with pseudo-archaic language. But even here we find in Gurney's childlike images an innocence and wide-eyed earnestness that rings true, in verse that is in effect little more than pleasant pastiche. He begins with the leafless winter trees, but the oblique shadow of war is subtly cast across this seemingly jocund little ditty.

Winter now has bared the trees,
Killed with tiny swords the jolly

Leafage that mid-summer sees,
But left the ivy and the holly.[45]

The opening is strikingly violent; winter is a murderer with multiple weapons, causing destruction with tiny swords. Bare winter trees are familiar and safe territory, but this has behind it the shadow of a war-torn landscape in miniature. And then we stumble upon the close juxtaposition of the killing and the incongruously festive 'jolly', without knowing who it describes. As our eyes travel from line to line there is a momentary mental jolt before we process that it is in fact the murdered 'leafage' which Gurney anthropomorphises and to which he attributes jollity. Later, in the third stanza, the distinctive adjective appears again, linked to the destruction of the first stanza. This time we are told it is *children* who are jolly: 'bright red berries and children jolly.' This is a carol that conjures up 'The Holly and the Ivy' as its ghostly predecessor, and we remember by association that the berry there is 'as red as any blood'. So now, by the deftest of strokes, blood, murder and destruction are linked, alarmingly, to children. When we remember that this is included in a collection of war poetry, the subtlety of the association becomes the more powerful.

As soon as Gurney received the confirmation from Sidgwick and Jackson that his manuscript was accepted, he wrote to Howells to report the good news.[46] Howells was at best a reluctant correspondent, and Gurney made a point of giving Howells what would soon be his new address with the 184th Machine Gun Corps in the body of the letter, drawing attention to his new status as he signed off, *and* also putting it on the envelope for good measure. Howells could not use Gurney's transfer as an excuse not to reply. Howells did reply, but trumped Gurney's publication triumph with the killer blow of his own award of a substantial annuity from the Carnegie United Kingdom Trust, a charitable trust which supported composers and published competition-winning works. Howells's resignation from Salisbury had left him with little money, a situation with which Gurney was wearily familiar. However, while Gurney could barely afford cigarettes, Howells was awarded a very generous salary of £150 per year by the Carnegie Trust, in return for editing Tudor church music. It was, as doctor's orders had decreed, to spare him from having to work, and to help him recuperate. Howells, whose sense of motivation was second only to Gurney's, spent the three salaried years writing prodigiously. He need not have gloated to his impecunious friend of his good fortune. Gurney was yet again obliged to write back congratulating Howells on his luck.[47]

He had written much of *Severn and Somme* with his comrades in mind. He had recorded their experiences, expressions and characters, and written of their suffering. Now, just as he could begin to imagine his book being passed eagerly from hand to hand, he was obliged to leave them for a machine gun corps. Still, it was not to be a total separation. The 184th Machine Gunners would be going into the line with the Gloucesters, and once he had completed his retraining he would at least be near them, if not sharing the same dugouts. On 27 July 1917 Gurney reluctantly moved away from the Buire au Bois orchards. He seemed both surprised and gratified to find that his comrades would miss him; they showed 'real regret at my leaving; though most thought I was lucky to get the chance'. It was a coveted transfer— machine gunners had the reputation of an easy and more interesting life than the average soldier ('and one can take a more impersonal interest in the slaying of Huns, like the Artillery').[48] Gurney hated the thought of hand-to-hand combat, of looking into the eyes of a man at bayonet-point. Aside from the emotional relief of being behind a machine gun, he also (perhaps overoptimistically) looked forward to better food, and a better quality of dugout. Machine gunners were required at the sides of the line, so he hoped to avoid going into the front posts, which were generally the worst and most dangerous positions to occupy. Full of cheerful expectations, he moved down south to Vaux, near Bapaume,

> a flat land of continual cultivation; whose cottages are cleaner than those of other parts; where one may see windmills with the old new delight and pride in man's cunning and masterful mind; where churches are a landmark and houses loom large; a country of faint continual haunting charm almost entirely of man's fashioning. A Scarlatti, early Mozartish atmosphere restful and full of home-sense, and heart-ache.[49]

He was deeply impressed by the French women who had remained to cultivate the farmland. While he spent his time being educated in the art of machine gunning, and practised throwing bombs, 'Dark women with proud features as of old coining' worked the land within yards of the explosions, apparently unperturbed by the danger. Gurney 'saluted the old honour unspoiled'.[50] The 'clumsy English in their daily doing of futile worrying things' could only watch in awe as these living reminders of the greatness of the French race continued as if nothing had changed in the last few years.

On 31 July the Third Battle of Ypres, otherwise known as the Third Battle of Passchendaele, began. Gurney, endeavouring to learn about the mechanism of his machine gun with a formidable Scotsman as teacher, received his instruction with the sounds of the explosions in the distance. It would not be long before he would be part of the attack. For now at least, he was having the quietest time of it since his hospital stay in Rouen. It had been a charmed spring; he had somehow managed only to be in the line once since April—and he knew his luck was about to run out. The scale of the bombardment was such that whilst he listened to the explosions, Scott, back in London, could hear the rumbling of the very same guns. This odd moment of kinship inspired the poem 'Rumours of Wars'. Whilst the fighting raged, Gurney took advantage of his final few days of safety to write 'The Immortal Hour' and 'Question and Answer'. On 14 August he revised the poem 'Beauty', retitling it 'Winter Beauty', and sent Scott 'Camps'. Gurney was anxious to get as much finished as he could and into Scott's safekeeping, and this final bundle of verse was sent just before he had to move up the line that afternoon. These were to be the last poems he would conceive on foreign soil.

Gurney's machine gun unit began to move north, rejoining the rest of the 2/5ths, and marching together back to Flanders, with the guns growing ever louder as the miles passed. The trenches had been in a desperate condition when they had last occupied them. Now, after further months of continuous fighting, conditions were deplorable. Gurney felt it was particularly bad luck to have been moved to such a cheerless place after the brief glimpses of hop gardens in the fertile landscape through which he'd just marched. Now he was packed with an unfeasible number of men into 'dangerous bivouacs by some ruined chateau' (six and a half kilometres south of Ypres). At least he did not have to contend with being frozen as well as half drowned in mud. As he later wrote, with a striking, rhythmically wrong-footing portmanteau locution, 'These were August, and more soldier—warmer happy days.'[51]

> The ground was waterlogged and the only way through it was by corduroy roads, which seemed well worn and had clearly often been repaired.[52] At the side of the track were many shell holes, full of stagnant green liquid and, here and there, a dead horse. A bogged down tank completed the picture of desolation.[53]

In such a landscape, any diversion was welcome. On 22 August Gurney could report a momentary excitement; a German plane had been shot down in front of him, supposedly by the French air ace George Guynemer. 'He fell not 30 yards from me. The only exciting, really thrilling thing I have seen in France!'[54] Arthur Benjamin, ever attracted to glamour and style, had left the army for the Royal Air Force, but had been shot down over Germany, and was, like Harvey, a prisoner of war. Gurney was envious. His own opinion was that if one must be killed, it would be much better to drop from the sky than to be blown into it from a hole. He was in fact one of the last to be able to claim proximity to the superstar Guynemer. Only two weeks later Guynemer went out on a mission and never returned.[55]

The possibility of death was everywhere, and mostly it was infinitely less glamorous than that of Guynemer. That night, whilst out on fatigue, Gurney himself came face to face with it, when a piece of shrapnel flew into his head from a nearby explosion. His head remained intact, but his helmet bore the dent. It was a very narrow escape. His good fortune continued. The next day his 'gun team is in the line, but I, a relief, am modestly in the rear at present, near the big guns. Fritz tries to bomb them at night, bless him.'[56] But his luck could not hold out. He had known that it was only a matter of time before he would be part of a major offensive, and in early September, his moment came.

The 2/5ths received instructions for a big attack, planning to take the high ground occupied by the Germans, which was known as Hill 35. The Gloucesters got into position in the first few days of September. Attacking higher ground rarely ended well, and previous attempts to take the hill had been unmitigated disasters. Every one of the 2/5ths would have known that such an action was tantamount to suicide. Even if the attack wasn't doomed to failure, Gurney could hardly have taken comfort from the fact that the life expectancy for a machine gunner during an attack was four minutes. After months of training, this was the moment he had both dreaded and anticipated. If his courage had failed him, and he had seized any chance to escape from likely death, not one of his comrades would have blamed him.

The Ypres Salient in the summer and autumn of 1917 was one of the myth-making fronts of the war. Like the Somme, it was every bit as bad as the popular conception of the war would have it—blood, mud and guts were very much in evidence, and Gurney could have claimed with some justification to have seen the very worst of the war that summer.[57]

He was spared going 'over the top' of the front line by being with the machine gunners, whose job was not to attack, but to be at the sides of any attack to cover the men's advance. They would usually set up a gun in a makeshift emplacement, perhaps hastily constructed in a shelled building if such a thing presented itself, although these were obvious targets for enemy artillery. A gun emplacement might alternatively be dug out from the existing trenches and filled with sandbags. The landscape was littered with abandoned tanks, an eerie sight, but useful for getting bearings in an area where all landmarks had long ago been obliterated. The ruins of Ypres were behind them, and ahead the battalion faced the impregnable ridge, with forests of barbed wire between them and the heavily fortified German line.

On 10 September, as the battalion waited for the attack to begin, the Germans released a gas cloud over the British lines just below the remains of the village of St Julien.[58] Gurney was carrying heavy machine gun equipment along the trench, with six other men from the Machine Gun Corps. If a gas alarm had sounded, they ignored it. Equally, there could have been gas left in the trenches and shell holes from a previous gas shell, which had not yet dissipated. Because machine gunners and operators of heavy artillery were less mobile than the common infantry, they were often obliged to remain in a gas attack for longer. They were issued with even more cumbersome and inconvenient masks as a result—respirators twice the size of the standard issue, with a huge, unwieldy box of charcoal attached. There was really no incentive to wrestle with one unless absolutely necessary, and neither Gurney nor his comrades wore theirs. Consequently, all seven men inhaled enough of the gas to necessitate removal from the line, although Gurney stuck it out in the line with his catarrh-like symptoms for a full week before he reported sick.[59] His delay in reporting his injury was either an act of bravery or an indication that his injuries were not severe.

Gurney was not inclined to be superstitious, but back in May he had felt a strong conviction that his return to the line would end in severe injury. 'Well, I think I shall come through alright in the end, but first, a pretty severe and painful wound.'[60] It was not a particularly cheering thought, but his sense that his war was nearly over might well have been wishful thinking as much as superstition. Did the conviction that he had done his time and that fate owed him a blighty lead him to escape the line with what appeared to be only a superficial injury? From as far back as Vermand, he had believed he would be wounded again. Now, his foreboding was proved right.

CHAPTER SEVEN

'A Touch of Gas'

Went sick for contrariety and gas symptoms;
Hoping a week's easy; with six others wheezy
(Though ready for the Line) and coughing discreetly,
(Who had walked through gas too lazy to do the easy
Thing—and wear gas masks, till it overdid us).[1]

Gurney's 'blighty' is shrouded in mystery, but his unexpected escape from the fighting is far from the desertion or breakdown it might appear to be. When he recollected the moment in an untitled poem from the 1920s (a section of it quoted above), he was clear about his intentions in reporting sick, 'coughing discreetly'. It is an easy narrative, and as such to be treated with not a little suspicion. His elision of motivations affords contrariety and gas symptoms equal weight, evoking a schoolboy wheeze; shirking duty out of laziness and not a little cheek.

The reality was not so glib or simple, although there may well have been an element of truth in this account. The temptation has been to assume that his gas symptoms were apparently so trifling that his 'injury' was merely a pretext for leaving the front because of another mental breakdown. If so, he would naturally have been reluctant to admit it, both for the sake of his friends' anxiety and for his own pride. He had hoped against hope that the war would cure his 'neurasthenia'. It would be a hard thing indeed to admit that, after fifteen months of suffering and danger, he was no nearer a state of mental stability than he had been when a depressed undergraduate back in London. Tempting though this reading of events might be, it is erroneous. Whether or not Gurney was in a state of nervous breakdown, the series of events that were triggered by his small exposure to gas were entirely standard, and in keeping with the Royal Army Medical Corps' policy on the treatment of gas effects at that time.

Gurney did not know what type of gas he had inhaled. He only knew that it was new, different from the gas he had been exposed to that winter on the Somme, which 'had a heavy hothouse Swinburnian filthy sort of odour—voluptuous and full of danger.'[2] As the box respirator was able to protect against chlorine and phosgene, the gases previously favoured by the Germans, they invented the even more unpleasant mustard gas (dichlorethyl sulphide), referred to in awe as the 'King of battle gases'. From July 1917 until the end of the war it was their gas of choice, causing 75 percent of gas casualties across the Western Front between July and November, and producing nearly eight times as many injuries as the average of all other poison gases in the war. It was such a feature of the fighting around Ypres that summer that it became known by the French as Yperite.[3] Mustard gas was named after its amber colouring, and after the mustardy smell, which was noticeable only when in high concentration. However, if only a small amount was present, then neither colour nor smell would be detectable.

Gas was, essentially, a weapon of terror. It was unpredictable and caused widespread panic, a feature as useful to the side who had released it as the injuries and (comparatively few) deaths it caused. Sometimes the gas released was simply smoke, or tear gas, but the confusion it caused was the same. Gas masks were cumbersome contraptions. They were hot, sweaty and difficult to see through—hardly an asset in trenches that were already hazardous and difficult to negotiate. The men hated gas attacks, but it was the medical officers who were the most terrified of them. The chemistry behind the new inventions moved at a tremendous pace, and no sooner had they learnt to predict the side effects of one gas, and decided upon the best courses of treatment, than they were faced with another new and untested kind. It was often not possible to tell what kind of gas it was, and there was a great deal of confusion around the different kinds being used by the Germans that summer. By the time Gurney was gassed, in September 1917, the British were still scrambling to keep up with the latest German toxic inventions.[4]

There is no record of the type of gas Gurney inhaled, if indeed anyone knew. His gas exposure left him with catarrh and a cough, which had both all but gone by the middle of the month. The gas had hurt his throat. Mustard gas was essentially a gas that burnt, rather than suffocated. It attacked and irritated the tissues of the lungs, causing them to produce fluid which filled the small air passages, preventing oxygen from reaching the blood. The effects of this would not be felt immediately. Had Gurney inhaled it, he might have recovered from the original irritation and coughing, and felt quite well, whilst still being at risk of death. Doctors had found that enough oxygen would reach a gassed soldier's blood so long as he remained absolutely still and quiet, but if he exerted himself in any way then the heart, trying to make up for the deficiency by working harder, could fail. This was true of severe cases, but their lungs and throat would have been so desperately damaged by burning and blistering that they would have been likely to die whether or not they remained still. This was not known, however, and the standard procedure at this point

FIG. 7.1: Lijssenthoek Casualty Clearing Station. By kind permission of the Lijssenthoek Project.

in the war for any gassed soldier, who, like Gurney, exhibited even minor symptoms, was total stretcher rest.

Gurney reported sick only after his symptoms had persisted for a week, but 'Delayed action' cases were greatly feared, despite the fact that most deaths from gas exposure actually took place within the first forty-eight hours. The doctor who assessed Gurney initially was dealing with a huge quantity of gassed soldiers, in every degree of distress. There was little time to observe all cases carefully, and even those who appeared to have only minor symptoms could potentially be in danger of heart failure. Gurney might have welcomed his escape from the line, but as far as the doctors were concerned, this was no 'wangle', as Gurney rather guiltily put it, but a necessary precaution.

He was sent back to the nearest casualty clearing station (either Brandhoek, Mendinghem or Lijssenthoek) to await his fate. He was delighted to be away from the incessant guns and the squalor, and with Tolstoy's short stories ('which are perfect') and Harvey's *A Gloucestershire Lad* for company. There he would probably have been confined to a stretcher, and treated with inhalations of boiling water and Friars Balsam, the standard remedy for gassed throats.[5] He was feeling quite upbeat, even though the possibility of going back to the front was far more likely than that of escaping to England. In fact, he was well enough to correct the proofs of *Severn and Somme*, which he had received just in time. By 22 September he had posted back his corrections to Scott. It was the first time Gurney had seen his book in its entirety.

Although the relief at escaping raised guilt at letting his comrades down, it was at this point only a temporary state; he had every expectation of being sent back to St Julien. He even talked about how he would feel were he to be awarded the DCM in the imminent battle. But it was to be another year before the Medical Corps realised that the recovery time for mild exposure to mustard gas was only four to six weeks. Instead of being sent back to Ypres, Gurney began the long journey back to Britain, still on his unnecessary stretcher. The hypochondria was on the part of the medics, not Gurney himself, but who was he to argue?

Two days after he left the battalion, on 12 September, the 2/5ths' long-awaited attack on Hill 35 was cancelled.[6] Despite this unexpected reprieve, Gurney had still had a timely escape, and he knew it. What is now known as the Third Battle of Ypres had already begun in the areas around him as he made the decision to report sick. He was transported from the hell of St Julien 'where sheer hideousness is the prettiest thing' to the literary paradise of Edinburgh in a matter of days, and could hardly understand his own good fortune.[7] But this was not merely an unexpected holiday. Whatever mental state he was in, he was not prepared to dwell on it in his correspondence. However, he could not avoid having his state of mind reflected alarmingly back at him as he looked around at the men with whom he was being shipped down the Seine from Rouen.

> I am not well of course, but the thing that struck me on the boat coming over was that noone looked well. There was not any more jollity than if it were merely Another Move. The iron had entered into their souls, and they were still fast bound; unable to realise what tremendous changes of life had come to them for a while.[8]

He was heading away from the guns and the mud, towards the air ships patrolling the sky at the mouth of the harbour of Le Havre. It had once been his first glimpse of France, and now it was to be his last. The complexity of emotions his reprieve engendered was incommunicable. Ironically, the enforced rest seemed to have disturbed him as much as the gas:

> Today we have been steaming down the loveliest river in the world, in the loveliest weather. Alack! gas or staying still has disturbed my anatomy so much that I could not [. . .] appreciate it at all worthily.[9]

He continued, before trailing off into silence:

> But how I should have liked to have you as confidante tonight—early! For everything seemed futile, save Beauty that was too high for me; myself a failure and prematurely worn; my friends poor trusting fools to be disappointed . . .

This bleak note of anxiety at the prospect of disappointing his friends and failing to achieve as an artist was a new one. Until now, the frustrations at underachieving had been temporary and circumstantial; he had looked forward to the 'revenge of joy' he would have once back in England and able to work at a fast and furious pace, and he confidently imagined being able to pour into his work all he had learnt through his suffering. Now, as the reality of returning was closer than ever, he seemed to be losing faith in his future, the one vision that had sustained him. As he looked at the stars from the deck of the hospital ship carrying him to England, with the 'blue and silver gleam of tossing sea-water' below, the waves seemed to mirror not only the night sky but his own inner turbulence, troubled by 'feelings of all kinds turning my distended breast.'[10]

The channel crossing was met by an ambulance train, from which, after a tedious twelve-hour journey, he was lifted by stretcher to take in his first sight of Bangour General Hospital. This would be his home for the next six weeks. As soon as the train had been emptied, another blast on the whistle was sounded and it was despatched south once more. The orderlies were so practised at their procedures that they prided themselves on being able to empty a train of three hundred patients in no more than ninety minutes. Gurney, still confined to his stretcher, lost a poem in the rush when his bag was dropped during the transfer.

He had been given a choice of destinations and had chosen Edinburgh for both practical and literary reasons. Of the hospitals on offer, it was the only one that could usually be guaranteed to have space, so was a safe choice. Even if he had specified Gloucestershire or London, he ran the risk of being placed miles from his friends and incurring a burden on them to travel out to visit him. Edinburgh, or 'Enbro', as it appealed to his romantic imagination to call it, was for Gurney the city of literary inspiration, of Robert Louis Stevenson and Walter Scott, and he imagined being able to commune with their spirits whilst nosing through secondhand bookstalls in the streets. He was not yet in a frame of mind to welcome visitors. Imagined encounters were the only ones for which he was currently fit.

> There is nothing the matter with me as far as I know save fatheadedness and unfitness and indigestion from doing nothing and eating too much. (I am in a horrid temper, so don't interrupt; Weltmuth and indigestion together.[11] Of course it *might* be gas. I only hope they keep me here till I am cured under that impression!)[12]

It might indeed have been stomach trouble induced by the gas, but for Gurney, this was a familiar symptom of mental disturbance; indigestion had gone hand in hand with depression back in London in 1914. With anxious friends kept at a distance, it was easier to make the contradictory claims that there was nothing the matter, whilst simultaneously admitting that he is in fact as 'Ratty as can be [...] So much France has done for me.'[13]

Bangour Village, as the hospital was previously known, had originally opened in 1906 as a lunatic asylum. It was built fourteen miles west of Edinburgh with a view to keeping patients out of the way of the metropolis, as much for their own peace and quiet as for society comfortably to turn a blind eye. It became the Edinburgh War Hospital in 1915. Set in its own woodland, the hospital had been designed to resemble a group of houses, or villas. They were all in typical Scottish grey stone with red roofs, attractive gables and rounded windows on the top floor, and large windows beneath. Since its wartime transformation, it had become a destination for the wounded of every kind, mental and physical. With three thousand patients to accommodate, it was beyond its capacity when Gurney arrived in 1917. A neighbouring field had been given over to tents for a camp hospital to treat the less serious cases. Gurney was directed to Ward 24, which was 'a nice clean room' in one of the villas. His condition was worse than he was letting on; he was considered too serious a case to be relegated to the overflow marquees.

Craiglockhart Hospital was only twelve miles away, which was to be made famous by Wilfred Owen's and Siegfried Sassoon's residencies, and which had been specifically earmarked since 1916 for 'neurasthenic officers'. As Gurney convalesced at Bangour, so Owen and Sassoon looked out over the same Pentland Hills. The landscape might have been the same, but their treatments were very different. Gurney was a private soldier, registered as gassed rather than shell-shocked, and so would have been less likely to receive any specific psychiatric help at Bangour than if he had been under the care of Sassoon's doctor, W.H.R. Rivers, who was so tantalisingly close. It is pointless to speculate how different the progression of Gurney's mental deterioration might have been had he received the benefit of a doctor such as Rivers, a pioneering psychiatrist and Freudian, who would have respected Gurney's literary qualities, and given him the time he needed to be heard and understood.

However, hospitalisation in any form brought with it the joys of clean sheets, no lice, and being able to shave in a real mirror. Ironically, Gurney felt more connected to the war's progress than he had in the thick of it, as for the first time since 1916 he had access to the daily papers. News was readily accessible, but there was a dearth of good quality reading material, to his intense frustration. Confined to bed in a hospital that was in the midst of the countryside, he was as far from the inspiration of Sir Walter Scott, R. L. Stevenson and the anticipated secondhand bookstalls as he had been in France. But there were many compensations. When literature did come his way, he had the leisure time to devour it. He was delighted by the characterisation in Vachell's *Quinney's Adventures* (1914), incorrectly predicting that it would become a classic: 'I can see it in the hands of people of 2005.'[14] At the beginning of October, Gurney was reading Charlotte Brontë's *Villette* (1853), and finding it a 'queer magical sort of tale.' He was particularly taken with the character of the author, pointing astutely to the similarities between Brontë and himself:

What an uncanny tortured otherworldly yet supremely real atmosphere she can bring one into! Was she one of the people who can find no peace on earth?[15]

He was still receiving the *Times Literary Supplement*, which Scott had faithfully forwarded on to him when he was in France, and was dismayed to come across a slating review of Harvey's second poetry collection, *Gloucestershire Friends*. Secretly he was in agreement with the reviewer, but his loyalty to his dearest friend ran deep. He was immersed in correcting the proofs of his own magnum opus, and it was impolitic (and perhaps too much like tempting fate) to be too smug at Harvey's misfortune.

Bangour was to be Gurney's first experience of residency inside an asylum. Away from the front, well fed and cared for, he felt this was the beginning of his new life. 'You remember F.W.H.'s parable of the man who was in Heaven and did not know it? Even so is it with me!'[16] Once he had recovered, he could look forward to using the knowledge and technical developments he had made as a poet to secure his place in history. There was always a chance he would be sent back, but in the meantime, he could read and think in peace.

As soon as he was allowed up, he spent two hours playing the ward piano. Unfortunately, it could not be Bach, as he had no music with him, but he settled (for now) for accompanying other patients, with tastes rather lower-brow than his own. He gritted his teeth, rifled through the sheet music available, and played 'The Rosary', by Ethelbert Woodbridge Nevin, a best seller in 1898, and Wilfrid Ernest Sanderson's 'Drake Goes West' and 'Friend o' Mine'. To his joy, he found that

> the effort to concentrate is a pleasure to me; which means that in so much neurasthenia is a thing of the past. And that what I have would go if I lived in my old life once again, with an added incalculable Joy added thereto. Rejoice with me my friend, for that which was lost is found; or shall I say rather—its hiding place is known.[17]

He felt that he was all but cured—his burning ambitions were finally to be realised, and his friends might yet be proud. But it did not take long for his mood to swing back to the creeping lethargy and 'thickness' that haunted him. Four days later the piano playing had become too difficult—his head was 'thick', and his fingers 'stiff' (possibly psychological as well as lack of practise, but it was still only five months after his bullet wound). The weather was dull, and he had read everything he could find. He was unfocused, unsatisfied and depressed. The doctors clearly did not share his confidence in his neurasthenia being a thing of the past, as he was still largely confined to bed, on a light diet, and despite regretting his lack of a convincing gas 'cough', there were enough symptoms to merit his being detained and his illness taken seriously.

As the initial euphoria slipped away, he searched around to find his salvation in others, and it was the Scottish soldiers in the ward who provided obvious idols to worship. Casting about for others in whom to invest when he himself felt he had

FIG. 7.2: VAD nurse Annie Nelson Drummond. © Peggy Ann McKay Carter.

little resilience left was a strategy Gurney had employed on a number of occasions. He had fallen in love with the Scots when he spent Christmas with the Black Watch out in France. Now, a 'bundle of oppressed nerves', he rather forlornly imagined aligning himself with them, trying to fit in (with only partial success) and hoping their wholesomeness would somehow rub off on him.

> Just to see the face of a Scot not 12 yards away, what a humiliation of weakness must I feel before such strength! I swear that if happiness and utility do not come to me after the war, I will first earn some money at picture-palaces and then go to sea with such men, whom I do admire so, and who take me along with them to some extent; in a rough life to live in free air, to work oneself clean out with the joy that comes from sticking it well to follow.[18]

This was clutching at straws. For the first time, he openly confronted the possibility that happiness and domesticity might permanently elude him.

It was in this mood of intense vulnerability that he first met the Scottish nurse Annie Nelson Drummond. The possibility of a relationship with her offered him a vision of domestic bliss that was hard to refuse, but he knew that he was susceptible on two accounts—he was desperate for security, and he had barely seen any women for months. He was still sore from the Chapman family's rejection of his ill-conceived advances to their teenage daughter Kitty before the war, and he warned himself against making another 'tragic blunder'. But it was no use; he could not help himself. Just as he tried to align himself with the burly Scots on his ward to absorb some of their strength, so by falling in love with Drummond he hoped he could find another way out of his own personal hell.

> She is 30 years o[ld an]d most perfectly enchanting. She has a pretty figure, pretty hair, fine eyes, pretty hands and arms *and* walk. A charming voice, pretty ears, a resolute little mouth. With a great love in her she is glad to give when the time comes. In Hospital, the first thing that would strike you is 'her guarded flame'. There was a mask on her face more impenetrable than on any other woman I have ever seen. (But that has gone for me.) In fact (at a guess) I think it will disappear now she has found someone whom she thinks worthy.
>
> A not unimportant fact was revealed by one of the patients at hospital—a fine chap—I believe she has money. Just think of it! Pure good luck, if it is true (as I believe it is). But she is more charming and tender and deep than you will believe till you see her.
>
> O Erbert, O Erbert. . . .
>
> I forgot my body walking with her; a thing that hasn't happened since . . . when?
>
> I really don't know.[19]

Annie was a warm, homely girl. The daughter of a milliner and a coal miner, she grew up in West Lothian. She was used to caring for others, having helped to raise her young brothers, and had turned to nursing as a vocation. Gurney was especially delighted to find that she had a keen appreciation of music, had had piano lessons, and was appreciative of nature. Gurney had witnessed Harvey's transformation when he had fallen in love in 1913. Harvey had found a temporary cure for his depression in the form of an Irish nurse, Sarah Anne Kane (known as Anne), whom he was to marry, after an interruption of nine years. Gurney knew that thoughts of Anne sustained Harvey through the dreary days in his prison camp. As so often in the past, Harvey proved a reference point for Gurney, a haunting presence influencing his actions. Now Gurney had the sympathy and friendship of his own nurse; it was natural he would assume that, like Harvey, he too could find his salvation in her. His relationship with Annie was to be his most significant love affair. Despite this, he does not talk of her in terms of physical arousal, other than repeatedly observing her 'prettiness'. Instead, her presence helps him to transcend himself, to 'forget his body', as he put it.

Gurney's sexuality is a matter for speculation, and guarded speculation at that. Arthur Benjamin, who was comfortably open about his own homosexuality, hinted that Gurney had confided in him secrets that he had not thought appropriate to share with others. There is little that is simple about Gurney, his personality, or his attachments. Gurney's correspondence shows that he saw his love for Harvey and Annie as equal and comparable, and that 'there are really only two people who matter to me'.[20] It was an extraordinary claim, considering his apparently close friendship with Howells, and Marion Scott's years of devotion. What was it that Annie, whom he barely knew, could offer him that could eclipse all others apart from Harvey? It appears from his correspondence with Harvey that whatever deep emotions he felt for his friend he might have sublimated temporarily into this new heterosexual relationship, which so closely mirrored that of the union between Harvey and his own fiancée. It is more likely that, rather than being a soul mate, Annie unwittingly represented a socially acceptable receptacle for an outpouring of far more complex emotion than she bargained for.

It seemed particularly important for Gurney to bring Harvey and Annie as close as possible, and for these two most treasured friends to appreciate each other, despite the geographical distance between Edinburgh and Harvey's prison camp in Germany. Gurney lent Annie his copy of Harvey's recently published second poetry collection, *Gloucestershire Friends*. He was far from blind to the weaknesses of the collection. The zenith of his faint praise was reserved for one poem, 'My Father Bred Great Horses', which if it were a little better 'would be first-rate'. But whether or not he approved of the quality, lending Harvey's verse to Annie was a way of introducing her to his world, and in particular to his greatest friend. Harvey's poetry was the nearest Gurney could get to 'communion with his undefeated, laughing spirit', as he put it.[21]

Annie was not greatly literary and was probably not particularly impressed, but Gurney was not in need of another literary friend. He craved inspiration and stability, and she was both attractive and sympathetic. They became increasingly close in early October, and with love came inspiration, in the form of the poem 'After Music': 'Why, I am on fire now, and tremulous / With sense of Beauty long denied'.[22] Apart from a few hours of playing Beethoven, he had had little quality music-making at Bangour Hospital, and had composed nothing. His new state of exhilaration drew him back to music, with this paean of praise for its redemptive power. Music's restorative properties result (in the poem) in Gurney's redemption. But this is far from a straightforward love song; there is an intriguing gender confusion at the end, as he imagines himself as Euridice:

> No Joy that's clean, no Love but something lets
>   It from its power; the wisest soul forgets
> What's beautiful, or delicate, or chaste.
> Orpheus drew me (as once his bride) from Hell.
> If wisely, her or me, the Gods can tell.[23]

Was it really music in the abstract that was responsible for drawing him from hell, or was it 'a certain sister', as he coyly described her to Marion Scott?

When he was not writing, Gurney found himself assigned tasks around the ward. Just as he had been frustrated with cleaning kit and endless inspections, so he quickly found the routines of domesticity tiresome. 'Yesterday I was wiping cutlery and plates and things after breakfast and dinner, and it tired me out. I hate that sort of thing so.'[24] The clearing-up might have been dull, but the meals were worth the bother; the patients ate better than civilians, with haddock and chips being a favourite, and a generous supply of cream and milk from the local farm.[25] Gurney's ward was known as the Ragtime Ward, as the nurses were uncommonly jolly. Theirs was the envy of many of the other wards, which were run by 'dragons and discipline'. The ward kettle was constantly on the boil, and on warm afternoons the nurses took the patients out for picnics in the grounds.

Ladies of Charity

With quiet tread, with softly smiling faces
    The nurses move like music through the room;
While broken men (known, technically, as "cases")
    Watch them with eyes late deep in bitter gloom,
As though the Spring were come with all the Graces,
    Or maiden April walked the ward in bloom.

Men that have grown forgetful of Joy's power,
    And old before their time, take courtesy
So sweet of girl or woman, as if some flower
    Most strangely fair of Spring were suddenly
Thick in the woods at Winter's blackest hour—
    The gift unlooked for—lovely Charity.

Their anguish they forget, and worse, the slow
    Corruption of Joy's springs; now breathe again
The free breath was theirs so long ago.
    Courage renewed makes mock at the old pain.
Life's loveliness brings tears, and a new glow.
    Somehow their sacrifice seems not in vain.[26]

This poem's well-behaved abab rhyme scheme contains within it the soft hum of excitement that accompanies the presence of these nurses, who 'move like music through the room.' They are everything Gurney holds most sacred; nature and art, so much so that the rather formal title, and the gift of 'lovely charity' they bestow seem curiously coy for such an intimate, effusive poem. We can sense Gurney practically hugging himself with the thrill of his new love, that has, as he hints, transformed his life like winter woods unexpectedly filling with blossom.

Alongside his burgeoning love affair with Annie Drummond, Gurney found a more cerebral friend in the hospital chaplain. He attended the Reverend T. Ratcliffe Barnett's lecture on the eighteenth-century Scottish philosopher Adam Smith on 3 October and was impressed by the chaplain's knowledge and literary credentials. He was an acquaintance of Wilfred Owen, and a musician and established author of books on folklore and travel.[27] Gurney exchanged books with Barnett as he had with his godfather Cheesman before, Barnett inscribing a copy of his *Reminiscences of Old Scots Folk,* 'my house an ever open door to you'. Gurney returned the compliment by sending him a copy of *Severn and Somme* a month after he had left the hospital, inscribing it 'To that Bon Chaplain and Good Friend'.

He was also taken with a musical coal miner, Private T. Evans, who possessed a beautiful tenor voice, and had done Prout's harmony exercises and Royal College of Organist test papers for fun for thirty years, when not working down the pit. Gurney gloried equally in his strength, his mind and his accent. He also sympathised with Evans, who was suffering from depression and gastritis. Evans had 'hardly any knowledge of fine music, but with fire, and a temperament that with his voice ought to go far.'[28]

Like Gurney himself, Evans was his own artistic master, learning and creating music for the sheer joy of hard work and creativity, rather than climbing the conventional career ladder. More cynically, the parallel Gurney would have been loath to make would have been that the odds of professional success were stacked against them both: a depressed and untrained miner finding his way in the classical music industry, and a penniless composer who was likely to be increasingly crippled by mental illness. Gurney had a high opinion of Evans's talent, and respected his ambition. Their friendship lasted beyond the duration of their convalescence. When Evans moved to London, Gurney wrote to Scott instructing her to look after his new friend, and he made sure Evans got to hear a performance of his Elizas. The following year, when Gurney was ill during the summer of 1918 in St Albans, Evans visited him in hospital. In 'The Miner', he captures something of the contradictions of his new friend's character. The title of the poem suggests Evans be defined by his occupation, but from the outset subverts expectation by painting a picture of a man prevented by social status and lack of education from expressing himself through the arts, holding in tension his 'indomitable energy', alongside his social awkwardness and passion for music.

The Miner

Indomitable energy controlled
By Fate to wayward ends and to half use,

He should have given his service to the Muse,
To most men shy, to him, her humble soldier,
Frank-hearted, generous, bold.

Yet though his fate be cross, he shall not tire
Nor seek another service than his own:
For selfless valour and the primal fire
Shine out from him, as once from great Ulysses,
That king without a throne.[29]

Ever since Gurney had been well enough to be out of bed, and had ventured to try the piano, he had been used as a slave-pianist. He was cajoled into accompanying ghastly drawing room ballads, for hours at a time, suffering:

The rapturous soulfulness that disdains tempo. The durchganging baritone that will not be stayed long by interludes of piano, whose eager spirit is bars too early for the fray.[30]

He weighed up the possible benefits of extending his stay at Bangour as a useful accompanist, evading the trenches but prolonging the musical torture, or forgoing the ballads and being sent back to France. Amateur music-making won—Ratcliffe Barnett managed to detain Gurney for an extra fortnight in the hospital, along with Evans, on the strength of their artistic contributions to hospital life. It was a good wheeze, and Gurney was delighted to see the effects of his music-making on the sick men around him, however badly realised by both inadequate instrument and performers. He tentatively began to inflict some higher-brow music on his undiscerning audience, and much to his surprise, found that they not only sat through the whole of Beethoven's D major Sonata, but also thanked him afterwards for playing it! The experience inspired the poem 'Upstairs Piano', in which he curses the wooden beast in 'ecstasies of wrath' for refusing to do justice to the greats. It is Gurney at his most endearing: witty, wrong-footing and eccentrically hyperbolic.

Upstairs Piano
O dull confounded Thing,
You will not sing
Though I distress your keys
With thumps; in ecstasies
Of wrath, at some mis-said
Word of the deathless Dead!

Chopin or dear Mozart,
How must it break your heart
To hear this Beast refuse

The choice gifts of the Muse!
And turn your airy thought
With clumsiness to nought.[31]

By the end of October, he was expecting to be moved out of the hospital. He had three more poems to his name as well as his first song for months, 'The Folly of Being Comforted'. It was one of his best, in his opinion.[32] He had a copy of W. B. Yeats's 'wistful, magical words', and had been particularly taken with the power of the final couplet ('Heart! O Heart! If she'd but turn her head, / You'd know the folly of being comforted'), and the sincerity of the poem. He had attempted a setting of 'When You Are Old and Grey' as far back as April 1909, which he had come across in his trusty *Oxford Book of English Verse*, and he had always held Yeats in the highest esteem. Yeats's verse, unlike Harvey's unfortunate *Gloucestershire Friends*, lived up to Gurney's ideal that 'The greatest test of Art—the Arts of Music, Writing, Painting anyway, is to be able to see the eyes kindly and full of calm wisdom that would say these things behind the page.'[33]

'The Folly of Being Comforted' was written in a single sitting, after he had been up all night helping on the wards, and set by memory. When he returned to his copy of the poem, he found to his consternation that he had left out two lines, upsetting the balance of his first draft. Even so, with the adjustments complete, he felt the song had a 'sorrow of wasting beauty and such tragic passion', and that it was more substantial than anything he had written, with the exception of 'By a Bierside'.

On 30 October, Gurney gave a recital at the hospital, arranged by the Reverend Barnett. The officers to whom he was performing listened 'beautifully', and Barnett was driven to transports of 'pure ecstasy', in Gurney's own modest summary. He played Bach, Beethoven and Chopin, and on Barnett's insistence included some of his own work. He premiered 'The Folly of Being Comforted', and performed 'By a Bierside', the first time he had heard it sung in public. He was clearly making a good recovery, and if he was well enough to carry off a recital, he was probably not ill enough to remain in hospital. On Bonfire Night, the day after Wilfred Owen had left Craiglockhart, Gurney was finally in Edinburgh after an emotional leave-taking from Annie. Had he been discharged only hours before, he could have bumped into Owen browsing the same bookshops around Waverley Station. But they were never to meet.

Gurney caught a train to London to see Scott. It was the beginning of ten days of leave, the first time he had had any official break from the army since he enlisted. He had not seen Scott since 1915, but had written to her nearly every day, charting a diary-like progress from training to the trenches, and now to convalescence. He had created a relationship on paper that was built around his insecurities and anxieties, ambitions and practical requirements, and depended upon her willingness to listen.

His slightly ambiguous comment from Edinburgh, meant as a compliment, that 'if there were no M.M.S. it would be necessary to invent one' might have given her pause for thought.[34] He had written to Harvey recommending that he make Scott's acquaintance if he made it back to London because she might be of material use to him: 'she is a most kind and interesting woman, who may be able to help you—but that is of secondary consideration.'[35] It may have been a secondary consideration, but it was the nexus around which Gurney's relationship with her was being built. She had become necessary to him as a literary editor, sender of parcels, and provider of emotional reassurance. The 'loveable egotist' required an audience, and patient older women were the ideal recipients of his angst.

We will never know whether Scott and Gurney felt awkward when finally in each other's company after such a long correspondence, but one topic that he was certainly not anxious to discuss with her was that of his new lover. Did Gurney suspect that Scott would have welcomed more than an intellectually stimulating exchange of letters, and might reasonably have felt she had earned first refusal on his affection? Whatever the emotional attachment Gurney had to Harvey, it did not preclude his taking delight in telling him, and Howells, of his new love. Gurney even boasted of it to the writer Ethel Voynich, a mutual friend of Scott's and his (best known for her novel, *The Gadfly*). Gurney's acquaintance with this 'lady-novelist', as he rather patronisingly referred to her, was not particularly intimate, whereas Marion Scott had shared his daily life with eager affection for years.[36] And yet it was Scott who was not to be told. However impractical it was to keep the news of Annie from her, Gurney certainly felt that his relationship with Scott, warm and affectionate though it was, needed to be based on selective information. The effort of remaining silent on the subject of his unofficial engagement must have been enormous. Even without a secret to keep, the atmosphere at her home was hardly conducive to relaxation:

> Never, O never, shall I be invited or accept an invitation to stay with the Scotts again. Marion's all right, Stella's all right. Mr Scott is (I think) all right. But . . . Oh well, I enjoyed myself pretty well on the whole, and have only realised since coming away what an upheaval I must have caused occasionally.[37]

There was some comfort to be had from evenings in Scott's music room, a nirvana to which he had often returned in imagination from the trenches. He made the most of the real thing, spending hours playing her piano, with the welcome byproduct of keeping time for questions about events in Edinburgh to a minimum.[38] But it was hardly the joyful reunion Scott must have hoped for. Gurney does not elucidate in what ways he caused upheaval, but it is reasonable to assume that, wild as he was before his war service, he would not have returned any more reasonable and amenable a houseguest. After a few uncomfortable days, Gurney moved on to the altogether cosier and more modest Chapman family home at High Wycombe, where he had spent many happy days before the war. He anticipated putting his feet (in disreputable slippers) up on the Chapman family's mantelpiece and making himself thoroughly at home. Unfortunately, things did not turn out quite as he envisaged. The children at High Wycombe were 'trumps of the aciest', but the matriarchs of the households were another matter. He found Mrs Chapman decidedly frosty, as Marion Scott's mother had been.

At the Royal College he saw the composer Thomas Dunhill briefly, and could finally thank him in person for the part he had played in helping Scott to arrange for the publication of *Severn and Somme*. Dunhill was a kindly man, but Gurney thought his songs weak, and lacking in colour: 'Poor chap, I fancy he takes some time to heat up, and that his character has made him a musician rather than his gift.'[39] Gurney was dismayed to find him looking 'fagged and thin'. This was the first time he had had the chance to see what toll the war had taken on his civilian friends, and it was a shock.

He met Howells and Benjamin in London, and then saw Howells twice more when on a brief visit to Gloucester. For the first time, he and Howells met as something like equals—when Howells talked about his fiancée Dorothy Dawe, Gurney could enthuse about his new love. He could listen to Howells's anxieties about his health, and how he was struggling to write as much as he would like, secure in the knowledge that he had himself another gem of a song in 'The Folly of Being Comforted', and that *Severn and Somme* was due out any day. Even with the threat of a return to France looming ever larger, things were going well for him. From his new position of comparative security, Gurney felt that he could become closer to his childhood friend and rival than ever before.[40] Although he was apart from Annie, and still suffering from slight indigestion (which he put down to the effects of the gas), he was happier than he had ever been, reacquainting himself with London and Gloucester, and full of tales of the trenches.

Orders came for a two-month stint at a command depot in the wilds of Northumberland before his return to the front. He parted company from Howells, who marvelled, as all his friends had done on his brief visit, at Gurney's energy and vitality. His love for Annie had transformed him, and Howells clung to the hope that both the relationship and Gurney's equilibrium would last. If he and Harvey had their reservations, they had the kindness to keep them to themselves.

PART III

Civilian

CHAPTER EIGHT

'To His Love'

Gurney arrived at Seaton Delaval station on 15 November 1917, nearly three hundred miles from London. He stepped out of the train with a motley assortment of Gloucestershire soldiers, all in need of convalescence or retraining, and found that he had been posted to 'surroundings that mock all beautiful dreams',[1] or as another private rather less poetically assessed it on first sight, a 'godforsaken hole'.[2]

Seaton Delaval was a large training camp, very like the institution Gurney had wandered around in his melancholy days in Rouen: 'a sort of Con: Camp in Khaki'.[3] It was permanently occupied by the Gloucesters' 4th Reserve Battalion, which had been there since March 1915 to defend the coast against invasion.[4] While they were waiting for a sighting of a German, they trained up and sent out to France an ineluctable stream of Gloucestershire men.[5] It was a standard route for retraining wounded Gloucesters from the 1st and 2/5th Regiments, and Gurney knew that his posting to C Company of the 4th Reserves was likely to be only a delay, rather than a final destination. This was a stepping stone on his way to the front.

On arrival, he found the depot to be a tightly run and well-disciplined camp. Accommodation was in long wooden huts or other requisitioned buildings in the grounds of the ancient Delaval estate. The land had been gifted to the Delaval family in 1080 by William the Conqueror for their services at the Battle of Hastings. In the early eighteenth century, Sir John Vanbrugh had built an impressive house there, which stood rather incongruously against the landscape of pit villages. Delaval Hall had lost its grandeur in 1822 when it was reduced to a burnt-out shell after a fire, and had been only partly shored up in the 1900s.

Camping in miserable weather next to partially ruined buildings was a home from home for those who had already served abroad, but here there was less free time than in France. The army, anxious to avoid idle hands, filled the troops' days with parades and drills, alongside physical exercise and signals training. Private A. Thomas, who was stationed there, recalled that

Smartness exemplar was the rule predominant, and woe betide the man who had so much as a piece of mud on his boots and as for brasses on our equipment, why their brilliance rivalled the sun.[6]

The trainees were housed in a barn and were marched to work every day along a path that ran by the seashore. At least Gurney had a view of the sea, and could dream of W. H. Davies's poetry and his own seafaring ambitions. But even for Gurney, romanticising this landscape was a challenge, as it was dotted with large gun emplacements and forests of barbed wire. The countryside was carved up by trenches and concrete bunkers, ready for any invasion that might come from the beach. The wind was fierce, and the walk back to camp at night was in pitch darkness. In his bleakest moments, he felt he might as well have been back at Ypres.

On Sundays, the troops were paraded and marched to church behind the band, which played 'Rock of Ages' and other rousing hymn tunes. Gurney did not record whether he took up his post of baryton player amongst their ranks. He certainly did not have his own instrument, so he may have kept quiet about his brief career as a brass player. On Sunday afternoons there was a little time off for exploring the nearby village of Seaton, four miles from camp, which boasted one hundred modest houses, a village green, a little church constructed in tin, a hall for concerts, a cooperative store and ten shops. The one amusement regularly available was the dog races, where the local miners put their pets through their paces.

There was nothing for it; Gurney simply had to stick it out. There was always the faint hope that the war would end during that time, or perhaps, as rumour in the camp had it, there might be transfers to Ireland. Determined not to be sent back to France, he considered applying for a commission in order to waste yet more time in training, but all applications had been stopped. There was no other option than to make the best of life and to embrace his training, which was a refresher course to return him to his original signalling duties. He knew that if the war continued, and it looked set to carry on forever, he would stand little chance of avoiding it for long. His health was assessed as a bewilderingly optimistic A3, certainly well enough to be sent back out to Ypres; and by this stage in the war, the army had become adept at finding ways to send anyone out, fit or otherwise.[7]

> There are two ways of getting unfit men to France. One is, putting him on the G.O.C's [General Officer Commanding] inspection—when he will be rejected by that potentate; then putting him in as substitute at the last moment. The other, by keeping him off the inspection, and putting him in after. An admirable example of soldierly honour. Of course the General knows all about it.[8]

His days at Seaton Delaval were brightened by a significant landmark; *Severn and Somme* was published on 16 November, the day after he arrived at the camp. For a first book from an unknown writer, it attracted a respectable amount of critical attention. Gurney had never been reviewed as a writer before, seldom if ever even as a composer, and he was very pleased with the critics' responses, especially the reviews in the *Daily Telegraph* and the *Morning Post*. *The Times* was positive, although he was frustrated at the tone of the review, which laid unnecessary stress on his 'being a Gloucestershire poet'. The implied provincialism stung, but Gurney's belief in writing from and about his roots was deeply held. Only two weeks before, the highest praise he could offer the Georgian poet W. W. Gibson's verse was that 'Nowhere save from the West Country could that have been taken; it is so sweet, so mature.'[9]

Local reception for *Severn and Somme* varied; the *Bristol Times* was impressed, but the *Gloucester Journal* was unfavourable, comparing Gurney with Harvey, rather than assess his work on its own merits. He dismissed the review as 'rather savage and very stupid; considering it necessary to praise FWH in order to decry me.'[10] Despite the attention, sales of *Severn and Somme* were modest, but Gurney put that down to bad timing; 'everyone being so fed up with everything'. He felt that enthusiasm for anything to do with the war was waning as the conflict dragged on and on. The public had taken Rupert Brooke readily to their hearts in 1915, but by 1917, poems about the war were rather old hat, and Gurney sensed that people would prefer to be distracted from it than read about it.

Harvey received his copy in Germany and wrote to say that he liked 'To the Poet before Battle' and 'Homesickness' best, choices revealing more about Harvey's own conservative style and tastes than about Gurney's talent.[11] 'To the Poet before Battle' was one of the first poems Gurney wrote, and probably one of the most inauthentic, being something of a Brooke pastiche. Arthur Bliss took the trouble to write from the Base Division of the Grenadier Guards to express his admiration for the book: 'That much of it which was beautiful in the book pleased me'—a rather curiously circumspect choice of phrase.[12]

Gurney's own analysis of the volume was self-deprecating, but astute. Just as he had identified failings in Masefield's verse that he himself shared, so his analysis of his first efforts as a poet showed his awareness of the uneven nature of the collection.

> My own opinion of the book is, that it is very interesting, very true, very coloured; but its melody is not sustained enough, its workmanship rather slovenly, and its thought, though sincere, not very original and hardly ever striking. For all that, the root of the matter is there, and scraps of pure beauty often surprise one; there is also a strong dramatic sense. Where it will fail to attract is that there is none, or hardly any of the devotion of self-sacrifice, the splendid readiness for death that one finds in Grenfell, Brooke, Nichols, etc.[13]

It is a telling statement. If he ever entertained one, he had now most certainly relinquished any sense of a heroic death complex. He had quickly lost interest in writing eager, wide-eyed patriotic poems. He was too cynical, and too realistic. He felt that although he had made the decision to fight, he had so much more he could offer his country alive, rather than as a human sacrifice. But as time went on, and the patriotic fervour faded, it was the moments of beauty that were to endure.

His anxieties about the book's appeal, even in the shorter term, proved unfounded. To his equal surprise and delight, the first (albeit modest) imprint sold out, even before he had seen a copy. 'A friend of the Hunts inquired at the *Times* Book club to hear that it was out of print, and had been selling like hot cakes, together with Harvey's two Books and *A Shropshire Lad*.'[14] It gave him an inordinate amount of pleasure to be able to class his own work on a level with Housman's collection, which, aside from being verse he revered, had been a publishing phenomenon.

Shortly afterwards, Gurney's name appeared again in the *Sunday Times*. This time it was as a composer. On 9 December the tenor Gervase Elwes had sung 'Sleep' in a concert at the Aeolian Hall in London, alongside songs by Vaughan Williams and Frank Bridge. Attendance was out of the question, and Gurney could only read about it in the paper, but he was gratified to see his work mentioned. It seemed that Gurney's star was in the ascendant; his songs were being heard, his poetry selling out, and for now at least, he was not in France. Annie was still his, as far as he knew, although by 17 November he had heard nothing from her: 'But still I feel that all is well, and feel that our hearts are conscious one of the other; which brings a kind of serenity after the heat'.[15]

Whilst he had been on leave in Gloucestershire, he had written her a love poem, composed to the rhythm of his bicycle wheels as he rode to Minsterworth at dusk one night:[16]

> My heart makes songs on lonely roads
> To comfort me while you're away,
> And strives with lovely sounding words
> Its crowded tenderness to say.

His affair with Annie was not just a relationship, it was a revolution; he was a new and different man. From being an observer of life, watching others' loves from the shadowy periphery, he was for the first time in the heady midst of his own passionate affair. Despite the lack of free time, and the absence of his love, his pen was running away with him that December. He was intoxicated, not so much by Annie herself, but by the new life his passion for her had given him. By accepting his advances, she had rescued him from his solitary half-life, and saved him from 'a lonely path through crowded ways'.[17]

Gurney had a dangerous amount invested in this fledgling relationship, but oddly enough, Annie was not the only woman in his thoughts. In Annie he found the anchor he needed to help him create a solid and stable place for himself in the world.

Marion Scott supplied the equally necessary intellectual and practical support—an utterly dependable lifeline, confidante and, to some extent, literary critic. But Gurney also needed an uncritical audience who would not question him, or expose his vulnerability. The pretty, fun-loving Chapman girls fulfilled the role admirably. He craved love, and he was not averse to its coming from a number of sources simultaneously.

He had corresponded with the Chapman family in High Wycombe since he had left for training in 1915. His ill-fated proposal had been to Kitty, the eldest, but Gurney probably did not realise the extent to which her younger sister Winnie, who was now sixteen, had been harbouring an adolescent passion for him. She had at some point obtained a lock of his hair, which she referred to as 'My Dearest Ivor's Curl.'[18] Gurney was nine years older than her, and not above flirting, writing teasingly:

> When will the days of peace and plenty and beaucoup ping pong once again return? Alack, man knoweth not. Nor young women either, in spite of their growing up, putting their hair up, putting on frills, and fine raiment, and generally startling and upsetting their humble adorers—of whom
>
> I am
>
> (Very affectionately)
>
> one of the wormiest and most enthralled
>
> Ivor[19]

To have a soldier nearly a decade older than herself claiming to be in her 'thrall' would be hard to resist, although he wrote to her in much the same childish tone as that with which he addressed her little brother Arthur, despite the fact she was now nearly the same age as her sister Kitty had been when Gurney had considered marrying her.

A match with Winnie would hardly have been a meeting of minds, or equals, but the flirting continued. During his relationship with Annie, he spent time with Winnie whilst on leave, and was very attached to her, coquettishly berating her for reclaiming her portrait. He had carried it in his pack throughout his time in France. That winter he obtained two copies of Wilfrid Gibson's *Friends*, a book that was very precious to him, in order to send her one. The other copy was also intended as a very personal Christmas present: for Annie. Gurney was clearly thinking of the little collection as one that would move Annie, as he set the poem 'Roses' for her that year. It was rather a poignant collection to choose to celebrate his relationship: the tone is set by a series of poems of love for Gibson's friends, but these are elegies. Rupert Brooke and the composer William Denis Browne had both been killed during the Gallipoli campaign.

By the end of November, Gurney was finding that the excitement of love and flirtation was not quite enough to keep up his spirits against the damp and cold. He

FIG. 8.1: Gurney with Kitty Chapman and her mother, 'La Comtesse', as he referred to her. © The Anthony Boden Private Collection.

admitted to Scott to being more unhappy in the dismal Northumbrian climate than he had been in the trenches. It was not just the rain and grey skies that depressed him. He sensed a coldness in his letters from Annie and was suspicious at their infrequency. He became restless and anxious, and the feeling of being confined in the camp oppressed him. He even started to miss the front; at least when there was danger, one felt alive. 'It is good to go to one's limit, and good to see men facing hardships well and coolly facing vile Deaths.'[20] Trapped in the safety he had so ardently desired, he found himself exhausted, after regular nocturnal exercises, and too depressed to read all the books he had requested from his friends. Christmas was a miserable affair, even in comparison with the previous year's, which had been spent behind the trenches near Thiepval on the Somme. This year, the moments of time off on Christmas Day gave him the chance to collect together some of his latest poems, and, despite his lethargy, he managed to produce a 'Housman song', probably 'On Wenlock Edge'. The stormy winds that blew in off the North Sea were the perfect metaphor for his own pent-up frustration and would have given him ample material to build into this turbulent musical depiction of trees heaving, bent double in the wind.[21]

By January 1918, it looked as if he might be able to stay for another five months, all the time hoping that the war might end before he got back to it. It was a miser-

Fɪɢ. 8.2: Portrait of Gurney, Christmas
1917. © Gurney Trust.

able time, but he consoled himself with the knowledge that whilst he was in
Northumberland and not in France, he stood at least some chance of getting to
see Annie. Whilst his euphoria at the height of his relationship with her had enabled him to write, the possibility of losing Annie crippled him with anxiety. This
was his first (and only) serious romantic relationship, and he was a woefully inexperienced suitor. He had done everything he could think of to secure his 'Princess';[22]
he had showered her with poems and even gone to the extravagance of having a
Gloucestershire regiment badge dipped in gold for her to wear as a brooch. He had
confidently imagined her as his wife, even going so far as to invite Harvey to stay
with them after the war. But although Gurney considered himself engaged, there is
no record that she felt seriously committed to a future with him. She might have
been fascinated by Gurney's ardour and enthusiasm at first, but perhaps she was
beginning to find this demanding young soldier a little too intense.

Song of Urgency

Sing in me now you words,
That she may know
What love is quick in me,
O come not slow!

Nor cold to me, but run
Molten, fiercely hot
Before Time carelessly
Make me forgot,

Or dull of image in
My dear Love's mind.
You words of power, of flame,
Hasten, be kind![23]

The urgency of the title speaks more of insecurity than romance. Gurney knew he must do everything he could to secure his place in Drummond's affections. In an anxiously pattering alternation between six and four beats, he exhorts inspiration to help him write a love poem strong enough to ensure she keeps him in the forefront of her mind. These short, breathless little lines are hardly the utterance of a lover secure in the knowledge of his beloved's affections.

On 16 January 1918 he managed to obtain enough leave to spend the weekend in Edinburgh, hoping against hope that seeing her again would salvage the situation. The weekend was taken rather on the quiet, so as not to offend Gloucestershire friends and family, but he poured out his heart to Howells, knowing that he would understand intuitively that Scott in particular must not be told. His sense of relief was overwhelming when, after the weekend with Annie, he could report that everything was as it should be, after all:

> Herbert Howells, it is just perfectly and radiantly All Right. I have reached Port, and am safe. I only wish and wish you could see her and know her at once. You and Harvey.
>
> My goodness, but it was a hot pain leaving her. We had a glorious Saturday afternoon and evening together. A glorious but bitterly cold Sunday evening. A snowy but intimate Monday evening. For the first time in ages I felt Joy in me; a clear fountain of music and light. By God, I forgot I had a body—and you know what height of living that meant to me. Well, I'll say no more. [...]
>
> But to get her and settle down would make a solid rock foundation for me to build on—a home and tower of light.
>
> Like you, I see in her first of all a beautiful simplicity—her very first characteristic,—As you see in Dorothy. The kind of fundamental sweet first-thing one gets in Bach, not to be described, only treasured.[24]

He had hardly been able to write poetry for weeks, but now, in a letter that carefully avoids any mention of his personal life, he sent Scott one of the most moving and powerful poems he was ever to write. 'To His Love' reflects back on the losses of the past two years. It gestures towards the pastoral elegiac tradition of poetry, setting death against a natural backdrop: the landscape to which the dead man belonged in life. The poem conjures up the ghosts of Milton's 'Lycidas' and Shelley's 'Adonais' which attempt to compel nature to console the bereaved and make sense of the death. However, Gurney's is an elegy that refuses to console.[25] It investigates the loss, and ends by attempting to use nature to hide the gruesome corpse in lines that make a good case for one of the most powerful ending couplets in English. He had looked to Heine's lyric poems and to Housman for inspiration for the bitter twist of his endings, and was justly proud of the final lines of poems such as 'Memory Let All Slip':

> Blue sky and mellow distance softly blue;
> These only hold
> Lest I my pangéd grave must share with you.
> Else dead. Else cold.[26]

And of 'The Fire Kindled':

> Here we go sore of shoulder,
> Sore of foot, by quiet streams;
> But these are not my rivers. . . .
> And these are useless dreams.[27]

In 'To His Love', however, the stress on the unexpectedly dehumanised 'red, wet / Thing' of the final lines, and the impossibility of forgetting its all too vivid, tactile wetness is portrayed with such directness that it far outstrips anything he had previously written.

To His Love

> He's gone and all our plans
>   Are useless indeed.
> We'll walk no more on Cotswold
>   Where the sheep feed
>   Quietly and take no heed.
>
> His body that was so quick
>   Is not as you
> Knew it, on Severn river
>   Under the blue
>   Driving our small boat through.
>
> You would not know him now . . .
>   But still he died
> Nobly, so cover him over

> With violets of pride
> Purple from Severn side.
>
> Cover him, cover him soon!
>   And with thick-set
> Masses of memoried flowers—
>   Hide that red wet
>   Thing I must somehow forget.[28]

The consolations of other pastoral elegies (the loved one being reconciled with the stars, or reborn through nature in some way) are useless here. Gurney's violets are inadequate, and the urgency of the cry 'Cover him, cover him soon', renders the gesture of loading a bleeding corpse with flowers both painful and grotesque. A policy was established early in the war not to repatriate bodies, so the presence of this abject 'thing' imagined in the landscape of home is doubly misplaced.[29] This is certainly his most modern and startling poem so far. He has dispensed with his established formula of 'transference', which until this point had been his main method: moving between the square shapes of Gloucester Cathedral to French fields, from French villages back to Gloucester villages, and from the sounds of war to the sounds of music. 'To His Love' represents a violent collapsing of this strategy: its horror lies in the impossibility of escape from one landscape into another—they collide in the abomination of the bleeding body. But who did this bleeding 'thing' represent? And to whom is this enigmatic poem addressed?

'To His Love' was to become one of Gurney's most famous poems and one of the most important poems of the war, holding its own with the best of Isaac Rosenberg, Siegfried Sassoon and Wilfred Owen. Since its publication it has been assumed to be an elegy for Will Harvey, the mention of their jointly owned boat *The Dorothy* placing him firmly in the frame. It is certainly a bitter response to the loss of a Gloucestershire friend, and if it is indeed Harvey, it makes sense to assume that the poem was written during the brief period over the summer of 1916 in which Gurney believed him dead. However, the only date to which we can link the poem with any certainty is 20 January 1918.[30] By this time Harvey had been in prison for a year and a half, and Gurney was back in England, blissfully in love, and hardly in a state of mind to have written this despairing, tender piece retrospectively. Why he would choose such a moment to write an elegy for Harvey, in the full knowledge that Harvey was alive and well, is a mystery.

Still, the link to Will Harvey is only part of the story. The pronouns are deliberately ambiguous—who is the 'you' that the poem addresses? The confusion opens the door to interpretations of the poem as a homosexual address. But this most loved and most misunderstood of Gurney's poems is neither an elegy for F. W. Harvey nor a statement of love—it may have drawn on the memory of his temporary grief for Harvey during his brief disappearance, but it is in fact far more likely to be addressed principally to the wife of Harvey's younger brother Eric.

Eric was to realise the prophecy of the poem, as he was killed by machine gun fire on 30 September 1918, eight months after the poem was written. He had married in October 1915 before he took up his commission for a second time with the Gloucesters, and he was to return home to Gwen, his new wife, only once, to recuperate from shell shock in the autumn of 1917. He was sent back to France in April 1918 and killed, leaving his pregnant widow to bring up his child alone.

Although Will was his dearest friend, Gurney had known Eric for longer and had formed a close friendship with him. They had been choristers together and became reacquainted during the many weeks Gurney had spent with the Harveys in the holidays. Eric would have had ample opportunity to accompany Gurney and his elder brother on some of their sailing trips on *The Dorothy* during these visits. Eric had been a comrade of Gurney's in the 2/5th Gloucesters, whilst Will had been away fighting in different locations with the 1/5ths; and when Gurney had been in hospital in Edinburgh, he wrote to Matilda Harvey particularly asking to be remembered to Eric.[31] Gurney and Eric were bonded together by their shared body of experience, including the misery of the move from Laventie to the Somme, that 'bleak wilderness of death.'[32]

If the poem's 'love' did indeed refer to the dead man's female partner, rather than to the recipient of Gurney's own affection, both Will's and Eric's partners could be candidates. Will had met Anne Kane, a beautiful Irish nurse with auburn hair, in 1913. Gurney could legitimately be addressing the poem to Eric's Gwen or to Anne, but Gwen was a far more obvious candidate. It would seem odd and insensitive to address such an elegy to Anne, confidently awaiting her fiancé's return from prison, when her future sister-in-law was waiting for her already damaged husband to be declared fit enough to be sent back to the front.

The Harvey brothers were particularly in Gurney's thoughts as he was writing 'To His Love'. Only ten days before he posted the finished poem to Scott, he had been spending time with Roy, the eldest of the three. Roy had been up at Seaton Delaval on 9 January with his wife Netta, who was not, apparently, to Gurney's taste (Gurney wrote of their visit that he had 'enjoyed myself as to him, but not his wife').[33] He had seen Roy recently when he had been on leave and stayed at the Harveys' home The Redlands that November, and they had sat up talking until 4 am. Eric had been there, convalescing, and Gurney had found him 'as nice as ever.'[34] Now, against the dreary backdrop of Seaton Delaval, he talked with Roy of the happy memories of the prewar years. They talked of Will, but also of Eric, and of their anxieties for him.

So much evidence would point to the poem's association with the Harvey brothers. But the letter in which the poem appears is not in fact concerned with

FIG. 8.3: Will Harvey and two other prisoners at Bad Colberg prison camp.
Courtesy of Michael Frankish.

either Will or Eric but devoted to discussion of another death of a Cotswold man—
Edward Thomas. (In 'Cover him, cover him soon!' we might perhaps hear an echo of
Thomas's 'Scatter it, scatter it!' in 'The Trumpet': a poem Gurney knew well and later
set to music). Thomas was in his mind, and he had been continually rereading his
verse. 'The exquisite art of the books, the loving subtlety, the half-lights, the deep-
in sadness of his lovable mind—are very striking', he writes, in the same letter in
which he encloses 'To His Love'.[35] This description might lend itself to his poem,
which is testament to Gurney's own 'deep-in sadness', and subtlety born of love.

Whether 'To His Love' was written for Eric, Will, or even Edward Thomas, directed to a female or a male love, is perhaps beside the point. The ambiguity of its
subject speaks of Gurney's perpetual need to seek out new sources of affection and
kinship. His life was marked by a continual stream of attachments, both to people
and to places. Few of these remained constant, and the fluidity of the poem's subject
is a powerful representation of the fragility of his loves.

Only a few days after writing out 'To His Love', he wrote a particularly poignant letter to Will Harvey in Bad Colberg prison camp (near Coburg in Thuringia, in the centre of Germany), where he was being held in solitary confinement as a punishment for trying to escape. Full of reassurance and affection, the letter adopts not only the same tone but the same phrases as the poem. In 'To His Love', Gurney had imagined that they will 'walk no more on Cotswold / Where the sheep feed / Quietly and take no heed'. Now, he imagines them back in their shared landscape, and the act of writing to Harvey comforts and renews him:

> Friend of orchard and river; drawing life from memories of blue and silver seen together and great sights of sunset from the little hill. . . . Dear chap, there's so much to talk about. I'll put my hand on your shoulder, and we'll wander about the fields and roads to talk of the *Georgian Book, No. 3*.[36]

Their joint presence in the landscape is a consolation and a source of solace, albeit still a precarious dream. 'To His Love' finds that the shared experience of the landscape is a common bond, but one that can no longer be enjoyed, with the presence of a polluting corpse. The poem seems to act as a bleak counter to the fantasy reconciliation described in the letter. In life, Gurney was transformed by his love for Annie: 'You would hardly know me now', he wrote to Harvey. In the poem, the dehumanised body is equally unrecognisable: 'you would not know him now'. The two sentences chime unmistakeably. Even the abject 'red wet thing' finds an echo, as Gurney boasted of his transformation from the 'white-faced thin thing' he had been in hospital to rugged health.

There is something a little ominous about these echoes between poem and letter. An antielegy that refuses to console undermines the fragile optimism of Gurney's own love, which he expresses in almost the same phraseology. The possibilities of exploring the Gloucestershire landscape one day with Will Harvey were still a source of hope and comfort. There was no such hope for Edward Thomas, and Eric was soon to be separated from his 'love' and his homeland. There was also, of course, always the strong possibility that Gurney himself would never see Gloucestershire again, and would become a corpse that Annie, his own new love, had somehow to forget. The amalgamation of all these tragedies, actual and potential, resulted in a masterpiece that laments on behalf of a generation, their lovers and their memory; a lament that refuses to look the other way and ignore the brutality of their deaths. Proleptically, the poem feels for those left with the corpse of a memory, the abandoned 'thing' (whilst at the same time, the 'thing' could also perhaps represent a composition in the making—a metaphor for life). It is the empathy and feeling for the universal experience that makes the poem work so deeply: the pathos of something left unfinished.

'To His Love' was one of a number of poems written that spring, exploring an almost obsessive concern for lost love and the fragility of relationships. With the possibility of being sent back to the front becoming ever more likely, he now reviewed his own fate, from Annie's point of view. He had never before had the possibility of a lover who might mourn his death, and he did not limit himself to investigating the theme through poetry. On 4 January he set to music 'The Lawlands o' Holland', an anonymous Scottish ballad in which a woman mourns the loss of her love at sea and maintains she will never be consoled. Gurney set it to a dark, undulating accompaniment. In the new year he set Housman's 'The Land of Lost Content', to which he would return a year later, incorporating it into his baritone song cycle *The Western Playland*. Between Housman's nostalgia for the 'blue remembered hills' of a past landscape, and the folk song's mourning for a love lost abroad, it is easy to see how his preoccupations combined to create the mood from which the masterpiece 'To His Love' had been born.

Gurney set another Housman poem in March, which was also to be destined for *The Western Playland* cycle: 'The Cherry Tree', a retitling of 'Loveliest of Trees', which he dedicated to Emily Hunt. As ever, Gurney did not limit himself to adoring one woman at a time. Whilst it was for Emily's sister Margaret that he had entertained a passion, it was Annie who was preeminent in his thoughts now. In his imagination, her 'eyes and lips are so bright in me this dull grey typically-Northern imitation of a morning'.[37] He had confidently reassured Howells that everything was, in capital letters, 'All Right', but his preoccupation with loss spoke perhaps of other possibilities.

The dedication of 'The Cherry Tree' to Emily was probably a result of renewing their acquaintance; he had returned to Gloucester on 12 February 1918 for a brief period of leave, as his father, the solid, quiet presence in the background of his turbulent life, had been taken suddenly ill and undergone an operation. Although the Gurney family knew it was serious, no one realised that it was the start of the cancer that was to kill him a year later. He appeared to make a good recovery, although as soon as he had recovered, another operation would be required.

David Gurney was adored by his children, but he also posed something of an enigma. Gurney's sister Winifred remembered how 'as a family we were mostly more reserved following my father's characteristics. Though my father was also extremely emotional. This together made him very difficult to understand, the conflict within him being strong'.[38] David appeared to Ivor and his siblings to be a haven of serenity, but he was repressed and troubled. He was a peaceful man, who tried constantly to intervene between Florence and her children. He was enormously long-suffering (*too* long suffering, Winifred thought). In order to find any peace, he would spend his evenings in the Conservative Club. When it was early closing on a Thursday, he would watch the rugby rather than go home. When Florence's disapproval of his habits became too much, he simply changed his sporting allegiances to a more respectable game of bowls rather than return home any earlier.

FIG. 8.4: Gurney's father David, shortly before his death. Courtesy of Noel Hayward, from the photograph album belonging to Dorothy Gurney.

Thus his sanity remained intact, but his children saw little of him. He was a keen angler, finding that the peace and quiet of the local canal was an ideal antidote to home life. Sometimes he would think up an expedition for his children's benefit. He occasionally borrowed a horse and cart from a customer who was slow to pay his bills and so owed him favours, and took them out of town in it for a treat. They remembered this, like much of the time spent in their father's company, with great fondness. David was a strict parent, but he had a keen sense of humour, unlike his wife, and whenever Florence was away, the usually gloomy atmosphere at home seemed serene and full of laughter.[39]

The children instinctively knew that he loved them, and also that this made their mother jealous. Winifred recalled:

> Father was very fond of romping with us [...] He often took us on his knees and shook us till our teeth rattled or chattered, and the worst thing I endured was what we knew as 'a rough shave'. He rubbed our faces with his rough chin. Still, we loved all this, and, like Oliver Twist, asked for more until play became painful.[40]

Despite Gurney's continued anxiety about his father, the Gloucestershire trip had left him full of the joys of spring. For so many months he had longed for the landscape that nourished him—and countless times in poems and letters had imagined his walks through the familiar places. Now, for a blissful three days, he could live out his dreams.

One of the chief attractions of home was the companionship of John (Jack) Haines; Gloucestershire solicitor by day, poet by night, and thirteen years Gurney's senior. Harvey introduced them to each other before the war, and almost as soon as they met they fell into the habit of long talks about poetry and music. Haines remembered Gurney as an imposing figure, 'handsome, powerful, crammed with vitality, excessively opinionated and somewhat violent in his critical views.'[41] Gurney was deeply impressed by Haines, and by his social circle; a good friend of Lascelles Abercrombie, he was connected to a world that was to become increasingly important to Gurney as his confidence in his own poetry grew. Haines knew Edward Thomas well and kept a photograph of the poet in his 'book room', a haven to which Gurney's thoughts had often turned in the trenches.

Haines seemed to have an encyclopaedic knowledge of English literature and was never without a quotation for any discussion. Only after some years of being deeply impressed by Haines's erudition did Gurney begin to get a little cynical. He greatly enjoyed Haines's company and conversation, but as his own confidence grew, he rather wickedly wondered if it were entirely a coincidence that many of Haines's poetic quotes and his opinions on various works bore an uncanny resemblance to those expressed in Saintsbury's *English Literature Manual*, something akin to an early twentieth-century Bluffer's Guide to books!

He had walked with Haines through the hills of the Forest of Dean, and Haines long remembered the ecstatic mood of his companion.[42] But Gurney was not simply happy to be back in his home landscape with a friend; his walks were therapy as well as enjoyment. Alone, he pushed himself hard, as if he were trying to walk any illness out of himself. He undertook '17 miles on a pint of beer and bottle of ginger beer, because I felt seedy',[43] and visited eleven different villages or hills: Maisemore, Hartpury, Ashleworth, Minsterworth, Twigworth, and Cooper's Hill— names to which his poetry would frequently return as touchstones of health and wholesomeness.

By the 18th of February Gurney was on his way back up to Seaton Delaval, managing to arrange to spend the train journey with Howells, who was traveling to Yorkshire to convalesce from the illness caused by his heart condition. The 'seediness' that he felt was bound up with the realisation that he was a step closer to being sent back to France; away, perhaps for ever, from Annie and Gloucestershire. The prospect of leaving the West Country in all its beauty to return to Seaton Delaval and imminent overseas service quickly became too much. The easiest way to avoid France, he realised, was to ensure that he was never considered well enough to reach its shores. There was no doubt that he was fighting the beginnings of some kind of episode of manic depression, his moods swinging from 'seedy' to overwhelmingly exuberant, but his decision to make a declaration of illness, a sudden return of his 'gas' injury, was at the very least judiciously well timed.

He had not mentioned gas symptoms for months, boasting instead of health that was better than it had ever been (although there were hints that this was not the whole story, and that he was feeling 'seedy' in some way). However, on his return to Seaton Delaval, just as he was about to be subsumed into the army machine once more, he reported sick. By the 25th he had been admitted to No. 1 General Hospital in Newcastle to be examined for the effects of gas. Gurney could certainly have been forgiven for finding himself more inclined towards hospital and a lengthy recovery than a return to being shot at in France, but his symptoms were no fiction, or 'wangle', to use a favourite word of his. He reported suffering an irregular heartbeat, a condition that was to plague him all that spring. Already known by the name of 'soldier's heart', it had become disordered action of the heart (or DAH) by the 1880s, and doctors believed that it was a condition caused entirely by external factors. Whilst shell shock is now firmly associated with the First World War, 'soldier's heart' is hardly remembered, although it was actually the more common complaint, and had been a major fixture in army medicine since the Crimea.[44] At the time Gurney reported suffering from its symptoms, it was considered a delayed result of gas poisoning, the heart being disrupted by the lack of oxygen reaching it from the lungs. It was only during the 1920s that it was found to be a psychosomatic illness, although quite beyond the conscious control of the sufferer.

There was a great deal of medical panic associated with gas injuries, as Gurney had seen at Ypres. In Gurney's case as with many others', the overcautious treatment of the patient could result in their developing an unnecessary anxiety about their own health and about delayed reactions, that often led to the onset of DAH. Gurney, of course, was not a straightforward case. His development of the condition was hardly separable from the bundle of complaints and symptoms that made up his general malaise. Whether or not he was aware of it, his case fitted a well-recognised trajectory. It was expected that the symptoms of DAH would often recur as the convalescing soldier got nearer the front again. This was a standard pattern; the soldier would realise his time in safety was coming to an end, and his body would rebel. His heart would beat irregularly and deep anxiety would be unconsciously translated into the symptoms of physical illness.

By the time Gurney was admitted to Newcastle, he felt he could not 'work, walk or sleep properly', but the doctors examined him not for mental disturbance but for the effects of gas. As far as the medical authorities were concerned, Gurney was reporting with a physical, not a mental, condition. It made sense, then, to have him admitted to a purely medical institution, as this was not a case for an asylum. Once it was confirmed he was being admitted to the hospital ward, he had a moment of blind panic, realising he had only two books in his pocket. To save himself from the desperation of having nothing to read, he made a quick dash into the town, and in ten minutes had procured a copy of Boswell's *Life of Samuel Johnson*. He then settled down to reading it in bed, drawing some comfort from the fact that Johnson apparently also had moments of blank despair when not able to write. He began to daydream about what his own career as a great writer was to entail, if he could only finish his war service and regain his health. As usual, he quickly turned to the other patients around him to find sympathetic characters and discovered a patient who shared his passion for Beethoven. He had a joyful two hours of piano playing for the benefit of his new friend, but mostly 'the act (if passivity be an act) of living bores me to tears'. Newcastle itself was, in his view, hardly conducive to inspiration: 'one loses the sense of wonder in the Army; which can be remade or aroused by Music, Quiet and Natural Beauty, of which things Tyneside is almost destitute.'[45]

After a week or so he was transferred to the nearby village of Brancepeth, a more aesthetically appealing prospect than Tyneside. Here Gurney found himself rather incongruously in a great gothic castle, complete with turrets and crenulations. It had been given over to the army to use as a convalescent depot, an auxiliary to the overflowing Newcastle hospital. It was only a temporary stay, with the expectation that his recovery would lead back to Seaton Delaval, in preparation once more for France.

Brancepeth was, as Gurney declared, 'a fine place', with metal beds cluttering up the luxurious rooms. Apart from the medical paraphernalia, the rooms were largely unchanged, and still retained their prewar grandeur. There were huge stone fireplaces surrounded by tapestries, and walls hung with hunting trophies and formidable portraits of ancestors. It was undeniably romantic. Parts of the castle were derelict, and it had strong connections with Alfred Lord Tennyson.[46] The saloon, dining room and hallways were full of beds, but the library and billiard room were left for the soldiers' entertainment. The grounds were still beautiful, if less well kept than they had been in happier times. Soldiers lounged on the antique armchairs, smoking and thumbing through the library's leather-bound volumes, or strolled in the rose garden in the weak spring sunshine.

Gurney was both suitably impressed and disdainful: 'This is a real old castle—with a picture gallery and armour and bloodthirsty inquisitive looking weapons on the walls. I should hate to live in such a place of barns, but there must be worse Convalescent places. The poor old piano sounds like a boiler factory in full swing because of the stone walls.'[47] The combination of the acoustics and the fact that warmth was out of the question in the cavernous, draughty rooms made life at Brancepeth far less enjoyable than might be expected in so picturesque a setting, and Gurney was too miserable to be inclined to appreciate the luxury. Safe and at leisure, he berated himself for grumbling when in London Scott was in more danger than he was because of an increase in air raids. He was not physically incapacitated, and even managed a nine-mile round trip to see Durham cathedral: 'to gaze on that magnificent group of buildings from across the river on the first day of Spring! O but it was a revelation, a vision beyond price!'[48]

Gurney was given a bed in a sectioned-off part of the great armour gallery. One end of the gallery was being used for entertainments, and also housed the piano.

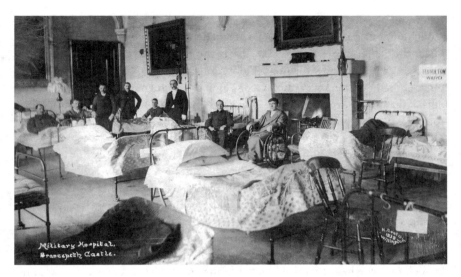

FIG. 8.5: Brancepeth Castle. By kind permission of
Lt. Col. Edward de Santis, US Army.

The gallery was normally an impressive sight, but during its requisition as a ward looked rather like a room of ghostly shrouds, as the suits of armour that lined the walls were covered up by white cloths. Games were set out for the patients at one end, but because of the drapery it was the only room in the house in which smoking was prohibited. Consequently, it was always deserted. As one of the nurses observed, 'not even all the "games in Christendom" set out there will tempt without my lady nicotine.'[49] Gurney might not have been in quite the frame of mind for games, but his admission was closely followed by two letters from Annie, so he began his residency in particularly good spirits. It was to prove an 'easy but dull time', but he was pining for his love and could not accomplish what he might have done had he been in a more settled frame of mind: 'my sense of shame, of reproach was considerably lessened by finding in a bookshop at Durham this sentence of Romain Rolland "Mozart could not compose save in the presence of the one he loved" and later that he could not play either. It is so with me. I take no delight in playing, walking, reading, existing by myself; and how many years is it I have been lonely now?'[50]

Work was not coming easily, although thoughts of Annie continued to provide creative inspiration throughout March and resulted in two love songs: 'Thou Didst Delight My Eyes' and 'Song of Silence', both dedicated to her. Gurney was not used to writing love songs based on his own emotions, and 'Song of Silence' is a curious failure. The theme of love had not inspired him to great poetic heights, and it may be that he chose not to sign his name as the poet with good reason.[51] Gurney could pour forth joy and emotion on the subject of his beloved when writing to his friends, but when it came to composing a love song, he retreated in bashfulness to a touching, but rather stilted, formal serenade, and the conservative harmonies reflect the rather conventional text. It has the formulaic air of a Victorian love song, with a Brahmsian sweeping melody, drawing perhaps on his early exposure to his godfather Cheesman's library of popular sentimental ditties. He admitted himself that he was writing more to prove to himself that he still could, rather than from true inspiration. 'My work is chiefly a Stunt at present, and done to preserve self-respect chiefly.'[52]

Brancepeth afforded him the time to experiment again with violin music. He had been writing for the violin since 1909, largely with the Hunts in mind, and he had attempted four violin sonatas between 1910 and 1914. Now, in March 1918, he returned to the form, more out of a sense of duty than inspiration, with an attempt at a violin sonata in A flat, but was forced to give up in disgust: 'Alas for the joyless fragment of a Violin Sonata! That annoys me to look at, merely.'[53]

At some point during that spring, his relationship with Annie came to an end. We do not know whether he received a letter from her, or whether the decision was mutual, which, considering the depth of both adoration and desperation on Gurney's part, is highly unlikely. Either way, the blow was profound, and combined with the ever-increasing likelihood of his return to the fighting, was enough to trigger a relapse in his psychosomatic heart condition. There had been an increasingly despairing tone to his letters, but on the 26th, having tried and failed to clear his head and improve his physical state with exercise, he wrote with startling vehemence to Scott:

My Dear Friend

Here's some news for you.

You know how a neurasthenic has to drive himself, though he feels nervy and his heart bumps in a disturbing but purely nervous fashion? Well, Ivor Gurney determined to drive himself. His heart certainly did not feel right, but that was imagination and he must go on—through Salisbury Plain, Laventie, Somme, Caulaincourt, Vermand, St Julien. He was tested once or twice, but doctors said nothing. They marked him A3 at Depot when he got there. It is true he never felt well, and had continual digestive and general nervous trouble, but that was presumably to be driven out. Which lands him at Depot getting weaker and fuzzier in the head without knowing why. On Friday he went to Durham 9 miles there and back, after which his pulse was waltzing irregularly like this as it is now

 ... That's my heart.

Surely a prostitute's job is cleanly compared to doctors who allow this and mark 'Debility' on a case sheet so that a man shall not know? Shall leave the hospital a little recovered and go on till he drops again? That's what they have done for me. By God, I'll do nothing more strenuous than clerical work for months, whatever they try to do with me, and *never* march again.[54]

Two days later, on 28 March, Gurney appeared to have deteriorated profoundly, and Scott received a deeply troubling letter:

And yesterday I felt and talked to (I am serious) the spirit of Beethoven.

No, there is no exclamation mark behind that, because such a statement is past ordinary ways of expressing surprise. But you know how sceptical I was of any such thing before.

It means I have reached higher than ever before—in spite of the dirt and coarseness and selfishness of so much of me. Something happened the day before which considerably lessened this and lightened my gloom. What it was I shall not tell you, but it was the strangest and most terrible spiritual adventure. The next day while playing the slow movement of the D major

I felt the presence of a wise friendly spirit; it was Old Ludwig van all right. When I had finished he said 'Yes, but there's a better thing than that['] and turned me to the 1st movement of the latest Ab Sonata—a beauty (I did not know it before). There was a lot more; Bach was there but does not care for me. Schumann also, but my love for him is not so great. Beethoven said among other things he was fond of me, and that in nature I was like himself as a young man. That I should probably not write anything really big and good; for I had started late and had much to do with myself spiritually, with much to learn. Still he said that he himself was not much more developed at my age (spiritually) and at the end—when I had shown my willingness to be resigned to God's will and to try first of all to do my best, he allowed me (somehow) to hope more, much more. It depends on the degree of spiritual height I can attain—so I was somehow let to gather. There! What would the doctors say to *that*? A Ticket certainly, for insanity. No, it is the beginning of a new life, a new vision.

. . . Don't think I am cracked. No you won't. I am a pretty level creature on the whole. My heart's bumping like anything. There's some indigestion— nothing else.[55]

His overwrought state is palpably clear—he could hardly let the letter go—adding addenda in a distracted manner, and then reading and rereading what he had written with an air of hysteria as he commented on its ludicrousness:

What a letter! I can't help laughing.
What a letter to deliver through the Post.

His repeated petitions to Scott not to find him mad clearly betray his own anxiety about his 'revelations': if he did not believe himself to be mad, he was at least aware that he would appear so, and that what he was experiencing had all the hallmarks of insanity. His hallucination speaks of a broader theme. Gurney often tried to create an order of affection among the Greats—which mirrored what he struggled to do in life with his various kinship groups. But this time he had crossed the boundaries between poetic imagination and reality. What he was describing were, over and above the symptoms of his anxiety and erratic heartbeat, the beginnings of a condition that falls broadly into the category of schizoaffective disorder.[56] It was to envelop him gradually over the next nineteen years. This was the first mention of an external voice or presence that he had experienced, although he would later claim that he had heard voices since his school days. By May he could describe it to Howells as a 'nervous breakdown from working too much', but even as he wrote, he must have known that the handful of songs and verses he had written at Brancepeth were not enough to lead to such a dramatic collapse. Could this have been the moment of his break with Annie? Howells had asked after Annie in April, a few weeks after the alarming correspondence with Scott. Gurney had replied that she was 'flourishing still in the North Countree'.[57] It would have been an odd little comment had they parted already (unless he was being bitterly ironic). But he may not have wanted to admit to Howells (or indeed himself) that his dream of domestic happiness was over. Howells was not a correspondent to whom Gurney wrote with absolute and unguarded honesty, and, it is possible he could not yet admit to him that the relationship had fallen apart, and that his mental health had been too precarious to survive the blow. The thought of Howells's and Dorothy's sympathy might have been too much to bear.

Whatever had triggered his collapse, he was in too serious a state for a convalescent depot, and the authorities at Brancepeth returned him to Newcastle General Hospital at the end of April. After a few days there, his mental state improved, at least to all appearances, enough for them to send him on to Seaton Delaval again. It was an overoptimistic move, as it quickly became clear that he was in no fit state to continue training. On 8 May the medical officer at the camp sent him to Lord Derby's War Hospital in Warrington. The implications were clear—Lord Derby's was a mental institution. This time, no one bothered to examine him for gas effects, as they had in Newcastle. He was a mental patient, and his admission was the beginning of a stigma that would never leave him.

CHAPTER NINE

'Rather Dead Than Mad'

Lord Derby's War Hospital, Warrington was a vast institution. It had been an asylum in peacetime and was recommissioned by the army as a mental hospital for the military when the scale of the mental casualties had started to become apparent. Gurney's sister Winifred remembered it as a 'bleak and depressing place'. It made her shudder even to think of it, and she erroneously but tellingly misremembered it as being an old prison.[1] Seemingly endless corridors painted in an unattractive brown and white echoed to the sound of footsteps on linoleum, the clanking of metal doors and jangling of keys in locks. There were rumours on the wards of secret rooms; padded cells, sound-proofed and covered in horse-hair matting. They contained soldiers tied into straitjackets, buried alive somewhere in isolation in the bowels of the huge building.

Like most other asylums at the time, it recognised that the mentally ill needed more treatment than could be administered by a doctor walking through the wards followed by his entourage once a day, but with an intake of around twenty-five hundred new patients every year, it rarely had the patient-staff ratio to attempt anything more. The only treatment they could offer Gurney at this point was to insist that he rested, and to encourage him to lie out on the verandas, in the hope that the fresh air might have a wholesome effect. This was a period in psychiatry when the distinction between clinical and mental illness was blurred. In lieu of any effective drugs, leading doctors worked on the assumption that if the body could be made as healthy as possible, then the health of the mind would follow. Thus, much of the treatment of the mentally ill followed lines similar to the treatment of an illness such as tuberculosis, and wards were run like sanatoriums.

From the first days of the war, Warrington had received wave upon wave of mentally ill servicemen, including those who never even reached the front. Many of them, particularly as the war ground on, were conscripted without the mental capacity to be anything but a liability in the front line and could not survive even the training without breaking down. Initially, many of these cases were treated at Warrington, but then moved elsewhere to make room for the floods of mental cases returning from abroad.[2]

FIG. 9.1: Lord Derby's War Hospital, Warrington. © countyasylums.co.uk.

The medical staff assessed Gurney and labelled him as suffering from dementia praecox. This diagnosis was commonly given at the time for symptoms that might come under the terms schizophrenia, bipolar or schizoaffective disorder. It was a common diagnosis for patients at Warrington, and a clear indication that something very serious was amiss. He was certainly not faking his illness. Had he only been suffering from disordered action of the heart, then rest and the reassurance of home service might have been enough. Dementia praecox was a different matter altogether. Very few of Warrington's patients with this diagnosis were discharged. Of the 127 sufferers admitted in 1917, only 35 were released to their families or judged fit for discharge within the year. It was not a heartening statistic.

In his 1978 biography of Gurney, Michael Hurd speculates that there might have been some kind of incident at Warrington in which Gurney was accused of malingering. There is no real evidence to support this, and whatever bullying he might have received from the poorly trained asylum attendants, the doctors at Warrington would have recognised the severity of his illness. It was highly unlikely that a malingerer would have got this far; the previous year their statistics recorded only 1 percent of their admissions of neurasthenics or shell-shock cases being without any mental symptoms.

Gurney lay, day after day, tucked into his narrow iron bed in a long line of men in varying states of distress, with little to distract him from dwelling morbidly on his situation. He lay, watching the nurses on their daily rounds, medicating patients, sedating others, occasionally calling for attendants to subdue anyone who had suddenly become violent. Doors clanged, footsteps echoed on the tiled floor, men moaned, and cigarette smoke hung in clouds around the ceiling of the ward. He longed for fresh air, exercise, and above all, Annie.

Here we must stare through glass
　　To see the sun—
Stare at flat ceilings white
　　Till day is done:
While you, sunshine, starshine,
　　May out and run.

Blow in and bring us all
　　Dear home-delight—
Green face of the Spring earth,
　　Blue of deep night.
Blot each of our faces
　　From the others' sight.[3]

Love may not previously have elicited the most profound poetry from him, but despair found a powerful directness of expression. 'In a Ward' succinctly captures the blankness of depression and enforced immobility, in an environment bled of colour. The patients' gaze is devoid of purpose and contrasted in the final stanza with the lusciousness of the spring earth, whose face has all the colour the patients' lack.

Gurney had mastered the art of the turn, the final couplet that throws the hardest punch. It is this very fresh, spring-like face that must occlude the patients from each other. The very act of witnessing each other's misery acts as a mirror, and the reflection is unbearable. The poem stands on the shoulders of 'To His Love', written six months previously, with its highly coloured invocation of nature, and a shocking attempt in the final lines to use the natural world to hide the unbearable. Gurney the poet was emerging as a strong, serious voice with the technical control to examine the abject and the painful with precision and clarity.

He might well have found the sight of the other patients distressing, but he could also pity them, and find some amongst their number with whom he could strike up friendships: 'Some very nice people were among that motley crowd and several I shall be sorry not to meet again. There was an old coster (with his "attempt-mark" still on his neck) a most sweet and plucky nature; who had continual longing for his folk and donkey cart. He has full expectation of my joining him in business after the War—with evenings spent fruitfully at the Picture Palace.'[4]

During the day he could fantasise about cinemas and socialising, but as the shadows lengthened, the silence after the ever-early lights out was punctuated by moans and cries. Gurney found himself tormented to distraction by the voices in his head. The area of the brain in which thought is processed is the same area in which auditory hallucinations are experienced. These voices were as real as those of the doctors and patients around him, and they were utterly terrifying. He felt as if he were in hell. They shouted: commanding, nagging, disapproving. They instructed him to kill himself, and he did not need much persuasion.[5] Death was surely preferable to a half-life as a tortured mental case. This was Gurney's first real taste of serious mental illness, and the terrifying loss of liberty that accompanied it in an asylum. By mid-June, he had decided that he could no longer continue. The misery of his situation was more than enough to render him suicidal, without needing an external event to compound his unhappiness. He knew his dreams of a life with Annie were now unrealisable, and he had lost the consolation he could previously have found in his army comrades' humour and support. To compound it all, Gurney could no longer even cling to his belief that the army might effect a cure for his 'neurasthenia'. Being accused of malingering was trivial compared with the very real possibility of insanity. Confined to the war, he had no other point of reference than his fellow patients, and what he saw was terrifying. In their distress he saw an image of what he himself was fast becoming.

By the 19th he had made up his mind. He wrote brief, matter-of-fact notes to Scott, to Parry and to his family.

> Dear Sir Hubert, I am committing suicide partly because I am afraid of madness and punishment, and partly because my friends would rather know me dead than mad.[6]

When he had ensured the notes would be sent, Gurney left the ward on the pretext of taking some exercise in the grounds of the hospital. When he was sure he was not observed, he slipped through the gates and walked quickly to the nearby river. He had every intention of jumping in. He had a great affinity with water; the River Severn was one of his abiding loves, and he had been happiest on board *The Dorothy*. It was natural now that he should choose a river as his means of escape. He imagined the sense of release, the

> mercy of Death—to feel close over
> The head, water; to know peace near, and the prover
> Of Courage

He imagined what it would feel like, the numbing of his senses, and hoped the afterlife was better than the misery he was suffering.

> Water, cool closing water—Death's weapon, water;
> Mercy of Death; End of hearing, touching, sight;
> Trusting in God for surer, well-deserved delight.
> New day; or calm night.
> Or Nothing, End of all; a close of consciousness
> On Ending quite.[7]

His head pounded. The cacophony of voices rose to a screaming pitch. He was desperate to make them stop, for the water to close over him and silence them. He stood, poised on the bank. But, somehow, looking into the dark, cold water, he could not make himself do it. He had routinely risked his life in France, but to take one's own life back in Britain seemed too difficult, and his courage left him. Instead of a merciful release, he had yet another failure to add to his list. He would live and relive this moment in years to come.

As soon as his absence had been noticed, attendants were sent out to look for him. They found him wandering pathetically by the side of the river in a daze, lost and hopeless. He was beyond any ability to hide himself or to protest. Barely aware of what was happening to him, he was escorted back to the hospital, and placed on suicide watch, to ensure that no second chance for suicide presented itself.

On the morning of 21 June, Scott received her note, and the one for Parry that Gurney had intended her to pass on. She immediately called both the local police and the hospital, but all the staff could tell her was that the matter was 'in hand', and that they would be 'writing further.'

Back in his room again, heavily sedated, and alone once more with the voices in his head, he realised that his friends would indeed now know him labelled as a madman. This was a hideous prospect. If death was not an option, then being sent somewhere that might be able to cure him was his only hope. He petitioned his medical officer for a transfer to a civilian asylum, hoping that this might, after all, be only a temporary illness.

Haines came to see him and found that Warrington was 'the most detestable place I have ever spent 6 hours in, without exception, and the place could drive me mad, despite my lack of genius, in a very few weeks.'[8] But Haines's very presence was a temporary comfort at least. The 'breath of Gloucestershire air' he brought with him spurred Gurney's return to the poetry of Edward Thomas, who had always been one of his chief loves. Gurney responded to Thomas's acute, almost existential sense of alienation, and intense appreciation of beauty. He recognised his own 'sickness of mind [. . .]—the impossibility of serenity for any but the shortest space' in Thomas, and might have been comforted to know that Thomas had also contemplated suicide and failed to take his own life.[9] Both Gurney and Thomas were plagued with the idea of cowardice, Gurney at 'funking' his suicide attempt and Thomas by the idea that he might be too terrified to complete the task. Gurney's decision to live was not entirely the result of the lack of courage to drown himself. His attempt had been an impetuous reaction to the tormenting voices, a moment of despair, but on calmer reflection he felt it was too early to give up hope of a cure. He had much still to achieve, and his ambitions, as well as his friendships, kept him alive.

As Gurney slowly reconciled himself to living, he turned to music, and in a rare burst of creative energy he wrote what was to be his first of nineteen Edward Thomas settings, 'The Penny Whistle'.[10] He also set the traditional ballad 'The Bonny Earl of Murray' and continued to write a steady stream of poetry, drawing on his experiences in France, on his childhood and Gloucestershire. Many of these poems, such as 'The Stone-Breaker', 'Down Commercial Road' and 'On Rest', came to be the backbone of his second poetry collection, *War's Embers*. He had assimilated something of Walt Whitman's energy and voice, after dabbling with his influence in *Severn and Somme*. 'On Rest' revels in the breathless heaping up of images that Whitman so often employs. There is no space here for the four-square, as Gurney began to experiment with a more conversational, freer line, structured by a declarative, repetitive rhetoric. Like Whitman, he is always at pains to be very specific about the details he holds up for inspection in his lists of impressions. (Gurney will not mention his excitement at drinking from a real cup without carefully qualifying it as being 'borrowed'.) Neither poet has traditional hierarchies; they do not prioritise but simply embrace. Here everything is valuable: birdsong, straw, bacon and eggs, and the cumulative effect recreates the exuberance of the moment. 'On Rest' begins:

> It's a King's life, a life for a King!
> To lie safe sheltered in some old hay-loft
> Night long, on golden straw, and warm and soft,
> Unroused; to hear through dreams dawn's thrushes sing
> 'Revally'—drowse again; then wake to find
> The bright sun through the broken tiles thick-streaming.
> 'Revally' real: and there's an end to dreaming.
> 'Up, Boys, and Out!' Then O what green, what still
> Peace in the orchard, deep and sweet and kind,
> Shattered abruptly—splashing water, shout
> On shout of sport, and cookhouse vessels banging,
> Dixie against dixie musically clanging.—
> The farmer's wife, searching for eggs, 'midst all
> Dear farmhouse cries. A stroll: and then 'Breakfast's up.'
> Porridge and bacon! Tea out of a real cup
> (Borrowed). First day on Rest, a Festival
> Of mirth, laughter in safety, a still air.[11]

This 'Festival of mirth', so vividly conjured into being from the past, is all the more poignant for its contrast with his joyless present. He showed it to Margaret Hunt, who had made the long journey to visit him, having heard about his suicide attempt. Her appreciation of his verse bolstered him considerably, as, keen to offer him what comfort she could, she made such favourable comments on his writings that 'the author might blush indeed at such praises'.[12] The visitors continued to come. Scott had visited immediately, and left Gurney with flowers. She gave instructions to the staff to take particular care of him. As a result, Gurney received a special visit from the matron, who had 'many ribbons on her breast, and a very pleasant smile and manner.'[13] Such a motherly figure was a comfort at a time when he felt so utterly lost. But as the days wound on, the question as to what was to be done with him became increasingly urgent. He was too far away to visit repeatedly, and too unstable to be released, but his friends were unanimous in condemning Warrington as a bleak and depressing institution. This might in some way have helped him survive his time there—they confirmed his sense that it was unbearable and offered him the hope of a transfer to other, more serene locations. Scott toyed with moving him to a smaller private hospital in Whitchurch, Gloucestershire (Haines thought the scenery would be to Gurney's liking there). Haines was against the idea of a mental institution, but sending Gurney back to his family was impossible: 'the father is too delicate and the mother too nervy.'[14]

Parry had been deeply distressed to receive his copy of the suicide note and had also been making enquiries on Gurney's behalf. He discussed Gurney's situation with Muir Mackenzie, the honorary secretary of the Royal College, who suggested a home for wounded soldiers run by Philip Napier Miles, a relation of his and an amateur composer. King's Weston House perched majestically on the banks of the River Severn near Bristol. It could have been just the environment Gurney needed to regain his stability, but it was not to be. On enquiry, Parry was informed that King's Weston did not cater for 'mental cases', and however generously Gurney's symptoms were presented, it would have quickly become apparent that a man plagued by voices exhorting him to suicide was not the right patient for a quiet convalescent home. Napier Miles suggested St Albans, which, he said, was better suited to mental cases. Oddly enough, his wife wrote only three days later, urging Gurney not to use up his chance of a transfer on the wrong institution. A serviceman in hospital was entitled to up to two transfers, and the move to Napsbury instead of King's Weston counted as his second (and therefore final) move. Despite the Napier Mileses' official reluctance to take him, she claimed they could offer him 'all sorts of things we know he could not get in a real hospital, and we should be so proud and glad to do it.' A private house, run by a musician and sympathetic to Gurney's personal case, could not, in theory at least, have been bettered, but it did not happen.

It was decided finally that Gurney should be transferred to the unit for mentally ill ex-servicemen at Napsbury War Hospital, St Albans, and he was moved to Napsbury by train on 24 July 1918.[15] This was a common transfer for patients who had found themselves returned from overseas and who were first held, inconveniently, in Warrington, with relatives many hours away who were unable to visit them. St Albans was closer to London, if still a distance from Gloucestershire. His friends were not convinced by this short-term solution; the crisis in June had demonstrated how critical it was that he received the most appropriate and compassionate care. To make the best of a bad job, Parry suggested that Gurney might perhaps stay at

FIG. 9.2: Napsbury War Hospital, near St Albans. © countyasylums.co.uk.

Napsbury until his mental crisis had subsided, and then be transferred to the more congenial King's Weston for his convalescence. When the case was reopened in October, however, it was too late.[16] By that time, he had been officially discharged from the army, and therefore was no longer eligible.

The move to Napsbury was not the disaster his friends dreaded. In fact, he found his stay at the hospital to be a great improvement on the abject misery of his time in Warrington. Here he was treated less like a straightforward mental case and more like a soldier in a temporary crisis. Such framing of his illness was crucial. If the institution communicated to him that it did not believe in recovery, then it was impossible for him to hope for it. Back in Newcastle, he had been mortified at being labelled a case of 'debility', and it rankled that he had been admitted as a 'mental' patient to Warrington's huge, bleak asylum. When the voices were at their most intense, he was so terrified that he had asked to be sent to an asylum in the hope that there would be psychiatric treatment to alleviate his suffering, but when in a less desperate mood, he knew he was not yet ready to accept the identity of madman.

Napsbury War Hospital had been the County of Middlesex Lunatic Asylum before the war. In 1915, 350 beds were requisitioned by the military for a mental hospital for privates, with the progressive thinking that by treating them as temporarily distressed, the patients would be allowed to recover without stigma, and lessen the chances that they would be certified and committed officially to asylums.[17] The mentally ill soldiers were kept separate from the civilian lunatics to avoid the shocking sights that were a daily part of asylum life, and to which Gurney had been so abruptly introduced at Warrington.

The other 349 patients with whom Gurney found himself consorting were a motley mixture of broken men, in various manners and degrees. Many who were labelled mentally defective were in reality wrecks of men, crushed by their own anxiety and constant exposure to horrors. Most, to a greater or lesser degree, were depressed and inarticulate. Many, like Gurney, were suicidal; some were convinced that they were to be court martialled and shot; others marched incessantly as though trying to make up for their inadequacies as a soldier; whilst others chose to hide beneath their beds.[18]

Gurney shared with many of the other patients both a sense of external persecution and a deep-seated belief in his own failure—as a soldier and as a musician. The very nature of his hallucinated promises from Beethoven spoke of his dilemma as to his own inadequacy—was it too late now to achieve greatness? Could he be allowed to hope? What, he asked himself through the fog of his delusions, was he worth? The impossible expectations placed upon ordinary and emotionally ill-equipped men in wartime resulted in a destruction of self-worth from which it was hard to recover. Gurney was hardly well suited to his military identity. As a child he had shared with his siblings a sense that he was never good enough, and he had struggled to win the love of his mother. As an adult he had few mental resources to draw upon to hold together his shattered confidence. It was no coincidence that the first really serious manifestation of voices, delusions and the symptoms that we might now call schizoaffective disorder began around the time of Annie Drummond's rejection of him. His worst and deepest anxieties and fears had been realised—he was indeed a failure, and a reject; she had confirmed it.

Despite his own inner misery, summer at Napsbury War Hospital was not altogether a bleak affair. Annie Drummond was many hours away in the north, but St Albans was near enough to Gloucester to feel that he had some connection to home through occasional visits from his friends. When the weather permitted, he was allowed to work on the farm in the grounds, hoeing and digging up potatoes. After the frustrations of being enclosed on the ward in Warrington, he could now watch the sky to his heart's content, delight in the poplars 'tossing their arms and heads violently to and fro in the wind', see flowers and hear birdsong.[19] The asylum doctors were evidently not categorising him as a suicide risk for now, at least. A handful of physically fit and comparatively stable asylum patients had been retained to run the farm and workshops when the other civilian patients had been scattered around the country to make room for the soldiers. Gurney worked alongside them, reaping dock leaves and thistles and hoeing mangels. This attempt to replicate normal rural employment proved therapeutic, and his self-respect began to return by degrees. The exhilaration of hard work in the fresh air found its way into a number of poems such as 'Mangel-Hoeing' and 'The Poplar'. Towards the end of August, as he worked with his hoe, a flight of starlings overhead put him in mind of the frequent flyovers of war planes heading for the front. His comrades were still fighting, and he imagined the gusts of autumn winds that blew across his mangel field reaching them also, perhaps in a far less congenial setting. The train of thought sparked by the conflation of starlings and planes resulted in 'Migrants', which he thought 'one of my best things—to the author's mind, at any rate.'[20] He captures, with the smallest and surest brush-strokes, all the colour, beauty and latent menace of Edward Thomas's poetry, and Gurney was right when he believed this to be some of his best work. Even if he still considered music to be his 'chief game', he was now writing verse that was more than worthy to hold its own alongside the poets he idolised.

> No colour yet appears
> Of trees still summer fine
> The hill has brown sheaves yet,
> Bare earth is hard and set;
> But Autumn sends a sign
> In this as in other years.
>
> For birds that flew alone
> And scattered sought their food
> Gather in whirring bands;—
> Starlings, about the lands
> Spring cherished, summer made good,
> Dark bird-clouds soon to be gone.
>
> But above that windy sound
> A deeper note of fear
> All daylight without cease
> Troubles the country peace;
> War birds, high in the air,
> Airplanes shadow the ground.
>
> Seawards to Africa
> Starlings with joy shall turn,
> War birds to skies of strife,
> Where Death is ever at Life;
> High in mid-air may burn
> Great things that trouble day.
>
> Their time is perilous
> Governed by Fate obscure;
> But when our April comes
> About the thatch-eaved homes,—
> Cleaving sweet air, the sure
> Starlings shall come to us.

Gurney layers his meditation on the starlings gathering in 'dark bird-clouds' (a beautifully condensed, compound image worthy of John Clare) with the war planes passing overhead. He conjures them both through shadow and sound: one a dark cloud, the other shadowing the ground. The whirring of the birds' 'windy sound' has a deeper note of fear above it, in a vertiginous blend of depth, height and pitch. It is unclear whether they are war birds or actual birds being considered in the final stanzas, but it emerges, as the starlings cleave the 'sweet air', that it is the wholesome birds who return. The terrifying prospect of those who may burn in midair is left only as a hint of the latent darkness and violence of both war and mental illness that surrounds Gurney, the ominously nebulous 'great things that trouble day'.

Much to Gurney's delight, the doctors took the risk of allowing him out alone, and he was able to send Scott a postcard of the magnificent abbey at the centre of St Albans. He had thrown himself down with a sheaf of manuscript paper on the grass outside, to begin work on a scherzo for violin and piano.[21] He found his sketch 'had too much of the old-fashioned Beethovenish smack about it to please me.'[22] Nevertheless, he was not wholly displeased with his efforts, and the fact that he was attempting it at all showed that he felt at peace enough not only to write but to attempt something on a larger scale than his war songs. No city could ever eclipse Gloucester in Gurney's affections, but he was enjoying his temporary status as a resident of St Albans: 'St Albans I like extremely—for its position on a hill and its own clean delightful self. The abbey is fine especially the tower, inside and out—not as good as Tewkesbury, but very good.'[23] High praise indeed.

To mark Gurney's birthday on 28 August, Howells sent him a score of the piano quartet he had composed that year. Gurney fell upon it and found it to be 'full of clouds and moving airs'.[24] His own head was full of his violin sonata in D major.[25] Having made various drafts of the scherzo, abandoning some sketches to start again with completely new material, he continued to work on the sonata during September and had almost finished it by midautumn of 1918, with the luxury of the use of a piano for an hour every evening. He completed it during the following autumn, his first writing for anything but voice since 1914. Howells found it to be a first-rate work and was extremely impressed. Gurney dedicated the sonata to Harvey and was desperate for him to hear it. He described it to him: 'the first movement is the cathedral and Gloucester, the second—Maisemore. Third: Cranham, Fourth: Crickley; and you may find (as I hope) pictures in it.'[26]

In September, at around the anniversary of his first encounter with Annie, Gurney sent her a copy of Poems of Today, inscribed rather stiffly 'To Nurse Drummond, with thanks for joy and best wishes for all things to come, September 1918, Ivor Gurney, from St Albans.' There is no record of whether she ever initiated any further contact with him, although he tried repeatedly to keep in touch with her through the 1920s. He could not have known that she had moved to Massachusetts with her husband, another patient of hers, admitted to Bangour in 1919 when he was being treated for a concussed eardrum. They were to marry just weeks before Gurney was to be certified insane in September 1922, and she was hardly likely to maintain a correspondence with a deranged ex-boyfriend whilst preparing for her own wedding. However, Gurney must have meant something to her: in a battered old leather suitcase she kept the poetry book he had sent her, along with a score of Gurney's set of Housman songs *The Western Playland*, which he was to dedicate to her years after they had parted.[27]

When the other women in Gurney's life found out about his affair with Annie, and the distress it had caused him, they were quick to see her actions as the cause of his breakdown. Ethel Voynich denounced her as a 'heartless hussy', and Scott later described her as 'the lively VAD who played fast and loose with Ivor til she drove him to desperation'. It was easy (and perhaps rather romantic) to attribute his breakdown to his disappointment in love, and Scott, of all people, was unlikely to be charitable towards a woman who had been the object of Gurney's adoration and rejected him.[28]

The combination of fresh air, hard work and the purpose and focus his violin sonata was affording him had improved his mental condition to such a degree that he was considered fit for discharge in early October 1918. The relief, both for him and for his friends, was enormous. His illness had been only a temporary breakdown, the result of overwork and the strain of the army. They need not consider him insane, or permanently damaged. Itching to get back to his familiar hills, which he felt he had almost forgotten, Gurney wanted to give himself a fresh store of images of beauty on which to draw. He assumed that this was no permanent freedom but that 'duty points to the Army again, and there I shall probably find my feet after a short time and write my best. Well, Time will tell, and the last part of my life may be the happiest. Well may it be—the first part has been bitter enough—bitter enough.'[29]

It may not have been obvious to Gurney, but it was certainly clear to the authorities that he was going to be of no further use as a soldier. Once the decision to have him decommissioned had been made, it was essential that the Ministry of Pensions recognised his illness as war-related, otherwise he could not secure a war pension on which to subsist. There were many thousands of damaged young veterans writing to the ministry to plead their case for a pension with which to support their family. Gurney's case was one of many, and the money could only be stretched so far. The pensions office looked for any excuse not to award a full pension, and Gurney had enough of a track record of prewar mental instability to allow them to classify his illness as 'aggravated but not caused by' his war experience. He was allotted only a partial pension of 12 shillings a week, despite Scott's rather desperate insistence on the term 'shell shock' when describing his condition.

He returned to 19 Barton Street, Gloucester, to what must have been a very uneasy family reunion. Gurney had, of course, assured the staff at Napsbury that his parents were willing to care for him, but even he, in his eagerness to return home,

Fig. 9.3: Gurney's brother Ronald in uniform, 1915. Courtesy of Noel Hayward, from the photograph album belonging to Dorothy Gurney.

had doubts about imposing himself on his father. After his operation in the spring, David's health had seemed to be improving and the prognosis was good, but it was by now becoming clear that he was still seriously ill. As well as the inevitable tensions between him and his mother, Gurney felt a great sense of guilt at having let his father down (as he perceived it). David Gurney had been 'more kind than almost any father about all the time I have wasted in the past'.[30] He did not specify what he believed this wasted time to be, but the phrase smacks of the weight of responsibility to make his parents proud. He had an ally in his little sister Dorothy, 'a first rate sister, and I am proud of her'.[31] She had recently started to write poetry herself ('some of it not so bad, either', Gurney rather patronisingly declared), inspired largely by her own friendship with the Harvey family.[32] Gurney even went out for the odd walk with his brother Ronald, whom he had hardly seen during the last four years, since Ronald had also signed up and had been serving abroad.[33] But Gurney could not feel at ease in his family's presence; he still felt he had a lot to prove to them all, and had not yet justified his father's belief in him.[34]

Florence had been the parent who kept Gurney's piano practise on track, shouting up from the shop floor when he raced through his pieces in order to have time to improvise (her well-intentioned discipline may have had the unlooked-for effect of turning the stubborn and perverse boy into a composer). But looking back on his childhood, Ivor felt that it was David Gurney who had always been the one with the real musical ambition for him. As a boy, Gurney's father had narrowly missed the opportunity to become a chorister himself. A local Maisemore lady with influence had spotted his talent and offered to send him to Gloucester Cathedral Choir, suggesting she would cover the fees herself, but David's parents refused.[35] When Gurney took up his own choristership there, he knew he was living out his father's dreams. Now the possibility that his father might not live to see the fulfilment of his son's early potential was a very real anxiety. Gurney was vastly improved since his suicidal and despairing days at Warrington, but a Board of Discharge's verdict that a patient is 'cured' was not a guarantee of their ability to function independently. There was intense pressure on beds in every hospital ward, and any ex-serviceman who appeared to be able to manage and had family to go to was discharged as soon as possible. Gurney was still unsure 'of his impulses', as he rather ambiguously phrased it, presumably referring to the voices in his head that continued to plague him intermittently.[36]

Almost as soon as he was home, he wrote to Napier Miles at King's Weston to see whether he could be admitted there immediately. He had spent months in Warrington and St Albans gazing longingly at postcards of Gloucestershire, but however much he might have missed his native landscape, he felt lost in it. He was not ready to be entirely alone there once more. Ironically, as his friends discovered, a transfer was now impossible. The army had washed its hands of him, and he must do the best he could in Gloucester. He spent as much time as possible with the Hunt sisters in Wellington Street, but the peace of their music room was no longer enough.

Two days after he'd returned home, he turned up in Haines's office unannounced. Haines was delighted to see him, but horrified by the state he was in. He saw before him a man in torment, besieged by persecutory voices. The swaggering, boisterous young genius had been transformed into a sunken figure, whose new quietness and humility were painful to see. After the initial shock, Haines found that Gurney's auditory hallucinations, if one ignored the fact that they were delusions, did make some kind of sense within their own terms. As Gurney was clearly not compatible with the working environment of a quiet solicitor's office, Haines decided that the only thing to do was accompany him out of his office and tramp about with him on the hills. Despite the foul weather, he abandoned his work and walked his friend around in the pouring rain until he himself was ready to drop. They walked to Birdlip and Crickley, visiting Gurney's favourite old haunts. The familiar places and exercise were enough to restore a sense of calm and rationality, and Haines left Gurney a happier man than he had been earlier. Haines was drained and exhausted. He found Gurney's attitude to every aspect of his life worryingly disordered and felt his behaviour was becoming unsustainable. 'His chief trouble is concerned with food—he would eat nothing all day. He asserts that if he gives way to the desire for food he is unable to stop: [. . .] if he has lunch he invariably goes out afterwards and buys large quantities of cakes and eats them and continues doing so as long as he has the money.'[37]

Whilst Gurney struggled on, hardly able to support himself on his pension and the mere pennies he was being sent for *Severn and Somme* royalties, his friends were also experiencing mixed fortunes. His two friends with the weakest constitutions, Howells and the frequently ailing Scott, were both struck down in November by the Spanish flu epidemic. The flu was a deadly insult after injury, sweeping through Europe just as the war was drawing to a close and killing more than the conflict itself had claimed. There was still a distinct feeling that Howells, even with flu, which had developed into pneumonia, was managing to have a better time than Gurney. 'Poor Herbert' was 'not feeling any too cheerful I daresay, in spite of his being at the house of his lady-love, at Churchdown under that little hill of Chosen he has loved so well.'[38] Will Harvey was certainly having a change for the better in his fortunes. Having spent the last twenty-nine months in seven German prison camps, often in solitary confinement as a punishment for his persistent habit of trying to escape, he had finally managed to get out of prison.[39] Gurney eagerly awaited Harvey's return to Britain. In the meantime, he had to keep himself occupied and find a way to earn money. He managed to secure some work in a munitions factory for a few weeks in October and November, which ended as the armistice was declared. 'I am better myself after a fortnight's hauling of heavy things about the Munitions works', he reassured Scott.[40] Temporary hard labour took his mind off his difficulties, and the dangerous nature of the work was hardly likely to bother a suicidal veteran.

Gurney had corresponded regularly with the Chapman family back in High Wycombe throughout the war, and now the father, Edward Chapman, came down to Gloucester to pay Gurney a visit. Like Haines, he too was shocked by the desperate state in which he found him. Gurney could not find peace, and his attempts to take control of his destiny were becoming increasingly extreme and bizarre. The night before Chapman arrived, Gurney had attempted to run off to sea. He had walked the twenty-three miles to Newport, intending to join a ship in the hope that life at sea and the hard physical work would restore his sanity. No ship would take him, and he returned home. It was a bizarre escapade, and his friends felt that he was desperate enough that it was surely only a matter of time before he would resort to suicide again as a means of escape. Chapman, not knowing what else to do to help, and being so distressed by the condition in which he found his young friend, took the dramatic step of offering to adopt him. It was a generous and extraordinary offer. Chapman was probably aware that Gurney had been at his happiest and most stable in their family home, and he reasoned that the security they could offer might just be enough to help him through his breakdown. This was November, and Gurney was expecting to resume his studies at the College in the spring, so a residency in High Wycombe, permanent or otherwise, would have made sense.[41] Unsurprisingly, Gurney's own parents were impressed neither by the offer nor by the insinuation that their protection was not enough for their own son.[42] There is no record of Gurney's response to Chapman's offer, but the matter was not raised again.

He was not stable enough to manage life in Gloucester, but he could still find inspiration in the city itself. He felt well enough to embark upon his second mature attempt at a string quartet, or 'quartett', as Gurney spelt it, in homage to Beethoven's streichquartetten. He had written one in the spring of 1912, his second year at the Royal College. Now, with the College once more in his sights, he began work on another that November (1918), finishing it the following March.[43] The quartett in A was inspired by the cathedral, when, in the wintry late November sunshine, 'St Nicholas Tower shone white in a pearly sort of fashion lovely to see.'[44] It was a very particular moment—glimpsed in the early days of the new, postwar world; Europe had become a different place altogether with the announcement at 11 am on 11 November that all hostilities would cease. The armistice was declared, and the war that was supposedly to end all wars was finally over. Gurney was, at least to all appearances, ecstatic. The Quartett was the result of his relief and enthusiasm, begun even before the violin sonata, his other homage to Gloucester, was complete. He wrote in very much his old tone of enthusiasm and sardonic humour to his friend the organist Sydney Shimmin, hoping that now, finally, the College's generation of 1914 might regroup:

> Thank Goodness the War's over; thank Goodness there is a chance we'll all be back again soon moving our fingers over black and white, and playing ecstatic sentimentalities on the Vox Humana the while the Vicaw [sic] surreptitiously chaws his last eucalyptus lozenge before commencing operations. [...]
>
> Have you heard that I have got my ticket? That means College soon I hope, and sounding loud timbrels, plucking resonant harps, tootling on sackbuts shawms, balaikas (or whatever they are) and other tuneful instruments of Musick. May you be there along soon! We'll sit in some inn parlour and chortle 'Widdecombe Fair' together for joy of return, reunion, mere existence— Joie de vivre, as the linguists say. Ho ho![45]

This wildly tongue-in-cheek, jovial picture of the future was hardly the whole story, but the fact that he could cling to it was probably one of the reasons he was impelled to carry on. The more reflective response to the armistice came in a long, introspective poem, 'The Day of Victory', which he published in the *Gloucester Journal*. On the morning of 11 November, Gurney had stood listening to the bells and cheering crowds in the rain-soaked streets of Gloucester as the 'dull skies wept, the clouds drooped soddenly'. The flags waved around him, and he found he could appreciate how a 'glory of spirit wandered the wide air through', without any lessening of the weariness and sorrow the war had left behind. He thought of his own suffering, the sights he had witnessed on the battlefields of 'too many lovely bodies racked too bitterly' and observed those around him who carried their own burdens; the mothers who had lost their sons, the widows, and fatherless children. Even theirs was, somehow, a message of hope:

Yet one discerned
A new spirit learnt of pain, some great
Acceptance out of hard endurance learned
And truly; wrested bare of hand from Fate.[46]

His thoughts ranged from those who would never return home, to the fates of those, like himself, who now had their own personal wars to fight to survive in a strange new civilian world. 'Will Peace bring me peace, though?' he had asked himself back in 1917.[47] The poignancy and bleakness with which he observed the victory celebrations indicate that the question was, at best, still unanswered.

CHAPTER TEN

'A Revenge of Joy'

During Gurney's time in France he had corresponded with the colourful and exotic author Ethel Voynich, and she had made Gurney her rather reluctant confidante and literary critic during the course of their letter-writing. Now, possibly after finding out from Scott something of Gurney's distress, Voynich invited him to join her and a group of friends and relatives spending Christmas 1918 at Zennor, in Cornwall. It was an inspired thought, and perfect timing. Although Gurney had rather mixed feelings about her novels, her exotic life of travel between Russia, America and England and her literary and musical connections made her stimulating company. Gurney joined her and two Cambridge students, her nephew Geoffrey Taylor and his friend Edgar Adrian. All were in festive and carefree mood. They had emerged from the shadow of a war that had so far dominated their short adult lives. Now, as the realisation dawned that what had begun to seem an endless conflict had indeed finished, they could turn their attention to their exceptionally promising careers. Taylor, only four years older than Gurney, was already a fellow of Trinity College Cambridge and had spent the war advising on the design of aeroplanes. He would be recognised as one of the foremost scientists of the century, receiving a knighthood for his services to physics. Adrian had just finished his medical degree when the war broke out, and spent the duration treating soldiers with shell shock (he was to be awarded a Nobel Prize in 1932 for his medical research on the nervous system). He would have had a very clear understanding of the conditions in which Gurney had been living during his time in Warrington and Napsbury.

It was a vivacious and illustrious company with whom to celebrate Christmas. Together they enjoyed a 'scrumptious' Christmas dinner (as Gurney gleefully put it) in a hotel. This was no café au lait and bacon cooked in an old tin over a makeshift fire, but many courses, with generous helpings sumptuously served. He was in heaven. When the party returned to their rented cottage, there were parlour games such as musical chairs and a winking game. The lighthearted atmosphere was ideal therapy for Gurney, who had been surrounded by disturbed, haunted men for too long. He was as keen as Taylor and Adrian to embrace the possibilities the future held. His place at the Royal College had been held open for him, and he felt he was ready to attempt a return in the spring.

In the meantime, he intended to make the most of his surroundings. He was particularly impressed with the sea around the rugged Cornish coastline. For the first time Gurney felt he understood why poets such as W. H. Davies and Masefield wrote of crashing and rolling waves. This was a world apart from the Gloucester docks, or the English Channel as seen from a troop ship. Here the sea was violent, treacherous and full of drama, and he internalised his impressions of these winter waves to draw upon in the future whenever he wanted to portray a romanticised vision of the sea.

The dramatic scenery delighted him, as did the romantic names of the places. Writing to Haines, who was back in Gloucester, Gurney enthused:

> You must know Cornwall someday, a grey land of blue sea and frowning cliffs of might. Boulders outcropping in all conceivable places. Skies wonderful enough. Violets in bloom (though not many) at Xmas. Great winds and dashing spray, clear stars, gulls, cormorants, rooks, a wishing well, old and dangerous-to-the-unwary-traveller pitshafts . . . Zennor Head, Carn Naun, Hell's Mouth, Rosewall, Tregenna. [. . .] You'd love the lot, and come back to stare at the ceiling through clouds of smoke—to see Armada clouds, huge breakers, wicked looking rocks and brown and grey moorlands . . . Surely the great Symphony in C minor will come out of this. (Pray that it may not resemble the Brahms!).[1]

The cold weather did not deter the party from spending the days walking and rock climbing, and Gurney gloried in the great chasms and lichen-covered granite, 'O a murderous but gloriously majestic place! The fear of men of the sea, but to poets a joy, a great memory after the seeing.' On the day after Boxing Day the party undertook a walk to Gurnard's Head, a little peninsula of rock that jutted out from the coastline. Gurney seemed particularly distracted. He had taken a thin little manuscript book with him, ideal for fitting into a trouser pocket, and threw himself face down on the grass to write ideas in it whenever the group stopped for a rest. Taylor later recalled the afternoon:

> When we got to Gurnard Head Adrian found a little chimney (ie a crack between 2 rocks) which led on to a little place which was otherwise inaccessible. We took I. G. up this place showing him where to put his hands and feet. Then we went back down the chimney and climbed round the rocks back to the grass neck which connects Gurnard Head with Cornwall. Adrian and Aunt Ethel and I were talking and did not notice that I. G. was not following till we got to the neck. It was then getting dusk. Adrian & I went back to look for I. G.

and finally found him at the top of the little chimney writing in the dark (it was dark by the time we got back to the chimney). He had gone back & climbed up by himself, but I very much doubt whether he could have got down by himself even if it had been light. We climbed up & brought him back in the dark to Aunt Ethel who waited for us on the neck connecting Gurnard Head with the mainland.[2]

The piece that had so distracted him was a setting of Francis Ledwidge's 'Twilight Song', which would become known as 'Desire in Spring'. It had been an extraordinarily dense week, and his memories of it were so colourful and vivid that they soon found their way into poetry. The cottage had been in remote countryside, and the stars in the winter sky untroubled by the glow of city lights had made a particularly strong impression. He drafted 'The Companions', drawing on images that he had jotted down in his holiday diary.[3]

The Companions

On uplands bleak and bare to wind
Beneath a maze of stars I strode;
Phantoms of Fear haunted the road
Dogging my footsteps close behind.

Till Heaven blew clear of cloud, showed each
Most tiny baby-star as fine
As any jewel of kings. Orion
Triumphed through bare tracery of beech.

So unafraid I journeyed on
Past dusky rut and pool alight
With Heaven's chief wonder of night
Jupiter, close companion.

And in no mood of pride, courteous
Light-hearted, as with a king's friend,
He went with me to the journey's end,
His courtiers Mars and Regulus.

My door reached, gladly had I paid
With stammered thanks his courtesy
And theirs, but ne'er a star could see
Of all Heaven's ordered cavalcade.
The inky pools naught held but shade,
Fine snow drove West and blinded me.

On his return to Gloucester, and with the move back to London and the Royal College looming ever nearer, he was soon 'down in the dumps,' again, as he wrote to Winifred Chapman, as he sat, overwhelmed, amongst the chaos of his packing. 'Can you send any hints on how to pack shirts, music, socks, books, coats, shoes, of enormous bulk into a box half the size of the combined mass?'[4]

By 16 January 1919, after a 'heartbreaking search' for cheap accommodation, he was in his new 'dingy diggings' in Sterndale Road, West Kensington, with his box unpacked, and his books having arrived that day.[5] From the trenches he had imagined his postwar life in London; sitting in congenial pubs sipping ale, humming folk songs and dispensing his newfound wisdom with joyful enthusiasm.[6] The reality was that life with hardly a penny to buy a pint, in a dismal corner of London in January, was not likely to be the idyll he had conjured up.

The College had been run by Hugh Allen since Parry's death in 1918, and he had made drastic changes in his first year, appointing some impressive new staff, including the young conductor Adrian Boult in February 1919. The message was clear; the prewar days of the Brahms-influenced, highly traditional composition teaching were over. Parry had led the College with his particular blend of charisma, determination and sensitivity, and he was much missed. His death, only a month before the end of the war, was tragically mistimed for a man who had spent the four years of the conflict worn down by grief and anxiety for his students. As Howells wrote, the war had been a 'scourge that cast a devastating shadow over Parry's mind and heart. . . . How many of us ever wished that death could have come to him a few months later than it did? Since by then the slaughter and the agony (both well-nigh universal) would have been at an end.'[7]

Gurney's emotions were mixed as he once more pushed his way through the heavy swing doors of the Royal College. Parry's absence was not the only shadow that fell over the institution. The plaque that now faces any visitor to the College with the names of thirty-eight of Gurney's fellow students who had not survived the fighting had yet to be erected, but he needed no monument or roll of honour to know how lucky he was to have the chance to resume his studies. Howells's great friend the viola player and composer Francis Purcell Warren had been killed on the Somme, aged only twenty-one. So had Kennard Bliss, Arthur's much adored, flamboyantly artistic brother. Two composers associated with the College, George Butterworth and Ernest Farrar, were also dead. Whatever he himself had endured, Gurney had at least returned. But alongside the excitement of this new beginning was the niggling anxiety: could he now, after his years of hard suffering, actually write the symphonies and great works that were never far from his mind? It was one thing to dream from the trenches of the masterpieces that he would create after the war, but quite another to have to realise the ambition.

Composition proved to be a halting affair. The quartett in A that he had begun just before Christmas was temporarily abandoned as it presented too many difficulties.

His bedtime reading, by candlelight, was a score of a Brahms quintet (along with some Edward Thomas), possibly with the hope of picking up some hints at structuring a large-scale chamber work.[8] Whilst he had begun some verse, it was only incompletely drafted out; however, he could take pride in the fact that *War's Embers*, his second collection of poetry, had been completed just before Christmas, and was now facing its fortunes with publishers.

Much to his delight, Sidgwick and Jackson (who had had a modest success with *Severn and Somme*) now accepted *War's Embers*. By 25 February he was correcting his proofs and once more admiring the smart appearance of his words in print. He had insisted that poetry was a temporary measure, expedient during the war, and that music was his real calling. At the same time, he was showing no sign of relinquishing his claim to being a poet. Just as soon as he had corrected the proofs for this second poetry collection, he was beginning on poems intended for a third. Poetry, whether he admitted it to himself or not, was as much a part of his identity now as composition.

War's Embers picks up where *Severn and Somme* had left off, charting the next stage on Gurney's journey as an experimental poet. At his best, his power lies in his ability to boil neologisms down to their essence, and to look unexpectedly at the mundane. *War's Embers* represents the next stage in his development of his hallmark ability to create juxtapositions that wrong-foot and surprise. The poems included in the collection continued to build on his wartime experiments, developing a syntax that draws on speech rhythms. His verse now resonated with the ebb and flow and often unexpected modulations and syncopations of music, although he still experimented with the strict limitations of a poetic form, as the opening poem, 'The Volunteer', testifies. Here, however, although the second and fourth line of every quatrain are carefully rhymed, we can already see his increased confidence in breaking out of the limitations of his neat little six and seven beat lines and 'aba' scheme, as the first and third lines experiment with a far looser assonance, rhyming 'curious' with 'against' and 'mud' with 'all'. The rather defiant, even cheeky volunteer would take on God, challenging both him and the old order. Gurney enacts this challenge, a tentative pull at the threads of tradition, within the structure of the poem itself.

> I would test God's purposes:
>   I will go up and see
> What fate He'll give, what destiny
>   His hand holds for me.
>
> For God is very secret,
>   Slow-smiles, but does not say
> A word that will foreshadow
>   Shape of the coming day.

Curious am I, curious . . .
  And since He will not tell
I'll prove Him, go up against
The naked mouth of Hell.[9]

War's Embers is a collection of growing confidence and individuality, but it suffers from being difficult to categorise. Gurney had become a 'nature poet' along the lines of his hero Edward Thomas, and (had he but known his work) John Clare, but the label only tells a fraction of the story. This is war poetry and nature poetry commingled, and while such a combination is possible for Thomas, Gurney's collection is a little too eclectic to claim a clear identity. Thomas's poetry was written before any firsthand experience of fighting, and draws on the natural world with the undertones of war as an unspecific shadow colouring its view. *War's Embers* shifts between poetry that is specifically concerned with war and peacetime nature poetry (even lines for a school song for Gurney's alma mater, the King's School Gloucester, at one point). The volume's defining feature is that whatever the subject matter, the poetry stems from a fascination with people-watching, attentive to nuances in shadow, and colour, and with an acute ear for the music inherent in landscape, trenchscape and cityscape. Nevertheless, it must have felt at least mildly discombobulating for its readers in 1919, who were increasingly keen to forget the war.

Harvey had finally returned to Gloucestershire, and Gurney found every excuse to leave London to see him, fuelling his passion for book-talking by spending as much of his time at Harvey's family home in Minsterworth as he possibly could. Many of Gurney's happiest memories of Gloucestershire would be of time spent with the Harveys. During the war, his longing for the countryside had been bound up with his separation from Harvey himself. Harvey was as essential to Gurney as the hills they had walked and the sunsets they had seen together. Gurney had found a temporary happiness when he had poured his love for his absent friend into his relationship with Annie, but now he was reunited, against heavy odds, with the original. The contentment they found in each other's company, tinged with the slight edge of competition, spurred both men on to work. Harvey had been back in the country for only a few weeks. He had left prison camp weak and malnourished, and had succumbed easily to the influenza epidemic.[10] He was still recovering, but was well enough to enjoy days and nights with his old friend, wandering the countryside or in the beautiful gardens of his home. Both men were convalescing in their different ways, and looking forward to a shared future was a tonic for them both.

On a cold, fire-lit evening in late February they decided to select some poems from Harvey's two collections for a song cycle. Gurney had criticised Harvey's 1916 *A Gloucestershire Lad* for being 'a careless book, often ill-wrought, often ragged', but now he kept his reservations to himself. He was very fond of some individual poems, 'In Flanders' for one, and both of Harvey's collections had redeeming features; he had few 'beautiful lines, but can write beautiful wholes.'[11] Now Gurney engineered it so that some of those 'beautiful wholes' found their way into the cycle.

His wartime setting of 'In Flanders' was already firmly established in his mind as one of his own compositional masterpieces and was an obvious choice for the opening of the new *Gloucestershire Lad* cycle. 'If We Return' was another of a select handful of Harvey's poems that Gurney felt he could not surpass with his own verse. The song cycle, a 'great stunt', as Harvey described it, was cobbled together quickly to be included in a poetry reading Harvey was to give in nearby Stroud only a week later. Gurney rushed the second song, 'Piper's Wood', and returned to it to rewrite it in September. His setting of 'The Horses' was already nearly finished, so did not pose any significant problems, and the other two, 'The Rest Farm' and 'Minsterworth Perry', he wrote just in time for Harvey to learn. They performed the cycle with Gurney at the piano. Harvey, despite still being 'weak in the gills and husky' after his influenza, did his best, and the evening was a success. The *Stroud Journal* recounted the audience as being 'charmed' by the humorous Lieutenant Harvey, with the glamour of his prison camp adventures still freshly attached to him.

The discipline of writing quickly, and with his closest friend to encourage him, left Gurney exhilarated. Haines, who had attended the recital, was delighted to find him 'wonderfully normal and well'; great progress, considering his anxiety about Gurney a year before.[12] Staying at The Redlands with Harvey meant wholesome family life, plenty of walking, music and conversation. He should have been composing in Kensington, but in Gloucester work was less of a strain, and he began to write prolifically. He wrote his only Alice Meynell setting, 'Song of the Night at Morn', and continued to set Harvey's verse, with a version of 'A Song', which was published as 'Walking Song' in 1928, and 'Praise of Ale', a poem Harvey was to publish that year in *Ducks and Other Verses*. The songs are hearty, simple and assured, reflecting the jocular tone of much of Harvey's most popular verse.

Gurney had already begun another violin sonata, in E flat major, in the weeks before *A Gloucestershire Lad*, and it dominated his work that spring, with a final revision of it in May 1919, whilst at Crickley Hill. It is a work shaped by the contours of the Gloucestershire hills, with a heavy dose of Brahms, and some surprising, Scriabinesque moments adding unexpected flashes of colour. He was thoroughly pleased with the outcome, and particularly with the exuberant, melodious first movement, which he felt was 'the best long movement I have done'.[13]

The sonata was part of a continuation of a flowering of violin music, building on his experience of writing his two violin sonatas the year before. Whilst still with the Harveys, he wrote a scherzo for violin and another little violin piece entitled 'The Apple Orchard'.[14] Over the next two years, two more violin sonatas in F were to follow, and a piece called 'Home Song'. Gurney's resurgence of interest in writing for the violin might have been a tribute to Margaret Hunt, who was to die unexpectedly that spring. Whilst Harvey had been convalescing from the 'flu epidemic, she had been fighting her own losing battle with the illness. Gurney visited Margaret regularly until her death on 3 March and spent almost every day with her grieving sister Emily in the weeks that followed. The two sisters had hardly ever been separated, and the loss of her sibling and companion was a heavy blow. Gurney took his work round to their house, and wrote at their Bechstein, keeping the bewildered 'Emmy' company whilst finding the peace he needed to compose. He had begun to set Edward Thomas's verse at a moment of personal crisis, when he had contemplated ending his life back in Warrington in the summer of 1918. As Margaret lay poised between life and death, he sat in her music room working on a setting of the powerfully nihilistic 'Lights Out', in which the speaker recognises that death is his only option but approaches it with dignity and humility.[15]

> I have come to the borders of sleep,
> the unfathomable deep
> Forest where all must lose
> their way, however straight,
> or winding, soon or late;
> They cannot choose.[16]

It was an aptly sombre tribute to the woman who had introduced him to art song, and to some of the greatest musical influences that shaped his development as a composer. She had supported him uncritically, and he had regarded her as one of his principal muses since his teenage years.

Although he was officially enrolled as a student, his heart was clearly not in his studies, and he had spent hardly any time in the College itself since January. But the more he wrote, the more Gurney began to feel that perhaps he could indeed manage life at music college once more. He had no wish to be seen as a damaged, mature student, returning haunted by memories the younger generation could not understand, and years behind in his work. He wanted to make his reappearance as a respectable composer who could hold his own as a contemporary of Howells and Bliss, who were forging ahead with their careers and had already established themselves as young composers to be reckoned with. With typically gung-ho enthusiasm, he started to 'catch up' by beginning work on a haphazard combination of an orchestral *Gloucestershire Rhapsody*, a symphony and a mass, alongside his songs. The symphony is missing, and it is unclear how far he got with it, but *A Gloucestershire Rhapsody* still exists: a single twenty-minute movement, with a curious, pseudomedieval section in the middle. He had begun work on it in West Kensington, in his 'dingy' book-filled temporary lodgings in January 1919, and finally completed it in March 1921.

He felt that the finished result was good enough for the College orchestra to perform, and Scott prepared the parts, ready for the premiere on 16 June.[17]

Gurney's musical aesthetic was expansive, free and quasi-improvisatory, and the *Rhapsody*, with its possibilities of a fluid form, gave him the opportunity to indulge his inclinations fully. It may be that it was rather too much freedom. He was a master of miniatures, but hardly yet experienced in orchestral writing, and the flexibility the rhapsody allows does not best serve a mind that needed structure and boundaries to focus its inspiration. The result is a beautiful but restless work that never seems to settle on any one theme: dances and a march passing by, before they have really been registered. It is as if Gurney were aiming to bind together a series of momentary glimpses, memories recalled, or sudden moments of beauty and emotion, as he had so often done successfully in his poetry.

The *Rhapsody* encompasses some memorably lyrical moments, opening with meandering triplets led by the cellos from their lowest open string, bubbling up through the orchestra. It begins in C major, but with such an emphasis on the sixth degree of the scale that it feels as if we are in the pentatonic world of Vaughan Williams's *The Lark Ascending*. There are fragments of melody, often in the flutes, redolent of the half-perceived impressions Vaughan Williams had painted into his *A London Symphony* in 1912–13 to evoke walking the streets of London before daybreak and after nightfall. At other points, Gurney's prominent trumpets may well be intended to invoke a military bugle. A jaunty folk song–inspired tune, led again by the cellos, swiftly transforms itself into a grandly symphonic Elgarian melody, sweeping surprisingly through the work.

In short, *Rhapsody* is a striking piece, bursting with emotion and with a real sense of movement, but the undoubtedly beautiful melodic lines follow each other in such surprising proximity that the listener is left with the impression of having undertaken a whistle-stop tour through Elgar's and Vaughan Williams's greatest moments, and of having heard a work that is unable to achieve a clear sense of coherence. Ironically, Gurney's poetic account of the piece seems more effective than the music itself. If the *Rhapsody* represented a poetic instinct attempting to become music, then it is more successful when translated back into words.

A Bit from My "Gloucestershire Rhapsody"

The trees talked it, and horses, went trampling by.
There is no end to glory when blood is high,
And we that are Gloucester's own, since She has gracious grown
Will take a day of April as it is meant in mind.

Cotswold called an infinite love from the deeps
Of Her—Severn remembered the galley sweeps;
Thought Dane—as Cotswold Roman—and lifted Her whole

Soul to the day; all the history and gossip keeps
She heard in twenty centuries of change, and strange people.

March with Her wind, which might be great, is kept friend;
For one day man is allowed equality, and of godlike mind
Comrade with March and Cotswold—Severn broadening all—grand.

All love from all memory called out—Beethoven, Belloc;
The Lament Song—and watching the scarred hills 'Puck
Of Pook's Hill'—and my own music surging up and up.[18]

Like the musical version, the poem is an exhilarating rush of ideas, quite literally a surge of inspiration, sweeping past trees, horses, Gloucester, Cotswold, Severn, and centuries of observers. Half-formed allusions whirl together in the March wind, in a crescendo of talking, trampling, rustling leaves, hooves and beating blood. This is poetry that is only a short step from musical composition, a score notated in words. The cacophony broadens out into a panoramic view of Cotswold and the arts, represented by Beethoven and Belloc, as Gurney's musical depiction of the windy landscape surges into a celebration of musical and literary creativity.

A Gloucestershire Rhapsody was a love song to the landscape that had kept his mind and soul nourished during his wartime exile, and he was unable to stay away from it for long. After five unhappy weeks at the College, Gurney was back in Gloucester, composing, walking and shuttling between his friends' various households. He spent a few idyllic weeks in April working on Dryhill farm, on the edge of the village of Shurdington near Cheltenham. The old grey Cotswold stone farm was a rambling affair, owned by a delightful and well-read farmer, and situated in a spot guaranteed to send Gurney into raptures. It was 'under a Roman camp near the site of a Roman villa where many things have been from time to time discovered' (Gurney had himself turned up a Roman coin, which he sent to Scott for identification). 'A place of thorn, oak, ash, elm, clear streams, a 500 feet-up place where one gets a sight of the Severn Sea, May Hill, and on clear days of the Welsh Hills, by looking out of a window merely or wandering out of a gate.'[19]

His gentle introduction to farm work at St Albans had whetted his appetite for agricultural life, and this seemed at first to be the ideal combination; the acquisition of new skills and the promise of a fresh start. '[B]ut O what a full competence and more of beauty! Aren't I lucky? Well, time will show whether this will be worthwhile to me. Meanwhile, the good earth and winds, sun and stars must restore me to some semblance of the old bodily sick but spiritually sound me.'[20]

By the end of April 1919, the relentlessly physical labour was becoming harder to romanticise, and Gurney was frustrated at not being trusted with the more interesting skilled jobs. He had tried to live out his own theory of the ultimate music education—that is, dispensing with study, and replacing it with plenty of hard physical work, fresh air and countryside. But he knew fundamentally that his place was not on a farm but back at the College in Kensington. On 9 May, as he and Emmy Hunt crowed over their copies of the newly published *War's Embers*, he had made up his mind. He would return to London for the summer term and knuckle down to disciplined study. The next day, his father died.

It was an irony typical of Gurney's misfortune that he was to suffer his worst personal losses in that spring of 1919, a year after the war had ended. His father's death at age fifty-seven occurred only two months after Margaret Hunt had been buried. David Gurney had never fully recovered from his operation in 1918, and after a year of pain, the cancer that the surgeons had failed to remove had finally overcome him. The loss came at a time when things were going comparatively well for Gurney. His compositions were becoming ever more musically ambitious and accomplished, and his second book was now in print. He had always wanted to convince his father that his faith in him had not been misplaced, and it was an added blow to lose him when he felt he was only just beginning to realise his ambitions.

Six years after his father's death, Gurney was to record his memories of him in the poem 'Petersburg'.

> My father looked on ploughland and willed me.
> His was the friendliness of every hill and tree
> In all the west Gloucestershire, in all west Gloucestershire
> Born of that earth, of like love brought to birth;
> Knowing the flights of birds, and the song of the smallest
> Bird—the names of flowers, and the likeliest place
> Where first Spring might bring Her lovely trifles in.
> So on a night when Orion ruled with majestic light,
> He remembered his past dreams, all broken, and hoped for grace
> Whereby a son should say what he had never never,
> Been able to say or sing of such beloved Earth.
> Walked to Maisemore, and made his vows as his father
> Had done before—So on the Day of one Master
> Of me I was born—Leo Count Tolstoi—to be
> War Poet, and lover, maker, server of earth, the born of Gloucestershire.[21]

It was his father who first instilled in him his love of nature and of walking. As such, it was his father's mantle he took on when he dedicated his life to writing and composing in honour of Gloucestershire. He felt himself to be his father's mouthpiece, educated and talented enough to articulate in words and music the beauty that David Gurney appreciated but could never express.

Gurney did not play the organ at the funeral—that job went to his cousin, Joseph, who was the organist at All Saints' Church. But Gurney wanted to take his leave of his father with his own music; as soon as the family returned home after the service, he went to the piano and played Chopin's 'Funeral March' in its entirety, with Winifred looking on 'and marvelling at this unusual performance.[22] It was his own tribute to the man for whom he had become a musician.

Nine days after the funeral, the atmosphere at home had become unbearable. The shadow of his father's absence hung heavily over the gloomy little household. His widow refused to be consoled. She was convinced that the business would collapse, despite Ronald's desperate reassurances to the contrary. Gurney could not bear it. He could be of no practical use to either of them and hastily returned to London. This time he boarded with Maggie Taylor, a mutual friend of his and Scott's in Clifton Hill, St John's Wood. He had hardly allowed enough time to grieve before throwing himself back into his studies, but at least in St John's Wood he was away from his histrionic, despairing mother.

Even if he had offered to stay on in Gloucester, Ronald would probably have encouraged him to leave, for everyone's sake. The atmosphere between Ivor and his mother had become poisonous, and Ronald had entirely run out of patience with him, wanting to give him 'a rattling good talking to'.[23] Gurney's self-absorption and instability meant that the full burden of continuing the family business fell to Ronald. As far as Ronald was concerned, Gurney had been the rather undeserving recipient of far too much attention, money and kindness. He had shunned his real family for his erudite friends and could be insufferably superior. Ronald was an intelligent, hard-working man, who had, in the face of his own struggles and the trauma of war service, become a deeply frustrated, defensive character. The focus for his vitriol was, perhaps inevitably, his overindulged and unreliable brother.

Ronald had taken the dramatic step of going to Bombay to 'better himself' (in the words of Winifred), around the time that Gurney was starting his studies at the College in 1911.[24] He lived there for three years whilst training to be a tailor, then moved to America, where he broke a record for the number of garments cut in one hour. He was, according to Winifred, every bit as brilliant as Gurney, but his talents were more practical than artistic. He may also have suffered from depressive moods in a similar vein to Gurney's own troubles. 'As a matter of fact I myself have travelled a long way down the same road that he has gone', Ronald wrote enigmatically to Scott when Gurney was incapacitated with his illness in 1922.[25] He understood his brother's mental struggles, but his jealousy and resentment of him was palpable, and Gurney did little to avoid inciting it. 'My advice to you is not to shout so damned egotistically about your being a better man than me. You are only shouting at the very one you depend on', Ronald chided him, taking a grim satisfaction in his brother's fall from grace.[26] The antipathy was mutual; Ronald had been accepted into the Welsh Guards when Gurney was initially rejected from the Gloucesters, and the slight on his masculinity and fitness must have rankled. It may be that the competitive nature of the relationship between the two was part of the incentive for Gurney to try enlisting a second time. If Ronald was good enough for the army, then so was he.

Army life, with regular pay and a distance from his family suited Ronald, and he had opted to remain a soldier after the armistice had been declared. Now his father's death meant that he was obliged to ask for his discharge to salvage what was left of the family business. This he managed with skill and his customary practicality, despite having to bear the brunt of his mother's difficult behaviour. As Winifred recalled, 'I think she must have been extremely jealous: she wanted to control, but not to have any responsibility. At times she would set out, showing a desire to help Ronald when he was busy, perhaps trying by staying up at night to get a morning order finished for the next day. But without much warning mother would leave what he thought she was going to finish and put her clothes on and go out and not return.'[27] The account could almost be an anecdote demonstrating Gurney's own capacity for egocentric and irresponsible behaviour.

From the safe distance of South Kensington, Gurney was translating his double loss of father and Margaret Hunt into music, with a setting of Walt Whitman's 'Reconciliation'. Whitman, like Edward Thomas, had altered Gurney's view of the possibilities of verse—his discovery of the poet had taken him 'like a flood' when he first read him in the trenches, and Whitman's pellucid text found its counterpart in a gentle, meandering melody that June.

> For my enemy is dead
> A man divine as myself is dead,
> I look where he lies white faced and still in his coffin,
> I draw near, bend down and lightly touch with my lips
> The white face in the coffin.

The image of the dead man must have been particularly resonant for Gurney. The memory of his own father lying in his coffin was still very fresh, as he set the poem only a month after the funeral. The gentle kissing of the white face is perhaps a gesture towards laying to rest the body that haunted Gurney's own poem 'To His Love': 'that red wet thing I must somehow forget'. Back in 1918 Gurney could only countenance hiding a body under piles of flowers, in the impotent hope of 'somehow' dulling the pain of loss. Now that he had buried both father and friend, he finally felt able to approach a poem which held out hope that the world might be washed clean. He set 'Reconciliation' at a time when tens of thousands of civilians and ex-combatants, along with Gurney himself, were trying to reintegrate themselves into postwar society, and attempting to make sense of the experiences they had undergone. It is a poem that offers what Gurney sorely needed: reconciliation, not only between enemies but with oneself.[28]

In June he returned to piano music, which he had not written seriously since before his College days. He began his second attempt at a piano sonata. The first had been written back in Gloucester in 1910, but he found it 'more difficult than is pleasant'. He made some substantial sketches at a sonata in D but gave up in favour of a prelude, a more manageable, concise form. Much of the summer holidays were spent with Harvey at Minsterworth, and it was there, during that August, that he finished his first prelude (in D flat). He had found it far more rewarding work than sonata-writing, and he quickly incorporated it into a set of five preludes that autumn. A prelude takes one or perhaps two ideas and develops them, but it is not long enough to demand a large-scale structure to be followed in order to make it cohere; it is the pianistic equivalent of a song, or a poem—a moment in time, a thought encapsulated in miniature, and as such, the form seemed to suit Gurney's compositional methods particularly well.

J. S. Bach, the greatest writer of preludes and fugues, had never been far from his mind during the war. In the trenches in March 1917 Gurney had dreamed that he might one day create his own equivalent to Bach's *Well-Tempered Clavier*. He had often deliberately summoned to mind Bach's forty-eight preludes and fugues, as mental background music to eclipse whatever he faced. They had become a form of emotional protection, but also a personal shorthand, each work loaded with a meaning that only Gurney could access. The A major Prelude (book II), for instance, encapsulated the innocence and spirit of Christmas carols.[29] In training at Chelmsford, when he felt his mind to be clear of depression, he found the 'Wedge' Prelude running involuntarily through it. Later, in the trenches, the G minor Prelude 'sticks to me in solemn moments'.[30]

As he sat at Harvey's piano, looking out over the beautiful gardens through the music room window, he may well have been leafing through Harvey's volumes of piano music. The preludes he wrote there do more than nod towards the great composers of piano preludes. In fact, they seem to try out other identities—to *become* Brahms, Scriabin, Chopin, or Rachmaninov. It is perfectly common for other composers' work to influence and even be heard in new pieces—Vaughan Williams was so intent on his French-inspired orchestration that he quoted some of Debussy's *La Mer* in his first movement of *A London Symphony* without even knowing he had done it. But Gurney's preludes do not just sound variously like the other composers of preludes: they actually *feel* like them. The keys in which they are set, the tactile experience of playing them, the layout of the hands on the piano keyboard, and the soundworld of the great composers are absorbed to an extraordinary extent in these pieces. The preludes are extremely effective as pieces in their own right, but they are also deeply felt acts of homage to Gurney's heroes.

In the years to come, Gurney's ability to inhabit others' identities would be construed as a symptom of madness. As a composer responding to others' poems, Gurney had to master the art of 'becoming' other poets; responding to their images and emotions and developing them through music. It was a necessary skill for any successful song composer, and in his preludes he continued the same process; instead of using a text, he drew inspiration from others' music, and moulded it into something new. His multiple musical inhabitings gave him scope for an infinite variety of voices, as he ranged freely out of himself to stand in the shoes of the great composers, whilst always retaining something of a musical atmosphere that was unmistakeably his own.

The preludes were quickly recognised as successes. Winifred MacBride (a promising young soloist who had recently graduated from the College) performed them at the Wigmore Hall a year later, on 29 June 1920, in a programme that included Howells and John Ireland.[31] Gurney was developing quite a profile at the Wigmore—then, as now, one of London's foremost venues for chamber recitals. On 13 June 1919, two of his new Thomas settings ('Lights Out' and 'The Penny Whistle') had been performed there by Walter Johnstone-Douglas, and an annual appearance was good going for any young composer.

During September, Gurney moved between the Harveys' house at Minsterworth and his other favourite haunt, the Chapmans' in High Wycombe, reluctantly resuming his post as organist at Christ Church. He did have his own lodgings near the station, but the comforts of the Chapman family home far outweighed any benefits of solitary living. Whilst at High Wycombe he continued to add to his burgeoning collection of preludes. When he was tired of composing, he found relief in the company of the Chapman children who were now becoming young adults, flirting with the girls and devouring the home cooking produced by their mother Matilda. When he had been at the front, the Comtesse (as he renamed her) had sent Gurney his favourite treats: oat cakes and scones made to particular family recipes. Now he could indulge in them fresh from the oven. As his body was nourished with ample good food and energetic games of ping-pong, so music of the highest quality continued to flow. Alongside his preludes Gurney had been working on a set of seven songs since late July. They were to be known as his 'Sappho' songs, setting recreations and translations by Bliss Carman of the Ancient Greek lyric poet Sappho's writings: 'Hesperus' (with which he was particularly delighted), 'The Apple Orchard', 'Love Shakes My Soul', 'The Quiet Mist', 'Soft Was the Wind in the Beech Trees', 'I Shall Be Ever Maiden' and 'Lonely Night'.[32]

When Gurney returned to the College in the autumn of 1919, commuting between London and High Wycombe, it was with a whirlwind of songs and piano preludes in his head. There was no shortage of inspiration, or motivation; he needed only encouragement, some gentle steering and the mental stability to write. The first

FIG. 10.1: Ralph Vaughan Williams, 1921.
© Vaughan Williams Charitable Trust.

two of these was to come from Hugh Allen's inspired new appointment, Ralph Vaughan Williams. Allen could not have found a better teacher for Gurney at this pivotal moment in his career. Vaughan Williams had come a long way. Back in 1910 when Gurney and Howells had heard his *Fantasia on a Theme by Thomas Tallis*, he had been a little-known 'odd fellow from Chelsea', as Herbert Brewer had described him to the Gloucester Cathedral Choir. Now he was a leading name in British music, with a long and illustrious career still before him. He had been demobilised from the Royal Army Medical Corps in February 1919 and had only recently returned to London to take up his post that September. We do not know whether Vaughan Williams asked for Gurney to be his pupil, or whether the move from Stanford was initiated by Gurney himself, but finally, after years of frustration with exacting and unsympathetic teachers, Gurney found in Vaughan Williams someone who understood and respected him and his work. He was a kind and dedicated man, who recognised both the frailty and the potential of his new pupil, and became a close ally of Gurney's, a supporter in public and in private, to whom Gurney would turn in times of crisis.

Vaughan Williams was a visionary. It was his influence that helped Gurney to become more harmonically experimental, encouraging him to move beyond the constrictions of Edwardian musical propriety. He believed in technique and was quietly insistent that a pupil must 'learn his stodge'—his rather lovely way of referring to harmony and counterpoint, in order to go on to develop an individual, authentic voice. (Gurney admitted that despite Vaughan Williams's best efforts, his harmony was 'shockingly slack' that first term.)[33]

Unlike Vaughan Williams, Stanford had become rather set in his ways by the time he was teaching Gurney in 1911, and had developed an approach that was rather inflexible. Both teachers knew Gurney was capable of genius, but Stanford had not been the man to help him channel it. Vaughan Williams was gentler and more willing to guide him. He and Gurney were particularly well matched musically, as both teacher and pupil had moved away from the major-minor hegemony to the freedom of the modes used in folk tunes. Gurney added a penchant for post-Wagnerian harmony, and a heavy dose of Chopin, Scriabin and Hugo Wolf. It took an open-minded teacher, who was himself on a lifelong journey of development and harmonic exploration, to oversee Gurney's own experimentation, and help him marry together such disparate harmonic worlds as those represented by Wagner and English folk song.

Gurney took a selection of his recent songs along to his first lesson with Vaughan Williams to ask for his thoughts. One was a setting of Walter de la Mare's 'The Scribe' and the other of Edward Thomas's poem 'Scents', drafted during the summer of 1918, but to which he had returned that summer. His new teacher worked on it in red pencil, which was rather alarming as such an ominous implement had been Stanford's weapon of choice for 'correcting' and condemning. But Gurney was relieved to find that, far from editing out his quirkier musical ideas, Vaughan Williams's few suggested changes opened up the song and showed him new possibilities to be explored.[34]

Gurney was heavily influenced by Vaughan Williams's quest to reinvent British music, and to forge an authentically English sound. The project of creating a self-consciously national music was one that was of central importance to composers both in the years preceding the war and in the 1920s. Conversely, whilst Gurney aspired to being 'English', he also distanced himself a little from the folk song–influenced school of composition. He respected the achievements of folk song–collecting composers such as George Butterworth, Holst and of course his new teacher, but felt that 'toujours I am sceptical about the lasting value of most English music. It is the ploughing of the ground, the preparing, and while one is grateful, there is too much as a general thing of excellence that so many clever people arrive at with their well-trained intellects and healthy minds and instincts.'[35]

Such a significant comment raises questions as to where Gurney saw his own contribution fitting into the panoply of English music. The answer may lie in Vaughan Williams's own insistence on music speaking for the composer's generation. Just as Gurney had written *Severn and Somme* to please the soldiers whose experiences it described, so he learnt from his new teacher how music might achieve a similar objective. It could be a mirror for society, a means of articulating the feelings of others who were not so able to translate their thoughts and emotions into sound. One of Vaughan Williams's great tenets, set out in a controversial little manifesto in the *RCM Magazine* back in 1912, was that a composer ought to develop his own authentic sense of Englishness through assimilating the sounds he heard around him into his work.[36]

Gurney wrote much of both Gloucester and London, attempting to capture the essence of the cities, observing details of life, however trivial or sordid, and elevating them to the status of the poetic. Vaughan Williams does the same in his *A London Symphony*, first heard in the Queen's Hall in March 1914.[37] Would Gurney have made the connection that Vaughan Williams's attempt to present a many-faceted vision of a city he loved in all its glory and grime was remarkably similar to his own poetic project? Vaughan Williams had intended to create a panoramic view of Edwardian London through the sounds of street sellers and jingling cabs, whilst Gurney's songs were becoming a sound-record of contemporary Georgian poetry.

That autumn Gurney set a plethora of Georgians, many of the poems having come into print only a few months before he pounced on the text. In September Gurney returned to John Masefield, with whose 'By a Bierside' he had had such a triumph during the war. It was, in his opinion, probably still his best song. His only other Masefield setting, the rollicking ballad 'Captain Stratton's Fancy', had found a different sort of popularity in 1917 amongst the many prisoners of war to whom Harvey had taught it. Now, knowing he had an affinity with Masefield, he attempted 'On the Downs', and 'The Halt of the Legion' at the end of September 1919.[38]

Gurney does not record what his new teacher made of these offerings, but there was certainly no interruption in the flow of compositions. He continued to set the Georgians throughout the autumn of 1919 with his first Edward Shanks setting: 'The Singer', which again had only been published that year. It was the first of five Shanks settings over the next two years at the College.[39] J. C. Squire, later to be a staunch supporter of Gurney, found his way into Gurney's music between 1919 and 1920 with two separate settings of his: 'The Ship' and 'You Are My Sky'.[40]

In the midst of this Georgian-dominated autumn, Gurney and Harvey managed to get themselves invited to lunch with John Masefield himself, at his house on Boars Hill, near Oxford. Masefield had been generous enough to send Gurney the 'most delightful of letters',[41] which he duly gloated over. Knowing Gurney's admiration for Masefield, Harvey had made contact with the poet in October on his behalf. Their meeting proved to be something of a miniature reception for Gurney; the other poets who had settled around Boars Hill had also been invited to inspect this new curiosity, and Gurney found himself greeted by an illustrious company of Roberts: Robert Graves, Robert Nichols and the poet laureate Robert Bridges, as well as Masefield and his wife. Masefield had already been very impressed with *War's Embers*, which had only been out since May (Gurney had probably sent him a copy). It was Gurney's first meeting with the great man, and he was keen to show what he could do as a composer, as well as to be respected by him as a fellow poet. Luckily, Masefield's house was equipped with a piano, so Gurney played whilst Harvey sang some of his Masefield settings, and then waited eagerly for the poet's reaction. It was mixed. He seemed particularly taken with 'Captain Stratton's Fancy' and Gurney's two recent settings of 'The Halt of the Legion' and 'Upon the Downs', but he was less impressed with 'By a Bierside'. His lukewarm response to Gurney's classic stung his pride considerably. Harvey, however competent a baritone, was perhaps not up to the grandeur, scale and solemnity that the song demanded. It was one thing to rattle out a rollicking tune with a pleasant singing voice, but quite another to do justice to so monumental a work. Nonetheless, the response overall was positive, and Masefield gave 'the Gloucestershire Lad' (as he fondly referred to Gurney) his official blessing to continue to set his texts. Meeting Gurney prompted a poem from Masefield himself. Meeting Gurney had brought to mind

> Notes that were comfort in the time of tears,
> Words that directed furrows of the plough

Masefield's appraisal summarised the motivation behind his work with a precision and clarity in which Gurney would have taken great pleasure, but he never knew that he had been the inspiration for a work by his hero.[42]

> Long since, after the weary war, you came,
> You, with a friend, to see me, and to sing
> Poems of yours and ballads of old fame
> Many a moving, many a merry thing.
>
> I thought of Blake, the English lad who sang
> To tunes too beautiful for tongue to tell,
> Of Allingham, whose country ballads rang
> Where Irish brooks, a winding river swell . . .
>
> And of old poets, long-forgotten now,
> Who, after singing, left, in country ears,
> Notes that were comfort in the time of tears,
> Words that directed furrows at the plough.
>
> Themselves, perhaps, but memory of a tone
> Of mirth, of sadness, never heard again,
> An unseen thing that like a fallen rain
> Or vanished warmth, has kindled a thing sown.[43]

Gurney was now on friendly enough terms with the influential poets of his day to accompany them to concerts. On 28 October he went to the Aeolian Hall with Edward Shanks and Harold Monro, the morose but influential owner of the Poetry Bookshop and publisher of the *Chapbook*. They had tickets to hear the tenor Steuart Wilson performing Vaughan Williams's cycle for piano, quartet and voice *On Wenlock Edge*. It had been written in 1909, but Gurney had not yet heard it. It made an immediate impression, just as the *Fantasia on a Theme by Thomas Tallis* had done back in 1910, and he declared it to be 'a fine strong piece of work'.[44] Gurney was particularly struck by the dramatic possibilities of combining the intimacy of song with the power of strings and piano. With Vaughan Williams on hand to offer guidance, he immediately set about a work for the same forces: tenor, quartet and piano, taking, as Vaughan Williams had done, A. E. Housman as his inspiration. The result was the song cycle *Ludlow and Teme*, completed over the course of two months. It was another example of Gurney's ability to inhabit others' work. He had turned his admiration for Vaughan Williams's cycle into his own version of the work, unmistakeably Gurney in sound, but identical to its model in conception.

Ludlow and Teme is one of Gurney's most significant achievements in terms of its success and enduring place in the repertoire. The cycle comprises seven poems: 'When Smoke Stood Up from Ludlow', 'Far in a Western Brookland', ''Tis Time, I Think, by Wenlock Town', 'Ludlow Fair', 'On the Idle Hill of Summer', 'When I Was One and Twenty' and 'The Lent Lily'.[45] Like his five war songs, it has the added interest of reflecting on the emotions of the moment; in this instance, the emotional aftermath of the war. Much of the cycle takes its dramatic tension from attempts to reconcile beauty with violence through sound, a rare, perhaps unique, parallel to his and the war poets' attempts to articulate war experience through verse.

The first song, 'When Smoke Stood Up from Ludlow', begins with an unsullied pastoral idyll and ends with a message of death. Gurney depicts a vivacious young yeoman, predominantly in the bright, confident key of A major, launching into the song with an upward-springing motif that characterises his youthful energy. The tension of the song exists in the imagined dialogue between the boy and a blackbird, who urges him to 'lie down . . . what use to rise and rise?' Life will end in death. Gurney depicts the blackbird's nihilistic voice in the darker, flat key of D minor, and illustrates his words with a startling and destabilising violence; far more than is present or called for in Housman's text. By the end of the piece, the two keys become confused, and the pervasive influence of the D minor undermines the pull of the original, life-affirming tonic key. This tension between two opposing impulses characterises much of the cycle, and at this early stage of the work Gurney refuses to allow them reconciliation. Here the piano has the final word, taking the yeoman's initial flourish that sprang the song into being, and slowing it down to end the song on an uncertain, questioning note, with none of the buoyancy of its first appearance. The song trails off with only the fifth, a bare E octave in the piano, setting up a musical question or challenge that is eventually taken up and resolved by the cycle's final song, 'The Lent Lily'.

'Far in a Western Brookland' depicts a lost idyll. The pastoral is a genre shaped by nostalgia: the distance between the present and memory, and the physical distance between the location of the writer and the absent landscape. Housman's landscape is imagined, and the poem is characterised by yearning. Gurney's setting combines a sense of mourning with expansiveness and serenity. Still, within the context of his cycle something more than the (real or imagined) loss of landscape is being mourned. Gurney writes with the sounds of war fresh in his mind: brutal, hammering figures characterise the setting of 'The Lads in Their Hundreds', which ends abruptly with two semiquavers and a quaver, a sputter redolent of machine gun fire. When the sense of human loss is too great for sound and fury, Gurney uses silence— the 'lads that will die in their glory and never be old' have their fate shouted emphatically at the audience by the tenor, with a dramatic absence of accompaniment, as the strings screech to a halt. The implications of these lads' deaths cannot be missed. There is more at stake in Gurney's reimagination of the poem than Housman could have anticipated, and Gurney's decision to cut the song off with a brief round of gunfire makes the point unmistakeably clear.

In 'On the Idle Hill of Summer' Housman is more ambivalent about the nature of war than elsewhere, but it is still apparently a foregone conclusion that taking part is a lad's destiny. Gurney reinterprets the poem in terms of a brutal military invasion of the countryside. In 'The Lads in Their Hundreds' Gurney had represented the military as thuggish and aggressive with grinding, marching figures, and the musical suggestion of a violent death. In 'On the Idle Hill of Summer', however, the music explores a different aspect of the soldier's relationship to the military. The idea of the army provokes a musical hysteria at times, but at other points the same tight, militaristic rhythms reminiscent of drumming or fanfares rescue the music from the point of disintegration.

The army both destroys landscape and induces madness, but as Gurney knew from his own experience, its regimentation and order could also, paradoxically, hold the soldier (and the song) together. But for how long? At the thought of the 'lovely lads and dead and rotten', the song's dotted, drumming rhythm becomes transmuted into a nightmarish perversion of the order it had previously imposed. The strings are silent, leaving exposed a highly complicated and rhythmically confusing piano passage in which neither piano nor voice have any reference to the beat. This is one of the rare moments in the text where corpses are directly contemplated, and both piano and vocal line are derailed by the thought, only to be redeemed by the inexorable military rhythms, which pick the song up and drive it on.

Military order, in the form of triplets, dotted rhythms and drums can rein in the uncontained imagination of the singer, saving him from musical and mental disintegration when contemplating horrors. But what kind of redemption is this? 'On the Idle Hill of Summer' ends with a curiously unfocused epilogue, suggesting a blank, emotional void in which both ex-soldier and composer struggle to find a language to express the inexpressible. It is only in the final song, the exquisite and serene 'Lent Lily', that Gurney offers the answer to the musical question left hanging at the end of the unbalanced first song, and allows the cycle finally to find peace, and a sense of real emotional and harmonic resolution.

However popular Housman appears to have been at this time, his rather ghoulish celebrations of premature death in war must surely have had a peculiar resonance for the ex-combatant. For Gurney as poet and composer, the musical expression of subject matter common to war poetry is something that would have appeared an obvious undertaking, and *Ludlow and Teme* interprets, embraces and attacks Housman's texts in the months after the armistice. A far cry from the patchy and hastily assembled *Gloucestershire Lad* set, *Ludlow and Teme* was Gurney's most substantial and sustained success to date. It was the work of a mature composer, who could, in his own style, condense the past years of suffering and wisdom into a coherent and forceful work, without losing the sense of beauty that he so valued.

He worked on it over Christmas 1919, which he spent very happily with the Chapmans, and the score was ready for its premiere in March. Gurney was becoming more ambitious. Spurred on by what he already sensed to be a great success, he attempted another large-scale work, a string quartet in F. He had written a quartet inspired by Gloucester over the winter of 1918, and another that Scott and her quartet had performed for him back in 1912. The experience had whetted his appetite for more. Having honed his skills as a quartet composer in the dramatic scoring of *Ludlow and Teme*, and with the confidence Vaughan Williams's guidance gave him, he felt ready to begin work on his third.

Gurney took breaks from his new quartet to help direct rehearsals of *Ludlow and Teme*. He was to be accompanying the tenor Steuart Wilson (whose performance of *On Wenlock Edge* had inspired him and who had the added distinction of having been a friend of Rupert Brooke). They were to join the distinguished Philharmonic Quartet for the premiere at a soirée at Marion Scott's house in March. It was to be the highlight of her 'Gloucestershire Evening' (which included works by Howells). The invited audience at Scott's Hyde Park home included Stanford, Arthur Bliss (now no longer a captain but gratefully back in civilian guise), and the composition teacher Thomas Dunhill, and they pronounced it a resounding success. When Gurney was called upon to take his bow, he had to be extricated from behind a bookcase in another room, overcome with embarrassment and emotion at their enthusiasm.

In May 1920 he was to hear *On Wenlock Edge* for the second time. He recorded his thoughts in the margins of his concert programme:

> Purely English words retranslated and reinforced by almost purely English music—the product of a great mind not always working at the full of its power, but there continually and clearly apparent. The French mannerisms must be forgotten in the strong Englishness of the prevailing mood—in the unmistakable spirit of the time of creation. England is the spring of emotion, the centre of power, and the pictures of her, the breath of her earth and growing things are continually felt through the lovely sound.[46]

Again, it spurred him on to write another Housman cycle, *The Western Playland*, this time for baritone. Unlike *Ludlow and Teme*, which was composed over a couple of intense months, *The Western Playland* was more of a conglomerate, putting together new work and versions of preexisting songs he had already written.[47] It does not have quite the coherent unity of *Ludlow and Teme*, with each song designed to complement and refer to the others, but it is still an enduringly popular and powerful cycle, with a sense of musical progression, and a dramatic and emotional coherence.

The Western Playland was to be performed by the baritone Topliss Green six months later, on 26 November 1920, with Gurney, rather unusually, conducting the ensemble. Gurney was delighted to have the work heard in the College's concert hall, an honour *Ludlow and Teme* had not yet had, but this was to be no ordinary performance. It was a major event in the College calendar, intended as the first of an annual fixture of concerts to celebrate and remember the service of Collegians in the war. The performers and composers featured had all played some active part in the conflict, and the concert itself was dedicated to the memory of the students who had not survived. Gurney's premiere was to appear alongside Bliss's mischievous *Madame Noy*, some songs for tenor by Vaughan Williams, George Dyson's Rhapsody No. 1 for quartet, and some organ solos by Ernest Farrar. The fact that Farrar himself had not survived to perform them added to the poignancy of the evening. The concert was rounded off with a patriotic and emotional rendition of Parry's 'Jerusalem': a reminder that there was one other important figure who had not lived to see the armistice.

Gurney stood on the podium with a packed and sombre auditorium behind him. It was a moment in which many thoughts and emotions converged (not least of which must have been his anxiety at his lack of conducting experience). In the trenches, he had dreamed of the major works he would write if only he could survive. Now he had two Housman cycles, piano preludes and his chamber music, and the dream was becoming a reality. He had escaped from the front against heavy odds, and even regained enough mental equilibrium to return to the College. His writing had attained a fluency and confidence of which he could previously only have dreamt. As the memorial concert continued, he listened to pieces such as the thoughtful slow movement of Francis Purcell Warren's cello sonata—one of only a handful of works Purcell Warren ever wrote. Poor 'Bunny' Warren would be destined to be forgotten; the impression his short life had made on the music world was too small, however large his talent. Gurney, however, had been granted the chance to consolidate his reputation as a musical 'war poet'. He knew that this was his moment, and the next few years would be critical in establishing him as the major musical voice he had always believed he was destined to be. But for the last six months he had hardly been able to bring himself to set foot in the College, the institution to which he had longed to return. He was constantly treading a precarious path between creativity and desperation. Could the 'revenge of joy' he had anticipated having on the musical and literary world really now take place?

CHAPTER ELEVEN

'Despairing Work Is the Noblest Refuge'

Nineteen twenty was the year Gurney should have been building up his network of contacts, and working to secure more high-profile premieres. The war had been over for nearly two years, and he had resumed his studies. Other veterans such as Arthur Bliss were already forging ahead, having their works performed across London, and receiving column inches in the press. Despite his determination to succeed, Gurney was already beginning to struggle. Vaughan Williams offered what support he could, but he found to his dismay that by the summer term of 1920, six months before the premiere of *The Western Playland* would take place, his new student was becoming increasingly erratic. He was spending less and less time in college. A blind eye could be turned to a certain extent, as composers were freer than most students to come and go. Wherever Gurney was, he was producing work of great quality, but Vaughan Williams could sense that this was more than the mere inclination to work from home or a desire for solitude.

Gurney found that he could only cope with life as a student in London if he could escape it regularly, and his lack of money coupled with a desire for strenuous exercise meant that his escapes were mostly on foot. Earlier that spring, a few weeks after completing his Quartett in F, he had walked from London to Oxford, and from there back to the farm at Dryhill, despite the freezing weather. He had loved the time he'd spent working there the previous spring, and sought the stability and peace he had briefly experienced in 1919. The old symptoms of disturbance were beginning to surface, and Gurney struggled to control them. His self-loathing and frustration manifested themselves in disordered eating. He vacillated between binges on cakes ('an appetite for cakes is an expensive thing', as he ruefully pointed out), and starving himself.[1] Matilda Chapman worried that his behaviour was 'very strange sometimes lately,' implying that he had been relatively stable until this point.[2] She did not say what about his actions troubled her—he had undertaken some extremely long walks, but that alone was hardly a sign of madness. After all, the 'super-tramp' W. H. Davies

was positively fêted for his equally eccentric habits. As Gurney was almost continually composing and writing, she assumed that his difficulties arose from overwork.

With one of the ironies that characterised Gurney's life, it was just as his health was disintegrating that the College at last began to recognise his success as both a composer and a poet. Reports of the premiere of *Ludlow and Teme* had made a very favourable impression on Parry's successor Hugh Allen, and probably led to the invitation to premiere his *Western Playland* there that November. In midsummer term, two of Gurney's poems featured in the *RCM Magazine*, prominently positioned straight after the President's Address. No doubt Scott had had something to do with the placing, but a very real interest in poetry existed in the College community, led by Allen himself, and the new president couldn't fail to recognise Gurney's talent.

Gurney's inability to settle was no reflection on the institution. He found the atmosphere at the College stimulating, and was thriving under Vaughan Williams's care, but it was not enough. He craved the happiness and stable domesticity that the Harveys and the Chapmans provided, and felt that if only he could replicate it himself, he would find some anchor. His fantasies around Annie Drummond had been centred as much on the rural domestic life she would be able to provide, as on her for her own sake. Now he felt he must continue to build his dream without her, and London was not the place to do it.

A year earlier, back in June 1919, he had seriously entertained the idea of buying his own small farm, and had asked Haines if he knew of any for sale (despite having

FIG. 11.2: Gurney's cottage at Dryhill. © Eleanor Rawling.

no savings). Now, his thoughts returned to the village of Cold Slad. He remembered seeing a little abandoned cottage there when he had been working nearby at the farm at Dryhill the year before. In May 1920, he resolved to rent it and try to live there alone.[3] He decided to give up the struggle for recognition in London and become a farmer, with the occasional visit to London for a concert or two. He shared his plan with Howells, who was at a loss to know whether to encourage him or not. He would, Gurney reassured him, have the farm labour to tire his body out, and the sense of mental equilibrium which seemed to come with physical labour would be more of a help to creativity than the stagnation that settled on him when he was cooped up in London.

His plan contained elements of common sense, but it was the fantasy of a desperate man. He was so close to realising his dreams; he had moved in the right literary circles, albeit briefly, had published two collections of verse, and had had many small successes with his songs. But he was still a long way from being a recognised establishment figure, and to distance himself from musical London at this critical point was not a move that would make his career any easier. All the while he knew he was fighting an illness he did not understand, which had previously driven him to contemplate suicide and could do so again. Perhaps the peace and serenity of the countryside was indeed the best option for him.

He secured his little cottage without much difficulty; it was in such a state of disrepair that there was no competition for it. When he had been stuck in the trenches, he had dreamt of just such a little home (although ideally with fewer holes in the floor and roof):

O for a garden to dig in, and music and books in a house of one's own, set in a little valley from whose ridges one may see Malverns and the Welsh Hills, the plain of Severn and Severn Sea; to know oneself free there from the drill-sergeant and the pack, and to order one's life years ahead—plans, doubtless to be broken, but sweet secure plans taking no account of fear or even Prudence but only Joy. One could grow whole and happy there, the mind would lose its sickness and grow strong; it is not possible that health should wait long from such steady and gently beautiful ways of life.[4]

Beguiling though Gloucestershire was in spring, there was more to maintaining a property and paying for it than being in love with the surrounding countryside, and Gurney was in no real position to live alone, or afford such a move on his inadequate army pension. Neither was it terribly practical, since at that time he was still supposed to maintain some kind of presence in South Kensington until the summer holidays at least, not to mention his weekly commitment in the organ loft at High Wycombe.

It requires a little explanation, does it not? Well, in one of my fits of not being able to stand it any longer, I wrote a letter to the chief churchwarden at Wycombe, arranged for the service to be taken, and came here—to find out what might be found out. An old Cotswold stone house with one pretty good upper room, but draughty. There are holes in the floor—to be dodged. There are two square places in the roof which will need stopping. The garden was long ago a ruin, the stream dried up, and weeds grew in it; no one came save the curious; and now under the shadow of the great rise of Crickley—here am I. I am a bit afraid, but hope to earn a little somehow, enough to carry on.[5]

He had a few money-making schemes in mind, should he find that things became too desperate. A pianist was always needed for the silent cinema in Gloucester, and if all else failed, he had befriended an amiable sea captain named Browcher, who had apparently promised to take him to sea. But for now, with the summer stretching ahead, Gurney's work was progressing better than ever. He dug in his wilderness of a garden and walked the country lanes, ate when there was food to be had, and went without when there was none, and the songs came easily, for a brief while at least.

Midnight

There is no sound within the cottage now,
But my pen and the sound of long rain
Heavy and musical, I must think again
To find so sweet a noise, and cannot anyhow.

The soothingness and deep-toned tinkle, soft
Happenings of night, in pain there's nothing better,

Save tobacco, or long most looked for letter. . . ..
The different roof-sounds. House, shed, loft and scullery.[6]

The last line is a delightful example of both Gurney's scrupulous honesty and his humour; although the rhyme dictates that the poem ought to end with 'loft' (to rhyme with 'soft'), he could not bring himself to lie. There was also a scullery, and so that is what he wrote. He could have reversed the two for the completion of the rhyme, but the extension of the line, the last four syllables running on with the triplet 'scullery', are beautifully evocative of running water, flowing from a roof, whilst being comically prosaic.

He finished the last Housman settings for *The Western Playland* in his new cottage, with the sounds of the recent performance of *On Wenlock Edge* still fresh in his mind. Annie Drummond was still in his consciousness, despite the affair having been well and truly over since March 1918, and the manuscript is dedicated to her, perhaps with a pang of regret that she was not by his side, arranging flowers in a jug on the kitchen table, or sitting in an armchair by the fire in the evenings.[7] He was alone, but at least he was working. He set his first poems by Robert Graves at the cottage in July, with Graves's new collection, *Country Sentiment*, being the inspiration for all but one of his seven settings. The book had been published only that year, and Gurney no sooner bought it than he began work setting some of the texts.[8]

His isolation was not entire; it was only a short walk (by Gurney's standards) to the Harveys' house and to home cooking. Once more, The Redlands proved to be a highly conducive atmosphere for work; Gurney's cottage lacked a piano, along with most other items of furniture, and so access to the Harveys' music room was essential. The family tolerated his eccentricities, and, in the company of his old friend, he wrote prodigiously. When he was not writing or composing, night walking became a regular pastime, and the Harvey family took to leaving a window propped open through which he could come and go, as if he were some kind of nocturnal family pet. Unfortunately, he did not limit his occupations to walking, but began playing the piano in the middle of the night as well. This was directly underneath the bedroom of Harvey's Aunt Kate, who, not unreasonably, objected. 'Oh, the world is full of Auntie Kates!' was Gurney's truculent response.[9]

Back in his tumbledown cottage, Gurney was really only playing at keeping house. He was not ready to forgo the College completely, and he was obliged, and perhaps a little relieved, to give up his tenancy in order to return to the College in October. His finances were becoming a little less desperate, which was a source of great relief. By the autumn of 1920 his songs were selling well, and he was justifiably buoyed up by the confidence (and income) that this gave him.[10] 'Winthrop Rogers is not only willing to back my songs pretty hard—to take many more, but he has sold out the first edition of some of the Elizas—already! Isn't this good luck?' Winthrop

Rogers, a generous man with a pleasant New England drawl, was particularly kind to Gurney, who in turn thought him 'the most engaging publisher that ever was'. He had even advanced Gurney £20 when he had entirely run out of money at one point over the summer.[11] He then committed himself to publishing six more of Gurney's songs, and the set of five piano preludes that had been performed at the Wigmore Hall that June.[12] Finally, with a little help, Gurney was beginning to earn a living as a composer: a far more satisfactory option than running off to sea, or vamping on a cinema piano.

He had been living with the Chapmans intermittently for most of the previous year, and it was a long time for any family to accommodate a guest, let alone one as demanding as Gurney. His presence placed the family under strain, however fond of him they might have been. Edward Chapman finally lost patience with Gurney when he sneaked in during the night unannounced, only to be discovered asleep on the couch under Chapman's own coat, surrounded by the crumbs of what had been an entire tin of biscuits. His company may have been amusing, but he was beginning to outstay his welcome, and his return to his London lodgings that autumn must have been accompanied by a sigh of relief. The family was deeply fond of him, as their previous adoption offer testified, but they were not saints. At this point, they found that the odd glimpse of him at weekends was more than enough.

Gurney had spent some of his time in High Wycombe that September setting more Georgian verse: his fifth Edward Thomas song, 'Bright Clouds'; and 'Time, You Old Gipsy Man', his only setting of Ralph Hodgson's verse, which he had found in the 1915 anthology *Poems of Today* (he had met Hodgson the previous autumn). Gurney had developed as both poet and composer in the shadow of the *Georgian Poetry* collections, but to this abiding love of the 'New Elizabethans' (as they were sometimes known) he now added another: the Elizabethans themselves.

The Elizas had been his first Elizabethan triumph back in 1914, and the success of their publication as individual songs with Winthrop Rogers that summer (1920) was still fresh in his mind. Now he turned again to the same era, with Thomas Campion's 'Thrice Toss These Oaken Ashes Up in Air', and later that term, 'Come, O Come, My Life's Delight', which he dedicated to Frederick Saxty.[13]

Gurney also set Campion's 'Thou Art Not Fair', and 'Silent Music' (otherwise known as 'Rose-Cheeked Laura'), after the new year. Two settings of John Dowland's words from his songs 'I Saw My Lady Weep' and 'Fine Knacks for Ladies' were written between 1920 and 1921. Dowland, along with Thomas Campion, was one of the few examples in the history of British music of a composer writing his own texts, and the parallel with his own career would certainly not have been lost on Gurney. Robert Herrick was also in favour in November 1920, with 'To Violets' and 'Charm Me Asleep'.[14]

Gurney's return to Elizabethan verse alongside immersion in the poetry of his own time was indicative of Gurney's postwar world-view. By drawing on a society he respected for its freshness and creativity, he could suggest an ideal vision for the world of the 1920s. Gurney was in good company in his interest in the Elizabethan era as a poetic Utopia; a time when poets worked as a community towards one common ideal. Rupert Brooke had turned to them for inspiration, as had the scholar Herbert Grierson.[15] In parallel to the literary interest, a committee of musicologists were busy editing ten volumes of *Tudor Church Music*, published during the 1920s.[16] Howells had drawn from the Elizabethans in his 'Elegy' for strings and viola in 1917, written to mourn the loss of 'Bunny' Warren. In fact, Howells felt so connected to Elizabethan culture that, as he put it, he 'had this strange feeling that I belonged to the Tudor period—not only musically but in every way'.[17]

There was a common belief amongst composers and poets that as England experienced something of a second musical renaissance, the first one was a valid example on which to draw. Both Gurney and Vaughan Williams were mavericks in their different ways and appreciated the Elizabethan lack of interest in following trends. Their rather romantic view of seventeenth-century creativity was the ideal model Gurney sought for his own life and work. He maintained that the Elizabethans

> knew nothing of international celebrities or of world movements in art. . . . They did not search Europe for the latest thing in novelty. They knew better than that: they knew they only had to go into the next street and call in Mr Byrd or Mr Weelkes or Mr Wilbye, who could set our own incomparable poetry to their own incomparable music.[18]

The source of many of Gurney's Elizabethan texts was a copy of A. H. Bullen's *Lyrics from Elizabethan Song-Books*. Bullen had compiled the anthology in 1888 and republished it in 1913. He had trawled through songbooks in the British Museum to compile lyrics set by composers such as Byrd, Dowland, Weelkes and Wilbye, as a complement to the preexisting anthologies of Elizabethan verse available. It was bound to appeal to Gurney, who had long fancied himself a New Elizabethan, and from Bullen's introduction Gurney could learn about the poet-composer Thomas Campion, whose achievements represented an excellent precedent for Gurney's own dual career. The poems in Bullen's anthology were variable in standard, but a search 'for something not wishy-washy yet settable' uncovered plenty to give him inspiration.[19]

Gurney's copy of Bullen was not a new acquisition; he had been using it since at least 1917. He had already set Thomas Morley's 'Sleep, O Sleep Fond Fancy' (1920–21) from his Bullen anthology, along with Thomas Weelkes's 'Summer and Frost', 'Brown Is My Love' from the original Italian by Torquato Tasso, and John Farmer's 'Who Would Have Thought That Face of Thine'. For other Elizabethan texts, Gurney largely used Quiller Couch's 1900 classic, the *Oxford Book of English Verse*. He was particularly drawn to Jonson and Shakespeare. Shakespeare came first, and Gurney worked on eight settings in his lodgings in Earl's Court in the autumn of 1920: 'When

Icicles Hang by the Wall', 'When Daisies Pied', 'Blow, Blow, Thou Winter Wind', 'Come Away, Death', 'Orpheus with His Lute', 'Take O Take Those Lips Away,' 'Clown's Song' and 'A Sea Dirge'. They are a particularly characterful set, frequently using the pentatonic (five-note) scale favoured by both Vaughan Williams and Howells, with its strong suggestion of folk song. Gurney used the scale to flavour his harmonies, often moving away from it as the song developed, as in 'Blow, Blow, Thou Winter Wind'. 'A Sea Dirge' combines the scale with his trademark Wagnerian flavour. The first chord is an inversion of the Tristan chord, an open-ended, noncommittal place to start. Gurney's harmonies often display a natural reluctance to commit to any one key (perhaps a metaphor for the man himself), and this song is a prime example.

One of the characteristics of Gurney's mature composition is his sensitivity to keeping rhythms alive and fresh, avoiding the predictably prosaic. In his poetry he might add a syllable or a feminine ending, or alter the metre of a line to illustrate a point, or simply to avoid too complacent a rhythm. So in his music he had become adroit at steering his songs in unpredictable, original directions.[20] In a salient note on one of his poems to Scott in 1917 he had written: 'I believe the long line in the "Song of Pain and Beauty" is quite all right. It is like 3/4 after 2/4.'[21] The line in question is in italics:

> That, out of difficult ground,
> *Spring like flowers in barren deserts, or*
> Like light, or a lovely sound.

The critic E. B. Osborne, reviewing *Severn and Somme*, recognised the connection between the subtlety of Gurney's verse and his musicality: 'But the musician comes out, ... in the subtle avoidance of all jog-trot, this-way-to-market, rhythms and in the artistic management of vowel-sounds, and in the use of the diminished double rhyme (honour ... manner ... praises ... faces, and so on), all of which gives his verse an air of distinction even when he has had no time to polish it.'[22] Osborne's was an astute and observant critique. One of the characteristics shared by both Gurney's music and poetry was his negotiation between balance and 'squareness', and ingenious new shapes that constantly surprise.[23] In musical terms, to describe a piece as four-square would be to criticise it for being overly predictable. This contradiction underlies much of Gurney's composition. On the one hand, he was constantly trying to achieve balance and create a structure, but on the other, this necessity was always in tension with his inclination to disrupt what he was crafting. He worked towards something well proportioned, but inevitably inflected it with vitality, seeking to escape from the expected and formulaic, whilst working loosely within the conventions of form and harmony.[24]

Gurney found his interest in the rhythms and musicality of poetry mirrored in Gerard Manley Hopkins's verse. Both poets studied musical counterpoint, which is an unusual bond. He had come across Hopkins's poetry in *The Spirit of Man* anthology back in 1916, and was intrigued and perhaps a little puzzled by the six poems of Hopkins he found there.[25] He later borrowed Haines's copy of Hopkins's *Poems 1918*, and immersed himself in a discombobulating, liberating new world.[26] Haines records that he lent him 'the books he desired to read, books which brought him in touch with the work of Edward Thomas and Gerard Manley Hopkins, the two modern poets he most admired and those who contributed most to his literary technique.'[27]

The parallels between Hopkins's and Gurney's use of language and rhythm are striking. Gurney's 'mature' verse, as his work from this period might be termed, seems to find its own idiosyncratic voice through a peculiar blend of the excesses of Whitman, and the restrictions of Hopkins. From Whitman, Gurney took his effusiveness, open textures and interest in minute and particular detail (a trait shared with Hopkins). He mirrored Whitman's fondness for poetic lists, his long, loosely structured lines, and his love of finding poetry in the commonplace. But Whitman's syntax is often far simpler than Gurney's. In Hopkins he found a voice that enabled him to move from Georgian to the experimental and modern (despite the fact that Hopkins, a misfit in his own time, died in 1889).

Hopkins was keenly interested in music, and theorised his poetic rhythm in musical terms in the preface to his poems, published posthumously in 1918. Gurney read his copy with much interest, and it is highly unlikely he would have passed over such a discussion of poetry and musicality. Hopkins described a concept he termed 'sprung rhythm', in which poetic feet should be counted not by the number of syllables but by stress only. 'The poems in this book', Hopkins wrote, 'are written some in Running Rhythm, the common rhythm in English use, some in Sprung Rhythm and some in a mixture of the two. And those in the common rhythm are some counterpointed, some not.'[28] Much of Gurney's earlier poetry naturally finds itself in what Hopkins describes as common running rhythm ('I watched the boys of England where they went / Through mud and water to do appointed things').[29] Even in his earliest work there is, as here, often an extra foot or an alteration to the rhythm, as we might expect from a man with an innate sense of musicality. As he became more adventurous, he found in Hopkins and Whitman the authority to break free of what Ezra Pound disparagingly called the 'tum pum' of regular metre. For instance, Gurney's poem 'War Books' begins, 'What did they expect of our toil and extreme / Hunger—the perfect drawing of a heart's dream?'[30]

Verse written strictly in running rhythm becomes 'same and tame', as Hopkins put it, so he set other rhythms against the established pattern to create a counterpoint, which, when it dominates, becomes sprung rhythm. For instance, 'The sour scythe cringe and the blear share come' is a heavy, strong, six-stress line.[31] But within the same poem is a five-stress line, with a triplet upbeat:

Finger of a tender of: O of a feathery delicacy, the breast of the
Maiden could obey so,[32]

Hopkins uses sprung rhythm to allow himself space and time without breaking the rules. Such a musical understanding of the fluidity of poetic rhythm was something that preoccupied Gurney as a song composer. By virtue of setting stresses in the text to different note values, he was already creating an effect similar to that of Hopkins's sprung rhythm; offering a rhythmic counterpoint in music against which the original rhythm of the line could work.

In his poem 'When from the Curve of the Wood's Edge', Gurney experimented with both his Hopkinsian rhythmic counterpoint and the 'crazy precious diction' that had intrigued him back in 1916. It ends:

Then under the skies I make my vows
Myself to purify and fit my heart
For the inhabiting of the high House
Of Song, that dwells high and clean apart
The fire, the flood, the soaring, these the three
That merged are power of Song and prophecy.[33]

The shapes of the lines bear a strong resemblance to the opening lines of Hopkins's sonnet 'To R. B.':

The fine delight that fathers thought; the strong
Spur, live and lancing like the blowpipe flame,[34]

As Gurney's poetry developed, his thoughts returned to the war, and around 1921 he began for the first time to set the war poets themselves to music. The war had cast a long shadow over *Ludlow and Teme* and *The Western Playland*, and his musical engagement with it did not stop at using Housman as an oblique reference point. Back in July 1917, in the midst of the conflict, Gurney had eagerly anticipated the new wave of war poetry that he might be able to set one day, in place of trawling through Palgrave and Bullen for inspiration. Now his first venture was Sassoon's 'Everyone Sang', opening with an effervescent, rising melodic line, capturing the welling up of emotion and sound as 'Everyone suddenly burst out singing, and I was filled with such delight'.[35] It is easy to see why Gurney was drawn to the text; Sassoon describes a moment of unexpected musical beauty in the trenches similar to that which Gurney himself had unwittingly anticipated in his own poem 'First Time In'.

Gurney wrote prodigiously for the next two years. but his fierce productivity pushed his friends' tolerance to the limit. 'I seem to have caused a lot of people a lot of trouble, but think that the whole lump of my songs is the best of any lump.'[36] Whilst old relationships were becoming strained, other friendships developed as his literary and musical standing began to increase. Harold Monro's new literary journal *The Chapbook* provided an unlikely source of musical support to Gurney over the winter of 1920–21.[37] Monro offered to publish the song 'Desire in Spring', Gurney's triumph written whilst stranded up in the rocks in Cornwall in the winter of 1918. It appeared in print in December 1920, a few days after he had conducted at the memorial concert at the College. Gurney was becoming friendly with Monro; the correspondence over 'Desire in Spring' had resulted in their attending concerts together, so it is more than likely that Gurney frequented the Poetry Bookshop, despite there being no record of his visits.

Monro's Poetry Bookshop was the centre of poetic life in London. On Tuesdays and Thursdays, the bookshop held poetry readings, attracting other writers and the general public. The resident cats and dogs would settle down by the fire, or sidle between the legs of the solemn Monro, who looked like a 'rather serious, one might almost say dejected Guards officer', as John Drinkwater described him.[38] It was Gurney's idea of heaven—books and firelight, poetry talk and unbridled creativity, and the company of Drinkwater, Walter de la Mare, Robert Bridges and W. B. Yeats. Monro welcomed Gurney. Despite being at the epicentre of literary London, Monro was remarkably uninterested in schools of poetry or groups and lived by the high ideal of poetry being above artistic politics.[39] Gurney, full of the same enthusiasm for creativity for its own sake, found that they shared the same fundamental belief in the importance of art. Neither Gurney nor Monro could countenance an existence without poetry (and in Gurney's case, music). Monro insisted that 'I only know one thing about myself for quite certain, which amounts to this: that if anyone can imagine an earth without poetry he need not imagine me one of its inhabitants'.[40]

During the autumn and winter of 1920, Gurney was taking every opportunity to introduce himself to these influential literary and musical figures. This felt like the moment at which his name might be made, and, uncharacteristically, he was consciously setting about trying to further his reputation with a flurry of networking. His abundance of settings of the Georgians translated itself into the beginnings of friendships with many of them, and meeting the poets whose work he had read so avidly in the trenches resulted in more song settings. With all the confidence of a newly published poet, he had begun to ingratiate himself with the key players in the Georgian poetry movement. He had met Robert Graves, Edmund Blunden—'a very nice chap, and a devil for work'[41]—and the amiable, music-loving W. W. Gibson that summer. He sent John Freeman a setting of 'Last Hours', written at the Chapmans' house in 1919. Freeman was not a musician and could not play it, but asked a friend for an opinion, and the song was pronounced 'as fine as heart could wish.'[42]

Gibson in particular took to Gurney and asked him to dine with him in October.[43] Gurney pursued the contact and invited him to lunch. Gibson subsequently became something of a regular, if still polite and distant, correspondent. On one occasion

Gurney had sung him some of his settings of Gibson's poetry, probably including the darkly atmospheric 'All Night Under the Moon' (1918). There was also 'Red Roses' (March 1918), which he had written in Brancepeth at the height of his relationship with Annie Drummond, and to whom it was dedicated. Gibson had thought Gurney's songs very beautiful but felt that Gurney himself did not do justice to them (he was never a strong singer after his voice broke). Gibson sent him a copy of his 1918 collection *Whin*, and Gurney set 'The Crowder' from it almost on receipt of the book. His admiration went far beyond the point of politeness. Gibson's verse had many points of contact with Gurney's own, as he had been a strong formative influence on Gurney's developing style. Both poets were drawn to the English landscape and a nostalgia for it, and some of Gibson's war poems, such as 'Otterburn', look at the conflict from the point of view of the soldier's memory of the landscape he has left behind.

> Though low he lies in Flanders
> Beneath the Flemish mud,
> He hears through all his dreaming
> The Otterburn in flood.[44]

This tangential approach influenced Gurney's own war poetry, which often avoids focusing on the actualities of war itself, allowing memories of nature and contrasts between the French countryside and that of home to do the work instead.

That winter Gurney was firmly under Gibson's spell, and equally in thrall to Walter de la Mare.[45] Although Gurney was capable now of far outstripping either of them in terms of experimental verse, he never lost his love for the Georgians. He always retained one foot in their world, whilst writing work that began to bear more relation to the experimentation of the modernists Pound and Eliot than his more conservative friends. This was in part because the Georgians held a particularly musical attraction for Gurney. He found that their unconvoluted verse, full of rural images, lent itself ideally to song setting. Gurney's own interest in writing about landscape has led to his being mislabelled as a backward-looking poet, tarred with the same brush as the Georgians, and his strong musical association with them, along with his personal friendships and initial infatuation with their work, is at the heart of the misconception. The simplicity of their verse, when reinterpreted through music, allowed him freedom for harmonic experimentation, and was a liberation rather than a restriction. In his settings of their words, he could experiment freely in sound, just as he was beginning to explore new territory in his own verse.

De la Mare was not a new departure for Gurney, his having set 'The Scribe' in 1918.[46] His next attempt had been 'An Epitaph' (1919), which he sent to de la Mare in the spring of 1921, accompanying it with an ambiguous comment that the song had been 'long considered but a failure still'. Both songs were chosen for publication by Oxford University Press in 1938, so his was not a universally held view of the piece. 'Winter' was set in 1919, but it was a meeting with de la Mare for the first time on 6 February 1921 that inspired Gurney to return to him in earnest, de la Mare's noble poem 'Alexander' bringing out the Schubertian musical dramatist in Gurney.[47] Gurney's own poetry was often at its strongest when exploring the possibilities of opposing and contrasting spheres—landscapes of war and peace, or the relationship between beauty and abjection. In his setting of 'Alexander', he translates into music-drama his understanding of the fundamental tension between two worlds at the centre of the poem. The gravitas of Alexander and the dead calm sea is represented by bell-like sonorities, with quavers and triplets illustrating the beguiling mermaids' song. The piano acts as narrator and propels the drama forwards, and the song ends (unusually for Gurney) with a substantial piano postlude with a character of its own. The piano has embodied the pull between Alexander's authority and the magic of the mermaids throughout, and has the final word, deciding upon Alexander's music at the end.

As part of his concerted effort to make connections with other literary figures, Gurney also renewed his acquaintance with C. K. Scott Moncrieff. Moncrieff himself had been badly wounded in the war, and had been greatly affected by the death of Wilfred Owen, to whom he had been intimately attached. Moncrieff's 'Song of Roland', a translation of an anonymous, eleventh-century French epic of knights, kings and death in battle, was dedicated to Owen. 'Roland' was published in 1919, and Gurney was deeply impressed by his 'magnificent translation . . . which is iron and ringing iron at that.'[48] It may also have been at the back of his mind that Moncrieff was a very useful person to know. He was the private secretary to Lord Northcliffe, the owner of *The Times,* and also wrote reviews for G. K. Chesterton's literary magazine, the *New Witness.* To covet favour with him was a strategically useful course of action for a poet and composer looking for public recognition.

It was not just Moncrieff's literary connections that interested Gurney, however. The weeks before Remembrance Sunday in 1920 were a time of intense national mourning and commemoration. Gurney felt he wanted to write his own memorial, a commemorative piece that would be his elegy to the war. He had his eye on 'The Song of Roland' as a possible text, but in the end he decided on a purely orchestral piece. He had begun an elegy the previous year, under the more generic title 'Funeral March'. Now, prompted by the remembrance celebrations, he returned to it, and began to turn it into a work specifically associated with the conflict. Gurney completed his *War Elegy* for orchestra that November, under the watchful eye of Vaughan Williams. He found it a particularly difficult piece to write; songs posed comparatively few problems, but this longer work, he reported on 6 November, was 'a hard and futile grind.'[49]

In the autumn of 1920, at a critical moment in Gurney's struggle to finish his march, a most unusual procession wound its way slowly through central London. Families all over Britain had had to grieve for dead sons and husbands without the presence of a body or grave as the focal point for their mourning. That November, up to a million people lined the streets around Westminster Abbey to welcome the symbolic return of one soldier, the 'Unknown Warrior', chosen from six bodies exhumed from the Somme, Cambrai, Arras, the Aisne, the Marne and Ypres. The body had been selected from the six by a blindfolded officer, so total anonymity could be preserved. This was both ghoulish and remarkably painstaking, but crucial to the purpose of the ceremony; if the unknown warrior could have come from anywhere on the Western Front then he could be every son, brother, lover, husband, father. Representing all those who would never return, he provided a focus for relatives' grief. It was a moment of pure theatre that captivated the nation and its composers, poets and artists. Composer Marion Arkwright wrote a musical account of the body returning on HMS *Verdun*, 'Through the Mist', and Alfred Noyes quickly wrote 'The Passing of the Unknown Warrior' for the *Daily Mirror* to publish the day after the event. Gurney's own views on Armistice Day were, like many others', a complex combination of relief, anger, sorrow and anxiety for the future. He was to write a number of poetic responses to the armistice, from his 1918 poem 'The Day of Victory' onwards. Now, two years later, he was moved to put his emotions into music.

The *Elegy* begins with a trudging figure, around which Gurney weaves a darkly subdued counterpoint in the strings, followed by a plaintively meandering melody, introduced by a solo clarinet. His eclectic influences make for some curious bedfellows on occasion; elements of modernism are absorbed into an Edwardian Elgarian style, alongside flirtations with European turn-of-the-century composers. The *Elegy* has the same inclination as Mahler, Nielsen and Sibelius to find its way through chromatic shifts; even at the beginning of the 1920s Gurney was prepared to entertain quite adventurous dissonance. The subject matter of war clearly evinces this, but Gurney must have been disappointed by Marion Scott's reaction. Scott had established a reputation as a music critic, but for all her championing of contemporary music and of Gurney himself, she found this new work too progressive for her tastes. Her verdict in print on the piece was uncharacteristically uncharitable:

> The themes are heartfelt and sincere, their treatment is grave and sensitive, and the opening and closing sections of the work are eloquent. Toward the middle, the music loses its grip and wanders around rather than holds the direct onward flow. It will probably gain by being rewritten.[50]

This was a rather unfair analysis. The *Elegy* is more successful than the *Rhapsody* largely because of its well-defined structure and fluent scoring, which is rich rather than heavy. Such statements as Scott's have contributed to the assumption that Gurney was incapable of structuring a longer work. *A Gloucestershire Rhapsody* does little to help the case for the defence, but the *War Elegy* and many of his chamber works demonstrate compellingly that this was not the whole story. We cannot date the *Rhap-*

sody more accurately than 1919–21, but if it was written before the *Elegy*, it might be tempting to see the latter as a reaction to the *Rhapsody*'s overly loose structure.

By January Gurney was back for the spring term of 1921, and writing two songs for violin and voice. Both took Elizabethan texts from his much-used *Oxford Book of English Verse*: Robert Wever's 'In Youth Is Pleasure' and Robert Herrick's 'Lullaby'. At the same time, he wrote 'May Carol' for violin, and further violin works followed, with a slow movement based on Webster's play 'The Duchess of Malfi'. Again he attempted a more substantial work, a sonata in G major.[51] The work owed a heavy debt to Brahms's G major sonata, being written 'in imitation more or less' of it, but 'if the imitation is so far below the model, yet there seems to me to be some Englishness in the music.'[52]

Gurney himself describes this sonata in G as his fourth. He had always been interested in writing violin sonatas, with three attempted as early as 1910–13 (only one exists now in full; it is unclear whether the other two were finished). Until Margaret Hunt's death in 1919, he had been able to write for the Hunt sisters as a violin and piano duo. He had returned to the genre whilst convalescing at St Albans in the summer of 1918, and his superb sonata in E flat had been finished under the first term of Vaughan Williams's supervision in 1919. There were numerous scherzos and single movements of sonatas dating from between 1918 and 1921 that indicate the beginning of work on more (there is no record of whether he finished them), but the existence of these movements shows that he remained consistently interested in writing major works for violin and piano throughout his career. Gurney is, of course, known primarily as a song composer, and this constant thread of violin writing is a largely overlooked aspect of his work. Yet he continued to write violin sonatas until as late as 1926—a violin piece was to be amongst the last of his works.

For now, the distraction of hard work was just about enough to maintain a fragile mental equilibrium. It was the one constant in his unsettled existence, and although composing larger works cost him a great deal of effort and heartache, the act of writing was cathartic. As he wrote to Harvey, when his sonata was nearing completion: 'Despairing work is the noblest refuge against other despairs after all.'[53]

Gurney turned to Harvey, both as provider of friendship and congenial accommodation and as a source of poetry to set. Now, early in 1921, as he wrestled with his violin sonata, he began Harvey's 'Riddle cum Ruddle' but abandoned the draft early on and wrote a melodious setting of 'Country Love Song' instead. He also set Harvey's 'Dinny Hill'. At the same time, he was thinking about writing some lighter songs, as a money-making enterprise. It might be that his return to Harvey's verse had given him the idea; when Harvey was in lighthearted and humorous vein, his poetry lent itself perfectly to 'popular' art song. Gurney reserved those poems of Harvey's such as 'In Flanders' and 'A Song of Walking' that referred to their beloved Gloucestershire for his serious settings—his adoration of his hills and meadows was no laughing matter. But he recognised that if Harvey could write witty, memorable verse that found instant popularity, then perhaps he could create the equivalent in music.

His setting of Harvey's 'Country Love Song' was a perfect example of a simplified art song—with the charm and accessibility of such enduringly popular (and lucrative) songs as Vaughan Williams's early success, 'Linden Lea'. 'Country Love Song' is a far simpler setting than Gurney's usual work. The first half of the song is completely nonchromatic, but, as if he cannot quite bring himself to write anything too banal, he builds in a descending chromatic line in the reprise to add some spice. He did not put his own name to it, deciding, for the first time, to try writing under a pseudonym. He was building up a relationship with respected publishers such as Stainer and Bell and Winthrop Rogers, and he was keen to distance himself from any less serious songs he might write. Gurney signed the score as John Winterton, toyed with altering his persona to Griffiths Davies, but then scrubbed out both and settled on Michael Flood. He then returned to his new alter ego Winterton to write a comic song with an Elizabethan text: Nicholas Udall's 'Ralph Roister Doister'. Posing as Michael Flood, he wrote 'At the Jolly Blue Boar', a poem by Kenniston H. Wynne, and 'Cowslip Time', with a text by Winifred Mary Letts.[54] Gurney also set 'The Fair' by Letts, this time expanding his new identity to give himself a rather ostentatious middle name: Michael Raphoe Flood.[55]

Back in 1917, when the battalion had been at rest in the beautiful orchards of Buire au Bois, Gurney had been particularly struck by the success of the 2/5ths' makeshift concert party troupe, the Cheeryohs. He had seen firsthand the pleasure their music hall songs had given the other men. He knew he could write music influenced by folk songs, and he had already turned his hand to ballads and sea shanties successfully. It was a natural progression of thought to turn to popular song, with an eye to the profits he might make. If his old organ loft accomplice Ivor Novello could make a fortune writing catchy tunes, then why not the other Ivor? He settled on the name of his godfather Cheesman's great friend Frederick Saxty (who had recently been working in America), and wrote a whole host of jazzy, accessible settings of Louis How's *Nursery Rhymes of New York City*. Seven date from 1921–22, and two from 1925. The poems are written as witty nursery rhymes, intended for adults, and Gurney matches the tone of the poems with harmonically simple settings.[56]

They are perfectly plausible and engaging songs with immediate appeal, but they betray Gurney's training and high musical and imaginative standards. They have never been published, so we cannot know whether they might have found success as the 'pot boilers' Gurney intended. However, they are clearly 'art songs', harmonically too interesting and quixotic to stand a chance of being taken up by any music hall, too mercurial and metrically a little too unpredictable. Fundamentally, the qualities that mark them out as works of quality are also those that might perhaps have doomed them to failure as trifles that would earn money, which was their purpose. Nonetheless, the songs, charming and characterful as they are, are testament to his versatility as a composer, and his ability to adapt his style convincingly.

Gurney's *Nursery Rhymes* may never have reached the public, but the 1919 song cycle *Ludlow and Teme* was now proving to be one of the biggest successes of his career. He had submitted the score to the Carnegie Trust in December 1920. Now, on 17 May, he found out that his submission had been successful and they would publish it, declaring that he had 'thoroughly entered into the spirit of the poem[s]'. It was an insightful comment that was bound to cause the composer much delight. They continued in their praise: 'The songs are tuneful, expressive and well contrasted, and should prove a valuable addition to the repertoire of the concert room.'[57] His pleasure was perhaps slightly tempered by his suspicions that Scott had had a hand in his being selected.[58] With or without Scott's lobbying (and there is no indication that she would have held any real influence over the panel), it was still a significant vote of confidence. Sixty-seven pieces had been submitted, and only seven, including Gurney's, were chosen for publication.[59]

This was the recognition he had long felt was his due, and had seemed to be endlessly forthcoming for Howells and others. Now Gurney's name was listed in the Carnegie's catalogues along with Bliss and Arnold Bax, and he could, momentarily at least, claim his place as a central figure in the new generation of British postwar talent. The boost to his confidence resulted in some more ambitious chamber music; in the last weeks of the summer term at the College, Gurney wrote a piano trio in C sharp minor, his first since a scherzo in 1913–14.[60] He was not to return to the medium for another two years. Around the same time, he branched out further, with his first of only two pieces for cello, a sonata in E minor.[61] His violin sonatas were often heavily modelled on Brahms's contributions to the genre, and so was this cello sonata. Gurney could not fail to be aware of the gloriously dark and stormy sonata by Brahms in the same key, but his own work bears little obvious resemblance to Brahms's, and is more sensitive to the difficult balance issues between cello and piano than the music of his hero. We do not know whether he finished the sonata, but only one movement now exists. It is attractive and interesting enough to have merited a place in the cello repertoire, had it been published.

Under Vaughan Williams's supervision, the songs had been flowing 'like buttermilk from a jug', as he had once described his newly found poetic talent. In output at least, he was a model composition student. But as a member of the Royal College's student body, he was an unpredictable liability. After a total of eighteen terms, both he and the College acknowledged that it would be best to end his studentship rather than continue his studies in such an erratic fashion. Gurney left the College officially at the end of the summer term of 1921, although really he had hardly been in attendance for months.[62] It was a respectable length of study—approximate to Howells's time there, and during his student years he had developed beyond recognition despite, or perhaps because of, the interruptions. He had first entered the institution in 1911 as an ambitious undergraduate with a bundle of compositions under one arm, ready to take on the world. Now, ten years later, he finally left for good; a wiser and more accomplished composer, but with no formal graduation, or any qualification. Nevertheless, he did not leave having been abandoned by the institution. In the brief time he had been his pupil, Gurney had firmly established his friendship with Vaughan Williams, and his teacher's support, both financially and emotionally, was to continue for the remaining sixteen years of Gurney's life. And Gurney would always have a direct link to the College through Scott, who, as president of the Royal College of Music Union, could keep him up to date with developments.

Gurney had given up his rented lodgings in Earl's Court and returned to Gloucester, but living at home again was hardly an enticing prospect. The fact that he had not even completed his degree was hardly likely to impress either his brother or mother. However, Gloucester still exerted its magnetic pull over him, wherever he found himself living: 'Gloucester is simply wonderful. . . . Home it is for anybody at first sight.'[63] The usual haven at The Redlands was the obvious option, but there was no Harvey there anymore; he was to marry his fiancée Anne Kane that April and was hardly about to ask Gurney to join them in their first few months of marriage. Harvey's changed status from bachelor to married man was a source of some consternation for Gurney. He liked Anne well enough, declaring her 'very nice and very Irish', but his reluctance to lose his closest confidante was palpable. He could only imagine Harvey 'stoically-cheerfully' contemplating the prospect of marriage, and a year later, when Harvey briefly returned home with his new family in tow, Gurney was painfully aware that he could no longer command Harvey's full attention. 'The baby was in bed, but he still is F.W.H. and is incomparable. It was an evening of friends, but not alone. The long evenings of music-and-book talk seem to have vanished—quite essential to any joyful making of art.'[64]

The loss of his unfettererd access to Harvey left an emotional void for Gurney, that could not easily be filled. His friendships with the Harveys and Chapmans were becoming increasingly strained, and Emmy Hunt was far too respectable to propose he live with her, despite her loneliness after her sister Margaret's death. Haines was a great companion but was not volunteering free accommodation. As luck would have it, an aunt stepped in. Aunt Marie (who was in fact an Edith, but not a fan of the name) was a warm-hearted, Welsh lady approaching sixty, who had lived alone since her second husband, Guy Gurney, died in 1913. She owned a little house in Westfield Terrace in the village of Longford, on the outskirts of Gloucester. Gurney's sister Winifred was already staying there for a brief interval before her training as a midwife began. Marie's quiet, unassuming hospitality was just what he needed, and Longford was intermittently to be his home until September 1922.

FIG. 11.3: Outside Aunt Marie's house in Westfield Terrace, holding his sister
Dorothy's dog. Courtesy of Noel Hayward, from the photograph album
belonging to Dorothy Gurney.

It was a sleepy little village, just far enough from Gloucester to feel separate from
home, but near enough for frequent visits to friends. Gurney could cycle out in any
direction and be in the landscape he loved within moments; on one side were the
Cotswolds, on the other the Severn flowed by. Aunt Marie's house was surrounded
by meadows, which in spring were full of daffodils, and Gurney had moved in at just
the right time to see them flower. It seemed, superficially at least, to be ideal, but
both nephew and aunt knew the arrangement was unlikely to be permanent. He was
painfully aware that he was prevailing upon her kindness, and the sense of debt ran
deep. His return to Gloucestershire should have been to his own little cottage, a
dream that had briefly seemed so close to realisation the previous summer.[65]

The tranquillity of the place gave Gurney the chance to work at some considerable
speed, although being surrounded by such countryside was a temptation and inspiration. He would often abandon work late at night to roam out into the fields or down to
the river, and revel in the sunrise, the slowly changing skies so much more beautiful than
the watery imitation of sunrise over London. His poem 'Longford Dawns' begins:

Of course not all the watchers of the dawn
See Severn mists like forced-march mists withdrawn

London has darkness changing into light
With just one quarter hour of any weight.[66]

Gurney was one of many unemployed, and he found an alternative community amongst them in which he could briefly feel accepted. At night men would fish for baby eels, as elvers were a favourite dish among the working-class households in Gloucester. This nocturnal community held the dual attractions of watery landscape and male comradeship for Gurney, and he wrote a brief account of it, unusually in prose rather than poetry:

> It was about half past two, when the stars were all hidden behind a curtain of cloud, that I first came down to the river between elms and willows and saw the candle lanterns shining up and down and making paths of light on the etched current.
>
> It was a stumbling sort of progress in the dark, but at last I reached two men by the remains of a fire, talking dolefully about the state of things, their nets held in position by short stakes.
>
> Elvers, it appeared, were swimming badly that night and all the cigarettes had gone. Unemployment was a dreary subject, even when the job missed was chain making—a hard thing. Their catch was very poor even after three hours of alternate sitting and rising up under that steep bank. Elvers are caught in a net rather like that used in lacrosse but larger. The thing is laid in shallow water for two minutes or so and then raised by a long handle, drained, turned over and emptied into a bucket. The price of these tiny things—mere bits of white string a couple of inches long—is 6d a pound just at present. It is easy to dispose of them: the poorer folk of Gloucester being very fond of such queer looking things: fried in bacon and much talked of. Men go round the streets with a barrel full of white seethingness crying 'Elvers O' and such folk as have no reputation for aristocracy to lose flock out and buy.[67]

Gurney was still obliged to put in the odd reluctant appearance at Christ Church, High Wycombe, and in July took up a temporary residence in a nearby inn called the Five Alls, in Studley Green, to make the commute a little easier. He found the organist post entirely disagreeable, but the Chapmans provided diverting company, as always. He was also in cycling distance of Robert Graves at Boars Hill and decided to pay him a visit. He turned up very late at night and was about to slink away after one knock, when Graves opened the door in his pyjamas. Instead of turning him away, Graves invited Gurney in and entertained him until past midnight with stories of Sassoon's great bravery during the war.[68] From the Five Alls, Gurney cycled the thirty miles into London to spend evenings with de la Mare, who was persistently bountiful in his supply of literary talk and books.

Gurney was in urgent need of work, as well as intellectual sustenance. Two school posts came to nothing, and he was trying to find employment at the docks. He had almost entirely run out of money despite his pension, and whilst Scott and Vaughan Williams could subsidise him, neither of them was prepared to support him entirely. He left his aunt's house for London that summer and managed to secure a thoroughly unprepossessing post as a casual labourer in a cold storage depot for meat. Jobs were scarce, with a generation of ex-servicemen trying to find employment, and Gurney was lucky to have the fortnight's trial. It was hardly pleasant work, surrounded by great swinging carcasses of animals, but it did have the small advantage of being right next to the Thames. He found lodgings with a Mrs Poole nearby in Southwark and alternated between day and night shifts. When resting, he spent his time observing the light changing on the water, as the river flowed 'boastfully under Cannon St Railway Bridge'. He could also acquaint himself with the underbelly of London life, the forgotten parts of society who congregated around the river at night, an urban parallel to his elver fishers who haunted the banks of the Severn.

The cold storage work was only ever a temporary stopgap, and he was soon back with Aunt Marie, as no further employment was to be had in London. All was 'not well' with him, as he admitted to friends in his letters, without being more explicit. Walks to places such as Crickley, where he had previously found peace, were the best medicine on offer, and Gloucester held the additional benefit of compassionate and concerned friends who had his best interests at heart. Jack Haines was keeping a close eye on him and became his guardian, walking companion and source of poetry talk. Since April, Jack Haines, Gurney and their mutual friend W. P. Kerr had been meeting regularly at each other's houses to talk poetry and to sing, with Gurney accompanying them. Kerr was, by profession, a tax inspector, but by inclination he was a witty writer: a published poet and literary journalist. This was Gurney's own musical version of the Dymock poets' prewar cosy coterie, of which Haines himself had been on the fringes.[69] After so many months wishing he could sit by the glow of a fire and enjoy the luxury of talking books and music with his friends, Gurney's chance had finally come, for however brief a span. These were sublime evenings. 'Praise God for Poetry—it is a good thing and fills up spaces in landscape and life with human interest and memory', Gurney had written to Haines from St Albans back in 1918.[70] Now he was at liberty to exalt in poetry to his heart's content. Haines later remembered how Gurney's eyes flashed when he began on his extravagant arguments, often so forcefully put as to be violent. 'There are only two poets in the English language, Shakespeare and Edward Thomas', he would contend, but with his formidable gift for conversation, he was able perhaps not to convince, but at least to have such extreme views seriously considered.[71] His opinions may have been idiosyncratic, but his friends agreed that he was a fascinating companion, and his conversation and passion for his subject enlivened their evenings together. Haines considered him to be the most 'dynamic creature' he had ever met.[72]

All four men were united by their poetic ambition, but in terms of professional standing, Gurney as an unemployed cold storage worker was most certainly the odd one out. The others were firmly white-collar professionals: Harvey and Haines were both respected solicitors, and Kerr was a tax collector. In 1921, they were enjoying varying degrees of success. Gurney now had two books to his name, and the added kudos of his compositions. Harvey had an impressive five volumes to his name, almost one a year since *A Gloucestershire Lad* in 1916. Kerr had been included in numerous anthologies, but had worked hard for his success, with Gurney sympathising with him in 1919 as the manuscript of his poetry collection was returned for the sixth time. He was a stimulating companion and in conversation had much in common with Gurney, who admired him as 'the most provocative and amusing of talkers (Quite reckless).'[73] Haines, older than the other three by some years, had the glamour of the Dymock poets and his friendships with Edward Thomas and Robert Frost to offer, as well as the kudos of his own *Poems*, published that year.[74]

There were, of course, the walks. Haines and Gurney often went on excursions, tramping for more than thirty miles at a time across the Welsh mountains, with Haines (a keen botanist) identifying wildflowers, just as he had done on his walks with Robert Frost, before Frost had returned to America. Although Gurney never met either Frost or Thomas, he knew he was close to both through Haines. Gurney admired Thomas's poetry to extravagance, and it may well have been an essay Haines had published on Thomas that first drew Gurney's attention to his verse. Haines had a photo of Thomas in his book room, at which Gurney would glance up adoringly during their evenings of literary discussion.

Gurney insisted that poetry was helped by walking and would often cite Wordsworth as having believed the same. Why was it, he would ask, that so few English poets walk?[75] When the countryside was not beckoning, he would sit at Haines's piano for hours with a poetry book on his lap, setting Robert Graves or some other fortunate to music. Spending so much time with Haines, it was inevitable, perhaps, that over the summer of 1921 he should start setting Haines's own verse. But it never appealed to him as much as Harvey's (of whose poems he set fifteen), and he set only two of Haines's, 'Fair Lady's Mantle' and 'The High Road'.

As the autumn of 1921 wound on, Gurney's poverty became more extreme. Jobs were hard enough to come by, and jobs in music were scarcer still. He tried his hand at reviewing, a line of work that Marion Scott had always found lucrative. He wrote a handful of reviews, including one of Lady Florence Darwin's six *Cotswold Plays*, which was published in March 1922 in the *Times Literary Supplement*, the publication that had sustained him in the trenches with its juicy titbits of contemporary poetry.[76] That December he managed to secure a post vamping away on a 'perfectly beastly' organ in a cinema in Plumstead, southeast London, with a respectable salary of £4 a week.[77] His relief was immense. Unfortunately, the appointment did not last long, although his dismissal after only the fortnight's trial did not come as a surprise to him. He had confided to Harvey that he was 'not sure of it', and that both he and his work were 'quite upset'. Clearly he was not functioning well enough to be able to do the job justice. He hung around in London until he ran out of money, and then, once again, was obliged to return to his aunt. He managed to find another post as a cinema organist. This time it was in Bude, and he was to commence in the new year. He moved down to Cornwall before the job started in anticipation of what looked to be a more permanent post. Walks along the coastline and the prospect of new employment combined to create ideal conditions for composition. Gurney wrote four of what would eventually be his *Five Songs of Rupert Brooke*: 'The Treasure', 'There's Wisdom in Women', 'One Day' and 'Song'.

He was delighted with his new life in the Cornish harbour town: 'Anything better than being a Bard among fisher-folk could hardly be imagined.'[78] But his enthusiasm was tempered by his recent experience, and he admitted he found cinema posts 'fearful to retain, easy to lose.'[79] He was right to have worried. The appointment lasted a mere week before he was summarily dismissed. He wrote to Harvey that 'it was for opening merely a dash for the first week; local talent took on afterwards', but whatever the justification, it was becoming only too obvious that Gurney was unemployable.[80] Even so, the trial period of only a week gave Haines the opportunity to act as Gurney's lawyer and win him £10 compensation for 'wrongful dismissal'.[81] Vaughan Williams, who knew what the appointment had meant to Gurney, wrote to him in sympathy: 'I'm so sorry Bude was a bad egg'.[82]

Gurney returned to live at his aunt's house in Gloucester, demoralised and penniless, but he did at least have his Thomas settings to show for the experience, and he wrote a setting of Rupert Brooke's 'Clouds' the following month. He had set Brooke's 'Heart's Pain' in the autumn the previous year and now rewrote it specifically for the set. He sent the cycle to Edward Marsh with a letter whose tone—a mixture of bumptiousness and despair—indicates his growing problems.

> I send under title of 5 Songs of Rupert Brooke, 4 settings, of which I do not think very much, but they are probably better than those of most folk. . . .
>
> If you care to get these sung to you, I can believe you would like them, though mere carpentry in the doing. I am fond enough of 'When Colour goes home' to wish to have done that with some sprite in me, but could not.[83]

Edward Marsh, generally known as 'Eddie', was at this time Churchill's secretary at the Colonial Office but continued his private role as a liberal patron and friend of contemporary arts and artists. He had been devoted to Rupert Brooke and had helped to bring about the volumes of *Georgian Poetry*. De la Mare had already discussed Gurney's increasingly desperate situation with Marsh, who was keen to help, but Gurney did not want charity; he hoped Marsh would be able to help him to a job. Marsh decided to offer financial help for now at least, and the Brooke settings may well have been a strategic choice, intended as a gesture of thanks.

The new year of 1922 began with what should have been a high point in Gurney's calendar. On 30 January Marion Scott, ever keen to promote Gurney's work, engaged the baritone Clive Carey to sing some of Gurney's songs for a musical soirée at her home. He premiered 'Walking Song', written in 1920, de la Mare's 'The Scribe' and James Stephens's 'The County Mayo' (both 1918). Harvey took part too, reading some of Gurney's poems. It was one of the few times that his music and poetry had been performed together, although it is curious that Gurney chose not to read himself. Harvey was perhaps the more theatrical and, considering Gurney's stage fright after the premiere of *Ludlow and Teme* at Scott's in 1920, they may both have felt it better if Harvey made the public appearance on his behalf. The evening was not a resounding success; Carey was not in good voice, and Gurney could report being pleased with only one or two of the renditions of his songs.

Gurney's mental stability was ever precarious, but the combination of his dire financial straits, continual scrabbling for work and summary dismissals was not helping. His health was deteriorating, and his increasingly shambolic appearance reflected his distress. His long-suffering aunt Marie had to put up with comments from her neighbours about her unsightly houseguest, coming in and out at all hours of the day and night. Gurney's mother was mortified at the state of her son. Florence had always been keen for the family to progress socially, and laid great store by appearance and respectability.[84] Now her much fêted composer-son had returned to Gloucester, and instead of the wunderkind of whom she had boasted, he appeared to be little more than an insane tramp. Winifred recalled how 'Gloucester people would form their own opinions seeing him about and knowing who he was, at a time when he was at his worst, not only in health but in appearance. In this he was difficult and a great worry.'[85]

However shocked his family might have been, they knew that this latest development was far from uncharacteristic. When asked in later life about Gurney, fellow chorister William Bubb recalled with conviction that 'Gurney had always been batchy—it wasn't the war' ('Batchy' is a charming Gloucestershire colloquialism for deranged, or bizarre).[86] Victor Curtis, a boy seven years younger than Gurney, who knew him through the community at All Saints' Church in Gloucester, remembered that 'we all knew him as Crazy'.[87] Winifred recalled her memories of her brother as a schoolboy: 'Ivor always seemed in a dream. More often than not he would be walking down the gutter as if looking for something, his cap all sideways, peak over one eye.'[88] Gurney had never had any desire to conform, even if he had had the ability to.

Even as a schoolboy he cultivated an aloof, bohemian identity, making as little effort to blend in as he would in institutions in years to come.

Marie was well aware that there was no one else within the family prepared to offer refuge to her eccentric nephew, but she was also aware of how grateful he was for her kindness. Gurney was always ready to take from friends and relatives, whether it was food, money or networking opportunities. But, to his credit, he was of a naturally generous disposition himself, and was always keen to express his thanks. He dug Marie's little garden by way of recompense for her hospitality. His mother Florence was hostile towards him, and Gurney was barely able to remain in the same room as her and her domineering criticism. In Marie he found a female relative who respected his need for freedom and allowed him the peace to write, whether or not she understood the work he produced. He would drink tea, write, smoke and lose himself in the Elizabethans. She would leave him to it and retire to bed, coming down in the morning

> fresh-cheeked for all her years,
> To find me writing, and I'd smile and talk my thanks,
> Lie down, covered with a rug for one hour, with eyes clear as on high
> Cotswold there.[89]

Marie was hardly a rich woman, and however generous she might have been, she could not be recompensed indefinitely by gratitude and gardening. By February 1922, Gurney was trying to find work as a labourer on a farm. Money was constantly on his mind. He was lost, but the irony was that his writing, particularly as a composer, was now consistently of the highest standard. Instead of fame and recognition, the last twelve months had brought home to him the humiliating truth that he had to depend on other people for even the basics of living.

Aid was to come from an unexpected source. Sir Alexander Kaye Butterworth wrote to Marion Scott offering £25 to help Gurney to continue further study. It was a gift given in memory of his own son, the talented young composer and Royal College graduate George Butterworth, who had been killed on 5 August 1916 at Pozières on the Somme, only a few miles from where Gurney had been stationed at Albert. The sector of trench that he had died holding had been named in his honour, but his body had been lost in the fighting. His father had nothing but his compositions, and a name etched on the 'missing' section of the Thiepval Memorial with which to remember George.[90]

Gurney's poor state of health was obviously common knowledge, since Butterworth wrote that 'I understand that Mr Gurney is still suffering from the effects of shell shock'. He also suggested that it would be best if Marion Scott took charge of disbursing the money (evidently aware that Gurney was not fit to manage his own finances). It was a generous and fitting gesture. George Butterworth's music had close similarities with Gurney's. Initially Sir Alexander had not supported his son's decision to become a composer, but after his death he championed his compositions, and came to recognise the extent of his talent. He would have seen in Gurney a young man developing a soundworld similar to that of his son, but struggling to reach his creative maturity. As Sir Alexander saw it, Gurney had the opportunity to continue the development that had been denied to George, and he wanted to help him.

Gurney was pathetically grateful for such handouts, but being supported by the combined charities of Marion Scott, Vaughan Williams and Butterworth was hardly conducive to self-respect. He was becoming increasingly anxious, 'living on charity being most dreadful'.[91] Considering Gurney's abilities and education, the menial nature of the jobs that he sought seems puzzling. However, even for those who were mentally stable and fully functional, it was difficult to obtain any sort of job in the postwar years. Gurney shared the national sense of disillusionment and postwar disappointment intensely, and it found its way into his poetry, as a sense of betrayal, or as he put it, a 'fierce indignation'.[92] He had spoken for the Gloucesters during the war through his verse. Now, inadvertently, he was becoming the poetic spokesperson for the unemployed, damaged and embittered ex-servicemen whose ranks he had been forced to join.

CHAPTER TWELVE

'Below the Horizon'

Gurney's inability to find any paid work was demoralising enough, but now distress came from another source, as he increasingly felt ignored and unrewarded as a poet. He had no part to play in the literary renaissance happening around him. The transition in his letters is stark. In 1919 his hopes for the future had been high:

> Don't the old book [*War's Embers*] read well in print though? Don't it look business-like, tight and right? Well I think we are both entitled to be pleased at the result of our 'doos'.[1]

Only three years later, he could dismiss any thoughts of a future in a single line:

> But had war hopes proved anything well,—Well it is no use thinking.[2]

There was one journal, the *London Mercury*, that would prove supportive of Gurney's work. Gurney had met its editor John Collings (or simply J. C.) Squire that autumn (1921), probably through their mutual friend, Haines. Squire had begun his editorship of the *London Mercury* in 1919, which aimed to represent some of the best contemporary poetry, and Gurney quickly realised he was a useful person to know. Squire had himself been published in Eddie Marsh's *Georgian Poetry*, and the *Mercury* endeavoured to continue something of the ethos of that hugely successful series. The periodical was a substantial volume, which divided itself between new poetry, book reviews, short stories and essays on literary subjects. Gurney first appeared in its pages with 'Encounters' and 'The March Past' published in the October 1922 issue.

Squire, who was to become so influential in literary circles that he was accused of managing a 'Squirearchy', was to remain faithful to Gurney. He would publish over two dozen of his poems in the *London Mercury*. But as Gurney had written ruefully to Marion Scott in October 1919 after a particularly painful meeting with Edward Shanks, who was then working as a reviewer for the *Mercury*:

Shanks told me that Squire thought me the best of the young men below the horizon, which led to a natural question as to why he had rejected so much lately.[3]

Below the literary horizon was all too accurate, and it was a position and a problem which was about to get worse than he could have imagined.

Gurney's biggest poetry project, and the one in which he placed most faith, was the collection of poems which he sent in May 1922 to his publishers Sidgwick and Jackson. He casually called the pages he posted to them '80 poems or so' (they were finally published under that title in 1997). His apparent nonchalance belied the investment he really had in the collection. His sister Dorothy had typed out a selection of his poems in April, and it was poems taken from this group that he sent to the publishers. They returned the sheaf of papers on the ninth of May— the very day they received it—and asked 'for revisions and reductions'. Frank Sidgwick's letter was not unreasonable:

> I am sorry to return this MS., but it won't do for publication, for several reasons. First, it is far too long, and the process of selection is your business, not ours. But more important, I cannot help feeling that the poems are unfinished, uncorrected, unpolished as they are certainly unpunctuated. These things should not be left to the reader. I don't care how hard you make the reader's *literary* difficulties, but you must place him in possession of the facts.
>
> Amongst the MSS. received this morning, which you sent with a letter which broke off in the middle of a word and forgot to sign, was a sheet headed 'Midnight' followed by the single line:—
> 'There is no sound within the cottage'
> What are we to make of that? If it is the whole poem, it strikes us as inadequate.
>
> I hope I don't write unsympathetically, but it is so clear that there is poetry lurking behind your work that it becomes more vexatious to find these brambles across the path. The whole MS. is more like a poet's notebook than a volume of finished poems.[4]

Gurney was clearly not functioning normally, and in the circumstances Sidgwick's response is kind and mildly encouraging. Although Gurney seemed to be trying to take his literary career into his own hands, he reported the rejection to Marion Scott, but still maintained 'O there's good stuff there!' and buckled down to correct and select from the poems.[5] He quickly got the poems ready for resubmission by the 10th of May, but did not like to seem too eager, and delayed 'for form and coyness sake'.[6] He sent them off as a collection of forty poems in June. It was to little purpose. Once more, Sidgwick rejected them:

> I am sorry to return again the MS. 'Forty Poems' but we are unable to see any improvement in it save for a slight reduction in length. The whole thing wears, to us, a haphazard appearance; the true stuff is there, but it doesn't shine out as it should, and much of it seems unmusical. I fear we cannot offer publication.[7]

Surely Sidgwick knew of Gurney's musical compositions, so the accusation of his poetry being 'unmusical' seems a deliberate slight on both Gurney's arts. He seemed to be applying a criterion which sat more happily with the, by then, rather outdated Georgian mode. Gurney's poems were much more unpredictable both rhythmically and in their language and associations, and thus far more in key with the latest of contemporary poetry than the Georgians, despite his respect for them. Sidgwick's notions of what was 'musical' were not the same as Gurney's, who was reaching for far more experimental and surprising ideas in both genres.

It was not that Gurney could not compose conventionally 'musical' verse. The manuscript of *80 Poems or So* contains numerous poems which have a wistful beauty, like the first stanza of 'Coming Dusk', which is draped in the same blue mists of the horizon as A. E. Housman's celebrated 'blue remembered hills':

> Blue is the valley, blue the distant tower,
> And Cotswold drapes in mist behind the azure;
> In April has there come November's hour,
> And there is melancholy beyond measure.

But what Gurney is introducing, and Sidgwick probably reacting against, is a much tougher line, and a more uncompromising attitude, encapsulated in the startling little poem 'April Gale', with its condensed images pared down to the bone, and its unexpectedly violent last line, which in only a handful of words gestures towards a world of pain and struggle:

> The wind frightens my dog, but I bathe in it,
> Sound, rush, scent of the Spring fields.
>
> My dog's hairs are blown like feathers askew,
> My coat's a demon, torturing like life.[8]

What is more, the people and city places which Gurney chose to describe were not quite acceptable in poetry, although there had been poets such as Gibson whose work had embraced such inelegant and gritty material even before the war. Gurney was, by now, much more than a rural poet. He had the images of the trenches seared into his brain, but also a thoroughly unsentimental appreciation of London and rural living, learned from night shifts at the cold storage depot, and sharing the hopelessness of the many ex-servicemen looking for work. Uncomfortable rough sleeping became matter-of-fact poetic material:

> Lockhart's shows lively up Whitefriars Lane,
> Sleepers beside the river change their pain,
> (Summer is better now the cloak's in pawn)
> And the first careful coffee-stall's withdrawn.[9]

Just as Eliot's *The Waste Land* was to jar with many readers, Gurney's lively excitement, both of versification and content of poems such as 'The Road' would have jarred with a more conventional editor:

> Or in one hour of joys
> When football plays
> Marvellous music on these jigging heart-strings,
> And one lucky kick brings
> Battle-winning in a Niagara of noise—
> Or some furtive
> Trick of professionalism
> Plunges a crowd in Hell's
> Own tumult and scorn and hot-alive
> Furious cataclysm—
> The referee quells.[10]

This was verse that had gone beyond the Georgian, nodding to Thomas, but proceeding in what seemed like a more random fashion with its own idiosyncratic, tempo-changing metre. It was a lonely place to be. Other poets such as Lawrence and Eliot were established enough to be given the benefit of the doubt in their rhythmic and structural experimentation. Gurney was not yet one of their hallowed ranks, and his irregular, challenging verse was too much for Sidgwick.

Gurney needed to look for reassurance elsewhere. He sent 'Tewkesbury', which had just appeared in the *Gloucester Journal*, to Eddie Marsh, with the note that 'it seems good enough to myself'.[11] It is marked by characteristic cross-historic juxtapositions, odd allusiveness and changes of direction, which must have startled Marsh's rather conservative tastes. There is no record of the response of the readers of the *Gloucester Journal* when they read this:

Tewkesbury

> Some Dane looking out from the water settlements,
> If settlements there were must have thought as I,
> 'Square stone should fill that bit of lower sky.

Were I a king and had my influence,
Farms should go up for this, flames make terror go high.
But I would set my name in high eminence.'
Forthampton walking, thinking and looking to Tewkesbury.
Where a cricketer was born and a battle raged desperate,
And mustard grew, and Stratford boys early or late
May have come, and rivers, green Avon, brown Severn, meet.
And Norman Milo set a seal on the plain,
'Here man rules; his works to be found here;
Acknowledges Supremacy, his strengths to be in vain,
And gathers by a sign the broad meadows in round here.'

What is best of England, going quick from beauty,
Is manifest, the slow spirit going straight on,
The dark intention corrected by eyes that see,
The somehow getting there, the last conception
Bettered, and something of one's own spirit outshow[n,]
Grown as oaks grow, done as hard things are done.[12]

Marsh devoted three pages to a critique of Gurney's poem. Unfortunately, we do not have his criticisms but one can imagine what they must have been like. Gurney rushed to his own defence, with a mixture of pride and apology.

As for 'Tewkesbury', if you can give so much time to criticising a small poem, you must have small time for yourself. It is very considerate to take so much trouble. Anyway, I am proud of the thing; as a picture it seems to me to be first-rate. There is one foot dropped in one line—altered to 'Here man does rule, his works to be found here.' Otherwise it is a sort of Chapman verse, and that I am content with, though the Miltonic verse may be far above that in technical achievement—yet Milton does so often achieve technique only.

The difference being as between Palestrina and Byrd that Byrd was always trying to do things with his modal counterpoint—not a pure thing perhaps, but far more likeable.

It is cockeyed, but Milton would have put a Corinthian pillar or two between the village Forthampton and Tewkesbury, couldn't have got the various hints in about the history—not in the time at any rate. I suppose my blank verse to be words set to a blank verse tune, but do like
    'And gathers by a sign the broad meadows in round here'

And do like the poem as a whole very much; do not think anyone else would have drawn Tewkesbury as well.

> I am sorry to reply in so contradictatorial a fashion, being very surprised to find three sheets devoted to me, but am so sat upon, that kicking seems right.[13]

Masefield, to whom he also sent 'Tewkesbury', was much more reassuring. He thanked Gurney for the poem, 'which I like very much', and said it had 'a strange, intriguing rhythm; it is one of your very best.' He went on encouragingly: 'I'm glad you are still writing poems, you have a lovely gift.'[14] Obviously Masefield could respond to the musicality of Gurney's verse, although he had not initially been taken with the setting of his 'By a Bierside', with its extraordinary inner pulse of lengthy silences, restrained grandeur, and sudden sweeping movement. But this private praise cannot have made up for the growing pile of public rejections.

As if to rub in the fact that others had *not* been rejected, the announcement was made in *The Times* of 30 June that Blunden had been awarded the Hawthornden prize. Both the award itself and the associations for Gurney of the name could not help but remind him of other failures: Hawthornden was one of his pet names for Annie Drummond.[15] Gurney wrote to congratulate Blunden, with a letter that included a sample of his own poems as if to claim value for his own work, and a grumble that 'hearts of stone have the editorships now'.[16] Soon afterwards he wrote again to Blunden, enclosing his poems and asking him to send them on to his publishers, Cobden Sanderson. He ended the letter with the clearest statement of his feeling of neglect:

> I am an unsuccessful and angry poet writing to a successful poet who has already done things for him.[17]

Gurney's meticulous sense of the justice of reward for all that he had done and suffered being sorely tried. Still, not everything was gloomy, as his essay 'The Springs of Music' was published in America in the *Musical Quarterly* for July 1922. 'The Springs of Music' was an eccentric, experimental prose-poem of an essay, destined to sit incongruously in the publication alongside such diverse articles as 'Eskimo Music in Northern Alaska' and 'The Music of the Peoples of the Russian Orient'.

> Since the springs of music are identical with those of the springs of all beauty remembered by the heart, an essay with this title can be little more than a personal record of visions of natural fairness remembered, it may be, long after bodily seeing.
>
> It is the fact that these visions were more clearly seen after the excessive bodily fatigue in France or Flanders—a compensation for so much strain. One found them serviceable in the accomplishment of the task, and in after relaxation. There it was one learnt that the brighter visions brought music; the fainter verse, or mere pleasurable emotion.[18]

These opening lines are enough to give a little of the flavour of this rhapsodic exploration, which he ends by calling a 'queer discursive essay-thing' and a 'mist of pretty words'. His stress on the importance of the transformation of nature into art recalls both his own insistence that experience 'must sink in to the very foundations and be absorbed' and Wordsworth's 'spontaneous overflow of powerful feelings recollected in tranquillity' (he refers directly to Wordsworth in the piece).[19] He connects bodily exercise and the 'visions', the insistence on an idea of compensation, and his prioritising of music above poetry. 'The Springs of Music', whilst it appears to be a manifesto of Gurney's creative life, has to be treated with a little suspicion. He did not always stick to the principles it states, and the bias towards music (at a time when his composition seemed to be achieving more success than his poetry) would be expected in a piece written for a musical audience of a music magazine.

'The brighter visions brought music; the fainter verse, or mere pleasurable emotion.' This statement has often been taken out of context as a hierarchy of genres—music first, poetry a poor second, but it was not necessarily as simple as that. The act of creating a poem is often to preserve a glimpse, a faint gleam, whereas in order to write a quartet, sonata, or even a song, a more sustained inspiration might be required. 'Mere pleasurable emotion' appears to be unformed verse, waiting to be written. He is quite clear about his own identity here. He is a composer, and poetry exists to serve him, and his art.

His meagre fee for the publication of such a wild, beautiful and honest piece was hardly enough to live on. Gurney had lurched between temporary posts and unemployment for months. All the while there had been in the back of his mind the possibility that there might be something more permanent; a vacancy in the Gloucester Office of the Civil Service, where Kerr was head of department in income tax. Gurney was hardly passionate about income tax, but any post with a salary was to be eagerly pursued.

After months of petitioning from Gurney and string-pulling from Kerr and Marsh, the position was finally secured. Whatever mixed emotions he might have had, Gurney duly set out from his aunt's house to report for duty on the first Monday morning in July, looking as tidy as he could manage. On the surface, it seemed an ideal opportunity; he could earn his day's pay and have free time in the evenings and weekends to write and walk. It was a model that worked for all Gurney's Gloucestershire poet friends: Kerr himself of course, and Harvey and Haines, who returned from their solicitors' offices in the evenings to write. Even T. S. Eliot worked reluctantly in a bank.

Predictably, it did not take long for Gurney to find he was far from happy in his new career. The experience of being dismissed from a string of less demanding jobs had done nothing to bolster his confidence, and this new position was not in the least suitable for his temperament. He had no experience whatsoever of tax, or even of office work, and he was being given the post in a climate in which there were plenty of far more competent men who would have been glad of such an opportunity. He must have known that the chances of its success were minimal, and within a

FIG. 12.1: Westgate Street, Gloucester. The Tax Office was on College Court, between Westgate Street and the Cathedral. © The Francis Frith Collection.

matter of days he was arriving at the office increasingly dishevelled, distracted and anxious. 'I have just received my second week's pay without outcry', he wrote to Marion Scott, 'so I suppose it is all right, but all things frighten me rather'.[20] His insecurity manifested itself in arrogance, at least in his correspondence with Marsh. Before he had begun, he had boasted that 'from the tales of ignorance shown by the girl clerks I should be worth the money I think'. He was not, predictably, worth the money.

He describes the tax office itself in the same letter:

The Taxes office is just on the Corner of College Court, quite a fine building with something of a staircase, and a view across to Malvern from higher window looks, and an interesting view across good slate roofs and honest 18th Century brick. The front is very fine Corinthian (or sort of) with well spaced windows. It is not so bad for Taxes; from which I have cribbed the best of Poetry Note Books.

Gurney's imagination was clearly straying towards the outside world. His focus was not on the papers on his desk, but on the surrounding architecture and the view from the window. He had spent months in the trenches imagining the landscapes of home, and he was to perfect the ability to be mentally elsewhere in the coming years. His 'wangling' tendencies of army days had obviously not left him.

His poem 'The Tax Office' gives a different account of the building and its functions, and shows him more sympathetic to those being taxed than to the life of the imprisoned clerk:

The Tax Office

Georgian with a stairway up to the roof
And banisters of carved and curious grace . . .
An Inspector saw it, liked light and open space.
Bespoke it. 'Office of Taxes' is the proof.
And puzzled country folk climb stair with forms,
Inquire of rebates, and fend imagined harms,
In the rooms some man planned as his poetry's mind so
Fancied—'In this way, and in this way my house should go.'
And here the Gloucester farmers bring State-dues in
What strength and cunning could from bare earth outwin.
Winter light shines rosy on the oaken stairway
As Summer floods with true gold universal day
Throwing slant light on forms and piles of stiff forms,
On polished surfaces and mixed-up heaped-like-hay
Envelope piles, drear walls and the mixed harms
Of three times fifty years.
Sunshine falls there
The imagined graces of West Country air
Are a loved thing there—
On clerks at worrying method into service order:
And on the border
Of the precincts of secrecy the line
Everchanging of iniquity-fearing
Liable citizens wearing
Faces of anxiousest mien
Turning to go out then, at last to return to
Real lands whose name in writing is sudden freedom
For clerks writing dumb;
Looking out suddenly on river or new
Cornland, or dry stubble as the new season leads
Figures of acres, records of deeds of meads
By Waltheof or Egbert held perpetually
(Since service paid) for some unfelt nominal fee.
Seeing beyond paper marked clerkly the history
Of rich flats of Severn or Uptons in writ-free

Poplar'd closes, May with dim November (and feast-time December)
Loves: they are at home there. They are loved equally.
Autumn hears talk there of June's breath-tossed wild hedge-roses;
And Autumn crocus dies not at March's violet loveliness.
The earth has such memory—nothing dies, nothing in thought does die.[21]

Gurney is writing up social and cultural anthropology in poetic form; a poem typical of his porous imagination, 'The Tax Office' reads as a sort of census in local cultural work and activity over the ages. It is a poem interested in contrasts: between the building itself with the poetic plans of its original owner and the very unpoetic and bureaucratic tax office; between the anxious citizens come to find out for what tax they are liable and their 'real' world on the farms; and between the clerk 'worrying method into service order' and the sudden freedom which he achieves by writing the magical names of the 'real lands'. Gurney the clerk sympathised with the iniquity-fearing farmers and dreamt of escaping his forms and order. The poplars are (in a Hopkins-inspired compound) 'writ-free'; no bureaucratic niceties control them, and Gurney, as if preparing for the confinement of the asylums, registers the importance of memory: 'nothing in thought does die.'

While he was at the income tax office, another blow to his self-esteem was being prepared at the Cathedral, only a few steps from his office door. When the Three Choirs Festival came to Gloucester that September, he found that he had no place in it. It was a hugely high-profile event, with 17,357 audience members; the highest attendance rate ever. The festival had stopped for the duration of the war, starting again in Worcester in 1920, and this was the first time it had come back to Gloucester. It had been a summer of seemingly endless rain, but, between the 3rd and the 8th of September, the rain miraculously kept off, and the whole city seemed to have turned out to hear the concerts.[22] The programme was particularly special. Devised by Herbert Brewer, Gurney's old director of music at Gloucester Cathedral, it was angled towards showcasing British talent, with twenty-seven works by British composers featured in the course of the week. Amongst these were three of Gurney's College colleagues: Bliss, Eugene Goossens and Howells, all of whom had been commissioned by Brewer (at the prompting of Elgar) to compose new works for the festival. When Gurney as a young organ scholar had relied on the festival for his musical education, he had been frustrated that with an endless repetition of *Elijah*s and *Messiah*s it hardly represented adventurous musical choices. Now, in a line-up into which Gurney naturally fitted, he was conspicuous by his absence.

Bliss, Howells and Goossens were all offering experimental pieces in a strikingly progressive idiom. Brewer was shocked by Bliss's *A Colour Symphony*, a dissonant, daring work with its movements inspired by the symbolic, heraldic associations of colour, and labelled purple, red, blue and green. Ironically, a work as beautiful as

Gurney's *Gloucestershire Rhapsody* would have been a welcome relief for the conservative Brewer, in contrast to the pieces he had unwittingly unleashed on a rather puzzled Gloucestershire audience. Goossens's work *Silence* was a technically brilliant but rather cold setting of a poem by Walter de la Mare, and Howells's *Sine Nomine*, a 'fantasy' for wordless soprano and tenor soloists, wordless chorus, large orchestra and organ, was thoroughly incongruous as a precursor to Mendelssohn's *Elijah*. It received no further performances during Howells's lifetime, even though he considered it to be one of his best works. Gurney had longed to hear Howells's new compositions when he was trapped in the trenches. Could he have borne to sit through these premieres? As he watched the preparations for the festival getting underway from his window in the tax office, it was with the knowledge that not a single note of his would be heard during the week. He was firmly 'below the horizon', even in his native Gloucester.

This pile of rejections and exclusions led, perhaps inevitably, to a crisis. Winifred Gurney had seen little of her brother over the last few years, having been busy with her own career, first as a teacher, then serving as a nurse during the war. Now, with the chance to observe him at close quarters, she was horrified at the wreck he had become. It was whilst they were both resident at Longford Terrace with their aunt that Gurney finally broke down completely. Winifred took a phone call from the local police station asking her to come and collect him. He had gone there asking for a gun.

Winifred escorted him off the premises, mortally embarrassed and worried for his sanity. At every step, she sensed his desire to run away from her. She knew how close he had come to attempting suicide back at Warrington, and now she feared he might really go through with it. Her one instinct to ensure he returned home without incident was to impress upon him how worried his aunt was. Now that his father was dead, his aunt was the sole member of the family who held any emotional power over Gurney. Sure enough, he followed her meekly back. Winifred had tried during the course of the walk to suggest to him that he was in need of medical help, but, as she could have predicted, he had taken no notice of her entreaties. She felt that he would have turned against her if she raised the subject again. There was nothing for it but to leave him to deteriorate.

He had managed a couple of months at the tax office, longer than any other employment, but he was now beyond the point of employability.[23] He had proved a most disconcerting colleague, turning up dishevelled and complaining of the wireless messages that tormented him. He had begun to starve himself for weeks at a time. In the end, he was ignominiously escorted off the office premises by his brother Ronald, who had been summoned for the purpose, and whose embarrassment and anger can only be imagined. He was furious that, yet again, Ivor had failed to get a 'grip on himself', while he, Ronald, had been obliged singlehandedly to drag the family business back from the brink of bankruptcy by his own skill and hard work. As far as Ronald was concerned, matters had gone too far, and he was determined that his irresponsible, overindulged brother should not continue to damage the family's reputation and be the cause of such outrageous scenes.

Ronald felt that Gurney was beyond the help of his aunt. He took charge of him, much to Marie's distress. Winifred remembered her subsequently having a nervous breakdown, as a result of 'failing' Gurney, but later corrected the memory. Whatever the truth of the matter, she was genuinely fond of her struggling nephew, and her sense of helplessness in the face of Gurney's rapid deterioration must have been profound. Handing him over to the pugnacious Ronald would hardly have allayed her fears for him.[24] Ronald wrote a less than reassuring letter to Marion Scott, who was desperately concerned but could do little from South Kensington. From his tone it was clear that he was genuinely alarmed by his brother's behaviour and out of his depth. Whatever well-meant intentions he might have had were concealed under his abrasive, aggressive attitude:

Dear Miss Scott,

I am very much obliged to yourself & Ivor's friends for their persistent help to rather an undeserving person.

Personally I myself as you know have never been over sympathetic to him, as I have always been convinced he was always being handled in the wrong way. As a matter of fact, I had thought he was slowly improving, when Mr. Kerr sent for me. I do not now live at home, as I have been married this 2 months.

This last business has rather broken my patience with the family in general, for the future, I intend the lot of 'em to do exactly as they are told. Not two of them will live together for the future.

As for Ivor, for the present he is going under the Pension's office to a country house near Bristol. (A neuresthenic Convalescent home). They think it best he should not be certified Insane for the present.

There is no reason under the sun that he should not become thoroughly well enough to be able to do his Music.

But it will only be done, by his being permanently under discipline & a definite stronger will directing his life.

Never again shall I permit kind but Lenient & letting him more or less having his way, class of people.

Please don't think I am directing that at London. The trouble began here, not there.

[...] For the present I shall need nothing. If Barnwood is ultimately necessary & inevitable I shall let yourself & the Dr. know & every possible effort shall now be made to deal with him.

Up to now I have never endeavoured to deal with him, but he will not again be allowed to drift.

Thanking you & hoping your own troubles will be soon right

Sincerely yours.

Ronald E Gurney[25]

The country house near Bristol was King's Weston, a return to the brief hope of 1918. Gurney's breakdown took place the week before this letter, around the 7th or 8th of September. Harvey and Marion Scott knew about it by the 14th. Scott's first move was to consult with Vaughan Williams, who promptly promised Ronald £100 to cover any expenses Gurney's treatment might incur. There had also been time to arrange a consultation with the chief mental expert of the Ministry of Pensions. He examined Gurney and concluded that the ministry must take responsibility, either for curing him or for providing him with a disability pension for life. Arrangements had been put in hand to send him to King's Weston the following week, from where he could be moved if it became necessary. Harvey reported that Gurney's own doctor, Dr Terry,

says that the delusions (now dangerous ones) are a direct result of undernourishment & that he could be cured now in 6 months by obeying the ordinary laws of eating and sleeping. There is nothing organically wrong with him.[26]

But Harvey did not seem to agree with the diagnosis:

Thank God I'm responsible for the legal side, <u>not</u> the medical! Of course we all knew that eating & sleeping normally was the cure; but what we (his friends) know, & the doctors apparently don't know yet, is that <u>something</u> behind the refusal to eat which is in reality—what? Devil Worship?

In a postscript, Harvey implies the same family problems which Ronald hinted at:

I have warned Kerr (who heard from V.W. that you had seen him) to say nothing to his brother mother etc.

Devil worship was perhaps a rather outlandish suggestion, but Arthur Benjamin also believed, with some evidence, that there was a deep secret that contributed to Gurney's breakdown. He believed that much of Gurney's trouble might stem from ambiguity about his sexuality:

I think that psycho-analysis is the only cure for him; but that, of course, would mean entire confidence on Ivor's part, which is doubtful. I used to know a good deal about Ivor and on that knowledge—the details of which it is impossible for me to discuss with you—I think that psycho-analysis is the only chance.[27]

There was clearly something that Gurney kept from most of his friends, but had shared with Benjamin, who was comfortable with his own homosexuality. Although the staunchly heterosexual Howells recoiled hotly at the very idea that his close friend was gay, many of the patterns of Gurney's life and relationships point to a conflicted sense of his own sexuality. Gurney's passionate attachments had been to men, to Howells, and particularly to Harvey, and his relationships with women had been limited to finding alternative mother figures, such as Margaret Hunt, and now Marion Scott. His one 'conventional' heterosexual relationship, with Annie Drummond, had been a gesture towards emulating the engagements of the two closest men in his life. It can, of course, be only speculation, but for two men to commune with each other through loving the same woman is a well-recognised phenomenon.[28] Gurney had repeatedly tried to draw Annie and Harvey together. Harvey had his nurse, and Gurney had found another, and anxiously tried to link her to his original love, as a repository for the emotions which he could not express to Harvey. Sexuality, particularly at a time when homosexuality was illegal, is a highly complex and grey area to say the least, and we cannot know how Gurney understood his own impulses. Benjamin was in no doubt that there was more to Gurney's distress than Scott knew, or was prepared to entertain, but whatever he had confided in his closest friends, psychoanalysis and, indeed, sexual orientation were never mentioned again.

Harvey, who perhaps knew Gurney better than anyone, offered some more exact observations on the source of Gurney's psychological troubles. The doctors thought his illness was caused by starvation and sleep deprivation; both Scott and Harvey knew better.

> The starvation is, as you rightly say, caused by something behind. Ivor's soul is ill, and how can he be healed? Do you believe it possible for a devil or evil spirit to come and rest in a body already belonging to a human being? I have sometimes fancied that Ivor MAY have thought he has been possessed by an evil spirit. Of course I know that more often people build up their own tormentors in their hearts, and there comes a point at which the lifeless image becomes a sort of Frankenstein imbued with the attributes of spurious life. Or is Ivor suffering from a split in his personality, by which one section of it has gained predominance over the rest. God alone knows. I only know that we have got to help him in the battle.[29]

On Friday the 15th, Kerr wrote to Marion Scott to report on progress, and mentioned that Dr Terry had said that Gurney had been suffering from 'physical delusions for a long time.'[30] He filled in some other details: that Gurney had been examined by a Dr Tomlinson, the pensions neurologist for the district, that the plan was to send him to a pensions hospital in Ewell (in Surrey), and that he 'is not certified a lunatic'. In complete contradiction to Ronald's opinions, Kerr noted that Dr Terry was going to make personal contact with the medical superintendent at Ewell and make three things clear to him:

(a) that he is an exceptional person & of great talent.

(b) that he must on no account whatever have him certified as a lunatic without consulting his friends

(c) that if any other treatment is advisable, his friends must be notified & he must be transferred for it.

Kerr seemed quite confident that he and Gurney's friends in London and Gloucester would have enough influence to secure good treatment for him in whatever institution he was finally placed, and he assured Marion Scott that he would be moved 'this week'.

In 1922 it was difficult to obtain psychiatric help without being certified.[31] There were practical penalties to certification. If he was certified, Gurney would lose control of his finances (such as they were). He would be denied the right to vote. These were all symptoms of society's loss of faith in the patient. But it was the stigma of certification that was the worst consequence, and would have been keenly felt both by Gurney himself and by his respectable middle-class friends. As lawyers, Haines and Harvey would be well aware of the implications of certification. The label was worse than a spell in prison, and should Gurney ever be released, they knew it would be impossible for him to find employment.[32] Perhaps most frightening of all, there was also the very real anxiety that once a person became a patient, they were entirely at the mercy of a bureaucratic, inflexible and unforgiving system. Neither friends, relatives nor patient had any say in the decision as to when, if ever, the institution would release its involuntarily held charge.

Mental hospitals at this time served quite a different purpose from medical hospitals. Their business was not necessarily to cure, but to maintain a patient indefinitely, protect them from themselves, and to protect society from them. It was by no means a foregone conclusion that a patient would eventually be released.[33] Kerr was doing everything he could to avoid Gurney's certification by trying to take control of Gurney's options for treatment. 'We got on to the Bristol people to expedite his removal to Ewell, & held out hopes of getting him to Ewell on Wednesday. Ronald will travel with him.'[34] Unfortunately, Ewell was full, and so was another place they tried, so they went back to Ewell to try to get them to take him as an urgent case. They were advised by the local doctor to leave it to the Pensions people who, said Kerr, would be only too glad to get out of their responsibility. Meanwhile Gurney continued to stay with Ronald, his wife and her daughter; an arrangement that suited none of them.

Ronald might not have admitted it to Scott, who made her intense dislike of him perfectly clear, but he had taken charge of his brother with the clear intention that he would have him institutionalised within 'a month or so' if he was not cured in the meantime. There may have been some element of brotherly kindness at the heart of his offer of sanctuary, but if there was, it was heavily veiled. Aunt Marie had sheltered Gurney since February; his residency with Ronald in August lasted only a few weeks. It was a move necessitated by desperate circumstances, but no one was under any illusions that a stay with his brother would be conducive to Gurney's recovery. Most of Gurney's literary and musical friends who had any dealings with Ronald found him to be a deeply unpleasant, pompous individual. Winifred later bitterly resented Ronald and his wife, and despised their treatment of Ivor. Her assessment of the couple was that they were 'two of the most self-centred, unsympathetic, callous individuals on top of the most conceited, self-opinionated nonentities.'[35] Clearly, a sibling who had fallen out with her brother was not likely to offer an objective character analysis, but the fact remains that Ronald, at the very least, was a character who divided opinion.

He is an intriguing, semisketched presence in Gurney's life story. He was highly skilled, being naturally very practical: the antithesis of his cerebral brother. Winifred gives some tantalising glimpses into Ronald's behaviour (without drawing any inference from her recollections). She remembered how he had greatly enjoyed dressing up in her clothes as a child, and had longed to be a girl. Later she recalled how Ronald had been 'in love' with a boy named George Romans, and had declared that he would not marry unless he could take George as his partner. Winifred believed that as children Ivor and Ronald had not hated each other, merely being very different characters who had failed fundamentally to understand one another. It was only now, in such desperate circumstances, that real conflict between them arose.[36]

What exactly happened after Gurney's breakdown is difficult to piece together, since contemporaneous letters must be balanced against the fullest later accounts, which come from Ethel Gurney, Ronald's new and thoroughly unsympathetic wife. Her accounts vary a little. Michael Hurd, Gurney's first biographer, set down a version of the events leading up to his committal which depended on her reminiscences:

> He began to imagine that 'electrical tricks' were being played on him. He felt pains in the head and the voices returned. He left his aunt's house and thrust himself, uninvited, on his brother, who had just married. Here his behaviour became intolerable. He would shut himself in the front room of their house in Worcester Street and shout for them to keep away. He would sit with a cushion on his head to guard against electric waves coming from the wireless. He refused to go to bed, or to eat properly. He sneered at his brother's orthodoxies: 'Only fools go to work—why don't you get somebody else to keep you.' He flew into violent rages. He threatened suicide and called at the police station to demand a revolver.[37]

When Ethel was interviewed for a radio programme broadcast in 1983, she gave a rather different account of Gurney's certification:

It was the police at the end. He used to go to the police and ask them for a re-volver as he wanted to commit suicide but the only way he would do it was with a revolver. And so the police came to my husband one day and said you'll have to have him seen to. You'll have to have him put somewhere where he'll have treatment. We had him put to Barnwood House first of all. It was a pri-vate place. Well, he got out of there twice [laughs]. And we thought it would be best to have him put right away somewhere where he couldn't get home. So he went to Dartford, was it? Yes, Dartford, that's it. And he died there, but he was there some time before he died.[38]

The 'some time' which she so casually and vaguely recalls was fifteen years, and one hopes that her cheerful dismissal of Gurney's tortured adult life masks some guilt at the part she played in his certification. Clearly, Gurney had been an impossible houseguest, but there is something chilling in Ethel's amusement at the thought of a desperate man repeatedly escaping from an asylum, as if he were a child shirking summer camp.

What is clear is that Gurney was in a very disturbed state, as everyone agreed: his friends, his family and his doctors. He had starved himself for six weeks and was a piteous sight; he was so weak he could barely walk. Ronald instituted strict rules, against which Gurney did not have the strength to protest. Bedtime in Ronald's household was rigorously enforced, and Gurney was made to sleep and eat, as far as Ronald could force the issue. The regime helped improve his physical health a little, but Ronald's infantilisation of his elder brother did nothing to assuage Gurney's sense of utter dejection and humiliation. Ronald administered a dose of sedative to his brother every morning before he cycled off to work, leaving the drugged Gurney, Ethel and Ethel's little daughter alone in the house together. Gurney routinely ig-nored the daughter, a treatment that, in her own home, was frightening and confus-ing for the child. At other times he would terrify Ethel by appearing in the middle of the night, covered in mud, peering over her by the light of a candle. On one occa-sion, he tried to gas himself, putting the whole household in danger. One morning, as a protest against his captivity, Gurney found the place in which Ronald hid his bottle of medicine, swallowed the lot, and waved the empty bottle triumphantly at his brother as he wheeled his bicycle out to set off for the family shop. Ronald phoned the doctor and was told that the dose was not fatal, but that Gurney would regret it for the next few days. He did, and was put on a deck chair in the garden with a bowl by his side to suffer the consequences.[39]

Neither Gurney nor Ronald and his family could tolerate such living arrange-ments for long. There was no one to stop Ronald, who was insistent that Gurney was to be labelled a lunatic. Scott was on holiday in Switzerland; Haines had been away during the critical weeks of September 1922 and was horrified at the state in which he found Gurney on his return. Winifred, who might have intervened, had recently begun her residential midwifery training. Gurney had initially stayed briefly with Harvey, but Harvey was not in a position to offer him any longer-term shelter, now he had a family of his own to consider. Despite his many friends, Gurney was essentially alone.

Gurney's friends agreed with Ronald in principle that some swift intervention was necessary, but Ronald's motivations for action might well have been more complex than the concern of Gurney's other well-wishers. Would he have been so ready to have his brother committed had Ivor not left him with total responsibility for the family in the wake of their father's death, regularly demanded money from him, and been continually superior about Ronald's lesser abilities and talent? There was an unpleasant triumphalism in Ronald's control of Gurney and in his haste to have him committed. Equally, Ronald hints at his own similar mental health problems. It may be that his own identification with Gurney's illness was too much for him to bear at close quarters, and that he felt the need to exorcise something in himself by disposing of his brother.

Whatever the motive, Ronald engineered matters so that the final betrayal came as a trap. He invited two local doctors, Gurney's Dr Terry and a Dr Soutar, along with a magistrate to the house. Gurney did not know who this fateful third party was, and so could not have been aware of the power of certification that they as a triumvirate wielded. The magistrate settled himself inconspicuously in a chair and pretended to read a newspaper, feigning lack of interest. Gurney gave no indication to the three men of being anything other than normal. But after a while he turned to the silent magistrate and uttered the question that was to seal his fate. He asked him whether he might borrow a revolver.

This was not a sign of madness; neither was it an admission of suicidal intent.[40] But it did not matter. It was enough to curtail his liberty forever. Only a few weeks before, Dr Terry had maintained that there was nothing wrong with him that a healthy routine would not cure. Now, under pressure from Ronald, he had apparently changed his mind. The paperwork was signed, Gurney was certified insane, and he was committed to Barnwood House asylum on 28 September.

He had had only four years of freedom from the artistic frustrations and limitations of the army. Now his liberty was to be limited to a degree he could never have imagined, and his access to the intellectual world and all its challenges and stimulations would be permanently cut off. A life spent as an asylum patient was a social and personal disaster for anyone. For an artist just reaching his maturity, it posed a particular set of difficulties. But for someone who relied on wider communities for his stability and his sense of identity, there could hardly have been a worse fate.

PART IV

Asylum

CHAPTER THIRTEEN

'Praying for Death'

Today, the site on which Barnwood House Hospital stood is an eerie place. All that is left of the large villa that once housed one of Gloucester's most exclusive mental health institutions is a crumbling stone wall, dividing the grounds from the modern cul-de-sacs incongruously surrounding it. Tall trees abound, many with rooks' nests and huge balls of mistletoe, and the only surviving building is the chapel, a plain but imposing Victorian structure half hidden by tall yew trees. The hospital was closed in 1968. Now the chapel is used as a gym, lit by unforgiving neon, with pounding music issuing from it. A simple crucifix still adorns the bare walls, and wooden holders display the hymn numbers from the last service that took place there. Despite the modern gym equipment, it is easy to see that it has only undergone superficial changes, and that it must have been a comfortless, bleak place.

Barnwood House itself was by no means comfortless, however. In fact, it was the most salubrious of the local provisions for the insane. Barnwood village was not a particularly prepossessing area—even by the late nineteenth century it had already been subsumed into the suburbs of Gloucester. But the asylum there was a far more enviable destination than the other local county asylums, which were enormous institutions, often full beyond their capacity. The nearby Old County and City Lunatic Asylum at Wotton held up to 1,200 patients, and Gurney would have stood little chance of any individual attention amongst such a crowd. Barnwood House was significantly smaller than any county asylum, with only 160 patients in residence.[1] Gurney thrived on conversation, and he needed to be surrounded by people who understood him and appreciated his talents. At Barnwood the doctors could spend time with their patients and build personal relationships. Another major advantage was that Barnwood was privately run, which meant that unlike a public asylum, affluent relatives had an influence on the treatment and progress of their loved ones and would have been allowed (or would have been in a position to demand) regular visiting hours.

Barnwood was more like a genteel retirement home for deluded generals than an asylum.[2] The interior of the house itself had the decor of a rather stifling, overfurnished

FIG. 13.1: Barnwood House Hospital, Gloucester. It has since burnt down, and only the chapel remains. © Gloucestershire Archives.

middle-class Victorian home. A great deal of energy was invested in the decoration of private asylums (which was certainly not the case in the county institutions). This was in part for the benefit of the patients, but also to sanitise insanity, making the institution more palatable for sensitive and wealthy relatives. There were Turkish rugs and carpets in most rooms, with an abundance of pictures and ornaments adorning heavy oak cabinets, and Japanese wallpaper in the corridors.[3]

The asylum was emerging from a scandal at the time that Gurney was placed there. The name of Barnwood in the early 1920s was synonymous with a famous poisoning case, and one resident, a Mrs Katherine Armstrong, who had been admitted two years before Gurney, was inadvertently at the centre of the enquiry. She was, by all accounts, a domineering woman, and her weak and resentfully subservient husband, a Welsh solicitor by the name of Major Herbert Rowse Armstrong, decided that he had had enough of her. He was also in debt to a business colleague, and thought it might be convenient to do away with them both at the same time.

Armstrong almost succeeded in killing his business rival Oswald Martin by sending him a box of poisoned chocolates. When that failed, he invited Martin to tea, handing him a scone laced with arsenic, with the immortal words ''scuse fingers'. His wife had been committed to Barnwood as her gradual poisoning had brought on symptoms resembling madness. She was returned home at Armstrong's demand, where he presumably continued her arsenic doses, and, weak and delusional, she died of heart failure soon after she had been released from the asylum. Oswald Martin only narrowly survived the poisoned scone, and Armstrong was found guilty in 1922, the year of Gurney's admission, of successfully poisoning his wife. He had been hanged at Gloucester Prison that May.[4]

Barnwood could also boast some rather illustrious residents. Sophie Brzeska was a resident and died in Barnwood in 1925. She had been the partner of the sculptor Henri Gaudier Brzeska, whose death at the front in 1915 had been mourned by Ezra Pound among other Modernist writers and artists. Just before the war, the suffragette Lady Christiana Herringham had been a resident at Barnwood, believing herself to be in a 'tangle' (a word that was to be favoured by Gurney in his descriptions of his asylum predicament) and experiencing smells of jasmine that haunted her room, along with knockings and suggestive voices. Her case bore some similarities to Gurney's. Both were delusional but could write coherently. Herringham, a friend of Roger Fry and a major force in the Edwardian art world, was an influential social critic, and wrote about her experience of Barnwood; many of her claims were ones Gurney was himself to echo in the coming months. She told her husband that her fellow patients had too little to occupy them, and that 'I can't help thinking that some have been sent by relations who found them troublesome.' She wrote to the physician Louisa Garrett Anderson (daughter of Britain's first female physician, Elizabeth Garrett Anderson), refusing to use the conventional language and call Barnwood a 'retreat' but insisting instead upon the more emotive term 'asylum': 'A very slight acquaintance with life in an asylum under very favourable conditions shows some extremely serious difficulties and defects.'[5]

For many, 'the life is difficult enough to make them worse and not better' (a sentiment that Gurney was repeatedly to echo). She was horrified to find that not only were some attendants and nurses untrained; they were also unreliable. One left her patients at night for hours when she should have been in constant attendance, or handed them over to a substitute.

> it is extremely difficult to be a patient—imprisoned—with a good deal in the life to make a sane person suspicious and even insane.

Barnwood certainly had its dark side. Most significantly perhaps for Gurney, Herringham claimed that doctors were overturning the Visiting Committee's recommendations for patients' releases, in order to maintain high numbers (and thereby high revenue) for the hospital. In order to be certified, two doctors needed to agree on Gurney's madness. His own doctor, Dr Terry, had not thought him mad. The other, Dr Soutar, who would now take over his care, worked for Barnwood. Gurney was clearly in great mental distress, but whether he was certifiable is a moot point. Dr Soutar knew that Gurney came with the financial support of his concerned friends. Would he have been so inclined to certify him had he not had a vested interest in bringing revenue to the hospital?

Either way, the fact remained that in September 1922 this outdated Victorian residence, home to genteel but distressed ladies, the remnants of Bloomsbury intellectuals and alcoholic clergymen, extended its welcome to Gurney. He was dishevelled and desperate, insisting both on his sanity and on his intention to commit suicide. For the first time, a full examination and report had to be made that could not be fudged by well-meaning friends, or attributed to delayed shell shock for the benefit of obtaining a war pension. The doctors at Barnwood decided he was suffering from the rather vague 'dementia paranoides', and 'systematised delusional insanity'. The duration of the present attack was given as one month, a surprisingly short time, and the cause put down to military service.

The symptoms and delusions Dr Soutar found on this first of many examinations were to vary little for the next fifteen years. The doctors found Gurney physically run down, starved, and with an irregular heartbeat (the same symptom that had been recognised as disordered action of the heart, and thought to have pointed towards a war-related trauma), but otherwise with no outward health problems. They probed him for information, and whilst he could answer coherently, the effort cost him dearly. His answers were always delayed, and he would press his head with his hands as if trying to free himself from painful thoughts before answering.

Eventually they discovered that Gurney believed he was being interfered with by wireless, and being fed electrical meals. He claimed that he could go without food for three months at a time. Voices, which he never named specifically, constantly tormented him through what he enigmatically referred to as 'electrical influence', which appears to have manifest itself as a gruesome combination of physical pain, verbal instructions and abuse that he could not escape. The voices forced him to take food against his will and prevented him from doing his work. They drove him to seek out a revolver or poison to end his misery. Gurney maintained that the voices were in fact sent by the Metropolitan and the Gloucestershire Police, and (rather ambiguously) he wanted to go and 'swear before them'. This desire to appear before the police was something he was to return to repeatedly over the coming years, but he never revealed the crime he was accused of committing that had brought about his punishment. He was an innocent man, imprisoned without trial. To see it as such was a way of both rationalising his incarceration and fuelling his burning sense of injustice. He was under sentence, and if he could only commute his 'sentence' to six months' imprisonment he would be justly punished for his mysterious 'crime'. He frequently suggested another alternative to prison, which was that he might be allowed to 'mark books' for the police. 'Marking books' is rather vague, something like community service perhaps, but he was in the coming years to spend many hours of his incarceration underlining sentences in whatever books he had at hand, much to the chagrin of his mother, who supplied them. It may be this that he had in mind; quite literally making his mark on literature. He was clear that it was the police with whom he was in trouble, and equally certain that if he could only make his punishment finite, it would be more bearable than an endless asylum residency. He began to protest in his letters:

All today I would gladly have prayed for Death.
Or imprisonment for past crimes or to clear fate.
Anything but to stay in electrical pain or influence.
'Mercy of Woolwich mud earnestly desired.'[6]

Gurney's electrical influence was both delusional and experienced as very real pain, usually in his neck and head, for which the doctors gave him aspirin. They could find no evidence of auditory or visual disturbances, but the delusions he described to them were a deeply bizarre series of nightmare images.[7] Gurney told them that the seasons had been changed, and that strange birds and insects had been sent to various places. He was apt to position himself as the tragic hero in his own life narrative, and this alteration of the seasons in sympathy would be a natural extension of his self-mythologising. He was electrically tormented not only by the police but by the 'International Society of Nations', presumably inspired by the League of Nations which was very much in the public consciousness in the early 1920s. His accounts of his physical torture are graphic: he felt his brains were being pulled away, he was regularly struck on the back, fed by wireless means and had his stomach evacuated by wireless (as he believed).[8] The doctors found that at any given moment he could tell them with absolute certainty which particular group of people were torturing him, and from which direction the 'interference' was coming.

Feelings of persecution and the belief that somebody of authority is interfering with and controlling a patient are both typical complaints for a schizophrenic patient, but also common delusions for a disturbed soldier. Wartime recruits who, like Gurney, were reluctant or unable to shed their civilian identity had found their very sense of self under threat in the army. The military regime was designed to render the individual passive, anonymous and controllable—a pawn in the great game of war. It was not for the soldier to understand his role, but to be trained to play his part, and to be dispensable. Few before 1914 could have had any idea of the psychic damage such an abnormal situation could wreak on ill-prepared civilians, enlisting out of a sense of civil duty or social pressure.[9]

This sense of being invaded and tampered with often has a connection with an erotic response in the patient, as it did in Gurney's case. Dirty and obscene thoughts are felt to be planted in the patient's mind, humiliating him, and leaving him crippled by a sense of guilt and self-disgust. Gurney later described being haunted by voices shouting sexual obscenities. He had displayed a bizarre fixation with enemas since his days at the Royal College, and had become obsessed with cleansing himself internally. Among his current delusions was the belief that he had somehow been inserted into the anus of a policeman; an image that brought together his sense of uncleanliness, anal fixation and preoccupation with the law and his supposed transgression of it.[10] A poem, written in December 1922, shows his continued preoccupation with feelings of guilt and dirtiness, ending 'O grant death, grant cleanliness to loathing in pain'.[11] If, as Arthur Benjamin believed, Gurney was attempting to supress any homosexual inclinations, then how much more frightening and powerful must it have been to be persecuted by these ordinarily repressed erotic thoughts, translated into external voices?

Gurney told the doctors that his mental troubles had started over twenty years ago when he was a schoolboy, and that he had been tortured by the Germans (by wireless) when at the King's School in Gloucester. This is the only record of a claim that his childhood had been disturbed by mental illness, and it may well be a false memory. He also told them that he had been sent to Warrington for nearly a year, which, although it was such a black time it may have felt that long, was really just under two months. His testimony reveals more about how he experienced and remembered his life at this point than about accuracy of time scales. However, the delusions that currently tormented him were certainly not a new phenomenon, as his suicide attempt at Warrington had been ordered by the same persecutory voices. Unsuprisingly, his time locked up in the hospital at Warrington, the nearest he had previously come to being an asylum patient, now loomed large in his thinking. He cursed himself for having failed to take the step off the riverbank when he had had the chance. He had known then that he would rather his friends mourned his death than witnessed his descent into madness. Not only had his worst fear now been realised, but he was sane enough to appreciate the full tragedy of his situation.

He may have been hazy about his past, but he knew where and who he was, and how he wanted to present his career to the medical staff, complete with embellishments. They duly recorded his musical and literary achievements, along with the rather more unlikely 'he has achieved a great reputation [. . .] especially in the drama of the times of Ben Jonson and Shakespeare.' Already, he was beginning to fit into the mould of the institutionalised patient. Reinventing a prepatient career with a degree of wish-fulfilment is typical behaviour for a patient, taken out of his past life and left with the task of defining himself within an institution.[12]

The staff at Barnwood won Gurney's respect. He found Dr Soutar to be a 'good man', despite his having been the one to sign his certification forms, and proclaimed the superintendent Dr Townsend a 'gentleman'.[13] The admiration seemed to be mutual, as Dr Townsend declared Gurney 'such an extremely nice fellow'.[14] Many of the attendants had been servicemen themselves. Asylums had been severely understaffed during the war, and so provided a source of employment for ex-servicemen when peacetime jobs proved scarce. Thus, by a curious twist of fate, the more fortunate ex-soldiers ministered to the war's casualties with little intervention from civilian society, and the bond drew patients and staff together. Gurney felt a particular connection with the ex-army staff, referring to them as he might have described his comrades in the 2/5th only a few years ago:

> the doctors are good men but conditions are not good. Pain bad sometimes. Attendants many ex-Service, very kind. But may I receive either freedom or chance of death. Dangerous service. Anything rather than to remain here.[15]

Indeed, a number of the attendants were probably demobilised members of the Gloucester regiment, given the locality. But however well he was looked after, to say that Gurney was unhappy in Barnwood would be an understatement. Initially, Gurney's horror at finding himself incarcerated eclipsed the oppression of his illness itself, and the institution supposed to effect a cure became, in his mind, the cause of his suffering:

> I cannot bear my pain. There is no reason for any such. Any fate but to remain in Barnwood House. Death at once is far better.[16]

Until recently he had been a free spirit, tormented and depressed perhaps, but able at least to act on every whim to tramp the fields at night, sleep in barns, and watch his beloved sunrises and sunsets. Now he was to experience the most extreme intrusions into his privacy. From the earliest days of his admission, he constantly implored the staff to allow him to die. The very fact of his continued breathing became a torture to him.

> I am praying for death, death, death,
> And dreadful is the indrawing or out-breathing of breath.[17]

The staff could not take any chances. He quickly found himself under constant surveillance, having been placed on suicide watch. His desire for death was by no means an affectation or figure of speech. Gurney had been committed to Barnwood not because he was insane, but because he was *suicidal*: a distinction that had a profound impact on his treatment.

At least one of two statutory requirements had to be satisfied in order for committal to take place: the patient needed to be a danger either to themselves or to the public.[18] In Gurney's case, it was the former. Any mental institution was obliged to treat a suicidal patient differently from other patients. On arrival, Gurney was placed upon the special suicidal list, or the 'SS'. This was often referred to as being 'certificated'. He was rarely allowed out of the sight of an attendant, even being followed into the toilet; any well-trained attendant knew that a bend in the pipe from a toilet cistern was a prime spot for attempted hangings.[19]

Gurney found himself being 'led about by an attendant', under 'strict orders'.[20] If the attendant had been doing his job conscientiously, Gurney would have been stripped naked every night to check for concealed weapons—a sensible precaution when he was making such disconcerting claims as 'I cannot cut my throat on a window pane is all that is the matter'.[21]

A medical handbook of the time records:

> A patient has been known to mutilate himself severely with a pen-nib. One moment's inattention or carelessness may lead to tragedy, and this fact cannot be impressed too strongly on the staff.[22]

It is very likely that Gurney was not allowed to use a pen for the first few months of his suicide watch. Indeed, almost all his manuscripts from around this time are in pencil, a medium he would never normally choose. In 1917 he had rather bumptiously declared that

> The man who would attempt to write verse with a pencil when a pen is handy and convenient to him would rob a church without more thought than he would give to the flicking of a cigarette ash.[23]

Gurney's writing was his lifeline; and the pen was the means by which he communicated his intellectual power to others. To deprive him of this medium was to strip him of his identity.[24]

During the war there was much that Gurney omitted from his letters, and what he chose not to tell his correspondents was just as revealing as the narratives he constructed. He had been anxious about boring his readers or talking too much about himself (although having apologised for doing so, his self-consciousness rarely stopped him). His poetry took his moments of epistolary solipsism further, as poems often arose out of monologues to Scott, developing his thoughts on death, comradeship, fear or beauty in a medium more conducive than a letter. Now, in the silence of the asylum, he returned to his vivid memories, and began to fill in much of the detail that he had omitted at the time. His thoughts returned to the everyday minutiae of army routine, to moments of humour or humanity; his new mental suffering also evoked memories of the suffering he had undergone during the war but chosen not to articulate in verse at the time. In poems such as 'Ypres War', written that October, a picture of the misery of much of his time as a soldier now belatedly emerged. His pain is viscerally felt through strangely angular couplets; a poetic parallel to the landscapes evoked through the surreal fragmentation and sharp, linear gestures of war artists such as Paul Nash.

> Horrible outlooks over toward Zillebeke,
> Sodden dreadful old time pastures, or culture
>
> Tanks stuck, war-wreckage—hard enough to endure
> Clean warfare the Romans had not safer to seek

If they loved War, rather than farms or the chase
Or walking, talking. But East Ypres it was

As spoilt a good as earth ever might see
All goodness denied there of Europe's age-motionry [. . .]25

His body of war poetry was to grow over the next few years, culminating in a
wealth of poems in 1925. For now, in the first few weeks at Barnwood, the doctors
found Gurney's concentration very impaired. After six weeks of starvation this was
hardly to be wondered at, but after a few weeks of regular meals he was again occupying his time with writing and music. Dr Townsend was pleased to inform Marion
Scott of this apparent progress. He did not trouble himself to read what Gurney was
actually writing. Had he read such despairing poems as 'My Life', he might have
speculated that Gurney's distress was as much the result of his incarceration as a
symptom of mental illness. His writing was a rebellion against his environment and
an attempt to insist on his own sanity, rather than a sign that he was settling down
and amusing himself.

I get up at eight o clock every morning, and smoke
Under or not under electrical influence
And great pain comes on me, and with horror, violence
Of worse things than before was guessed. The dreadfullest yoke
Of terror and pain, and pain suffered to extremes
And an after follow of afternoon fatigue and desire
To be out awhile free in the freer air
Of fields and roads, as once was desire of dreams
Past desire of death many times gone and there seems
Absence absolute of God; absolute absence
While pain and terror of different kinds in violence
Or wearingness come on me and I am gone
Out of myself into pain, into delirium alone.
And my mind is tortured and my tale changed,
Truth itself turned against truth and ranged
Against itself, everything worthy gone
To a past that's pain, and now all's clear alone.26

'My Life' is a curious amalgam of a diary entry and a poem. In his urgency to record his story, to chart his life and how he had gotten to this point, he had created a new
form of autobiographical, confessional poetry. The result is one of the most illumi-
nating descriptions of what it actually felt like to suffer from Gurney's illness. Evidently, one of his concerns was that his history and his memory were affected, that
his 'tale' could be 'changed', and 'truth itself turned against truth and ranged against

itself.' This urgent imperative to set down his story, for posterity and for his own sanity, becomes the principal driving force for the rest of Gurney's life. What clearer or more urgent motivation could there be for the repeated writing and rewriting the facts of his life which from now onwards was to occupy so much of his time, or for mining every memory, every moment of his past life, for poetic material?

Such a candid poem detailing Gurney's routine and the specifics of asylum life is very rare. The experience of incarceration and extreme illness was still relatively new to him, and for this short time he explored his symptoms and ruminated on his predicament in poetry. Soon he would reduce all mention of his condition to broader strokes, such as 'there is such hell within me', or describing himself repeatedly as being subject to 'torture'. As the realisation began to dawn on him that being locked up was perhaps a permanent state, the writing of appeals started in earnest. So began what would be such a frequently used formula that it would develop into a whole genre of his writing—the 'appeal poems'. The more he wrote, the more he rehearsed a broadly similar structure. He would begin with memories of his former life, or of the landscapes of Gloucestershire, London and Flanders. The poem would, having reminisced, then turn to the present, appealing for release or for death to end his 'current pain'.

This formulaic structure was yet to be set in stone, however. His writing in 1922 still offered a brief window into his perspective on his illness as he attempted to work out his relationship to his situation through his verse. He wrote of his sense of moral obligation to appeal against his torture, not necessarily against his committal, but against the illness that he was experiencing as a wireless influence burning and hurting him. This new and desperate need to put pen to paper necessitated not necessarily a lesser, but a *different* form of literature: poetic letters and autobiography in verse, rather than conventional poems. He wrote, as he would rarely do after these initial weeks at Barnwood, of the anxiety at his loss of his own history, of the mental confusion he experienced when suffering an attack of 'wireless', and the difficulties of sustained, creative thought:

> All, and other thought
> Worries at my own, and so is consciousness
> Brought to confusion, and then is utterly
> Mixed up inwoven, thought broken, and the free
> Spirit broken utterly and the memory
> Not used, so as the pain do not return.
> And I have peace, and nothing does hurt or burn.[27]

This is poetry born of the need to understand and articulate his own mental state. These improvisatory poetic testimonies can work it out as they go, tease away at something difficult to pin down. They can contradict and negotiate with themselves. How else to express how it feels to have your consciousness 'mixed up inwoven' than these exploratory sketches dramatising and enacting the confusion they describe?

His poetry had begun as a diverting occupation inspired by the 'lesser sparks of imagination'. Now it had become a matter of life and death. To write was to exist, to have his voice heard, if only by himself. He wrote in the final lines of the appeal poem 'There Is a Man':

what is better is the finding
of any ease from working or changing free
Words between words, and cadences in change
But the pain is in thought, which will not freely range.[28]

Gurney was no longer at liberty, and so looked to the free and unlimited arrangement of words to find solace. He wrote of the pain between words, the silence that constituted thought, and his work now became an attempt to fill that unbearable silence with music and sound. But he was caught in an ambiguous double bind: although he found comfort in creativity, the very act of creative thought caused pain, whether literal or metaphorical.

By mid-October Gurney had been in Barnwood for a month, but from the moment of his admission he had been looking for an opportunity to escape. On the 14th his chance came. For some reason, the midday changeover of staff was more relaxed than usual. At a quarter past twelve, Gurney found himself momentarily unguarded, whilst taking his obligatory exercise in the grounds. He quickly climbed over the railings and walls and ran. His freedom was not to last long, however. By 2:30 pm attendants had caught up with him in the neighbourhood of Sandhurst, a little over four miles away. When they questioned him as to where he thought he was going, he explained rather vaguely that the wireless voices had told him he must report to a place some distance away. He was escorted back to his room, and the attendants tightened up their surveillance. For a few weeks he seemed to have settled down, or so the superintendent thought. His doctors could find no outward sign of distress, despite his descriptions of terrible symptoms, but his eating and sleeping were still irregular.

He was merely biding his time, and on 8 November he escaped again. This time it was rather more planned than opportunist. He knew his only chance of evading the ever-watchful attendants was to wait until the evening, after the depressingly early asylum bedtime at 8:30 pm. As soon as he was unsupervised, he hurled a large clock through the window, and jumped out after it, cutting his hands and feet badly in the process.[29] It was a desperate act, but Gurney was so desperate that he was indifferent to bodily harm. His intention was not to remain free, but to escape in order to kill himself, as he recounted in a letter to Harvey:

Under spell of E.I. [electrical influence] of various sorts I escaped at night. Dared not stay at the Railway. Left letter at Palace and Deanery. Made for railway. No use. Made for river. Could not do it. Made for Police station, where later was handed to Hospital Authorities. Would have taken Railway, or Shot, but it was not possible. Could not face river. Kindly treated by authorities on the whole. Would ask for death or freedom. Or imprisonment to cover small crimes. Railway denied by chance. No trains at critical moment.[30]

In a gesture of total futility, he reported to a police station only an hour after his escape. The police detained him until the asylum staff could collect him. He had lost a lot of blood in his escape, both on the broken glass and on barbed wire, and this time he was in no position to walk far, having badly bruised his feet. When the head attendant finally reached him, he was greeted by a pathetic spectacle: Gurney was limping, soaked in blood and in a state of severe shock. Dr Townsend had to write to Scott advising her to defer a planned visit until he was more presentable. Barnwood was not a high-security asylum—they knew they were not equipped to deal with such a volatile and dangerous patient, and they did not want the responsibility of his death on their hands. It was becoming clear that he was both too unsettled and too unsettling a presence at Barnwood, and that his residency could not continue.

It was only two months since his admission, but the now already familiar debates about Gurney's future were underway once more. Scott and Vaughan Williams had travelled down to visit him, but it was a long way from London. Scott felt that Gurney was her responsibility, and ought to be moved to be nearer to her. She was a naturally possessive woman when it came to relationships, but equally, she was the most devoted friend Gurney could have wished for, and her practical help was infinitely more valuable than anything his family had offered him. Haines was of the opinion that Gurney ought to remain where he was, despite the fact that being in Gloucestershire meant unhelpfully histrionic visits from his mother.[31] He was near his hills and the landscape that meant so much to him, even if he was not at present at liberty to enjoy it. And the fact remained that Barnwood was the lesser of many evils; Gurney loathed his incarceration, but Barnwood was infinitely more civilised an institution than most. The staff had had enough, however, and welcomed the suggestion of a move for this difficult patient. The windows had barely been reglazed by the time Dr Townsend was writing to Scott, politely suggesting that Gurney might be better off away from the Gloucestershire area.[32] Holloway Sanatorium in Virginia Water was suggested, possibly by Scott, but almost immediately ruled out, and Dartford was mentioned for the first time, as Dr Townsend had a personal link to the superintendent, Dr Steen.[33]

Ronald, in charge of the family's precarious finances, had other responsibilities to weigh up alongside his brother's potential happiness. He was already of the opinion that Barnwood was too expensive for the family, and had obtained a list of private asylums from the Ministry of Pensions that charged less than Gurney's current fees.[34] The rest of the family was suggesting Cardiff, and even Gurney himself joined in the debate. His thoughts turned to Napsbury, where he had been relatively happy. He took it upon himself to write to the hospital, which had returned to its asylum status after its brief stint as a military hospital. The letter was never posted; it was the beginning of what he found would be the fate of all asylum patients, whose voices and opinions were resolutely unheard.

Whether or not Gurney's opinion was sought, Dartford soon became the preferred option, and arrangements were made for a transfer before Christmas. Gurney knew little about the institution, but he fervently hoped that life there would be more bearable.[35] He anticipated the same kind of relief he had experienced when he had moved from the misery of Warrington to the comparative civilisation of Napsbury. He even wrote a pathetic little prayer-like note to the superintendent before the move:

> To Dr Steen Dartford Kent.
> Asking him to take him and save him.
> Ivor Gurney[36]

The thought of the move back to London inspired a number of London poems, as he imagined familiar haunts such as Ludgate Hill and Blackfriars once more. Dartford was, of course, not strictly London, but it was officially the City of London Mental Hospital, and 'near London' was close enough to be worth petitioning London to save him from the stagnation he was experiencing in Barnwood.

'If I am left here any longer I shall go mad', he wrote in December with no sense of the irony of the claim, whilst writing poems romantically idealising the 'mornings of bright London'.[37] There was very little chance that a huge county asylum such as Dartford would be a place of redemption, but at this early stage of Gurney's career as a patient there was still some hope that his predicament was temporary, and that somehow the right institution would effect a cure.

CHAPTER FOURTEEN

'Asylum-Made Lunatics'

Merely to confine the insane is not to treat them, and certainly not to cure them, except by accident. It is to leave them to recover or not, just as may happen. But it is even more than this. It is in many cases to aggravate their condition, to manufacture, in the late Dr. Maudsley's striking words, 'asylum-made lunatics.'[1]

The pianist/composer Arthur Benjamin was still very much involved in Gurney's crisis, and had been party to the anxious correspondence shuttling between Gloucester and London. He offered the loan of his car to drive Gurney up to Dartford himself, but this was deemed rather too informal an arrangement for a patient who had a penchant for desperate escape attempts. Instead, a car was hired, and flanked by two attendants, Benjamin accompanied Gurney for the journey on 21 December 1922. They set off first thing in the morning and arrived at Dartford in time for lunch. Looking out of the car window, Gurney silently watched as the contours of the familiar hills disappeared behind him, lit by the rising sun. He would never again see Gloucestershire. From now on, it was to become a landscape of the imagination, to be brought alive only through his writing.

By midday, Gurney's hills had been replaced by the industrial estuary of Dartford. The approach took him up a winding road through the village of Stone, to a complex of austere Victorian red brick buildings that overlooked the great, grey stretch of river below. The hospital itself was dominated by an imposing water tower,

FIG. 14.1: The City of London Mental Hospital, Stone House, Dartford.
Courtesy of Francine Payne.

surrounded by impressive buildings, but to Gurney it presented a cheerless spectacle. This was the City of London Mental Hospital, or Stone House; the institution
he had looked to for his salvation. At first sight, it was far from reassuring. Barnwood
had resembled a genteel retirement home, with its ornaments and aspidistras. Stifling as that had been, now he saw that it had been replaced by something far worse.
The entrance hall looked grand enough, decorated for the benefit of visitors, but as
the patient progressed further into the building, instead of corridors bedecked with
paintings and Persian rugs there was cold, echoing linoleum, chipped whitewashed
walls and barred windows. Stone House, as its name implied, had all the charm and
allure of an enormous prison.

As Gurney gradually gained familiarity with his surroundings, he came to find
that there were some redeeming features; the asylum did at least have the advantage
of being surrounded by acres of grounds, leading down through woodland to the
reed beds surrounding the River Dart. In the first few months, Gurney managed on
occasion to get attendants to walk him around the grounds of the asylum and would

stand gazing down at the estuary below him, with a mixture of awe and horror at the industrialisation that even in 1922 was well underway.[2]

Like many large asylums, Dartford had its own farm within the grounds, which immediately attracted Gurney's attention. But for now at least, the outdoor attractions of Dartford were all out of bounds to him. The car drew up outside the front doors, and Gurney was ushered into the hospital. Benjamin stood on the doorstep alone, watching the back of his friend disappear up the long corridor, flanked by the two attendants. He returned to London choked with emotion. Gurney was taken to the office of Dr Steen, the hospital's conscientious, earnest superintendent. Despite a crippling workload, Steen made a point of undertaking all the hospital's admissions assessments in person. His neat, tiny handwriting recorded that his new patient was 5 ft 8 ¾ inches tall, and weighed only 10 st 3 lb. Apart from a brief initial weight gain, he would spend most of his life at Dartford gradually losing weight, until his emaciation became painful to see, his woollen suits hanging off his shrunken shoulders.

Dr Steen recorded his initial conversations with Gurney:

> Patient states that the electrical tricks have been very much worse since last August. But in looking back he can see that all his life he has been subjected to electricity. When studying at the RCM he felt the same thing but did not realise it at the time.
> Patient has been ill (mentally) off and on since 1917.
> No hist. of alcohol, T.B. or insanity in family.
> Patient was of a reserved disposition, steady in his habits (almost teetotal).
> Patient had ulceration of stomach some years ago.
> During the war Patient suffered from Shellshock. Was gassed and wounded.
>
> Mental Condition
> Patient is strange in his manner. He has delusions that he is being tormented by electricity—he says he is a tangled police case and is being treated as a medical case. He has auditory hallucinations.[3]

This interview with Dr Steen would be the high point in the medical staff's interest in Gurney. Even this first assessment was fairly cursory. The admissions form in which Dr Steen's comments are written gives inadequate space for a satisfactory case history, and the details recorded are superficial and perfunctory. This was all the information upon which the doctors could base their decisions about diagnosis and treatment, and determine choices about Gurney's accommodation, restrictions in routine, and diet.

It was universally acknowledged among medical professionals that admission, even transfer from one mental hospital to another, was traumatic for the patient. The usual procedure for a newly admitted mental patient was to keep them separate

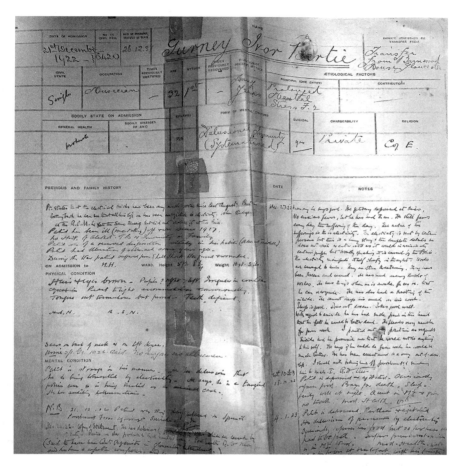

FIG. 14.2: Gurney's medical notes. Courtesy of Nicholas Anderson, from his father's private notes on Gurney's case.

in a specially designated observation ward, thereby shielding them from other potentially distressing patients, until a diagnosis could be made and a treatment plan worked out. This interim period was designed to help the patient acclimatise to his new environment. Dartford simply did not have the facilities or space to make admission easy for its new patients.[4] Gurney was put in a bed in the general male hospital ward, along with an eclectic assortment of patients with a variety of illnesses and behavioural problems. If he felt that his incarceration in Barnwood was unbearable, the inadequate admission process he encountered at Dartford would have shattered any final illusions that this institution would be an improvement. As soon as he had access to paper, he politely thanked Scott for her efforts on his behalf, but

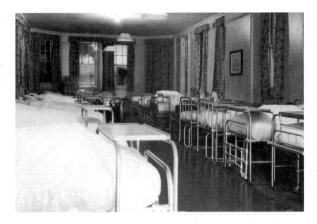

Fig. 14.3: A ward at Stone House, Dartford. Courtesy of Francine Payne.

his disillusionment was perfectly clear. Dartford was, in fact, 'a place one cannot be happy in'. 'What have I here to hope for, save death?'[5]

Now Gurney was one of many on a ward, and one of 744 patients in total. To attend to this number, the asylum could muster only two doctors, overseen by the superintendent, who himself had to spend the majority of his time engaged in administration, rather than treating patients. Only ten days after the move, it was already clear that his prayers had not been answered. Dartford was worse than Warrington, hitherto the benchmark of hideousness. He had already given up on Dr Steen as his potential saviour, and implored Marion Scott to rescue him.

> Will not Miss Scott decide on something? Since this place is so flat a failure, so much a humiliation?[6]

The use of the word 'humiliation' is revealing. Life in the asylum, aside from the stigma of being there in the first place, was organised with little regard for the dignity of the patient. Communal washing, shared towels, and a total lack of privacy in the open wards all combined to strip the already vulnerable patients of their sense of self-regard and individuality.[7] The general indignities of asylum life were made far worse for Gurney by the transfer of his status as 'suicidal' from Barnwood. Dartford was more used to dealing with suicidal cases than Barnwood, but was equally keen to avoid them achieving their goal. Suicides reflected badly on the institution. They not only necessitated inquests and reports to committees who might very well raise difficult questions but were also bad for the morale of other patients.

During the course of Gurney's residence at Dartford, there were six suicides recorded. Shortly before Gurney arrived, a female patient had thrown herself down a fire escape and died of her injuries. Disillusioned and increasingly despairing in his bleak new environment, Gurney could not be trusted to be unsupervised.[8] Nevertheless, Dr Steen was a reasonable man and prepared to take risks with his patients' interests in mind. When Gurney, desperate to get outside, promised not to try to harm himself, Steen decided to revoke his suicidal status only six days after his admission. 'He pleads very much for farm work', he wrote.

> I pointed out my position as regards to suicide and he promised me that he would not do anything to himself. He says if he could do farm work he would be much better. He has been accustomed to a very out-of-door life. I shall risk taking him off parchment and sending him to M1 [Male Ward 1].[9]

Steen was taking a considerable risk. Gurney was still advocating his own death in the course of the very same conversation. Nevertheless, he was rational enough to appreciate the special lengths to which Dr Steen was prepared to go on his behalf, and reported the conversation to Marion Scott:

> I shall hardly be able to work here. Though Dr Steen has suggested kindly that I shall be allowed on the poultry farm.[10]

The record of the interview with Dr Steen affords more detail as to Gurney's state of mind at the time:

> 27 December: Memory he says good. He gets very depressed at times; no anxious fears, but he has had them. He still fears every day the suffering of the day. The nature of the sufferings is this electricity. The electricity is sent by certain persons but this is a long story and the complete details he does not wish to enter into as it would incriminate certain people but broadly speaking it is caused by the police. The electricity manifests itself chiefly in thought. Words are conveyed to him. They are often threatening. They have been obscene and sexual. He has had many kinds of voices. He sees things when he is awake, faces and co [sic] that he can recognise. He has also had a twisting of the inside [presumably a verbatim record of Gurney's description of his experience, not an actual physical symptom]. He cannot keep his mind on his work. Sleep is good. Does not dream. Takes food well.

Gurney's position looked much bleaker the next day, despite his move from the restrictive hospital ward to the open male ward (referred to as M1), where patients were allowed a little more freedom:

> 28 December: Patient is depressed and agitated. Occasionally refuses food. Prays for death.

Gurney felt as if he had been in Dartford for so long he had already lost count of time. He was only ten days into what would be fifteen years of incarceration. In

December there was still the forlorn hope that Dartford was a temporary nightmare, and that there was a future outside the asylum to look forward to, but the Christmas of 1922 was nevertheless an unimaginably depressing affair for Gurney. The asylum did its best; it prided itself on its entertainments, and when he had arrived, Gurney had found that the cavernous dining hall with its cheap, institutional furniture was decorated with strings of Chinese lanterns and flags. There were competitions for the best decorated wards, which many patients entered into enthusiastically.

There were pianos on most of the wards, and Gurney found some consolation in playing carols for the patients. He was assessed again on Boxing Day:

> He has delusions of persecution by 'voices' which are caused by electricity.
>   Pains are also produced in a similar way. Poor health.
> (Said to have been Asst. Organist in Gloucester Cathedral.)
> And has been a capable composer, and an approved poet.

Gurney's medical notes give a telling glimpse of how little the doctors knew, either about Gurney's condition or about his past life and achievements. His composing and writing are noted, but his past achievements are treated with scepticism. One of the many great difficulties that beset an asylum patient was the suspicion with which any kind of personal achievement or testimonial was treated; he was 'said to have been Asst. Organist'.

A madman's voice could not be trusted. Often, it went entirely unheard. No wonder Gurney was to spend the best part of fifteen years rehearsing his life story over and over in his writing. There were to be doctors who listened; who understood and respected his work, and became deeply involved in his case. But for now at least, despite Dr Steen's apparent kindness, he was still patient number 6420 to the medical staff, not a genius who craved indulgence and intellectual stimulation. Marion Scott lost no time in attempting to befriend Steen on behalf of his new charge and invited him and his wife to a concert (possibly including Gurney's music) within a few weeks of the transfer. She was clearly determined to impress upon them that Gurney was more than another case or statistic.

Gurney's poem 'Sights' was published in the *London Mercury* (edited by the loyal J. C. Squire) in January 1923, but such small triumphs could do little to alleviate the gloom, and the new year did not hold out much promise of improvement in Gurney's condition. He was under orders to spend his days mostly in bed on the ward, his health being described as only 'moderate'. He was deeply unsettled by his environment, with no change in the pains in his head or the delusions of 'persecution by electricity' that were to be a fixed point for the rest of his life. His eating was still disordered and he was constipated, a common ailment in asylums due to the combination of heavy medication and stolid food. He hated the regular meals, but continued refusal to eat would simply result in forcible feeding. Negotiation was not an option. A procedure that had been condemned as torture when it was inflicted on imprisoned suffragettes was a frequent and unremarkable occurrence in Dartford. Although there is no record of its having been deemed necessary for Gurney, the overworked doctors did not record everything that took place in the hospital, and it is possible that he would have been subjected to it. In the first days of January he managed to cut his fingers at breakfast with his knife and required stitches, only a few weeks after his injuries from the escape through the window at Barnwood had healed. Was this an unfortunate accident (as the hospital records claim), an impotent gesture of protest at the enforced meals, or a result of the drugs affecting his coordination? We do not know, and the doctors may not have stopped to ask.

Gurney was allowed out of bed for a walk on the afternoon of 6 January 1923 with another private patient, a Dr Glanville, who was articulate and responsible enough, so the authorities thought, to be trusted as a chaperone. Gurney had been taken off the suicidal list only ten days earlier, and it was the first time he had been outside unsupervised. The opportunity for escape was too good to pass up. He must have told Glanville of his plans, because, as they started to make their way back to the hospital for tea, Gurney slipped away, leaving Glanville to return alone in the gathering winter darkness. Dr Steen had taken a gamble on his suicidal patient, and it had not paid off.

'Losing' patients was by no means uncommon in Dartford. Dr Steen, by nature an optimist, was remarkably lenient about allowing the less seriously ill patients out of the grounds. As many as forty of the men and fourteen of the women were allowed parole beyond the asylum gates at any one time.[11] As a result of this policy, patients were frequently 'lost', often leaving for a few days and refusing to readmit themselves. Gurney was very far from being a patient who was convalescent and ready to be returned to society. He would still have been considered a potential danger to himself, and possibly to others. What is more, he had a track record of escapes, however badly executed, and he had learnt his lesson from his attempts to escape from Barnwood. This time there would be no voluntary handing himself in to the police. Instead, he walked for nearly thirty miles, seeking out Squire at his house in Chiswick. He had justifiably lost all confidence in the authorities as his allies—both police and doctors seemed repeatedly to let him down and betray him. The only people he could turn to now were his friends. Surely Squire, who was publishing his poem, could be relied upon to be an ally? He turned up unannounced at his house. Squire did not hand him over to the authorities, but whatever he expected from Squire, it seems he did not get it. Either Squire could not countenance Gurney staying the night or Gurney left of his own accord. He spent the night alone, sleeping rough on Paddington station. Perhaps he meant to throw himself under a train, as he had intended when he escaped from Barnwood. Perhaps he was toying with the idea of boarding a train to Gloucester, despite having no money. Or as Howells had found in the early, homesick days of their student lives, the very link with his home county, watching the trains depart for a destination he longed for, could have been enough to draw him there.

The next morning he walked to Cheyne Walk in Chelsea, the home of Ralph and Adeline Vaughan Williams, his other most loyal supporters. By nature a generous and compassionate man, Vaughan Williams never deserted Gurney. Having been involved in the difficult decisions about Gurney's treatment, it must have been a considerable shock to open the front door and find his deranged pupil standing there. What course of action could he possibly take? His decision left him feeling, as he later put it, like a murderer, but he had little choice other than to turn him over to the police.[12] The couple took him to the nearby Work House Infirmary in Hounslow, and he was returned to Dartford by the evening, to the palpable relief of his doctors, and to the lasting agony of both pupil and teacher.

The incident was quickly hushed up, the watch around Gurney was intensified, and the episode forgotten. It was not so easily dismissed for either the patient himself or for Vaughan Williams. For as long as Gurney lived, Vaughan Williams supported him. He continued to help financially, and began to visit regularly, fitting in trips to the asylum around his demanding schedule of conducting, teaching and composing. His visits were motivated by extreme kindness, but also perhaps by the need to compensate for a nagging sense that he had betrayed him.

Gurney's spell of solitary confinement had left him with insomnia by the end of January. He was given Sulphonal and Dial, mind-numbingly strong sedatives, which appear to have helped him to sleep.[13] The combination of such heavy medication and his own deep depression led to days confined to bed, being allowed to sit up and smoke only after a week. During this enforced leisure, he could do nothing but write. He had appealed to his friends in person, and the strategy had failed. Now the only power he had was through his pen, and so the steady flow of what would be literally hundreds of letters and poems appealing for release began again in earnest. The volume was such that James Glover, the chief male nurse, was obliged to ask Scott if she would prefer the letters be sent weekly or daily.

Day after day, almost until the end of his life, Gurney wrote combinations of appeals and poetry, in which the boundaries between forms seem to dissolve.[14] Poems become appeals, and appeals become letters, essays or autobiographies, in a complex, repetitive and obsessive pattern. In Barnwood, they had largely been addressed to his friends, and literary or musical contacts. He had established that that was clearly not working, so he widened his net, and began to address more distant figures of authority such as the war prime minister and, repeatedly, the Metropolitan Police.[15]

If his voice was to stand any chance of being heard, it was dependent on his cherished ability to create. The appeal literature is generally not well constructed, and the letters and poems are formless, and often rambling. Nevertheless, written alongside poems and songs that are among his best, the appeals have moments of considerable beauty. For instance, even as late as 1935, he can convey wistfulness with a powerfully compact image:

> Perhaps Autumn has come—but it may need Edward Thomas poems to
> carry it through
> however shut up it is difficult to know land news.[16]

The appeals also show a loss of boundaries, expressing their maker's struggle to distinguish between delusion and reality. They may often be highly repetitious to the point of tedium, but within these parameters they convey the pathos of the maker who cannot now create.

The appeals occupy a space somewhere between poetry and prose. They are peculiar, poignant manifestations of his mental state and document his feelings on his imprisonment. They rage, protest, exhort and demand sympathy. Gurney's reconstructions of his life read as if he were repeatedly writing and rewriting his own obituary; they are the nearest thing possible to a posthumous autobiography. Appeals usually describe a life that, to its writer in the asylum, has become as inaccessible as it would be after death. The paradox is that the appeals represent a kind of repeated resurrection, and a resistance to the curtailing of that identity. 'To the City Besançon' is a typical letter of appeal written three years after Gurney's committal. Its structure and content, and the many other similar appeals, speak of the tension between this fiercely defensive vivacity and suicidal despair, and mirror the shifting definitions of self-identity in the asylum. Here are the first and last stanzas of this epic poem.[17]

To the City Besançon

It is not many that have belief in friend of blood
With Briton Roman—found in night walking, when
I'd steal out of bed; as silent as sleep; and tread
The creaking stairs with fears till my work was done.

Of lacing boots; getting hat overcoat, all unheard;
And close the door to watch upward; stars a million,
the very stars of Gloucester, found in Beethoven.

Then, after stealth—walking hard on ways too nearly common,
Pass the old places, climb, panting till the Roman
Camps of Maximus many a name unheard
of Legion; panting at last, I stood highest on.

[. . .]

Never let recover strength of body; nor any good the
Hurt thing asks—they trapped now to a Hell incredible
For sin—but to sin was all their power—all they were able.
Having England's first right, right of the love of France.
Belgium—Love of Scotland and of all Ireland;
Thus by Labour—and a high right of labour unseen . . .
Denied seeing. . . .
      Evil unthought clawed me to a den
Where it might have it's [*sic*] way with a bloodless clear hand . . .
And torture till Hell spoke in those hideous men;
Hell spewed up again. . . .
          Ivor Gurney

What at first sight might appear to be a jumble of bizarrely unrelated ideas are often references to themes, people and times of particular significance to Gurney. The references have become condensed through recurrent usage and familiarity, and are dropped into the text, often without explanation or apparent connection. He is trying to build his own system of signs and signifiers into a compressed and knotty form of notation. He is revisiting 'the old places'—ancient sites of culture as well as his own historical and cultural reference points—as a sort of wandering Roman sentinel. He is an observer both of history and of his place in it.

Gurney's admiration of Elizabethans, shared by many of his contemporaries, becomes translated in line 150 of 'Besançon' into a rather unexpected non sequitur:

But never post could gain
(Lover of Elizabethans.) the fine musician . . .

In Gurney's mind, such a love was a badge of distinction, a sign of his integrity and taste as a creative thinker. All the more outrageous then, the poem implies, that he could not find employment. He notates himself in parenthesis to underscore his own sensibility and refinement in the midst of such humiliating debasement—stripped of his attachments to culture, friends and resources. Gurney's cryptic use of allusion could in part be a result of his lack of communication with others. The asylum precluded 'normal' social interaction and limited the critical reception of Gurney's work. But this is not the full story. The difficulties and quirky awkwardness of Gurney's style are not to be explained away by incarceration alone. Even if such condensing of thought and image were a result of his isolation, it makes for some of his most intriguing poetry. 'Iliad and Badminton' (written between 1925 and 1926) commingles historical figures, times and places in a sweeping spectrum of allusion. Here he places Gloucestershire cricketers (his own personal heroes) alongside Homer's Hector to give a deeply personal, rather whimsical view of what glory and heroism might mean, from the *Iliad* to the modern day. It is not a poem concerned with its readership, any more than Ezra Pound concerned himself with whether the reader might follow all his allusions in *The Cantos*. Both, on vastly different scales, are works that aim through a patchwork of allusion to present a picture of an ideal society, a 'textbook for Princes', as Pound described his monumental work. Gurney had not read Pound but worked in parallel with him and Eliot in experimenting with fragments, references and allusion to draw together work that was singularly uncompromising in its challenges.[18]

Iliad and Badminton

Men hurl no more the quoits, or bend bow in Tothill
Fields, but a sight of Jessop at his crouch and act—
Stays with me still, though my arm with the rudder have racked.
Shot a hole through a German maybe, Vermands hill.
Hobbs and Strudwick—they keep the long thoughts like Shirley
Of so clear line—and of Boswell, I saw the burly
Past Cricket figure of him, W. G. of Graces.
Out soon—a venerable figure—as from Froissart merely;
Hector was valiant all, but Townsend defied courage,
Would glide where Hector smote, not noted ever on page.
They talk of Kreisler and Ranjitshinjhi, both princes.
Delicatest McNeill Whistler; etching like Paliaret surely—
Glory enough for one—neither glory for others nor wage.
From dead Shrewsbury, as from the younger Grace memory winces—
But Gloucester, Cheltenham's way, with August stays clearly;
Troilus walks white, Cressida truer watches him;
Agamemnon takes brute ease in the half crown gallery—
Priam tells tales of Merton, Thornbury,—doleful since his
Brothers of Troilus—loved son—finished dim
His sight by Richebourg—and bats no more fourth man,
Or takes a bowling turn, drawing eyes of Helen.[19]

'Iliad and Badminton' reads as a photographic set of illustrious cultural figures we roam past on a self-improving Grand Tour of Gurney's life. He delivers his lecture here as a sequence of scenes and characters (in the tradition of James Boswell, whose work he had requested). In an environment where almost every liberty was prohibited and strict parameters were imposed on all aspects of his life, Gurney developed a poetic style that allowed him to range with an extraordinary freedom, in imagination at least. Whilst cultivating such mental and poetic liberty was a logical response to his circumstances, it is also very likely that this growing tendency to allude in shorthand to an eclectic range of material was informed to some extent by his deteriorating condition. This is not to reduce the difficulties of Gurney's work to eccentricity and madness, more to suggest that his work was (unsurprisingly) both influenced by and written in response to his illness. For a while, the balance between creativity and mental disintegration seems to have been such that a freedom of thought was possible that would have been inaccessible to a writer in more conventional circumstances. However dreadful life in the asylum was, much of Gurney's work written between 1922 and 1926 is among his best, ranging and experimenting, as in 'Iliad and Badminton', with a fearlessness that might only come from the removal of 'normal' social, cultural and linguistic barriers. On the edge of reason, and on the edge of society, Gurney can observe and make connections that the 'sane' world might miss.

Reading Gurney's asylum work as 'mad' does him a grave disservice and results in a blinkered understanding of some of his best poetry. In the grand tradition of Schumann and Beethoven, such mature, ambitious work can better be understood as 'late' rather than 'mad'. Late work is often difficult and uncompromising, requiring greater effort from the reader or listener, as it explores previously uncharted territory. Here the many layers of Gurney's allusions, his habit of seeing history from the ancient world to the present in one glance, and his Hopkinsesque style all combine to be initially off-putting.

Gradually, however, as Gurney's distress increased, so the quality of his work deteriorated. One of the symptoms of schizoaffective disorder can be the slow degeneration, or at least alteration, of the patient's use of language. Psychiatrists have a number of terms to describe the different stages of this disintegration. One such phase is commonly referred to as 'derailment'. This can be described through the analogy of a journey: buying a train ticket from Paddington to Oxford, but going via Sussex, for instance.[20] The journey makes sense in its own terms—there is a train ticket, a journey is undertaken by train, and the metaphorical traveller arrives, but the route might appear incomprehensible to an external observer. The metaphor might easily be applied to many of Gurney's appeals and poems, 'Iliad and Badminton' being a prime example. A point is made, a thesis is set out to be presented, but the information included and the structure of its argument is eccentric. It does, however, make sense within its own logic, and a level of perception is sometimes possible that a single-minded journey from A to B would not have afforded.

Gurney's changing relationship to language is of course critical to understanding him as a poet, but it is erroneous to assume that his poetry would necessarily be the worse for it. Whatever criteria we use to judge quality, a poet experiencing such mental changes, able inadvertently to record the process through his writing, leaves a valuable record. In Gurney's case, his work is far more than an unusually articulate chart of his mental deterioration. It is a creative response to a changed state of the perception of the connections between thoughts and ideas. His efforts to draw his thoughts together, to keep control of language, results in writing that is challenging, often unpolished, but invariably wholly original, profound and devoid of any affectation. He had come a long way from the early pseudo-Georgian, Rupert Brooke–inspired poetic efforts of 1915. Gurney was beginning to chart new poetic territory (with the voices of Whitman and Gerard Manley Hopkins still somewhere in the background). It is one of the many ironies of his life that, in the midst of his prolonged agony, his poetry and later his music were to experience golden years in which articulacy and true musical and linguistic adventure were combined. It was only in the 1930s that his grasp on language deteriorated profoundly, and his artistic voice was silenced.

His technique of oblique association of events and places and his increasingly idiosyncratic use of language were a combination of a creative response to his situation, and part of the schizophrenic element of schizoaffective disorder. It was also informed by the new poetic voice that he (like some of the other war poets) had been compelled by circumstance to develop to express the unprecedented experience of the trenches. Broadly speaking, poets such as Sassoon, Edward Thomas and Owen had enlisted in the early years of their poetic careers and would have developed their mature voices during this period with or without the intervention of the war. But the extremities the war poets faced often necessitated a condensing of the process and quickly gave many a maturity beyond their years and poetic experience.

In the asylum, Gurney found himself for a second time in an extreme situation that demanded expression through poetry. He was faced with the challenge of finding a language to explore both incarceration and the experience of delusions and impending madness. Now, with more time to write than the war had afforded, but just as much misery and longing to express, he built on the maturity his poetry had already begun to develop.

He may have begun to write some of his finest poetry, but it is hard to make a case for the appeals being among his greatest achievements. They are certainly among his most bizarre. In fact, the appeals are so odd, so lengthy and rambling and directed to such unlikely recipients, that we might assume such a genre is unique to Gurney, and a by-product of his illness. In fact, they belong to a long tradition of similar literature, written by desperate inmates of asylums, from John Perceval's indignantly titled *A Narrative of the Treatment Experienced by a Gentleman, During a State of Mental Derangement* (1838) to 'Beat Generation' writer Seymour Krim's *Views of a Nearsighted Cannoneer* (1961).[21] Nearer in time to Gurney, a female asylum patient, writing under the pseudonym of Rachel Grant-Smith, described years of fruitless letter-writing to authorities in *The Experiences of an Asylum Patient* (1922).[22]

Asylum rules relating to patients' letters dictate that the institution should treat all written correspondence by patients with a marked degree of formality and respect. Whilst the verbal ravings of patients might be discounted, the act of writing apparently lent gravitas to their words. Some of the envelopes of Gurney's appeal letters are preserved. A large proportion of them are not stamped or post-marked, suggesting that they were withheld by the asylum. It is possible that they were handed to Marion Scott on her visits to the asylum to post, or perhaps she requested that they were held back for her to intercept. Equally, they may have been collected together, and sent to her in one big envelope. Whilst we cannot know precisely what happened, each of these possibilities would have constituted a serious breach of the rules. The minutes of the Visiting Committee's meetings record that patients' letters 'detained by order of the Medical Superintendent' must be submitted to the committee, but there is no record in the minutes of such letters, and it is highly unlikely that they ever saw Gurney's withheld correspondence.[23] There is a letter from Marion Scott to Harvey, dated 12 January 1929, which implies that the authorities were withholding his letters either on the grounds of the insanity of their contents or simply because of the impracticality of some of the addressees:

> I came upon some papers which Ivor had written, but which the Hospital would not send to the addresses thereon, and instead of destroying them they passed them on to me: it seemed to me that perhaps I had better investigate these derelict envelopes. In one addressed to the Secretary, King's College, and the Women's Club I found the contents appeared to be for you, so I send them, though I think they must have been written some time ago.[24]

Scott's striking use of the word 'derelict' to describe the envelopes indicates the breakdown in meaning and communication such unreceived letters represent. Gurney's appeals were often addressed to figures of authority, such as the London Metropolitan Police and the prime minister. Others such as 'To Old New England', 'To the Army of Bapaume', 'To the Old Vic', or 'The University of Durham' are all to institutions, people or places Gurney respected, or that featured in his life.[25]

Gurney's appeals have been described as being addressed to 'obviously impossible' recipients (he cites the London Metropolitan Police Force as an example), the implication being that such letters, however lucid in the early years of incarceration, are a symptom of his madness.[26] However, the act of addressing authority in order to secure release was not as eccentric as it might appear. Letter-writing, however ambitious, was the right of all asylum patients, as they were legally entitled to appeal to certain figures of authority. All asylums were instructed to advertise this by posting a copy of the Lunacy Act of 1890 (Sect. 41) on the walls wherever private patients were in residence:

> The manager of every institution for lunatics shall forward unopened all letters written by any patient and addressed to the Lord Chancellor, or any Judge

in Lunacy, or to a Secretary of State, or to the Commissioners or any Commissioner, or to the person who signed the order for the reception of the lunatic, or on whose petition such an order was made, or to the Chancery Visitors or any Chancery visitor, or to the Visiting Committees of any institution in which such lunatic is detained.[27]

This remarkably long list of potential recipients shows Gurney's own appeals to bodies of authority in their proper context. He walked past a poster telling him of his right of appeal to such figures as the secretary of state every day for fifteen years. What appears an act of lunacy was in fact no more than a rather desperate attempt to follow proper procedure.

The monotony of asylum life was unrelenting. Initially at least, Gurney was keen to try anything that would alleviate the boredom. Indoor activities took precedence during the dreary winter months. There were parties on the wards, sometimes in fancy dress. As the weather improved, there were garden parties, motor drives and picnics. Dr Steen claimed, with some justification, that Dartford led the way nationally in the provision of entertainments. The hospital was proud of its status as the first in the country to purchase a cinematograph (Steen had to work hard to persuade the more conservative members of staff that it would not start fires, or cause widescale panic amongst patients).[28] It proved to be a good investment; the hospital held weekly events, involving some combination of dancing, recital or film viewing. Gurney's medical notes mention that he made at least one attempt not only to attend but to take part in an event. On 17 February 1923 he was 'present at "Pictures" serving in a musical capacity, but needed much watching, and appears as yet hardly fit for such entertainment.'[29] Drawing on his short-lived career as a cinema pianist at Plumstead and Bude, Gurney was either attempting to provide background music for the films or providing musical interludes between screenings. Whether or not he agreed with Dr Steen's verdict that he was 'hardly fit for such entertainment', his clearly questionable success probably did not deter him from making his performances in the cinematograph evenings a regular event.

There was an asylum chapel, and concerts of religious music took place there on most Sunday evenings. They were well attended by visitors and 'especially popular' with patients.[30] Whether or not he performed in these informal recitals, Gurney's piano playing soon became a familiar feature of the wards. He was by nature gregarious and outgoing, and even in the depths of his misery, he still attracted people to him. The asylum employed a young upholstery apprentice, a local lad called Charlie Day, who joined the asylum staff at the age of seventeen to mend the soft furnishings. He was also responsible for the more frivolous aspects of asylum life, such as making Christmas decorations and fancy dress costumes. He became close friends with Gurney and would visit him for long chats after his working day had finished. In his recollections of their friendship, Day recalled how Vaughan Williams was a

FIG. 14.4: Some of Dartford's better-behaved patients on an outing.
Courtesy of Francine Payne.

frequent visitor to the asylum, often bringing a troupe of musicians from the Royal College with him. Day's reminiscences are vital evidence in challenging the myth of Gurney the 'lost' composer, writing into a vacuum.

Vaughan Williams himself left no record of these musical sessions with Gurney. As a result of this omission, books such as Robert Edric's fictionalised account of the asylum years, *In Zodiac Light* (2008), have portrayed a misleading image of Gurney composing obscure and rambling works alone, unable to hear any performance of his music, and becoming increasingly out of touch with reality.[31] Edric pictures Gurney insistently showing the doctors his 'compositions'—page after page of spidery black blobs slipping off wobbly staves—a striking but entirely inaccurate image of a mad composer. In total contrast, Day described witnessing a scenario more like an early version of a university outreach scheme, with regular composition workshops on Gurney's work. 'In the dining hall on the grand piano they would play the songs Ivor had written since his last visit. Patients and staff could wander in and listen.'[32] In effect, Gurney's studies were continuing, and whilst he could not be part of College life in person, Vaughan Williams could bring a taste of the College to Dartford. It was a serious commitment for Vaughan Williams, and a lifeline for Gurney.

Day's brief recollection of Vaughan Williams's visits has significant implications for the way in which the still largely unpublished asylum compositions should be judged. Idiosyncrasies in both music and poetry have frequently been attributed not only to his illness but also to the lack of an audience, performance opportunities and intellectual stimulation. Far from being dashed off in a deranged frenzy, Gurney's asylum compositions were thoughtfully conceived, worked and reworked. They were then played through and discussed by musicians who took Gurney's asylum work seriously.

Despite Vaughan Williams's support, Gurney was too depressed for 1922 to be a year of prolific composition. He produced only a handful of songs, concentrating his efforts on poetry to express his new and shocking predicament. It was as if music had failed him, temporarily at least (although by 1925 he would be composing as prolifically as he had been in the years after his demobilisation). One aspect of music-making was permanently out of bounds to Gurney, and it was a loss that would cause him immense pain. He was never again to witness a live orchestral performance of quality. In the poem 'Watching Music', he poignantly articulates his frustration at his inability to attend performances—musical scores can indicate the pitch and duration of notes, but never capture their sound. Without the possibility of performance, they are impotent; 'poor unmouthed creatures', as he poignantly describes them elsewhere.[33] The poem begins:

> Watching music—guessing the sounds set down.
> How on the real instruments they would sound, when
> Gathered in a small room, lit with gold firelight thrown
> Lovely about the room, the gloom riching again.
> Strings should sound all man's heart ever found,
> Or piano dearly touched tell truth's tale of pain
> Or beauty . . .
> Seeing the black
> Notes on the page, cursing the sounds' lack
> To tell such imagination its true creation
> To realise sound's beauty under the look
> Of crotchet, minim, quaver on the page,[34]

Music cannot be heard, and so he creates the sonorities of instruments through the musicality of his language. The warmth of the vowel sounds in 'lovely about the room, the gloom riching again' complements the sinuosity of 'Strings should sound all man's heart ever found'. His brief recreation of the sounds of instrumental music is interrupted by the spitting anguish of the present, the bitterness of the 'black' . . . 'cursing the sounds' lack'. Music 'looks' at itself. Gurney records the appearance of music notated on the page, but with no sound. This is a poetic record of his own musical deprivation.

It was no substitute for live performance, but he did at least have access to some recorded music and to the radio. The asylum owned a record player, which received occasional donations from record companies to supplement its collection.[35] In 1921 the hospital was also the first to introduce a wireless to its recreation room. Both were well used and appreciated by the patients. More wireless sets were purchased for the wards and dining hall, to liven up the dinner times and dull winter evenings. Despite Gurney's conviction that it was 'wireless' in the abstract that was torturing him, he frequently made use of this link to the musical world, searching the *Radio Times* for broadcast concerts of particular interest to him. He had to negotiate both with the wishes of other patients who may not have been such fans of classical music, and with the inflexible asylum regime. He later complained to Adeline Vaughan Williams that the best music was broadcast after the unreasonably early hospital bedtime.[36] Clearly the lenience shown by Dr Steen over revoking Gurney's suicidal status did not stretch to extending his listening hours; later bedtimes meant paying staff overtime.

When in London, Gurney had taken full advantage of the vibrant music scene and had been present at historic premieres. The live concerts the asylum itself put on were of a very different quality, however. Now, in place of *A London Symphony* or the *Fantasia on a Theme by Thomas Tallis*, Gurney was offered a far less palatable diet of amateur concerts comprising exclusively light music, much of it frequently repeated. Despite its limited repertoire, the asylum's instrumental ensemble was very popular, lending a sense of occasion to the annual fancy-dress dances for staff and patients, and accompanying the more regular dance evenings and parties on the wards.[37]

To supplement the home-grown entertainments there were occasional visiting troupes, offering lighthearted plays or cabaret of highly variable standards. Some were so dreadful that when the superintendent pasted the programme into the scrapbook in which the events were recorded, he wrote a heartily underlined 'never again' underneath it. And just in case he forgot, he added N. B., and underlined that. Three times. The well-meaning performers of 'Oh Susannah—A Farcical Comedy' were unlikely ever to strut the boards of Stone House's stage again.[38]

A perusal of the entertainments scrapbook gives the impression that life in the asylum was a flurry of cream teas, parties and brass bands. What the scrapbook does not record, of course, were many more days that were endlessly monotonous. Even on the days of a social or musical event, many more hours of the day were dominated by dreary routine and the fight against energy-sapping, debilitating medication. It is also not clear from the records who was permitted to attend these events. There were many patients who would not have been in a fit state to sit without disrupting a performance, and these diversions were for the benefit of those who were not so seriously ill. Those who needed it most would have had very little contact with the outside world, or any distraction from their predicament.

At first the uneventful days had merged into each other, as Gurney waited to be told he could leave. By March 1923, however, he was starting to understand the importance of marking time. Like so many other long-term prisoners, he began to count the days. The margins of his manuscripts record the tally: six months confinement, then six and a half months, and so on, as the days dragged on. He wrote to Dr Harper, who had been his physician whilst in London, complaining that a stay in the hospital that should, he believed, have only been six weeks had now extended to eight and a half months.[39] For Gurney, Dartford was no therapeutic holiday camp, as his continual writing to any person or body of authority asking for release or 'chance of death' testifies. His forays into cinematograph evenings and possible attendances at dances and concerts could at best only serve as minor distractions from his mental suffering.

The days wound on, and it became increasingly clear to Gurney that this forbidding prison was to be his home. He experienced an increase in the wireless interference he believed was torturing him. He found himself in an impossible situation; the more miserable he was, the more his delusions increased, and the more he suffered, the more he despaired. Gurney was, both literally and metaphorically, trapped in a 'house of dull pain',[40] as he expressed it, whilst outside the daffodils and cherry trees flowered. He ached for the Gloucestershire countryside.

As the spring blossomed, he cried repeatedly for 'free death by river',[41] campaigning for his own death in his almost daily appeals. He found some distraction in an escape into others' verse, and was reading poetry prolifically. He frequently requested whole boxes of books from his exasperated mother and Marion Scott, most of which he destroyed by obsessively underlining the text. Disgusted at the waste, his mother eventually gave up sending them. There was an impressively large library at Gurney's disposal, which was a major feature of asylum life.[42] Around fourteen thousand books were on loan within the asylum at any one time, and a trolley was pushed around the wards daily to bring books to bedridden patients.[43] The titles stocked are not recorded, though they probably erred on the side of the popular. A 1920 pamphlet entitled *Life in a Madhouse* describes the average asylum library as being too lowbrow for intellectual patients, with 'poor novels . . . of no earthly use to one who had ransacked the BM [British Museum] in years gone by.'[44]

Gurney could also use the reference library, which was set up with desks for patients to write letters in more privacy than the wards afforded. It stocked most periodicals and newspapers, giving Gurney access to the latest published poetry and book reviews, but Scott also kept him well supplied with his own personal copies of the *Times Literary Supplement*, the *Christian Science Monitor* (an odd choice, but explained by the fact that she wrote as a critic for them), and the *Radio Times*. He also requested the *Manchester Guardian*. In short, she ensured that he kept in touch as much as possible with external events. Just as he had done in the trenches, he followed news of publications with interest, and gleaned tasters of poetry collections from quotes in reviews. He was physically shut off from literary and musical London, but it had not dampened his interest in its progress. Whilst he advocated his own death, he was not yet ready to renounce the intellectual world, and certainly had not relinquished his grip on his place in it, tentative though his hold might have been.

Of the two hundred or so poems written during the first year of his incarceration, many focus on his predicament, powerfully articulating his despair and frustration. Others exhibit a startling detachment. He was more than capable of stepping out of his immediate misery and, in moments when the voices in his head were subdued, he began to write some of his most exquisite poems to date, with no hint at the circumstances in which they were written. 'Hedges', for instance, dates from January 1923, and is an appreciation of the artistry of hedge-laying, comparing it to the art of making music.[45] Its language has a vigour and quirkiness (lines such as 'Green lopped-off spear-shaped, and stuck notched-crooked up' are a delight to savour and proof enough of Gurney's idiosyncratically musical feel for language). A world away from depression and suicidal thoughts, Gurney weaves together Mozart's Piano Concerto No. 23 and his unusual simile as deftly as the hedge layer weaves his 'wonderful patterns of bright green', the poem itself an exercise in counterpoint.

Other poems written that spring draw on subject matter that was familiar Gurney territory: he ranged from the Romans to London, and repeatedly returned to Gloucester and its countryside. His work variously began to investigate his relationship to Gloucestershire in retrospect, to mourn its loss, and to be concerned for its preservation. He used nature as a metaphor to express his feelings about his situation as a patient, and began to develop a rich combination of bitterness, despair and affection for the landscapes that existed only in his imagination.

'Cut Flowers', written during this first year in Dartford, offers an interesting parallel to the technique used by poets such as Blunden, who had mastered the art of yoking together the unspoilt pastoral and war's destruction for effect. This binary between nature and the unnatural acts of man, freedom versus captivity, was a theme present in Gurney's writing before the asylum. Now, from within Dartford, the 'steely yoke' that destroys in swathes is a postwar threat, and, just as cut flowers must be condemned to wither and die, so must the poet, having been plucked cruelly from his own landscape.

The poem begins:

Not in blue vases these,
Nor white, cut flowers are seen
But in the August meadows
When the reaper falls clean—

And the shining and ridged rows
Of cut stalks show to the eye
As if some child's hand there
Had ranged them, and passed by
To other rows, other swathes.[46]

Gurney was familiar with Edward Thomas's superbly bleak poem 'Rain', in which the 'myriads of broken reeds, all still and stiff' offer an oblique image to substitute for the many dead. Gurney's own message is clear, separated only by a space at the very end of this long, thin, stalk-like poem. The poem ends with the single line: 'gather them, pluck not, please'. It is best not to be collected up at all, whether it be by the grim reaper or the asylum authorities. Cut off from his natural habitat, he explored within the confines of his metaphor what better options there might have been: anything other than the 'intolerable . . . four walls' of the asylum.[47] The question as to where Gurney might flourish was one that exercised many of his friends on his behalf, and their responsibility for his enforced incarceration would haunt some of them for the rest of their lives.

CHAPTER FIFTEEN

'Dark Fire'

'Out from the dim mind like dark fire rises thought'[1]

Apart from a brief stir amongst the staff when two male nurses were dismissed for playing cards on duty, little happened within the asylum community in the early summer of 1923. Gurney continued to write volumes of poetry, both alongside and intertwining with his appeals, but he still did not feel able to touch composition.

Instead, he was amusing himself by reading a great deal of French poetry. He even tried his hand at translating the poem 'France, Mère des Arts, des Armes et des Lois' by Renaissance poet Joachim du Bellay.[2] It is easy to see why it attracted his attention. 'To France' bears many similarities in tone to the appeal poems, berating the Mother Country for neglecting its child (or lamb, in this analogy), and lamenting the writer's tragic life.

Without the original text, it would be easy to assume that the poem had been written by Gurney himself, and that this was an invention of his, an appeal poem dressed up as a translation, under the assumed identity of a Renaissance poet. But 'To France' is in fact a surprisingly faithful rendition of Bellay's text. The only slight variation was the addition of an exclaimed 'Aie Me!' by Gurney for added affect.

Four years later, he was to become far bolder in his experiments with other literary and musical personas, frequently 'becoming' Beethoven, Shakespeare or Brahms, trying out their identities for size, and rewriting their work. This translation seems like an early example of this; Gurney, in everything but name.

Translation is perhaps the acceptably sane version of Gurney's later habit of 'becoming' other writers. By translating from French to English, he could legitimately make another's words his own. By July he was writing in French, having renamed himself 'The poet of St Julien à Vermand', a fictional saint, an amalgamation of the two locations at which Gurney was injured.[3] He sent a translation of a Victor Hugo poem, 'Waterloo', to his sister Dorothy, in the hope that she could get it published in the humble *West Ham Weekly News*.[4]

On 18 August, this period of relative calm and productivity was violently disrupted. Dr Templeton, an ambitious young medical officer who had recently joined the staff, decided to replace Gurney's head pains and voices with something far worse. He gave him malaria. As a patient in a large county asylum, Gurney was an all-too-likely recipient of any experimental treatment thought fit by doctors, with less external accountability than would have been required in a smaller private institution. The malaria experiment deliberately induced delirium, in the hope that the high fever might drive out the mental illness (rather like leeching in the seventeenth century). There was some evidence that malarial fever might have beneficial effects, although the research on its effect on the mentally ill was very much in its infancy. The hospital authorities would not have needed to do much to persuade Ronald to sign the permission form, as he was generally in favour of anything that seemed like punishment for his truculent brother. Marion Scott also agreed to the treatment without any apparent reservations. Scott's health was never robust, and she had been suffering from nervous exhaustion. She was hardly in a position to take a positive, interventionist approach to the matter.

> The world in general is not a very noble or inspiring place just now, and against this general background there was the particular problem of Ivor's insanity. For months I had been dashing my thoughts and energies against the problem. Almost uselessly it seemed and my heart could only cry out in rebellion at the whole horrible torture of insanity, and revolt at the routine of acquiescence to which its continual sight has reduced physicians.[5]

Scott decided she needed a retreat in the Swiss alps with Sydney Shimmin and another friend, Gertrude Eaton, to help her face the 'misery of Dartford'. Gurney, for whom the misery represented not an occasional depressing visit but an unrelenting reality, had no brisk mountain walks to perk him up. As Scott was about to depart for her holiday, she sanctioned the experiment on Gurney as a no doubt well-meant parting gesture. Scott's affection for him, and her anxiety on his behalf were genuine and deeply felt, but even Gurney must have found it hard to be grateful for this latest use of her authority over him.

The malaria treatment has sparked an ongoing debate as to whether Gurney was suffering from syphilis, contracted perhaps in France. On admission to the asylum he would have been routinely suspected of having syphilis, not merely because of his psychological symptoms but because of its incidence in the general population, and the heightened anxiety about troops returning infected from foreign service. Sir Malcolm Morris had addressed the Royal Institute of Public Health at their London Conference in 1919, citing demobilised soldiers importing infection and warned of the danger of passing it on to British women.[6] This incidence (around 3 million diagnosed cases in the UK in 1916) did little to counter the view that insanity was the product of moral degeneracy.[7]

Whilst it is perfectly possible that Gurney had contracted syphilis or gonorrhoea, it was certainly never diagnosed.[8] The speculation stems more from a fundamental misunderstanding about the purpose of the mysterious malaria treatment than from evidence. Syphilitic patients were labelled by asylum doctors as suffering from 'general paralysis of the insane', which appears repeatedly in asylum records as a cause of death.[9] The asylum's doctors were thoroughly accustomed to diagnosing syphilis, as when a patient's illness progressed to the tertiary stage, an asylum was their usual destination. Asylum patients lost all vestiges of dignity and reputation on admission to the institution, so the doctors were not concerned with hushing up any diagnoses that might cause embarrassment. Had they thought Gurney was suffering from syphilis, it would certainly have been unflinchingly recorded. However, his diagnosis was that of 'delusional insanity'; the term 'general paralysis' is never mentioned in relation to his case. Furthermore, Gurney and the other nineteen patients chosen for the malaria experiment were all inoculated with the same serum syringe, and the records of the experiment state that the syringe was not used on any syphilitics. In short, the staff were as certain as they could reasonably be that none of these twenty patients, including Gurney, were sufferers.

Malarial treatment was a nationally debated topic in the 1920s and '30s. In January 1924, the *Journal of Mental Science* published an article entitled 'The Effect of Malarial Fever upon Dementia Praecox Subjects'. It was written by W. L. Templeton, who until shortly before the date of writing, had been second assistant medical officer at Dartford, and had been responsible for the experiment on Gurney. He had learnt of the possibilities of malaria treatment whilst in Vienna and had introduced it to the hospital. In his article, Dr Templeton claimed that producing fever artificially in acute mental conditions resulted in an improvement in the state of mind of the patient, their temporary illness acting as a purge. He records his experimental treatment (clearly at Dartford, although the institution is not named) of twenty male dementia praecox cases. Templeton confidently concludes that the patients, once recovered, were much improved from their original condition. His gamble had been an unmitigated success, he claimed, and some of the men were as good as cured. No patients are named, but it is certain that one of these twenty was Gurney.[10] Gurney's response to the treatment is recorded briefly in his medical notes, and is somewhat at variance with Templeton's enthusiasm:

August 18th Patient is now having daily paroxysms of malaria fever. He is extremely restless and anxious [. . .] in bed on account of fever says his chart
is faked. Health poor.
August 29th 1923 Mentally he is depressed and prays for death. [. . .] He is in
weak health.

Gurney somehow found the energy to write a lucid letter to Scott on the 29th,
the day after his birthday, for which he had received a none-too cheering visit from
his brother. Just as he had become accustomed to do in his wartime correspondence, he omits any mention of the true misery of his situation. Anxious not to spoil
Scott's holiday, he hoped that Scott was enjoying her break, recounting that he had
been reading Shakespeare's history plays 'with great admiration'.[11]

September 6th Patient's malarial paroxysms have terminated and he is improving in health but there is little or no change in his delusions. He however
expressed himself as willing to give a promise not to escape. Health fair.

The notes read as if this is a promise extracted after torture. It was not far from the
truth. The margins of the notes also record the patient's weight. During the period of
treatment, Gurney dropped from 10 st 9 lb to an emaciated 9 st 1 lb by 16 October.
Twenty-one days after Gurney's treatment ended, Templeton abruptly resigned.
No adequate reason for his departure was given, and he never returned to psychiatry.[12] His almost defensively upbeat published account of the experiment appeared
in print after his dismissal. The malaria experiment was never repeated at Dartford.
The Annual Report for 1924 merely states that 'Malaria treatments have not been
continued as the results were disappointing.' The psychological effects of the malarial treatment on the other Dartford patients can only be guessed at, but a telling new
behavioural trait is recorded in Gurney's notes at this time:

November 5th: Still asking for discharge or death. Adopts an emotional
prayerful attitude from time to time.

In the midst of his misery that autumn, Gurney's thoughts turned repeatedly to
the armistice, as a focus of his anger at his betrayal. During the war, he had clung to
the hope, however desperately, that England would pay the debt she owed him and
his comrades. On previous armistice days, he had taken part in the public acts of
memorialising, and even written works such as his orchestral *War Elegy*. Now, three
years after he had written it, he was half-starved, ill and despairing. This 11 November found him praying on his knees, and not as an act of remembrance for his
friends. The armistice celebrations were a national act of 'honour'—a term bitterly
resonant for Gurney. Honour was precisely what he had sought and lost; the indig-
nity and pain of the malaria experiment were simply the final insult.

He might have been stripped of his dignity, but his delusions were still intermittent, and only total madness could take from him his knowledge of the war. War poets are inherently truth tellers—his insights gained through suffering gave Gurney, he believed, the right to speak. Just as he had admired Sassoon for telling a truth (if not a profound truth, Gurney thought), so he began to insist on his own cultural right to tell of what he knew. In his appeals, the idea of the war poet as the tag to which he might cling for a sense of self-identity had become increasingly important during the spring and summer of 1923. That a handful of his poems had been included in *The Muse in Arms* in 1917, one of the earliest anthologies specifically collecting war poetry, gave him the legitimacy he needed. His inclusion was official recognition that he was, indeed, a war poet. As society looked back at the conflict, trying to understand how it might memorialise, mourn or try to forget, the war poets began to take their place as cultural icons—spokespeople for a time of overwhelming sorrow and intensity, voices to warn future generations, and Gurney, rightly, knew that he had much to offer alongside them.

He drafted three different versions of an Armistice Day poem, all seething with betrayal; furious on behalf of the dead, but primarily on behalf of the tortured living.

Armistice Day

The dead, that died for Englands honour only
Had not been pleased on this grave day to know
(Lying in mingled graves, or in sombre lonely)
That crowds would dare stand for honour, to give
Homage, while twenty miles off one of Five
War Poets, called in torment to honour of England
And prayed a doctor not to remain alive.
England. One of Five. . . .
Their blood, their wish, their spokesman England, remember.
(Believe in God) One of Five.
    I. B. Gurney
D. Steens.
Demanding Free Life
   or Free leave
     of death by
      River
       at once[13]

In his verse he had repeatedly returned to the trenches since he had moved to Dartford. Now, as his incarceration dragged on, he was becoming increasingly invested in his self-coined title, War Poet. His 'selected army Verses are best of any', he believed. Sitting alone in his room, he could try out his name alongside those he admired, and see how well it fitted in the list of the other poets who had emerged from the war.[14] He began to give them a running order: Nichols first, with Brett Young coming in second, and F. W. Harvey third. He was, as he put it in 'Victory Night', 'one of five', but he did not mark who the last of his 'five' chosen poets was, or whether he classed himself fourth or fifth. Modesty was not one of Gurney's chief virtues, insecure though he often felt about his work. In addition, one of the very few advantages to his isolation was that there were no other intellectual voices to disagree with his opinions. By September 1924 he was promoting himself to 'first war poet, he thinks'.[15] It was a big claim, but considering the quality of the war poetry he had written that year, it was one that stood up well to criticism.

The status of war poet was not an anachronism for Gurney: it was a continuing reality. His insistence on the term First War Poet served to give him a sense of belonging, a category into which he could claim he fitted, but it was more than this. He had begun to use the unlooked-for opportunity the asylum afforded as a chance to recollect, if not in tranquillity, then at least at leisure. He could recall and assess the events and memories he had not had the chance to write about in the less conducive conditions of wartime.

During the war, he had recorded his thoughts as letters and poems out of mental necessity, as an outlet for his creativity, and to order his often traumatic experiences by shaping them quickly into art.[16] They were hasty vignettes, in essence and intention more like the sketches and poems in the *Gloster Gazette,* that were designed to resonate with the troops, to amuse or move them, and not necessarily written with an eye to posterity. Now, with the infinite leisure and thinking time that Dartford provided, these first war poems (which he felt to be jottings made on the spot) could be improved upon, and the real process of crafting words could begin. Gurney could use the lessons and disappointments of the postwar years to inform and crystallise his thoughts on the conflict, without resorting to the clichés which some of his earliest and most hasty wartime attempts had employed. He was already involved in his own retrospective.

It was a grand aim, but one that, had he known it, was absolutely in keeping with other writers who had had the good fortune to have survived to rewrite their experiences. Blunden, Graves, Aldington and Sassoon all spent the 1920s fashioning their emotional responses and recollections into memoirs that came to form the canon of war literature, a decade after the conflict had ended. *Undertones of War, Goodbye to All That, Death of a Hero* and *Memoirs of an Infantry Officer* all shaped the way the war was viewed for the rest of the twentieth century. It seemed that, just as composers such as Arthur Bliss felt the need to write large-scale monuments exorcising their wartime experiences and losses ten years after the event, so writers also had

Fig. 15.1: 'Killing the patient sack'—The 2/5ths engaged in bayonet training.
© Soldiers of Gloucestershire Museum.

a psychological need to bid 'goodbye to all that' through their writing. Only Gurney continues as a war *poet*, however—the others refigured their memories as memoir.

During the war, he was aware that such experiences would be best written about when fully digested. He believed that the immediacy and anger of Sassoon's verse was detrimental to its quality, and now, just as other poets were moving away from the war as subject matter, Gurney had the opportunity to return to it with objectivity and a more dispassionate approach. With his combination of hindsight, and the poetic lessons learnt from Edward Thomas, Whitman and Hopkins, Gurney was now far better equipped to write of the war than he had been when learning his craft in the trenches. There had been flashes of brilliance, particularly in *War's Embers*, in which he encapsulated a truth in lines that sung, such as the gloriously ridiculous final couplet of 'At Reserve Depot':

The passers-by carelessly amused will see
Breakfastless boys killing the patient sack.[17]

Now he could sustain a poem on the most difficult of subjects with an honesty and immediacy that was both disarming and wrong-footing. A poem about the smell of rotting bodies and the repulsion of burying what was left of your friends would not have found favour with the reviewers of *Severn and Somme,* who had expected wholesome verse from a Gloucestershire lad following in Harvey's footsteps. Neither was it an aspect of the war that his comrades would have wanted to dwell on. Now, with no one to please but himself, he could return to such repugnant memories from the benefit of distance.

North French air may make any flat land dear and beautiful
But East of Ypres scarred was most foul and dreadful
With stuck tanks, ruined bodies needing quick honour's burial,
But yet sunset, first morning, hallowed all, awed, made mysterious
The ugly curves of land running to eastward; the Front of us,
Worse things of conflict not yet hidden unseen underground.
Shall we also fall stricken by one steel shard, sicken
The air with stenches, that were of the Gloucestershire villages,
Be buried with haste, horror; by those were comrades before,
Lie, covered, rot, with no hope but to make meadows quicken
When Time has cleaned this dreadful earth of infinite brute carnages;
And left some clean stuff; earth, beautiful—as once bodies were?[18]

His asylum war poetry is scrupulously honest, and reads like documentary, but it is not exclusively concerned with horror and degradation. In his poem 'The Curses', he presents a portrait of himself as poet-soldier, ludicrously incompatible with his appointed task. He is laden down with literature, both literally and metaphorically, shedding books as he goes.

Curses on packs that weigh a ton too heavy!
(Comrade you carry books; one sticks out, believe me!)
Curses on marching cobbles the left hand man.
(True, one needs his legs unequal, a difficult plan.)
Curses on halts that disappear like mere seconds.
(You should take your watch out, measure it all—each tick, reckoned.)
Curses on shoulders that will not settle to steady
To bear the weight of equipment, the spirit ready.
(Yes, but when you have parcels, and there's half of a cake
In your haversack, and Cobbett, Borrow and William Shake-
speare in your left pack, in your right Walt Whitman;
Spirit of Man–an anthology, and a bit, man,
Of that remarkable author William Wordsworth.
In your trenching tool cover, Keats, yet the child of earth.
A chess set hidden somewhere, and the Everyman Century
of Essays stuffed in your tunic out of harm's way.
Really, really, you must fill your head with your learning,
Until no more the blisters on your feet are burning).[19]

As he repeatedly returned to his months in the trenches, he looked from many angles at the experience, embracing humour, friendship and the ridiculousness of it all as well as the misery. Cumulatively, the body of his war poetry written during these years offers a detailed picture more powerfully vivid and original than almost any other war poet.

Robert Graves and (in music) Arthur Bliss wrote at least in part to rid themselves of their nightmares and to negotiate a future around or despite the memories that haunted them. Gurney did not continue to write as a war poet because the act of bearing witness helped him. He wrote of the war in peacetime to establish his own presence, and the validity of his experience. By writing of the war in the years after the armistice, he could convince himself and others that he had been a war poet worthy of consideration (a continual source of anxiety for him), and could maintain his claim on society, citing his war service as his part of the bargain. Not only had he fought, he had, then and now, documented his service and created art from it. Surely the more he wrote, the more his country must honour and hear him, and free him from his captivity?

In the asylum, Gurney's future was limited to a reliving of his past. His war writing was impelled by a need to hold on rather than let go. Gurney's sense of his calling as one of the chosen spokespeople of the war gave him the focus that was needed to create some of the most significant songs and poems to emerge from the conflict. Haines felt that Gurney's post-1922 poetry was the start of a new era for him. He had acquired 'a style of his own and a certainty of touch quite different and they are fresh and original and strikingly modern for the early twenties.'[20]

It is one of the most profound ironies of Gurney's years in the asylum that just at the point at which the doctors were recording his mental state as deteriorating, Gurney was managing to produce an extraordinary quantity of verse, and was about to couple it with a return to music, work in both genres that was balanced, dispassionate, and well crafted. He was, in fact, working his way up to the most prodigiously creative year of his life.[21]

Gurney began to create new work at an increasingly ferocious pace, but he was also looking back over older manuscripts. The two disciplines of revision and new writing began increasingly to merge, and to inform one another. Preexisting work frequently spawned what were essentially new poems with the same or similar titles, born during the process of revision, but with more difference than similarity to the original. 'First Dawn' is a charming poem capturing a moment of stasis in the trenches, with the smell of bacon in the air and nothing happening other than soldiers looking forward to the mail arriving. Gurney developed it from its predecessor 'Laventie Dawn'.[22] By 1924 Gurney's poems were entities of continual growth and development. Just as he was returning to the same themes, time and time again—London, Gloucester, honour, dawn, walking, wartime experiences—he was also developing them in countless different poems and guises. It did not matter whether there was repetition, or whether poems used the same phrases (he overuses the word 'azure', for instance, to the point of obsession). Gurney's creative process was one of a huge-scale cross-fertilization between past and current work, giving the impression that his writing by this point was one vast poetic thought, that happened to be divided up into individual poems.

Take the third line of 'First Dawn', for instance—'While in the trenches, men forgetting nights dolours'—which chimes with the third line of the similarly titled 'Smudgy Dawn': 'across low meadows misted still with the dolours of night—'. As the two poems were written around the same time, to see them as entirely separate pieces seems an artificial distinction. But there is also great variety within this ongoing development of ideas and images across the corpus of his work. These are two very different 'Dawns'—one over the trenches, and one in Gloucestershire. 'Smudgy Dawn' is in itself a rewriting of a poem beginning with the title words of a separate poem, 'Spring Dawn'.[23] These are not so much improvements as a theme and variations, developed over a period of time. A panoply of experience is represented through dawn in wartime, dawn at home, and dawn remembered from the asylum.

Another subject for development and variation, explored over a number of poems, is Gurney's admiration for the art of hedge-laying: of weaving together the same branches to create a pattern, through craftsmanship. It is an image that provides a useful metaphor for his own approach to his poetry. Now, after nearly a decade as a poet, Gurney could look back over his work as a vast and ongoing exercise in counterpoint. By putting his poems into dialogue, he is, effectively, weaving together loose strands, adjusting branches that were perhaps not bound in tightly enough, adding others, and exercising a little judicious pruning. This interlinking of theme and image sets up a subtle rhythm across the individual poems: a kaleidoscopic pattern of colour, sound and image. In fact, Gurney's poetic voice is characterised by one long gathering together and interweaving of fragments. Two years before, T. S. Eliot described 'a heap of broken images' in *The Waste Land*. The fragmentary nature of the poem gave the impression of disjointed splintering, even as Eliot claimed 'these fragments have I shored against my ruins'. Eliot had been recovering from a breakdown in 1921–22; both poets were writing at least in part to restore their mental equilibrium. Gurney, however, could not afford for his fragments of memory to be left in a heap or to be disparate and discarded—for the sake of his own sanity he had to connect events, images and memories, weaving himself a protective shield of words to safeguard his own mind from the illness that threatened increasingly to erode it. For Gurney, poetic coherence was synonymous with health.

A year into his incarceration, Gurney was still far from being ground down entirely, but his physical suffering was acute. During the winter of 1923 he complained increasingly of pains in his neck and head. They had always been a symptom of his condition, but now in the new year of 1924 they were becoming unbearable, and an osteopath was engaged to try to give him some relief. After seven visits, Dr Cyriax had to admit defeat. No one seemed certain what was causing them, or whether they were indeed a physical manifestation of his delusions of wireless interference, in which case even the most skilled osteopath could be forgiven for being at a total loss.

Shortly before Christmas, he received a very rare visit from Herbert Howells. Marion Scott believed he should visit, although his reluctance was palpable. 'Ivor is so agonisingly sane in his insanity that he feels every thread of the suffering all the time', she wrote.[24] He would certainly not have overlooked Howells's anxiety, and could hardly have taken comfort from it. Howells made every excuse from the moment of boarding the train with Scott. He had to leave early, as he had a party to attend. Perhaps they ought to cut the visit short—he felt he might be coming down with the flu. When they arrived, they sat on the asylum's cane chairs in a corner of the dining hall. Gurney stood awkwardly before them. They watched as other patients were brought in, to be seen by their visitors. Scott recalled an attendant she recognised leading one of the other ex-service patients to meet his family.

> He might have been twenty-five or so, and had evidently been in the war. He had lost one leg, some fingers on his left hand, he was totally blind, and he was insane. O my God—how can men make war? [. . .] I shall never forget that group. The sightless boy, at one side, the Naval man, talking quietly to him—perhaps purposely trying to give the old man time to control his voice—and the latter standing there crimson and trembling, his left hand clutched across his right wrist to still its shaking, his tongue protruding, his whole being convulsed with utter grief. Herbert wisely kept his back turned. Even I, accustomed to seeing tragedy there, nearly broke down.[25]

The visit was miserable, and as soon as Howells could, he made his excuses and fled, weeping. Howells was a sensitive, emotional man, and it was painful for him to see his childhood companion reduced to such degradation and misery. Unlike Gurney, he had the luxury of leaving Dartford to return to a consoling wife and family.

By March Gurney was miserable and uncooperative, his mental condition apparently worse, and he was refusing to get out of bed. He spent the days reading and writing, lying in a bed that had been set up for him on the ward veranda. It was common practise to encourage patients to spend much of the day in the open air, however freezing the conditions. Psychiatry at the time modelled itself closely on the treatments for physical illnesses, whether or not they had any benefit for the mentally ill. Thus, the open-air treatment for a condition such as tuberculosis found its way into mental health practise. It did no demonstrable good, but it happened to suit such a spirit as Gurney's. Being bedridden in the hospital grounds was hardly a substitute for tramping twenty miles over the Gloucestershire hills, but it was at least a taste of the outdoors, and he could see the sky and the edge of the woods from where he lay, propped up on pillows.

During this time, he received the news that Stanford had died of a stroke (on 29 March 1924). Gurney wrote a fond and generous reminiscence of his teacher which was published in the July edition of the journal *Music and Letters*. Stanford had been 'a stiff master, though a very kind man; difficult to please, and most glad to be pleased. England will bury many in the Abbey of Westminster much lesser than he'.[26]

Perhaps his poetic muse had temporarily dried up between January and June as a result of his excruciating headaches, or the work from this period of his life was among a number of boxes of manuscripts that were subsequently destroyed. Either way, he was devouring whatever books came his way. Gurney was very specific in his literary requirements, placing an order with Scott in August for Skelton, Kipling in French, Dolben, Meredith, Drummond of Hawthornden, Blunden, Clare, Sassoon, Hardy, Plutarch, Wilfred Owen.[27] He was certainly writing copious poems by June 1924, as well as arranging the fruits of his labours throughout the summer and autumn of 1924 into seven poetry collections: *Rewards of Wonder; Dayspaces and Takings; Ridge Clay, Limestone; La Flandre, and By-Norton; Roman Gone East; London Seen Clear;* and *Fatigues and Magnificences.* The titles themselves reflect Gurney's by now predictable preoccupations: the war, Gloucestershire, Romans, London and nature. He also collected his own personal favourites of his work, filling a solid little brown and blue book with board covers with a collection of his *Best Poems:* eighty-five of his greatest achievements to date.[28]

The first months of 1925 produced another flood of collections, of which *To Hawthornden* was the first. Hawthornden had been his pet name for Annie Drummond. The memory of her image still served as a muse and a focus for his work, despite having had no contact with her since the end of their relationship in 1918. He had written to Annie in November 1924, and Scott had tried, on his instruction, to track down her address. He wanted to tell her that he had completed '8 books' and to send some of his new work for her approbation, including the poetry collection named in her honour. He felt that the more he wrote, the more he could convince her that he was not a failure. His writing justified him, and Annie was the imagined judge of his worthiness. In fantasy, she served a valuable purpose, giving him something to live for, someone to strive to please. In reality, Gurney never received any reply from her. Scott probably did not pass on to him the news that Annie's mother had written back, saying her daughter had emigrated to America, was married and had a son.

To Hawthornden was closely followed by another two poetry collections in January and February 1925, entitled *Pictures and Memories* and *The Book of Five Makings.* The five makings (as always, Gurney is scrupulously honest) refer to the five occasions on which he returned to his pink marbled hardback book of poems to revise them. One of the suppositions as to why so much of his work did not find publication during his lifetime was that there was a fundamental lack of care being taken over his writing. Gurney produced a prodigious quantity of work in the asylum, with no external reception for it, and therefore no need to please critics. It is easy to assume that he could be as slapdash as he chose. The accusation has stuck, fuelled partly by the incident back in 1922, in which the manuscript of his proposed collection *80 Poems or So* had baffled Sidgwick and Jackson, who returned the verdict that the poetry was sloppily presented and needed careful revision. However, the manuscripts of the *Book of Five Makings* give the lie to this commonly held view of Gurney's unpublished work. On close inspection, we find that instead of hasty scribblings, there are careful and logical revisions. From the drafts it is possible to chart the progress of the poems, the additions, and the care taken over the precision of language.

Memories of Honour follows the *Book of Five Makings*. This short collection which he describes as 'Infantry Poems' dates from March 1925, as does his *Poems of Gloucesters, Gloucester and of Virginia*, which is largely focused on wartime experiences, but also branches out to include thoughts on America, and on Gurney's relationship with his father. There are historical links to authors and past battles, but these poems often seem rather rudderless in comparison with the revisiting of the war years. It is here that his poetry truly comes alive. Now, with the benefit of the experiences distilled, he could recall the humour and the surprising, trivial details of life. In one poem he appeals to China (as the suppliers of tea) to intervene, since what was served as tea in a dirty Dixie in the trenches was not worthy of the name. In another, he remembers the women near Vaux, who continued their work in the fields despite being practically in the firing line for his bomb-throwing exercises. These are poems lamenting the lack of chocolate, and the absence of beer, and others recall wine that was so poor it was interchangeable with ale. The tastes, smells and textures of trench life emerge in surprisingly sharp focus. At other times, the images of his wartime experiences flash by, sometimes dwelt on in detail, others a series of glimpses: his surprise at finding violets when marching past a wood, remembrances of drinking water from the well at Omiécourt. There are moments of sublime serendipity, alongside those of sheer terror, such as:

> Lay up against the wires, with the dark night cloaking
> everything from sight, save fire's gleam and like blood-
> Shine of red flares chucked over for chance of charging.[29]

He fondly remembered the consolation to be found in café au lait when available, and fondly recalled the beauty and pride of French women. Gurney was far from oblivious to the charms of women, however hapless his physical relationships with them might have been. In 'Mirror of Suzanne', he remembers a girl's grace and poise as she is obliged to walk past the staring Gloucesters on the road. It is presented as a passing moment, but as the title intriguingly implies, Gurney knew her by name. Whether or not his connection to her went any deeper than temporary muse, the memory of her reflection in the waterlogged potholes inspired a particularly beautiful poem, some ten years after the event. A world away from the anguished autobiographical asylum letters, it is a poem written by a man in total control of his faculties. Gurney skilfully manipulates our gaze from the beautifully intimate image of the girl 'loved by autumn water' that reflected her, to the poet, undertaking 'some absurd exercises', awkwardly gauche in her presence. We see their stolen glance at each other reflected in the water. It is a poem firmly rooted in the romantic tradition, tightly contained within its rhyme scheme.

Mirror of Suzanne

A French girl passed a Company of Gloucester Infantry,
And kept dignity, and erect gait, with bent head . . .
We were off to some absurd exercises in some field near by . . .
But it had rained, there were round pools left on the road;
And, I after regarding her youthful dignity
Looked down also, and saw mixed with blue high and cloud
The reflection of her form loved by autumn water;
So slim and self-possessed, as of Europe to be proud.
Which was again a new-old marvel, again the
Eternal differences between races declared,
Could Gloucestershire have so passed by much of Picardy?[30]

Gurney put together another collection, *The Book of Lives and Accusations,* on 29 March, and intended to post it to 'The American Rhodes Scholar at Christ Church, Oxford University' (it is not clear whether he knew who was holding the scholarship at the time). The collection covers many of Gurney's favoured topics: 'Resurrection' describes priests gathering daffodils and Easter flowers, with strong overtones of Housman's 'The Lent Lily' (Gurney was revising *Ludlow and Teme* at around this time, and 'The Lent Lily' concludes the cycle). 'Voces Intimae' takes the title of a Sibelius string quartet that he particularly loved, moves swiftly on to Crickley and its ancient earth works, and follows these with a roll call of heroes. The brilliantly minimalist and daring poem 'Walt Whitman' compresses syntax to convey the vigour and punchiness of his idol's use of words:

He not wrote, but cleft the earth
Some truth known to the manhood of all earth.

Not fashioned, but wrought iron
With the cost of his own spirit in sparks giving.[31]

At the same time that he was engaged in compiling his prodigious number of poetry collections, Gurney also began composing in earnest once more, with a quartet in D minor, *A London Meditation* for piano trio, and another piece of the same title for quartet. Since 1918, hardly a year had gone past without Gurney writing some chamber music, and it was a genre as natural to him as song. This was a confident and ambitious return: *A London Meditation* is a successful, characterful work, with a sense of austerity, and its own particular, bell-like sonorities, echoing the peals from London church towers.

Gurney began to write songs again in December 1924, and from then on he barely paused for breath. In 1925 alone he wrote fifty-four songs with piano, three others with quartet accompaniment, five choral works, two organ pieces (this marked the beginning of a particular flowering of organ works in 1926), a piano sonata and a prelude, five works for violin (including a potential four sonatas), and a formidable eleven string quartets. Many of the asylum manuscripts are lost, either destroyed by the institution or mislaid by his friends. Most of these compositions are among the missing, and we know tantalisingly little about them. Of the above, only the 1924–25 string quartet in D minor survives, owing to the fact that Scott performed it with her quartet at Dartford in 1925, and had copied out the parts for the players. Gurney wrote the quartet in November 1924, and then returned to it with substantial revisions, probably in January 1925 as a result of her performance.

Written in four movements, the D minor quartet is a work dominated by a two-note figure that echoes throughout each movement, passed between the four voices in various different guises as the piece develops. The quartet begins in C minor, giving its sudden shift into D minor an air of freshness and spontaneity. The first movement is thickly textured and relentlessly energetic, as Gurney allows the players little chance to catch their breath. The C major second movement comes as something of a relief, offering the light and shade that the first movement withholds. It is the heart of the work: intense, and calmly ecstatic.

The third movement is a scherzo in 6/8, in which he references a cello solo from his 1919 A major quartet, whilst exploring a tripping staccato semiquaver/quaver figure which bounces between the open fifths and octave of G–D. The work closes with a fiercely playful allegro molto. As a general rule, Gurney writes chamber music with the ear of a composer whose natural tendency is to think in terms of a keyboard and vocal line. The first violin is almost always predominant, and the other three parts are often either paired or used to support the melodious, frequently highly pitched first violin. When fragments of melody are allocated to the rest of the quartet, it tends to be in the manner of a flourish up or down a keyboard, as Gurney passes scalic or triadic motifs fluidly around the group. Gurney's quartets quickly emerse us in their dense, top-heavy soundworld. As a result, when he does alter the texture and division of labour, it is all the more striking to the listener. In the final movement of the D minor quartet, he shines a spotlight on the other three instruments, with moments of solo and sparser textures as the first violin occasionally takes a back seat to allow for a more equal conversation.

There were a further eight chamber works, from trios to clarinet quintet movements, and Gurney apparently even completed the first three movements of a symphony.[32] By anyone's standards, it was an impressive haul. As the manuscript books filled up, he relished returning at last to his identity as a composer, whether or not anyone would be commercially interested in the works over which he had spent so much of his time. As so often, one art form merged into another, and in the poem 'Masterpiece', written at the time of his first draft of the quartet, he observes himself composing. The new intensity of his composition in the asylum became a Proustian moment of recall to the many days he had spent writing music in Gloucester and London, and working through the night at his aunt's house, 'wondering what neighbours may be thinking'. He had set out his approach to poetry-writing in a letter to Scott from the trenches, back in 1917. Now 'Masterpiece' endearingly describes a musical equivalent. In both instances, he notes the necessity of quickly jotting down the flash of inspiration, phrase or tune that rises 'like dark fire' from the 'dim mind'. Then he must return to it, perhaps at night, to work more methodically to develop the initial idea, to shape his 'square work'.

Masterpiece

Out from the dim mind like dark fire rises thought,
And one must be quick on it . . . or scratch sketches, a few . . .
And later, three weeks later, in fashion sedater,
See, the night worker writing his square work out,
Set to the labour, muscle strained, his light hidden under:
Half-past two? Time for tea . . . Half-past, half-past two . . .
And then by degrees of half hours see how it shows:
The pages fill with black notes, the paper-bill goes
Up and up, till the musician is left staring
At a String Quartett nobody in the world will do . . .
And what Schumann would say there's no one to be caring.

Now, had it been a joke or some wordy windy poem
About Destiny or Fatal-Way or Weltmuth or Sarsparilla,
London would have hugged to it like a glad gorilla . . .
Happy to know its deepest heart told out so:
Deepest conviction, or maxim driven so home
(To the next door neighbour). But since the new making is still a
Mere Quartett for Strings after the Beethoven way,

With no aspiration to say more than ever was said
By Beethoven; expecting such treatment and casual pay;
The musician is left to turn over Shakespeare and to find
Favourite passages when the dim East shows blind.
Get rid of his drink how he may, blamed for such drinking;
Leave his MS there, wondering what neighbours may be thinking
Of people who work a week through without end.
And neither Lyons, Lipton or the London String Quartett
To care much what high glory from the light glory came to command.
Or—see . . . how the two tunes into one English picture came linking.[33]

The final line could serve as a mission statement for Gurney the creative artist. His work was perpetually in search of new structures in two genres, that might frame and unify his many references and allusions, weaving them into 'one English picture'. This is a poem about composition and the search for a complete form. The poem is the product of his revelling in the resurgence of his chamber music composition, knowing full well that the chances of anyone other than Vaughan Williams or Scott hearing or playing the new works were slim. This knowledge, set out with a combination of such poignancy and tongue-in cheek humour, struck a different tone from that of his attempts to find commercial favour in 1921–22. Then he had tried to produce popular songs for the public to hug to themselves 'like a glad gorilla' (as he so colourfully put it). He knew now he could neither beat them nor join them. Instead, he continued in his own way, unashamedly highbrow, and depressingly unpublished.

In the new year of 1925 he began to write a quartet in G minor. It had a vocal part rather adventurously added to the slow movement, and was dedicated (with no clue as to the connection) to the American Women's Club of Baltimore, Maryland.[34] Continuing the American theme, it was closely followed by a 'New England' quartet in E minor, which he sent to Vaughan Williams for his thoughts in February 1925.[35] He wrote:

> The Quartett was written in such hell of electrical influence—besides torture— (and after accused on) that its originality is doubtful to the writer (they torture in such ways). If original it is of the finest of the world—a very big one, and fit to play after the Rasumovskies.[36]

He kept returning to it, and by April, presumably with the comments and criticisms of his teacher to mull over, he decided it would benefit from the rather unorthodox addition of a fifth movement. This was clearly a major work, along with the many other missing manuscripts. It was the first of a trilogy of quartets, all now lost to posterity, that were intended as an answer to Beethoven's three magnificent quartets written for Prince Rasumovsky in the early 1800s.

Just as Gurney was increasingly turning to America for poetic inspiration (although we can only speculate as to why America now held him in thrall), so he returned to Walt Whitman for texts to set to music. Whitman had always held a hallowed place in his imagination. Now he provided inspiration for four songs and a baritone song cycle with quartet and piano, the same forces as *The Western Playland*, all written in 1925.[37] Only two of the songs now exist, the atmospheric 'Ethiopia' and 'In Cabin'd Ships at Sea'. Whitman's influence crept into his chamber music, inspiring a *Fantasy Quartett* in F minor.

Vaughan Williams had written two orchestral pieces with Whitman texts, which Gurney knew well, and a song cycle with quartet in some way bridged the gap between chamber music and poetry, but *Fantasy Quartett* takes the identification between poetry and music one step further. It was a piece for purely instrumental forces, with Whitman absorbed into the composer's bloodstream; no need to rely on a text on which to hang a song. The manuscript is lost, and we know only that Gurney apparently had inflections of Bach in the slow movement. We can only speculate as to whether this quartet was Gurney's impression of how Whitman would sound had he been a composer. Because Gurney had such a powerful identification with Whitman's work in one genre, it is hardly surprising that there are some similarities between Whitman's verse and Gurney's later composition.

Whitman often employed the technique of moving from image to image to create a whole, formed of a conglomeration. Gurney's more adventurous postwar compositions often tend to move from the starting point of the tonic through a catalogue of unexpected harmonies that venture far from the opening. His harmonic journeys are Whitmanesque: unpredictable voyages that build cumulatively a picture of many colours and layers of meaning. On the page they can look rather startling, as Gurney travels breathlessly through dissonance after dissonance— for example, his 1924 trio *London Meditation* and his 1925 setting of Yeats's 'Song in the Night' both experiment with harmony and unexpected expansions and contractions of rhythm.[38] On the page, they appear to be unfocussed and harmonically obscure, but make perfect aural sense.

Gurney also turned to Europe for inspiration in his fantasy travels. He had received some French books during his Francophile phase in December 1924, and now he returned to them in March for three settings of French and Catalan poems. 'À la Flandre' (which would become one of his *Three French Songs)* inhabited the world of the French romantic poet so enthusiastically that Gurney even wrote his pedal instructions ('toujour les pedales à supporter') in French.[39] 'À la Raço Latino' is a song that offers a prime example of the parallels between Gurney's compositional and poetic structures. Just as he can contain disparate elements within a poetic structure, or by the strength of a narrative, so here Gurney ingeniously uses the repetition of one musical phrase to embark on a tonal journey, contained within the boundaries of an intensely structured work with musical rhymes at the ends of phrases, the equivalent of poetic feminine endings.

There is a powerful tension within the song between a conscious sense of classical balance (formally and in terms of tonality) and the fact that the stabilising elements actually act as the destabilising device. For instance, much of the music circles around a B flat, which Gurney treats variously as either a problem to negotiate in a variety of different ways or a gateway note, a portal to other distant harmonic worlds. As this negotiation and experimentation continues, Gurney avoids the music becoming rambling through the clarity of the sequential construction of the melody. This is, in short, a masterpiece of a song: impassioned and intense, and working on a complex harmonic level.

Gurney's armchair travels were a rich part of the annus mirabilis that was 1925. Sitting in his bare little room, he had travelled the world in imagination, inhabiting other languages, flavouring his music with other musical cultures until their sights and sounds became as real to the listener as they were to Gurney. To the attendants passing his open door, he was a man sitting all day in silence. In his mind, a riot of harmony, image and colour was almost continually taking place, and the result was a breathtaking quantity of work. All three Catalan and French songs are paeans of love to different geographical places. Considered alongside his relatively new fascination with America, his innate adoration of the Gloucestershire landscape had perhaps become so divorced from the reality he had not seen for three years that it had become a transferable allegiance, or at least a passport to the ability to understand and inhabit others' love of place. It was an unsatisfactory form of consolation, but it was all he could manage.

CHAPTER SIXTEEN

'The Patient Believes He Is Shakespeare'

In the midst of all this fantasy globe-trotting and constant composition, an event took place in the asylum that was to be a landmark in Gurney's uneventful routine. In striking contrast to the usual light music evenings performed by musicians who were more enthusiastic than accomplished, a high-quality classical concert took place on 27 March 1925. The tenor Alfred Capel Dixon, accompanied by Arthur Benjamin, performed two of Gurney's most upbeat and popular compositions to a mixed audience of patients and medical staff: 'When I Was One and Twenty', his Housman setting from *Ludlow and Teme*, and 'Captain Stratton's Fancy' (a popular crowd-pleaser, as Harvey had found when it became a favourite in his prison camp). It was an accessible, folksy introduction to Gurney's work and guaranteed to impress the staff.

The rest of the programme consisted of movements from Mozart and Beethoven trios and a variety of folk songs, including two Percy Grainger arrangements. The programme was suitably undemanding, but still significantly elevated above the usual standard of asylum music-making. It was to be the only time that Gurney's music was performed publically within the asylum, and unfortunately there is no record of the audience's response. Dr Steen made no note of the particular significance of the occasion, simply writing, 'excellent all through' underneath the programme when he glued it into the entertainments scrapbook. We do not know what thoughts he had as he heard for the first time the boisterous, ebullient music that his taciturn patient had written. Perhaps he complimented Gurney in person. The only record of his response is his brief note, which was his standard comment on many events. It may have been just another concert for the asylum staff, but for Gurney it represented one brief punctuation in what would be fifteen years of anonymity within Dartford.

We do not know whether the event enhanced Gurney's status in the asylum, or boosted his self-respect, but it could not help but remind him of the status he might have been enjoying as a force to be reckoned with in British music. Such glimpses of an alternative fate, seeing his name written in the programme alongside Mozart and Beethoven, might have helped strengthen his resolve to continue working. He was not yet entirely forgotten, and the brief moments of public recognition were just enough to maintain his hope that his work would not be overlooked. The BBC had undertaken to broadcast a performance of *Ludlow and Teme*, and in August preparations were underway for the recording on the 25th.[1] Gurney anxiously attempted to follow the progress from Dartford, writing to the tenor Osmond Davies to alert him to revisions he had made to the cycle the previous year. He wrote that he wished it were the revised version being performed; he was grateful that the piece was being heard, but he should have been present at the rehearsals, directing the ensemble, and talking the players through the changes in the score. His frustration was overwhelming; he had no say in the matter, and his revisions were being ignored.[2]

The Carnegie Trust, who had published *Ludlow and Teme*, had also agreed to publish *The Western Playland*; it was a considerable honour. By June 1925 he was anxious to see a proof copy of the score: 'But O when will my not all redeemed "Western Playland" arrive? Why did they take those flats out in "The Aspens"?'[3] The final corrections to the score would be one of Gurney's last musical endeavours, in late April 1926. By the time it was finally published, on 27 February 1927, he would have stopped writing music altogether.

For now at least the work continued, helped by a particularly auspicious appointment to Dartford's staff. Dr Robinson, who had previously treated Gurney, had been promoted to superintendent, and his vacancy as medical officer was filled that May by a young Canadian doctor, Randolph Davis. Davis appeared for the first time on the wards just as Gurney finished work on the proofs of *The Western Playland*. Each medical officer had a number of patients allotted to him. He represented the only professional involved in that patient's case and wielded a considerable influence over a patient's state of health. Davis's residency at Dartford was to be short-lived, but he developed a particular rapport with Gurney. He believed in the therapeutic value of exercise, and whenever his timetable allowed, would walk in the grounds with him, discussing their shared interest in music. As Davis gained his trust, he began to probe deeper into Gurney's past, his childhood and relationships, to try to discern recurring patterns of behaviour.

> I remember so well the afternoon Gurney and I spent along the river and sitting on the grass in the roadside. It was the sympathy which he showed for things which I told him concerning my own experiences in different parts of the world which impressed me so profoundly with the fact that he was sane. Insane people invariably never show sympathetic interest in the experiences of others.[4]

Davis believed that Gurney's ability to empathise and relate to others was proof that he was simply distressed, rather than fundamentally ill. This was an erroneous conclusion. There is no reason why a sufferer of schizoaffective disorder might not be able to relate emotionally to others, and when Gurney was not suffering under the intermittent delusions that tortured him, he was indeed sane enough not only to converse, but to write some of his greatest poems and songs.

'The great reason why I can do for Gurney what others cannot is because Gurney likes me, not because I particularly like him.' Davis was a compassionate and intelligent man, who could see he was making some progress with Gurney. It was, he was keen to establish, not a friendship born of pity, but a therapeutic relationship, built up dispassionately and in order to facilitate a 'talking cure'. 'Understanding him, I know I can cure him', he wrote confidently to Scott.

Gurney needed to talk, but he also needed to get out of Dartford. Although he had spent three years railing against his incarceration in the asylum, Davis believed that the inevitable depression it had caused was not yet a permanent state. It was not too late to rescue him.

> It is what a man thinks of himself that counts not so much what others think of him. Once a man loses faith in himself all is lost until he recovers that faith no matter what others may try to do for him.[5]

Despite working within the asylum system, Davis understood that patients like Gurney might well thrive outside the walls of the institution, and that their incarceration simply added to their distress. Gurney shared his view. Ironic though it was, a lengthy stay in a county mental hospital probably provided the circumstances least conducive to recovery for an insane person. There were a number of other options for a patient with financial means: residency in the house of a doctor, private supervision by a personal attendant, or a stay in a smaller private institution. Any of these possibilities would have entailed more individual attention and flexibility for Gurney. With a staffing ratio of one doctor per 450 patients, there was little Dartford could do for him even if psychiatry had advanced to a point where beneficial treatments and therapies were available.

Whatever the exact nature of Gurney's illness, it is likely that his incarceration hastened his demise. Only ten days after his transfer he had written: 'a ward twenty-five yards long is not fair play to the human being.'[6] And again, in the long appeal poem 'Chance to Work': 'but here I am walking a ward'.[7] The asylum forcibly contained a spirit whose every fibre resisted restriction, and the claustrophobia was enough in itself to drive him to despair.

Gurney had appealed to Haines back in 1922 to let him live in the hut in his garden as a rather desperate alternative to Barnwood.[8] Now Davis provided the hope of a more practical alternative to the asylum. He had rented rooms in a London boarding house run by a Mrs Hay, with the intention of living there with Gurney as a private patient. Gurney would inhabit the front room, and with the assistance of regular payments from Scott and Vaughan Williams, Davis would devote all his time and expertise to curing him. It was an extremely tempting offer, and better than anything that had so far arisen. Scott was worn down by the constant petitions from Gurney to rescue him. She felt she had no choice other than to ignore them. But the longer she refused his pleas to find an alternative, the longer she prolonged his miserable existence in the asylum. She genuinely wanted to do what was best for Gurney, and cared deeply for him, but he resented her refusal to intervene.

> . . . how to get
> Free is not possible, my friends swiftly forget
> Or do not know what pain in the mind can be.
> But four walls surround and the influence continues
> And thought is spoilt.[9]

How much more pleasant life would be, Scott felt, if she could find a guiltless solution to end his misery. Her friendship with Gurney would be much more uncomplicated if she could prove to him that she had not 'swiftly forgotten' his suffering. If she took Davis up on his offer, she could visit unhampered, Gurney could entertain his friends, and it might even prove cheaper than maintaining him at Dartford. Initially, she jumped at the chance Davis was offering. She visited the rooms with Vaughan Williams, but reservations quickly started to creep in. Gurney would have to live in very close quarters with other boarders. This was hardly as distressing as living with the clinically insane, but to Scott it was a stumbling block. 'You would be thrown a great deal with the Hays and their [paying guests]—who are of a different stamp from you and Ivor Gurney', she wrote to Davis, who failed to see the problem.[10] Scott found the conversion of the front room inadequate—the wardrobe would have been in the hall, and there was no gas meter. These were extraordinary objections on behalf of a man who had slept in trenches and barns across France and Flanders, and now inhabited a bare room with barred windows and no wardrobe at all. However, for Scott, who rarely crossed paths with those of a 'different stamp' in her smart corner of Kensington, such issues were a sticking point.

Davis tried to deal patiently with Scott's concerns, but the tone of his letters became irritable and impatient. For all Scott's devotion to Gurney's well-being, she was beginning to drive away the one real hope for his salvation that had presented itself. It had been a tragic mistake on her part that, when she decided he needed to be taken out of the far more congenial atmosphere of Barnwood, it had been to one of the most depressing environments she could have found. At any point over the last three years she might have investigated the possibility of finding a doctor who would care for him as a private residential patient, rather than keeping him at Dart-

ford against his will. Such a scenario was relatively common. Now, when the opportunity presented itself to her, she created obstacles. She objected to Davis's requesting £75 for three months' board and expenses in advance. It was a thoroughly
unreasonable objection; the sum was hardly extortionate, and she only succeeded in
alienating him further by accusing him of taking Gurney to get to his money. Davis
retorted that the sum 'will not any more than pay expenses [. . .] if there is anything
left after 3 mos. of the £75 I will return it to those who give it. You may be sure if I
wished to take him for gain I should never think of 75 pounds for 3 months all my
time. It would be nearer 750 pounds. [. . .] Personally I think I have done a great deal
in offering to help Mr Gurney and have done so only because I understand him and
feel that he can be helped. Otherwise I should never have considered the matter.'[11]

It transpired that £75 was in fact a sum that Davis owed, and that he was waiting
for money to reach him from selling a property in Canada. He needed the money
urgently, and that had prompted him to insist upon Scott paying in advance for Gurney's care. This, of course, was hardly impressive, and he confessed the rather embarrassing situation to Scott. He sincerely wished to help Gurney and believed that
he could provide a better environment for him than his current miserable surroundings. Scott, who was protective of Gurney to the last, would not part with
money to a man she felt she could not trust, and the plan for Gurney's release was
abandoned.

Davis remained committed to his welfare and continued to write to Scott suggesting alternatives that might suit Gurney better. He suggested Gurney could be
transferred to Bethlem Hospital, where Davis now worked, having left Dartford. He
would have been able to take him out for walks around Southwark for a couple of
hours every day, which would be infinitely preferable to his loneliness in Dartford.
Scott's instincts had been right when she had suspected Davis of being financially
motivated, but this time there were no monetary dealings involved. It would have
meant a straightforward transfer from asylum to asylum. Nevertheless, Scott dismissed the idea out of hand. Instead, she made the rather half-hearted gesture of
engaging a Harley Sreet psychiatrist for a single visit to Gurney. As Davis pointed
out to her, such a cursory introduction to his case could hardly result in a diagnosis,
let alone any beneficial treatment. It might have made her feel that she was being
useful, but it was of no material benefit to Gurney.

There is no evidence Scott had consulted Gurney over the two options offered by
Davis, or that he had any idea of the part she had played in blocking his chance of
release. One of the many unfortunate aspects of Gurney's situation was that whoever was kind enough to assume responsibility for him wielded an enormous power
over his future. Scott could only act as she saw best in difficult circumstances, with
nothing but a layperson's understanding of mental illness to inform her choices.
Had she not decided at this point that the situation was entirely hopeless, and that

he would never see life outside the asylum gates, his story might have been dramatically different. She could have investigated the possibility of finding a residency with another doctor, perhaps more trustworthy than Davis, now the idea had been entertained. Instead, believing she was acting in Gurney's interests, she left Gurney in the unhappy position in which Davis had found him.

Davis disappeared from Gurney's story, but was replaced by another young psychiatrist, a Dr Edward William Anderson (known by his friends as Teddie). Anderson's appointment was a stroke of great good fortune. Gurney had faced being left entirely alone, with no member of the asylum staff to take a particular interest in his now chronic case. Doctors were not encouraged to favour individual patients. Davis's departure could easily have triggered a quick decline in Gurney's state of mind, but it so happened that Dr Anderson was equally humane and compassionate. In his first few weeks on the wards, he found that there were so many patients it was difficult to remember who was who. But he quickly realised that there was something extraordinary about Gurney. It was Anderson's first job after medical school in Edinburgh. His youth (he was eleven years younger than his patient) and his gentle Scottish accent would have appealed immediately to Gurney. Memories of his beloved Scottish soldiers, and of his painful but precious time with Annie Drummond would have been invoked by this young doctor. Anderson, in turn, was drawn to his new charge, and became far more interested in him than professional standards demanded.

Anderson was both a literary and a musical man, and spent his hours off from work practising the flute. He discovered that when he engaged his patient in conversation about music, he could glimpse the man he had been, before illness and the asylum had taken their toll. When animated on the subject of the arts, Gurney became coherent and could converse normally. Gurney the musician was still very much intact, as he was writing copious songs and chamber works, and Anderson enjoyed their conversations about his works in progress, as well as using them as a means to engage with him. In turn, Gurney was grateful for this artistic, intellectual man's company, and gave him copies of his songs to mark their friendship.[12]

Dr Anderson was deeply moved by Gurney's work. He read his poems avidly and played his songs. He was in awe of his patient's achievements and was intrigued and honoured to be shown the manuscripts on which Gurney was working from day to day. For the first time in three years, Gurney's mental health began to improve. The support and respect of first Davis and then Anderson played a significant part in alleviating his depression and stabilising his condition. Subsequently, the creative surge with which the year had begun could continue, and under their care he felt able to write some of his highest-quality work in both genres.

Anderson respected Gurney's stubborn determination to fight his illness with poetry and music. Although his employment at Dartford was unfortunately short-lived, he never gave up on his formidable patient. All through the 1920s he con-

FIG. 16.1: Dr Edward William Anderson in 1923. Courtesy of Nicholas Anderson.

cerned himself with Gurney's case, and, like Davis before him, always believed that there was the possibility of redemption.

Contrary to the impression given by the cursory medical notes, Gurney had by no means been written off by the staff at Dartford, even if the official visits from the doctors became more and more infrequent as the years went on. It was asylum policy to leave months between medical assessments for a chronic patient. The case notes do not record the many walks and evenings spent with Anderson, who lived on site and invested a huge amount of time and energy in befriending his charge.[13]

The memory of Gurney was to haunt Anderson throughout his career. Of the thousands of patients he treated, Gurney's case notes were the only ones of which he retained a copy. Anderson was a progressive psychiatrist, and after he left Dartford went on to work at the Maudsley Hospital in London, which had a reputation for being at the very forefront of psychiatric medicine. He later founded the first centre for psychiatric studies, based at Manchester University.[14] His experience with Gurney fostered in him an academic interest in great literary and musical minds, and madness. He wrote a paper on the playwright August Strindberg and his mental illness, which drew on his experiences with Gurney, and revealed the intelligence and subtlety with which he approached his treatment of him.[15] Perhaps he felt that something more could have been done for him, or perhaps it was simply the tragedy of the situation, but throughout his life, Anderson always spoke about his work with Gurney with an air of sadness.

Gurney was languishing in the most unconducive environment for creativity, fighting the 'torment' and 'torture' he intermittently experienced. Nevertheless, his creativity seemed to be unstoppable. Among numerous other songs and chamber pieces in the spring and summer of 1925, Gurney wrote five settings of Robert Bridges's poetry in June. He returned to Bridges's *The Spirit of Man*, which had become so significant when Harvey lent it to him in the trenches as a parting gesture just before he was captured. It had lost none of its attraction for Gurney, who declared the anthology 'so wonderful like natural light after blinded scorching dark. [. . .] The cool immortal book The Spirit of Man as giving ever love of God. Truly "democracy—the average man".'[16]

Bridges himself had sent him a translation of Virgil, and he repaid him with a setting of his 'A Love Lyric', which he dedicated to the memory of Margaret Hunt. He followed this with further settings of Bridges: 'My Spirit Kisseth Thine' and 'The Hill Pines Were Sighing'. Scott copied both out to send to Bridges as Gurney's writing was too difficult to decipher. This deterioration was partially on account of his illness, but also simply the result of his habit of resting the paper on his knee to write. Many of Gurney's song manuscripts are hard to decipher from this period, with notes becoming something like sticks, on which it is hard to tell where the dot is intended to be. On some manuscripts, flats tended to be written as an *s*, and his tendency to favour often unreasonably flat keys resulted in manuscripts that resembled a flock of birds, with *s* or *ss* against almost every note.

An impressive volume of music was being written in a short space of time, but Gurney's compositions were neither rushed nor poorly thought through, however idiosyncratic his handwriting was becoming. Had he been at liberty, he would have had to spend hours of every day in some kind of employment. Doubtless he would have swapped his fate in an instant, but whilst the asylum denied him stimulating experiences, it did afford him long uninterrupted periods without distraction. With Vaughan Williams's visits to look forward to, he was not working entirely in a musical vacuum. Vaughan Williams played through some of the wealth of manuscripts as Gurney wrote them, offering criticism and encouragement. He was also giving him the confidence to push harmony, form and texture further than he could ever have dared to do at the Royal College. These songs, still almost all unpublished, are among Gurney's most sophisticated work, and it is on these unheard works that his reputation as an experimental and progressive composer ought to rest.

By 1925 Gurney's use of harmony was certainly advanced, but he had no intention of writing music that was particularly new or stylistically innovative for the sake of it. In comparison with some of his more avant-garde contemporaries (Arthur Bliss, for instance), he still ranks among the more conservative of his generation. However, dramatic innovation is not necessarily an indication of quality, and what

FIG. 16.2: A late asylum manuscript, the song 'Snowflakes' (May 1925).
© Gurney Trust.

Gurney's asylum songs offer in abundance is the ability to manipulate harmony in unexpected ways for emotional effect.

His harmonic experiments might not always work, and there must, by definition, be the odd occasion when such experimentation, straining at the bounds of conventional harmony, does not quite come off. One such example might be his September 1925 setting of Yeats's 'Song in the Night', which is decidedly odd throughout, although it has its own internal sense of logic.[17] It seems that here his previous com-positional patterns have been shuffled, in a manner akin to a kaleidoscope. Instead of going through the routines he has rehearsed many times before, he twists them slightly, rendering them unpredictable and odd, but not necessarily dysfunctional. The song visits unexpected keys without fully establishing them, moving swiftly through them to other, unrelated keys. Gurney is attempting something adventur-ous and distinctive, despite the fact that Yeats's mildly melancholic words do not call for such an extreme harmonic setting. However, a text and its musical setting need not be an exact mirror of each other, and considering his circumstances, this partic-ular text might well elicit an angst-ridden interpretation.

> All the words that I utter
> And all the words that I write
> Must spread out their wings untiring
> And never rest in their flight,
> Till they come where your sad, sad heart is,
> And sing to you in the night,
> Beyond where the waters are moving,
> Storm-darkened or starry bright.

For a man whose only recourse is to words and notes, and whose writing is unpub-lished and even unposted, such a text might well have a peculiarly tragic resonance.

Alongside the songs and the chamber music, Gurney had returned in imagina-tion, and perhaps even in reality, to the organ loft. There is no record of whether he had any contact with the chapel music-making at Dartford, but in 1924 and 1925 he repeatedly turned his mind to choirs, having barely written any choral music until that time. There had been a handful of choral pieces and organ preludes between 1919 and 1922, but over Christmas 1924 he had started to write for the very specific combination of violin, cello, baritone, chorus and organ, creating a 'Collect for the Nativity of Our Lord', and a 'Latin Motett', for which he had found the text in the *Daily Mail* the day before Christmas Eve. It was followed early in the new year by a 'Sevenfold Amen'. In June and July 1925 he returned again to choral music, with a motet for double choir with a text by Robert Bridges, 'Since I Believe in God', and 'Lord, Thou Hast Been Our Dwelling Place', for six soloists, choir and organ.

These were works for choirs of cathedral standard, requiring an ability to sing complex music in eight parts. He intended his 'Lord, Thou Hast Been Our Dwelling Place' for York Minster (Gurney might have known Edward Bairstow, the director of music there, as they had shared a teacher in Walter Alcock). Gurney had already met with some encouragement from Henry Ley, the organist of Christ Church, Oxford, who had been shown 'Since I Believe in God' and been impressed enough with the work to ask for parts to be made so the choir could perform it. It is an intriguing piece, slow paced and monumental, with the thick textures Gurney so often used in his piano parts spread across all eight vocal parts. It owes an obvious debt to Parry's great double choir motet 'Lord, Let Me Know Mine End', but with far more harmonic adventuring than Parry would ever have entertained.[18] Gurney seems to take a lesson from Vaughan Williams's architecturally conceived *Fantasia on a Theme by Thomas Tallis*, as it has long rests built in to allow the acoustics of the building to echo after the end of phrases. It was certainly not the asylum chapel or its choir that Gurney imagined when he thought of its premiere. There is something both brave and poignant about those gaps—Gurney had created silences on the page for a cathedral's acoustic that he would never again hear, imagining the echoes reverberating in a performance he would not attend.

Gurney does not record any thoughts on his religious beliefs during the asylum years. It may be that he was so used to the association of choral music with religion that these explicit statements of faith were not intended as any more than words suitable for cathedral choirs. But references to God, even when they might be a cry of anguish that God had deserted him, are frequently to be found in his poetry. Gurney's god was a god of inspiration, as much associated with Bach as with conventional Christianity. Back in 1915, he had written to Scott that

> People who find their Faith shocked by this war, do not need a stronger faith only, but a different one, without blinkers. The whole question is summed up in the last line of [Bach's] A flat Prelude, 2nd Book. There you will find a complete and compendious summary of all necessary belief.[19]

Bach provided Gurney with a different faith, and with spiritual nourishment. Having 'found' not God but Bach in the trenches, he prayed to his musical deity from the asylum:

> 'O Bach, O Father of all makers, look from your hidden
> Hold where you are now, and help me, that am so hard hurten.'[20]

Gurney's motet 'Since I Believe in God', a form dominated by Bach's legacy, might well have been a work of homage to the 'Father of all makers', as much as to God himself.

In October 1925, in the midst of his most creative period, Gurney received a visitor he had never met before. He generally had few interruptions to his regime of writing and composing, and only Marion Scott and Vaughan Williams made frequent appearances. Despite his long-standing friendship with Gurney, Harvey rarely visited, and Howells made so many excuses that Scott gave up trying to cajole him into accompanying her to Dartford. This visit was to be the first of at least two from Helen Thomas, Edward Thomas's widow, who knew Gurney by reputation alone.

Gurney had been working on his set of Thomas songs, 'Lights Out', back in June. Scott had approached Helen Thomas to ask her permission for Gurney to set two more poems to complete the work. In the course of their correspondence she had described Gurney and his situation, and Helen had determined that she would meet him in person. As she walked up through the village of Stone towards the huge complex of red brick Victorian buildings, she would have been forgiven for thinking that she was approaching a prison rather than a hospital. The warder unlocked the first of many doors and led her through seemingly endless bare corridors, their drabness broken only by the shafts of autumn light which found their way through the barred windows. Marion Scott, who was accompanying her, was unperturbed by the asylum's oppressive atmosphere and chatted with the staff. Helen was clutching a bunch of flowers and had worn her most colourful hat, in an effort to make a cheerful appearance. She felt as incongruous as she looked, against the backdrop of white-washed walls and bare linoleum. She waited, awkward and unsure what to expect, until at the end of the corridor she saw a gaunt, dishevelled figure of a man, in pyjamas and a dressing gown.

Gurney took her hand in silence, staring intensely into her face, before leading the way to a little cell-like bedroom, furnished with only a bed and a chair. Helen noted that there was nothing of beauty or comfort. The flowers she had brought had to be put on the bed—a vase was out of the question, as Gurney was allowed nothing that he could use to harm himself or to escape. The two women began to talk about poetry, in an effort to engage the alarming, silent figure before them. Helen talked of her husband, his habits and his love of walks, in the hope that her memories might animate Gurney.

Helen's visits were the only distraction in months of tedium, and provoked intense emotion in Gurney. He wanted her to hear his work—to appreciate who he had been, and what he could still achieve. He was keen for her to hear his homage to the husband she had lost. Thomas had been killed in an explosion in 1917. He lived only in Helen's memories of him, and in the words he had written. By taking his verse, inhabiting it and recreating it as song, Gurney could breathe fresh life into it. In the midst of his own death-in-life, he could offer her something new of her lost husband.

He had determined to play to her, and silently led Helen and Marion Scott into the adjacent ward, where an old battered upright piano stood, with a bird cage on a stand positioned next to it. The other patients in the room sat in silence on hard benches ranged against the walls. Gurney had hardly spoken to either woman, but now he began to play, singing softly under his breath.

Hopeless and aimless faces gazed vacantly and restless hands fumbled or hung down lifelessly. They gave no sign or sound that they heard the music. The room was quite bare and there wasn't one beautiful thing for the patients to look at.[21]

But the patients and their attendants did listen. Even the canary, incarcerated behind his own bars, trilled along to his playing. Gurney chose to play his setting of Thomas's 'Lights Out'; a suicide note of a poem, and one in which, faced with the prospect of imminent death at the front, Thomas had embraced the end of his life with a mixture of pain and resignation. It was a far cry from the performances at the Wigmore Hall or even Scott's private Kensington soirées, but it was a recital that neither woman would ever forget.

By the end of the visit Helen felt that she had won something of Gurney's confidence, but that conversation was not the way to reach him. He had offered her his music, and shared with her their joint love of Edward's words. She wanted to share something of her husband with him in return. On her journey home, she hit upon the idea of taking Gurney some of Edward's maps, so he could follow the routes he had loved to walk across the Cotswolds. It was a way in which Gurney could quite literally follow in Thomas's footsteps.

> This proved to have been a sort of inspiration, for Ivor Gurney at once spread them out on his bed and he and I spent the whole time I was there tracing with our fingers the lanes and byeways and villages of which he knew every step and over which Edward had walked. He spent that hour re-visiting his beloved home, spotting a village or a track, a hill or a wood and seeing it all in his mind's eye. He trod, in a way that we who were sane could not emulate, the lanes and fields he loved, his guide being his finger tracing the way on the map. It was deeply moving, and I knew that I had hit on an idea that gave him more pleasure than anything else I could have thought of.[22]

As 1926 progressed, the quantity of Gurney's high-quality work began to dwindle. Few could sustain such a schedule for long, and Gurney, whilst more driven than most, was still only human. Dr Anderson, Gurney's one real ally within the asylum, left after only a year. The poetry continued throughout the spring of 1926, alongside far fewer songs: two in January, and two more in March. It was a pale imitation of the productivity of the previous year (if we assume that these were indeed his last songs, and that other, later manuscripts were not lost). The quality of his work had not deteriorated, but these last surviving songs represent a curious departure for Gurney. Until this point he had chosen to set an eclectic but always intelligently selected combination of Elizabethans, a smattering of Romantics, Walt Whitman, and the Georgians. Some of his choices were of relatively little-known poets, but they were always published, attributable texts. His last songs set unknown and untraceable texts, as if he were wandering out of the constraints of poetry anthologies into an unknown literary territory. Most probably these poems were written by Gurney himself, as in some cases the manuscripts' corrections show him writing the text even at the same time as he was writing the music. He seemed to be wandering away from the canon of published poetry and into uncharted territories, either losing his way or perhaps finding it: in setting his own words to music, he was embracing his own voice, creating work that was in its very essence his own.

Gurney had only occasionally set his own texts in the past, a fact that in itself is puzzling. We might assume that the practise would be far more common for a man who was writing poetry and song often on the same day, and who was so influenced by the troubadour poet-composers of the Elizabethan era. In the trenches, he had created the exquisite 'Severn Meadows' from his little poem 'Song', and had again turned to his own verse in a love song to Annie Drummond during their brief affair. But aside from these isolated cases, he had shown remarkably little inclination to use his own poetry. Now he began to merge his poetic and compositional voices in earnest, with twelve songs to his own words being written between 1925 and 1926.[23] He probably did not know that these would be his last songs; the end came (if indeed it did) because he began to find writing too much of a mental strain, and not through his own choice. But although he did manage a further handful of piano and chamber pieces, these settings of his own poems represent a fitting end to his career as a song composer. His last musical breaths were something of a triumphant ending, merging his voices as musician and poet, doing away with others' work, and relying entirely on himself to create. It was, in a sense, a swan song that represented the culmination of all he had aimed to achieve—a truly Elizabethan synthesis of words and music.

Taking a glance at a handful of these final twelve songs, the manuscript of 'Song' is very hard to read and seems to have been written at speed. The text has all the qualities and familiar themes of Gurney's poetry and life, and, perhaps significantly, addresses the idea of a male lover directly (there is no evidence that the speaker is female):

> If I call my lover high then where the pine forest clings and sighs
> Shall I find his arms at evening round me as my heart now calls for in the
>   valleys
> As the silence droops softly as the starred heavens show more clear
> then my heart sings of my lover where farmlands are.
> Comes the sweet and lordly daylight and small meadows sweet light.

'Lament' is based around the same harmonic shape as 'Song', although it appears to have been written less hastily, as the score has the luxury of tempo markings (poco adagio) and dynamics. The manuscript shows that the text and melodic line have been crossed out in places, and the words altered, suggesting either that he was writing from memory or, more likely, composing both words and music simultaneously on the page as he wrote. The result is an exquisite miniature, his words a blend of A. E. Housman and Edward Thomas, carefully structured around a series of internal and end rhymes.

> The scent of earth breathes
> from the wood near dark[.]
> May we not bring, ere Spring, the life
> that lies in each dim music spark?
> Hear the horn call far on hill
> Now darkling show the wood edges;
> the tales of age on age are breath
> in the cold air sweet in death.

Like 'Song' and 'Lament', 'Over the Ridge' is also probably Gurney's own text. Its creeping modulations descend inevitably into flatter keys, a trademark of many of the asylum songs, and particularly appropriate here as he depicts the descent of darkness: 'the long shadows fall and softly break the breeze blowing from the wall that shows to Eastward'. Like 'Lament' and 'Western Sailors', 'Over the Ridge' is a short vignette, not articulated in sections but composed in one continuous stream, with figuration in the piano that remains steady throughout. These last songs often seem to be drawn towards expressing one brief musical idea. Each has its own coherent identity, making perfect musical sense with no sign of a failure of ability or technique, but its parameters are narrower. These songs are a single musical idea, a thought captured in miniature.

Gurney was not yet ready to be silenced. His abiding passion for close identification with great writers and musicians still compelled him to experiment, and as he turned away from composition, he began to investigate a new channel of self-expression: drama. This departure might have been prompted by a trip to the theatre, organised by Scott. Private patients were allowed out for a drive if the asylum authorities felt they were well supervised, and she had occasionally taken Gurney out in the spring of 1926.[24] Now she became daring and suggested a more ambitious trip: to see a play at the Old Vic in April or May. There is no record of what they actually saw, but it was probably either Shakespeare or opera; the Old Vic were performing *Rigoletto* and *Il Trovatore* alongside the plays in repertory. As Gurney showed little interest in romantic opera but was obsessed with the Bard, it was much more likely that Scott would have hit upon a performance of *Much Ado about Nothing* as an ideal outing for him.

The fact that he was capable of making such a trip might seem to indicate his normality, but this was by no means an impulsive social event. Scott was obliged to reserve a box at stage level, as the new superintendent Dr Robinson advised, 'so there would be no risk of Mr Gurney precipitating himself from an height.' It would have been a theatrical way to achieve the suicide for which he had longed for years.[25]

This expedition, the most exciting event in Gurney's almost empty calendar for the last three years, could not fail to make a lasting impression. He had always been intensely interested in drama, and now with the memory of a live performance still vivid in his mind, he started to experiment with writing his own plays. The results were *The Tewkesbury Trial* and a fragment of a *Gloucester Play*. He also intended to write a third play to be dedicated to Harvey. Only a title page remains, and we do not know whether *Play of Winter* ever progressed further than this.[26]

The *Gloucester Play* is written loosely in iambic pentameter, with such a heavy debt to Shakespeare that it feels like a tribute or even pastiche.[27] It is set in Gloucester in 900 AD, in the time of King Alfred. The first scene opens in Gloucester's Great Hall, with the mayor and a sailor named Nicholas Cridlan making grand speeches in front of assembled guests about the beauty and nobility of Gloucester.[28] Much of their speech material is recognisable as stemming from Gurney's pet themes: the beauty of the daffodil fields surrounding the town, the importance of praising Gloucester itself. But it is by no means a Gurneyesque ramble dressed up in prose. The speeches are beautifully written, and the dialogue is generally poetic and quite compelling, for instance:

> Stephen Coleford: And lady, saw you the meadow floods today,
>   all dark and gleaming against the hills removed.
>   Azure and patterned enchanting with willow
>   never so white Gloucester . . .
>
> The Mayoress: I could not go
>   will not dare speak of a thing unseen that
>   delights Master Coleford still in the tale telling.

The play is perhaps more interested in the poetry of its language and images than in the pace of the drama, which begins slowly with set speeches, building its own momentum as the play develops. The fragment ends before the end of act 1, scene 4. There follows a sobering reminder of the fluctuation of Gurney's state of mind from focused and creative to distracted and delusionary. On the next page of the manuscript we might expect notes for the continuation of this serious drama, but instead, a turn of the page reveals handwritten lists of body parts. He gave his lists the apparently arbitrary heading 'the young Tennessee', and returned to his long-standing preoccupations with guilt and forbidden anal activity with the rather startling instruction 'To forbid the use of anus for passage'.

Mary of Tewkesbury is an unfinished play, longer than the *Gloucester Play*, and dates from April 1926. Elsewhere he retitles a second draft *The Tewkesbury Trial*. It begins with remarkable similarity to the *Gloucester Play*, opening in the meadows surrounding a Gloucestershire town, but this time outside Tewkesbury, in 1422. It is supposed to take place just after Agincourt, with ongoing fighting in France, and Henry V still on the throne. It concerns itself with construction of a lady chapel for Tewkesbury Abbey, in memory of Richard, Earl of Warwick, who had just been killed fighting in France. Gurney is showing us, in his *Mary of Tewkesbury*, how commemoration of the war dead should be done. Through his didactic drama we learn that the correct way to honour death in war is through beautiful architecture, much music and talk of the glories of Gloucestershire.

The play itself is too derivative to be described as successful, but a poem written at the same time on the same theme sheds some light on the point of the scenario it describes. 'To Tewkesbury Abbey' is an appeal poem, written on Lady Day (the day dedicated to the Virgin Mary, particularly apt for the Mary chapel of Tewkesbury). It could almost function as a coda or epilogue to *Mary of Tewkesbury*. It begins:

> The prayers that raised stone which called prayers
> Here at least should have saved men from the dares
> Of evil coveting insult to most high God.—
> But nothing, not the older things have availed.
> Not soldiers buried crowded, nor their wives cares . . . [29]

Grieving widows such as the Lady Isabella take centre stage in Gurney's drama. Now, in his appeal poem, not only are they not recognised but the prayers that have been said in such sacred spaces as Tewkesbury are found to have been in vain. This is the dystopic reality of the 1920s. The Earl of Warwick's glamorous commemoration featured in his drama is about as far from Gurney's ignominious decline as could be imagined, which is precisely why he writes of it.

Gurney's plays show him practising what he preached, working out his literary theories in his own work. At around this time he wrote that the purpose of setting Shakespeare to music should be to provide a counterpart to the text, 'the look of England and the history of England' being the prime considerations.[30] Here, writing plays so heavily Shakespearean that they are almost a literary fantasia on a theme by Shakespeare, he concentrates on both the look and history of England, in a world steeped in Shakespeare's influence.

As he was working out these ideas in play form, he was simultaneously experimenting with similar subject matter in other pieces of prose, which are somewhere between the essay and the short story. Between May and June 1926 he wrote two essays, 'Transference' and 'After Agincourt'. He takes as his subjects the destruction of the chapter house at Hereford Cathedral in 1713, and a musical festival which he imagined taking place after the soldiers had returned to Gloucester from Agincourt. Gurney's work in any one genre, whether it be poetry or song, or now drama or essay, was always only one part of a bigger picture. Gurney's career is characterised by his unique ability to view the themes and ideas dear to him through a multitude of lenses, whilst ranging across genres. His work, when viewed as a whole across the different media he chose, offers a richly nuanced picture as a result.

Gurney was not alone in returning to 'Old England' as a Utopian ideal of civilisation, although he probably did not know it. Blunden wrote essays in the late 1920s and early '30s such as 'The Preservation of England', which contributed to a drive to save the countryside from encroaching modernity, and a move further towards nostalgia. In 1933, F. R. Leavis and Denys Thompson published *Culture and Environment*, which upheld, as do Gurney's plays, the myth of 'Old England' as the 'England of the organic community'.[31]

Gurney clearly enjoyed writing dialogue, and the stronger passages of his plays tend to be those that take up Shakespeare and develop his words and sentiments with evident relish. He is at his best when engaged in pastiche, and seems to have little interest in developing his own plots over and above creating an event or scenario on which to hang his pseudo-Shakespearian dialogue. Rather than representing an attempt to reinvent himself as a dramatist, his plays are the precursor to the natural next step. Gurney would 'become' Shakespeare himself. Within a few months, he had moved from creating his own plays, in the shadow of Shakespeare, to rewriting Shakespeare's plays themselves.

This wasn't the first time that Gurney had stepped out of his own skin and into that of one of his idols. Back in Bangour War Hospital in 1917, he had been just as egotistically happy to improve great artists such as Beethoven. He had rewritten three bars of the first movement of Beethoven's D major Sonata for Scott's benefit in perfect sanity ('I have one or two striking improvments [*sic*] to offer').[32] It was not a sign of madness, but an indication of his living relationship with musical and literary works, as both interpreter and creator. Now, in 1927, he began to move into a brave new world. His work was still coherent, and of literary merit, but exploring a strange, highly experimental new territory, where boundaries between fantasy and reality, and between himself and others were disconcertingly fluid.

By inhabiting Shakespeare's text and rewriting it from the inside, he could allow himself the freedom to enjoy writing what are often very accomplished lines, without having to worry about the overall direction of the drama. This move, from emulating Shakespeare to becoming Shakespeare, coincided with a marked deterioration in his condition. He could, in effect, use his writing to combat his increasingly 'derailed' identity by hanging on to the structure and plot Shakespeare's plays provided.

He had been well enough to continue his drives with Scott through the summer of 1927, and had written poetry prolifically alongside his plays. By September, he was again showing signs of increasing agitation, and by December his doctors found him to be severely deluded. As his illness took a stronger hold, so the revisions of

Shakespeare's plays began in earnest, as did the claims to *be* Shakespeare, Hilaire Belloc, Beethoven and Haydn, among others.

One of the most extraordinary things about his work from these later asylum years was that so often what might appear deranged, and was certainly creativity informed by and expressing illness, had its roots and parallels in 'sane' art. What could be more bizarre than presuming to know better than Shakespeare? The Georgian poets had in fact tried it, and might even have given Gurney the idea; Gordon Bottomley had published his own version of *King Lear* in the second volume of *Georgian Poetry*.[33] Such literary experimentation as Bottomley's was not held against him as an indication of insanity. Instead, Bottomley's *King Lear's Wife*, reimagining the original Shakespeare in realistic, rough and coarse language, was absolutely key to what Marsh saw as the Georgians' achievements.

In Gurney's 1927 version of *The Tempest*, he created this speech for Prospero:

Be sure this is pleasure to me, though they have sinned
And cast me out—yea, beastly from my adored City . . .
Cast me, as t'were a beggar, out of all my cares
Rare as prayer—books, virginals, clarinet, embraced—
To lose my power in a night, to go oversea, hidden, stowed-under . . .
Duke of the time's treasures, to lie in a dark hold, reft
Of all, friends gone from me, in danger—with no light: till
At sea, safe from anger and courtesy, they (these)
Led by some sorcery past all prayer or detection
(Dazzled by lying promise) Set down me
And my dear daughter.[34]

This is loosely based on Shakespeare's lengthy dialogue between Prospero and Miranda in act 1, scene 2, in which he tells his daughter the story of their betrayal and exile to the island. There are obvious parallels with Gurney's own retellings of his life story: Prospero is betrayed by his brother, and Gurney was committed to an asylum by his. Shakespeare's Prospero is a master of the 'liberal arts', valuing his library 'above his dukedom'. Gurney attributes specifically musical gifts to his Prospero (virginals, clarinet) as well as literary skills that he had offered a society to which he had been deeply attached.

Both Shakespeare's and Gurney's Prosperos are profoundly bitter men, keenly aware of their grievances and of a miscarriage of justice. Shakespeare gives some account of the motivation behind the betrayal of his Prospero. He had neglected his dukedom, and his brother, greedy for power, had him removed by force. Gurney's Prospero has no sense of a narrative to explain how his exile came about. For reasons he cannot fathom, he is deserted by his friends, forcibly cast out into an alien environment. He is poor, with no place or function in society ('as t'were a beggar').

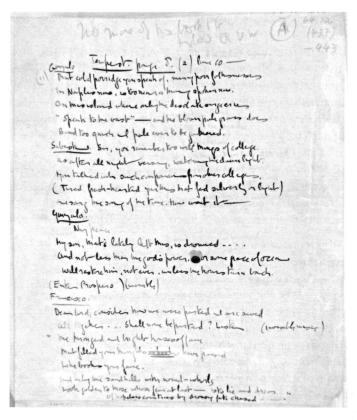

FIG. 16.3: Manuscript of Gurney's rewriting of Prospero's speech. © Gurney Trust.

His lack of status and burning sense of injustice are markedly like Gurney's own. He never reconciled himself to his incarceration, or to his friends' refusal to rescue him. Five months after his rewriting of *The Tempest*, his medical case notes recorded:

> Seen to-day by M.O.P Medical Officer. He maintains that he wrote the greater part of Shakespeare, Thakaray [*sic*] and Hilaire Belloc amongst others and that Beethoven and Haydn never existed, Patient having composed all their music. Very much more obscure in speech at times completely incomprehensible. Mentally worse.[35]

Many of Gurney's letters appealing for release from the asylum register a similar combination of vulnerability and bitterness to that which he attributes to Prospero. Whilst his doctors found his speech to be at times incomprehensible, he was writing narratives based on his own life story that, within their own terms, make perfect sense. Shakespeare represented a solid institution; something strong enough to withstand the act of revision and to remain recognisable to Gurney's readers (even if, since Anderson's departure, he had no actual readers in the asylum). But at the same time, by rewriting the familiar work of Shakespeare, he was threatening the very institution upon which he depended. Paradoxically, writing Prospero's speech was both an act of defiance—placing himself in the position of the magus figure, granted the power to attack and redevise the tradition of literature from the outside—and a plea to be recognised and accepted within that very tradition. It is also a plea to be part of ordinary society, where people are free to read and watch Shakespeare, and to live their lives outside the walls of an asylum. Gurney's writing was a direct response to the pressure an institution such as an asylum puts on an individual's sense of identity. It was part of Gurney's tragedy that such work has so often been read as confirmation of his madness.

Gurney was clearly not Shakespeare, or Prospero, and this is not altogether sane writing. But we might consider something the entirely sane poet Robert Graves wrote: that we can know a writer, almost inhabit their skin, through a pathologically close relationship to their work. Graves was talking about the long dead poet John Clare (who, like Gurney, wrote from within an asylum):

> [Clare's] poems are still alive. I find myself repeating some of them without having made a conscious effort at memorisation. And though it was taken as a symptom of madness that he one day confided in a visitor: 'I know Gray—I know him well', I shall risk saying here, with equal affection: 'I know Clare; I know him well. We have often wept together.'[36]

Gurney had said as much to Scott back in 1916, in a statement that was entirely 'sane':

> If I can set 'La Belle Dame Sans Merci' well, the reason is; that there is something in me of Keats. . . . They must not be Keats' thoughts only, but mine also.[37]

Such strong identifications are not just madness, for Graves or for the two asylum poets. Though Gurney's madness *is* madness, there's indisputably method in it. Becoming others is a natural part of being a poet and, for Gurney, simply presented itself as a particularly rich set of possibilities in an extreme situation in which boundaries become redefined. It could also be read as an extreme form of the sympathy which Gurney felt he himself failed to receive.

Gurney's fluidity of boundaries between literary figures and their work has strong parallels with the process of writing a song. Songwriting is, in essence, concerned with breaking down barriers between poet and composer. Gerald Finzi, hugely influenced by Gurney's songs, wrote of the need for a 'creative identification' with someone else's text being the starting point for a good song setting. And what is creative identification if it isn't becoming Shakespeare? Gurney the songwriter was capable of a kind of creative identification with his poets that allowed him not only to inhabit their verse, but also to question their work from the inside and take their texts to task, both embracing and attacking their meaning. It was perhaps the ultimate way for a composer to understand his text: to become the author. Now, in the liminal space between 'sane' creativity and an uncharted territory of experimentation and mental disturbance, Gurney took his training as a song composer to another level, revealing a fascinating and disconcerting new landscape. It presented endless possibilities, but also began to step beyond the nebulous boundary between imaginative experimentation and madness.

CHAPTER SEVENTEEN

'A Fear of Obscurity (My Own)'

The final decade of Gurney's life charted a gradual process of silencing: first music, then poetry, and finally prose. His investigations of his own identity through inhabiting others' was a rich seam to mine, and he had only just begun to explore its potential. The second half of the 1920s was a period of his literary development that yielded some bold and daring results, but to develop the artistic possibilities of his fluid identity he needed the mental stability to continue to work. This was a struggle that he was beginning to lose.

By 1927, he had become emotionally volatile. He could be violent and was frequently aggressive, and on one occasion he actually assaulted the superintendent; a heinous crime by asylum standards, tantamount to striking God himself. But he did not entirely lose control of himself, and when female visitors were present it was noted that he was suitably docile and quiet. Adeline Vaughan Williams found him to be gentle, and remarkably sane. She refused to believe he was beyond rescue, and in February 1927 she arranged for him to begin a course of treatment with a Mr Lidderdale, a Christian Science practitioner. This was rather a long shot, given that the treatment was based on prayer, and so far Gurney's prayers had singularly failed to be answered. Even Lidderdale himself thought it best that the 'treatment' was not mentioned to the hospital authorities, who would certainly not have approved. The plan was for Lidderdale to visit Gurney regularly for a period of time, and take him out for drives, which had generally proved a success whenever he had gone out with Scott. During their excursions Lidderdale would pray for Gurney, with or without his knowledge. Any visitor and change to routine might be welcome, as there could often be months of loneliness between Scott's trips to the asylum. Such a well-meaning routine might have been beneficial had Lidderdale been someone whom Gurney felt inclined to trust. At the very least he was offering a change of scene, prayer or no prayer. Unfortunately, Gurney took a violent dislike to him, and refused to leave the grounds in his company.

Lidderdale's analysis of the situation only confirmed what Scott, Adeline and Ralph Vaughan Williams had known for years; that Gurney would be better off anywhere than in the 'atmosphere of hopelessness' in Dartford. Lidderdale made it quite clear to Scott that the institution to which she had had Gurney transferred was as much a factor in his depression as his illness, but neither Lidderdale's prayers for a cure nor Gurney's petitions for release were answered. Scott was adamant that Gurney would stay at Dartford, whether or not it destroyed him. She was under pressure from all concerned and from Gurney himself to make decisions on his behalf, and she felt burdened by the situation. She decided that all she could do for Gurney was to continue her visits, despite her own often poor health.

It was a controversial decision, although it must be noted that few others took further initiatives to help Scott find an alternative. Howells found the asylum so distressing he could hardly bring himself to go there, and so stayed away; a great loss to Gurney. Gurney's mother repeatedly appealed to Scott to have her son moved. Florence was hardly a positive force in Gurney's life, but on this issue her interference might have been beneficial. Both Dr Davis and Lidderdale recognised that the asylum was a destructive environment for him. Dr Anderson, despite any loyalty as an employee, could see that his patient was lost in such a huge, dismal institution. Everyone around Scott who had any experience of the situation said the same thing. Even Adeline, Scott's ally and another devoted visitor, wrote, 'He gets no help at all for his mind from his surroundings, [...] He also spoke of his loneliness "No one comes to see me." How I longed to take him away!'[1] Adeline might have wanted to remove him, but she did not, and her wishes were of no practical benefit to Gurney.

Locked away in Dartford, Gurney's loneliness was compounded by knowing himself to be a misfit amongst the other patients, although they represented a social group he had no aspirations to join. He buried himself in his reading as a retreat from those around him, but found himself persecuted for it.

> Only when I can read the Spirit of Man (or L van Beethoven sometimes) am I at touch with right possibility [...] was it my fault these books stay here—unread? Or that I am mocked by those I hate—lonely, silent, the only reader of books?[2]

Gurney was considered to be a chronic patient, which meant that he was now rarely assessed. Even on the few occasions that a medical reassessment took place, it was largely a futile exercise, as from 1926 onwards he refused to allow anyone to examine him properly. It was clear to both staff and patient that his was now a life sentence rather than a hospital stay. The Christian Science treatment offered no improvement, and it was given up in April 1927, with his mental condition being recorded as 'very confused'. Despite his apparent confusion he was still writing. The attendants set up a table for him to sit at in the hospital grounds when the weather permitted. He had long ago lost the energy to try to escape and sat at his improvised writing desk with a sheaf of paper, writing for hours at a time, interrupted only by mealtimes. Now his work was almost exclusively in prose, and he alternated the usual letters of appeal with essays and revisions 'correcting' Whitman's verse.

Although the medical profession had largely given up on him, outside the asylum he still had his own modest triumphs to help keep his name in the public eye, on however small a scale. In late June Vaughan Williams sent him a copy of *Music and Letters'* special edition dedicated to Beethoven, on the centenary of his death. It included Gurney's poem, 'Beethoven, I Wronged Thee Undernoting Thus / Thy Dignity and Worth', which he felt, with some justification, was 'pretty good'.

Stainer and Bell published Gurney's setting of Robert Graves's 'Star Talk' at the end of the month. He had written it in 1920 and had revised the manuscript in his feverish period of creativity and revisions in July 1925. He had altered it again just before it went to the publishers in 1927. Such milestones were significantly better than nothing, but the publication of both his verse and music was far too infrequent to make any kind of lasting impression on the general public. Gurney had only had three poems published in two years, and the number of performances of his music from incarceration until the year of his death could be counted on the fingers of both hands.[3]

There is no record of Gurney's writing music after 1927. He had written a piano piece that January, with the rather intriguing title 'Si J'etais Roi', and at some point during the year he apparently wrote a 'Comedy Overture' intended for *Twelfth Night*, but both have disappeared.[4] He might have lost the stamina to compose, but he had not lost his sense of self-worth as a composer, or the dogged insistence on his abilities that had borne him through the war, and much adversity since. In the trenches, he had repeatedly imagined a happier time when he would be able to fulfil his potential. Now, he wrote of himself in the past tense, as if writing his own obituary. 'England has much to thank—that Ivor Gurney was musician as well as poet'.[5]

It appears to have been a conscious decision to end his composing career here. He tried to sketch the beginnings of a string quartet in late June 1927, but wrote to Scott that 'Yesterday and the day before I made sketches in revenge of a SQ [string quartet]—but terrible is their elimination.'[6] He was still requesting scores, and regularly asking for more books. During the war he had written encouragingly to Harvey in his prisoner-of-war camp of how they would one day walk together, talking of literature. Now, from within Gurney's own prison, the habit of talking books died hard. Most of his closest relationships had been built on discussions of music and literature. He was still writing to Harvey about books in 1927, even though in his discussion he himself had become Shakespeare, and his godfather Cheesman was apparently really the American author Henry David Thoreau.

Although Gurney no longer wrote any of his own songs or chamber music, he expressed a particular interest in studying the scores of songs by Strauss, Reger and

Wolf. In the new year of 1929 he asked to be sent the music for Brahms's violin sonatas, the models for his own contributions to the genre. Books and music were still a lifeline. And his desire for them showed that he was still lucid enough to be able to find inspiration in the arts. He had not quite given up, but his letters acknowledge a tone of resignation. Fundamentally he knew that there was, in fact, 'no escape', either from the asylum or from the total madness that threatened at times to consume him, and against which he had fought for so long.[7]

His self-imposed studies were becoming increasingly difficult. He struggled to see, and his eyes hurt him. Ophthalmic investigation failed to make any diagnosis, and no one could decide whether his symptoms were the result of a physical ailment or due to his mental distress. Around Easter 1927 he was 'half blind—usually unable to read', and greatly distressed at his predicament.[8] He found it too difficult to read music, although he continued to request scores, and he was obliged to give back the key to the main hall where he usually practised the piano. But this gesture of relinquishment was too final for him. Despite struggling to read music, he was not yet ready to give up his status as musician, and in October was campaigning for the return of his piano key.[9] There is no record of whether the privilege was resumed, and considering his generally hostile attitude, it is possible that he was now forbidden access to the piano on the grounds of his behaviour. He did have access to the mediocre pianos on the wards, but they came with complications because attendants and patients either were annoyed by the constant music or insisted he play their requests. The attendants had, in Gurney's view, 'awful favourites'. Whatever else he had lost, Gurney still had his sense of intellectual superiority.[10]

As his eyes began to fail, the BBC became increasingly important to him. Radio offered a vital link to the outside musical world, and he had eagerly made use of it since his first months in the asylum. He had never given up on his development as a musician, and listening to the radio was one way in which he continued to learn. He listened voraciously to an eclectic range of composers, and even wrote to the BBC in May, petitioning them to play a revealingly modern list of works, including chamber music by Scriabin, Reger, Ravel and Howells, and symphonies by Dunhill, Parry, Glazunov and Rachmaninov.[11] His was no conservative musical palate. He was delighted to find broadcasts of Schubert, Scriabin, Bach and Mozart to be 'silver minted with great clear design: and yet as if ploughed up out of the earth'; an image similar to his earlier poetic descriptions of turning up Roman coins in the soil of Gloucestershire.[12] It was his shorthand for something rare and beautiful that speaks of its heritage but retains a freshness and immediacy. He listened to broadcasts of Stravinsky conducting *The Firebird*, and to the mezzo Isobel I'Anson singing Schubert. He even wrote to her congratulating her on her performance, although, as was the usual fate of Gurney's correspondence, the letter was never posted.

In April 1929 he wrote to the Royal College, asking rather incongruously for money, tea and coffee; basics with which Scott normally kept him supplied. He added a rather enigmatic little comment, that he was 'still away from music—unable to bear the pain'.[13] It is unclear whether being 'away' from music meant abstinence from composition, from practical music-making, or from both. He may have been referring to the physical pain of his eyes, as well as his mental anguish. His physical discomfort may not have been permanent or entirely disabling. He could still write coherent letters and study scores, and so although his piano work 'Si J'etais Roi' of January 1927 is the last surviving composition manuscript, we cannot assume that it was in fact the last piece of music Gurney ever wrote, or was physically capable of writing.

The practical and physical difficulties associated with playing the piano might have contributed to his increasing exploration of other media. He had first dabbled with essays in 1922, just before he was committed to Barnwood, and one, his delightful 'The Springs of Music', had been published in the *Musical Quarterly* at the time. The essay had been one of his last successes before the asylum doors had closed, and he may have felt that as it was a form in which he had previously had some success, it was one he might now be able to return to and develop. Back in October 1922 he had written a poem in honour of the great essayist Hazlitt, just as he himself had begun to develop his own essay writing. Now, in the second half of the 1920s, as the music and poetry had begun to dwindle, he had turned again to essays. In an extension of the impulse behind his playwriting, he attempted to emulate Hazlitt's ability to 'speak in words so plain' the mood or essence of his most beloved writers and composers.[14] His essays reveal as much about his own creative instinct and the development of his musical and literary voice as they do about his subjects.

'On a Dictionary Quotation' and 'On a New Project' were both written in May 1926. The first discussed the meaning of orchestral colour, and the second was inspired by a newspaper review of a translation of the texts of Bach's cantatas. In April 1927 Gurney mused on the compositional process of Brahms's *Handel Variations*, writing from the point of view of Brahms himself, and wrote a similar piece from Beethoven's perspective telling of the composition of his second Piano Sonata. Brahms and Schumann featured heavily in his choices of subject matter, including an imagined diary entry, written in response to Schumann's daughter Eugenie's memoir. It had just been published that year, and had been sent to him, presumably by Scott. Perhaps it was the example of Scott, whose career largely involved writing essays for journals and musical publications, that inspired this burst of musicological musing. She was publishing her journalism in the *Christian Science Monitor*, and posting him copies, so it would have been an obvious model. He even intended one of his earlier 1926 pieces to be specifically for the *Monitor*, making the link explicit.

He saw his essays as a kind of literary scrapbook, a 'sticking in book', as he called it. As the 1920s progressed, and Gurney's health deteriorated, the essay began to take on a new significance in his constant fight to maintain his identity. It was a medium in which to record his views; a book in which he could paste his many fragments of memory before they were lost altogether. His essays are among the last surviving fragments of his work.

It has been thought that Gurney wrote a poem as late as 1929, entitled 'The Wind'. It is copied out in his handwriting in March of that year and attributed to Valentine Fane, a poet now so entirely forgotten that the name has been taken as another of his pseudonyms, common enough in his recent compositions.

The Wind

All night the fierce wind blew—
All night I knew
Time, like a dark wind, blowing
All days, all lives, all memories
Down empty endless skies—
A blind wind, strowing
Bright leaves of life's torn tree
through blank eternity:
Dreadfully swift, Time blew.
All night I knew
the outrush of its going.

At dawn a thin rain wept.
Worn out, I slept
And woke to a fair morning.
My days were amply long, and I content
In their accomplishment—
Lost the wind's warning.

If this is indeed Gurney, then it is a lucid and well-structured poem, belying the usual assumptions that his mental condition was degenerating rapidly at this point.[15] However, the subject of the poem does not fit with Gurney's general profile. It was a source of constant regret that his opportunities to achieve his potential had been cut short by his illness. 'The Wind' gives the impression that the writer is optimistic enough by day to believe that there is time to create, despite the wind's warning at night. Gurney, desperately frustrated and thwarted by the asylum to the point of hardly being able to bear playing music, was unlikely to write that he was 'content' in the 'accomplishment' of his days. This was a man who, according to his medical notes, believed the hospital was surrounded by his persecutors at night. His nocturnal torments stretched far beyond the very real possibility that he would not achieve his goals. The tight structure of the poem, its line lengths and rhyme scheme are also more redolent of Fane than Gurney. It is far more likely that Gurney came across the poem in one of the many publications available in the reference library of the asylum, and that elements of the poem appealed to him enough to copy it out.

The last years of Gurney's life were punctuated only by Scott and Vaughan Williams's occasional visits, and the publication of a slow trickle of poems written in previous years. For the majority of the time, days merged into weeks. Gurney read, played the asylum pianos when he could, and all the while retreated further and further into his memories. On 14 March 1929 Scott arranged a trip to Gravesend and Rochester at Gurney's request. She had not visited him for months, and he was desperate to 'get out of the torture for the afternoon'. It was a grey and bitterly cold day. At Gravesend, Gurney stood on the promenade in a greatcoat donated by Arthur Benjamin, and gazed silently out over the Thames estuary. Rochester was especially bleak, with the cathedral standing gaunt and majestic 'like King Lear' as Gurney commented. Perhaps Lear's hopelessness, crazed and alone, was at the back of both his and Marion Scott's mind as Gurney stooped in the wind, hugging the ill-fitting coat around him.[16]

Every morning Gurney had been in the habit of looking at his small atlas, imagining the journey between England and America, tracing the marches he remembered so well across Flanders and Northern France. It was a routine he had devised in 1925 (perhaps as a response to Helen Thomas's visit). Now he told Scott he wished she might buy him a 'Phillips 1/—Atlas', but they could not find one in the Rochester shops, and he had to make do with an edition of Shelley instead. He and Scott proceeded to read it aloud to each other. Gurney began to read 'Hymn to Intellectual Beauty' to Scott, and then fell into silence. He handed her the book, following the words with his finger as she read, 'I vowed that I would dedicate my powers / To thee and thine; have I not kept the vow?' They were both silent. It was an ambiguous, intense moment. 'Did he mean music or me?' Scott wrote. 'Both I think. Ivor the poet with his own poetry locked within him, unable to utter it, speaking through the words of another English poet. We were very happy.' It was the nearest thing to a declaration of love that she would ever receive from him. It is noticeably incongruous that Ivor, with his poetry 'locked within him'—a tragic, frustrated mute—might take delight in such a moment. The 'we' must be taken as an extension of her own feelings.

A blustery trip to Dover followed in September 1929. The Channel was the nearest Gurney would get to France, and the host of memories its shores held for him. Scott took a photograph of him staring out to sea, lost in his own thoughts. Seaside trips seemed to strike a particular chord with Gurney, and in May 1930 Scott took him on a trip to the town of Sheerness, on the Kent coast, where the River Medway joins the sea.

FIG. 17.1: Gurney on a trip with Marion Scott, taken at Dover, 1929. © Gurney Trust.

This uneasy combination of industrial town and seaside resort was hardly a thrilling destination, but Gurney's walk along the modest seafront and pier was the nearest he could now come to happiness, despite being flanked all the while by his attendant. From Dartford he could look down the hillside to the estuary and beyond, and bemoan the failure of his attempt back in Gloucester in 1920 to escape to sea. Perhaps, had he been able to immerse himself in the hard physical work on board a ship, it might have been his salvation. He would certainly have welcomed the camaraderie that he might have found amongst the sailors, but even at the time it had been an unrealistically romantic notion. Sheerness's muddy estuary was to be the last time he would ever glimpse the sea.

In 1929 he had noted:

> to have written of the sea so much, and perish so far in hell, is hardly recountable—It is time I write to narrow limits. So unsure my pen—it is time I trust to Churches—[...] so much of the rest—with a pen that wanders where the grief of poetry failed—[17]

If only Gurney had slipped so far into incomprehension that he was unaware of his own distress. In painful fragments he articulates his sense of his own tragedy that is, as these anguished utterances testify, 'hardly recountable'. He had not lost the desire to *try* to recount it, however, to write in order to draw his boundaries closer. He might have lost the control of his earlier poetry, 'so unsure my pen', but he could still attempt to articulate what his poetry had left unsaid, with 'a pen that wanders where the grief of poetry failed'.

By August 1930 his sight was sufficiently restored to allow him once again to live vicariously through books of every genre. Scott occasionally took him on day trips in the asylum's car (always in the company of at least one attendant), and they returned for a final trip to the Old Vic.[18] But the majority of his days were spent reading. He was enjoying some 'grand' Milton, and studying Hilaire Belloc's 1923 collection of essays entitled simply *On*. He was clearly still engaged with the idea of developing his views on essay-writing. He requested Pears's *Cyclopaedia*, in which he had found solace over the previous year.[19] He became fascinated with natural history, remarking on falcons, ravens and bees.[20] It may perhaps have taken him back to his early days in Gloucester, poring over books on British wildlife with Cheesman, and marvelling, on walks with him or with his father, at the plants and birds. After so many years, nature had lost none of its freshness and appeal for Gurney. As his own horizons narrowed, the varied colourful articles in Pears captured his starved imagination. The *Cyclopaedia*, a substantial hardback volume, falls open naturally at the atlas in the centre. Here he could trace every country, and look at a map of London.

Maps had come to mean a great deal to him in the asylum. They symbolised the possibility of travel and freedom, ranging across counties or continents, if only in imagination. After the dictionary and encyclopaedia sections, the *Cyclopaedia* includes a section of brief dictionaries on specific subjects. The first is a dictionary of wireless, full of the glamour and excitement of the discovery of radio, which had only been around for thirty or so years.[21] It must have made fascinating reading for a man who fervently believed he was himself the victim of wireless interference, and that it was electricity that tortured him. At other points during the twentieth century, schizophrenics have often claimed that the television, and later aliens were interfering with them, depending on the current anxieties or discoveries of the time. It is not hard to see from this celebration of wireless as a powerful, dangerous new medium with seemingly limitless possibilities how Gurney might unconsciously have hit upon it as the source of his own interference.

When he was not reading, his mind returned repeatedly to his memories of the war, 'these tales of 1914–1917 come in such torture', as he remarked in a letter addressed to the Cathedral at Amiens.[22] This was a revealingly confessional remark from England's self-professed First War Poet. Gurney relished his memories of the war, crafting them into poetry, and reliving the brief moments of comradely acceptance and camaraderie. But as Sassoon and many others also found, the very happiness of such memories of friendship was now acutely painful, not to mention the remembrance of abject terror and misery.[23] Amiens Cathedral had miraculously remained undamaged during the war, unlike many of the men who had fought near it. Perhaps this confession to it was a plea not only for relief from the torment of the present, but for healing from the pain of the past; the unscathed cathedral was a survivor. Gurney's appeal to it was a plea for a return to the state of resilience and strength that the building itself symbolised.

Forgetting the war was a wish Gurney could not risk fulfilling. His war experience tortured him, but his status as a war poet was gradually becoming recognised. Two of his poems were published in *An Anthology of War Poems* in 1930, collected by the veteran and author Frederick Brereton, with an introduction by Edmund Blunden.[24] It was an imposing collection, with a large coloured picture of the cenotaph on the cover. As if speaking out from inside the famously symbolic empty tomb, the poets whose work was chosen to represent the war came to be the canonised few whose names were indelibly associated with the war's literary legacy.

It was not only his war poetry that was finding an audience. The following year, 1931, saw two poems published in *The Mercury Book of Verse*, a compilation of the poetry the *London Mercury* had published between 1929 and 1930. 'Tobacco' and 'Encounters' found their place there alongside a poem of Rupert Brooke's, along with a generous helping of Blunden, some de la Mare, W. H. Davies and Robert Bridges. They were all heroes of Gurney's and the inspiration for many of his song settings. A year later, in November 1932, J. C. Squire included Gurney in his anthology *Younger Poets of Today*. After years of aspiring to join the ranks of the Georgians he could now see his name listed alongside them at last.

In the first weeks of March 1932 Gurney's thoughts turned to birdsong, both in Gloucestershire and on the Somme. Through the barred window in his narrow room he could see the grounds of the asylum and observe the blossoming of the few spring flowers that had been planted. He had been allowed access to the grounds for a number of years, but now, for unfathomable reasons, he felt he could not bear to venture out into what he had come to see as a travesty of nature. Perhaps he felt that Dartford's grounds were a pale imitation of the landscape he longed for. The springs he had known in Gloucestershire meant orchards overflowing with blossom and walks through the daffodils in the meadows around Longford. Dartford's neat and anodyne flower beds with their dull rows of polyanthus and geraniums were an insult to the riot of wildflowers he knew he was missing. The comparison was altogether too painful, but the alternative was imprisonment inside the building, which led to a claustrophobia that became overwhelming. He begged Scott to take him on another trip, 'Rochester, or elsewhere'. Anywhere but Dartford. Scott duly responded, and took him for a couple of drives, and a trip to Eltham to visit her friend Hester Stansfeld Prior, then president of the Society of Women Musicians. Prior had laid out musical scores in the hope that they would catch Gurney's interest. They did, and he picked up an orchestral score of Brahms's Fourth Symphony and took it to her piano. He score-read the slow movement flawlessly.

His letters are the only remnant of his voice from this time. They map the final stages of mental and linguistic deterioration as his illness finally began to take over. His medical records describe his speech as incomprehensible from as early as 1926. Gurney was speaking and writing mostly in what psychiatric practise today might refer to as 'word-salads' (a term for a random association of words that appear to be gibberish). It is not a permanent state, and he would have been able to move out of it back into coherence, but the very fact that such extremes were being recorded indicates that a marked deterioration had taken place.[25]

The extended flights of fancy that characterise the asylum writing from the late 1920s (becoming Shakespeare, or being Brahms for the length of an essay, for instance) are imaginative, and obviously eccentric, but they make some kind of sense. Now Gurney entered a new phase in which he could sustain nothing more than a series of miniature ideas that were at best only loosely connected. The same themes to which he had always returned continued to haunt his thoughts: his familiar roll call of literary and musical figures, the references to Gloucester and his war experiences, the moments of autobiographical recollection, and the appeals against torture. Now, increasingly, they became fragmented, jostling with each other with only the faintest sense of a narrative. Reading his manuscripts from this period is an experience akin to reading a document torn into small pieces, thrown in the air and pieced together in the order in which the pieces fell. A glance at a page of Gurney's writing shows a striking number of dashes and aposiopesis, as thoughts fail to cohere, or are abandoned. These leaps from one idea to another without connection might now be termed symptomatic of schizophrenic desultory thought.[26] An extract from a three-page letter addressed to the May Queen of London is typical:

William Shakespeare / writings fraying and racked up and down in Hell—
    occasionally trying to write tea tavern gossips of Joh: Brahms without success—being also (sometimes brilliantly) tangled in the coloured-paper jugglery at sea of hot glue that the newspaper thrust one into—but were Hazlitt, Kapp. or Hanslich . . . and Ferris is a fraud . . .
    Since the one who writes created the whole (perhaps) of the Elizabethan legend—as it shows in Marlowe and Shakespeare and Lamb . . . he may write to the May Queen or any . . . but should be thinking of Franz (Peter) Schubert, or Anton Dvorak—hearing them played in Warwickshire or Berkshire . . . in wood and stone . . . that legend also (in past) his—against a wireless that

asked (as the threat) happy life and with a tradesman's content . . . respectabil[i]
ty (parsimonious) and a Presbyterian acceptance. . . .

They tortured for it . . . and only prayer to God got Schumann's and Schubert's
end in . . .

(Like the rest. see the fragmentary and magnificent 'Walkure' Schott's
piano score)

The son of David Gurney, that in poisoned overfed sexual illness forgot at
times to honour his father . . . (forgetting ill, all but the net) writes after reading so much difficulty. (yet very funny) and yet so bravely done—of the Reference books; and scraps: as master of all the things of desire, perhaps.[27]

Gurney was losing his ability to structure thought, although he was still haunted
by the same preoccupations—the relationships between great works of music and
literature, and his conflicted sexuality. The phrase 'poisoned overfed sexual illness' is
surely suggestive of a sense of shame. We can only speculate how much of this is
culturally reflected, a response to the obscene thoughts that the voices in his head
were apparently giving him, or a reflection on the 'secret' at the heart of Gurney's
conflicted nature to which Arthur Benjamin had alluded.

Now, rather than structure his thoughts within the limitations of a poem or essay,
he began to use dates, scores and similar measures of time or achievement as a tool to
attempt to impose order and coherence in what was increasingly becoming mental
chaos. Letters from 1927 include such phrases as 'Ivor Gurney in Hell 17—27—
writes', 'In 3333—11etc. torture' and 'This Hell is 3 1/2—5 1/2—x'.[28]

Gurney read the *Daily Mail* and took an interest in sports results (although whatever his state of mental health, he had not yet lost his appreciation for quality journalism. In 1933 he wrote, 'I am sorry 'the Daily Mail' is so awful. [*sic*] and prefer the
football scores').[29] He had for the last few years been in the habit of recording football scores in the margins of poems, songs, and in letters. Whilst many of these are
likely to be fictional, some could also very well be from the matches that took place
in the asylum grounds. The hospital organised football and hockey teams in winter,
and two cricket teams and a tennis club in summer. They frequently played matches
against local Dartford teams, part of Dr Steen's strategy for bringing the outside
world into the hospital grounds.[30]

The numbers Gurney records that are actual sports reports are in the minority,
however. More often, his numbers, fractions and dashes reflected his own system for
recording the regularity with which he felt the clouds of delusion gathering. His nu-
merical systems gave him a means of recording the voices and pains that plagued
him. In some letters these episodes are recorded as frequently as three to seven
times a day. He was measuring his own balance between sanity and madness. At
times he estimates a painfully low percentage, and the odds seemed stacked against
him: 'sanity is 3 ½ over 41 here sometimes.'[31]

FIG. 17.2: At Knole Park, photographed by Marion Scott, c. 1930. © Gurney Trust.

Alongside his mysterious calculations, the locations that inspired so much of his poetry began to take on their own voices.

> This is a Salford 46 + Widnes 5 day. (Sir Richard Cary of Widnes House. . . .) And Dunfermline regards the North with American victory. and all the Latin caution—As Albert Palatinate deep under might labour for victory, or Breslau now claim the triumph of Bavaria.[32]

They populated his letters like amiable phantoms: chatting to each other, responding to literature, and playing football matches together. His world, now so empty of friends, had become peopled by places. Letters included oblique references such as '(Knole 140. Horace 43.)', which presumably referred to his memories of a visit to Knole Park in Kent on one of his drives with Marion Scott. He weighed up the experience in relation to his appreciation of the poet Horace (for no apparent reason). Five days later, he continued to balance his thoughts and memories, putting them into pairs as if they were being scored, or compared: 'and of Dulwich Hamlet and of èè victory. and of the Kent Map / Horace victory. and of North Italy's true hopes. (This day thus far).'[33]

He wrote to Scott over the Christmas of 1933 like a child sending his thank-you letters, still sensible of the demands he made on her. He thanked her, rather stiffly, for her present of the *Daily Mail* yearbook, and for her 'services through the year'.[34] It is an oddly formal little note; his grip on the etiquette of relationships and the finer points of social interaction was beginning to slip. That Christmas, and throughout 1934, he was drawn back to modern poetry, declaring in October that 'poetry can be very great'.[35] Hardly an incisive comment compared to his analyses of his contemporaries' work in previous years, but he had at least not lost the capacity to find pleasure in literature.

The actual events to which Gurney could now look forward were pitifully few, but he was not yet so apathetic that he had lost touch with anniversaries from his past life. Since the early 1920s society had learnt to mark the war through a series of annual commemorations. So Gurney, in his own way, was beginning to focus his personal memories around particular dates. It was an odd example of private memory being adapted to conform to public memorialising. For a society intent on moving on, the occasional date to focus the national consciousness was useful. Gurney's war memories were more vivid than his present, and every part of the year resonated with the memory of a wartime event. He was continuing to live the war in parallel to the 1930s. The spring reminded him of the great victory in Arras in 1916.[36] He marked 19 November as the anniversary of a victory in the Baltic in 1915, as if it were taking place on the very day he was writing. He 'salutes' the victory of Loos, and Remembrance Sunday.[37] His anniversaries seemed all to be victories, or reimagined as triumphs, far removed from the experience of the drudgery of war as he had actually lived it.

Gurney continued to rehearse every moment of his war years in his letters, living in the continuous present of his memories. It is a curious paradox that the more he tried to keep his past alive, the more his recollections began to morph into moments of history. As his narratives became defined by dates, they took on an air of being so far removed from the present that the Battle of Trafalgar and the Battle of the Somme might be talked about in the same breath. He asked Scott to send him 'little 3d [roughly 1p] books of the dates of the war', conscious of the fact that as the years progressed, 'only anecdotes are left of a tale meant to be told'.[38] He knew that, whatever it cost him, it was his calling to tell the story of the war as he had seen it. It was a position of both privilege and pain, and one that required an ordering of memories and a certain distance. But whilst he could attempt to contain his memories within the parameters of anniversaries, his own fight had not ended in 1918. He marked 15 September, the day of his incarceration in Barnwood, along with the great battles of the war. It was his personal tragedy, the anniversary of a battle that had not yet ended, and of which the outcome was still uncertain.

FIG. 17.3: Reading outdoors, late 1930s.
© Gurney Trust.

In May his condition deteriorated. The doctors left him alone, as he had forbidden them to come near him. His reasoning was that the medical staff might better spend their time investigating under the floorboards, rather than taking his temperature and weighing him. It was the machines under the floor that were torturing him. For months on end he sat in his bare room, reading, and producing reams of letters.

In 1934, twelve years after his committal, he admitted to Scott a 'fear of obscurity (my own)'.[39] This had always been a very real fear for Gurney. Previously, it could have been allayed by the thought of the work he could still produce that would secure his reputation. Even in 1925 he had been able to write prolifically, and his work was broadcast, performed and published. There had still been a hope, however faint, of a cure or at least a life outside the institution. Now, as the walls closed in around him, he was under no illusions as to the course the rest of his life would take. He had had his chance, and his reputation must stand or fall by the work he had completed— the grand plans for music dramas and completed plays would never now come to fruition. He knew he had written works that would ensure he had a place, however small, in musical history: he was confident enough to know that songs such as the Elizas, 'By a Bierside' and 'The Folly of Being Comforted' were miniature masterpieces. His poetry was beginning to get the recognition it deserved, but was it enough? Had he really achieved the dream he and Howells had shared so many years ago back in Gloucester when they had planned to change the face of English music? The dream had most certainly come true for his friend. As the days passed in often unbroken monotony, Gurney might well have wondered whether Howells really was always too busy to visit.

Scott and Vaughan Williams had not deserted him, even if few others came to visit. Emily Hunt wrote to him, and occasionally received replies. Gurney still wrote to Harvey, whose visits to Dartford were at best only occasional in these last years.[40] Gurney's mother kept up a keen and desperately anxious correspondence with Scott over her son's welfare, and both she and Winifred visited him, although the difficulty and expense of travelling from Gloucester to Dartford was prohibitive.[41] Winifred sent him Christmas presents, with chatty little notes containing snippets of family news.[42] On her final visit to him, Gurney surprised her by asking about something she had written in a letter a while before. She was taken aback both by the total lucidity of the question and by his memory.[43] However disjointed his thinking appeared on paper, he was still clearly capable of considered conversation.

Other friends on the outside of the asylum walls were working to ensure that what Gurney had achieved would not be forgotten. Squire at the *London Mercury* was ever loyal, printing four of Gurney's poems in December 1933, following them with six more in January 1934, and a further six between May and August. Scott's own career was flourishing, with the publication of a short biography of Beethoven, which went on to be reproduced in at least twelve different editions. Scott kept up her visits irregularly, but they were becoming increasingly difficult and strained on both sides. Since 1928 Gurney had, rather unreasonably, begun to resent her visits as intrusions (despite campaigning by correspondence for her to take him out for trips). She interrupted his routine of smoking and reading (he chose not to remember who had supplied both cigarettes and books). On one occasion she committed the apparently unforgiveable faux pas of visiting him on St Michael's Day (29 September), which seemed to outrage him, although he does not say why the date caused such offence. Perhaps, knowing that St Michael was the defender against Lucifer and the dark forces, Gurney felt that he needed to devote the day to praying for protection.

> and Miss Scott's last visit ended me—for I wish to be courteous. She denied my having written save under my own name. I ask my affairs free from them—terribly sorry—for she visited on St Michael's Day. I in torture asking only to talk and smoke—and she denied all good. It is not my fault there are articles in the papers against them: since I always struggle in a mine of hell any more is it that I am unable to read—or my bed shakes. Unable to decide their status-of-right I left that considerable—Torture by the House Internal. From such

thoughts, and far worse—the Spirit of Man rescues me for a few moments—
and she knew this, on St Michaels Day— . . . I have appealed often enough—
for the one who has visited me most—the shame in it is terrible. (6th year
shame).[44]

Not long ago he had been desperate for her to take him out of the asylum for trips,
but now something changed. In December 1935, for either her benefit or his, Gurney
politely but firmly requested she should stop visiting him altogether. She had asked
Dr Robinson if she might take him out for a drive in July, but he refused, giving the
deterioration in his patient's behaviour as his reason. Gurney seemed to be closing in
on himself, and Scott must have found the ban deeply hurtful, after so many years of
solicitous friendship. She had always taken pains to ensure that Gurney felt supported
and knew that he could rely on her friendship. Now he appeared not to want it. Alone
at Dartford, he vacillated between being abusive and hostile and being sullen and
depressed. All such behaviour was duly recorded in his case notes as symptoms of
madness. In another context, extremes of aggression and apathy might well have
been seen as justifiable reactions to his gnawing frustration at his situation, rather
than as symptoms of his systemic illness. But, as ever, an asylum patient's words and
behaviour were not his own; self-expression became a set of symptoms to be noted
and observed by dispassionate medical professionals. Exuberance could be interpreted as mania, and any outburst of anger was surely the result of a lack of emotional
control. In fact, it was remarkable that Gurney had not turned against Scott earlier,
considering she had the power to end his imprisonment and did not do so. No matter
how catastrophic her decisions had been for him, he knew she was unfailingly loyal,
and he also knew that he was forced to depend on her for his practical needs. He was
trapped. He could not help but resent her as the years dragged on, but he remained
respectful (if distant) towards 'dear Miss Scott' to the end.

Whilst Gurney no longer desired Scott's presence, he never suggested that she
stop sending him supplies, and the stream of comestibles, money and reading matter
continued. The need for poetry still gripped him violently, even if he had no more
use for human contact. The new year found him returning to *A Shropshire Lad*, presumably reawakening memories of France and Flanders, and of the little volume of
Housman that had accompanied him through much of his war service. In April he
was thinking about Robert Frost. Gurney's ban did not entirely deter Scott, and she
visited him at Christmas 1936, lending him her copies of Shelley, Wordsworth
(which was, he emphatically declared, 'dreadful') and the *Palgrave Golden Treasury,*
that stalwart of poetry collections from which he had drawn so many texts for songs
in previous years.

The visit was not a success, and in March 1937, when she suggested returning, Gurney wrote to deter her. 'Is it Spring? Is it of A. E. Housman's honour?' he tentatively

wondered, concluding his letter with 'Please don't come to visit this dreadful place. But I should like money.'[45] The money duly continued, and in a rare surviving example of Scott's side of the correspondence, we read her sorrow for him: 'I feel so sad to think of your long days and nights of pain . . . I only wish I could bring any happiness, and comfort for sorrow, to you.'[46] But her presence was not required. Again, in November 1937, he implored her not to visit.

Scott's role as ministering angel seemed to have ended. If she were to continue to help Gurney, she needed to turn her attention to other ways of being of use to him. He himself was apparently now beyond her reach, but his reputation was still to be consolidated. Banned from seeing him in person, Scott proceeded with plans for the promotion of his work, prompted by the enthusiasm of a young composer, Gerald Finzi.

Finzi never actually had the chance to meet Gurney, and his lifelong commitment to publishing and editing Gurney's songs is all the more impressive considering he had no personal relationship with him. He had been inspired to find out more about this mysterious Gurney, having been deeply moved by a performance of 'Sleep'. He made contact with Scott in 1935, suggesting the idea of a symposium on Gurney's work, to be published in the journal *Music and Letters*. Scott agreed, and they began making plans. It would be two years before it saw publication.

Finzi could not have known that becoming embroiled in Gurney's affairs would turn into a project that would take many years and require the patience of a saint. Luckily, he was both long-suffering and diligent, and he devoted an extraordinary amount of time to working on Gurney's behalf. In June he began by typing out a selection of Gurney's poems. In April, he and Scott had persuaded Walter de la Mare to write an introduction for an edition of Gurney's poems, and the project was well underway.

Now entirely alone, Gurney sank deeper into a delusional state from which he would never fully emerge. He lived in what appears to have been a permanent state of reverie. In September 1937 thoughts of France were, as usual, mingled with literature. He was 'remembering Laventie with utmost thanks and relief—and writing straight on to praise Vermand.'[47] The memory of these places seemed to give him a certain sense of release. Recalling trenches he had struggled through and places at which he had been wounded now became a source of solace. As he finally turned away from the world, it would be comforting to hope that he had found some vague sense of peace through his many workings and reworkings of his war years. However, Gurney's memories could only ever provide the thinnest thread of comfort to a man who never reconciled himself to his situation, and was now all too painfully aware that his faculties were slipping away from him. He was finding even letter-writing to be increasingly difficult, and channelled what little energy was left to 'praise books and music' as a substitute, singling out Masefield, Housman, William Hurlstone and George Butterworth for the purpose.

Gurney had had a bad cough since the summer, severe enough to cause Scott to remark on it in her letters that August. By the autumn it had become apparent that he was seriously ill. His cough plagued him, and a pain stabbed him in the chest whenever he gasped for air. He was frightened enough to allow the doctors to listen to his chest, and on 23 November they concluded that he was suffering from pleurisy and tuberculosis. His letters from 1937 had begun to have a new serenity about them, despite being increasingly nonsensical. However, this was not a man slipping into a peaceful oblivion but fighting for each breath. Where moments of lucidity remain, the impression is largely one of deep unhappiness.

There is a widely held but groundless belief that gas patients, because of their damaged lungs, were especially prone to tuberculosis. However, gas victims were actually less likely to contract it than those who had not been exposed. Either way, the amount of gas Gurney had inhaled in 1917 was small enough that there would have been no permanent damage. Bilateral pulmonary tuberculosis was a common killer in asylums. Dartford was huge, underheated and draughty, and Gurney was so emaciated that he did not possess either the physical strength or the mental determination to fight an illness so overpowering. There were no antibiotics to treat it. The best the asylum doctors could offer were sulphonamides (the precursors to penicillin), which had become available only in 1932, but it was not enough to effect a cure.

The fifteen-year nightmare was nearly over. As the weather became colder and wetter, Gurney slipped gradually beyond the point of recovery. Scott knew it, and visited him at the end of November 1937, despite his protestations. He was so ill he could barely speak. She found him desperately thin and barely aware of his surroundings; a spectral, coughing figure slumped in a chair. On the way back from the asylum, having been able to do no more than sit with him in silence, she cast about impotently for some way to show her affection. At Dartford station she found a fruit stall, bought him some oranges, grapes and grapefruit, and had them sent up to the asylum. It was a pitifully small gesture, but what could be done in the face of such utter wretchedness? When she arrived back home, she found the proofs of the special edition of *Music and Letters* waiting for her. A whole section of the journal was dedicated to celebrating Gurney's work. There, in a bundle, was the affirmation and recognition Gurney had so fervently sought, year after year. J. C. Squire, Vaughan Williams, Howells, de la Mare—all had written a tribute to him. Scott requested a copy of the proofs for Gurney, and immediately sat down to write to him. It has been assumed that he never managed to open the proofs, simply murmuring, 'it is too late'. That, however, is apocryphal. He might have been too exhausted to talk for any length of time, but he was lucid enough to read and write, even to observe such nice-ties as to remember to thank Scott for his fruit:

> so many thanks for the oranges which were magnificent. The grapefruits, I think the office will see to—they gave me one flaming drink of 4 ginger beer strength / fine men but <u>too</u> surprising.
>
> Thank you so much—(Lichfield) I read the life of Dr Samuel Johnson in Lit/Biog (Dent) this morning—much admiring the book. But how huge noble and amazing seemed the two-vol- Everyman (great) present. . . . I hope the postal orders arrived back (to you). . . . (I am very ill) but rejoice in AEH x fashion, and of the o m T's . . .
>
> May I be allowed to send best wishes to Miss Scott?
>
> To Miss MM Scott: much troubled . . . I accept the notepaper—but am lost. With best wishes (honour) Ivor B Gurney.[48]

It was probably the last letter Gurney wrote. He may have been aware that this was the end of the many years of correspondence with Scott, as he seems to be writing a remarkably coherent final goodbye to her. We can never be sure whether he did indeed read and understand the significance of the symposium. The 'notepaper' to which he refers could be a thanks for an addition to his supply of writing paper, but it could also be a reference to the package of papers, and an admission that he was too 'lost' to make sense of it.

The crucial first pages of this letter are lost, however, and it would surely have been in those that he would have made direct reference to so important a parcel, if he was indeed capable of recognising its significance. He was in a lucid enough state to talk, to be whimsically amused by the staff, and to enjoy books, so there is a high chance that he did indeed see and appreciate the articles written about him. If he had been able to read them, he would certainly have understood what an accolade it was to have the most eminent composers and writers of the time singing his praises in the preeminent music journal.

It was by now quite clear that he could live for only a matter of days. He lay alone, with no visitors, in the cold hospital ward with its rows of iron beds lined up along the whitewashed walls. Gasping for air and desperately weak, he drifted between sleep and wakefulness. The only indication he had that it was Christmas were the paper chains and lanterns that were hung intermittently around the ward.

Gurney survived the night but died on Boxing Day morning. His lungs had haem-orrhaged, and he choked to death. The trees outside the hospital ward were white with frost when his body was carried out, to be returned, finally, to Gloucestershire.

Scott had arranged for the funeral to be conducted at Twigworth parish church. On 30 December the Reverend Alfred Cheesman received the coffin which enclosed

FIG. 17.4: Gurney's gravestone in the churchyard at Twigworth.
Courtesy of Pamela Blevins.

his godson. Gurney was only forty-seven, but his body was that of a haggard, elderly man. Scott insisted he should have a burial that 'befitted a poet', and had ordered an oak coffin, lined with elm and cushioned with white satin. She must have been sensible of the irony that Gurney would not have touched such a luxurious fabric for fifteen years.

In 1912 Cheesman had become the vicar of the Parish Church of St Matthew's, Twigworth, a village just outside Gloucester. During his breaks from College,

Gurney had spent many happy hours in the vicarage there, talking of his plans, ambitions, and reading poems aloud with his godfather.

Twigworth Vicarage
(To A.H.C.)

Wakened by birds and sun, laughter of the wind,
A man might see all heart's desire by raising
His pillowed sleepy head (still apt for lazing
And drowsy thought)—but then a green most kind
Waved welcome, and the rifted sky behind
Showed blue, whereon cloud-ships full-sailed went racing,
Man to delight and set his heart on praising
The Maker of all things, bountiful-hearted, kind.
May Hill, the half-revealed tree-clad thing,
Maisemore's delightful ridge, where Severn flowing
Nourished a wealth of lovely wild things blowing
Sweet as the air—Wainlodes and Ashleworth
To northward showed, a land where a great king
Might sit to receive homage from the whole earth.[49]

Cheesman had been one of the first to recognise the potential in Gurney when he befriended him as an impetuous, warm-hearted child, and he had helped to shape his progress from boy to man. He had witnessed Gurney's moments of greatness, his courage during the war, his musical and his literary triumphs; and he had been broken-hearted as he watched him decline into madness. Now, only two years before his own death and after years of estrangement, he was to bury the boy he had christened.

It was as bleak an ending to the year as could be imagined. On the morning of New Year's Eve, Gurney's friends and family assembled for the service. The little church was still decorated with Christmas holly, incongruously festive for the task in hand. Gurney's coffin stood in the centre of the church, covered with a large floral cross. There were at least six wreaths, from Scott, the Gurney family and the Haineses, among others. Gurney's mother did not attend, owing to a rather ambiguous 'indisposition.' Vaughan Williams, too, was unable to come. Scott sat with the chief mourners, taking the place of Gurney's mother alongside Winifred, Ronald, Dorothy, and one of Gurney's aunts (Aunt Marie was not present), while the Chapmans and the Harveys joined the ranks of the congregation. Haines was there, and so was Emily Hunt. Gurney's days at the College were represented by Sydney Shimmin, the organist Herbert Sumsion, and Howells. Representatives from the British Legion were present, as well as men who had fought alongside Gurney in the 2/5th Gloucesters. Even the old boys' representative from the King's School was in attendance, along with Gloucestershire dignitaries—finally Gloucester was beginning to recognise the achievements of its son and posthumously accord him the 'honour' he had craved for so long.

Cheesman recounted his memories of the many hours he had spent with his godson. He remembered Gurney's generosity, recalling how he had spent the first guinea he had ever earned on a book, intended as a present for his godfather.

> He was so full of joy and beautiful things, because he loved beautiful music and poetry. He loved all things—the Severn country, the distant hills, the fields, and streams and flowers.[50]

Cheesman concluded with the epigraph to Thomas Gray's 'Elegy in a Country Churchyard', which began, fittingly, 'Here rests his head upon the lap of earth / A youth to fortune and to fame unknown.' Cheesman went on to blame the war for Gurney's deterioration. He stressed the physical toll it had taken on him, and claimed that being wounded, gassed and shell shocked had reduced him to becoming one of war's embers, like the prophetic title of his poetry collection. It was a rather convenient narrative that would be disingenuously taken up by Scott. It was easier and less stigmatising to portray Gurney as a victim of a global, not an individual, tragedy.

Howells played adaptations of 'Severn Meadows', and 'Sleep' on the little organ. Harvey presumably did not feel able to sing as he had done so many times with Gurney at the piano. Howells also played a fourteenth-century French chanson, which Gurney had loved, and an arrangement of Elgar's 'Angel's Farewell' from *The Dream of Gerontius*. The group of mourners filed out of the church to the strains of Parry's 'Elegy', gathering around the newly dug grave in the wintry morning light. The whole event had a double sorrow for Howells—Gurney was to be buried at the foot of the grave of Howells's son Michael, who had died two years before, aged only nine.

In 1918, at the height of his passion for Annie Drummond, Gurney had picked violets from Harvey's garden. It was a symbolic gesture and marked one of the happiest times of his troubled life. The flowers were for Annie, by way of bringing her closer to Will. He had sent her the flowers, imagining how he and his love would have Harvey to stay when they were married. Perhaps Harvey remembered this touching, sentimental gesture, a secret that only he, Gurney and Annie shared, as he picked some rosemary from the same garden that Gurney had loved. The grave was to be heaped with the elaborate floral tributes, garishly bright in the flowerless winter graveyard, but just before the soil was replaced, Harvey leant over the grave and dropped the little nosegay onto the coffin. He had tied a scrap of paper to it that read, 'Rosemary for remembrance.'[51]

To Ivor Gurney
By F. W. Harvey

Now hawthorn hedges live again;
    And all along the banks below
Pale primrose fires have lit the lane
    Where oft we wandered long ago
And saw the blossom blow.

And talked and walked til stars pricked out,
    And sang brave midnight snatches under
The moon, with never a dread nor doubt,
    Nor warning of that devil's wonder
That tore our lives asunder.

And left behind a nightmare trail
    Of horrors scattered through the brain,
Of shattered hopes and memories frail
    That bloom like flowers in some old lane
And tear the heart in twain.

This hawthorn hedge will bank its snow
    Spring after Spring, and never care
What song and dreams of long ago
    Within its shade were fashioned fair
Of happy air.

But you within the madhouse wall,
    But you and I who went so free,
Never shall keep Spring's festival
    Again, though burgeon every tree
With blossom joyously.

Not that I fear to keep the faith;
    Not that my heart goes cravenly;
But that some voice within me saith
    'The Spring is dead!' yea, dead, since he
Will come no more to me.

It needeth but a tear to quench
    The primrose fires: to melt the snow
Of Spring-time hedges, and to drench
    With black the blue clear heavens show . . .
And I have wept for you.

CHAPTER EIGHTEEN

Afterword

On a particularly dark night during the Second World War, Winifred Gurney was stopped by a policeman to have her identity papers checked. The policeman inspected her card and remarked on her surname. 'Are you any relation to Ivor Gurney the song writer?' he asked. 'I have all his songs.' Winifred had always assumed that her brother's songs were hardly known and too difficult to have any kind of popular appeal. She was thrilled, gratified and speechless. 'I have always felt a sense of shame that I could not make some reply, but this emotional make up just paralyses my speech so I rode off in silence.'[1]

In a grand poetic flourish, Edmund Blunden wrote that Gurney

> perished, one many say, from the merciless intensity of his spirit both in watching the forms of things moving apace in the stream of change and in hammering out the poetic form for their just representation and acclamation.[2]

Gurney had perished, although whether the 'merciless intensity of his spirit' was the cause is debatable, but his legacy had to be managed—the vast swathes of unpublished work assessed, edited and published, and his estate administered—if the memory of this 'very distinguished poet and composer', as Vaughan Williams described him, was to be kept alive.[3]

When Finzi realised how much needed to be done to help promote Gurney's works, he decided to undertake the editing of some of his songs. In due course, he came to regret having to deal so closely with Scott, who, as the years progressed, became increasingly possessive of the manuscripts that had been hers for so long. Finzi's letters show his respect for her, and recognition of the enormous amount of work, time and money she had expended on Gurney's behalf for so many years. He recognised that had there been no Marion Scott, however difficult to deal with, few of Gurney's manuscripts would still exist at all. Despite this, even the mild and polite Finzi found it hard at times to stop a note of angry frustration creeping into his correspondence with her. Scott, for all her benevolence, had always had an inclination towards the territorial, and Gurney had been *her* beloved protégé. After his death she was left with his papers as her only remembrance of what she felt had been something akin to an unspoken marriage between the two of them. Her relationship with Gurney had largely been conducted by letter, and she was reluctant to relinquish her control over her precious manuscripts. Gurney's poems and songs were the children of their fictional union—Gurney once even described *Severn and Somme* to Scott as their foster child, 'carefully reared and baptised by you.'[4] How difficult it must have been for this lonely woman to surrender her babies up for adoption when Finzi demanded it. Haines and his wife observed Gurney in the company of Scott, and got to know Scott independently, and were firmly of the opinion that her attachment to him was purely maternal.[5] Winifred Gurney might have been nearer the truth when she suspected that Scott's relationship to her brother had been far more intense at least in fantasy than it had been in reality. When there was talk of a biography in the 1950s, Winifred fancied that 'Miss M Scott is afraid of a biography because she was in love with Ivor definitely . . . If Ivor was in love with Miss Scott he stuck rigidly to his own opinions regarding his music and poetry and as one reads he would alter nothing.'[6]

Scott had taken over Gurney's estate in 1938. She remained in control of it until she died of cancer on Christmas Eve 1953, leaving her flat full of manuscripts relating to him. They were, it seemed, strewn in every drawer and wardrobe. Some were even locked away in her local bank. The task of sorting them was gargantuan and would need months of painstaking work. It seemed natural that Finzi should take on the responsibility, but Ronald Gurney, in a wholly unexpected move, decided that while he had tolerated Scott's control whilst she was alive, now she was dead, he would intervene. His attitude struck fear into the hearts of all those who had an interest in preserving Gurney's documents.

> I now regard it that there is nothing left worth bothering about publishing and that Miss Scott's work was completed and the reasons for her administration are satisfied. Therefore, I direct that the administration of my brother's affairs must now return to me.[7]

Ronald had no genuine interest in his brother's affairs or work, but enjoyed the power he could now wield over the London intellectuals who had always seemed so aloof and superior. He resented 'the fact that Miss Scott thought and behaved as if my brother's estate was hers and only hers and that I only was consulted when a rubber stamp was required.' He was quite open about his interest in making money from the estate. If his brother's work didn't pay, it was, in his eyes at least, useless.

Miss Scott herself said that the poetry was not expected to pay for itself—there will be no more on that basis. . . . As regards the future of the MSS—I am not prepared to discuss that at present with anyone—perhaps I shall become hard up and need fuel for warmth.[8]

Unfortunately, he was not aware of the fact that as Gurney lay dying, he had been asked what he wanted to do with any money his work might make. He directed that it should be given to the poor (an odd choice considering his debt at the time of his death to Scott). This was a verbal, not written instruction and as far as Ronald was concerned, any money his brother's work might generate, however paltry, was to be his.[9]

To Ronald, Gurney's music was a 'dead horse' that was being flogged, and his poetry, despite looking impressive in a new collection by Edmund Blunden, still appeared to him in 1953 to be a 'sea of words'. It did not help matters that one of the large boxes of manuscripts Ronald had insisted on obtaining had been rather damningly marked 'useless and of no value'. Howells, Finzi and finally Vaughan Williams all pleaded with him, but by the time both Vaughan Williams and Finzi went to Gloucester for the 1955 Three Choirs Festival, only one box had been given to the Gloucester Library, and most of Gurney's songs were still in danger of Ronald's threat to turn them into kindling.

No wonder, then, that so few of Gurney's songs were assessed and published in the decades succeeding his death. If Finzi had been able to take over where Scott had left off, our knowledge of Gurney's work would now be entirely different. The legacy of this fatal delay in being able to obtain the manuscripts is still only slowly being rectified. Ronald's obstinacy meant that Finzi, despite having both ample expertise and good will, did not have the chance to work for any length of time on Gurney's songs. He was to die in 1956 aged only fifty-five, and Vaughan Williams, who might have stepped in to defend Gurney's work, died two years later.

At this point, Oxford University Press had published only thirty of Gurney's songs.[10] Ronald reluctantly allowed another collection of ten songs to be published in 1959. In the same year he finally relented to the pressure from London and handed over his boxes of manuscripts to the library. He did not, however, relinquish his stranglehold on their publication, and while he might give permission for the odd music collection to be published, he was adamant that the poetry, which never made money, would not be seen in public. Gurney's reputation must stand or fall by the little that was in the public domain, he insisted. It was all his brother deserved.

Winifred, being more reasonable than Ronald, proposed two possible reasons for this unkind recalcitrance. She found his wife Ethel to be 'wicked' and believed that Ethel resented the fact that if any of Gurney's work made money, it would go to his siblings, not to Ethel herself. Winifred also hinted at the possibility that Ronald was becoming rather unhinged; 'Ethel did say once that she thought Ronald was a bit that way.'[11]

Edmund Blunden compiled an eclectic collection of Gurney's poems with Hutchinson in 1952, leaving out much that was mellifluous because of the trend against anything associated with the Georgians. This proved to be a bad choice, and the book did not sell well (Blunden later described it as having been 'still-born').[12] After Gerald Finzi's death, Joy campaigned in the early 1960s for a collected poems, canvassing support for the volume from eminent musicians and poets associated with Gurney. The poet and critic Leonard Clark (a Gloucestershire man and friend of Harvey) chose three hundred poems from the possible one thousand in manuscript, which were looked over and approved by the now very elderly John Masefield. It was, as Clark pointed out to Joy, an opportune moment, as the major war poetry anthologies were beginning to emerge, and Gurney was woefully underrepresented in them.[13] If he could not take his place fully alongside the already extensively published war poets, a volume dedicated to his work would go some way to redress the wrong. However, Joy struggled and repeatedly failed to find a publisher. She also had to wrangle with Ronald, who continued to insist that none of his brother's verse deserved publication. On one visit to Gloucester to plead with him, he simply slammed the door in her face. But eventually, a decade after she had begun the campaign, her efforts paid off. After Ronald's death, a shortened version of the manuscript Clark had assembled was published by Chatto and Windus.[14]

In the 1980s, P. J. Kavanagh published a more comprehensive *Collected Poems*, which is still the touchstone for studies of Gurney's writing. His collection has shaped what we know of Gurney's verse, but this was still only a limited selection. The majority of Gurney's work is still unpublished. His growing reputation at the end of the twentieth century was based on less than a third of his work, in both music and poetry.

In the last twenty years or so, Gurney's star has undoubtedly been in the ascendant. Michael Hurd's short, moving biography *The Ordeal of Ivor Gurney* (1978) helped to put Gurney on the map, and to raise awareness of the driven and tortured figure behind the well-known handful of songs and poems. His biography encouraged a steady trickle of academics to investigate Gurney's story further, and Pamela Blevins's dual biography of Gurney and Scott has done much to resurrect Scott's achievements.[15] Kelsey Thornton's *Collected Letters of Ivor Gurney* (1991) remains a bible for the Gurney enthusiast. It offered for the first time, in one volume, an almost daily account of Gurney's war and the years leading up to his incarceration, allowing the 'loveable egotist', as Howells called him, to speak for himself. In his letters we find his humour, his struggles and his compelling drive to achieve exuding from every page.

Gurney had written despite, and often because, he felt himself to be 'beaten down, continually beaten down' by fate.[16] In a letter to Scott, outlining the inspiration behind the song 'By a Bierside', he told how he had imagined 'some Greek hero' laid out in death: heroic and tragic in equal measure. It might have been a premonition of how he was to see himself in later years: the young hero, a victim of the gods' cruelty. Gurney's life is characterised by his 'heroic' perseverance, and the sense that he, still somehow the young schoolboy full of promise, was left behind in the shadows while his contemporaries went ahead of him to achieve greatness. As his speech written into *The Tempest* demonstrates, he saw himself as both Prospero and Ariel, the fettered spirit and the frustrated magus. His determination to find joy in shadows is beginning to earn him the recognition he craved and which he so richly deserved.

Appendices

These catalogues are included with grateful recognition of the work of Philip Lancaster, who has dated and collated many of the manuscripts of both the musical and literary works. Much of Gurney's work remains unpublished, and this is the most accurate record to date of all Gurney's work, both extant and lost.

Appendix A

A CHRONOLOGICAL CATALOGUE OF GURNEY'S MUSICAL WORKS

ABBREVIATIONS AND PUBLISHERS

F.p.:	first (known) performance
FS:	full score
GF:	annotation, or date recorded, by Gerald Finzi
IGSJ:	Ivor Gurney Society Journal
RCM:	Royal College of Music
B&H:	Boosey & Hawkes
OUP:	Oxford University Press
S&B:	Stainer & Bell
WR:	Winthrop Rogers (now Boosey & Hawkes)

PUBLICATIONS

S&B, 1926:	*Lights Out*
OUP, 1938:	Ivor Gurney, *Twenty Songs* [published in two volumes of ten songs]
OUP, 1952:	*A Third Volume of Ten Songs*
OUP, 1959:	*A Fourth Volume of Ten Songs*
OUP, 1979:	*A Fifth Volume of Ten Songs*, ed. Michael Hurd
OUP, 1997:	*Ivor Gurney: 20 Favourite Songs*, comp. Neil Jenkins
Thames, 1998:	*Eleven Songs*, ed. Michael Hurd
Thames, 2000:	*Seven Sappho Songs*, ed. Richard Carder
Thames, 2004:	*Preludes and Nocturnes for Piano*, ed. Richard Carder

Publications from the same publishers dated otherwise are single-issue works.

c. 1904–7		Sketchbook containing various sketches and fragments, one dated retrospectively, 'about December 1904', but including song dated 1907 ('Passing By'). From these sketches can be distinguished:

Saw Ye Him Whom My Soul Loveth? [Voice and organ]
Words: Song of Solomon, chs. 3 & 5. Incomplete. Possibly associated with 'I Am the Rose of Sharon', below.

Mandalay. Song.
Words: Rudyard Kipling. [c. 1904] Incomplete.

Who Hath Desired the Sea. Song.
Words: Rudyard Kipling. 'about December 1904'. Incomplete.

Reverie. [Piano or ?organ.]

I Am the Rose of Sharon. [Voice and organ]
Words: Song of Solomon, ch. 2. Incomplete. May be associated with 'Saw Ye Him', above.

Recessional. [Organ]

Prelude. [Organ]

Omar Khayyam. [?Piano solo]

1907

Passing By. Song for voice and piano.
Words: 'Robert Herrick' [sic: Thomas Naogeorgus, trans. Barnabe Googe].

The Answer. [Piano] Fragment.

Caprice. [Piano]

Minuet. [Piano] Fragment.

[?Violin Sonata]
Unfinished sketches of violin part for short three movement work.

November

On Your Midnight Pallet Lying. Song for voice and piano.
Words: A. E. Housman. Publication: Thames, 1998.

1908

Since Thou, O Fondest and Truest. Song for voice and piano.
Words: Robert Bridges. Dedication: 'To Robert Bridges in gratitude'. Dated retrospectively in 1925, '?1908'.
Publication: Boosey & Co., 1921; Thames, 1998.

Gulls in an Aëry Morrice. Song for voice and piano.
Words: W. E. Henley. Incomplete.

The Sea. 'after Edward MacDowell'. Solo piano.

February

Dearest, When I Am Dead. Song for voice and piano.
Words: W. E. Henley. 24 February 1908.

March

I Dreamed the Peach-Trees Blossomed. Song for voice and piano.
Words: Rosamund Marriott-Watson. 3 March 1908. Incomplete.

The Full Sea Rolls and Thunders. Song for voice and piano.
Words: W. E. Henley. Dedication: 'To C. G. G. B.'.

April

The Starlings. Song for voice and piano.
Words: Charles Kingsley.

May

The Sea Is Full of Wandering Foam. Song for voice and piano.
Words: W. E. Henley.

	June	Dear Hands, So Many Times. Song for voice and piano. Words: W. E. Henley.
	August	Chanson Triste. Violin and piano.
	September	In September: An Idyll for violin and piano. 14–26 September 1908.
	October	I Would My Songs Were Roses. Song for voice and piano. Words: Heinrich Heine [trans. J. W. Oddie].
	November	Nocturne in A flat. Solo piano. 29 November 1908. Publication: Thames, 2004.
1909	February	In August: Second Idyll for violin (and piano). January–February 1909.
		Sehnsucht. Solo piano. 27 February 1909. Cf. '[Three Pieces]', October 1909.
	April	A Visit from the Sea. Song for voice and piano. Words: R. L. Stevenson. 5 April 1909.
		When You Are Old and Grey. Song for voice and piano. Words: W. B. Yeats. Incomplete.
		Romance for violin [and piano].
		Revery. Solo piano.
	May	The Crown. Song for voice and piano. Words: Elizabeth Barrett Browning. 6–8 May 1909.
		A New Child's Garden. Suite for solo piano. i. A Child's Song. Remaining movements unknown and missing.
	June	Nocturne in B flat. Solo piano. 19 June 1909. Publication: Thames, 2004.
		The Hill Pines. Song for voice and piano. [first setting] Words: Robert Bridges. Dated June–December 1909.
		Looking Glass River. Song for voice and piano. Words: R. L. Stevenson. 'Summer 1909'.
		The Country of the Camisards. Song for voice and piano. Words: R. L. Stevenson. 'Summer 1909–July 1910'.
	August	Song of the Summer Woods: An Idyll for piano. Dedication: 'To Margaret Hunt'.
		Late Autumn Woods: Sketch for piano. Dedication: 'To Margaret Hunt'. 14 August 1909.
		A Picture (Zuneigung): Sketch for piano. Dedication: 'To Margaret Hunt'. 30 August 1909.
	September	Legende. Violin and piano.
	October	[Three Pieces]. Solo piano. i. Sehnsucht; ii. Rumination in an Old Cowhouse; iii. Revery. i. composed February 1909; ii. 22 October 1909; iii. 28 October 1909.
		A Folk Tale for violin [and piano]. Dedication: 'To Emily Hunt'. [c. 1909]
		Humoreske. Violin and piano. [c. 1909]
		Despair. Solo piano. [c. 1909]

		Lament for piano. [c. 1909]
		Theme and Variations for piano. A theme and twenty-one completed variations and unfinished twenty-second. [c. 1909–10]
1910	February	Two Fantasies for solo piano i. Fantasy in F sharp major; ii. Fantasy in F major. Dedication: 'To Margaret Hunt'.
	April	First Sonata in G major for violin and pianoforte. Three movements. End of iii. revised 13 December 1910.
	July	I Will Make You Brooches. Song for voice and piano. Words: R. L. Stevenson. 18 July 1910.
	October	When June Is Come. Song for voice and piano. Words: Robert Bridges. 3 October 1910.
		Dear Lady. Song for voice and piano. [first setting] Words: Robert Bridges. Dedication: 'To F.W.H[arvey]'s mother?' (GF) [1910]
	December	Sonata in C minor. Violin and piano. Three movements. Dedication: 'Written for and dedicated to E[mily] & M[argaret] H[unt]'. October–December 1910.
		Two Sea Pieces for piano. i. Ocean Legend (November–December 1910); ii. Sea Joy (April 1909–December 1910).
		Sonata in F minor. Solo piano. Three movements. May–December 1910. Dedication: 'To M. H.' [Margaret Hunt].
		Coronation March. For Orchestra. ('March in B flat for full orchestra'). Piano score: December 1910–2 January 1911. FS completed 8 February 1911. F.p. Gloucester Cathedral, June 2012.
1911	January	Song and Singer. Song for voice and piano. Words: R. L. Stevenson. 18 January 1911.
	June	Song of Ciabhan. Song for voice and piano. Words: Ethna Carbery (pseud. Anna MacManus). Publication: OUP, 1979.
		I Praise the Tender Flower. Song for voice and piano. Words: Robert Bridges. [c. December 1911?]; revised February 1916. Publication: OUP, 1952 & 1997.
		I Love All Beauteous Things. Song for voice and piano. Words: Robert Bridges. [c. 1911–12] Missing, except title page.
		Violin Sonata in E minor. Violin and piano. Two movements, i. incomplete. [c. 1911–13]
		Fate. Song for soprano and piano. Words: Bret Harte. 'Summer term 1911–Lent term 1912'.

1912		Poems for piano.
		i. Autumn; ii. Wind in the Wood. [c. 1912?]. ii. incomplete.
		Heretics All. Song for voice and piano.
		Words: Hilaire Belloc.
	June	String Quartett in A minor.
		Four movements. January–June 1912. F.p. Society of Women Musicians, Winter 1912–13.
		West Sussex Drinking Song. Song for voice and piano.
		Words: Hilaire Belloc. Dedication: 'To F. W. H[arvey] (comrade to many in captivity)'. Publication: Chappell, 1921; Thames, 1998.
		[unknown]
		Words: F. W. Harvey. Missing.
		Title/words unknown, but known to have been written, June 1912.
1913	August	The Night of Trafalgar. Song for voice and piano.
		Words: Thomas Hardy. Publication: OUP, 1979.
	December	Five Elizabethan Songs. For mezzo-soprano, 2 fl, 2 cl, hp, 2 bsns. [Also arr. piano.]
		i. Orpheus with His Lute (Shakespeare); ii. Tears (Fletcher); iii. Under the Greenwood Tree (Shakespeare); iv. Come, Sleep (Fletcher); v. Spring (Nashe).
		FS of v. only extant. Dedication: 'To Emmy [Emily] Hunt'. F.p. Idwen Thomas (soprano), [before June 1916]. Publication (piano score): B&H, 1920; 1983.
[1913–14]		Violin and piano sonata in G major.
		First movement only extant. [c. 1913–14]
		Isabel. Song for voice and piano.
		Words: John Skelton. [unknown date, ?c. 1913–14]
		String Trio in G major.
		One movement. [c. 1913–14]
		Scherzo for string trio.
		One movement. [c. 1913–14]
1914		The Dreams of Peace: waltz. Solo piano. [c. 1914]
		Dreams of the Sea. Song for voice and piano.
		Words: W. H. Davies.
		Kennst du das Land? Song for voice and piano.
		Words: J. W. von Goethe. [First stanza only; in German]
	Summer	The Twa Corbies. Song for baritone and piano.
		Words: Trad. Border Ballad. Revised August 1915. Dedication: 'To Sir Hubert Parry'.
		F.p. ?Gertrude Higgs, RCM, 27 June 1916.
		Publication: Music and Letters, vol. 1, no. 2 (March 1920); OUP, 1928 & 1979.
		Chant for Psalm 23. SATB choir.
		Dated 'Summer term, 1914'. 'Used at Fauquissart, July 1916'.

	October	Choral Prelude on 'St. Mary'. For organ.
	November	Edward, Edward. Song for voice and piano. Words: Trad. Scottish Ballad. 6 November 1914. Dedication: 'To A. H. Cheesman'. Publication: S&B, 1922; Thames, 1998.
1915	September	March for Gloucester Regiment. [for military band.] Missing.
1916	August	By a Bierside. Song for contralto and piano. Words: John Masefield. 'Trench Mortar Emplacement, France, August 1916'. Dedication: 'To Marion Scott'. F.p. in orchestration by Herbert Howells: Frederick Taylor (baritone), Charles Stanford (conductor), RCM, 23 March 1917. Publication: OUP, 1979.
1917	January	In Flanders. Song for voice and piano. Words: F. W. Harvey. [Thiepval], 11 January 1917. F.p. in orchestration by Herbert Howells: Frederick Taylor (baritone), Charles Stanford (conductor), RCM, 23 March 1917. Publication: OUP, 1959.
	March	Severn Meadows. Song for contralto (or baritone) and piano. Words: Ivor Gurney. Caulaincourt, March 1917. F.p. Society of Women Musicians, Wigmore Hall, 24 April 1918. Publication: OUP, 1928, 1979 & 1997.
	May	Time ('Even such is time'). Song for voice and piano. Words: Walter Raleigh. Publication: OUP, 1959 & 1997.
	June	On Wenlock Edge. Song for voice and piano. Words: A. E. Housman. Dated 'Near Arras, June 1917 / Seaton Delaval, January 1918', having not been written out until returned from France. F.p. Society of Women Musicians, Wigmore Hall, 24 April 1918.
	July	Captain Stratton's Fancy. Song for voice and piano. Words: John Masefield. Dedication: 'To F. W. Harvey, singer of this song in many prison camps.' Publication: S&B, 1920; Thames, 1998.
	October	The Folly of Being Comforted. Song for contralto (mezzo soprano) and piano. Words: W. B. Yeats. Publication: OUP, 1938.
1918		If We Return. Song for voice and piano. Words: F. W. Harvey. [c. 1917–18] Incomplete. Publication, completed by Richard Carder, *IGSJ*, vol. 5 (1999).
		The Scribe. Song for voice and piano. Words: Walter de la Mare. Dated '1918'. F.p. Clive Carey (baritone), Thornton Lofthouse (piano), Westbourne Terrace, London, 30 January 1922. Publication: OUP, 1938 & 1997.
	January	The Lawlands o' Holland [first setting]. Song for voice and piano. Words: Trad. Ballad. 4 January 1918.

For G ('All night under the moon'). Song for voice and piano.
Words: Wilfrid Gibson. F.p. Society of Women Musicians, Wigmore
Hall, 24 April 1918. Publication: OUP, 1938 & 1997.

The Land of Lost Content. Song for voice and piano.
Words: A. E. Housman.
Revised/incorporated into 'The Western Playland', May 1920 (as 'The
Far Country').

February   The Lake Isle of Innisfree. Song for baritone and piano. [first setting]
Words: W. B. Yeats.

March   Thou Didst Delight My Eyes. Song for baritone and piano. [first
version; cf. April 1921]
Words: Robert Bridges. Dedication: 'To A[nnie] N[elson] D[rummond]'.

The Cherry Tree. Song for baritone or contralto and piano.
Words: A. E. Housman. Dedication: 'To E[mily] H[unt]'.
Revised/incorporated into 'The Western Playland', May 1920 (as
'Loveliest of Trees').

Song of Silence. Song for baritone and piano.
Words: Ivor Gurney. Dedication: 'To A[nnie] N[elson] D[rummond]'.
Publication: *British Music* [Journal of the British Music Society], vol.
15 (1993).

The White Cascade. Song for voice and piano.
Words: W. H. Davies.
Dedication: 'To Dorothy' [IBG's sister].

Red Roses. Song for voice and piano.
Words: Wilfrid Gibson. Dedication: 'To A[nnie] N[elson]
D[rummond]'.

Violin Sonata [?in A flat]. Violin and piano.
In progress, March 1918. Missing.

April   The Fiddler of Dooney. Song for voice and piano. [first setting]
Words: W. B. Yeats. F.p. Walter Johnstone-Douglas, Wigmore Hall, 13
June 1919.

June   The Penny Whistle. Song for voice and piano.
Words: Edward Thomas. June–July 1918.
Dedication: 'To the 2/5th Gloucesters'.
F.p. Walter Johnstone-Douglas, Wigmore Hall, 13 June 1919.
Publication: S&B, 1926.

July   Fain Would I Change That Note. Song for voice and piano.
Words: Tobias Hume.

Sowing. Song for voice and piano.
Words: Edward Thomas. Dedication: 'To H[erbert] N. Howells'.
Publication: S&B, 1925; Thames, 1998.

O Happy Wind. Song for voice and piano.
Words: W. H. Davies.

The Bonny Earl of Murray. Song for baritone and piano.
Words: Trad. Scottish Ballad. 'Summer 1918'. Dedication: 'Mrs Waterhouse'.
Publication: WR, 1921; B&H, 1950; Thames, 1998.

September   The Cloths of Heaven. Song for voice and piano.
Words: W. B. Yeats. F.p. Steuart Wilson (tenor), 32 Gordon Square, London (British Music Society meeting), 13 February 1919.
Publication: OUP, 1979 & 1997.

The County Mayo. Song for voice and piano.
Words: James Stephens (after ó Raifteiri). Dedication: 'Mrs [Margaret] Taylor'.
F.p. Clive Carey (baritone), Thornton Lofthouse (piano), Westbourne Terrace, London, 30 January 1922. Publication: WR, 1921; Thames, 1998.

Violin Sonata in D major. Violin and piano.
Four movements. Dedication: 'To F. W. Harvey'. c. August–September 1918.

O Tall White Poplar. Duet [for two sopranos].
Words: Ivor Gurney (variant of poem, 'The Poplar' (September 1918; War's Embers). Fragment.

December   Epitaph on an Army of Mercenaries. Song for voice and piano.
Words: A. E. Housman.

Is My Team Ploughing. Song for voice and piano.
Words: A. E. Housman.
Revised/incorporated into 'The Western Playland', May 1920.

To E. M. H.: A Birthday Present from Ivor. Solo piano.
'Christmas 1918'. Dedication: [Margaret Hunt].

Twilight Song ('Desire in Spring'). Song for voice and piano.
Words: Francis Ledwidge. [c. 23–30] December 1918.
Dedication: 'To E[thel] L. V[oynich]'. Publication: The Chapbook (A Monthly Miscellany), no. 18 (December 1920); OUP, 1928, 1979 & 1997.

1919   Praise of Ale. Song for voice and piano.
Words: F. W. Harvey. [1919]

The Eagle. Song for voice and piano.
Words: Alfred Tennyson. [c. 1919]

Nocturne. Song for voice and piano.
Words: Vivian Locke-Ellis. [c. 1919]

February   An Epitaph. Song for voice and piano.
Words: Walter de la Mare. Publication: OUP, 1938, 1985 & 1997.

A Gloucestershire Lad. Song cycle [for baritone and piano].
Words: F. W. Harvey.
i. In Flanders; ii. Piper's Wood; iii. The Horses; iv. The Rest Farm; v. [Song of] Minsterworth Perry.
25–26 February 1919 except 'In Flanders' (1916). ii. revised September 1919.

F.p. F. W. Harvey (baritone) and Ivor Gurney (piano), Stroud, March 1919.
Missing, except i.

When on a Summer's Morn. Song for voice and piano.
Words: W. H. Davies. [c. February–March 1919]. Incomplete.

The Apple Orchard. For violin and piano.
F.p. Isolde Menges (violin), Howard Ferguson (piano), February 1938.
Publication: OUP, 1940 (as no. 1 of 'Two Pieces', with 'Scherzo' (March 1919)).

March   Scherzo. For violin and piano.
F.p. Isolde Menges (violin), Howard Ferguson (piano), February 1938.
Publication: OUP, 1940 (as no. 2 of 'Two Pieces', with 'The Apple Orchard' (February 1919)).

[String] Quartett in A.
Three movements [iv missing or unwritten]. [Late November 1918]– March 1919

Lights Out. Song for voice and piano.
Words: Edward Thomas.Dedication 'I.M.–M.H.' [in memoriam Margaret Hunt].
Publication: *London Mercury*, November 1924; S&B, 1926.

Song of the Night at Morn. Song.
Words: Alice Meynell. Missing.

Kathleen ni Houlihan. Song for voice and piano.
Words: W. B. Yeats. Publication: OUP, 1938.

Anthem of Earth. Cantata for baritone solo, chorus and orchestra.
Words: Walt Whitman. Begun March 1919. In progress to ?c. 1921.
Incomplete; short score.

Mass. [for choir]
Words: Communion Service. [in progress, March–April 1919] Missing.

April   Maid Quiet. Song for voice and piano.
Words: W. B. Yeats.

May   Violin Sonata in E flat major. Violin and piano.
Four movements. Composed late 1918 (ii)–May 1919 (iv). i. revised July 1919.

June   Reconciliation. Song for voice and piano.
Words: Walt Whitman.

Sonata [no. 2] in D for piano.
Three movements. i./iii. incomplete.

July   Today I Think ('Scents'). Song for voice and piano.
Words: Edward Thomas. Publication: S&B, 1926.

Prelude in D. Solo piano.
Dedication: 'To Winnie' [Winifred Chapman]. 'Summer 1919'. F.p.
Winifred MacBride, Wigmore Hall, 29 June 1920. Publication: WR, 1921 ('Five Preludes for Piano': V); Thames, 2004.

Hesperus. Song for voice and piano.
Words: Bliss Carman, after Sappho. Publication: Thames, 2000.

August The Apple Orchard. Song for voice and piano.
Words: Bliss Carman, after Sappho. Publication: OUP, 1979 & 1997;
Thames, 2000.

Love Shakes My Soul. Song for voice and piano.
Words: Bliss Carman, after Sappho. Publication: OUP, 1959; Thames,
2000.

Prelude in D flat. Solo piano.
Publication: Thames, 2004.

Prelude in F sharp major. Solo piano.
Dedication: 'To Sir Charles Stanford'. F.p. Winifred MacBride,
Wigmore Hall, 29 June 1920. Publication: WR, 1921 ('Five Preludes
for Piano': I); Thames, 2004.

Prelude in D. Solo piano.
'Summer 1919'/'Autumn 1920' Publication: Thames, 2004.

September I Shall Be Ever Maiden. Song for voice and piano.
Words: Bliss Carman, after Sappho. Publication: OUP, 1952; Thames,
2000.

Once You Lay upon My Bosom. Song for voice and piano.
Words: Bliss Carman, after Sappho. Incomplete.

Lonely Night. Song for voice and piano.
Words: Bliss Carman, after Sappho. Publication: Thames, 2000.

The Halt of the Legion. Song for voice and piano.
Words: John Masefield.

On the Downs. Song for baritone and piano.
Words: John Masefield. Publication: OUP, 1959.

The Quiet Mist. Song for voice and piano.
Words: Bliss Carman, after Sappho. [c. September 1919] Publication:
Thames, 2000.

Soft Was the Wind in the Beech Trees. Song for voice and piano.
Words: Bliss Carman, after Sappho. [c. September 1919]
Publication: *IGSJ*, vol. 5 (1999); Thames, 2000.

Prelude in A minor. Solo piano.
Dedication: 'To Gerald James'. Publication: WR, 1921 ('Five Preludes
for Piano': II); Thames, 2004.

Prelude in D flat. Solo piano.
Dedication: 'To Mrs Chapman'. 'Autumn 1919'. F.p. Winifred
MacBride, Wigmore Hall, 29 June 1920. Publication: WR, 1921
('Five Preludes for Piano': III); Thames, 2004.

October Last Hours. Song for voice and piano.
Words: John Freeman. Publication: OUP, 1938.

Album Leaf. Solo piano.
Dedication: 'For Micky' [Marjorie Chapman]. Publication: Anthony
Boden, *Stars in a Dark Night* (Alan Sutton, 1986).

November   Winter. Song for voice and piano.
Words: Walter de la Mare.

The Singer. Song for voice and piano.
Words: Edward Shanks. Publication: OUP, 1938 & 1997.

'Symphony slow movement'. Orchestra.
[Autumn term 1919] Missing.

December   Ludlow & Teme. Song cycle for tenor, string quartet and piano.
Words: A. E. Housman (*A Shropshire Lad*).
i. When Smoke Stood Up from Ludlow; ii. Far in a Western
Brookland; iii. 'Tis Time, I Think; iv. Ludlow Fair ['The lads in their
hundreds']; v. On the Idle Hill of Summer; vi. When I Was One and
Twenty; vii. The Lent Lily. November–December 1919.
F.p. Steuart Wilson (tenor), Philharmonic Quartet, George Thalben-Ball
(piano), Westbourne Terrace, London, 19 March 1920. Dedication: 'To
the memory of Margaret Hunt'. Publication: S&B, 1923 (Carnegie
Collection). Revised 1925; published in new edition, S&B, 2011.

Sonata in F. Violin and piano.
Slow movement only extant. Autumn–Winter [1919].
F.p. Nigel Leat (violin), Peter Blackwood (piano), Huntingdon
Centre, Bath, 28 May 1987.

[1919–20]   Carol of the Skiddaw Yowes. Song for voice and piano.
Words: Edmund Casson. [c. 1919–20]
Dedication: 'To J. W. H[aines]'.
Publication: Boosey & Co., 1920 & 1925; B&H, 1977.

The Ship [first setting]. Song for voice and piano.
Words: J. C. Squire. [c. 1919–20]

Prelude in F sharp. Solo piano.
[c. 1919]. Publication: Thames, 2004.

Prelude in F sharp minor. Solo piano.
Fragment. [c. 1919–20]

Prelude in F. Solo piano.
Fragment. [c. 1919–20]

Fugue in G major. Solo piano. [c. 1919–20]

The Birds. Song for voice and piano.
Words: Hilaire Belloc. [c. 1919–20]

A Sword. Song for voice and piano.
Words: Robin Flower. [c. 1919–20] Publication: OUP, 1938.

[1919–21]   The Dying Patriot: Day Breaks on England. Song for voice and piano.
Words: James Elroy Flecker. [c. 1919–21]

A Piper. Song for voice and piano.
Words: Seumas O'Sullivan. [c. 1919–21] Publication: OUP, 1959 &
1997.

Christmas Folk Song. Song for voice and piano.
Words: Lizette Woodworth Reese. [c. 1919–21]

Chorale Prelude on 'Longford'. Organ. [c. 1919–21]

Chorale Prelude on 'Jerusalem My Happy Home'. Organ. [c. 1919–21]

Chorale Prelude on 'Rockingham'. Organ. [c. 1919–21]
Publication: Arr. piano by Stephen Banfield, *IGSJ*, vol. 13 (2007).

Home Song. Violin and piano. [c. 1919–21]

Violin Sonata in A minor. Violin and piano.
Three movements. [c. 1919–21] i./iii. complete; ii. violin part only.

1920   Star Talk. Song for voice and piano.
Words: Robert Graves. '1920'. Revised July 1925.
F.p. Clive Carey (baritone), Thornton Lofthouse (piano), Westbourne
Terrace, London, 30 January 1922. Publication: S&B, 1927; Thames,
1998.

London Song. Song for voice and piano.
Words: 'John Daniels' [Ivor Gurney].
Dated '1920' and '1925'; no 1920 source extant. '[A]ll rewritten',
[November] 1925.

A Lyke Wake Carol. Song for voice and piano.
Words: Arthur Shearly Cripps. 1920.

Most Holy Night. Song for voice and piano.
Words: Hilaire Belloc. 1920. Publication: OUP, 1959 & 1997.

The Happy Tree. Song for voice and piano.
Words: Gerald Gould. [c. 1920] Publication: OUP, 1952.

Bright Clouds. Song for voice and piano.
Words: Edward Thomas. 1920. Publication: S&B, 1926.

Cradle Song. Song for voice and piano.
Words: W. B. Yeats. 1920. Publication: OUP, 1959.

I Will Go with My Father A-Ploughing. Song for voice and piano.
Words: Joseph Campbell. [c. 1920?]
Dedication: 'Miss Marion Scott'. Publication: Boosey & Co., 1921 &
1925; B&H, 1977.

When Rooks Fly Homeward. Song for voice and piano.
Words: Joseph Campbell. [1920]

Prelude in C. Solo piano.
[c. 1920] Publication: Thames, 2004.

Fugue in F sharp minor. Solo piano. [c. 1920]

The Darling Black Head (Cean Dubh Deelish). Song for voice and
piano.
Words: Samuel Ferguson. [c. 1920]

A Song of Walking ('Cranham Woods'). Song for voice and piano.
Words: F. W. Harvey. [c. Summer–Autumn 1920]
Publication: OUP, 1928, 1979 & 1997. F.p. Clive Carey (baritone),
Thornton Lofthouse (piano), Westbourne Terrace, London, 30
January 1922.

['Anthem'. 'of war truly'] [SATB choir]
Words: [Digby Mackworth] Dolben. 1920. Title, text and scoring
unknown. Missing.

February   [String] Quartett in F.
Four movements. [?February 1920]

April   John Day. Song for voice and piano.
Words: William Kerr.

Counting Sheep. Song for voice and piano.
Words: William Kerr. [c. April 1920]

May   The Western Playland. Song cycle for baritone, string quartet and piano.
Words: A. E. Housman (*A Shropshire Lad*).
i. Reveille; ii. Loveliest of Trees; iii. Golden Friends; iv. Twice a Week; v. The Aspens; vi. Is My Team Ploughing; vii. The Far Country; viii. March. Composed May 1920, except ii., vi. and vii., which were adapted from earlier settings (see 1918). Revised 1925 as *The Western Playland (and of Sorrow)*. Dedication: 'To Herbert Howells' [1920]; 'To Hawthornden' [Annie Drummond] (1926). F.p. Topliss Green (baritone), RCM Union, 26 November 1920. Publication: S&B, 1926 (Carnegie Collection); new edition, S&B, 2020.

Sonata in F for violin [and piano].
?Four movements.
Slow movement [c. 1919–21]; possible associated scherzo [c. May 1920; incomplete].
Sketches of possible outer movements [Autumn 1920].

July   Two Songs from *Country Sentiment*. Voice and piano.
Words: Robert Graves. i. Nine of the Clock-O; ii. Goodnight to the Meadow.
Publication: OUP, 1938 (i); 1952 (ii).

Song ('The boat is chafing'). Song for voice and piano.
Words: John Davidson. Publication: OUP, 1938.

If Death to Either Shall Come. Song for voice and piano.
Words: Robert Bridges. Publication: OUP, 1938.

The Sea Poppy. Song for voice and piano.
Words: Robert Bridges. July 1920 score incomplete.
Later version only fully extant (June 1925).

The Even Darkens Over. Song for voice and piano.
Words: Robert Bridges. [?July 1920]. Missing.

Brittle Bones. Song for voice and piano.
Words: Robert Graves. 'Summer 1920'.

Loving Henry. Song for voice and piano.
Words: Robert Graves. [c. Summer 1920]

August   The Latmian Shepherd (Song from an unwritten play). Song for voice and piano.
Words: Edward Shanks. Publication: OUP, 1938.

September   I Have Loved the Flowers That Fade. Song for voice and piano.
Words: Robert Bridges.

Autumn (c. Sept–Nov)

Down by the Salley Gardens. Song for voice and piano.

Words: W. B. Yeats. September–October 1920. Publication: OUP, 1938 & 1997.

As I Lay in the Early Sun. Song for voice and piano.
Words: Edward Shanks.

You Are My Sky. Song for voice and piano.
Words: J. C. Squire. Publication: OUP, 1938.

Prelude in F sharp [D sharp minor]. Solo piano.
Dedication: 'To Sydney Shimmin'. 'Autumn 1920'. Publication: WR, 1921 ('Five Preludes for Piano': IV); Thames, 2004.

Brown Is My Love. Song for voice and piano.
Words: [Torquato Tasso, trans. Nicholas Yonge]. Publication: OUP, 1959 & 1997.

The Happy Townland. Song for voice and piano.
Words: W. B. Yeats. [c. Autumn 1920]

Heart's Pain. Song for voice and piano. [first setting; cf. December 1921]
Words: Rupert Brooke. [Autumn 1920]

Aspatia's Song ('Lay a Garland'). Song for voice and piano.
Words: Francis Beaumont & John Fletcher.

When Icicles Hang. Song for voice and piano.
Words: William Shakespeare.

When Daisies Pied. Song for voice and piano.
Words: William Shakespeare.

Blow, Blow, Thou Winter Wind. Song for voice and piano.
Words: William Shakespeare. [c. Autumn 1920]

Since to Be Loved Endures. Song for voice and piano.
Words: Robert Bridges. [Autumn 1920]

When My Love Was Away. Song for voice and piano. [first setting]
Words: Robert Bridges. [Autumn 1920] Incomplete.

The Shadow. Song for voice and piano.
Words: Edward Shanks. [Autumn 1920] Incomplete.

Prelude in C minor. Solo piano. Sketch.

Thrice Toss These Oaken Ashes Up in Air. Song for voice and piano.
Words: Thomas Campion.

Time, You Old Gipsy Man. Song for voice and piano.
Words: Ralph Hodgson.

Come, O Come, My Life's Delight. Song for voice and piano.
Words: Thomas Campion. [c. late 1920–21]
Dedication: 'To Frederick Saxty'. Publication: Boosey & Co., 1922; Thames, 1998.

November

War Elegy for orchestra.
F.p. Patron's Fund concert, Adrian Boult (cond.), RCM, 16 June 1921.

Piano Sonata [no. 3] in D minor.
Two movements completed.

Children's Sonata in G. Violin and piano.
One movement. [November 1920]

To Violets. Song for voice and piano.
Words: Robert Herrick. Publication: OUP, 1959 & 1997.

The Crowder. Song for voice and piano.
Words: Wilfrid Gibson. [Late] November 1920

The Mugger's Song. Song for voice and piano.
Words: Wilfrid Gibson. [c. late 1920]

Sam Spraggon. Song for voice and piano.
Words: Wilfrid Gibson. [c. late 1920]

Thou Art Not Fair. Song for voice and piano.
Words: Thomas Campion/Philip Rosseter. [1920]

My Lady's Lips. Song for voice and piano.
Words: Anon. [John Wilbye, Madrigals]. [c. 1920]

Who Would Have Thought That Face of Thine. Song for voice and
piano.
Words: John Farmer. [c. 1920]

[1920–21] Burning of Auchindown. Song for voice and piano.
Words: Trad. Ballad. [c. 1920–21]

Against Weeping. Song for voice and piano.
Words: Henry King. [c. 1920–21]

Sleep, O Sleep Fond Fancy. Song for voice and piano.
Words: attrib. Thomas Morley. [c. 1920–21]

I Saw My Lady Weep. Song for voice and piano.
Words: John Dowland. [c. 1920–21]

Fine Knacks for Ladies. Song for voice and piano.
Words: John Dowland. [c. 1921]

Everyone Sang. Song for voice and piano.
Words: Siegfried Sassoon. [c. 1920–21]

Come Away, Death. Song for voice and piano.
Words: William Shakespeare. [c. 1920–21]

Orpheus with His Lute. Song for voice and piano. [second setting]
Words: William Shakespeare. [c. 1920–21]

Take O Take Those Lips Away. Song for voice and piano.
Words: William Shakespeare. [c. 1920–21]

Dover's Hill. Song for voice and piano.
Words: Edward Shanks. [c. 1920–21]

Meadow and Orchard. Song for voice and piano.
Words: Edward Shanks. [c. 1920–21]

The Fields Are Full. Song for voice and piano.
Words: Edward Shanks. [c. 1920–21]
Publication: OUP, 1928, 1979 & 1997.

The Three Hills. Song for voice and piano.
Words: J. C. Squire. [c. 1920–21] Incomplete.

Summer and Frost. Song for voice and piano.
Words: Thomas Weelkes. [c. 1920–21]

Weep You No More Sad Fountains. SATB choir, unaccompanied.
[second setting; cf. Tears, Five Elizabethan Songs, 1913]
Words: John Fletcher. [c. 1920–21] Incomplete.

Come Sleep. SATB choir, unaccompanied.
[second setting; cf. Five Elizabethan Songs, 1913]
Words: John Fletcher. [c. 1920–21] One stanza only.
F.p. St Cecilia Singers, cond. Jonathan Hope, Three Choirs Festival, 3 August 2019.

Five Country Sketches for piano.
i. Minsterworth Reaches; ii. Meredith; iii. Longford Meadows; iv. Poplars at the Sluice; v. Wainlodes. [c. 1920–21] Missing.

[Untitled] ('Poco allegro'). Solo piano.
[c. 1920–21] Incomplete.

Goddess of Night. Song for voice and piano.
Words: F. W. Harvey. [c. 1920–21]. Publication: *IGSJ*, vol. 4 (1998).

Dinny Hill. Song for voice and piano.
Words: F. W. Harvey. [c. 1920–February 1921]

On Sussex Hills. Song for voice and piano.
Words: Hilaire Belloc. [c. 1920–early 1921]

Apples and Water. Song for voice and piano.
Words: Robert Graves. [c. 1920–early 1921]

Black Stitchel. Song for voice and piano.
Words: Wilfrid Gibson. [c. late 1920–early 1921] Publication: OUP, 1938 & 1997.

Blaweary. Song for voice and piano.
Words: Wilfrid Gibson. [c. late 1920–early 1921] Publication: OUP, 1938.

1921   Silent Music. Song for voice and piano.
Words: Thomas Campion. Dated '1921' in 1925 version/revision. No earlier source.

The Town Window. Song for voice and piano.
Words: John Drinkwater. [1921]

Traveller Turn a Mournful Eye. Song for voice and piano.
Words: Iolo Aneurin WIlliams. [1921] Incomplete.

The Full Heart. Song for voice and piano.
Words: Robert Nichols. [1921] Incomplete.

Clown's Song. Song for voice and piano.
Words: William Shakespeare. [1921]

The Ship. Song for voice and piano. [second setting]
Words: J. C. Squire. [1921]

The Little Waves of Breffny. Song for voice and piano.
Words: Eva Gore-Booth. [c. 1921]

Consolatur Afflictorum. Song for voice and piano.
Words: F. W. Harvey. [1921]

Elvers. Song for voice and piano.
Words: F. W. Harvey. [1921] Incomplete.

Darest Thou Now. Song for voice and piano.
Words: Walt Whitman. [1921] Fragment.

Ha'nacker Mill. Song for voice and piano.
Words: Hilaire Belloc. [1921] Publication: OUP, 1938.

Poor Henry. Song for voice and piano.
Words: Walter de la Mare. [c. 1921] Incomplete.

Bread and Cherries. Song for voice and piano.
Words: Walter de la Mare. [1921] Publication: OUP, 1938.

Song from 'The Sad Shepherd'. Song for voice and piano.
Words: Ben Jonson. [1921] Publication: OUP, 1952.

Song from 'Epicœne'. Song for voice and piano.
Words: Ben Jonson. 1921.

Echo's Lament of Narcissus. Song for voice and piano.
Words: Ben Jonson. [c. 1921]

A Sea Dirge. Song for voice and piano.
Words: William Shakespeare. [1921]

Minuet. Solo piano.
[1921] Fragment.

Praeludium in D minor for organ.
[1921] Incomplete.

Sonata in E minor for cello and piano.
One movement. [c. 1921]

Song from 'The Land of Heart's Desire'. Song for voice and piano.
Words: W. B. Yeats. [c. 1921]

The Trumpet. SATB choir [and orchestra]. [first setting]
Words: Edward Thomas. Short score. [c. 1921]
F.p. (with piano) The English Choral Experience, cond. Paul Spicer,
Abbey Dore, Herefordshire, July 2007.

Five Western Watercolours. Solo piano.
i. Twyver River; ii. Alney Island; iii. The Old Road; iv. Still Meadows;
v. Sugar Loaf Hill. [c. 1921]
Dedication: 'To Miss Marjorie Chapman'. Publication: S&B, 1923.

Slow movement on 'The Duchess of Malfy'. Violin and piano. [c. 1921]

Charm Me Asleep ('To music for calm'). Song for voice and piano.
Words: Robert Herrick. Dated 1921/1925; no 1921 source extant.

January   Snow. Song for voice and piano.
Words: Edward Thomas. Publication: OUP, 1952 & 1997.

May Carol. Violin and piano.

Pity Me. Song for voice and piano.
Words: Wilfrid Gibson. [January 1921]
Composed as 'Griffiths Davies'.

Pedlar Jack. Song for voice and piano.
Words: Wilfrid Gibson. [c. January 1921]

Old Meg. Song for voice and piano.
Words: Wilfrid Gibson. [c. January 1921] Fragment.

Ralph Roister Doister. Song for voice and piano.
Words: Nicholas Udall.

Riddle cum Ruddle. Song for voice and piano.
Words: F. W. Harvey. [c. January 1921] Fragment.
Composed as 'John Winterton'.

Country Love Song. Song for voice and piano.
Words: F. W. Harvey.
Composed as 'John Winterton' and 'Griffiths Davies'; amended to 'Michael Flood'.

February   In Youth Is Pleasure. Song for voice and violin.
Words: Robert Wever.

Lullaby. Song for voice and violin.
Words: Robert Herrick.

All That's Past. Song for voice and piano.
Words: Walter de la Mare. [Autumn 1920–early February 1921]

Beware! (Exile). Song for voice and piano.
Words: Walter de la Mare. [Autumn 1920–]February 1921.
Publication: *IGSJ*, vol. 4 (1998).

Hawk and Buckle. Song for voice and piano.
Words: 'John Doyle' (Robert Graves). [c. February 1921]
Publication: OUP, 1938.

Thy Voice. Song for voice and piano.
Words: Captain H. Rippon-Seymour. [c. February–May 1921]
Composed as 'Michael Flood'.

Cowslip Time. Song for voice and piano.
Words: Winifred Letts. [c. February–May 1921]
Composed as 'Michael Flood'.

The Fair. Song for voice and piano.
Words: Winifred Letts. [c. February–May 1921]
Composed as 'Michael Raphoe Flood'.

At the Jolly Blue Boar. Song for voice and piano.
Words: Harry Kenniston Wynne. [c. February–May 1921]
Composed as 'Michael Flood'.

Old Friend. Song for voice and piano.
Words: Noel Ferris [untraced. ?Gurney] [c. February–May 1921]
Composed as 'Michael Flood'.

March	A Gloucestershire Rhapsody for orchestra.

March   A Gloucestershire Rhapsody for orchestra.
1919–21. Completed January–March 1921.
F.p. Three Choirs Festival, 12 August 2010. Philharmonia Orchestra, cond. Martyn Brabbins.

April   Thou Didst Delight Mine Eyes. Song for voice and piano. [second version]
Words: Robert Bridges. [Substantial reworking of March 1918 song.]
Publication: OUP, 1952.

The Cherry Trees Bend Over. Song for voice and piano.
Words: Edward Thomas. [April 1921] Publication: OUP, 1952.

The Bridge. Song for voice and piano.
Words: Edward Thomas. [(c. April–May?) 1921]

The Gallows. Song for voice and piano.
Words: Edward Thomas. [(c. April–May?) 1921]

Cock Crow. Song for voice and piano.
Words: Edward Thomas. [(c. April–May?) 1921]

Adlestrop. Song for voice and piano.
Words: Edward Thomas. [(c. April–May?) 1921]

The Owl. Song for voice and piano.
Words: Edward Thomas. [(c. April–May?) 1921]

The Mill-Pond. Song for voice and piano.
Words: Edward Thomas. [(c. April–May?) 1921]

In Memoriam. Song for voice and piano.
Words: Edward Thomas. [(c. April–May?) 1921]
Publication: *IGSJ*, vol. 15 (2009).

Out in the Dark. Song for voice and piano.
Words: Edward Thomas. 1921. Revised slightly, 1925.

Spring. Song for voice and piano.
Words: Katarina Boganoff [untraced; Gurney pseudonym?]. [c. April–May 1921]
Composed as 'Michael Flood'.

June   Tarantella. Song for voice and piano.
Words: Hilaire Belloc. [June–July 1921] F.p. Clive Carey (baritone), Thornton Lofthouse (piano), Westbourne Terrace, London, 30 January 1922.

String Quartett.
[In progress, June–July 1921]. Extant 'Slow movement' ('Allegro' [*sic*]) possibly from this quartet. Incomplete. Otherwise missing.

July   Piano Trio in C sharp minor. For violin, cello and piano.
Two movements. i. incomplete.
F.p. ii. The Framilode Trio, Bristol, 24 November 1990.

Five Pastorals (Children's Pieces). Solo piano.
i. Green Lane Paddock; ii. Windy Reach; iii. Dryhill Shepherd; iv. The Crocus Ring; v. The Lane to Nowhere. [c. Summer–Autumn 1921]

September   Symphony. For orchestra.
Missing. March 1921: in progress. September 1921: slow movement nearing 'final form'.

Fair Lady's Mantle. Song for voice and piano.
Words: John W. Haines. July–September 1921.

The High Road. Song for voice and piano.
Words: John W. Haines. [c. July–September 1921]

November   It Was the Lovely Moon. Song for voice and piano.
Words: John Freeman.

December   Five Songs of Rupert Brooke. Voice and piano.
i. The Treasure; ii. There's Wisdom in Women; iii. One Day; iv. Song [second setting. Cf. 'Heart's Pain', 1920]; v. Clouds. v. appended in January 1922.

[1919–22]   Prelude in F minor. Solo piano.
[c. 1919–22] Incomplete.

Ploughman Singing. Song for voice and piano.
Words: John Clare. [c. 1920–22]
Dedication: 'To Edmund Blunden'. Publication: OUP, 1952.

The Ghost. Song for voice and piano.
Words: Walter de la Mare. [c. 1920–22]

Epitaph in Old Mode. Song for voice and piano.
Words: J. C. Squire. [c. 1920–22]

To a Snow Flake. Song for voice and piano.
Words: Francis Thompson. [c. 1920–22]

[1921–22]   To the Muses. Song for voice and piano.
Words: William Blake. [c. 1921–22]

The Waggoner. Song for voice and piano.
Words: Edmund Blunden. [c. 1921–22] Missing.

Carol ('When the herds were watching'). Song for voice and piano.
Words: William Canton. [c. 1921–22]

The Cuckoo Sings in the Heart of Winter. Song for voice and piano.
Words: Norah Chesson [Norah Hopper]. [c. 1921–22]

Early Morn. Song for voice and piano.
Words: W. H. Davies. [c. 1921–22]

Farewell. Song for voice and piano.
Words: Walter de la Mare. [c. 1921–22]

Alexander. Song for voice and piano.
Words: Walter de la Mare. [c. 1921–22]

The Ruin. Song for voice and piano.
Words: Walter de la Mare. [c. 1921–22]

Mary Murray ('Murray Hill'). Song for voice and piano.
Words: Louis How. [c. 1921–22]. Composed as 'Frederick Saxty'.

Castle Garden. Song for voice and piano.
Words: Louis How. [c. 1921–22]. Composed as 'Frederick Saxty'.

Columbia Heights. Song for voice and piano.
Words: Louis How. [c. 1921–22]. Composed as 'Frederick Saxty'.

Gramercy Park. Song for voice and piano.
Words: Louis How. [c. 1921–22]. Composed as 'Frederick Saxty'.

Riverside Drive. Song for voice and piano.
Words: Louis How. [c. 1921–22]. Composed as 'Frederick Saxty'.

Williamsburg. Song for voice and piano.
Words: Louis How. [c. 1921–22]. Composed as 'Frederick Saxty'.

God Mastering Me. SATB choir and organ.
Words: Gerard Manley Hopkins. [c. 1921–22]

Faith. Song for voice and piano.
Words: Margaret M. Radford. [c. 1921–22]

It Rains. Song for voice and piano.
Words: Edward Thomas. [c. 1921–22]

We Who Are Old. Song for voice and piano.
Words: W. B. Yeats. [c. 1921–22]

Aria after Bach. Violin and piano.
[c. 1921–22] Incomplete.

[Untitled] ('Tempo di valse'). Solo piano.
[c. 1921–22] Incomplete.

[Untitled] ('Largo'). Solo piano.
[c. 1921–22] Incomplete.

Preludes (Third Set). Solo piano.
i. Prelude in C minor; ii. Prelude in F sharp major. ii. incomplete.
Remainder unwritten. [c. 1921(–24?)]
Publication: i. Thames, 2004; ii. *IGSJ*, vol. 5 (1999), completed
Richard Carder.

1922	January	Clouds. Song for voice and piano. Words: Rupert Brooke.
		Violin Sonata in G major. Violin and piano. Three movements. March 1921–early 1922.
	April	[String Quartet]. Missing.
	May	[String] Quartett in A minor. ('Second quartett') Four movements. April–May 1922.
	June	[String Quartet] ('last of Three String Quartetts'). Missing.
		Will You Come? Song for voice and piano. Words: Edward Thomas. 1922. Publication: S&B, 1926.
		The Moon. Song for voice and piano. Words: W. H. Davies. 1922.
		Macbeth: Dark Woods. [unknown ensemble] [c. 1921–22]. Incomplete piano sketch.
		[String] Quartett in E major. First movement only. [c. 1922]

Change Should Breed Change. Song for voice and piano.
Words: Drummond of Hawthornden. [c. 1922]

O Dreamy, Gloomy, Friendly Trees. Song for voice and piano.
Words: Herbert Trench. [c. 1922?]

Voices of Women. Song for voice and piano.
Words: Frank Prewett. [c. 1922–1925]

1923 —

1924 Quintett in F for piano and strings.
Four movements. '1924'. Missing.

String Quartett in A major.
One movement. [1924]. Missing.

A London Meditation. For string quartet.
[?1924 (unrelated to piano trio of June 1924)]

June A London Meditation. For violin, cello and piano.

Slow movement for violin and piano.

July A Bird's Anger. Song for voice and piano.
Words: W. H. Davies. Dedication: 'For W. H. Davies'.

August This Is a Wild Land. Song for baritone, string quartet and piano.
Words: Robert Graves.

November String Quartett in D minor.
Four movements. [c. October–November 1924] Revised
August 1925.

December The Peasant's Confession. Song for voice and piano.
Words: Thomas Hardy. Dedication: 'With homage. To (m) T.
Hardy O.M.'

Ethiopia Saluting the Colours. Song for baritone, string quartet and piano.
Words: Walt Whitman. Missing.

Delicate Cluster. Song for baritone, string quartet and piano.
Words: Walt Whitman. Missing.

['Latin Motett']. For violin, cello, baritone, chorus and organ. Missing.

[The Collect for the Nativity of Our Lord].
For violin, cello, baritone, chorus and organ. Missing.

County of Peebles. Song for voice and piano.
Words: R. L. Stevenson.

In the Black Winter Morning. Song for voice and piano.
Words: Thomas Hardy.

Bonnie George Campbell. Song for voice and piano.
Words: Trad. Ballad.

I Am Not As My Fathers Were. Song for voice and piano.
Words: unknown; quoted in essay by Hilaire Belloc. 'New years eve
1924'.

'Violin Sonata movement in E minor'. [Violin and piano]
1924 or 1925 (GF). Missing.

1925

Stillness. [Song.]
Words: James Elroy Flecker. 1925 (GF). Missing.

The Phantom. Song for voice and piano.
Words: Thomas Hardy. [1925]

The World's great age begins anew. Song for voice and piano.
Words: P. B. Shelley. [1925]

After the Ceremony. Song for voice and piano.
Words: Ivor Gurney. [1925]

Song ('On the wide lakes now'). Song for voice and piano.
Words: [?Ivor Gurney]. [c. 1925]

To Do This If Not Old. Song for voice and piano.
Words: Ivor Gurney [after W. H. Davies]. [c. 1925] Incomplete.

The Pear Tree. Song for voice and piano.
Words: Edna St. Vincent Millay. 1925.

3 fold Amen. SATB choir, unaccompanied.
[?Gurney; unknown hand] 1925.

Fantasy String Quartett in A minor.
1925 (GF). Missing.

String Quartett in E flat.
Four movements. 1925 (GF). Missing.

String Quartett in A.
Seven movements. 1925 (GF). Missing.

Piano trio movement in C minor.
1925 (GF). Missing.

Sonata for Organ in F sharp major.
'Slow movement'. 1925 (GF). Missing.

Prelude in D minor for organ.
1925 (GF). Missing.

Danish Sonata. Violin and piano.
Four movements. 1925 (GF). Missing.

Prelude for violin solo.
1925 (GF). Missing.

Sonata in A minor for violin and piano.
Three movements. 1925 (GF). Missing.

January

String Quartett in G minor. [with voice]
Three movements known.
GF: 'A voice part appears in the [slow movement]'. Missing.

Sonata in C sharp minor for cello and piano.
[Slow movement known to have existed.] Missing.

Piano Trio in E minor. Missing.

Sevenfold Amen. SATB choir. 8 January [1925].

String Quartett in E minor: 'New England'.
Four movements. Missing.
[Cf. note to String Quartett in C: 'Gloucestershire', [c. May 1925] below.]

On Eastnor Knoll. Song for voice and piano.
Words: John Masefield.

Farewell Rewards and Fairies. Song for voice and piano.
Words: Richard Corbet. Dedication: 'To Mrs M. Chapman'.

The Idlers. Song for voice and piano.
Words: Edmund Blunden.

Blows the Wind Today. Song for baritone, string quartet and piano.
Words: R. L. Stevenson. Missing.

By the Bivouacs [fitful flame]. Song for baritone, string quartet and piano.
Words: Walt Whitman. Missing.

Rhapsodic Quintett for clarinet and strings.
One movement. Missing.

February   In Cabin'd Ships at Sea. Song for baritone, string quartet and piano.
Words: Walt Whitman. Missing.

To the Leaven'd Soil They Trod. Song for baritone, string quartet and piano.
Words: Walt Whitman. Missing.

Love Song ('Love's Pattern'). Song for voice and piano.
Words: [?Ivor Gurney].

When My Love Was Away. Song for voice and piano. [second setting]
Words: Robert Bridges.

The Douglas Tragedy. Song for voice and piano.
Words: Trad. Scottish ballad.

Fifth Avenue. Song for voice and piano.
Words: Louis How.

Woolworth Building. [Song for voice and piano.]
Words: Louis How. Missing.

March   Gai Nel. Song for voice and piano.
Words: 'Chanson de Tarois (Picardie et Artois)'; French; untraced (possibly ed. Gurney). 3 March 1925.

À la Flandre. Song for voice and piano.
Words: Léon Bocquet. 3 March 1925.

The Heart's Prevention. Song for voice and piano.
Words: Robert Bridges. 11 March 1925.

Dear Lady. Song for voice and piano. [second setting]
Words: Robert Bridges.

Merciles beaute: I. (Captivity). Song for voice and piano.
Words: Geoffrey Chaucer. 23 March 1925.

La Lengua Catalana. Song for voice and piano.
Words: Justin Pépratx; Catalan. Incomplete.

April   À la Raço Latino. Song for voice and piano.
Words: Frédéric Mistral; Provençal French. 17 April 1925.

Einar Tamberskelver. [Song]
Words: H. W. Longfellow. Missing.

The Sea Hath Its Pearls. Song for voice and piano.
Words: H. W. Longfellow. 21 April 1925.

Song of the Canadian Soldiers. Song for voice and piano.
Words: Ivor Gurney. 25 April 1925.

Overture to *The Tempest*. String quartet and piano. Missing.

Prelude in C minor. Solo piano.

Trio in C sharp minor. [?String trio]
Two movements. [?c. April] 1925 (GF). Missing.

May   Snowflakes. Song for voice and piano.
Words: H. W. Longfellow. 5 May 1925.

Birds in the High Hall-Garden. Song for voice and piano.
Words: Alfred Tennyson. 11 May 1925.

Heraclitus. Song for voice and piano.
Words: Callimachus, trans. William Cory. 15 May 1925.
Dedication: 'To the memory of John Fletcher'.

Come You Whose Loves Are Dead. Song for voice and piano.
Words: Francis Beaumont & John Fletcher. 16–18 May 1925.
Dedication: 'For the Poet of Rye on the Tercentenary of John
Fletcher 1925'.

Snow-buntings. Song for voice and piano.
Words: Frank Prewett. [c. May 1925] Fragment.

String Quartett in F: 'Virginia'.
Four movements. [c. January–May 1925] Missing.
[Cf. String Quartett in C: 'Gloucestershire', below.]

String Quartett in C: 'Gloucestershire'.
Five movements. [c. January–May 1925] Missing.
[The three missing quartets, in E minor (January 1925), F, and
C—named 'New England', 'Virginia', and 'Gloucestershire',
respectively—were intended as a group, modelled on and honouring
Beethoven's three Rasumovsky quartets.]

June   A Love Lyric. Song for voice and piano.
Words: Robert Bridges. 1 June 1925. Dedications: 'To Margaret
Hunt'; 'To Dr. R. Bridges. O.M. With most grateful humble homage
for [his] Virgil translation.'

The Hill Pines Were Sighing. Song for voice and piano. [second
setting]
Words: Robert Bridges.

My Spirit Kisseth Thine. Song for voice and piano.
Words: Robert Bridges.

Lo, Where the Virgin. TTBB unaccompanied.
Words: Robert Bridges. 8 June 1925.

Since I Believe in God the Father Almighty. Motett for double choir.
Words: Robert Bridges. Publication: The Ivor Gurney Trust, 2018.

Aftermath. Song for voice and piano.
Words: H. W. Longfellow. 18 June 1925.

To the Memory of Max Reger with Homage. Song for voice and piano.
Words: [Ivor Gurney].

Annan Water. [Song.]
Words: Trad. Scottish Ballad. Missing.
[date unknown. Mentioned in letter of June–July 1925]

July   [Two song settings of Edward Thomas]
[i.] Words; [ii.] The Trumpet [second setting].
Written for proposed publication of a set of Thomas settings.
Publication: ii only, S&B, 1926.

Lord, Thou Hast Been Our Dwelling Place. Soli, choir and organ.
Words: Psalm 90.

Quartett in A for piano and strings.
Four movements. Missing.

I Heard a Soldier. Song for voice and piano.
Words: Herbert Trench.

The Lawlands o' Holland. Song for voice and piano. [second setting]
Words: Trad. Ballad. 20 July 1925.

August   Off Trafalgar. Song for voice and piano.
Words: Robert Browning.

Quartett movement in F minor. Missing.

W[alt] Whitman Fantasy Quartett in F minor. Missing.

World Strangeness. Song for voice and piano.
Words: William Watson.

September   Wassail Chorus at the Mermaid Tavern. Song for voice and piano.
Words: Theodore Watts-Dunton. 'Truly for String Quartett and Piano'.
1 September 1925.

To Paumanok. Song for voice and piano.
Words: Walt Whitman. 6 September 1925.

By Broad Potomac's Shore. Song for voice and piano.
Words: Walt Whitman. 7 September 1925.

The Song of Chicago. Song for voice and piano.
Words: Walt Whitman. 14 September 1925.

The County of Mayo. Song for voice and piano.
Words: George Fox. 15–16 September 1925.

Cashel of Munster. Song for voice and piano.
Words: Samuel Ferguson. 19–20 September [1925]

The Death of Nelson. Song for voice and piano.
Words: Samuel Arnold. 22 September [1925]

All the Words That I Utter. Song for voice and piano.
Words: W. B. Yeats. 26 September 1925.

The Fiddler of Dooney. Song for voice and piano. [second setting]
Words: W. B. Yeats.

The Lake Isle of Innisfree. Song. [second setting]
Words: W. B. Yeats. Vocal line only extant.

Violin Sonata in E flat major. Violin and piano.
Four movements. [August–September 1925] Missing, ?except slow movement.

Symphony in E major. For orchestra (written in short score).
Four movements. Missing.

String Quartett in A minor.
Four movements. Missing.

October For the Lands and for These Passionate Days. Song for voice and piano.
Words: Walt Whitman.

November Heroic Elegy in E minor for piano and strings. Missing.

The Dead at Clonmacnois. Song for voice and piano.
Words: Thomas Rolleston. 13 November 1925.

[Slow movement for piano and string quartet]
[Begun: 17 November] 1925. Missing.

Lament. Song for voice and piano.
Words: [Ivor Gurney]. [c. 1925–26]
Publication: *British Music* [Journal of the British Music Society], vol. 15 (1993).

Violin Sonata in A major. Violin and piano.
[c. 1925–26] Incomplete.

Piano Sonata [no. 4] in G minor.
Four movements. 1925 (GF). Missing.

[1925–26] Song ('Where shall I who weary wander'). Song for voice and piano.
Words: Heinrich Heine [trans. Margaret Armour]. [c. 1925–26]

1926 Over the Ridge. Song for voice and piano.
Words: [?Ivor Gurney]. [c. 1926]

Sonata in G sharp. Violin and piano.
1926 (GF). Missing.

January The Late Rider. Song for voice and piano.
Words: [?Ivor Gurney].

February The First of Lent. Song for voice and piano.
Words: [Ivor Gurney].

March Western Sailors. Song for voice and piano.
Words: [Ivor Gurney].

Heroic Prelude [for organ]. Missing.

Easter Rhapsody [for organ]. Missing.

April Organ Sonata in F sharp minor.
Two movements known to have been completed. Missing.

July 'St Anne Hymn'. [unknown]
In progress, 2 July 1926. Missing.

September [Incidental music for Shakespeare plays]. [unknown]. Fragments. Numerous sketches and fragments for instrumental parts for plays, some labelled (*Macbeth*; *King Lear*; *Hamlet*; *Cymbeline*; *Timon of Athens*; *Henry VI*), with some characters named and lines of text given (?as cues).

Violin Sonata in A. Sketch.

O Sweet O Lovely (Salute for Beauty). Piano solo. Sketches.

Song of North ('In a land of the aspens'). Song.
Words: [?Gurney: 'Is this mine of old?'] Sketch of vocal line.

Preludes. [?Piano] Sketches.

November Scenes from the Kalevala. [unknown]. Missing.

Piano Quartett in D.
Three movements. Missing.

1927 January Si J'etais Roi. Piano solo.

A Comedy Overture (*Twelfth Night*). [unknown]. Missing.
GF: 'piano score', 1927.

Unknown date Scherzo in G minor. String quartet. (GF) Missing.

A new version of 'God Save the King'. [Chromatic respelling] Written in Marion Scott's autograph book. [c. 1911–22] Scott transcription.

'Then Hercules who felt within his breast'. Bass recitative.

Words: Untraced. ?Translation of Classical text. GF transcription. Fragment.

Appendix B

A Chronological Catalogue of Gurney's Literary Works

Note: Names of works are poems unless otherwise stated. Those poems that were not titled by Gurney are identified by their first lines, given in single quotation marks. In the works of 1924–25 it can be difficult to separate poems and appeals, some appeals being written (at least nominally) as poems. These are therefore included in the numbers given. Significant publications are detailed (first, and collections), but are otherwise only listed when a published poem is otherwise unknown in the manuscript record. Approximations arise from the margins for error in the dating of the large amount of undated material, the recognition of fragments and how they might relate to other poems, and in the vague determination as to whether a new version of a poem constitutes a new poem in itself. Poem numbers detailed include incomplete or partially missing poems. Further poems are known to have been written, with a number of late writings known to have been destroyed, particularly after 1927, when the archival record practically ceases except for some preserved correspondence. The figures and details therefore largely represent what is extant, excepting a few titled collections of 1924–25 that are now missing but which are named by Gurney in his correspondence. This catalogue should, however, give a useful guide to the extent of Gurney's output, and the patterns of literary activity.

1907	Easter	To A H Cheesman from Ivor [dedicatory verse; first extant writing]
1912	*c.* May	The Irish Sea
1913	August	'The rough hewn rocks that Neptune's hosts defy'
		'My tears are near the top, and welly' [light verse]
1915	*c.* July/August	To the Poet before Battle
	September	[A Ballad of the Cotswolds]; Satan above the Battle; Afterwards
	November	Carol ('Winter now has bared the trees')
	December	2 short verses
		FIRST POETRY PUBLISHED: 'Afterwards' & 'To the Poet before Battle', *RCM Magazine*, vol. 12, no. 1 (Christmas term 1915)
1916	January/early February	Essex
	March	My feet—the mud doth stick 'em [light verse]
	Late June—July	5 poems, incl. To England—A Note; Strange Service; To Certain Comrades
	August	Serenity; 'The careless writer' [light verse]
	September	'Who peers in his own anatomy' [light verse]
	October–November	14 poems/verses, incl. The Fire Kindled; Robecq; Bach and the Sentry; Sawgint; Requiem [x3]; The Signaller's Vision; Acquiescence; The Mother; The Colonel
	December	To an Unknown Lady; The Strong Thing

1917	January	15 poems, incl. Scots; Purple and Black; Song and Pain; Communion; Song ('Only the wanderer'); West Country; The Estaminet; Time and the Soldier; Influences; Hail and Farewell; Firelight; After-glow
	February	9 poems, incl. 4 of the 5 'Sonnetts 1917'; Ballad of the Three Spectres
	March	5 poems, incl. Song of Pain and Beauty; June to Come; Trees
	May	5 poems, incl. England the Mother [Sonnetts 1917]; Spring. Rouen, May 1917
	June	11 poems, incl. 5 Triolets; Song at Morning; Depression; Contrasts
	c. June–July	Dicky; 'I have loved children, and the lonely places'
	July	The Old City; 'To think that Belgium'; The Immortal Hour; Question and Answer; Rumours of Wars
	August	6 poems, incl. Camps; Eternal Treasure; Ypres; The Volunteer; To M.M.S.
	September	The Plain; The Sentry
	October	6 poems, incl. To the Prussians of England; 'Annie Laurie'; The Target; Memory Let All Slip
	October–November	8 'Hospital Pictures' [of an eventual set of 9 poems], incl. Ladies of Charity; Upstairs Piano
	November	7 poems, incl. The Battalion Is Now on Rest; Toasts and Memories; April Anthem
	15 November	PUBLICATION OF *SEVERN AND SOMME* (Sidgwick & Jackson)
		[46 poems, selected from work written between July 1915 and May 1917]
	c. November–December	4 poems/verses, incl. Song of Urgency
	December	11 poems/verses, incl. Dust (addition to 'Hospital Pictures')
	c. December–January	The Sun Burns Gold; Holyrood
1918	January	To His Love
	February	At Reserve Depot; Above Ashleworth
	March	Song of Silence [as song; see catalogue of musical works]
	July	23 poems, incl. Down Commercial Road; 'On Rest'; Crickley Hill; In a Ward; Ypres–Minsterworth; The Farm; The Stone-Breaker; From Omiécourt; The Lock-keeper
	August	c. 22 poems, incl. De Profundis; Migrants; Twigworth Vicarage; Hidden Tales; Omens; Fire in the Dusk
	September	c. 12 poems, incl. Toussaints; 'O Tree of Pride'; 'We came to ruined Caulaincourt'
	October	Pilgrimage; The Revellers

	November	Passionate Earth; Old Martinmas Eve; The Day of Victory
	c. November–December	Day Boys and Choristers
	December	The Harper; The Valley; Stout Cortez; At Zennor Head; 'On the high cliffs'
1919	*c.* December (1918)–March	16 poems, incl. To the Mothers of Them; London Visitor; Equinoctial; The Shadowed Place; 'No words his comrades spoke'
	c. January–May	The Ploughland; Blessings; Supposition; Maisemore Again; What Shall Remain
	January	The Companions; The Patroller
	February	8 poems, incl. Fine Rain; The Bugle; I Love Chrysanthemums
	c. February–March	Blanket of Dark; Town-Thoughts from Severn; Moor and Ocean; Before Resurrection; The Crocus Ring
	March	'Poor Madge must lie so still'; 'When God from the heart of the storm cloud'; The Eve of Passing [song text for Rupert Erlebach]
	c. March–April	My County; The Ship
	April	Equal Mistress; April 20 1919; Schubert
	May	PUBLICATION OF *WAR'S EMBERS* (Sidgwick & Jackson) [58 poems, selected from work written between June 1917 and December 1918]
		7 poems, incl. Beethoven; Spring's Token; The Hedger; The Bramble Patch
	c. April–June	On a Concerto
	June	Break; High St.—Charing Cross; Song of the Old King
	July	8 poems, incl. Threads; I Love Trees; She Laughs; The Bonfire; Dawn
	August	11 poems, incl.: Between the Boughs; 'If I walked straight slap'; 'Some men the blossom and the skies may love'
c. 1919–20		'When from the curve of the wood's edge'; To the Eastward
1920		
	September	The Trees Are Breathing; Legs
	c. October	October Wind; I Heard a Sickle Rustle
	November	First of Flood; October Noon, Brompton; Michaelmas; Defiance; [St] Paul's Rules the City
c. 1921–22		53 poems of indeterminate date that formed part of the submission to Sidgwick & Jackson, in May 1922, since published as *80 Poems or So*. Incl. The Road (Beyond Aldgate); Above Maisemore; April Gale; Bronze and Misted Moon; Compensations; Smudgy Dawn; There Is a Valley; Coming Dusk.

		269 poems brought together in three notebooks collated or written in 1921–22: a green hardcover exercise book, a pink marbled book, and a black hardcover exercise book. The books were sent to Edward Marsh in September 1922. The black exercise book also contains fair copies of earlier poems (not included in the number). The green and pink exercise books later became the basis of *Rewards of Wonder* (1924), incl. The Tax Office; Tewkesbury; Longford Dawns; Encounters. The pink marbled book includes Bach—Under Torment.
1922		Essay: The Springs of Music. Written for, and published in, *Musical Quarterly*, July 1922.
	January	Essays: On Sailing a Boat on Severn; By Ashleworth; On Earth Pines Like the Sea
		Publication: This City. *Gloucester Journal*, 7 January 1922.
		Review: *Six Cotswold Plays* [by Lady Florence Darwin]. Published in the *Times Literary Supplement*, March 23, 1922.
	April	Publication: On a Two-Hundredth Birthday. *Gloucester Journal*, 15 April 1922.
	c. April–May	c. 16 poems, incl. Above Dryhill; Western Sky-Look; Water Colours; On Foxes
	May	Collection [*80 Poems or So*] submitted to, and turned down by, Sidgwick & Jackson
	c. June–July	The Lock-keeper; First Time In; One Had Thought; Thoughts of New England
	September	Sonnet ('Fierce indignation'); Sonnet ('When I think of the Danemen')
	October	35 poems, incl. On Somme; Old Times; After 'The Penny Whistle'; The Shame; Ypres War; Kite by Wood
		Publication: Encounters; The March Past [c. 1921–22], *London Mercury*, vol. 6, no. 36.
	November	10 poems, incl. Roman; In God's Name; Why Do Men Torment?
	December	35 poems, incl. To God; There Is a Man; By Dartford Once; There Is No Need; My Life
1923	January	24 poems, incl. The Dream; Hedges; To R. W. Vaughan Williams; The Music Gathering; Chance to Work
	March	7 poems, incl. Appeal of a 'War Poet'; Light on Water; Confinement
	April	43 poems, incl. After War; The Salty Grass-Earth; Memory; The Incense Bearers; Cut Flowers
	May	5 poems, incl. Lines (to J. C. Squire)
		Publication: Advice [c. 1922–23?], *London Mercury*, vol. 8, no. 43.
	June	8 poems, incl. An Appeal of a Writer of France—Belgium; To Good Men of Guard; It Is Not Wise

July	17 poems, incl. Looking over Bridgewall; To the War Prime Minister; Three Centuries Back; By Mansion House; War Pain; two poems in French (Merville; Une Piece)
August	25 poems, incl. Stepney Causeway; Hospitalities; London in Rain; a set of four 'Verses of one IB Gurney / An Infantryman Writer of Verse'; After Reading Victor Hugo; a translation of Hugo's 'Waterloo'
September	12 poems, incl. Laventie Line; Quiet Front–Tired; On Men of the North
October	7 poems, incl. To England—Greatly Accusing; All Hallows Eve, London; 'Who will praise Aran now Synge is laid in earth?'
	Sketches of Gloucester: 10 poems written in a book of drawings of Gloucester by A. Ward, incl. That Tower; Old Houses; On Workers
November	34 poems, incl. Armistice Day; Past High [St] Paul's; War Poets; 18 very short appeal poems
December	Snow in London; Selkirk; Territorials Marching
1924	Collection: *Dayspaces and Takings*. c. 1924. Missing. Contents unknown.
	Collection: *Ridge Clay, Limestone*. c. 1924. Missing. Contents unknown.
	Collection: *La Flandre, and By-Norton*. c. 1924. Missing. Contents unknown.
	Collection: *London Seen Clear*. c. 1924. Missing. Contents unknown.
	Collection: *Rewards of Wonder: Poems of Cotswold, France, London*. 1924, collated with revisions from the contents of the green hardcover manuscript book and pink marbled book of 1921–22, with an additional poem. 102 poems. Published by Mid Northumberland Arts Group & Carcanet, ed. George Walter, 2000.
	Collection: *Fatigues and Magnificences*. 1924. Missing. Contents unknown.
	Collection: *Roman Gone East*. 1924. Missing. Contents unknown.
June	Of an Earth's Honour; First Morning; Dark Are the Ways
c. June–July	New England; Third Soldiers Song
c. July–August	9 poems, incl. Farewell; Thoughts of New England; Smudgy Dawn; What Time Brings
August	To the Memory of President Lincoln; Dryhill Camp; The Reward; Chance Meetings
c. August–September	The Golden Room

c. September–October	7 poems, incl. Somme Winter 1916; Dawn Comes Up on London; The Great Grief
c. October–November	6 poems, incl. To County Mayo; 'O dear fields of France'; two poems after Whitman
c. November–December	10 poems, incl. Masterpiece; poems after Whitman
December	More Thoughts of New England; War Poet

1925

3 poems written as songs, c. 1925: After the Ceremony; Song ('On the wide lakes now'); To Do This If Not Old [after W. H. Davies]. See music catalogue.

January	Collection: *To Hawthornden*. 18 poems, incl. Snow; March; The Awakening; The Love Song; The Sea Borders; The Motetts of William Byrd

Collection: *Pictures and Memories*. 50 poems, incl. First Framilode; Crickley Cliffs; To the City Worcester; Twyver Begins

10 single poems, incl. Laus Veneris; To the Memory of a (Great) Poet [Longfellow]; The City of Birth

February	When the Minds Dumb

Collection: *The Book of Five Makings*. 52 poems (plus variants), incl. First Poem; Like Hebridean; Varennes; Epitaph on a Young Child; Christopher Marlowe; Song of Autumn; The Nightingales; Dawns I Have Seen. Published with *Best Poems*, ed. R.K.R. Thornton and George Walter, Mid Northumberland Arts Group & Carcanet, 1995.

c. 7 poems added to the green hardcover manuscript book (c. 1921–22), when revised February 1925, in parts substantially (hence c.). [In addition to the separate revision of the contents of this book for *Rewards of Wonder* (1924)]

March	c. 15 single poems, incl. To Old New England; Watching Music; William Byrd; The Folly of Being Comforted; Good Friday; Merciless Beauty

Collection: *Poems of Gloucesters, Gloucester and of Virginia*. 5–6 March. 28 poems, incl. Moving Up to Ypres; Rejoining Battalion; The Women Working; The Mirror of Suzanne; Gloucesters Depot Rouen. 1917; Open Country; The Curses; Petersburg

Collection: *Memories of Honour: Infantry Poems and of the State of New York*. 23 poems, incl. Butchers and Tombs; Before the Somme; Le Rime; Serenade; The Stokes Gunners; The Battle; Don Juan in Hell; Regrets after Death; The Bohemians

Collection: *Poems to the States (The United States of North America)*. 8 poems

Collection: *Poems in Praise of Poets. Poems of the States*. 17 poems, most addressed to a different US poet; e.g., Clemens, Emerson, Longfellow, Thoreau, Whitman, Whittier

	Collection: *The Book of Lives and Accusations*. 15 poems, incl. Resurrection; Voces Intimae; Walt Whitman; And My Music
	Collection: *Six Poems of the North American States*. 7 poems (6 + 'interlude')
April	59 poems, incl.: The Son of Europe (Beethoven); Five [sic: 6] Poems to the Memory of Leo Count Tolstoi; The Retreat; To the City Besançon
May	15 poems, incl. To Germany; Last Song of the War Poet; Spring; To Virgil
June	33 poems, incl. After Reading Robert Bridges; The Saga of the First War Poet of England [4 poems]; Eight Poems [sic: 7]; Schubert
August	10 poems, incl. To Framilode; To Sodden Depths; Before Valmy
September	30 poems, incl. To Clare; Of September; To the City of Gloucester; Autumn Coming
October–November	Collection: *Best Poems*. 65 poems, incl. The Silent One; The Lightning Storm; Felling a Tree; Iliad and Badminton; The Noble Wars of Troy; Sounds; War Books
	23 additional poems amongst drafts and related materials for *Best Poems*, incl. It Is Near Toussaints; 2/5 Gloucesters; A War Poet's Grave; Before the Attack; Victory Night 1925; Vermand Coppices
November	Collection: *New Drum Taps*. Missing. Some contents likely extant in *Best Poems* and other single manuscripts of this time. It is possible that Gurney's mention of this collection may in fact be referencing *Best Poems*. [After Walt Whitman's *Drum Taps*]
	The Year's Change; Hymn for St. Hugh's Day; All Hallows. 1916. Robecq
December	8 poems, incl. To the Memory of Walt Whitman; Electrical; Near Christmas; Extemporization; Carol
1926	Over the Ridge [as song: see musical works]
	Play: Gloucester Play [unfinished: opening scenes of act 1 only drafted]
January	The Late Rider [as song: see musical works]
February	26 poems, incl. The First of Lent [as song: see musical works]; Music Room; Early Winter; The Depths; 8 new versions of poems first written in 1919
March	Western Sailors [as song: see musical works]; Lady Day 1926; To Tewkesbury Abbey
c. March–April	The Royal Visit. Published in *Gloucester Journal*, 17 April 1926.
April	After the Day of the Death of Johannes Brahms
	Play: The Tewkesbury Trial: a 'trudgi–commodity' in five acts [first draft titled 'Mary of Tewkesbury']

	May	c. 10 poems, incl. Age Old Caerglow; Ruined Farm on the Retreat 1917
		Short story: The Great Galleon
		Essays: On a Dictionary Quotation; On a New Project; The Move Forward
	June	c. 16 poems, incl. J.S.B. on St Peter's Day; Franz Schubert
		Essays/tales: Transference; 'After Agincourt . . .'
	July	c. 45 poems
	August	c. 52 poems, incl. The Wood of August; Musers Afar Will Say; Clouds of Albion
	September	c. 108 poems, incl. Sea Marge; What Was Dear to Pan; several poems based on Shakespeare's *King Lear*
	October	c. 72 poems, incl. a number of verses for insertion into several of Shakespeare's plays; The Organ Sounds; When to Mediterranean the Birds' Thoughts Turn; Soft Rain
		Essay [untitled; for *Christian Science Monitor*]
	November–December	c. 29 poems, incl. The Lost Possessions; December Evening; No, Come Not, Swallows; Going Outwards; The Pedlar's Song
		Essay: 'The Chestnut Merchants' 1600
1927		Rewritings or additions to Hilaire Belloc, *The Four Men* 3 poems by H. W. Longfellow William Shakespeare: *Much Ado about Nothing*; *The Tempest*; *A Midsummer Night's Dream*; *Henry VI*, pt. 1; *As You Like It*; *Two Gentlemen of Verona*; *All's Well That Ends Well*
	April	14 essays, incl. On the Treasures of Art; On Certain Familiar Things; Jonson in After Easter Week; Notes from a Pocket Book; L. van Beethoven
	c. April–May	Essays: Joseph Haydn; Mr. Uriah (Sandwich) Heep
	c. April–June	10 essays, incl. Fable by Leo Count Tolstoi; letters from/to various well-known figures, including to Whitman from Edward MacDowell, to Hanslick from Brahms, and to Thoreau from Longfellow
	May	3 essays, incl. Notes on 'The Walkure' Rewritings of, or additions to, numerous poems by Walt Whitman, including 'Song of Myself'
	June	Essay: Of Dior
1929	March	The Wind [signed as Valentine Fane]

Notes

Prologue

1. See David Kathman's entry in the *Oxford Dictionary of National Biography*, 2004, https://doi
.org/10.1093/ref:odnb/76084.
2. From 'My Life', December 1922, Gurney Archive, Gloucester Public Records Office, G.15.74.
All manuscripts held in this archive are hereafter cited by the code (G followed by a numeri-
cal reference) the Records Office has given them.
3. To Marion Scott, 28 March 1918, G.70.6. *Collected Letters of Ivor Gurney*, ed. R.K.R. Thornton (Ashington: Carcanet, 1991)

Chapter 1. 'The Young Genius'

1. Herbert Howells, 'Ivor Gurney the Musician', *Music and Letters*, vol. 19, no. 1 (January 1938),
p. 14. Howells describes Gurney as 'the most gifted man that ever came into [Stanford's]
care . . . he [was] the least teachable.'
2. Michael Hurd, *The Ordeal of Ivor Gurney* (Oxford: Oxford University Press, 1978), p. 29.
3. Winifred was born in 1886, Ivor in 1890, Ronald in 1894, and Dorothy in 1900.
4. Fuller Maitland, music critic for *The Times*, wrote that the *Fantasia* offered something 'wonderful because it seems to lift one into some unknown region of musical thought and feeling.
Throughout its course one is never quite sure whether one is listening to something very old
or very new'. Maitland's review for *The Times*, repr. in Gustav Holst's obituary for Vaughan
Williams, *Sunday Times*, 31 August 1958.
5. Howells, 'Ivor Gurney the Musician', p. 14.
6. Pamela Blevins's research into the lives of the Hunt sisters can be found in 'Ivor Gurney:
Missing Links: The Hunt Sisters, Winthrop and Calista Rogers, and Valentine Fane', *Ivor
Gurney Society Journal*, vol. 17 (2011), pp. 33–56.
7. 'Parry heard with delight of these enterprising gatherings, and clapping one of the promoters
on the back asked in evident hope of an affirmative answer, "Do any of you young fellows
talk wild?"' H. C. Colles, *The Royal College of Music: A Jubilee Record, 1883–1933* (London:
Macmillan, 1933), p. 34.
8. To Marion Scott, 10 January 1918, G.41.163.
9. In a postscript to Marion Scott, summer 1913, G.46.30.9.
10. Emily Hunt reminiscence, quoted in Hurd, *The Ordeal of Ivor Gurney*, p. 28.
11. Winifred Gurney to Don Ray, December 1950, G.78.24. (Don Ray was an academic interested in writing a biography of Gurney. It never happened, but he donated his correspondence to the Gurney Archive.)
12. A quotation from Marie Corelli's 1896 popular novel *The Murder of Delicia*.
13. Gurney described Howells as being 'fond of natural things and simplicity' in a letter to Marion Scott, 13 May 1917, G.41.92.
14. Winifred Gurney reminiscences, recorded by Michael Hurd, c. 1970, G.57.

15. Only the title and first three notes of Gurney's setting of 'Mandalay' survive. Cheesman owned two musical settings of 'Mandalay' which could well have been Gurney's inspiration.

16. Paul Spicer, *Herbert Howells* (Wales: Seren Books, 1998), p. 54.

17. Gurney wished Scott to remember him to Wood and Walford Davies whilst absent in the army.

18. To Marion Scott, 31 August 1913, G.41.3, p. 8.

19. Arthur Bliss, *As I Remember* (London: Faber and Faber, 1970), p. 28.

20. Paul Hindmarsh, 'Frank Bridge: Seeds of Discontent', *Musical Times*, vol. 132, no. 1775 (January 1991), pp. 695–696.

21. Edgar Bainton, 'Sir Charles Stanford and His Pupils', *RCM Magazine*, vol. 20, no. 2 (Easter term 1924), pp. 55–61.

22. Hindmarsh, 'Frank Bridge', p. 695.

23. 'Stanford was a great teacher, but I believe I was unteachable. I made the great mistake of trying to fight my teacher.... The details of my work annoyed Stanford so much that we seldom got beyond these to the broader issues . . . there was no time left for any constructive criticism'. Vaughan Williams, 'A Musical Autobiography', in *National Music and Other Essays* (Oxford: Oxford University Press, 1934; 2nd ed., Oxford: Clarendon Press, 1996), p. 185.

24. 'Charles Villiers Stanford: By Some of His Pupils', *Music and Letters*, vol. 5, no. 3 (July 1924), p. 200.

25. Arthur Benjamin, 'A Student in Kensington', *Music and Letters*, vol. 31, no. 3 (July 1950), p. 201.

26. For more discussion of Harvey's personality, see Frances Townsend, *The Laureate of Gloucestershire: The Life and Work of F W Harvey, 1880–1957* (Bristol: Redcliffe, 1988), p. 7.

27. F. W. Harvey, opening lines of 'Ducks', published in his anthology of the same name, 1919.

28. In a retrospective assessment of the state of war poetry, four years after the armistice, Gurney wrote to Marion Scott: 'Our young Elizabethans didn't know the old ones, or the war verse would have been a very different thing; in four years that has so faded. Wilfred Owen's "Strange Meeting" has come off best, I think. But F. W. H. and myself stand high among poor stuff.' 9–10 April 1922, G.61.23-6.

29. The first two of three stanzas of 'F.W.H. (A Portrait)', published in the Gloucesters' trench journal the *Fifth Gloster Gazette* (April 1916), then in Harvey's poetry collection *A Gloucestershire Lad at Home and Abroad* (London: Sidgwick and Jackson, 1917).

30. Benjamin, 'A Student in Kensington', p. 200: 'I at once introduced myself to Howells—slight and small, young looking even for his age, with a beautiful head—asked him about himself and suggested luncheon together. So began a long friendship.'

31. The only detailed account of his compositions was written by Thomas Dunhill in 1926, after they were performed in a chamber concert in Warren's hometown of Leamington. See 'Francis Purcell Warren, 1896–1916', *Music and Letters*, vol. 7, no. 4 (October 1926), pp. 357–363.

32. Harry Plunket Greene and Marion M. Scott, 'Ivor Gurney the Man,' *Music and Letters*, vol. 19, no. 1 (January 1938), p. 3.

33. Emily, twenty-six years older than Gurney, and Margaret, sixteen years his senior, were both old enough to be his mother.

34. Winifred Gurney reminiscences, recorded by Michael Hurd, c. 1970, G.57.

35. Winifred Gurney to Don Ray, 23 April 1951, G.78.18.

36. Winifred Gurney to Don Ray, late November 1951, G.78.25.
37. Marion Scott notes in manuscript held in the Royal College of Music Archive, quoted in Pamela Blevins, *Ivor Gurney and Marion Scott: Song of Pain and Beauty* (Woodbridge: Boydell and Brewer, 2008), p. 85.
38. Extract from lines 5–6 of the unpublished poem 'Time Back', written in early April 1923, G.4.166.
39. This was published by Oxford University Press in 1979.
40. To Marion Scott, February 1913, G.46.30.12. Only two movements survive, and another single movement of a violin sonata in G major, written during the following year (between 1913 and 1914).
41. 'I was ill at Fulham, and that makes all things gray'; the first line of 'Time Back'.
42. To Marion Scott, summer 1912, G.46.30.8.
43. Quartett in A minor (unpublished). Gurney always favours the double *t* in his spelling of quartet.
44. To Marion Scott, February 1913, G.46.30.12.
45. 'The Irish Sea' was sent in a letter to Harvey, early June 1912, G.61.394.
46. To F. W. Harvey, early June 1912, G.61.394.
47. To Marion Scott, February 1913, G.46.30.12.
48. Lines from the first, shorter version of 'The Lock Keeper' as published in *War's Embers and Other Verses* (London: Sidgwick and Jackson, 1919), p. 99. Ellipses in brackets here and elsewhere are my own.
49. Lines 37–38 of 'Rappahannock', in Gurney's unpublished collection of poems *Gloucesters, Gloucester and of Virginia*, written 5–6 March 1925, G.52.2, pp. 72–80.
50. To Marion Scott, May 1913, G.53.57.
51. The shorter version of 'The Lock Keeper' was published in Gurney's collection *War's Embers*, and the longer by Edmund Blunden in his collection of Gurney's verse entitled *Poems, Principally Selected from Unpublished Manuscripts*, with a memoir by Blunden (London: Hutchinson, 1954), and again by P. J. Kavanagh in *Collected Poems of Ivor Gurney* (Oxford: Oxford University Press, 1982).
52. An extract from a nine-page unpublished appeal poem beginning, 'My head burnt, my eyes burnt, in torture', mid-June 1925, G.44.47.
53. Unpublished poem 'The Dream', written in Dartford, January 1923, addressed to 'The London Metropolitan Police Force', G. 44.49.

Chapter 2. 'A Waste of Spirit in an Expense of Shame'

1. To Marion Scott, 7 June 1916, G.41.25.
2. 'West Sussex Drinking Song' was later dedicated 'To F. W. H[arvey] (comrade to many in captivity)'. It was published in 1921.
3. To Harvey, early June 1912, G.61.394.
4. To Marion Scott, June 1913, G.46.30.13.
5. To Marion Scott, summer 1913, G.46.30.9.
6. To Marion Scott, summer 1913, G.46.30.9. Gurney described to Scott how he would 'stare at blank paper till I was sick at heart!'
7. To Harvey, 17 August 1913, G.61.389.a.
8. To Harvey, early June 1912, G.61.394.

9. To Harvey, 17 August 1913, G.61.389.b.
10. The violin sonata would be in G major. Only the first movement exists.
11. 7–12 September 1913.
12. Benjamin to Howells, 2 August 1913, Royal College of Music Archive, 7832/27a.
13. See Christopher Palmer, *Herbert Howells: A Centenary Celebration* (London: Thames, 1992), p. 267.
14. 28 November 1913. It was the College's third performance of the work; the other two were in 1896 and 1908.
15. Greene and Scott, 'Ivor Gurney the Man', p. 2: 'Parry was greatly excited over Gurney's M.S. composition and was pointing out to his colleagues the similarity in idiom and even in handwriting to Schubert, when Gurney was called. As he walked into the room Parry said, in an awestruck whisper, "By God! it *is* Schubert!"'
16. See Howells, 'Ivor Gurney the Musician'.
17. J. P. Muller, *My System* (London: Athletic Publications), p. 31. It appears to have been translated and published in London between 1904 and 1905 and reprinted as a 'special learner's edition' in 1912–13, which is most likely the edition that Gurney bought.
18. To John (Jack) W. Haines, spring 1914, G.84.8.
19. To Harvey, early 1914, G.61.242.
20. For discussion of the physical and haptic in war poetry, see Santanu Das, *Touch and Intimacy in First World War Poetry* (Cambridge: Cambridge University Press, 2005).
21. The first six lines of the sonnet 'Bach—Under Torment', written c. 1921–22, G.64.1.
22. They were performed by the Society of Women Musicians in 1916 and published individually by Boosey and Hawkes in 1920. (Gurney titles his most famous song 'Sleep', but the poem's actual title is 'Come, Sleep'. He later uses the fuller title for a choral setting of the same poem.)
23. Frederick Kiddle to Gurney, 21 November 1920, G.acc. 41091.
24. To Harvey, written in Fulham, early 1914, G.61.242.
25. He had taken the two quotes from W. H. Davies's 'The Wonder Maker' from his collection *Foliage* (1913) and Alice Meynell's 'In Early Spring' from *Preludes* (1875).
26. To Harvey, early 1914, G.61.242.
27. To Marion Scott, 23 February 1917, G.41.68.
28. To Marion Scott, 14 April 1917, G.41.85.
29. W. H. Davies, the author of 'Dreams of the Sea', was a self-styled 'super-tramp'; a friend of Edward Thomas who was welcomed in artistic circles perhaps as much for being a shocking and exciting raconteur of adventures as for his poetic skills. Ever since Gurney had been shown Davies's *Nature Poems,* he had been a fan, rather extravagantly declaring Davies's verse the 'finest lyric poetry in English'. His volume of Davies had accompanied him in London and Gloucestershire, and would be tucked into his pack in France. 'Dreams of the Sea' was the first of a trickle of settings of Davies's work—approximately one per year between 1918 and 1924. Later, Gurney was to be particularly proud of this song, singling it out along with 'O Happy Wind', and 'The Moon', which he sent to Davies in 1922.
30. Bliss, *As I Remember*, p. 30.
31. Lines 1–4 of the poem 'Of an Earth's Honour', June 1924, G.46.1.2.
32. Poems such as 'England the Mother', the final sonnet of his first poetry collection, *Severn and Somme* (1917), for example.
33. 'Servitude', sent in a letter to Marion Scott, 14 February 1917, G.41.64, published in *Severn and Somme*.

34. Winifred Gurney reminiscences, recorded by Michael Hurd, c. 1970, G.57.
35. Colles, *The Royal College of Music*, p. 43.
36. In Gurney's opinion, his successes to date were 'Edward', 'The Twa Corbies', 'The Sea' and 'Kennst du das Land'. The manuscript of 'Kennst du das Land' had already been lost by Gurney as early as June 1915. 'The Sea', as he calls it, is probably a shorthand for 'Dreams of the Sea', but there is always the possibility that an entirely different song with that name existed and has also been lost.
37. At the outbreak of the war, the battalion consisted of eight companies: A and B—Gloucester, C—Stroud, D—Tewkesbury, E and F—Cheltenham, G—Dursley and H—Chipping Campden.
38. To Howells, 8 April 1915, G.3.3.
39. 'A Look into the Past' by A. A. Faville, DCM (from a typed article in a scrapbook in the Regimental Archive of the Soldiers of Gloucestershire Museum).
40. To Marion Scott, 9 May 1915, G.41.4.
41. To Marion Scott, 9 May 1915, G.41.4.
42. To Harvey, February 1915, G.41.1.
43. An excerpt from John Masefield's 'Biography', published in *Georgian Poetry 1911–12*, ed. Sir Edward Marsh (London: The Poetry Bookshop, 1912).
44. To Harvey, February 1915, G.41.1.
45. Although Private Henry Irving Done of the 2/4th Gloucesters claims in his diary that it was a hutted camp, when he was there in early 1915. Held in his archive in the Soldiers of Gloucestershire Museum (GLRRM:04493).
46. Anonymous, *1914–1915: An Undated Diary, written on the spot, as circumstances permitted*, p. 2. Held in the Regimental Archive, Soldiers of Gloucestershire Museum.
47. *1914–1915: An Undated Diary*, p. 2.
48. Extract from the diary of Lance-Corporal A. J. Long, 1/4th Gloucesters, 1914–15, 22 August 1914, Soldiers of Gloucestershire Museum archive.
49. *1914–1915: An Undated Diary*, p. 3.
50. *1914–1915: An Undated Diary*, p. 3.
51. To Marion Scott, 9 May 1915, G.41.4.
52. The 2/5ths could usefully watch for zeppelins and report their approach, but they were highly unlikely to have been able to shoot one down themselves with a standard infantry rifle, which was their task. Zeppelins flew too high, and were generally invulnerable to small arms fire, unless incendiary bullets were being used.
53. Sir Hubert Parry to Marion Scott, Royal College of Music Archive.
54. Performances were by Dorothy Higgs, with Howells accompanying her.
55. To Howells, 8 April 1915, G.3.3.
56. The performance took place on 27 June 1916.
57. To Marion Scott, 5 July 1916, G.41.30.
58. To Marion Scott, 16 June 1915, G.41.6.
59. To the Chapman family, 29 June 1915, G.45750.
60. To Marion Scott, 28 June 1915, G.41.5.
61. To Marion Scott, 28 June 1915, G.41.5, misquoting Henry VI, 'brave peers of England, pillars of the state'. Gurney had been particularly moved by Brooke's two sonnets 'The Soldier' and 'The Dead' back in Chelmsford, when they appeared in a review of *New Numbers* in the *Times Literary Supplement* on 11 March.
62. Harold Monro, *Poetry and Drama*, vol. 2 (September 1914), p. 252.

63. To Ethel Voynich, c. 12 August 1915, G.41.14.
64. To Marion Scott, 3 August 1915, G.41.7.
65. See Anthony Boden, *F. W. Harvey: Soldier, Poet* (Phillimore & Co. [an imprint of The History Press], 2016; orig. pub. Alan Sutton, 1988), pp. 101–102, for 'Ballade of Beelzebub—God of Flies'.
66. To Ethel Voynich, c. 12 August 1915, G.41.14.
67. To Marion Scott, September 1915, G.41.10.
68. Sent in a letter to Scott, along with 'Afterwards' and 'A Ballad of the Cotswolds', September 1915, G.41.10.
69. In the same letter Gurney wrote out Harvey's 'In Flanders', as it appeared in the *Fifth Gloster Gazette*, making it increasingly likely that the song he gave to Scott was in fact his setting of 'In Flanders', and that he set it as soon as the poem appeared in the *Gazette* in mid-August/September 1915.
70. To Marion Scott, September 1915, G.41.10.
71. Boden, *F. W. Harvey*, p. 113.
72. The other clue that makes this first army song likely to be 'In Flanders' is that when Gurney retrospectively cannot remember when he wrote it, he suggests August or September 1915 as possible periods. This is the only song written on active service before 'By a Bierside', which was a year later, in August 1916.
73. To Sydney Shimmin, November 1915, G.76.2.
74. To Marion Scott, 22 February 1916, G.41.18.
75. To Ethel Voynich, late February 1916, G.41.19.
76. To Howells, late February 1916, G.3.33.
77. To Howells, late February 1916, G.3.33.
78. To Ethel Voynich, late February 1916, G.41.19.
79. To Ethel Voynich, late February 1916, G.41.19.
80. 17 February 1916, G.61.144.
81. To Howells, late February 1916, G.3.33.
82. See Hurd, *The Ordeal of Ivor Gurney*. He quotes the extract from a letter from Florence Gurney to Marion Scott in his first full chapter, 'Gloucester: 1890–1911'.
83. To Marion Scott, 25 April 1916, G.41.24.
84. To Marion Scott, 25 April 1916, G.41.24.

Chapter 3. 'First Time In'

1. The battle took place between 18 October and 11 November 1914. Major and Mrs Holt's guide to Ypres and Passchendaele (Tonie and Valmai Holt, 1988; repr., Barnsley: Pen and Sword, 2008) quotes the British casualty statistics as 2,350 officers and 55,800 men.
2. To Howells, 24 May 1916, G.3.14.
3. A. F. Barnes, *The Story of the 2/5th Battalion, Gloucestershire Regiment* (Gloucester: The Crypt House, 1930; 2003), p. 32.
4. Barnes, *Story of the 2/5th Battalion*, p. 32.
5. Whilst in training in Chelmsford, he lists a setting of another Davies poem, 'The Sea', as among his work that would survive his death. However it is not clear whether it was lost or a sketch, or still existed in 1915; there is no manuscript surviving, and Gurney's mention leaves its status ambiguous: 'Anyway there's the Elizabethan songs, Edward, The Twa Corbies, the Sea, and Kennst du das Land—two of which seem to be lost and one a sketch.' To Marion Scott, 16 June 1915, G.41.6.

6. Barnes, *Story of the 2/5th Battalion*, pp. 34–35.

7. To Catherine Abercrombie, June 1916, Hurd manuscripts, Gurney Archive, D10828; see *Collected Letters*, p. 91.

8. Barnes, *Story of the 2/5th Battalion*, p. 158.

9. Very lights were a coloured flare, fired from a special pistol, to light up the sky at night.

10. Ploegsteert Wood, or Plug Street Wood, as it became known to the soldiers there, was the location for the writing of both Harvey's poem 'In Flanders' and Charles Hamilton Sorley's 'In Flanders Fields'.

11. Barnes, *Story of the 2/5th Battalion*, p. 37.

12. Written in the first few weeks of his residency in Barnwood House, autumn 1922, G.64.1.23, published in *Collected Poems*, p. 203. An alternative typescript of the poem exists and was included in *Poems of Ivor Gurney*, with a bibliographical note by Leonard Clark (London: Chatto and Windus, 1973).

13. To Marion Scott, 7 June 1916, G.41.25.

14. To Marion Scott, 7 June 1916, G.41.25.

15. To Catherine Abercrombie, June 1916, *Collected Letters*, p. 91.

16. To Ethel Voynich, June 1916, G.41.28. These first letters were only the beginning of his literary engagement with the experience—he went on to write three different 'First Time In' poems.

17. To Marion Scott, 7 June 1916, G.41.25.

18. This version of 'First Time In' is the second of those written in Gurney's pink marbled book, c. 1921–22. He added the last three lines in 1924, when he selected it for his poetry collection *Rewards of Wonder*. This is as it appears as the first of two poems entitled 'First Time In', *Rewards of Wonder*, p. 62. For an account and full transcript of the other 'First Time In' poems, see Lynn Parker, 'The Whole Craft and Business of Bad Occasion', *Ivor Gurney Society Journal*, vol. 5 (1999), pp. 11–30.

19. To Marion Scott, 7 June 1916, G.41.25. Maconochie (misspelt by Gurney) was the brand name for a type of tinned stew, which could contain potatoes and carrots and/or meat. It was a regular feature of soldiers' diets in both the Boer War and the First World War, and was widely criticised for being revolting, especially when unheated.

20. 'The Great Years of Their Lives,' *The Listener*, vol. 86, no. 2207 (15 July 1971), p. 74. Quoted in Eric J. Leed, *No Man's Land: Combat and Identity in World War One* (Cambridge: Cambridge University Press, 1979), p. 126.

21. Ford Madox Ford, *Parade's End* (*A Man Could Stand Up*, 1926), part 2, ch. 6 (London: Penguin, 1982), p. 637.

22. To the Chapman family, June 1916, G.45750.

23. Barnes, *Story of the 2/5th Battalion*, p. 38.

24. Barnes, *Story of the 2/5th Battalion*, p. 38.

25. C. V. Burder, *Hell on Earth: My Life in the Trenches 1914–1918* (repr., Big Ben Books, 2010), p. 96.

26. 'Out There' (one of two poems with this title), lines 5–12, 1923, G.44.14.

27. Arnold Bennett, *Over There: War Scenes from the Western Front* (London: Methuen, 1915), p. 185.

28. From 'Ypres', written when he returned to the Ypres salient, and was stationed at Vlamertinghe, c. 20–24 August 1917. Published in the *RCM Magazine*, vol. 14, no. 2 (Easter term 1918), p. 48.

29. An estaminet was the French term for a bar or café, generally fairly unostentatious.

30. Final stanza (lines 37–42) of 'The Estaminet', mid-January 1917, published in *Severn and Somme* (1917; repr., London: Sidgwick and Jackson, 1987), pp. 34–36.

31. On average, eight hundred men per month were admitted to hospital with one or other form of sexually transmitted disease. To contract one was an offence against army discipline, and punishable by imprisonment. See *War on the Western Front*, ed. Gary Sheffield (Oxford: Osprey, 2007), p. 123.
32. To Marion Scott, 22 June 1916, G.41.26.
33. 'The Estaminet', *Severn and Somme*.
34. A Tommy cooker was a compact, portable stove fuelled by solidified alcohol.
35. Winifred Gurney recalled how 'Money was short in so far as to afford books and the like that he [Gurney] would go without food for too long, then get hungry and eat ravishingly which more and more weakened his health'. To Don Ray, late November 1951, G.78.25.
36. To Marion Scott, 7 June 1916, G.41.25.
37. To Marion Scott, 5 July 1916, G.41.30.
38. To Matilda Chapman, 22 June 1916, G.45750.
39. From 'To the Poet before Battle: Sonnet', sent to Scott on 3 August 1915, G.41.7; printed in *Severn and Somme*, p. 23.
40. To Marion Scott, 22 June 1916, G.41.26.
41. To Marion Scott, 22 June 1916, G.41.26.
42. To Marion Scott, 22 June 1916, G.41.26.
43. See Gurney's poetic accounts of his 'First Time In' for other examples of this phenomenon.
44. To Marion Scott, 22 June 1916, G.41.26.
45. Quoted in Philip Knightley, *The First Casualty: The War Correspondent As Hero and Myth-Maker from the Crimea to Kosovo* (Baltimore: Johns Hopkins University Press, 2002).
46. To Marion Scott, 22 June 1916, G.41.26.
47. Privates E. Skillern and J. Hall both died on 21 June 1916 and are buried three graves apart from each other, in the Royal Irish Rifles Graveyard at Laventie, near Ypres.
48. 'To Certain Comrades' was printed as the first poem in *Severn and Somme*, pp. 21–22.
49. To Howells, 2 May 1916, G.3.21.
50. To Marion Scott, tentatively dated by Thornton as 21 June 1916. It must have been shortly before the night of the attack on 20–21 June, G.70.2.
51. To Howells, 21 June 1916, G.3.28.
52. To Marion Scott, 29 June 1916, G.41.27.
53. Charles Carrington, *Soldier from the Wars Returning* (London: Hutchinson, 1965), p. 87.
54. 'Strafe', written out in a letter to Marion Scott, 11 June 1917, G.41.101.
55. To Marion Scott, 29 June 1916, G.41.27.
56. To Marion Scott, 29 June 1916, G.41.27.
57. To Marion Scott, 29 June 1916, G.41.27. Gurney is referring to Whitman's 'Song of Myself' here.
58. 'To England—A Note' was posted to Scott the following day.
59. From 'To England—A Note'. Printed in *Severn and Somme*, p. 28. This is the sestet of the sonnet.
60. To Marion Scott, 29 June 1916, G.41.27.
61. To Marion Scott, 5 July (Gurney only managed to send the letter on 9 July) 1916, G.41.30.
62. To Marion Scott, 5 July 1916, G.41.30.
63. Barnes, *Story of the 2/5th Battalion*, p. 41.
64. Barnes, *Story of the 2/5th Battalion*.
65. See Grimwade's 'War History of 4th Battalion, London Regiment' (London: HQ of the 4th London Regiment, 1922) for details.
66. Burder, *Hell on Earth*, p. 53.

67. This song was probably written at the same time as the poem 'To the Fallen'.

68. To Marion Scott, 17 July 1916, G.41.31.

69. Gurney's exact location was nine kilometres northeast of Béthune, near Richebourg–St Vaast, on the immediate right of Neuve Chapelle. The village merged with Richebourg L'Avoué in 1971. This is a perpetual problem when trying to trace smaller locations mentioned in regimental war diaries—some villages were never rebuilt, but a number that remained standing have since changed their local area boundaries, and often their names, as in the case of Riez Bailleul, for example.

70. The village was never actually taken by the Germans but was within 1.6 kilometres of the front line at certain points during the war.

71. Edmund Blunden, *Undertones of War* (1928; repr., London: Penguin, 2000), pp. 56–57. The 2/5ths found themselves inheriting trenches that had just suffered a major attack—the Battle of the Boar's Head, which had taken place the week before (on 30 June), in which the three attacking Southdowns Battalions of the Royal Sussex Regiment had suffered huge losses. There was no escaping the smell, the debris and the carnage left behind.

72. Unpublished diary, 8 July 1916, held in the Regimental Archive, Soldiers of Gloucestershire Museum.

73. To Marion Scott, 17 July 1916, G.41.31. He mentions washing in a biscuit tin to Winnie Chapman, August 1916, G.45750.

74. The 61st Division (of which the 2/5th Gloucesters were a part) sustained 1,547 casualties, some 50 percent of their attacking strength, while the Australians suffered 5,533 casualties, over 90 percent of their infantry involved in the attack.

75. The Moated Grange area had been heavily fought over in March 1915, as part of the previous year's attack on Aubers Ridge. The Grange itself had changed from being in No Man's Land to having German trenches running through its outbuildings. It had already been largely destroyed by the time Gurney reached the area, as it was too advantageous a position for snipers to be allowed to remain intact. Miraculously, parts of its original moat still endure today, around new farm buildings.

76. Boden's biography of Will Harvey records that Will and Eric were summoned back to England in April 1916, training at Park House Camp in Salisbury with Gurney, then going back over to France with him and the 2/5ths (p. 136). Will Harvey was certainly with the 2/5ths when he was reported missing in August, but there is no record of him training at the same time as Gurney, and the war diary reports a Harvey transferring to the 2/5ths at Moated Grange. Also, Gurney says that when he visited Harvey's mother at the end of his time in Salisbury, she had three sons fighting.

77. To Marion Scott, 27 July 1916, G.41.32.

78. Printed in *Severn and Somme*, pp. 26–27.

79. He was to take the practise of embedding an ambivalent approach to a poem into its setting to a masterly level in his 1919 interpretation of Housman's 'The Lads in Their Hundreds', and was about to apply a similarly psychologically complex approach to his setting of Masefield's 'By a Bierside'.

Chapter 4. 'Most Grand to Die'?

1. To Marion Scott, 1 August 1916, G.41.33.

2. To Marion Scott, 1 August 1916, G.41.33. In *Collected Letters*, Thornton explains 'cory' as either trench French or schoolboy Latin for 'heart'.

3. Winifred Gurney reminiscences, recorded by Michael Hurd, c. 1970, G.58.
4. Dorothy Gurney reminiscences to Don Ray, 13 March 1951, G.71.5.
5. 'Stepney Causeway', lines 17–20, unpublished asylum poem, August 1923, G.15.215.
6. To Ethel Voynich, 28 August 1916, G.46.32.3.
7. Gurney found the text for 'By a Bierside' in the anthology *Poems of Today* (Sidgwick and Jackson, for The English Association, 1915). He quotes the version of the poem reproduced in the volume exactly, so must have had a copy of the anthology amongst his belongings.
8. The line 'Think on me too, O Mother, who wrest my soul to serve you' is from the 'Strange Service', *Severn and Somme*, p. 26.
9. To Marion Scott, 13 September 1916, G.41.38.
10. To Marion Scott, 1 April 1917, G.41.83.
11. To Marion Scott, 14 April 1917, G.41.85.
12. To Marion Scott, 1 August 1916, G.41.33.
13. To Howells, 24 August 1916, G.3.26.
14. 'After-glow', *Severn and Somme*, p. 39.
15. To Marion Scott, 16 August 1916, G.41.34.
16. To Marion Scott, 24 August 1916, G.41.35.
17. A quote Gurney takes from Keats's 'When I Have Fears That I May Cease to Be'; see letter to Marion Scott, 16 August 1916, G.41.34.
18. To Marion Scott, September 1916, G.41.37.
19. To Marion Scott, 13 September 1916, G.41.38.
20. To Marion Scott, 19 October 1916, G.41.43.
21. To Marion Scott, 25 October 1916, G.41.45.
22. To Marion Scott, letter misdated 8 October 1916 (he says that he is in rest, but he only reached Robecq at 2:30 on 27 October, and he includes a poem about the place in the letter), G.41.41.
23. Both from 'From Laventie Line', version 1, *The Book of Five Makings*, compiled February 1925, p. 98.
24. To Marion Scott, 8 October 1916 (misdated), G.41.41.
25. To Marion Scott, 29 September 1916, G.41.39.
26. 'The Glad Time', final lines, *The Book of Five Makings* (G.64.2), p. 110.
27. To Marion Scott, 9 December 1916, G.41.49.
28. For a description of the leaning Virgin and the poetry and mythology it inspired, see Paul Fussell, *The Great War and Modern Memory* (Oxford: Oxford University Press, 1975), pp. 131–133.
29. 'The Mother', *Severn and Somme*, p. 28.
30. From 'What Time Brings', c. July–August 1924, G.44.132–136.
31. This line was quoted after the war in Sassoon's 1918 poem 'Dead Musicians'.
32. Barnes, *Story of the 2/5th Battalion*, p. 53.
33. Captain Sinclair's account in Barnes, *Story of the 2/5th Battalion*, pp. 55–56.
34. See comment to Shimmin, early January 1917, *Collected Letters*, p. 179: 'The Cold upset my belly and other parts that may be veiled under a descent [*sic*] obscurity (as they usually are actually) and that has landed me into a Soft Job, just for the present'.
35. To Marion Scott, 22 December 1916, G.41.50.

36. To Marion Scott, 7 January 1917, G.41.53.
37. Fred A. Farrell, *The 51st Division War Sketches* (Edinburgh: E. C. Jack, 1920).
38. To Marion Scott, 7 January 1917, G.41.53.
39. Gurney describes the evening in his postwar poem 'New Year's Eve', from which this is a quotation. *Collected Poems*, p. 131.
40. Gurney had forgotten when he had originally conceived the song, writing, 'This valuable fragment dates anywhere between April 1916 and now. Or is it September or August 1915? Goodness knows.' To Marion Scott, 11 January 1917, G.41.55.
41. To Marion Scott, 11 January 1917, G.41.55.
42. Howells, 'Ivor Gurney the Musician', pp. 14–15.
43. To Marion Scott, 7 February 1917, G.41.63.
44. To Marion Scott, 3 February 1917, G.41.58, and to Ethel Voynich, late September 1915, G.41.11.

Chapter 5. 'The Fool at Arms'

1. For more detail on Haig's plan of campaign at this time, see Lyn Macdonald, *1914–1918: Voices and Images of the Great War* (London: Penguin, 1991) p. 190.
2. To Marion Scott, 17 January 1917, G.41.54.
3. 'Scots', sent to Marion Scott, 4 January 1917, G.41.52, printed in *Severn and Somme*, p. 31.
4. 'Purple and Black' was written on 7 January 1917 and sent to Marion Scott in a letter that day, G.41.53.
5. 'Communion' was sent to Marion Scott 7 January 1917, G.41.53, printed in *Severn and Somme*, pp. 37–38.
6. To Marion Scott, 1 August 1916, G.41.33.
7. From Walt Whitman, 'Song of Myself' (1855), final line of section 15.
   'And these tend inward to me, and I tend outward to them,
   And such as it is to be of these more or less I am,
   And of these one and all I weave the song of myself.'
8. To Marion Scott, 7 January 1917, G.41.53.
9. Published in *Severn and Somme*, p. 36.
10. To Marion Scott, 1 February 1917, G.41.57.
11. Sent to Marion Scott, 3 February 1917, G.41.60, published in *Severn and Somme*, p. 34.
12. The German translates as 'Here lies a brave Englishman'. To Marion Scott, 2 April 1917, G.41.80.
13. Written between June and July 1917, published in Gurney's second poetry collection, *War's Embers*, in 1919, pp. 91–92, and in the joint edition of *Severn and Somme* and *War's Embers* (Northumberland: Carcanet, 1987).
14. To Marion Scott, 3 February 1917, G.41.60.
15. The triolet was a favourite form of Harvey's. He had also published triolets in the May and October 1915 and February 1916 issues of the *Fifth Gloster Gazette*.
16. To Marion Scott, 3 February 1917, G.41.58.
17. Taken from the published version, which is slightly amended from the original Gurney sent to Marion Scott on 3 February.
18. To Howells, 13? February 1917, G.3.29–30, *Severn and Somme*, p. 40.

19. To Marion Scott, 14 February 1917, G.41.64.
20. To Ethel Voynich, February 1917, G.41.6113. Gurney had read that Woodrow Wilson had ended diplomatic relations with Germany on 3 February. America was to declare war on 6 April.
21. To Marion Scott, 14 February 1917, G.41.64.
22. To Marion Scott, 7 February 1917, G.41.63.
23. To Marion Scott, 7 February 1917, G.41.63.
24. He also titles a poem 'After-glow'.
25. 'England the Mother', to Marion Scott, 29 May 1917, G.41.96, later published in *Severn and Somme*, p. 51, the final poem of five 'Sonnets 1917' (as with many of his published poems, the initial version sent back to Scott differs slightly from the edited published version. I have reproduced the final versions throughout).
26. To Marion Scott, 14 August 1917, G.41.119.
27. 'Still, I chose this path, and do not regret it; do not see what else I could have done under the circumstances; and if the Lord God should have the bad taste to delete me
"Deil anither word tae God from a gentleman like me".'
To Marion Scott, 16 June 1915, G.41.6.
28. Preface to *Severn and Somme*, and letter to Marion Scott, 14 February 1917, G.41.64.
29. To Marion Scott, 23 February 1917, G.41.66. This letter is probably misdated—Gurney went back into the trenches at midnight on 16 February as the letter describes, so this is probably more accurately dated as around 17 February.
30. Owen wrote his first draft of 'The Chances' at Craiglockhart in August–September 1917.
31. The government had issued the recently developed box respirator to all troops in January, so technically the 2/5ths ought to have had complete protection as long as they were wearing it. There was no protection against the element of surprise, however. A second lieutenant and five privates, one of whom later died, did not manage to fit their helmets in time and were badly gassed.
32. To Marion Scott, 17 February 1917, G.41.62.
33. Barnes, *Story of the 2/5th Battalion*, p. 58.
34. To Marion Scott, 7 March 1917, G.41.76.
35. First of three stanzas of 'Song of Pain and Beauty', published in *Severn and Somme*, p. 42.
36. To Marion Scott, 26 March 1917, G.41.81.
37. Published in *Severn and Somme*, p. 48.
38. To Marion Scott, 23 March 1917, G.41.73.
39. To Marion Scott, 22 March 1917, G.41.72.
40. To Marion Scott, 22 March 1917, G.41.72.
41. To Marion Scott, 1 April 1917, G.41.83.
42. To Marion Scott, 1 April 1917, G.41.83.
43. To Marion Scott, 1 April 1917, G.41.83.
44. To Marion Scott, 18 May 1917, G.41.94.
45. To Marion Scott, 25 March 1917, G.41.81.
46. From 'What Time Brings', c. July–August 1924, G.44.132–136.
47. The lad in question was probably twenty-two-year-old dairy worker Corporal James Chappin, who was the only one of those killed that night who was not from Gloucestershire but from Long Marston near Tring, Hertfordshire, near Buckinghamshire.
48. To Marion Scott, 14 April 1917, G.41.85.
49. To Marion Scott, 18? May 1917, G.41.93.
50. 'The Retreat', lines 162–end, 23 April 1925, G.4.151–157.

Chapter 6. 'Even Such Is Time'

1. No. 8 General Hospital was a tented and hutted British military hospital in the north of the town. Nothing of it remains, and the site is now taken up with modern development.

2. *Your Daughter Fanny: The War Letters of Frances Cluett, VAD*, ed. Bill Rompkey and Bert Riggs (Newfoundland: Flanker Press, 2006), 8 June 1917, p. 82.

3. Gurney does not mention the orchestra, or any other musical activity that took place to distract him, but it may be that his stay was so brief that it did not coincide with any concerts.

4. I extrapolate that it was to the convalescent depot, or camp, as Gurney refers to it, that he was eventually sent. Although he doesn't name a hospital, and there were many in close proximity to each other at Rouen, he mentions on 30 April that his correspondence 'has been left at Con: camp and sent to the Batt.' To Marion Scott, 30 April 1917, G.41.88.

5. To Marion Scott, 30 April 1917, G.41.88.

6. *War Letters of Frances Cluett*, p. 111.

7. *War Letters of Frances Cluett*, p. 100.

8. Lines 1–5 of the poem 'Gloucesters Depot Rouen. 1917', intended for his unpublished poetry collection *Poems of Gloucesters, Gloucester and of Virginia*, 5–6 March 1925, G.52.2, p. 49.

9. To Marion Scott, 19 April 1917, G.41.86.

10. To Marion Scott, 31 August 1913, G.41.3.

11. To Marion Scott, April 1917, G.41.84.

12. To Marion Scott, April 1917, G.41.84.

13. To Marion Scott, 9 May 1917, G.41.90.

14. To Shimmin, 24 April 1917, G.76.7.

15. Gurney heard of Howells's quartet being selected on 24 April 1917.

16. To Marion Scott, 1 April 1917, G.41.83.

17. To Marion Scott, April 1917, G.41.84.

18. Howells was only at Salisbury from mid-February to mid-May 1917.

19. To Howells, 18? May 1917, G.3.22.

20. Quoted in Spicer, *Herbert Howells*, p. 33.

21. Stephen Banfield, *Gerald Finzi* (London: Faber and Faber, 1998), p. 64.

22. To Marion Scott, 18? May 1917, G.41.93.

23. To Marion Scott, 29 May 1917, G.41.96.

24. To Marion Scott, 4 May 1917, G.41.89.

25. To Marion Scott, 4 May 1917, G.41.89.

26. To Marion Scott, 9 May 1917 G.41.90.

27. To Marion Scott, 4 May 1917, G.41.89.

28. To Marion Scott, 29 May 1917, G.41.96.

29. Quotes taken from lines 16–18 of 'Rejoining Battallion [*sic*]', intended for *Poems of Gloucesters, Gloucester and of Virginia*, p. 49.

30. To Marion Scott, 18 May 1917, G.41.94.

31. To Marion Scott, 8 July 1917, G.41.108.

32. The final stanza of 'The Old City—Gloucester', *Collected Poems*, pp. 31–32.

33. Barnes, *Story of the 2/5th Battalion*, p. 151.

34. To Marion Scott, 12 July 1917, G.41.105.

35. To Marion Scott, 8 July 1917, G.41.108.

36. To Marion Scott, 15 July 1917, G.41.106.

37. Boden, *F. W. Harvey*, p. 172.

38. R. B. McKerrow (from publishers Sidgwick and Jackson) to Marion Scott, 9 June 1917, G.61.259–60.

39. The opening line of 'To the Poet before Battle', *Severn and Somme*.

40. First of nine stanzas, 'Spring. Rouen, May 1917', printed in *Severn and Somme*, pp. 42–45.

41. To Marion Scott, 3 August 1915, G.41.7.

42. 'After-glow', lines 5–6, *Severn and Somme*, p. 39.

43. 'Requiems', in *Severn and Somme*, pp. 48–49.

44. The first three lines of 'Afterwards', published in *Severn and Somme*, pp. 24–25.

45. The first four lines of the first stanza of 'Carol', published in *Severn and Somme*, pp. 25–26.

46. To Howells, 31 July 1917, G.3.6.

47. Spicer, *Herbert Howells*, p. 62.

48. To Shimmin, 23 July 1917, G.76.12.

49. To Marion Scott, 27 July 1917, G.41.110.

50. From 'The Women Working', part of the unpublished *Poems of Gloucesters, Gloucester and of Virginia*, pp. 38–39.

51. 'Moving Up to Ypres', line 17, from *Poems of Gloucesters, Gloucester and of Virginia*, pp. 19–21.

52. This was the practise, begun in Roman times, of laying logs covered in sand perpendicular to the road, to make heavily damaged or muddy roads more passable.

53. Edwin Campion Vaughan, *Some Desperate Glory: The Diary of a Young Officer, 1917* (London: Leo Cooper, 1985), p. 221.

54. To Marion Scott, 23 August 1917, G.41.123.

55. In these very early days of air combat, Guynemer was one of the first celebrity pilots; a national hero in France, he was attributed with shooting down more than fifty German aircraft. He was reported missing on 11 September 1917. Gurney rarely mentions the still comparatively rare presence of aeroplanes, but two references can be found in letters from 4 June and 14 August 1917 (*Collected Letters*, pp. 268 and 303).

56. To Marion Scott, 23 August 1917, G.41.123.

57. See Daniel Todman, *The Great War, Myth and Reality* (London: Bloomsbury, 2014), p. 4.

58. This has been misdated by Gurney himself, who on 17 September writes that he was gassed '5 days ago'. However, on the 12th itself, he writes of an already existing gas injury: 'My throat is still sore from gas; it is just (or was) as if I had had catarrh, but only an occasional explosion of coughing is left now.' To Marion Scott, 12 September 1917, G.41.135.

59. The war diary of the 184th Machine Gunners lists eight men; Gurney himself remembers seven.

60. To Marion Scott, 18? May 1917, G.41.93.

Chapter 7. 'A Touch of Gas'

1. A section from an undated asylum poem (c. 1925), quoted in Hurd, *The Ordeal of Ivor Gurney*, p. 110.

2. To Marion Scott, 12 September 1917, G.41.135.

3. James Kendall, *Breathe Freely! The Truth about Poison Gas* (London: Bell, 1938), p. 38.

4. Dr L. F. Haber, 'Gas Warfare 1915–1945: The Legend and the Facts', The Stevenson Lecture 1975, Glasgow University, p. 6.

5. *War Letters of Frances Cluett*, p. 110.

6. Hill 35 is near the village of St Julien.

7. To Marion Scott, 29 September 1917, G.41.138.
8. To Marion Scott, 26 September 1917, G.41.137.
9. To Marion Scott, 22 September 1917, G.70.10.
10. To Marion Scott, 22 September 1917, G.70.10.
11. The meaning of 'Weltmuth' is unclear—it is most likely to be a misspelling of 'mut', meaning spirit or zeitgeist, perhaps referring to a kind of world weariness.
12. To Marion Scott, 1 October 1917, G.41.140.
13. To Marion Scott, 1 October 1917, G.41.140.
14. To Marion Scott, 26 September 1917, G.41.137.
15. To Marion Scott, 1 October 1917, G.41.139.
16. To Marion Scott, 26 September 1917, G.41.137.
17. To Marion Scott, 26 September 1917, G.41.137.
18. To Marion Scott, 1 October 1917, G.41.139.
19. To Howells, January 1918 (this is an approximate date; I suspect it might have been written earlier), G.3.32.
20. Gurney to Harvey, c. March–April 1918, F. W. Harvey Archive, Gloucester Public Records Office, D12912/1/2/33.
21. Gurney to Matilda Harvey, October 1917, Harvey Archive, D12912/1/2/22.
22. First two lines of 'After Music', in Gurney's second poetry collection, War's Embers, p. 78.
23. Last five lines of 'After Music'.
24. To Marion Scott, 16 October 1917, G.41.146.
25. See W. F. Hendrie and D.A.D. Macleod, The Bangour Story (Aberdeen: Aberdeen University Press, 1991), with details of ward life taken from Nurse Effie Day's account, pp. 23–24.
26. Written at Edinburgh, sent to Marion Scott on 17 November 1917 from Seaton Delaval, published in War's Embers, pp. 80–81.
27. Tantalisingly, Owen's stay at Craiglockhart overlapped with Gurney's residency at Bangour; Owen left Edinburgh on 4 November, and Gurney on the 5th. For more detail on Gurney's relationship to Barnett, see Pamela Blevins's article 'Ivor Gurney, Wilfred Owen and T. Ratcliffe Barnett in Scotland', www.musicweb-international.com.
28. To Marion Scott, 26 December 1917, G.70.13.
29. 'The Miner', written in October 1917, is the third of Gurney's 'Hospital Pictures'. Published in War's Embers, p. 83.
30. To Howells, 2 October 1917, G.3.12.
31. Finished in Gloucester, November 1917, sent to Scott on 3 January 1918, G.41.161, and published as the sixth of 'Hospital Pictures', War's Embers, pp. 83–85. The first two of eight stanzas are reproduced here.
32. It was published by OUP in 1938.
33. To Marion Scott, 23 October 1917, G.41.148.
34. To Marion Scott, 26 September 1917, G.41.137.
35. Gurney to Harvey, October 1916, Harvey Archive, D12912/1/2/15.
36. 'I have actually condescended to read a lady-novelist', Gurney wrote (with tongue in cheek) to Marion Scott, 31 August 1913, G.41.3.
37. To Shimmin, November 1917, G.76.4.
38. He recalls playing the piano for hours in a letter from St Albans, 27 August 1918, G.41.175.
39. To Marion Scott, 27 August 1918, G.41.175.
40. To Marion Scott, 29 November 1917, G.70.12. Gurney describes feeling 'more intimate than ever before' with Howells.

Chapter 8. 'To His Love'

1. To Howells, January 1918, G.3.20.
2. *Private Papers of A. Thomas*, Imperial War Museum Archive, Item no. 11427.
3. *Private Papers of A. Thomas*.
4. At its busiest, the battalion contained over two thousand men.
5. This was a training camp run by what had been the 3/5ths, as they were formed in March 1915, first as a depot company, and later as a reserve battalion to the first and second lines. They did not go abroad but were amalgamated in September 1916 with the 3/4th and 3/6th Battalions as the 4th Reserve Battalion. In July 1917 the battalion was transferred to Seaton Delaval, where it remained until it was disbanded.
6. *Private Papers of A. Thomas*.
7. A1 was the highest level of fitness—Gurney had been enlisted as C3, so this was something of an unlikely promotion.
8. To Marion Scott, 12 December 1917, G.70.8.
9. To J. W. (Jack) Haines, 17 November 1917, G.83.3.
10. To Marion Scott, 12 December 1917, G.70.8. Jack Haines wrote to the paper to object to its unfair assessment of *Severn and Somme*.
11. Gurney told Haines that Harvey had sent a postcard listing these as his favourites, 16 March 1918, G.83.5.1–2.
12. To Marion Scott, 28 September 1918, G.61.22.
13. To Marion Scott, 27 July 1917, G.41.109.
14. To Marion Scott, 10 January 1918, G.41.162.
15. To Howells, 17 November 1917, G.3.25.
16. 27 December 1917, Harvey Archive, D12912/1/2/26.
17. 'The Change', line 6, Seaton Delaval, c. November–December 1917, unpublished, G.52.1.
18. Anthony Boden, *Stars in a Dark Night: The Letters from Ivor Gurney to the Chapman Family* (Gloucestershire: Alan Sutton, 2005), p. 52.
19. To Winifred Chapman, June 1915, G.45750.
20. To Marion Scott, 29 November 1917, G.41.156.
21. He was certainly composing during this Christmas period, although he had not yet tried anything on a piano by the first few weeks of January. He also wrote a setting of Gibson's 'For G' that January.
22. As he touchingly (if rather tritely) refers to her in a letter to Howells, 17 November 1917, G.3.25.
23. 'Song of Urgency', written at Seaton Delaval, January 1918, G.52.1, in *Complete Poetical Works of Ivor Gurney*, ed. Tim Kendall and Philip Lancaster (Oxford: Oxford University Press, 2020), vol. 1, p. 61.
24. To Howells, 16 January 1918, G.3.20.
25. For further discussion of Gurney's use of the pastoral elegy, see Kate Kennedy, '"But Still He Died Nobly": Gurney's Re-interpretation of the Pastoral Elegy', *Ivor Gurney Society Journal*, vol. 15 (2009), pp. 117–154. For a discussion of nonconsolatory elegies, see Jahan Ramazani, *Poetry of Mourning: The Modern Elegy from Hardy to Heaney* (Chicago: University of Chicago Press, 1994).
26. 'Memory Let All Slip', final stanza, written in Bangour, October 1917, *Collected Poems*, p. 33.
27. 'The Fire Kindled', final stanza (lines 21–24), October 1916, *Severn and Somme*, p. 22.
28. In a letter to Marion Scott, 20 January 1918, G.41.164.

29. Gurney was not always so bleak on the subject—after reacquainting himself with the spring flowers (including violets) of the Gloucestershire countryside, he wrote what could have been a motto for the pastoral elegy: 'The earth of Glostershire sorrows for its dead, and February flowers come of its great pity'. (To Marion Scott, 18 February 1918, G.70.16.) The dichotomy between the regenerative, beautiful landscape and the abject dead (in itself a trope of much Great War soldiers' verse) was still playing in his mind weeks after 'To His Love' was completed.

30. The letter in which he writes it out to Scott is signed 'Seaton Delaval, Northumberland Jan. 1917', which is a new year's slip, as the poem was completed in early 1918. G.41.164.

31. Gurney to Matilda Harvey, c. September–October 1916, Harvey Archive, D12912/1/2/13.

32. Barnes, *Story of the 2/5th Battalion*, p. 53.

33. To Marion Scott, 10 January 1918, G.41.162.

34. To Will Harvey, 30 April 1918, Harvey Archive, D12912/1/2/31.

35. To Marion Scott, 20 January 1918, G.41.164.

36. To F. W. Harvey, February 1918, G.61.390. I estimate that the letter was written after 11 February, as he is on leave visiting his father in Gloucester at the point of writing.

37. To Howells, 12 March 1918, G.3.23.

38. Winifred Gurney reminiscences, recorded by Michael Hurd, c. 1970, G.57.

39. Winifred Gurney to Don Ray, December 1950, G.78.24.

40. Winifred Gurney to Don Ray, December 1950, G.78.24.

41. Haines to Don Ray, 19 March 1951, G.74.1.

42. Haines to Don Ray, 19 March 1951, G.74.1.

43. To Marion Scott, 18 February 1918, G.70.16.

44. In the Crimean War it had been considered to be a side effect of enteric fever.

45. To Marion Scott, 3 March 1918, G.70.17.

46. The daughter-in-law of the owner of the castle was Tennyson's aunt, and it was rumoured that Tennyson, who had visited the castle on a number of occasions, had written 'Come into the Garden, Maud' in its grounds. (From 'A Brief History of Brancepeth Castle', courtesy of Brancepeth Archive and History Group.)

47. To Marion Scott, 12 March 1918, G.70.20.

48. To Haines, 16 March 1918, G.83.5.12.

49. From an undated note in a photograph album belonging to Una Tomlin Keast (née Hunter), a nurse at Brancepeth. From the private collection of Lieutenant Colonel Edward de Santis.

50. To Marion Scott, 22 March 1918, G.70.7.

51. Gurney told Harvey that he was himself the anonymous author of the text. Gurney to Harvey, c. March–April 1918, Harvey Archive, D12912/1/2/33.

52. To Marion Scott, 22 March 1918, G.70.7.

53. To Marion Scott, 5 April 1918, G.70.18.

54. To Marion Scott, 26 March 1918, G.41.166.

55. To Marion Scott, 28 March 1918, G.70.6.

56. Attempts to diagnose Gurney's condition from the distance of a century are, inevitably, of limited value. Opinions vary between the two most commonly used current diagnostic terms: bipolar disorder and schizophrenia. What we understand by these terms changes depending on the decade in which the diagnosis is made, and the discipline of the health professional making the diagnosis. A psychiatrist and a Jungian psychotherapist are unlikely to agree on the same language with which to summarise the condition of a patient, as I found

when taking Gurney's case notes and work to a wide range of health professionals to consult their opinion on his illness. After consultation with Professor Kate Saunders of Oxford University's Psychiatry Department, I am using the term 'schizoaffective disorder', as it is a term that encompasses elements of both bipolar disorder and schizophrenia, and as such, is the most accurate description of Gurney's changing condition. However, it would not have been a term that Gurney's doctors recognised, and so is of limited value to us, and in this instance I use it as a shorthand for describing an array of symptoms.

57. To Howells, 22 April 1918, G.3.1.

Chapter 9. 'Rather Dead Than Mad'

1. Winifred Gurney to Don Ray, December 1950, G.78.24.
2. Figures from the year before Gurney's admission show that of the 1,652 admissions of soldiers from France, the most common diagnoses were melancholia (309), delusional insanity (242), mental deficiency (232), confusional insanity (179), mania (135), dementia praecox (127), neurasthenia (99) and shell shock (63). All statistics on Warrington taken from 'A Record of Admissions to the Mental Section of the Lord Derby War Hospital, Warrington, from 17 June 1916 to 16 June 1917', by R. Eager MD, Major RAMC (T), Officer in Charge of Mental Division LDWH and Senior Assistant Medical Officer Devon County Asylum.
3. Last two of four stanzas of 'In a Ward', written in Warrington, July 1918, G.82.6, published in War's Embers, p. 62.
4. To Marion Scott, 27 August 1918, G.41.175.
5. Letter from the hospital to David Gurney, 22 June 1918, G.4.132.
6. Copy in the hand of Marion Scott, G.4.1.
7. Taken from the closing section (lines 87–89) of an unpublished manuscript, 'Lines (to J. C. Squire)', May 1923, G.42.3.
8. Haines to Marion Scott, 1 July 1918, quoted in Hurd, The Ordeal of Ivor Gurney, p. 125.
9. To Marion Scott, 29 November 1917, G.41.156.
10. When he conceived the idea of arranging some of his Thomas settings into a cycle in 1925, 'The Penny Whistle', written in June–July 1918, was to be the first song.
11. First lines of 'On Rest', War's Embers, ed. R.K.R. Thornton (Ashington: Carcanet, 1987), pp. 89–90.
12. Hunt's views on his poems are mentioned in a letter to Scott, early August 1918, from Napsbury (G.41.183). He was only then sending the notebook containing them to Scott, and it is unlikely that he wrote them all out for Hunt, and that she had sent him back comments on them, as he had only just finished writing the notebook. It is more likely that, given the dramatic nature of events, Margaret had visited.
13. To Marion Scott, late June 1918, G.41.181.
14. Haines to Marion Scott, currently undated, estimated to be between 1918 and 1919, G.4.105.
15. Formally known as the Middlesex War Hospital.
16. M Muir Mackenzie of the RCM to Marion Scott, 20 July 1918, G.4.136, and 11 July 1918, G.4.137.
17. For more detail, see Peter Barham's excellent study of the fate of mentally ill ex-servicemen, Forgotten Lunatics of the Great War (New Haven and London: Yale University Press, 2004), p. 55 onwards.
18. For details of individual case studies, see Barham, Forgotten Lunatics of the Great War, ch. 3.

19. To Haines, 4 September 1918, G.83.7.1–2.
20. To Haines, 4 September 1918, G.83.7.1–2. The poem was sent back to Scott on 27 August 1918 in letter G.41.175, and published in *War's Embers*, p. 77.
21. To Marion Scott, 24 August 1918, G.70.41b.
22. To Marion Scott, 27 August 1918, G.41.175. The manuscript exists but is unpublished.
23. To Haines, received 11 September 1918, G.83.1–6.
24. To Haines, 4 September 1918, G.83.7.
25. The scherzo of August–September 1918 at St Albans was written for, or at least became a part of, the D major sonata.
26. Gurney to Harvey, 1918, Harvey Archive, D12912/1/2/36.
27. Her daughter found them in her effects after her mother's death in 1959.
28. Written by Scott on the corner of an undated letter from Drummond's mother Margaret to Scott, probably from 1924, Gurney Archive.
29. To Marion Scott, c. 21 September 1918, G.61.1–2.
30. To Marion Scott, 22 July 1918, G.41.173.
31. To Marion Scott, 22 July 1918, G.41.173.
32. Gurney to Harvey, 1918, Harvey Archive, D12912/1/2/34.
33. Gurney to Harvey, 1918, Harvey Archive, D12912/1/2/36.
34. To Marion Scott, 22 July 1918, G.41.173.
35. Winifred Gurney to Don Ray, 16 April 1951, G.78.16.
36. To Marion Scott, 17 October 1918, G.41.177.
37. Haines to Scott, 1918, G.4.99–4.115, quoted in Hurd, *The Ordeal of Ivor Gurney*, pp. 130–131.
38. To Marion Scott, 2 November 1918, G.41.178.
39. By 17 October Harvey had reached the safety of Holland.
40. To Marion Scott, 2 November 1918, G.41.178.
41. He mentions his intention to begin at the Royal College again in January in a letter to Winifred Chapman, November 1918, G.45750.
42. Boden, *Stars in a Dark Night*, p. 177.
43. Like much of Gurney's chamber and instrumental music, it has never been published.
44. To Shimmin, 30 November 1918, G.76.15.1–2.
45. To Shimmin, 30 November 1918, G.76.15.1–2.
46. 'The Day of Victory', lines 30–33, c. 11/12 November 1918, published in the *Gloucester Journal*, 11 January 1919, and subsequently in *War's Embers*, pp. 92–94.
47. To Marion Scott, 7 February 1917, G.41.63.

Chapter 10. 'A Revenge of Joy'

1. To Haines, Boxing Day 1918, G.85.8.
2. Geoffrey Taylor to Scott, 23 October 1937, G.53.70.
3. Philip Lancaster makes this connection in his article 'The Sea's Redemption: Gurney in Cornwall', *Ivor Gurney Society Journal*, vol. 15 (2009), pp. 99–108, which is further substantiated by the draft's appearing in the same notebook as Gurney's diary. 'The Companions' is published in Gurney's collection *80 Poems or So*, ed. George Walter and R.K.R. Thornton (Ashington: Carcanet, 1997), p. 111.
4. To Winifred Chapman, January 1919, G.45750.
5. To Haines, 16 January 1919, G.83.10.1–2.

6. To Shimmin, 30 November 1918, G.76.15.1–2.
7. Quoted in Christopher Palmer, *Herbert Howells: A Study* (London: Novello, 1978), p. 22.
8. To Haines, 16 January 1919, G.83.10.
9. The first three of five stanzas of 'The Volunteer', the opening poem of *War's Embers*, p. 57.
10. Boden, *Stars in a Dark Night*, p. 178.
11. To Marion Scott, 25 August 1917, G.41.127.
12. Boden, *Stars in a Dark Night*, p. 180.
13. To Marion Scott, March/April 1919, Hurd transcript, Gurney Archive.
14. They were first performed in February 1938 by Isolde Menges and Howard Ferguson, and published separately two years later by OUP.
15. He revised the song a number of times between 1919 and 1926.
16. First stanza of 'Lights Out', Edward Thomas, 1917.
17. It was to be the only performance until 2010, despite his repeated suggestions in 1925 that it might be included in a Patron's Fund concert at the College.
18. Published in *Best Poems*, pp. 72–73.
19. To Marion Scott, 22 April 1919, G.46.30.7.
20. To Marion Scott, 22 April 1919, G.46.30.7.
21. 'Petersburg', from *Poems of Gloucesters, Gloucester and of Virginia*, p. 61.
22. Winifred Gurney reminiscences, quoted in Hurd, *The Ordeal of Ivor Gurney*, p. 133.
23. Ronald Gurney to Marion Scott, 13 May 1919, Gurney Archive.
24. Winifred Gurney reminiscences, recorded by Michael Hurd, c. 1970, G.57.
25. Quoted in Hurd, *The Ordeal of Ivor Gurney*, p. 157.
26. Ronald Gurney to Ivor Gurney, 12 November 1922, Gurney Archive.
27. Winifred Gurney reminiscences, recorded by Michael Hurd, c. 1970, G.57.
28. Gurney felt that Whitman's work deserved more expansive treatment than was possible in a song, and his next setting was an ambitious version of 'Anthem of Earth', written for baritone solo, chorus and orchestra in 1921.
29. In a letter to Ethel Voynich, November 1915, G.41.15, Gurney writes, 'How the A major Prelude (Book II) of Bach seems to be born of the spirit that makes Christmas Carols!'
30. To Marion Scott, 22 June 1916, G.41.26.
31. They were published by Winthrop Rogers in 1921.
32. The last was left incomplete, and the set was not published as a group until 2000, although a handful were published by Oxford University Press in the 1950s and 1970s.
33. Gurney to Harvey, 15 December 1919, Harvey Archive, D12912/1/2/39.
34. Both manuscripts with Vaughan Williams's changes are in the Royal College of Music's Gurney archive.
35. To Marion Scott, 4 May 1917, G.41.89.
36. 'Who Wants the English Composer?', *RCM Magazine*, vol. 9, no. 1 (Christmas term 1912), pp. 11–15.
37. We have no record of whether Gurney heard the work, but he was certainly aware of it and held it in great esteem. When he heard it was published by the Carnegie Trust, alongside Howells's Piano Quartet in A minor that had been dedicated to him, he was delighted by the news.
38. He was only to return to Masefield's verse once more, in 1925, with 'On Eastnor Knoll'.
39. He was to follow it at Gloucester in the summer and autumn of 1920 with 'The Latmian Shepherd', 'As I Lay in the Early Sun', and between 1920 and 1921, 'Dover's Hill', 'Meadow

and Orchard' and 'The Fields Are Full'. 'The Singer' and 'The Latmian Shepherd' were published by OUP in 1938, 'The Fields Are Full' in 1928.

40. 'You Are My Sky' was published by OUP in 1938, and the second setting of 'The Ship' in 1952. He continued to set Squire between 1919 and 1922, adding 'Epitaph in Old Mode' (published by OUP in 1938) and 'The Three Hills' (unpublished) to his collection.

41. Reproduced in Boden, *Stars in a Dark Night*, p. 104.

42. It appeared in the collection of Gurney's poetry edited by Leonard Clark at the prompting of Joy Finzi and published by Chatto and Windus in 1973, *Poems of Ivor Gurney, 1890–1937*. Joy, the wife of the composer Gerald Finzi, did a great deal to enable Gurney's work to be published after his death.

43. Masefield entitled his Gurney-inspired poem 'Of One Who Sang His Poems'. It was printed as the frontis to Clark's 1973 collection of Gurney's poetry.

44. To Jack Haines, 11 November 1919, G.82.17.1–2, *Collected Letters*, p. 499: 'And one evening the [Edward] Shanks, [Harold] Monro and myself went to hear Steuart Wilson sing the Wenlock Edge Cycle of Vaughan Williams—a fine strong piece of work.' However, on second hearing Gurney qualified his praise: 'sometimes one tires of the foreign mannerisms, or wonders why certain verses were set in such a manner' (G.8.36, handwritten comments by Gurney on his concert programme, from a performance of *On Wenlock Edge* at the First Annual Congress of the British Music Society, 5 May 1920. The performers were Gervase Elwes and the London String Quartet).

45. In *A Shropshire Lad* these poems are untitled, and are given the numbers VII, LII, XXXIX, XXIII, XXXV, XIII, and XXIX respectively. For further discussion and analysis of the cycle, see Kate Kennedy, 'Ambivalent Englishness: Ivor Gurney's 'Ludlow and Teme', *Ivor Gurney Society Journal*, vol. 12 (2006), pp. 41–64.

46. Unpublished notes on Gurney's concert programme, 5 May 1920, G.8.36.

47. Four songs were written for the cycle at the College that May, the others back at Dryhill in Gloucester, but three were reworkings of much earlier Housman settings, returning to some of his earliest settings from 1908.

Chapter 11. 'Despairing Work Is the Noblest Refuge'

1. To Marion Scott, September 1919, G.61.148,150–151.

2. Matilda Chapman to Marion Scott, 25 February 1920, G.61.136.

3. To Haines, May 1920, G.83.14.

4. To Marion Scott, 11 May 1917, G.41.91.

5. To Marion Scott, 13 May 1920, Hurd transcript, Gurney Archive.

6. Published posthumously in Gurney's poetry collection *80 Poems or So*, p. 112.

7. The manuscript held at the Royal College of Music shows another dedication, to Howells.

8. The first two settings he conceived (rather unusually) as a pair: 'Nine of the Clock-O' and 'Goodnight to the Meadow'. There was also 'Brittle Bones', which he sent to Graves himself almost as soon as he had finished it. Graves had his sister play it for him and was much impressed. 'Loving Henry' and 'Star Talk' were probably from the same summer and may even have been included in the letter to Graves. That summer also saw 'If Death to Either Shall Come' (published in 1938) and 'The Sea Poppy', both by Robert Bridges. He did not complete 'The Sea Poppy' at the time but returned to it in his spate of editing his own work whilst resident at the City of London Mental Hospital in 1925.

9. Brian Frith reminiscences, quoted in Boden, *F. W. Harvey*, p. 271.

10. Gloucester Archives, Acc. no. 41091, p. 75. Gurney writes in a note to Edith Harvey (cousin to Will and Eric), in an album of correspondence collected by Edith.

11. To Haines, 10 October 1920, G.83.21.1–2.

12. Gurney lists 'Kathleen ni Houlihan', 'The County Mayo', 'The Penny Whistle', 'Today I Think', 'Brittle Bones' and the 'Fiddler of Dooney' in a letter to Haines, October 1920, G.83.22.

13. Saxty was, as Winifred Gurney delicately describes the relationship, 'a very intimate friend' of Gurney's godfather Alfred Cheesman, who 'would be often in his company' (Winifred Gurney to Don Ray, 13 February 1951, G.78.5). There is much speculation about Chees-man's friendships with boys, ranging from Pamela Blevins's incendiary article 'There Is Dreadful Hell within Me . . .' (*British Music Journal*, vol. 19 [1997], pp. 11–27), to Rolf Jor-dan's defence of Cheesman's reputation in '"A Good Man, Kind and Gentle": The Reverend Canon A. H. Cheesman' (*Ivor Gurney Society Journal*, vol. 19 [2014], pp. 7–38). Debate con-tinues, but there is no existing evidence that Cheesman had anything other than a deep affec-tion for boys and adolescent men.

14. 'Charm Me Asleep' was written in 1921 and revised in 1925.

15. Noted in Arthur Knowles Sabin's unpublished autobiography *Pilgrimage*, and referred to in Joy Grant, *Harold Monro and the Poetry Bookshop* (London: Routledge and Kegan Paul, 1967), p. 19. Rupert Brooke had written a thesis on Webster and Elizabethan drama, and there had been a good deal of scholarly work on the Elizabethans and Metaphysical poets by academics such as Edward Arber and Herbert J. C. Grierson.

16. *Tudor Church Music*, 10 vols., published by Oxford University Press between 1922 and 1929, and edited by musicologists including Sylvia Townsend Warner and Percy Buck.

17. Autobiographical notes, quoted in Palmer, *Herbert Howells: A Study*, p. 11.

18. Vaughan Williams, 'Elizabethan Music and the Modern World', *Monthly Musical Record*, vol. 63, no. 752 (1933), pp. 217–218.

19. To Howells, 31 July 1917, G.3.6.

20. There are numerous examples of this, especially in his more mature work, but here for in-stance, in the second verse of 'Blow, Blow, Thou Winter Wind', as the music begins to repeat itself, it is extended with the insertion of a triple-time bar as a way of signalling the end, and interrupting the predictability of the rhythm.

21. To Marion Scott, 25 March 1917, G.41.81.

22. Osborne was the editor of *The Muse in Arms* (1917), one of the first anthologies of war po-etry, and one that Gurney had read many times. Here he writes in a review for the *Morning Post*, November 1917, G.61.76.

23. As mentioned in chapter 1, Gurney admired the square tower of Gloucester Cathedral, and the image frequently recurs as a benchmark for craftsmanship. 'The squareness of west Gloucester pleases me. The spires and square places' (a fragment, quoted in *Collected Poems*, p. xxxiii).

24. The wrong balance of the two can result in a work that is too rambling if there is not enough clarity in the phrase structure. This is rarely the case, though the unpublished 1925 Beau-mont and Fletcher setting of 'Come You Whose Loves Are Dead' might be one such exam-ple. More often, Gurney achieves the right balance between ingenuity and structural coher-ence, and a song that is vigourous and unpredictable is created.

25. 'Spring and Fall' (Bridges only gives the titles in the notes), the first stanza of 'The Wreck of the Deutschland' with some alteration by Bridges, 'The Candle Indoors', 'In the Valley of the Elwy', 'The Handsome Heart' and 'The Habit of Perfection'.

26. *Poems 1918* was published posthumously by Robert Bridges.
27. From J. W. Haines, 'An Hour with Books: Mr. Ivor Gurney, A Gloucestershire Poet', *Glouces-ter Journal*, 5 January 1935. Reprinted in '"A Combination of Don Quixote and D'Artagan": John Haines on Ivor Gurney', *Ivor Gurney Society Journal*, vol. 1 (1995), pp. 59–68.
28. Hopkins, author's preface to *Poems 1918*.
29. The opening couplet of 'To England—a Note', *Severn and Somme*, p. 28.
30. 'War Books', in *Best Poems*, ed. R.K.R. Thornton and George Walter (Ashington: Carcanet, 1995), p. 83.
31. From stanza 11 of Hopkins's 'The Wreck of the Deutschland', in *Poems 1918*.
32. From stanza 31 of 'The Wreck of the Deutschland'.
33. Gurney wrote this poem between 1919 and 1920. Published in *Collected Poems*, p. 44.
34. Hopkins's 'To R. B.', lines 1–2, in *Poems 1918*.
35. Opening line of Sassoon's 'Everyone Sang', published in 1919.
36. To Edward Marsh, June 1922, New York Public Library Berg Collection, *Collected Letters*, p. 535.
37. It began as *The Monthly Chapbook* (Poetry and Drama New Series). It later became *The Chapbook: A Monthly Miscellany*, in January 1920.
38. Grant, *Harold Monro and the Poetry Bookshop*, p. 3.
39. See Grant, *Harold Monro and the Poetry Bookshop*.
40. Harold Monro, 'How I Began', *T.P.'s Weekly*, no. 21 (4 April 1913), p. 419.
41. To Haines, October 1920, G.83.22.
42. Freeman to Gurney, 17 May 1921. Transcription of an original letter in a private collection. Gloucestershire Archives, Gloucester Public Records Office, SR.8.8.2.
43. To Haines, October 1920, G.74.77.
44. Second stanza of Gibson's 'Otterburn', in *Whin*.
45. The weeks leading up to and over Christmas were spent setting a number of Gibson's poems: a rollicking ballad setting of 'The Mugger's Song', an angry complaint of a jilted smuggler, followed by 'Sam Spraggon' and 'Black Stitchel'; in the early new year of 1921, the Gibson settings continued, with 'Blaweary', 'Pedlar Jack', 'Old Meg' and 'Pity Me'. Gibson might have been impressed with Gurney's interpretations of his work, but the songs found less favour with publishers. Stainer and Bell rejected his setting of 'Pedlar Jack', and although it is un-clear whether he tried to find publishers for any of the others, of Gurney's eight Gibson set-tings, 'Black Stitchel' was the only one published anywhere near his lifetime: in 1938, the year after his death. All the rest remain unpublished.
46. It was to wait until a private concert at Scott's house the following year (1922) for its pre-miere, with Clive Carey.
47. Gurney set a further eight poems in February 1921 and in 1922, which were to be his last settings of de la Mare's verse: 'All That's Past', 'Beware! (Exile)', 'Poor Henry', 'Bread and Cherries', 'The Ghost', 'Farewell', 'Alexander' and finally 'The Ruin'. Only 'Bread and Cher-ries' has been published (in the 1938 OUP collection).
48. To Edith Harvey, October 1920, G.74.75.
49. To Haines, 6 November 1920, G.83.23.1–2.
50. Marion Scott, 'Recent Music in London Rehearsal', *Christian Science Monitor*, 16 July 1921.
51. Gurney began the G major sonata in spring 1921 and finished in winter 1922, when he was already an asylum patient.
52. To Marjorie Hayward, solo violinist and chamber music player, who was a professor at the Royal Academy of Music and leader of the English String Quartet. Gurney enclosed the

score of the first movement of the G major Violin Sonata with his letter. Gurney wrote the work in spring 1921–early 1922. He had sent the score of the slow movement to Hayward in September 1921. The first movement was completed in early 1922, so the letter to Hayward, although undated, must have been written in 1922 (G.23.4).

53. To Harvey, possibly early 1922, G.70.44.

54. Winifred Mary Letts is now often included in anthologies as a female war poet. She knew Stanford, and six of her poems were set by him, including this one in 1913.

55. Raphoe, a historic town in Donegal, might have been a gesture towards his Gaelic texts, as Letts was half Irish. Gurney had been drawn towards Irish poetry, from as early as his teenage years, marking Seumas O'Sullivan's poem 'The Twilight People' in an index, with the date 16 January 1908. This date might perhaps imply he had set it to music that January, but if not, at the very least it demonstrates his interest. After the war, the Gaelic interest resumed with James Stephens's 'The County Mayo' in 1918, two settings of Joseph Campbell, and Samuel Ferguson's 'The Darling Black Head', all in 1920. He was to return to Irish poets in his next burst of compositional creativity in the asylum in 1925, with another Samuel Ferguson setting, 'Cashel of Munster', and Thomas W. H. Rolleston's 'The Dead at Clonmacnois'.

56. All were written in 1921 apart from 'Fifth Avenue' and 'Woolworth Building', which he wrote from Dartford Asylum in February 1925 to add to the set. These last two were written at a time in which he was drawn to other poems invoking foreign places (Provence and Flanders); and the image of Gurney, trapped in his asylum room, embarking on a musical tour of Europe and New York is particularly poignant.

57. *New Works by Modern British Composers*, series 2: A description by Percy Scholes, 1924. *Ludlow and Teme* appeared in print in October 1923.

58. He wrote to her a year later as he corrected the proofs of the cycle 'for whose inclusion in the Carnegie list I suspect your party to have been sole mover' (To Marion Scott, 10 May 1922, Hurd transcript, Gurney Archive).

59. The Carnegie United Kingdom Trust was funded by Andrew Carnegie, a Scotsman who had made his millions in the American steel industry. The scheme had been running only since 1917. It aimed to 'encourage British composers in the practise of their art' by publishing between one and seven original compositions annually, which they considered to be 'the most valuable contributions to the art of music.' Over the course of the competition, it facilitated publication (by Stainer and Bell) of works by Holst, Edgar Bainton, Frank Bridge and Vaughan Williams. The list of successful applicants in Gurney's year included Arthur Bliss, Gurney's illustrious contemporary, who had been forging an increasingly successful career since his demobilisation.

60. Two movements of the trio exist, but it is not clear whether more were written.

61. The second was the slow movement, and possibly more, of a sonata in C sharp minor, written in the asylum in 1925.

62. There is some controversy over this date; however, this is the date in the Royal College records.

63. To Marion Scott, 7 April 1921, G.61.17.

64. Three quotes taken from letters to Marion Scott: 19 April 1921, G.61.18–19; 26 April 1921, G.61.20; and 9–10 April 1922, G.46.30.6.

65. In the years following, he repeatedly returned in his asylum writing to the theme of Marie's generosity and his gratitude.

66. From 'Longford Dawns', c. 1921–22, G.64.4, f.27v.

67. This essay, which Gurney called 'By Ashleworth', was discovered only recently amongst Joy Finzi's papers. 'By Ashleworth' was written in 1922. Gloucester Archive Acquisitions 11715, Gloucester Public Records Office.
68. Gurney to Harvey, 'Two nights ago I was out to see Robert Graves', (1921), Harvey Archive, D12912/1/2/60.
69. The Dymock poets, so known as they lived in and around the village of Dymock on the border of Gloucestershire and Herefordshire between 1911 and 1914, included Edward Thomas, Robert Frost, Lascelles Abercrombie, W. W. Gibson, Rupert Brooke and John Drinkwater.
70. To Haines, received 20 August 1918, G.83.9.1–2.
71. Haines to Don Ray, 1951, G.72.5.
72. Haines, 'An Hour with Books', p. 63.
73. To Marion Scott, 15–16 April 1919, G.61.9–11.
74. Published in 1921 by Selwyn and Blount.
75. 'On Earth', unpublished essay, 1922, G.64.12.457–461.
76. Gurney's review was published anonymously on 23 March 1922, p. 187.
77. Gurney to Harvey, written from Plumstead, December 1921, Harvey Archive, D12912/1/2/63.
78. To Edward Marsh, January 1922, New York Public Library Berg Collection, *Collected Letters*, p. 525.
79. To Edward Marsh, December 1921, New York Public Library Berg Collection, *Collected Letters*, p. 523.
80. Gurney to Harvey, January 1922, Harvey Archive, D12912/1/2/64.
81. Haines to Don Ray, 19 March 1951, G.74.1.
82. Letter in possession of Brian Frith dated 11.3.22, Gloucester Public Records Office, SR.8.8.13.
83. To Edward Marsh, early 1922, G.29.41. The four songs he sent were 'The Treasure' (i.e., 'When Colour Goes Home'), 'There's Wisdom in Women', 'One Day' and 'Song' ('All Suddenly the Wind Comes Soft'). The fifth song would have been 'Clouds'. A version of 'Song' entitled 'Heart's Pain' has been published in Stephen Banfield, *Sensibility and English Song* (Cambridge: Cambridge University Press, 1985), pp. 197–199, but the others are unpublished.
84. Winifred Gurney to Don Ray, 25 April 1951, G.78.22.
85. Winifred Gurney to Don Ray, 25 April 1951, G.78.22.
86. In *The Ordeal of Ivor Gurney*, Hurd claims that Gurney's friends called him 'batty Gurney' (p. 17). The granddaughter of William Bubb claims Hurd had mistranscribed the phrase from a letter from her grandfather, and that the term was in fact 'batchy'. From a letter from Ruth Bubb to the author, August 2014.
87. From a letter from his grandson to the author, July 2014.
88. Winifred Gurney to Don Ray, late November 1951, G.78.25.
89. Final lines of 'The Elements', written from within the asylum, October 1925, *Collected Poems*, p. 255.
90. Butterworth to Marion Scott, 22 February 1922, G.4.84.
91. To Walter de la Mare, early June 1922, New York Public Library Berg Collection, *Collected Letters*, p. 534.
92. A phrase taken from his 'Sonnet—September 1922' (see chapter 12).

Chapter 12. 'Below the Horizon'

1. To Marion Scott, 25 and 26 February 1919, G.53.24–27.
2. To Marion Scott, November 1922, G.84.12.1.

3. To Marion Scott, 10 October 1919, G.46.30.5.
4. Oxford, Bodleian Libraries, MMS Sidgwick & Jackson 52, folio 993.
5. To Marion Scott, 10 May 1922, Hurd transcript; *Collected Letters*, pp. 531–532.
6. *Collected Letters*, p. 532.
7. Oxford, Bodleian Libraries, MMS Sidgwick & Jackson 53, folio 265.
8. 'April Gale', published in *80 Poems or So*, p. 50.
9. 'London Dawn', lines 8–11, *80 Poems or So*, p. 63.
10. 'The Road', lines 34–44, *80 Poems or So*, pp. 65–67.
11. To Edward Marsh, June 1922, New York Public Library Berg Collection, *Collected Letters*, p. 536.
12. The above transcription is based on the manuscript G.64.12.4, not the published version in *Collected Poems*. The page is torn at the end of the penultimate line, hence the editorial addition.
13. To Edward Marsh, June 1922, New York Public Library Berg Collection, *Collected Letters*, p. 537.
14. Copy of letter in Gloucestershire Archives, Gloucester Public Records Office, SR.8.8.14, undated.
15. William Drummond (1585–1649), known as Drummond of Hawthornden, was a Scottish poet who hosted Ben Jonson for two weeks. Gurney probably knew about Drummond of Hawthornden from his reading about the Elizabethan and Jacobean poets and playwrights, and had attached the name 'Hawthornden' to Annie Drummond.
16. To Edmund Blunden, early July 1922, Blunden Archives 1909–1970, MS-0426, Harry Ransom Research Center, University of Texas in Austin.
17. To Edmund Blunden, late July 1922, Blunden Archives 1909–1970, MS-0426, Harry Ransom Research Center, University of Texas in Austin.
18. 'The Springs of Music', opening paragraphs, published in *Musical Quarterly*, vol. 8 (July 1922), pp. 319–322.
19. To Marion Scott, 3 August 1915, G.41.7.
20. To Marion Scott, July 1922, G.53.19–21.
21. *Rewards of Wonder*, pp. 32–33.
22. For more information on the festival, see Anthony Boden, *Three Choirs: A History of the Festival* (Gloucestershire: Alan Sutton, 1992).
23. W. P. Kerr to Marion Scott, 15 September 1922, G.4.118.
24. Winifred Gurney to Don Ray, late November 1951, G.78.25.
25. Ronald Gurney to Marion Scott,14 September 1922, G.4.96.
26. Harvey to Marion Scott, 14 September 1922, G.4.98.
27. Arthur Benjamin to Marion Scott, 15 September 1922, G.61.130.
28. See, for example, Eve Kosofsky Sedgwick's reading of gender asymmetry and erotic triangles, in *Between Men: English Literature and Male Homosocial Desire* (New York: Columbia University Press, 1985), pp. 21–27.
29. Marion Scott to Harvey, 16 September 1922, Harvey Archive, D12912/1/2/86.
30. Kerr to Marion Scott, 15 September 1922, G.4.118.
31. It was in fact Stone House in Dartford, the hospital where Gurney was eventually to end up, that in 1925 managed to press for a government bill allowing uncertified voluntary boarders into hospitals. Until then, being certified was the only means of securing a place in a mental institution, but brought with it considerable problems and had very significant repercussions for the patient.

32. See Barham, *Forgotten Lunatics of the Great War*, for detailed accounts of many such cases.
33. In most large county hospitals, the numbers each year of discharged patients were roughly equivalent to the numbers who died incarcerated; a forbidding statistic, even if the numbers of elderly dementia cases are taken into account. This is the case in Stone House, City of London Mental Hospital in Dartford, the hospital in which Gurney would live for the next fifteen years.
34. The 'Bristol people' here must have been the Pensions Headquarters rather than the convalescent home, since he was 'now staying with Ronald'. Kerr to Marion Scott, 22 September 1922, G.4.119.
35. Winifred Gurney to Don Ray, 5 March 1951, G.78.8.
36. Winifred Gurney to Don Ray, 23 April 1951, G.78.21.
37. Hurd, *The Ordeal of Ivor Gurney*, pp. 145–146.
38. Transcribed from documentary 'Child of Joy: An Appreciation of Ivor Gurney', broadcast BBC Radio 4, 9 August 1983, British Library Sound Archive, NP7138.
39. Ethel Gurney's personal reminiscence, 1976, quoted in W. H. Trethowan, 'Ivor Gurney's Mental Illness', *Music and Letters*, vol. 62, nos. 3–4 (July–October 1981), p. 302.
40. Winifred Gurney to Don Ray, 5 March 1951, G.78.8.

Chapter 13. 'Praying for Death'

1. This includes around eight voluntary boarders.
2. See Barham, *Forgotten Lunatics of the Great War*, pp. 223 and 256.
3. Barnwood was visited by the superintendent of York's forward-looking asylum The Retreat in 1896, and he recorded his impression of its décor.
4. It is possible that Dylan Thomas had the famous poisoning case in mind when writing his first version of what was to become *Under Milk Wood* thirty-two years later. In the play, Mr Pugh, weak and downtrodden, and secretly reading 'Lives of the Great Poisoners', dreams of doing away with his bullying wife.
5. For more information on Christiana Herringham, see Mary Lago, *Christiana Herringham and the Edwardian Art Scene* (London: Lund Humphries, 1996).
6. To Dr Harper, December 1922, G.10.20. Woolwich mud could be a reference to a favourite spot for suicides, or a reference to the prison hulks that were moored there, and mentioned in Dickens's *Bleak House.*
7. Recorded in Case Book K, Gurney's Barnwood House medical notes, September 1922, Gloucestershire Archives, Gloucester Public Records Office.
8. Gurney could not have known it, but his description of the sensation of having his 'brain pulled away' is curiously similar to the poet John Clare's experience of mental illness. An eminent historian named Agnes Strickland told Clare that she was glad he could amuse himself by writing. '"I can't do it," he replied, "Why, they have cut off my head and picked out all the letters in the alphabet—all the vowels and all the consonants and brought them out through my ears—and then they want me to write poetry! I can't do it."' Quoted in Jonathan Bate, *John Clare* (London: Picador, 2003), p. 524.
9. For further discussion, see Barham, *Forgotten Lunatics of the Great War*, p. 69.
10. Gurney's Barnwood House medical notes, September 1922.
11. The final line of the unpublished poem 'There Is No Need', 1922, G.15.69.
12. See Erving Goffman, *Asylums: Essays on the Condition of the Social Situation of Mental Patients and Other Inmates* (New York: Doubleday Anchor, 1961), for a discussion of this tendency.

This is not an isolated incident. Gurney also exaggerated his status as an expert in all things Elizabethan by describing himself as an Elizabethan drama scholar. See, for instance, a letter to Sir J. Forbes-Robertson, c. September–October 1924, in which he calls himself 'a scholar of sorts: Great lives of Elizabethans, German music, much French verse' (G.15.90).

13. In a letter from Gurney to Dr Terry that resembles a poem in (very) loose iambic pentameter, November 1922, G.70.55.

14. Arthur Townsend to Marion Scott, 16 December 1922, G.4.10.

15. To Dr Harper, November 1922, G.84.10.

16. To Marion Scott, November 1922, G.10.62.

17. 'To God', lines 12–13, c. late September–December 1922, *Collected Poems*, p. 156.

18. Montagu Lomax, *Experiences of an Asylum Doctor* (London: George Allen and Unwin, 1922), p. 152.

19. John Macarthur, *Mental Hospital Manual* (London: Frowde and Stoughton, 1921), p. 95.

20. To Marion Scott, 9 December 1922, G.10.76, and December 1922, G.10.62.2.

21. To Marion Scott, Barnwood House, December 1922, G.10.20.

22. Macarthur, *Mental Hospital Manual*, p. 95.

23. To Marion Scott, 8 October 1917, G.41.142.

24. He was still not allowed to use a pen in Dartford Asylum by May 1923, as he continued to be on suicide watch. See a comment in the margins of the poem 'Student Time': 'Please to excuse pencil. None else allowed to write with' (G.44.138).

25. Lines 1–8, 'Ypres War', October 1922, G.64.12.155. Nash's painting 'We Are Building a New World' (1918), for example, shows a dystopic landscape devoid of people, with a harsh, sharply lined sunrise and blasted tree trunks, set in a deep foreground of churned-up mud and trenches.

26. 'My Life', December 1922, G.15.74.

27. Lines from 'I Get Up Every Morning', December 1922, G.15.76.

28. Last lines of 'There Is a Man', G.15.78.

29. A letter from Townsend to Marion Scott, 9 November 1922 (G.4.6), relates the circumstances of Gurney's escape.

30. To Harvey, November 1922, G.84.10.

31. Haines to Marion Scott, 18 November 1922, G.4.97.

32. Townsend to Marion Scott, 23 December 1922, G.4.5.

33. Townsend to Marion Scott, 1 December 1922, G.4.8.

34. Letter from Ministry of Pensions to Ronald Gurney, 30 December 1922, G.4.168. That autumn the bureaucracy surrounding Gurney's finances rumbled on, as his friends tried to sort out what kind of pension Gurney would receive, and who would pay his expenses. A letter of 11 October from Townsend, the new superintendent of Barnwood, told Marion Scott that they had decided that they would maintain him without payment until the pension decision was known (GA.4.1). It was not sorted out until the 7th of November, when the Pensions Office agreed to pay 40 shillings (£2) a week to Barnwood House. When he transferred to Dartford, the Visiting Committee of the City of London Mental Hospital agreed to take him for two guineas (£2.10) a week, plus £2 a quarter for laundry. At this point, Marion Scott agreed to become financially responsible for him.

35. Townsend to Marion Scott, 20 December 1922, G.4.10.

36. To Dr Steen, December 1922, G.10.63.2.

37. A letter to Marion Scott, 21 December 1922 (G.10.79), reads in its entirety: 'Dear Miss Scott If I am left here any longer I shall go mad.'

Chapter 14. 'Asylum-Made Lunatics'

1. Lomax, *Experiences of an Asylum Doctor*, p. 39.
2. See his unpublished December 1922 poem 'By Dartford Once' (G.15.236), which begins:
    By Dartford once the old ships went to sea,
    To clearer waters than now, to further harbours,
    That were more beautiful with paven floors
    Than in this uglier modern age they would seem to be.
3. Gurney's medical notes, part of the City of London Mental Hospital Archive, held at the London Metropolitan Archives, Farringdon.
4. The facilities for admission were far from ideal. New patients were accommodated indiscriminately alongside severely ill, possibly distressing cases in the infirmary: 'Owing to lack of accommodation, it is still necessary to receive new admissions into the large infirmary wards, and we do not see how this arrangement, which is not one of the best, can be altered until a hospital is erected for all such cases' (Board of Control Annual Report, 1925, London Metropolitan Archives).
5. To Marion Scott, 26 December 1922, G.10.8 and G.44.192.
6. To Marion Scott, 31 December 1922, G.10.26.
7. All such details of the minutiae and routines of asylum life taken from reports, minutes of meetings and registers and accounts books in the City of London Mental Hospital Archive, London Metropolitan Archives.
8. To Marion Scott, Barnwood House, December 1922, G.10.20.
9. Being taken 'off parchment' means to revoke a patient's formal status as a suicide risk. Gurney's case notes, 27 December 1922, held uncatalogued in the London Metropolitan Archives.
10. To Marion Scott, 26 December 1922, G.10.8.
11. Commissioner's Report for 1923, London Metropolitan Archives.
12. Recorded in Ursula Vaughan Williams, *R.V.W: A Biography of Ralph Vaughan Williams* (Oxford: Clarendon Press, 1964), p. 216.
13. He was prescribed Sulphonal and Dial on 21 January and was still taking them by the time of his medical check on 9 February.
14. Many of the appeals were destroyed after Gurney's death, some by the composer Gerald Finzi's widow, Joy, as she was 'sorting out' trunks of Gurney's papers. Joy was to prove a great advocate for Gurney. She worked tirelessly to secure publication of his poems after his death, but the loss of such a volume of work is regrettable, to say the least. We will never know what clues and information were lost in this breathtakingly misguided tidying spree, and we can never say with absolute accuracy when he stopped writing or composing, as so many manuscripts are missing from his archive.
15. This has an interesting parallel in Virginia Woolf's creation of the traumatised ex-serviceman Septimus Smith, who believed he ought to inform the prime minister and the Cabinet of his visions (Woolf, *Mrs Dalloway* [London: Hogarth Press, 1925]).
16. To Marion Scott, 10 September [1935], G.10.1.
17. The poem is 189 lines long; only a portion of it is reproduced here. The small French town of Besançon is a puzzling choice; it cannot easily be connected with anywhere Gurney had been or had contact with. It is situated in the foothills of the Jura mountains, close to the Swiss border, and is not without literary connections, although we do not know which, if any, Gurney was aware of. Gurney's interest in all things Roman might have led him to

Caesar's account of it in his *De Bello Gallico*. Equally, he was passionate about French literature: Balzac's novel *Albert Savaron* takes place in Besançon, and Colonel Sainte-Hermine, the fictional hero of Alexandre Dumas's *The Last Cavalier*, is a native of Besançon. In the poem 'Les Feuilles d'Automne', Victor Hugo evokes his birth in Besançon, and if Gurney had read Stendhal, then he would have known it to be the place where Julien Sorel is imprisoned in *Le Rouge et le Noir*, and he might well have felt the similarity in their circumstances.

18. Donald Davie makes a compelling, if perhaps a little overstated, case for revising our conception of Modernism in the light of Gurney's late work. He writes: 'This Gurney was a prodigious poet; beside his achievement, Wilfred Owen's and Edward Thomas's seem slender at best. And Eliot? And Pound? Why yes, take them too in, say, 1925, and Gurney had outdistanced them— in the range of first-hand experience he could wrestle into verse, and even in the range of past masters in English whom he could coerce and emulate so as to digest that experience.' Davie, 'Gurney's Flood', *London Review of Books*, vol. 5, no. 2, 3 (February 1983), pp. 6–7.

19. 'Iliad and Badminton', c. November 1925–April 1926, *Best Poems*, pp. 52–53.

20. This is the analogy Professor Edgar Jones of the Maudsley Hospital, Institute of Psychiatry, King's College, London uses to describe this particular state. He finds Gurney's poetry of this time to be synonymous with many cases of verbal derailment in schizophrenics he has treated (in discussion with the author, 2013).

21. John T. Perceval, *A Narrative of the Treatment Experienced by a Gentleman, During a State of Mental Derangement* (London: Wilson, 1838), and Seymour Krim, *Views of a Nearsighted Cannoneer* (New York: Excelsior Press, 1961), pp. 59–75, deal specifically with their authors' experiences in mental hospitals.

22. Rachel Grant-Smith, *The Experiences of an Asylum Patient* (London: Allen and Unwin, 1922), p. 77: 'The Lord Chancellor's Office can prove how many and frequent were my appeals to him both on my own behalf and that of others'. There are a number of other instances of appeal writing recorded in Roy Porter, *A Social History of Madness: The World through the Eyes of the Insane* (London: Weidenfeld and Nicholson, 1987).

23. Visiting Committee Minutes, Tuesday, 19 September 1922, London Metropolitan Archives.

24. Marion Scott to Harvey, 12 January 1929, G.70.45.

25. 'To Old New England' (G.4.151–157), 'To the Army of Bapaume' (G.4.161), 'To the Old Vic' (G.10.81.1), 'The University of Durham' (G.10.66).

26. Hurd, *The Ordeal of Ivor Gurney*, p. 159.

27. Lunacy Act, 1890, Section 41, 66.

28. The cinematograph was purchased in 1911 and run by the head engineer of the hospital.

29. His appearance at the cinematograph evening is recorded simply because it was still early enough in his stay to have regular notes made about his behaviour. As there was no official requirement to keep a record of which patients attended social events, there is no reason to assume that his participation did not continue. After a few months, doctors' notes on a chronic patient were made so infrequently that any attendance at an event would almost certainly go unnoted.

30. Dr Navarra's Report to the Board of Control as Acting Superintendent, 1925, London Metropolitan Archives.

31. Robert Edric, *In Zodiac Light* (London: Doubleday, 2008).

32. Francine Payne, *Stone House: The City of London Asylum* (Dartford: DWS Print Services, 2007), p. 154.

33. The line can be found in his poem 'And My Music', G.44.50.6.

34. The first stanzas of 'Watching Music', *Collected Poems*, p. 256.

35. In September 1922 the Gramophone Company Ltd. is thanked by the Visiting Committee for a gift of records.
36. Letter from Adeline Vaughan Williams to Marion Scott: 'he spoke of real grievances, i.e. that the best music comes on too late on the wireless and he has to miss it.' Quoted in Hurd, *The Ordeal of Ivor Gurney*, p. 166.
37. The director of music for the asylum, an organist who rejoiced in the name of Pratt, performed an organ recital on 11 April 1926. It marked his thirty-year anniversary as director of music for the hospital, and when the record of entertainments stopped in 1930, H. S. Pratt was still in post. His monopoly of the musical activities might suggest that there was little room for another organist/composer, whether or not Gurney's mental health would have allowed him to participate.
38. On another occasion, the superintendent's comments written underneath a programme from an entertainments evening offered by 'The Ladybirds' read: 'They had some excellent voices in the company, and we could have done with more of them, less of the others.' Entertainments Scrap Book, London Metropolitan Archives.
39. Appeal to Dr Harper enclosed with a letter to Marion Scott, late July 1923, G.10.42.1–3.
40. From the poem 'Allowed', March 1923 ('It is allowed to confine a man, but not / So as their manhood ever be forgot.' Transcription by Marion Scott only extant, G.12.10.
41. From a poem-letter of appeal to 'The Owner of [Thomas] Carlyle's House', late March 1923, G.15.167.
42. Payne, *Stone House*, p. 87.
43. There were 14,139 books recorded as being out on loan in 1935. On 4 January 1923 (the day on which Gurney cut his hand), the Visiting Committee decided to award a grant of £5 for the purchase of books for the asylum library during the current year. By 18 January, the Visiting Committee had decided that this was a miserly amount and increased it to £10. Visiting Committee Minutes, London Metropolitan Archives.
44. 'Ernest Parley', *Life in a Madhouse*, Independent Labour Party Pamphlets, no. 27 (London: Independent Labour Party, 1920), p. 24.
45. 'Hedges' is published in Kavanagh's *Collected Poems* (p. 201) but misnamed 'Hedger' (Gurney's handwritten manuscripts are extremely difficult to decipher).
46. Published in *Collected Poems*, pp. 210–211. These are lines 1–9 of 53.
47. From 'To God', December 1922, G.15.86.

Chapter 15. 'Dark Fire'

1. From 'Masterpiece', *Collected Poems*, p. 214.
2. Written in April 1923, G.64.11.123.
3. Two poems and an appeal, written in French, inscribed to 'Le Telegramme du Nord', office of publication. Gurney describes himself as 'Un soldat Anglais—et poéte de St Julien à Vermand'. G.15.302.
4. To Dorothy Gurney, 1923, G.70.37.
5. Marion Scott's journal, 1923–1930, G.47.
6. *The Lancet*, 5 July 1919, pp. 17–18.
7. Colonel L. W. Harrison, in 'Evidence to the Royal Commission on Venereal Diseases in 1916', estimated 3 million cases of syphilis in the UK, and stated that since gonorrhoea was four to five times more common, 'a good many more millions [were] suffering from it'. Quoted in letter from A. Reid to *The Lancet*, 22 November 1919, p. 945.

8. The population of the UK at the 1921 census was approximately 44.9 million, of whom 3 million were said to be infected by syphilis (6.7 percent, or a little over 1 in 20). However, the incidence of gonorrhoea was said to be four times higher (circa 12 million).

9. Sir Robert Armstrong-Jones, *Textbook of Mental and Sick Nursing: Adapted for Medical Officers and Nurses in Private and Public Asylums* (London: Scientific Press, 1907).

10. W. L. Templeton, 'The Effect of Malarial Fever upon Dementia Praecox Subjects', *Journal of Mental Science*, vol. 70 (January 1924), p. 94. The connection with Gurney is strengthened by Templeton's endnote, thanking Dr R. H. Steen (Gurney's superintendent) for permission to report on the cases.

11. To Marion Scott, 29 August 1923, G.10.69.

12. Fifty-Eighth Annual Report of the Visiting Committee, 1923. In 1941, his services were to be called on by the government, and this time, his experiment worked. He discovered that the aural administration of potentised mustard gas and rhus toxicodendron could significantly improve the terrible lesions on the skin caused by exposure to mustard gas. He had been of no help to Gurney, but, four years after Gurney's death, soldiers in the next war were to benefit from his research.

13. 'Armistice Day', G.15.161. There are other, equally interesting poems relating to Armistice Day in the archive: G.44.91, G.44.193 and G.52.6.

14. G.44.89. A single sheet on which are written eight short poems and, at the head of one side, a list of 'War Poets at a guess', November 1923. He lists Graves, Sassoon, Harvey, Robert Nichols, Brett Young, Wilfred Owen, Julian Grenfell, Charles Hamilton Sorley, Peter Quennell (mistakenly) and Rupert Brooke (in brackets, as Brooke of course never reached the fighting). Quennell had been included in Marsh's Georgian verse anthologies at the tender age of seventeen but had not fought in the war.

15. Between September and October 1924, all of Gurney's appeal letters include the claim 'The first war poet of England he thinks'. For instance, this wording appears in appeals to The Poetry Editor of the 'New Statesman' (G.44.9), The Editor (Poetry) of the *Saturday Review* (G.44.8), and Sir J Forbes Robertson (G.15.90). It continues into October–November but starts to lose the 'he thinks'.

16. When, back in March 1917, he learnt that Robert Bridges was to be looking at some of his poems, he was mortified. 'The news that my poor versifications are to be shown to R. B. gives me no pleasure at all. I did not want technical criticism, being quite aware that good stuff does not come out of such a one as myself in a hurry. It would need quiet and continued thought—whereas the things that are finished as quickly as possible: often finished in one go; things like the "Signaller's Vision" are meant to appeal to such people as are in this room with me—not to the experimenters in Greek metres' (To Marion Scott, 24 March 1917, G.41.79).

17. From 'At Reserve Depot', *War's Embers*, p. 66.

18. The first half of 'Ypres', from *The Book of Five Makings*, ed. R.K.R. Thornton and George Walter (Ashington: Carcanet, 1995), p. 134. Walter has reproduced the manuscript in as conscientious a manner as possible, with Gurney's crossings out replicated, and layout on the page indicated with dashes. It is a useful reminder that much of *The Book of Five Makings* was still work in progress, but for the purposes of replication here it is distracting, so I have chosen to omit their editorial markings.

19. First lines of 'The Curses', reproduced in *Ivor Gurney: Poems of War*, ed. R.K.R. Thornton (Newcastle upon Tyne: Rectory Press, 2014).

20. Haines to Don Ray, 19 March 1951, G.74.1.

21. See the poem 'Territorials Marching' for a typical example (G.10.85.1).
22. 'Laventie Dawn' was to be published posthumously in the collection *Rewards of Wonder*, p. 28.
23. 'Smudgy Dawn' appears in *Rewards of Wonder*, p. 59; 'Spring Dawn' in *80 Poems or So*, p. 46.
24. Marion Scott's journal, 27 December 1923, G.47.
25. Marion Scott's journal, 27 December 1923, G.47.
26. 'Charles Villiers Stanford: By Some of His Pupils', p. 200.
27. To Edward Marsh, August 1924, G.52.11.137.
28. *Best Poems* was only published in 1995, in an edition including Gurney's other collection, *The Book of Five Makings*. It was edited by R.K.R. Thornton and George Walter. *Rewards of Wonder*, another of Gurney's collections from this time, was edited by George Walter and published in 2000.
29. 'Open Country', from *Poems of Gloucesters, Gloucester and of Virginia*, pp. 52–53.
30. *Poems of Gloucesters, Gloucester and of Virginia*, p. 472.
31. First two stanzas of 'Walt Whitman', G.44.50.3.
32. Many of these songs exist only in the archive and are unpublished. Most other manuscripts are lost, although a portion of the chamber music exists.
33. 'Masterpiece', c. November–December 1924, G.44 (189–191), published in *Collected Poems*, p. 214.
34. Gurney has no obvious connection to the club, which was founded in 1898 as a small social club for the community of Roland Park, Maryland. It may be that Marion Scott had some link to it, but why it was at the forefront of Gurney's mind is not clear.
35. Both the E minor and G minor quartets are now lost, although Finzi records seeing three movements of the E minor quartet.
36. To Miss Winthrop Rogers, 10 February 1925, G.46.2.1.
37. He made an attempt at setting Whitman's 'Darest Thou Now O Soul' in 1921, but there is no evidence that he finished it.
38. The harmony of *London Meditation* is quite distinctive. Gurney alternates between major and minor triads on the same root, as a way of constantly modulating. In bar 7, he starts to alternate F sharp and F natural in the strings; then he slips from D minor down a third into B flat (bar 9), into B flat minor in the following bar (this is the parallel minor); into the relative major, D flat (system 3, bar 3); then again into the parallel minor (D flat minor, the bar later); then again down a third (enharmonic equivalent of a third) into A major; and so on. Yeats's 'Song in the Night' is discussed further in chapter 16.
39. Grouped as *Three French Songs* by Finzi.

Chapter 16. 'The Patient Believes He Is Shakespeare'

1. At 8:40 pm, 25 August 1925, the BBC National Service broadcast a performance of *Ludlow and Teme*, with Osmond Davies singing, the Kendal Quartet and Anna Mukle.
2. To Osmond Davies, 15 August 1925, G.13.1.29.
3. To Marion Scott, c. late April 1925, G.10.40.
4. Randolph Davis to Marion Scott, 30 December 1925, G.4.25.
5. Davis to Marion Scott, 30 December 1925, G.4.25.
6. To Marion Scott, 31 December 1922, G.10.26.
7. From 'Chance to Work', 1923, G.55.13–26, published as an undated poem in Hurd, *The Ordeal of Ivor Gurney*, pp. 171–178.
8. To Haines, November 1922, G.84.9.

9. Unpublished asylum poem beginning 'I Am Not Now', G.15.77.
10. Marion Scott to Davis, 1 December 1925, G.4.23.
11. Davis to Marion Scott, 22 December 1925, G.4.28.
12. Anderson's son Nicholas recollected in an interview with the author that his father had been given music by Gurney as a gesture of friendship. Unfortunately, there is no record of what these pieces or songs were, so we cannot know if these were works by Gurney that we now know nothing of. It is likely that they were lost works, as he did not have the means to make second copies of most of his asylum manuscripts, and these are likely to have been originals.
13. From Nicholas Anderson's information given in interview with the author, 2014.
14. It was Anderson who had interested Professor Trethowan in Gurney. Trethowan was his second in command at Manchester University, and conversations with Anderson led to Trethowan's highly influential study of Gurney's illness, based on Anderson's recollections, which has shaped our understanding of Gurney's illness ever since. See Trethowan, 'Ivor Gurney's Mental Illness' pp. 300–309.
15. Published when Anderson was professor emeritus of psychiatry at Manchester University, 'Strindberg's Illness', *Journal of Psychological Medicine*, vol. 1, no. 2 (1971), pp. 104–117.
16. Appeal to Sir J. Forbes Robertson, c. September–October 1924, G.15.90.
17. Yeats's subtitle for the poem was 'Song in the Night', which Gurney misremembers as 'Songs'. It is also known by its first line, 'All the words that I utter'.
18. From Parry's set of motets *Songs of Farewell*, written between 1916 and 1918. The final motet, 'Lord, Let Me Know Mine End', is a double choir setting of Psalm 39.
19. To Marion Scott, September 1915, G.41.10.
20. Lines 13–14 of 'Bach—Under Torment', G.64.1.
21. Helen Thomas, 'A Memoir of Ivor Gurney', *RCM Magazine*, vol. 16, no. 1 (1960), pp. 10–11.
22. Thomas, 'A Memoir of Ivor Gurney', pp. 10–11.
23. The songs that are likely to be settings of texts written by Gurney for the purpose are 'Severn Meadows' (March 1917) and 'Song of Silence' (March 1918), an incomplete setting for two sopranos of a version of his 'The Poplar' (*War's Embers*) entitled 'O Tall White Poplar' (c. 1918–19), 'London Song' (1920 / November 1925), 'Love Song' (February 1925), 'Song of the Canadian Soldiers' (25 April 1925), 'To the Memory of Max Reger with Homage' (June 1925), 'After the Ceremony' (1925), 'Song' (1925), 'To Do This If Not Old' (c. 1925), 'Lament' (c. 1925–26), 'The Late Rider' (January 1926), 'The First of Lent' (c. 1926), 'Over the Ridge' ('Song') (c. 1926) and 'Western Sailors' (March 1926).
24. Dr Steen records with particular pride that patients taken out on a trip to an exhibition of the Queen's Dolls House at Wembley were permitted to jump the queue. We can only surmise as to whether this was courtesy on the part of the general public or anxiety at the patients' bizarre behaviour.
25. Dr Robinson to Marion Scott, 5 April 1926, G.4.60.
26. This dates from autumn 1926.
27. The *Gloucester Play* can be found in the archive at G.52.3, and the two versions of *A Tewkesbury Trial* at G.52.4 and G.42.8.
28. He had probably taken the name Cridlan from a wartime friend, Basil Cridlan.
29. 'To Tewkesbury Abbey', 1926, G.45.147.
30. In an essay 'On a Dictionary Quotation', 22–23 May 1926, G.15.39.1–3.
31. See William Stafford, 'This Once Happy Country: Nostalgia for Pre-modern Society', ed. Malcolm Chase and Christopher Shaw, *The Imagined Past: History and Nostalgia* (Manchester: Manchester University Press, 1989), pp. 33–46.

32. To Marion Scott, 23 October 1917, G.41.148. This is the opening of Beethoven's Piano Sonata no. 7, op. 10, no. 3 in D major. Whilst Gurney has the audacity to 'improve' Beethoven, the only changes he makes are in terms of dynamics and articulation; he does not alter any notes.
33. Gurney had read some of Gordon Bottomley's plays in the *Georgian Poetry* anthologies, and Bottomley had sent him a book of his plays which Gurney was rather surprised to find he very much enjoyed. They had wiled away some of the time he had spent locked up alone after his escape in the spring of 1923, and he had even written a poem about them (G.15.45).
34. Unpublished manuscript, G.64.12 (438) (B).
35. Gurney's case notes, 8 December 1927, London Metropolitan Archives.
36. Robert Graves, 'The Road to Rydal Mount', *The Crowning Privilege* (London: Cassell, 1955), p. 51.
37. To Marion Scott, 8 October 1916 (misdated), G.41.41.

Chapter 17. 'A Fear of Obscurity (My Own)'

1. Adeline Vaughan Williams to Marion Scott, G.61, quoted in Hurd, *The Ordeal of Ivor Gurney*, pp. 166–167.
2. From a series of notes, probably intended for Will Harvey, 6 October 1927, G.15.194.
3. Oxford University Press published 'Walking Song', 'Desire in Spring', 'The Fields Are Full', 'Severn Meadows' and 'The Twa Corbies' in 1928; a major milestone. Gollancz considered publishing a collection of Gurney's poems in February 1928, but it came to nothing.
4. 'Si J'etais Roi' is the title of a popular mid-nineteenth-century French opera by Adolphe Adam, but it is not clear why Gurney was thinking of it.
5. From an appeal letter to Cheltenham Parish Church, G.15.178–179.
6. To Marion Scott, late June 1927, G.10.13A.
7. From an appeal letter to Cheltenham Parish Church, G.15.178–179.
8. From an appeal 'To Kings College London', 7 October 1927, G.15.198.
9. From a series of notes, probably intended for Will Harvey, 6 October 1927, G.15.192.
10. Notes for Harvey, 6 October 1927, G.15.191.
11. Letter addressed to the BBC, May 1929, G.15.24.
12. To the 'May Queen of London', 1 May 1927, G.15.23.1–3.
13. To the Royal College of Music, 19 April 1929, G.15.37.
14. Published in *Collected Poems*, p. 209.
15. No printed version of this poem has yet been found, and the real Valentine Fane did not publish a collection. She published poems for *Punch* in the 1920s, with such unpromising titles as 'The Lonely Mermaid' and 'To One Who Did Not Come to Luncheon', and published the serious poem 'Life's Treasures' in the *Fortnightly Review* in 1925. Gurney could have come across her work in either publication, as the asylum stocked both. 'Life's Treasures' is similar in tone and scope to 'The Wind', suggesting that Fane could well be the author of both. The copied-out version replicated here is in Gurney's archive.
16. Details of account taken from Marion Scott's journal, 1923–1930, G.47.
17. In a letter to Amiens Cathedral, G.15.203.
18. Marion Scott arranged these trips with Gurney's doctor, Robinson, in his London consulting rooms. They took place, according to Robinson, on
16 January 1930 (Old Vic Theatre)
1 March 1930 (Old Vic)

2 June 1930 ('for a drive')

30 November 1930 ('drive')

1 February 1931 (to Eltham [probably to visit the Palace and Gardens there])

17 July 1931 ('drive')

9 October 1932 ('out for tea')

18 December 1932 (visit to Hester Stansfield Prior)

10 July 1934 ('drive')

11 September 1934 (to visit some of Scott's 'friends')

19. He writes of 'Admiring "Pears"' in a letter to the Royal College of Music on 19 April 1929, G.15.37.

20. To Marion Scott, October 13, 1930, G.10.6. In the collection of notes presumably intended for Will Harvey, 6 October 1927, G.15.190–197 (193), he remarked that he thought Pears's *Cyclopedia* to be 'great' (with much enthusiastic underlining), but also disappointing. In Gurney's opinion, the last part, after the dictionary of gardening, ought to be left out. The part Gurney took objection to includes a dictionary of domestic pets, a dictionary of sports, and a 'ready reckoner: From one-sixteenth of a penny to twenty-one shillings'—a bewildering series of tables of calculations (G.15.191).

21. The first patent for wireless was filed in 1896.

22. To Amiens Cathedral, G.15.199–204.

23. See, for instance, Sassoon's poem 'Dead Musicians', in *Counter-attack and Other Poems* (1918).

24. These were 'To the Poet before Battle' and 'Song of Pain and Beauty'.

25. In the opinion of Professor Edgar Jones in consultation with the author.

26. For a list of such terms, including loosening of association, derailment, and knight's move thinking, see Ashley Rule, 'Ordered Thoughts on Thought Disorder', *The Psychiatrist*, vol. 29 (2005), pp. 462–464.

27. To the May Queen of London, written in 1927, G.15.23.1–3.

28. 18 May 1927, G.15.186; 27 June 1927, G.46.24; and 7 October 1927, G.15.198.

29. To Marion Scott, 29 November 1933, G.10.37.

30. Dr Steen, Annual Report, 1922, London Metropolitan Archives.

31. From a series of notes, probably intended for Will Harvey, 6 October 1927, G.15.193.

32. To Marion Scott, 29 November 1933, G.10.37.

33. To Marion Scott, 15 and 20 November 1937, G.10.56 and G.10.55.

34. To Marion Scott, 23 December 1933, G.10.43.

35. To Marion Scott, October 1934, G.10.9.

36. To Marion Scott, 16 March 1932, G.10.51.

37. To Marion Scott, 10 November 1932, G.10.27.

38. To Marion Scott, 23 August 1930, G.10.39.

39. To Marion Scott, 1934, G.10.13B.

40. In his biography of Harvey, Anthony Boden writes: 'From time to time, Will travelled down to Dartford to visit his dear friend Ivor Gurney in the City of London Mental Hospital. He found a tortured soul pleading for liberty or death. 'Get me out of here, Willy!' he would say. Will would promise to do his best, but knew that any idea of release for his friend was useless.' *F.W. Harvey*, p. 331.

41. Winifred Gurney to Don Ray, 12 February 1951, G.78.4.

42. Winifred Gurney to Ivor Gurney, Christmas 1936, G.10.77.

43. Winifred Gurney to Don Ray, 25 April 1951, G.78.19.

44. From a collection of notes likely intended for F. W. Harvey, 6 October 1927, G.15.192.
45. To Marion Scott, 20 March 1937, G.10.10.
46. Marion Scott to Gurney, July 1937, G.10.59.
47. Appeal to St Clements Danes, 11 September 1937, G.10.18.
48. To Marion Scott, 10 December 1937, G.10.36. It is unclear what 'o m T's' refers to. It may be a shorthand reference to the proofs that Gurney had received with this letter, or perhaps some kind of reference to the fruit that Scott had left for him. This letter is in part written on the verso of the letter from Scott with which the *Music and Letters* proofs were enclosed. It was written by her 26 November and received by him, with the proofs, on 27 November.
49. Published in *War's Embers*, pp. 79–80.
50. Recounted in the local newspaper coverage of Gurney's funeral: 'Mr. Ivor Gurney Buried, Moving service at Twigworth', *The Citizen*, 1 January 1938, p. 6.
51. Boden, *Stars in a Dark Night*, p. 204.

Chapter 18. Afterword

1. Winifred Gurney to Don Ray, December 1950, G.78.24.
2. The closing lines of 'Concerning Ivor Gurney', Blunden's introduction to *Poems by Ivor Gurney* (London: Hutchinson, 1954), p. 19.
3. Vaughan Williams to Ronald Gurney, 17 May 1955, G.8.1.52.
4. To Marion Scott, 27 November 1917, G.41.159.
5. Winifred Gurney to Don Ray, 11 April 1951, G.78.15.
6. Winifred Gurney to Don Ray, 13 February 1951, G.78.5.
7. Ronald Gurney to Gerald Finzi, 1954, G.8.1.
8. Ronald Gurney to Gerald Finzi, 1954, G.8.1.
9. Winifred Gurney to Don Ray, 13 February 1951, G.78.5.
10. OUP published two volumes the year after his death, and another in 1952.
11. Winifred Gurney reminiscences.
12. Edmund Blunden to Joy Finzi, 8 August 1964, CF 12.
13. In anthologies such as *Up the Line to Death: The War Poets, 1914–1918*, ed. Brian Gardner (London: Methuen, 1964), and *Men Who March Away*, ed. Ian Parsons (London: Viking, 1965).
14. The collection was published in 1973. For a detailed discussion of Joy Finzi's struggle to see Gurney's poetry published, see Anthony Boden's account of events in the *Ivor Gurney Society Journal*, vol. 15 (2009).
15. Blevins, *Ivor Gurney and Marion Scott*.
16. Lines from 'The Interview', September 1923, G.15.295, *Collected Poems*, pp. 198–199.

Index

150: charm